Southern Biography Series
Bertram Wyatt-Brown, Editor

WINNER OF THE JULES AND FRANCES LANDRY AWARD
FOR 2001

Published with the assistance of the
V. RAY CARDOZIER FUND
an endowment created to support
publication of scholarly books

John Marshall *and the* Heroic

Age *of the* Supreme Court

R. Kent Newmyer

LOUISIANA STATE UNIVERSITY PRESS
Baton Rouge

Copyright © 2001 by Louisiana State University Press
All rights reserved
Manufactured in the United States of America
First printing
10   09   08   07   06   05   04   03   02   01
5   4   3   2   1

Designer: Amanda McDonald Scallan
Typeface: Sabon
Typesetter: Coghill Composition Co., Inc.
Printer and binder: Thomson-Shore, Inc.

Library of Congress Cataloging-in-Publication Data

Newmyer, R. Kent
    John Marshall and the heroic age of the Supreme Court / R. Kent
Newmyer.
        p. cm. — (Southern biography series)
    Includes bibliographical references and index.
    ISBN 0-8071-2701-9 (cloth : alk. paper)
    1. Marshall, John, 1755–1835.   2. Judges—United
States—Biography.   3. United States. Supreme Court—Biography.
I. Title.   II. Series.

    KF8745.M3 N49   2001
    347.73'2634—dc21   2001001766

Frontispiece: Portrait of John Marshall by Henry Inman, 1831. Courtesy of Philadelphia Bar Association.

The paper in this book meets the guidelines for permanence and durability of the Committee on Production
Guidelines for Book Longevity of the Council on Library Resources.♾

In Memory of My Parents
Doris Young Newmyer
Dan K. Newmyer

An institution is the lengthened shadow of one man.

—*Ralph Waldo Emerson*

Contents

Illustrations

Frontispiece
Portrait of John Marshall

Following page 266

Thomas Marshall
Mary Keith Marshall
John Marshall at age forty-three
Mary ("Polly") Marshall
Marshall home, Richmond, Virginia
William Cushing
Samuel Chase
William Paterson
Alfred Moore
Bushrod Washington
Trial of Aaron Burr
Bushrod Washington
Trial of Aaron Burr
William Johnson
Thomas Todd
Gabriel Duvall
Joseph Story
Henry Brockholst Livingston
William Pinkney
Daniel Webster
William Wirt
John Randolph of Roanoke
John Taylor of Caroline

Preface

Several years ago—more then I care to mention—Bill Cooper, then editor of the Southern Biography Series, asked me if I might be interested in doing a book on John Marshall. He thought a one-volume "interpretive biography" of four hundred or so pages was needed—something between the short biography by Francis Stites and the jurisprudential studies by Edward Corwin and Robert K. Faulkner, on the one hand, and the life-and-times biographies by Albert J. Beveridge and Leonard Baker on the other. In full agreement with his assessment, I blissfully set out in search of John Marshall. What I didn't know was how long it would take me to find him, if indeed I have. I had no way of knowing either that an avalanche of fine scholarship was coming down the mountain.

Several factors (other than my ignorance of forthcoming Marshall studies) settled my mind. First, I was under the impression that my teaching and previous scholarship prepared me for the job. As it turned out, I knew a lot less than I thought I knew—or needed to know. I was also emboldened by the ongoing publication of *The Papers of John Marshall* at the College of William and Mary. The work done by the editors of these papers—as I knew from having written about someone whose papers were *not* published—would greatly ease my labors. And indeed it has. Equally important, having a definitive scholarly edition of Marshall's papers invited me to take a fresh look at his life and juristic labors. I even had some questions that wanted answers, along with a paradox or two demanding resolution. How was it possible, I wondered, that a man so deeply engaged in the divisive constitutional controversies of his age could have been so universally respected and admired, even by his opponents? Why was it that Marshall seemed so different from the other great men of the founding generation—from Washington, who was his model statesman; from Jefferson, his lifelong adversary; or from John Adams, who appointed him to the Court; or Joseph Story, who was his dear friend and colleague on the Court for twenty-four years? It also tantalized as well as frustrated me that Marshall left such a comparatively slender corpus of personal papers. Why did a man so deeply engaged in making history appear to care so little how future historians would treat his efforts? This modesty, along with his sense of humor, intrigued me, as did the contradictions I came to see in his career his biographers had not addressed. For example, how could someone so democratic in his personal relationships be so politically conservative? How could Marshall the political conservative sit so comfortably on the radical cutting edge of nation making? How did his nationalism comport with his deep love of Virginia and its people, which continued even after they embraced the states' rights ideology he hated and feared? How did Marshall's Virginia experience as a lawyer and Federalist politician influence his work on the Supreme Court? By what feat of leadership did he as chief justice unify the Court and make it into a major force in American government? And how, finally, was it that Marshall, the Supreme Court, and the Constitution became so inseparable—in fact and in historic memory?

Here then are some of the questions that tempted me to undertake an interpretive biography of Marshall—and here, as a guide to readers, is a brief statement concerning my approach to interpretation. First, this is not a narrative biography in the traditional sense of that term, nor is it simply a study of Marshall's jurisprudence. Rather I have attempted to combine the two forms. While I have been mainly concerned about Marshall's life in the law and the nature of his work as chief justice, I have also treated his private life and his pre-Court career. This I have done mainly in chapters 1 and 2, though references to his private life are sprinkled throughout the book. In the interest of brevity, if a book of five hundred–plus pages can be said to be brief, I have emphasized mainly those aspects of Marshall's personal experience and personality that directly influenced his work as a jurist. Accordingly, his marriage, his family, his rich social life in Richmond receive less attention than the formative impact of the American Revolution, which I treat here as a uniquely constitutional war. Before that transforming event, young Marshall seemed to be on his way to a comfortable life as a member of the Anglo-Virginia gentry. Fighting for independence, in addition to making him a traitor to England, made him a patriot citizen of the new Republic. He was present at the creation of a nation and made its preservation the central mission of his life: as a state legislator in the 1780s and 1790s, as a champion of the new constitution at the Virginia ratifying convention in 1788, and as a Washington-Adams Federalist in states' rights Virginia in the 1790s. Events of that uniquely formative decade, I argue, identified the great constitutional questions he would face as chief justice—and the answers to those questions as well.

Since I focus on Marshall's judicial career, a few remarks on my approach to that subject are in order, especially regarding Marshall's judicial opinions. The latter, especially those dealing with constitutional law, are not only his main claim to fame but they constitute the most important and revealing part of his written legacy. Not to focus on these opinions would be a bit like covering Shakespeare without the plays. But there were problems and challenges, too—one being the difficulty of writing legal-constitutional history so that the general reader interested in early national history can understand it. All I can say here is that I recognized the issue and did my best to ease the way. Another serious problem stems from the fact that his opinions, with the exception of those on circuit and his lone constitutional dissent, were to some extent collective in nature. In the absence of relevant court papers and personal correspondence, the chief way of separating Marshall's constitutional ideas from those of the other justices is to consider his opinions collectively and sequentially, to look for pattern, design, in the tapestry of his law. As a common lawyer doing constitutional law, as the chief justice of the nation's highest appellate court, he was concerned that his opinions, and the Court's decisions, added up to a coherent body of rules and principles for the guidance of lower federal courts, for state courts in many instances, and for the American people. Treating Marshall's separate opinions as part of an unfolding exposition of working principles of law, I hope, helps avoid some of the pitfalls of the great-case approach. This is the way I have approached his Contract Clause decisions; his constitutional opinions dealing with federalism, and his ongoing exposition of judicial review.

My concern has been not just to understand Marshall's constitutional thinking, but to locate it and him in the context of history—"in the circumstances which, in fact, were his," to quote Oliver Wendell Holmes Jr. Part of this historical context was itself legal in nature. Consequently, Marshall's constitutional system has to be seen as part of the common-law tradition, which in turn was part of the larger English cultural inheritance Americans of the Revolutionary War generation so readily appropriated to their own uses. Marshall's common-law-oriented constitutional jurisprudence, however, was also fashioned in response to the great political, economic, and ideological forces unleashed by the American Revolution. Given the case-and-controversy foundation of American public law, it was inevitable that private controversies between parties in litigation should reflect the cultural conflicts of the age. Very often, given the federal nature of the Republic, those conflicts pitted state against nation—and state legislatures and state judges against federal judges. One aspect of that struggle was economic, which I treat hereafter as part of the emergence of a national market. Marshall was also sucked into the vortex of early national politics as the Republic gradually cast off the deferential political culture of the eighteenth century in favor of party-based democracy, especially as it developed in the legislative branch of state governments. By the 1820s, I argue, state and local resistance to the emerging market economy merged with states' rights constitutional theory. Led by Virginian theorists, cultural localists mounted an all-out assault on Marshall and his version of constitutional nationalism. This struggle, particularly as it was embodied in the personal and ideological rivalry between Marshall and Jefferson, is one of the book's main interpretive themes. At the basis of their disagreement was a dispute over the meaning of the American Revolution and the nature of the new nation it brought into being.

This in brief is the interpretive matrix of what purports to be an interpretive biography. My goal is not merely to sum up the legal and institutional accomplishments of Marshall but to capture something of the nuanced texture of his reasoning, the complexity of his mature jurisprudence, and the affinities and tensions between his system of law and the transformative age in which he lived. As much as we might need to think so, his jurisprudence did not emanate full blown and perfect from the brow of Jove. Rather, it was the end product of an ongoing dialectic with his states' rights opponents both on and off the Court. Marshall's goal—as he saw it and as I try to depict it—was to maintain the national Union generated by the idealism of the Revolution and institutionalized tentatively and against the odds in the Constitution of 1787. Contemporary critics of Marshall, and some modern biographers as well, have tended to depict him as an aggressive, perhaps even excessive, nationalizer in this cultural war. I see him (as he saw himself) more as a beleaguered champion of an increasingly fragile union. To save the Framers' Constitution from the resurgent forces of democratic localism and states' rights theory, he helped put the Supreme Court, the weakest of the three branches in 1800, at the epicenter of the constitutional government in America. As chief justice he gave new meaning to that office and, in the process, identified himself with the Court over which he presided—to the enhancement of its authority and of his own reputation. For reasons I hope to show, John Marshall remains America's representative jurist: a judge for all seasons.

Acknowledgments

Writing history is solitary work, but at the same time it can be a remarkably collective and collegial enterprise. Doing this book has driven the lesson home. At every step of the way I've leaned on my friends and colleagues and on the work of other historians past and present, most of whom are strangers to me. Those who went out of their way personally to assist me deserve special thanks—with deep apologies to anyone I have inadvertently forgotten to mention and, of course, total absolution to all for any of the book's shortcomings. At the top of the list are two teachers and scholars who did not live to see my book but who were instrumental in its gestation. The late Kenneth Rossman, Doane College, Crete, Nebraska, taught me to love history and how to write it; he was the best teacher I have ever seen and one I have always tried to emulate. The late Paul Murphy of the University of Minnesota inspired me, as he did dozens of other students and colleagues. His generous encouragement many years ago led me to pursue my interest in the Marshall Court. I regret deeply that I cannot thank him over a friendly cup of coffee. I also want to thank my former colleagues in the history department at the University of Connecticut, whose insights into their own fields of study did so much to inform my own. My compatriots at the University of Connecticut Law School, where I am now privileged to teach, have also added greatly to my understanding of the world of law—a world that over all the years they still share with John Marshall. I am especially indebted to professors and former deans Phillip Blumberg and Hugh Macgill for their support and for generously sharing their love of books, history, and law.

I would also like to thank the following friends and fellow historians for their help. Kitty Preyer generously shared her deep knowledge of early American legal history with me, as she has done over the years. Her keen critical reading of the manuscript early on was immensely helpful. G. Edward White generously took time from his busy schedule to give me a trenchant critical appraisal of the entire manuscript, one that helped me avoid some embarrassing errors. I am also grateful to my former student and friend Harlow Sheidley, professor of history at the University of Colorado, Colorado Springs, for her thoughtful appraisal of the manuscript. My thanks, also, to James Banner Jr.; Don Higginbotham; Richard Kay; and Charles Hobson, editor of *The Papers of John Marshall*—all of whom read select chapters. I will discuss Hobson's contributions to Marshall scholarship in the Essay on Sources. But let me extend a note of special thanks to him here for making available the unpublished papers of Marshall he and his staff have so painstakingly assembled at Williamsburg, Virginia, and for patiently answering my innumerable queries about our mutual friend. Talking with Chuck Hobson about John Marshall is about as close as one can come to talking to the old chief justice himself.

Also it pleases me to extend thanks to Maureen G. Hewitt, editor-in-chief of LSU Press, and to editor Jean C. Lee for preparing the manuscript for production; to William Cooper, former editor of the Southern Biography Series, who suggested the biography to me; and to Bertram Wyatt-Brown, present editor of the series, for his encouragement and support along the way. Working with them has been a real pleasure. I am especially grateful to my friend Sydney Landon Plum, who took time from her own writing to copyedit mine and to do the index as well. Working with her has been a privilege and a pleasure. Several of my students helped me over the years, and many more listened patiently to my enthusiastic babble about the lost world of John Marshall. To all of them go many thanks. The same goes to Savina Lambert, who helped me with the illustrations, and to Tim Ruggieri and Geoffrey Meigs, my in-house computer consultants. A special note of gratitude goes to Sarah Devotion Garner for helping me cite check the manuscript.

A generous research grant from the NEH helped immensely, as did financial support from the University of Connecticut Law School Foundation and the University of Connecticut Research Foundation. For permission to use previously published articles, thanks go to the *Connecticut Law Review* and the *John Marshall Law Review*.

To my wife, Denise Merrill, who uncomplainingly indulged the solitary habits of a would-be scholar, I send my thanks—and my love.

John Marshall *and the* Heroic Age *of the* Supreme Court

CHAPTER ONE

Young Man *of the* Revolution

> Our resistance was not made to actual oppression. Americans were not pressed down to the earth by the weight of their chains nor goaded to resistance by actual suffering. . . . The war was a war of principle against a system hostile to political liberty, from which oppression was to be dreaded, not against actual oppression.
>
> —*John Marshall to Edward Everett, August 2, 1826*

I AM A CHILD of the revolution," exclaimed Governor Edmund Randolph during the opening debate in the Virginia ratifying convention. So he was, and so was each of the other delegates who gathered that dusty June in Richmond to determine the fate of Virginia and the federal Union. So most assuredly was John Marshall, the thirty-two-year-old delegate representing Richmond and Henrico County. It may seem paradoxical that Virginians young and old, established statesmen like Randolph and aspiring ones like Marshall, should all have been children of the Revolution. But that simple fact makes a telling point: generations are not defined by statistical calculations but by the shared experience of history. The more intense and profound the historical moment, the stronger the generational bond.[1]

---

1. *Ratification of the Constitution by States: Virginia*, edited by John P. Kaminski and Gaspare J. Saladino, in *The Documentary History of the Ratification of the Constitution*, 2: 971

Perhaps no other event in American history educated those it touched more profoundly than did the American Revolution—if by education we mean the manner in which a culture conveys and transforms itself from one age to the next. No other generation of Americans witnessed the birth of the nation. Never before or since would the reasons for war or the possibilities of peace be so thoroughly and brilliantly discussed by so many. And never would the principles of government settled on be so deeply rooted in the simultaneous acts of thinking and fighting and lawmaking. Never would principles be so thoroughly tested in the laboratory of real politics as during the years between independence and the ratification of the new Constitution. These common characteristics of the age did not, of course, mean that Revolutionary-era Americans agreed on the meaning of their Revolution, but only that the ideas derived from the age were apt to be personalized and internalized and, when the occasion permitted, translated into public institutions and cultural truth with a capital *T.*

So it was with John Marshall's republican education. For twenty of his first thirty-two years, he was bombarded from every side with the cultural messages of the Revolution. As a youngster under his father's tutelage, from 1765 to 1775, he followed the transforming debate in Virginia over liberty, power, and empire. For six years he soldiered, as an officer in the Virginia militia and then in the Continental line, to protect the principles of liberty agreed upon in the debate. For another six, as a novice lawyer and member of the Virginia legislature, he labored to implement those principles in the context of state politics shaped by the Articles of Confederation. During the debate over the ratification of the Constitution in Virginia in 1788, Marshall stepped forth on the national stage as a champion of the new order. The experience invited him, as it did others at the convention, to distill years of thinking, fighting, and legislating into a public philosophy that informed his life's work. This is not to say he never grew or never changed his mind. He did both. But when Chief Justice Marshall died in 1835 at the age of seventy-nine, he remained what he had always been: a young man of the Revolution.

Frontier Republican

John Marshall joined the Revolution in late summer 1775, when he arrived at the muster field for the Culpeper minutemen, located near Germantown in the

---

(the Virginia volumes are hereinafter cited as VRD [Virginia Ratification Debates]). On the generational theme, see Stanley Elkins and Eric McKitrick, "The Founding Fathers: Young Men of the Revolution," *Political Science Quarterly* 76 (June 1961): 181–216.

frontier county of Fauquier, Virginia. He walked ten miles to get there from his family's place at Oak Hill—not much of a chore for a lanky nineteen-year-old frontiersman. We know he came with high resolve. His purple-dyed hunting shirt and beaver hat marked him as a member of one of Virginia's numerous militia units that had sprung to life as the struggle with Great Britain heated up. The tomahawk, which hung at his side, was a symbol of his resistance to British authority. The rifle he carried indicated better than words that he meant business. There were words, too, though they come down to us secondhand. After greeting his fellow soldiers, some of whom most likely were friends and acquaintances, he informed them that commanding officer Captain William Pickett would not be there. Recently commissioned Lieutenant Marshall would stand in his place "for want of a better." Marshall passed on the news of fighting from Lexington and Concord that had just reached Virginia, which he had no doubt heard from his father, Thomas, who was already busy organizing a company of volunteers and who as a friend of Washington was instrumental in securing a commission for his eldest son. Lieutenant Marshall went on to say what was obvious enough, but what was in its fusion of individual and national rights remarkably revealing. As he put it, they were gathered there "to defend their country and their own rights and liberties." The job at hand was to "brighten their fire-arms and learn to use them in the field." That said, he ordered the sergeant to deploy the men in a single line and proceeded to instruct them in the "new manual exercise." After that there was more conversation about the cataclysmic events unfolding in Massachusetts, some friendly banter, a few foot races, and a game of quoits. Then the newly minted citizen-soldiers headed their separate ways home.[2]

Two months later they were together again as part of the Culpeper Minuteman Battalion, called into active duty by Colonel Patrick Henry, commander of Virginia's provisional army. The Culpeper troops marched south to Williamsburg in October 1775. From there a detachment of about two hundred, including Lieutenant Marshall, was ordered to the Norfolk-Hampton area to

---

2. Marshall's speech comes down secondhand via Horace Binney's eulogy of 24 September 1835 at Philadelphia, reprinted in *John Marshall: Life, Character, and Judicial Services as Portrayed in the Centenary and Memorial Addresses and Proceedings throughout the United States on Marshall Day, 1901,* comp. and ed. John F. Dillon (Chicago, 1903), 2: 287–88. David Scott Robarge argues persuasively that the muster probably took place in late summer 1775 rather than in May. "John Marshall and His Times: A Virginia Lawyer and Southern Federalist in the Early Republic, 1755–1801" (Ph.D. diss., Columbia University, 1995), 74 n. 8.

repel marauding British regulars operating under orders from Lord Dunmore, who still claimed to be the rightful governor of Virginia and who was trying to mobilize former slaves and loyalists against the patriots. The skirmish between the untested Virginia minutemen and British regulars took place at Great Bridge outside Norfolk on December 9. It was the first military action since Bunker Hill, and relative to the number of troops involved, it was one of the bloodiest battles of the war. Marshall would later join Washington and other officers of the Continental line in criticizing the reliability of militia fighting units. At Great Bridge, however, they all but annihilated the seasoned British regulars as the British attempted foolishly, with manifest contempt for the patriot-soldiers, to attack over a narrow causeway directly in front of the American positions. The great issues of empire, the talk of liberty and constitutional rights had suddenly translated themselves into an elemental proposition: kill or be killed.[3]

Lieutenant Marshall joined in the bloodletting and in the process was transformed from a boy into a man, from a citizen of the British Empire into an American traitor. These transformative personal matters were not mentioned at all when he wrote about the battle many years later in his biography of Washington. He did acknowledge ever so subtly, however—as a tribute from one fighting man to another—the courage of Captain Fordyce of the British army, who, though badly outnumbered and assailed with fire from two sides, "marched up with great intrepidity, until he fell dead within a few steps of the breast work." Marshall wrote these words when he was chief justice, but he was thinking and feeling as a soldier. In important ways, he never ceased doing so.[4]

What Marshall did at the battle of Great Bridge and in the campaign of burning and pillaging that followed in and around Norfolk, where the militia did *not* distinguish itself; what he did at Monmouth Court House, Brandywine, and Germantown, the major battles in which he took part, was radical in the extreme. He pledged to defend the rights of the American people and the American nation before either had come into existence. Though he had never fired a shot in anger, he backed his pledge by his willingness to fight and die if necessary. Literally, since it was British custom to hang traitors, he bet his life

3. Marshall writes about the battle in his *The Life of George Washington*, 2d ed., rev. and corrected (Philadelphia, 1832), 1: 68–70. Unless otherwise indicated all citations to Marshall's biography of Washington are to this edition.
4. Ibid., 69.

on the future of the nation and ventured forth with rifle in hand to create one. John Marshall's first great constitutional decision—one that illustrates the linkage between the actual fighting of the Revolution and the constitutional ideas that emerged from it—was to take up arms for America.

Marshall never explained his radical decision to support the Revolution so early on—or why he stuck with the cause when so many imbued with the *rage militaire* in 1775 soon thereafter lost their *rage*. Like most of the young men who fought America's wars, his motives for fighting were undoubtedly complex. The simple fact that his father Colonel Thomas Marshall was in the forefront of Virginia's mobilization was reason enough for an adoring son. There was also the matter of personal honor. In a society that celebrated the quality, a member of Virginia's gentry, like young Marshall, fought because not to do so was unmanly. A sense of adventure and empowerment at the prospect of shaping the destiny of country and empire may well have moved a young man who had not yet left the wilderness county in which he was born.[5]

This said, the case is strong that Marshall was moved mainly by principle—though to say so runs the risk of adding to, rather than penetrating, the mist of hagiology that surrounds him. His youthful speech to the Culpeper minutemen about the rights and liberties of America is, not surprisingly, replete with noble sentiment. More to the point was the length of his military service, first in the militia and then, after July 1776, as a lieutenant, then captain in the Eleventh Virginia Regiment of Washington's Continental line. When Marshall praised the "principled soldiers" of the Revolution in his biography of Washington, he spoke from experience. And what he said comports with his statement to Edward Everett nearly half a century after the event, that the American Revolution must be understood as a struggle not against oppression but for constitutional principle. So also must his jurisprudence, which from beginning to end was permeated with the constitutional lessons he traced to Washington's constant struggle to fight a war when thirteen separate states were fighting Congress and themselves. Colonial wars for independence are likely to be constitutional by definition. Lieutenant Marshall was learning on the job while he was fighting.[6]

---

5. Charles Royster discusses popular attitudes in his *A Revolutionary People at War: The Continental Army and American Character, 1775–1783* (Chapel Hill, N.C., 1979), ch. 1.

6. On the broader social, constitutional significance of the Revolutionary War, see John Shy, "The American Revolution: The Military Conflict Considered as a Revolutionary War," in *Essays on the American Revolution*, eds. Stephen G. Kurtz and James H. Hutson (Chapel Hill, N.C., 1973); also Shy's *A People Numerous and Armed: Reflections on the Military Struggle for Ameri-*

Still, questions remain as to why he decided to fight in the first place. How, one wonders, did the notion that liberty was worth dying for reach young Marshall in the remote reaches of Virginia's northwest frontier? And what cultural values and ideas did the young soldier blend with his wartime experience to produce the vision of the republican nation for which he ended up fighting? Though the details about it are scanty, the answers in part lie in Marshall's education. Using Bernard Bailyn's broad cultural measure, it appears to have been less haphazard than was once thought. True, Fauquier County had little to offer by way of schools. In fact, there were none at all until 1777. Marshall's parents, however, were unusually committed to education, each in his or her own way. There is distressingly little in Marshall's writings about his mother, Mary Keith Marshall, and we can only infer her influence on him. Married at the age of seventeen, she had her hands full giving birth to fifteen children and attending to basic matters of caring for them. And matters were indeed basic. Germantown was hardly more than a frontier post when the Marshalls first settled there, and the place Marshall was born and spent his first years was a simple frontier cabin. Frontier fare was the order of the day, as Marshall recalled, and sometimes there wasn't much of that either. Things improved when the family moved from Germantown to Leeds Manor in the early 1760s, but Mary had her hands full. There is good reason to assume that as the daughter of a minister she appreciated literacy and learning. It is possible she shared responsibility with her husband in seeing that her young brood acquired the basic skills of reading and writing. Her most lasting impression on their eldest son, however, had to do not with book learning but with courage and character. Marshall seems not to have escaped the assumption of his place and age, that a republican woman's place was in the home. More than most, however, he acknowledged the intellectual equality of women and argued for improving their educational opportunities. Writing many years later in regard to James Mercer Garnett's *Seven Lectures on Female Education,* he concluded "that national character, as well as happiness, depends more on the female part of society than is generally imagined." Reading history backward, it is hard not to conclude he learned that lesson first from his mother.[7]

---

can Independence, rev. ed. (Ann Arbor, Mich., 1990). Don Higginbotham, *War and Society in Revolutionary America: The Wider Dimensions of Conflict* (Columbia, S.C., 1988); James K. Martin and Mark E. Lender, *A Respectable Army: The Military Origins of the Republic, 1763–1789* (Arlington Heights, Ill., 1982).

7. Bernard Bailyn, *Education in the Forming of American Society: Needs and Opportunities for Study* (Chapel Hill, N.C., 1960); Marshall to Thomas W. White, 29 November 1824, *The Papers of John Marshall,* eds. Herbert A. Johnson et al. (Chapel Hill, N.C., 1974–), 10: 124–25

Marshall's brief formal education began at the age of fourteen, when his father sent him to Campbelltown Academy in Westmoreland County. Though billed as an academy, it was only a small boarding school run by the Reverend Campbell, an Anglican clergyman trained in Scotland who had some proficiency in the classics and a penchant for stern discipline. After a year Marshall returned home having acquired some new friends (including James Monroe), further proficiency in the basic skills, and an introduction to Latin. It was at this point his father procured the live-in tutorial services of James Thomson, a thirty-year-old Anglican priest-in-training. Thomson came from Scotland to assume duties in the newly organized Episcopal church for the parish of Leeds, which was coterminous with Fauquier County. As a leading member of the Leeds vestry, Thomas Marshall had been instrumental in choosing Thomson for the church position. It would appear Marshall may well have had his son's education in mind when he did so. Family tradition has it that he wrote directly to a friend in Edinburgh requesting a man who "must be a gentleman, a college graduate, especially well versed as a Greek and Latin scholar, and an Episcopalian." During his first year in Fauquier, Thomson resided in the Marshall home and tutored the Marshall children. During this period, John gained a solid mastery of Latin grammar, along with a lasting affection for Livy, Horace, and Cicero. Thereafter, with only a grammar and dictionary and "his own unassisted diligence," he went on to master the classics on his own.[8]

This brief period of study with the Reverends Campbell and Thomson, along with a brief stint at the College of William and Mary during a lull in the war, was the extent of Marshall's formal education. What else he learned—and it was *most* of what he learned—was on his own, with guidance from a doting father who had ambitious plans for his eldest son—first as a Virginia gentleman of standing in British North America and then as a Virginia gentleman of standing in the new American nation. Thomas Marshall was a man of no mean ambition himself and imparted that singular trait to his eldest son. Such influence was not unusual in the patriarchal social order of late eighteenth-century

---

(hereafter cited as PJM). In addition to Johnson, Charles T. Cullen and William C. Stinchcombe edited select volumes in this admirable series. Beginning with vol. 5 (1987), Charles F. Hobson has served as editor.

8. Marshall's brief recollections of his early education in *An Autobiographical Sketch by John Marshall . . . ,* ed. John Stokes Adams (Ann Arbor, Mich., 1937) is amplified by Joseph Story in his "Life, Character, and Services of Chief Justice Marshall" in *The Miscellaneous Writings of Joseph Story,* ed. William W. Story (Boston, 1852), 639–97. The procurement of Thomson (or Thompson as he spelled it) was recounted by Thomas Marshall Smith (Marshall's great-grandson) to John Dillon in Dillon, ed., *John Marshall,* 1: lvii n. 1.

Virginia. In the Marshall family, however, the well-drawn lines of patriarchal authority were supplemented, if not supplanted, by affection and respect. Joseph Story, Marshall's friend and colleague on the Supreme Court, was touched by the way Marshall constantly spoke of his father "in terms of the deepest affection and reverence" and how, in the privacy of their friendship, the chief justice often "broke out with a spontaneous eloquence" and "in a spirit of the most persuasive confidence" concerning his father's "virtues and talents." In his *Autobiographical Sketch,* Marshall proudly confessed that his father was "a far abler man than any of his sons" and "the solid foundation of all my own success."[9]

Part of that foundation was practical (for example, his surveying and mathematical skills), part character (his patriotism, his personal strength, and the courage and decisiveness under fire he displayed as commander of the Third Virginia Regiment at the Battle of Brandywine). A substantial part of Thomas's legacy to his son, however, had to do with book learning, not a familiar commodity even among well-to-do Virginians, especially those in the frontier counties. Thomas Marshall may have cherished education because he had so little of it himself. Possibly he was influenced by his neighbor, Thomas, Lord Fairfax, who brought the best of English culture to the Virginia frontier, and by his neighbor and friend George Washington, who in turn emulated Lord Fairfax. With such models in mind, the father set out to educate his eldest son to rise in the social hierarchy of late colonial Virginia, which is to say John Marshall's education was markedly English. He never alluded to the theological aspects of this education if such there were. Neither was he given to biblical quotations. But his father was a deacon in the Anglican church, and his mother was the daughter of an Anglican minister. This, plus the fact that both of his tutors were Anglican divines, makes it all but certain that the Bible and the prayer book were regular fare. English literature, poetry, and history certainly were. Milton, Shakespeare, Dryden, and Pope were among his favorites. The latter's *Essay on Man* left a special mark in part because, as Marshall remembered, he was required at the impressionable age of twelve to copy large portions of it. Oliver Goldsmith and George Crabbe were also favorites of his then and later. Story remembered Marshall's fondness for poetry, and in fact Marshall tried his hand at it, though somewhat late in life. In a different vein entirely, and much more influential in giving direction to Marshall's life, was his early en-

9. Story's recollections appear in Story, *Miscellaneous Writings,* 642–43; Marshall's in Adams, *Autobiographical Sketch by John Marshall,* 15.

counter with William Blackstone's *Commentaries on the Laws of England* in four volumes. It speaks loudly as to Thomas Marshall's ambition for his son that he was one of the first subscribers to the 1772 American edition. At Thomas Marshall's urging his son took a plunge into the *Commentaries* before going off to a war that aimed to unseat the authority of the British constitution the great Tory jurist praised as the best and fairest in the world.[10]

Reading English literature and poetry was a lifelong pleasure, and the Latin classics were a solace that helped John Marshall weather the early death of four children and the devastating loss of his wife. Reading also served as a relief from the pressures of work and the tedium of living in the culture-starved wilds of Washington City. In a more practical vein, Marshall's distinct style of writing was also traceable in part to his passion for English literature. Especially influential, as Marshall's most distinguished biographer explains, was Alexander Pope, whose crisp, precise writing was a model for Marshall. Horace and Livy also left an appreciable mark, as did Blackstone, who taught generations of lawyers who had suffered through *Coke on Littleton* that clarity, eloquence, and legal learning were not mutually exclusive. Marshall's lifelong respect for the written text, for the meaning of language, was also clearly traceable to the influence of the *Commentaries*. And so, most probably, was his conviction that the tens of thousands of judicial decisions over the centuries added up to a coherent system of jurisprudence.[11]

What else Blackstone and the great literature of England and republican Rome meant to a young frontiersman whose experience was bounded by forest, stream, and mountains is hard to say. The beauty of northwest Virginia could itself be an education, and we hear from Story, who heard it from Marshall, that nature left an indelible impression. The glory of the Blue Ridge Mountains probably inspired Marshall to poetize as much as did Goldsmith and Dryden. As a young man he learned what Emerson and Thoreau later preached: that inner feelings and outward nature and books could define truth and inspire the creative imagination. And as Lincoln later did, he came to cherish what he had little of. The isolation of the frontier—the scarcity of books, leisure, and learning there—rather than depriving Marshall of an education, deepened his appreciation of it. The northwest frontier also left another more practical mark: the desire to own a large piece of it. Following his father, John Marshall spent his mature life consolidating extensive land holdings in and

10. On Thomas Marshall and Blackstone, see PJM, 1: 39 n. 5.
11. Jean Edward Smith, *John Marshall: Definer of a Nation* (New York, 1996), 33–35.

about the Northern Neck and on into the valley of Virginia—for his own peace of mind and for the security of his growing family.

Frontier-inspired book learning, important as it was, affords few clues to the main question posed earlier regarding the source of Marshall's revolutionary "principles" and his decision to fight for them. Indeed there is more than a little irony in the fact that Marshall was educated in the literature of the nation whose authority he rebelled against. The paradox might be resolved if we knew for sure what young Marshall actually learned from Blackstone, or whether he prepared himself for war by studying the radical Whig tracts of James Burgh, Joseph E. Priestley, and *Cato's Letters,* by John Trenchard and Thomas Gordon—the staples of the revolutionary intelligentsia—or the writings of John Locke concerning the right of revolution. He did mention in his *Autobiographical Sketch* that on the eve of war he was more devoted to "the political essays of the day, than to the classics or to Blackstone." Possibly the knowledge of Cicero, Tacitus, Livy, and Horace imparted by the Reverends Campbell and Thomson informed his notions of republican liberty. If so, he makes no reference to them in this regard. The books he did mention and admire, moreover, were either nonpolitical or decidedly unrevolutionary. The rational, orderly, and moral world of Pope seems light years removed from the fratricidal realities of a bloody revolutionary war. Shakespeare understood blood well enough and described those human foibles that led to the shedding of so much of it. But Lieutenant Marshall assuredly did not rally under the Bard's banner at the Culpeper muster. Of all Marshall's reading, it was perhaps the conservative Blackstone who was most relevant to the revolutionary soldier. True, the staunch Tory lawyer sang the praises of a sovereign Parliament, whose authority Marshall fought to repudiate. But Blackstone praised even more the rights of property, which he conflated with liberty—the same Americans felt was being denied them by corrupt and misguided English politicians. To understand Marshall, we need to contemplate the possibility that conservatives could be revolutionaries—and possibly, even, were revolutionaries *because* they were conservatives.[12]

In searching for the educational roots of Marshall's revolutionary behavior, there is one other point to consider: namely, that by studying to become one of

12. Adams, *Autobiographical Sketch by John Marshall,* 5. For a discussion of the impact of radical Whig tracts on late colonial society see Bernard Bailyn, *The Ideological Origins of the American Revolution* (Cambridge, Mass., 1967). The general impact of the classics on the Revolutionary generation is discussed in Richard M. Gummere, *The American Colonial Mind and the Classical Tradition: Essays in Comparative Culture* (Cambridge, Mass., 1963).

God's Englishmen, he and other American patriots-in-the-making were learning to think of themselves as deserving of fair and equal treatment. When they were treated instead as inferior colonials, they branded the English as radicals for having repudiated their own constitution. By this line of reasoning, Marshall could become a revolutionary dedicated to the establishment in America of the values of liberty under law the British had taught him, but which they forgot. By the same token, if England should return to her senses, Marshall might feel free to reaffirm the taught tradition of English culture. This is precisely what happened in the 1790s when Americans grappled with the dangers of the French Revolution abroad and social radicalism at home. Marshall's comparison of good and bad revolutions—the American and the French—led him to embrace English conservatism and work it into the fabric of American politics and law.

In truth, this process of cultural amalgamation had begun long before the 1790s and before the Revolution, too. To understand why the Marshalls, father and son, were so quick to take up arms, we need to understand that the Anglo-Virginian culture they knew was as much or more American than it was English. They were prepped for battle, one might say, by having viewed the unfolding crisis of empire from its periphery. Viewed from the Blue Ridge Mountains, where the King's writ did not strike fear (if it ran at all), British authority was amenable to resistance, as young George Washington learned when he witnessed Braddock's defeat by the French and Indians in 1755. More importantly, the English culture the Marshalls and other Virginians admired was from the beginning attenuated by distance and mixed inextricably with a peculiar New World version of self-interest. To put the matter plainly, they were less English than they imagined and more American than they knew. To understand John Marshall's decision to fight and to evaluate the impact on his ideas fighting had, we have to understand this increasingly American amalgam.

Thomas and Mary Keith Marshall bequeathed to their first son a strong measure of Englishness. These intrepid American pioneers left no written paeans of praise to the British Empire, to which they belonged as colonial Virginians, but what they thought was clear from what they did. When they packed the wagons and ventured from the settled sanctuary of Westmoreland County into the wilds of northwest Virginia, they did so in order to recapitulate the Anglicized culture that had taken root along the tidal rivers of eighteenth-century Virginia. Land, slaves, and public office were the measures of social success in this world. Judging by what he accomplished, first in Fauquier

County and then in the new state of Kentucky, Thomas Marshall was very much a part of it.

God's Englishman was also an American pioneer. When Thomas Marshall arrived with his new wife in the outer reaches of Prince Edward County in 1754, there were no institutions of government, no churches or schools. Germantown, as it later came to be called, was nothing but a few scattered cabins. Indian incursions were still a threat. Indeed in 1755, the year John was born, serious uprisings threatened to halt the advance of English settlement. Twenty years later, on the eve of the Revolution, the frontier was no longer raw. And Thomas Marshall was no longer the planter of slender means his son once described him as being. True, his estate was long on land and short on slaves, the surest measure of wealth. Compared to the plantations of Virginia's first families—the Byrds' Westover, the Lees' Stratford Hall, or Robert Carter's Nomini Hall to mention some—Oak Hill was modest indeed. Still, the elder Marshall had by dint of ability and ambition established himself as a man with whom to reckon. As a measure of his new status and the English trajectory of his career, he became sheriff of Fauquier County, which had split off from Prince Edward in 1755; a vestryman of Leeds parish, organized in 1769; a justice of the peace; and a member of the House of Burgesses. All of those offices were English derivatives. So was Marshall's friend and neighbor Thomas, Lord Fairfax, who brought English culture to the Northern Neck and inspired others to do the same. Among Lord Fairfax's proteges was an upwardly mobile young gentleman, also Thomas Marshall's neighbor and friend, by the name of George Washington. At this time in his life, the future commander of the patriot forces was busy implementing *Rules of Civility and Decent Behavior in Company and Conversation,* his homespun version of English gentility, and aspiring to a career as an officer in the British army. Thomas Marshall was not so prominent as his two neighbors, nor so Anglicized. But he aspired to make it in a system permeated with English values, institutions, and culture and was on his way to doing so.[13]

13. Adams, *Autobiographical Sketch by John Marshall,* 3–4; Albert J. Beveridge, *The Life of John Marshall* (Boston, New York, 1916–1919), 1: 1–68, treats Marshall's family and early life in Fauquier County. Ch. 1 in Robarge's dissertation contains a thoroughly researched and concisely written account of Marshall and his family in the frontier setting, which corrects Beveridge's romantic view of Marshall's frontier origins. Robarge, "John Marshall and His Times." On Lord Fairfax, consult Stuart E. Brown Jr., *Virginia Baron: The Story of Thomas, Sixth Lord Fairfax* (Berryville, Va., 1965); on Washington's genteel ways, see W. Guthrie Sayen, " 'A Complete Gentleman': The Making of George Washington, 1732–1775" (Ph.D. diss., University of Connecticut,

Why then did he and his son suddenly turn against the mother country that had nourished them so plenteously? Part of the explanation was that success gave the Marshalls something to lose. Because this was so, the English constitutional rights Blackstone wrote about in his *Commentaries* and Thomas Marshall talked about as a member of the House of Burgesses in the 1760s became pressingly relevant. But there was something else working against English authority, especially for John Marshall. At the very time his family was beginning to acquire the trappings of English gentry, it was becoming un-English. The Blue Ridge country left its mark in ways other than inspiring the young man to emulate Pope and Goldsmith. Augustan England was a distant planet to the people living on the marches of empire. Even Williamsburg, where English ways were supported by the presence of the royal governor and his colonial entourage, was much farther away than the four or five days time it took to travel there. Living was arduous in Fauquier County, even for aspiring gentry. The grueling labor on the Marshall farms was done by slaves, but the oldest son, John, was no doubt involved in the rigorous work of planting and harvesting and marketing. He assisted his father in surveying, too. Hunting and fishing and other outdoor activities went with the territory. So did walking, which according to Story contributed to "that robust and vigorous constitution, which carried him almost to the close of his life with the freshness and firmness of manhood." Lieutenant Marshall thought nothing of the twenty-mile hike to and from the muster field. Later he would hike two hundred miles to and from Philadelphia to get vaccinated against smallpox. As chief justice he was the chief walking companion and confidant of President John Quincy Adams. Only a few years before Marshall's death, Edward Everett reported seeing the old chief justice still walking to the Court on a bitter March day with no hat and his coat blowing in the wind—a scene that prompted the puritanical New Englander to wonder how a man who had sown some wild oats as a youth could justly reap such a harvest of good health in his old age.[14]

One wonders why, in a culture that celebrated horsemanship, Marshall

---

1998). Rhys Isaac describes the Tidewater society (to which the Marshalls did *not* belong) and much else relevant to understanding Virginia culture in *The Transformation of Virginia, 1740–1790* (Chapel Hill, N.C., 1982). On the Anglicization of Virginia culture, see John Murrin, "The Great Inversion, or, Court versus Country: A Comparison of the Revolution Settlements in England and America," in *Three British Revolutions: 1641, 1688, 1776,* ed. J. G. A. Pocock (Princeton, N.J., 1980), 368–453.

14. Story, *Miscellaneous Writings,* 646; Edward Everett to Mrs. Everett, 25 February 1831, Everett Papers, Massachusetts Historical Society, Boston.

walked so much. He did ride, of course, and had a small stable at his Richmond residence. He knew horses, too, at least well enough to bet on them regularly at the Richmond track. But great Virginia horsemen, like Washington or John Randolph of Roanoke, would never hike to Philadelphia and back when they could ride. One can rest assured the elegant Randolph would not be caught dead either riding a mule, as Marshall reputedly did to his Chickahominy farm. Walking, we might speculate, like his disregard for stylish dressing and the uncultivated twang in his speech (gently derided by John Randolph), was a vestigial attribute of frontier living. It distinguished him from the Anglicized gentry of the Tidewater and reminded him that he was not born to the purple.[15]

Small matters, perhaps, but they suggest that John Marshall's frontier was a middle landscape between the Anglicized Tidewater and the outposts of English settlement where survival called the tune. There was much about the Tidewater aristocracy that appealed to Marshall—the most conspicuous thing being land and the most pervasive being power, which he duly celebrated at the Virginia ratifying convention in 1788. But the cultural pull of Fauquier County was more to the west than it was to the east, and the gravity of Old England could hardly be felt at all. If the beauties of frontier Virginia could seduce an Old England man such as Thomas, Lord Fairfax into becoming a Virginian at heart, think what it could do to a young man who had never seen the Old Country or much of the Tidewater version of it either. Later in Marshall's life, when the ideological winds blew strong and the duties of office weighed heavily, he would return for peace of mind and perspective to "the upper country." His Virginia home and his family gave him peace of mind. But the perspective he got from the Blue Ridge looking west was American not English. To borrow a notion from Robert Frost's poem "The Gift Outright," the Marshalls started out owning land (the more the better); by the time of the Revolution, the land "possessed" them.

The point is one that Frederick Jackson Turner would make a century later: life on the frontier—an experience Marshall would share with millions of other Americans—instilled a set of cultural values that was not English or exclusively Virginian either. With a modification or two, Marshall could have been a youthful version of Hector Saint John de Crèvecoeur's new American man, "who, leaving behind him all his ancient prejudices and manners, receives new

15. William C. Bruce, *John Randolph of Roanoke, 1773–1833: A Biography Based Largely on New Material* (1922; reprint, New York, 1970), 2: 128.

ones from the new mode of life he has embraced." The qualification was that Marshall did not really leave behind the English ideas he learned from his father and his tutors and from his books. Frontier living did not divest him of his English inheritance, but rather taught him a version of individualism and freedom that imparted special meaning to the English-Lockean-Blackstonian ideas of life, liberty, and estate—a meaning they could not have in the land-scarce, class-bound Sceptered Isle. It would not be a stretch to speculate that his experience on the frontier, where common sense regularly trumped theory, had something to do with his later affinity for the "common sense" Scottish philosophers Thomas Reid and Dugald Stewart, whose ideas were popular in the early Republic. It was Reid's contention that nature rightly observed might yield knowledge and that common-sense reasoning was self-validating and open to all. It is doubtful that young Marshall read Reid's *An Inquiry into the Human Mind on the Principles of Common Sense,* the bible of common sense philosophy. However, both of his tutors were university-educated Scots during the time Reid taught moral philosophy at the University of Glasgow, so it seems likely Marshall was familiar with common sense ideas.[16]

If Marshall and his fellow Americans came to like common sense philosophers, it was for the same reason they resonated with John Locke: because these intellectuals refined and legitimated what they learned from experience. Marshall, like others of the founding generation, would draw on the Old World to govern the New. But he would do so on his own terms and in his own voice. In more ways than the frontier drawl, Marshall's language, like Lincoln's later, never lost its native character. His maiden speech at Culpeper muster, his speeches at the Virginia ratifying convention, his hard-hitting diplomatic reports to President Adams in the XYZ affair, his speech about Jonathan Robbins in the House of Representatives in 1800—all bear the markings of an American plain style William Wirt would praise in 1803 as simplicity and logic raised to the level of eloquence.[17]

This is not to argue that Fauquier County instantly transformed the young man into an American. English ideas and Tidewater models were always close by, but in almost every instance, the leveling effect of the frontier could be seen.

16. J. Hector Saint John de Crèvecoeur, *Letters from an American Farmer* (1782; reprint, New York, 1926), 43; Richard B. Sher and Jeffrey Smitten, eds., *Scotland and America in the Age of the Enlightenment* (Princeton, N.J., 1990); Richard Beale Davis, *Intellectual Life in Jefferson's Virginia, 1790–1830* (Knoxville, Tenn., 1964).

17. William Wirt, *The Letters of the British Spy* (1803; reprint, Chapel Hill, N.C., 1970), 178–85.

Thomas and Mary Keith Marshall were not role models for the English country gentry. Thomas Marshall did teach his son to cherish family and to assume the role of patriarch. Family was all-important to John Marshall, but it was family with a distinctively democratic twist. There is no evidence that he attached any great significance to his Randolph ancestry, as his friend John Randolph of Roanoke did. While he showed great interest in the welfare of his family and kin, he showed little interest in family genealogy. Never, in word or deed, did he even hint that bloodline should be preferred over ability in the scale of social advancement. He had no truck either with the English doctrine of primogeniture and entail—the legal system whereby family unity was maintained by providing that the estate would pass unbroken to the first son. Neither, judging from their wills, had Marshall's forebears. As the oldest of fifteen children, John did assume responsibility for the collective well-being of his younger brothers and sisters—a duty he generously performed the rest of his life. But primogeniture for him was a matter of responsibility, not legal privilege. It was patriarchy in a democratic context. If Thomas lavished special care on his first son in education and in the technique of surviving and prospering on the frontier, it was with the notion that he would pass the lessons he learned on to his younger brothers and look to the well-being of his sisters. This peculiar American variant of an English idea made John Marshall the center of an extended network of brothers, sisters, nieces and nephews, and grandchildren—even family slaves. Not surprisingly, the patriarchal motif is also found in his jurisprudence, most conspicuously as regards Native Americans, and in his approach to judging itself.[18]

One final attribute of English aristocracy that lost its meaning on the American frontier was entail, the legal principle and social concept that the landed estate of a family cannot be diminished and must descend to the eldest son. Entail didn't make legal sense in America, where land was abundant. As a social concept it made no sense either, at least to Thomas Marshall and through the father to his son. Acquiring land, as we shall see, was a lifelong obsession Thomas Marshall passed on to his son. Indeed the Marshall family land operation—composed of the elder Marshall, his sons John and James Markham, and later their brother-in-law Rawleigh Colston—was one of the most effective

18. For Marshall family wills, see William McClung Paxton, *The Marshall Family* (1885; reprint, Baltimore, 1988), 10, 14, 23–24. For John Marshall's revised will of 9 April 1832, see PJM, typescript, Williamsburg, Virginia. Christopher L. Doyle explores the concept and practice of patriarchy in Virginia in "Lord, Master, and Patriot, St. George Tucker and Patriarchy in Republican Virginia, 1772–1851" (Ph.D. diss., University of Connecticut, 1996).

land-getting operations in Virginia. Its objective, however, was not to amass a single landed estate that could descend through the ages from eldest son to eldest son. Thomas Marshall's dream, like that of his son later, rather was to acquire enough land so every family member could inherit a hefty share. Buying and selling and moving on, as Tocqueville would later observe, was a peculiarly American trait. Indeed, it was a trait that made sense only in the American setting, where land was for the taking. Thomas Marshall took. While the Revolutionary War was still being fought, the colonel took time off to check prospects west of the Alleghenies. In 1785 he moved west with his family, as he always had—first from Westmoreland to Fauquier, then to the rich bottomland of Fayette County, Kentucky, where he staked out a large piece of choice land for his home place. In his pursuit of his New World dream, Thomas Marshall no longer needed Old England. He and his son took what the mother country had to offer, and when she demanded something back, they quickly turned away.[19]

Even before they marched off to war, Thomas Marshall and his son had acquired the habit of viewing the British Empire in Virginia from the American frontier. After the Treaty of Paris of 1763 ending the French and Indian War, the prospect was expansive indeed. Like most other Virginians, Thomas Marshall was proud when Britain expelled Catholic France from the Ohio Valley, when Britain lessened the danger of Indian attack, and when (at least until the Proclamation of 1763) it opened new lands for speculation in the trans-Allegheny west. On the other hand, with the French gone and the Indians in retreat, the need for British authority was significantly diminished, leaving only habit and sentiment to take the place of necessity. Those qualities were in short supply, especially in places like Fauquier County. In that distant corner of the empire, there were no shared social moments with royal officials to deepen the affection for the king or respect for British authority; no fox hunting with royal governors, no musical evenings at the governor's palace in Williamsburg (as Jefferson enjoyed as a young student). Absent the social and symbolic trappings of royal authority, what remained as the main link to England was an intellectual affinity to English culture and especially a tenacious attachment to

19. Rhys Isaac relates the boom in land speculation in the region between the Chesapeake and the Blue Ridge to new social mobility and the rise of the ethos of individualism. *Transformation of Virginia*, 311–12. Regarding the land speculations of John Marshall and his family, I am greatly indebted to the editors of *The Papers of John Marshall* for their exacting scholarship. PJM, 1: 100–4. Thomas Marshall's move to Kentucky and the beginning of his land speculation as surveyor of Fayette County is recounted briefly in Paxton, *Marshall Family*, 21–24.

English constitutional rights. The rights of Englishmen, including those in North America, coupled with a deep attachment to home and hearth and to perceived self-interest was an explosive, indeed, a literally revolutionary combination, as events after 1765 would show. Americans-in-the-making like Thomas Marshall were English enough to assume they deserved to be treated as Englishmen; they were enough non-English to look at English concessions with the calculating eyes of those who had something to lose. The moral outrage supplied by radical Whig ideology was grounded on perceived self-interest. When it came time to shoot and kill, Americans like the Marshalls discovered that the binding ties were already frayed beyond mending.[20]

This mixture of British culture (some radical Whig ideas, a touch of Blackstone, an instilled love of property and liberty) and the Latin classics, along with abundant native American experience, transformed John Marshall into the "principled soldier" he took pride in being. The principles he fought for were to a large degree constitutional in nature. What made them so was the decade-long debate in Virginia about the rights of Virginians under the British constitution, beginning with the Stamp Act crisis in 1765. Here in the tiny colonial capital of Williamsburg, in the House of Burgesses, which had audaciously begun to think of its powers as resembling those of Parliament, the great question of imperial home rule was contested and also the question of "who should rule at home." At issue were fundamental questions concerning the location of authority in a federal system, the relationship of constitutional law and self-interested politics, and, indeed, the rule of law itself. The man who brought home the lessons of this debate was John Marshall's father. The elder Marshall was a member of the House of Burgesses from 1761 to 1767, 1769 to 1773, and again in 1775 until he volunteered for active military duty. Thomas Marshall either witnessed or participated in those defining events wherein colonial self-interest came to be seen by a newborn class of Virginia statesmen as a matter of rights—first English and then American. He was one of the burgesses who voted resolutions of protest against the Stamp Act of 1765 and who protested the Declaratory Act of 1766, in which Parliament contemptuously declared its absolute sovereignty over the colonies. These events charted the course of escalating revolutionary sentiment in Virginia, and through his father the son was, from the youthful age of six on, a vicarious participant. By bring-

20. John M. Murrin, "A Roof without Walls: The Dilemma of American National Identity," in *Beyond Confederation: Origins of the Constitution and American National Identity*, eds. Richard Beeman, Stephen Botein, and Edward C. Carter II (Chapel Hill, N.C., 1987), 333–48.

ing the struggles of empire home to the Blue Ridge, Thomas Marshall taught the future chief justice his first lessons in constitutional history.[21]

Thomas Marshall also first acquainted his young son with a cast of Virginia heroes, ones the young man could readily match to the orators and statesman he read about in his study of the Latin classics. One such giant was Patrick Henry, who put Virginia in the patriot vanguard and inspired a generation of young men like Marshall to follow suit. (The two men would meet again as friendly adversaries in the courts of Virginia; as not-so-friendly political opponents in the Virginia ratifying convention and in the 1790s; and finally, in 1799, as allies against radical states' rights in Virginia.) More influential still in Marshall's life—as model, patron, and friend—was George Washington. Marshall's father and Washington were not social equals, nor were they intimate friends, though unsubstantiated family tradition has it that Washington hired Marshall as a surveyor. However, they were Northern Neck neighbors, which meant they shared a political/economic outlook common to that region. Both were avid land speculators, which fact also signified a common entrepreneurial outlook. In the 1760s, they were patriots-in-the-making, jointly caught up in the events that led to the Revolution—enough so that John Marshall could view the father of his country and his own father as comrades-in-arms. As delegates to the House of Burgesses in 1765, both men supported Patrick Henry's Stamp Act resolutions. Neither Washington (for certain) nor Thomas Marshall (in all likelihood) had given up on a peaceful settlement of disputes with England at this early date. But Washington correctly perceived what John Marshall later came to believe, that the conflict between England and its colonies was constitutional in nature—that it was a clash between the colonists, who demanded self-government in matters of internal taxation, and the British, who claimed absolute sovereignty over the colonies, which claim they implemented in the Townsend duties of 1767 and the Tea Tax of 1771. Virginia's opposition to these measures was by no means united, but it was particularly strong in the Northern Neck counties. Among those who grew increasingly radical (along with Washington) was Thomas Marshall. He returned to the House of Burgesses in 1770, when the conflict boiled up again. He was there

21. For revival of the once prominent notion that the Revolution was constitutional (and legal) in nature, see John Phillip Reid, *Constitutional History of the American Revolution,* 3 vols. (Madison, Wis., 1986–1993). See also Reid, *Constitutional History of the American Revolution: Abridged Edition* (Madison, Wis., 1995). Jack Greene commented on "The Significance of John Reid's Scholarship," at the 1997 meeting of the American Society of Legal History in Minneapolis, Minn., and related Reid's work to that of others who have mined the field.

in March 1775, when the House of Burgesses voted to create a new provisional Virginia militia. He was one of the sixty-five burgesses to vote for it, as against sixty in opposition, and he was one of the first to organize a militia unit under its authorization. When John joined the ranks in the summer of 1775, he cast his vote as well.[22] John Marshall was a principled soldier in a constitutional war; he was a republican one as well. If the war was fought for the good of all and the rights of all, as he said it was in his short speech at Culpeper, then joining the fight made him a *res publica,* a public vessel. Indeed, it was no huge leap of imagination to get from the noble Romans in Plutarch's *Lives* to Patrick Henry, Washington, and his own father. Old ideas took on new meaning. History vouched for by Thomas Marshall boiled down to a compelling proposition: that men of honor and republican virtue should stand and fight for their constitutional rights and the principles of liberty. In the fighting, the notion of honor and the ideology of republicanism would be sanctified by blood.

"Principled Soldier" in a Constitutional War

Logically speaking, waging war and creating a government based on the rule of law are incompatible undertakings. This logic may explain why, until recently, constitutional historians ignored the actual fighting and why military historians generally ignored constitutional developments. John Marshall, as biographer of George Washington and military historian of the Revolution, did not, however, separate military and constitutional history. His massive five-volume work (1805–1807) has been dismissed as derivative, excessively worshipful, and lacking in analysis—all with some justification. One key point that Marshall did *not* miss about the Revolution, however, was the one Karl von Clausewitz would later put to words: that "war is simply the continuation of policy by other means." Daniel Webster made the same point later when he marveled that Americans "went to war for a preamble" and "fought seven years for a declaration." Even after the Declaration of Independence and, indeed, while the armies were in the field, Americans continued to debate constitutional issues as they struggled to develop working institutions of government

22. For Thomas Marshall's involvement in the pre-Revolutionary debates in Virginia, I've drawn on Beveridge, *Life of John Marshall,* 1: 58–65. On Washington's pre-Revolutionary constitutional ideas, see Glenn A. Phelps, *George Washington and American Constitutionalism* (Lawrence, Kans., 1993), ch. 1.

sufficiently energetic to wage a long war. Constitutional debate also took place at the state level. Faced with the necessity of reconstituting themselves as self-governing political societies outside the empire, every state but two revised their constitutions. In the process they institutionalized the great constitutional principle of the Revolution: that the people are sovereign and speak constitutionally only in organic convention. To say that the adoption of the Constitution in 1788 completed the Revolution—which Marshall's contemporaries and modern historians agree was the case—is only to reassert the obvious: that military, political, and constitutional history were inextricably connected in the War for Independence. It is not simply that colonial wars of independence are constitutional by definition, but that mobilizing for war, negotiating treaties with allies, and keeping an army in the field raise fundamental questions of governance. In running the army, George Washington learned something about running the country. John Shy put the matter aptly when he said that the Revolution "was a political education conducted by military means."[23]

The war was a constitutional education for Marshall because it was a colonial revolution that was justified by legal arguments and that had as its objective the creation of a nation under law. Marshall listened to the constitutional arguments that preceded the fighting; he took part in the constitutional arguments that followed it. Strange as it may seem, he was also educated constitutionally by the fighting itself. In the course of the war, he observed the fighting from several vantage points: as a militiaman; as an officer in the Continental line; and with his appointment in November 1777 as a deputy judge advocate attached to Washington's staff. Though not a combat hero like fellow Virginians Daniel Morgan and Light-Horse Harry Lee, Marshall stood his ground when the bullets were flying. After the bloody Battle of Great Bridge, he skirmished with British regulars again at Iron Hill, Delaware. In the Pennsylvania campaign during 1777, he fought at Brandywine Creek, at Chadds Ford on September 11, and at Germantown on October 3 and 4, where he was wounded slightly in the hand. As part of a unit assigned to protect artillery, he witnessed the American retreat at Monmouth Court House in June 1778. He

---

23. Marshall, *The Life of George Washington*, 5 vols. (Philadelphia, 1804–1807). The story of Marshall's authorship, one of the most fully documented aspects of his life, is treated admirably in vol. 6 of the PJM. Marshall spent most of the rest of his life revising and correcting the first printing, an effort that culminated in the previously cited revised and corrected 2d ed. Webster is quoted in Hannah Arendt, *On Revolution* (New York, 1963), 68. For the constitutional dimensions of fighting, consult the following: Higginbotham, *War and Society*; Shy, *A People Numerous and Armed*, especially ch. 10; also see Shy's "The American Revolution," in *Essays on the American Revolution*, eds. Kurtz and Hutson.

was on the field during the memorable confrontation between Washington and Charles Lee during that engagement, which ended with Lee's acquittal on formal charges of cowardice and his subsequent resignation from the army. When others went home, he stayed. He endured the grim winter bivouac at Valley Forge in 1777–1778 and the almost equally devastating one the following winter. In July 1779 in New York, he was part of the support unit that backed Anthony Wayne's assault on Stony Point. He also served in the force sent to relieve his friend Henry Lee after the Battle of Paulus Hook, August 19, 1779.[24]

Unlike Oliver Wendell Holmes Jr., the other great American justice whose ideas about law were shaped by soldiering, Marshall left no reminiscences about his military experience. Probably it was true, as Story later observed, that "amidst the din of arms, he found no leisure to study the science of government." Still, in the long stretch between battles, Marshall had time to ponder some experiential truths regarding the practical art of governance. One such had to do with human nature itself. As a soldier at ease, he appreciated the temptations of the flesh and joked about them later in a letter to his friend Thomas Posey. We must assume that as a combat soldier Marshall felt the rush of fear and exhilaration. At the Battle of Great Bridge, he saw bravery and praised it, even when it credited the enemy. He witnessed cowardice as well; saw and condemned treachery and deceit—saving his harshest blast not for British spy Major John Andre but for American-turned-redcoat Benedict Arnold. As associate judge advocate, Marshall meted out the harsh punishments of martial law, perhaps with the same conviction about maintaining discipline that prompted Washington to deal harshly with young men who deserted. In the unfortunate clash between Washington and Lee at Monmouth Court House—if Marshall's account of the episode in his biography of Washington provides a clue—he came to understand, in a Shakespearean sense, how good men could clash, how pride could destroy what talent wrought. If he looked very closely, which he did, he saw that pluck and blind chance often counted as much as planning. Judging from his account of Washington's leadership, Marshall also concluded that moral stature, courage, and the sheer will to win could trump contingency and maybe even beat the relentless cycle of history that was supposed to doom republican governments.[25]

24. Beveridge discusses Marshall's military career in *Life of John Marshall*, 1: ch. 3.

25. Story, *Miscellaneous Writings*, 651. Marshall jokingly alludes to "our Camp Ladies" in his letter to Thomas Posey, 1 September 1779, PJM, 1: 34. He praises British captain Fordyce in his *Life of George Washington*, 1: 69, and condemns Arnold as "a sordid traitor," *Life of George Washington*, 1: 381–82. For Marshall's balanced view of the Lee-Washington confrontation at

Marshall not only saw Washington in action—"the greatest Man on earth," he called Washington in 1784—but observed the American people at war. The contrast put his youthful vision of a virtuous citizenry to the test. When he marched off to war he was, as he later recounted, full of "wild and enthusiastic" notions about the virtues of the people. During the first year of war, as the *rage militaire* swept over the country, this faith seemed well placed. When the hope of a sudden glorious victory turned into the prospect of a long, bloody war, when the human and financial costs of war became reality, however, patriotism turned into bickering, dissension, and desertion. Enlistments declined, and many who signed on came late and left early. Those willing to fight increasingly preferred short-term militia duty, which, as they understood it, would keep them close to home and free to tend crops and family between battles. As Marshall would observe at the Virginia ratifying convention, the militia, which Patrick Henry was praising as the backbone of republican virtue, was often not there when it was most needed. The "spirit of liberty," another of Henry's favorite phrases, alone did not turn the tide at Chadds Ford or Germantown. At Valley Forge, where his comrades went without shoes and food while the sunshine patriots in nearby Philadelphia traded much-needed supplies for British specie, Marshall learned about the meaning of patriotism—and the lack of it. It is a good guess that he agreed with the sentiments of his friend and fellow soldier Henry Lee, who noted at the Virginia convention that talk was cheap and action dear, that those who jawed most eloquently about "the goddess liberty" were often not on the field of battle to defend it.[26]

One hastens to add that Marshall was not disillusioned with military action as an instrument of politics. What appalled him was not war but the war *effort*. Experiencing a lack of it, he distilled some hard lessons about the limits of human perfectibility, which figured prominently in his conservative interpretation of American republicanism. His conservatism, however, was not sunk in doom and gloom. In his scheme of things, hope, faith, optimism—those mysterious qualities Marshall got from a hearty constitution nourished by the frontier—did not disappear. He also retained the aristocratic lesson his age, and his father, taught him: that some men were more virtuous than others and some were born to lead and others to follow. His military experience confirmed what

---

Monmouth, see *Life of George Washington*, 1: 253–54. For Marshall's likely role as judge advocate in the court-martial of Sergeant Athanasius Farber and Private John Burk, see PJM, 1: 15 n. 2.

26. Marshall praised Washington in his letter to James Monroe, 3 January 1784, PJM, 1: 113. See also Adams, *Autobiographical Sketch by John Marshall*, 9. For Lee's remarks, see VRD, 2: 1072–73.

culture taught: that Americans did not rally en masse to the war effort or queue up to bolster Washington's depleted ranks when things got desperate in 1777 and 1778. Ninety thousand on paper, two thousand in the field, said a lot about human nature to those inclined to listen.

So, too, did the shortsighted behavior of the state governments throughout the war. Elected by the most liberal franchise in the western world and claiming sovereignty under the Articles of Confederation, these governments regularly failed to supply Washington with the men and supplies he desperately needed and constantly pleaded for. In his biography, Marshall let Washington speak for himself about the dangers of state provincialism. As a fighting man, Marshall *felt* the problem and what he felt took a serious toll on his early idealism. Like the leading Federalist theorists, Marshall readily acknowledged that the people were the ultimate source of power in a republic; as chief justice he would connect the Supreme Court to them. Whether the people had the necessary wisdom and virtue to *actually* govern was far less certain in his view of things. How they could be sovereign and *not* at the same time govern directly would be a central problem in his jurisprudence as well as in American political theory.

Closely connected to the question of popular government was that of leadership. Here, too, the lessons of war for Marshall were conservative in nature—but with a decided twist of frontier egalitarianism. Military rank was not an obsession with him, as it was with some Virginia gentlemen who harassed Washington and impeded the war effort by their hankering for promotion. As a junior officer in a line company, he was far removed from Washington's staff, though as deputy judge advocate he met Hamilton and possibly the general himself. Judging by his actions at Valley Forge, Marshall chose to gain the respect of his men not by pulling rank or social class, but by outracing and outjumping them and by treating them equally and honorably as befitted fellow citizens in the new Republic. While he was highly respectful of rank, he did not see the officer corps as a permanent class and would surely have been repelled by the arrogant pronouncement of the Marquis de Crenolle in 1776, that "officers are the 'purest part of the nation.'" Here as in many other areas of Marshall's personal life, frontier democracy saved him from the arrogance of Tidewater aristocracy.[27]

Still there was much in Marshall's wartime experience to confirm the con-

27. Beveridge makes much of Marshall's Valley Forge experience in *Life of John Marshall*, 1: ch. 4. Crenolle is quoted in Higginbotham, *War and Society*, 87.

servative lesson of Virginia's elite political culture: that it was the moral obligation of the "best" men to lead, just as it was the civic duty of the rest to follow. With him, however, noblesse oblige was more oblige and less *noblesse*. That deferential arrangement was also built into the Revolutionary military establishment at a number of different points, but most conspicuously in the Continental line. Washington's major fighting force was not a standing army in the British and European sense of the word, since the idea was anathema to republican principles of individualism and liberty. From the beginning—and in contrast to the state-based, democratically oriented militia—the nation's army emphasized the need for order and discipline. Those in charge—Washington, his field generals at the top who established the system, and line officers who administered it—came almost exclusively from the ranks of the well-off and wellborn. Their responsibility for maintaining order and punishing theft, drunkenness, and disobedience in the ranks, even maintaining a certain amount of religious decorum, was not unlike the traditional duties assumed by the colonial gentry. Commanding was a form of governance. Although most Revolutionary officers did not see themselves as a permanent professional military class, they did think of themselves as natural leaders—in peace as well as in war.[28]

Such was the reasoning of the officers who organized the Order of Cincinnatus and who drew on the bonds forged by "virtuous suffering, in danger and in glory," as Marshall put it, to create a strong national government. There is no evidence Marshall joined the order, but he believed emphatically that those who led in battle deserved a place of honor in times of peace. His experience in the war, one might say, confirmed the lessons of classical history and validated the deferential structure of late eighteenth-century Virginia government and society. Given this connection between fighting and governing, it was natural that his biography of Washington gave so much prominence to military history and that the narrative moved so easily from Washington the general to Washington the president. Indeed, it was General Washington who embodied the meaning of the Revolution. This was true for a whole generation of Americans, but it was especially true for Marshall. The great man took the young man under his wing. When Washington made Lieutenant Marshall deputy judge advocate during the war, when he offered Marshall the attorney generalship of the United States and backed him for Congress in 1799, Washington

28. On the army during and immediately following the Revolution, see Royster, *A Revolutionary People at War,* especially ch. 2 and 8.

acted not just as a patron but as a deeply revered friend and neighbor. Put simply, Washington was Marshall's Cato. "Be Cato's friend," as Trenchard and Gordon put it in *Cato's Letters* to the young men of the American Revolution, and "he'll train thee up to great and virtuous deeds." Virtuous deeds, for Washington and for Marshall, included constitution making and nation building. Washington in fact was a serious constitutional thinker, and orchestrating the war effort helped make him so. He built on a realistic assessment of human nature, both its limits and its strengths. He knew that good leadership, properly advertised, brought out the best in people. And he came to see that the energy of inspired leaders might be imparted to government itself. No less important was the distinction he drew, even when invited to think otherwise, between government and those who governed. He could probably have taken America in the direction of a constitutional monarchy. Instead he championed constitutional government, in which law ruled and not men—not even virtuous men such as himself.[29]

The most immediate lesson Washington learned, and imparted to his young admirer, was the danger of self-interest and ambition when linked to localism and state sovereignty. Judging from the letters Marshall would quote in his biography, Washington spent nearly as much energy fighting a weak-kneed Congress and self-centered states as he did the British army. He came to believe, and lived to embody, what Edmund Burke expressed so powerfully in his statement about the revolutionary agitation in America in 1770: "that no men could act with effect, who did not act in concert; that no men could act in concert, who did not act in confidence; that no men could act with confidence, who were not bound together by common opinions, common affections, and common interests." Men bound together by "some great, *leading, general principles,*" to use Burke's words, were essential to the survival and well-being of the new nation. What bound Marshall's "principled soldiers" of the Revolution together was a shared "devotion to the union, and to a government competent to its preservation." After a half century the message of that glorious age imparted was still vivid in his mind. Marshall's brief statement sums up the continuity and the change that came over his mind as he grew from a boy to man, how a glass that had been half empty on the eve of the Revolution became half full by its conclusion. In his words:

29. Cato as quoted in Garry Wills, *Cincinnatus: George Washington and The Enlightenment* (Garden City, N.Y., 1984), 27. For Marshall's moving statement about Revolutionary officers, and about the Order of Cincinnatus, see his *Life of George Washington,* 2: 71–73, 77.

I had grown up at a time when a love of union and resistance to the claims of Great Britain were inseparable inmates of the same bosom; . . . when the maxim 'united we stand, divided we fall' was the maxim of every orthodox American; and I had imbibed these sentiments so thoroughly that they constituted a part of my being. I carried them with me into the army where I found myself associated with brave men from different states who were risking life and everything valuable in a common cause believed by all to be most precious; and where I was confirmed in the habit of considering America as my country, and congress as my government.[30]

Federalist in the Making, 1781–1788

Looking back over the war years and forward to the nineteenth century, Benjamin Rush observed to his friend John Adams, "The War for Independence is over: but this is far from being the case with the American revolution. On the contrary, nothing but the first act of the great drama is closed. It remains yet to establish and perfect our new forms of government, and to prepare the principles, morals, and manners of our citizens for these forms of government after they are established and brought to perfection." How prescient he was. Recent scholarship has shown that there was hardly an aspect of American society that was not touched by the dislocating forces accompanying the violent separation from England. Without the restraints imposed by English mercantilism, American entrepreneurs explored new markets and new economic ideas as well. Old ideas, such as those of John Locke, took on new meaning. Vast and unintended social change accompanied economic independence as traditional relationships between husbands and wives, parents and children, and between classes were recast in light of republican ideology. Established religion felt the tremors of egalitarian ideas. So did the institution of slavery. Most pressing, Americans were forced to reconstitute existing colonial governmental institutions and ideas to fit the needs of a newly free and independent people. In depth, sophistication, and the degree of popular engagement, the ensuing debate over consti-

---

30. Edmund Burke's *Thoughts on the Cause of the Present Discontents* (1770) is quoted in Richard Hofstadter, *The Idea of a Party System: The Rise of a Legitimate Opposition in the United States, 1780–1840* (Berkeley, Calif., 1969), 31–32. For Marshall quotes, see *Life of George Washington*, 2: 77; Adams, *Autobiographical Sketch by John Marshall*, 9–10.

tutional government was unique in American history. Nowhere was the debate more profound or the results more far-reaching than in Virginia.[31]

Marshall listened to and participated in this great debate—as a private citizen, as a rising lawyer in Richmond in the 1780s, as a member of the House of Delegates, and in 1788 as a delegate from Richmond and Henrico County to the state ratifying convention. Progressively during these years, his inchoate ideas about governance learned before and during the Revolution took concrete form. The challenge here is to explain why, and how, in a period of six or so years after leaving the army, Marshall should emerge in 1788 as a forceful spokesman for the new Constitution—one that cut significantly into the power of his own state, which he loved dearly, where he had been both happy and successful, and where he planned to, and would, spend the rest of his life.

The challenge is even more difficult and intriguing when it is recalled that other distinguished Virginians who had served their country ably in the Revolution came to sharply different conclusions about what it meant in terms of government. Marshall could have chosen, as did many of Virginia's most prominent leaders, to strengthen the national government by amending the existing Articles of Confederation. He could have made ratification contingent on prior amendments guaranteeing states' rights, or he could have demanded a second constitutional convention to address the problem. He chose instead to defend the new Constitution without reservation, this in the face of serious misgivings and bitter opposition by fellow Virginians, many of whom were friends and professional colleagues. For a second time, this young conservative-in-the-making chose the path of radical reform. The question is why?

Marshall's own answer to the question was beguilingly simple. Looking back near the end of his life on this period of constitutional gestation, he accounted for his unwavering support of the Constitution in plain language: "I partook largely of the suffering and the feelings of the army, and brought with me into civil life an ardent devotion to its interests. My immediate entrance into the state legislature opened to my view the causes which had been chiefly instrumental in augmenting those sufferings, and the general tendency of state politics convinced me that no safe and permanent remedy could be found but in a more efficient and better organized general government." And so it was.

31. Adams's letter to Rush is quoted in Bailyn, *Ideological Origins*, 230. Gordon S. Wood, *The Radicalism of the American Revolution* (New York, 1992) is the leading book on the transformative nature of the Revolution.

Soldiering made him a nationalist, and serving in the Virginia legislature in the 1780s confirmed what the war taught.[32]

Still the question of motivation is not fully answered. To understand why Marshall drew nationalist conclusions from the Revolution when others experienced it as a validation of states' rights takes us beyond republican virtue, of which Marshall had plenty, and into the area of perceived self-interest. This is not to deny the truth of his own explanation or to gainsay the possibility that principle alone can move men to action. Nor does it diminish the connection often made by biographers between his wartime experience and his jurisprudence. Anachronism invites simplicity. We need to remind ourselves that the young lawyer who grew increasingly distressed with states' rights politics in Virginia in the 1780s was not the future chief justice of the United States, or even yet the budding statesman who championed the Constitution at the Virginia convention. Legislative experience at the state level clearly influenced his nationalism, as it did James Madison's. But the manner in which Marshall interpreted that experience was influenced by the fact that he was a returning veteran who wanted to make up for lost time and a privileged young man whose taste of the good life inspired him to want more of it. He wanted more because he was in love with a socially well-placed young woman whose hand he wanted to win and whose family he needed to impress. It is not that Marshall's public philosophy was merely a reflection of his own interests, but rather that the two things cannot be separated, except by disregarding the complexity and contingency of human behavior. Self-interest and public interest were not mutually exclusive in his developing view of constitutional nationalism, nor would they be in his mature jurisprudence.[33]

Marshall returned to civilian life in 1781, the year Washington's army defeated the British at Yorktown. He could now go to work for himself, and there

32. Adams, *Autobiographical Sketch by John Marshall*, 10.

33. The tendency of recent scholarship, with which I agree, is to put liberalism (capitalism) back into the republican age. Among those whom I have consulted on the issue are: Joyce Appleby, *Capitalism and a New Social Order: The Republican Vision of the 1790s* (New York, 1984); Lance Banning, "Jeffersonian Ideology Revisited: Liberal and Classical Ideas in the New American Republic," *William and Mary Quarterly* 43 (January 1986): 3–19; Joyce Appleby, "Republicanism in Old and New Contexts," *William and Mary Quarterly* 43: 20–34; Michael Merrill, "Putting 'Capitalism' in Its Place: A Review of Recent Literature," *William and Mary Quarterly* 52 (April 1995): 315–26. Steven Watts, *The Republic Reborn: War and the Making of Liberal America, 1790–1820* (Baltimore, 1987), weighs in on the side of those who depict liberal capitalism as a key feature of the early Republic.

was much catching up to be done. His life had been on hold for six years, during which he had witnessed a sharp dislocation in his family's fortunes, which were not all that great to start with, especially when divided by fifteen. At the age of twenty-five, he was desperate to recover lost ground: to get himself a profession, to make some money, to bring some honor to his family name, all of which would permit him to do what above all else he most earnestly wanted to do, which was to make Miss Mary Ambler his wife.

The two young people met at Yorktown sometime in the winter 1779–1780, when Mary, or Polly as she was familiarly called, was only fourteen. Captain Marshall, on extended furlough waiting to be reassigned (which he never was), had gone there to visit his father. Colonel Thomas Marshall, commander of a garrison of Virginia troops stationed in Yorktown, was headquartered in a house next to where the Amblers were living temporarily. Mary Ambler was the second of four daughters of Jaquelin and Rebecca Burwell Ambler. Both the Burwells and Amblers were "first families," though Jaquelin Ambler's considerable fortune had been seriously diminished by the war. Most likely, Thomas Marshall knew Jaquelin before the war, but in any case, while at Yorktown, he served as a kind of guardian to Mrs. Ambler and the girls during the frequent absences of Mr. Ambler. He also helped the Ambler family relocate to Richmond in 1780, when Jaquelin, his fortunes on the rise, assumed duties as state treasurer.

Whether at this early stage Thomas Marshall weighed the advantages that would accrue to his son by marrying into the Ambler family, we don't know. Given his ambition for John's advancement and the customary Virginia habit of marrying up when the opportunity occurred, the possibility is good that Thomas did. In any case, he appears to have shared his son's letters with the Ambler girls, no doubt adding a proud father's gloss on them. Thus Captain Marshall's reputation as a dutiful son and a courageous soldier arrived before he did. Indeed, so attractive was the resulting image of the dashing hero that it set up a friendly rivalry among the sisters as to who would win his heart. When the young man himself showed up at the Christmas ball in ill-fitting frontier garb, with some plain manners to match, the race ended before it started— except for Polly. Family legend has it that the young lady had already "set her hat" at Captain John.[34]

34. Adams, *Autobiographical Sketch by John Marshall*, 6–7. The quote comes from Francis Norton Mason, *My Dearest Polly: Letters of Chief Justice John Marshall to His Wife, with Their*

In truth, much of the pursuing was done by Marshall himself, and it was not, by his own recollection, all smooth sailing. Still, things did look up after his lackluster debut at the Christmas ball. He lingered on in Yorktown until spring and, it seems clear, was a welcome guest at the Amblers', where he court-ed Polly and generally ingratiated himself with the family. Polly was very much on his mind, too, during the months of May and June 1780 while he was at-tending George Wythe's law lectures at the College of William and Mary in nearby Williamsburg. Whether John Marshall decided to attend the college to be near Polly is not clear, but Williamsburg was only twelve or so miles from Yorktown, an easy hike for a young man energized by love. Polly and her fam-ily seem to have visited Williamsburg, too, during his attendance at the college.

Marshall's introduction to the law at college was formative, despite its brev-ity, as we shall see. But judging from the marginal jottings in his commonplace book compiled during this period, Polly more than held her own against the "jealous mistress of the law." Alongside his dutiful entries on "action qui tam," "arbitrament & award," "bastardy," and "bills of sale" were heartfelt marginal references to "Miss Maria Ambler," "Miss Polly Am.," or more hopefully, "Miss M. Ambler—J. Marshall" and "John Marshall, Miss Poly Am." or simply "John, Maria." Dreams of love continued after Marshall left the college to begin law practice in Fauquier County. With Marshall at home at Oak Hill and the Ambler family in Richmond, courting was difficult, precar-ious as well. Marshall recalled later that for a couple of years he was alter-nately happy or miserable depending on Polly's "affection" or "coldness." One of the happy times was when he visited Richmond to "play Ma and Pa," as he humorously put it. One of the not-so-happy times was when a rival suitor, one "Captain Dick," appeared on the scene. The low point came when Polly re-jected his first proposal for marriage, sending the young suitor off in a huff. Except for the intervention of Polly's cousin, who took a lock of Polly's hair to Marshall as a peace offering, that might have been the end. All ended well, however. The lovers married on January 3, 1783, and set up housekeeping in Richmond. Unfortunately, we know very little of the details of this long mar-riage and sadly almost nothing of Mary herself. John Marshall's own "Dearest Polly" letters, written during his frequent absences on judicial duties, reveal

---

Background, Political and Domestic, 1779–1831 (Richmond, Va., 1961), which is the basic source of information about Marshall's domestic life. See also Robarge, "John Marshall and His Times," 132 n. 30.

what his friend Joseph Story attested to: that Polly remained at the epicenter of Marshall's life and that he remained, till the end, an incorrigible romantic in love.[35]

He was also a clearheaded realist with a driving ambition, a young man in a great hurry. He hurried to get out of the army. He hurried through his college education without graduating, which he probably could have afforded to do. He also hurried through his formal legal education, with a mere four months between his entry into Wythe's class and his admission to practice, not counting time off for courting. He hurried to practice law and did it with single-minded dedication so that he could make money, make life secure for his growing family, and enjoy the pleasures of Richmond society. And Richmond in the 1780s, it should be noted, was not all that hard to conquer, especially if one was the son of a well-placed, if not rich, planter and the son-in-law of one of the highest officials of the new state, who was anxious to help his daughter get the things in life she was accustomed to.

Like so many other places in America, Richmond was a small village with huge aspirations. The population when the Marshalls set up housekeeping numbered in the hundreds and included many slaves. The city was not much larger in 1788, when the ratifying convention met there. There were a few dozen wooden houses, one of which the Marshalls rented, and one church, Episcopal, which they immediately joined. There were no public buildings of distinction, no paved streets, and no amenities. Compared to Williamsburg, Richmond was rude and crude; there was no comparison at all to urban centers such as Philadelphia. The promise Richmond had in abundance—and it fit Marshall's upwardly mobile aspirations perfectly—was that things would get better. It was advantageously located on the fall line of the James River. This meant that goods brought from the western country on wagons could be transported by water to the coast and from thence to other coastal ports, to Europe, and the West Indies. A handful of English tobacco factors, the middlemen between Virginia growers and English markets, stayed on after the Revolution, forming an entrepreneurial nucleus, and they were soon joined by American merchants and businessmen. While the city depended heavily on the slavehold-

---

35. Marshall's marginal jottings are discussed in Beveridge, *Life of John Marshall,* 1: 159–60. Marshall's "Anniversary Eulogy to Mary W. Marshall," 25 December 1832, PJM, typescript, is a moving tribute to his wife. His letters to Polly, some of which reminisce about their courtship and life together, are printed in Mason, *My Dearest Polly.* Marshall's sister-in-law recounts his courtship in Elizabeth Ambler Carrington, "An Old Virginia Correspondence," *Atlantic Monthly* 84 (1899): 535–47.

ing countryside, the growing commercial and small manufacturing establishments operated within an expanding network of market relationships that transcended local and state boundaries. As of 1780, Richmond was also the capital city of the Old Dominion. The state legislature met there in a ramshackle wooden structure, which bore not the faintest resemblance to the governor's palace in Williamsburg. All of Virginia's superior courts were located in Richmond, too: the General Court, the High Court of Chancery, and the Court of Appeals.[36]

Unlikely though it seems, tiny Richmond was the economic, political, and legal center of the richest and most powerful state in the new nation. On top of that, it was the home of Mary Ambler. On both counts, Marshall wanted to get there posthaste. Wisely, however, he put down his bucket where he was— that is, in Fauquier County where his father's reputation and his own could help him get launched. There he was licensed to practice law by Governor Jefferson and on August 28, 1780, was admitted to the bar of the Fauquier County Court. Following in his father's footsteps, he was also elected to the House of Burgesses in April 1782. Legislative duties took him back to Richmond, where he quickly plunged into the political and social life of the capital. During the session he took up quarters at Formicola's Tavern, where he consorted with a lively group of legislators and lawyers who would go on to shape the destiny of the state. Leisure hours were spent courting Polly and planning the upcoming wedding. The long-anticipated event took place on January 3, 1783, in a makeshift Episcopal chapel, "with all the appurtenances of a wedding of Virginia aristocrats." According to entries into the Account Book, the newlyweds apparently rented, then in 1786 purchased a house, and finally in 1790 built their own house on the corner of Ninth Street, where it still stands. During this period Marshall acquired land in Fauquier—by purchase and as a gift from his father—but clearly Richmond was home. It would also be what Boston would be to young Daniel Webster, Salem to Joseph Story, Baltimore to Roger Taney, and Springfield to Abraham Lincoln—a window on life and law in America.[37]

36. On Richmond, see Virginius Dabney, *Richmond: The Story of a City* (Garden City, N.Y., 1976); John P. Little, *History of Richmond* (Richmond, Va., 1933).

37. The wedding is described in Mason, *My Dearest Polly,* 19. For Marshall's admission to the bar and early practice, see PJM, 1: 41, 108, 292, 291–92, and PJM, 5: 3–6. For Marshall's social, professional, and domestic life during the 1780s and early 1790s, the key source is his Account Book (September 1783–1788), PJM, l, and (July 1788–December 1795), PJM, 2. On the significance of the Account Book, see the editorial comment, especially PJM, 1: 289–92.

His life there in the 1780s, much of it marked by brief entries in his Account Book, was punctuated by much happiness and deep tragedy—and by uninterrupted social advancement. Happiness came with the birth of two sons: Thomas on July 21, 1784; Jaquelin on December 3, 1787. Within four years, however—from 1789 to 1792—the Marshalls also lost four children, two by early death and two by miscarriage. Polly went on to have four other children—Mary, John, James Keith, and Edward Carrington—but she never fully recovered. Whether her illness was a form of "insanity," as Jefferson called it privately, or an acute form of chronic depression, the fact is she became progressively fragile physically and emotionally until her death on December 25, 1831. As a result, Marshall assumed a larger share of domestic decision making than he otherwise would have done. In big things as well as small, his concern was to make life secure for his children and comfortable and entertaining for Polly. There were gloves for her hands, ribbons for her hair. When the neighbor's dogs kept her awake all night, he intervened diplomatically to silence them. When sons took to running out at night, he had a couple of walls removed so as to keep them under a gentle surveillance. And despite Polly's illness, she made their Richmond home a place where friends and family gathered happily and where spirited talk and fine wine from a well-stocked cellar flowed in abundance. Marshall presided over his table as he presided over his family, and later the Supreme Court of the United States—with gentle authority, humor, and generosity. In time, the circle of Marshall's gentle paternalism would include not only his immediate family but his brothers, sisters, in-laws, and cousins, and later his and Polly's several grandchildren.[38]

While ministering to a growing family, Marshall also entered fully into the life of the community, assuming a variety of public duties becoming to a republican citizen. He served in the House of Delegates, first from Fauquier County, then Richmond and Henrico. He served, to the chagrin of some, on the governor's Council of State and more humbly as a recorder of the Richmond Hustings Court, the city variant of the Virginia's famed county courts. He was a member of Richmond Masonic Lodge no. 10 and served two years as grand master of the Virginia Grand Lodge, a position he resigned in 1795. He attended Saint Johns Episcopal Church, and later the Monumental Church, but was never confirmed and never partook of the Eucharist. In his early years at

---

38. Supplemented and often corrected by *The Papers of John Marshall,* Mason's *My Dearest Polly* contains a running account of Marshall's social and domestic life. Also useful is Paxton, *Marshall Family,* though its emphasis is genealogical.

least, he was much more enthusiastically involved in Richmond's gentlemen's societies such as Formicola's Tavern Club, the Jockey Club, and the Quoit Club. As a mark of his social status, he also joined the ranks of Richmond's slaveholders. When fire decimated downtown Richmond in 1787, he contributed generously to the town benevolent fund. Indeed, even before assuming residence there, he joined in the futile effort to repel Benedict Arnold's 1781 attack on the capital, the same that drove Governor Jefferson out of town. Later he was part of the local military force organized to restore order after the abortive Gabriel slave uprising in Richmond in 1800.[39]

Long before becoming chief justice, then, Marshall was a local figure to reckon with, which may explain why he continued to be revered even after Richmond became the intellectual capital of southern states' rights. Lawyering also put him at the center of Richmond's life—both political and social. More will be said later about the details of his law practice—how he learned law by practicing it and how practicing in state and local courts was a form of governance with vast implications for his later ideas about judicial review. But for now, note the ways his legal practice prepared him for the role he would soon play at the ratifying convention. Several points are germane. The first is that by the time of the convention, Marshall was already recognized as one of Virginia's up-and-coming lawyers. Making it to the top of his profession did not, of course, make Marshall a nationalist, but his reputation increased the likelihood that he would be chosen to go to the convention. Experience in the competitive legal environment of Virginia's superior courts also provided him with skills of advocacy that would be put to good use once he got there, often against the same lawyers he knew socially and regularly confronted in the courtroom. Most important perhaps, the fact that Marshall chose to be a full-time lawyer meant that he did *not* choose to be a full-time slaveholding planter, which he might well have become. Being a professional lawyer freed him from the kind of life that would have inclined him, as it did most other Virginian slaveholders, to travel the road of states' rights. Being a successful lawyer with close professional associations in the business community may also have conditioned him to see the wisdom of a constitution that would facilitate Virginia's involvement in the growing national and international markets.[40]

39. See Mason, *My Dearest Polly,* 42–43, which culls from the Account Book. After 1796 Marshall was no longer actively involved with the Masons. His Masonic career is summarized conveniently in PJM, 2: 129 n. 6.

40. On Virginia legal culture, I have relied on A. G. Roeber's *Faithful Magistrates and Republican Lawyers: Creators of Virginia Legal Culture, 1680–1810* (Chapel Hill, N.C., 1981).

To put the matter simply, Marshall's social, professional, and economic circumstances in the 1780s prepared the way for his reception, and perception, of the new Constitution. He developed not so much a constitutional philosophy, which would come later, but an *attitude* that inclined him to accept and welcome change and progress. If the opponents were, as Cecelia Kenyon aptly said, "men of little faith," then Marshall was a man of great faith. A victorious war against all odds had taught him that lesson. He also believed in the special genius of "the wise and the good," a term he often used, and imbibed the Enlightenment principle, that wise men backed by a virtuous republican citizenry might control their collective destiny. But he also believed in himself; in his ability to succeed and prosper in the new age under the new Constitution. This was true professionally, and it was also true regarding his venturesome and highly successful career as a land speculator. In his case, land, and the entrepreneurial attitude he developed in the acquisition of it, shaped many things in his life, including his preference for John Locke, his distrust of state government, and his interpretation of the Contract Clause of the Constitution. In 1788, land added another compelling reason to champion the new Constitution.[41]

It would be difficult to overemphasize the importance of land greed in American history—or in Marshall's life. Land was America's most abundant and most sought-after resource. For the better part of two centuries, the vision of cheap land was the magnet that attracted millions of immigrants. It was billed as "free," but it never was. First, it had to be wrested from the Native Americans, which brutal process Chief Justice Marshall would try to mitigate; from the Spanish and French, who sold out; and from the Mexicans, who were forced out. It was fought *over* by the rich and powerful to see who could get the most and the best. It was fought *for* by the poor, who wanted a little piece of the action and who, unlike the large buyers and sellers, were willing to put their lives on the line to get it. (Chief Justice Marshall would have occasion to rule on their efforts, too.) It was the inspiration for a distinctive national literature and culture and simultaneously the starting point intellectually and economically for those who would carry America into the commercial age. For Virginians it was the backbone of the economy, the foundation of a way of life, and the measure of social status.[42]

41. Cecelia M. Kenyon, "Men of Little Faith: The Anti-Federalists on the Nature of Representative Government," *William and Mary Quarterly*, 3d ser., 12 (January 1955): 3–43.

42. Allan Kulikoff, *The Agrarian Origins of American Capitalism* (Charlottesville, Va., 1992) is especially suggestive regarding the impact of land on American culture in the late eighteenth- and early nineteenth-century United States.

Marshall shared land madness with others of his time and place, but he did so on his own terms. He enjoyed his Chickahominy "plantation" as a respite from law and judging, but he did not philosophize or rhapsodize about the republican virtues of grubbing in God's good earth. He was one of the most astute and aggressive land speculators of his day, but he had no desire to live as a great planter. What land promised him was social status, security for his family, and a legacy for his children. While his most extensive dealings came in the 1790s, he laid the foundation for a lifelong involvement in speculation in the 1780s. Indeed, one might even say that he inherited the land craze from his father. And it was natural that his first major acquisition during this period was title to the family estate of 850 acres at Oak Hill, a gift from his father, who had moved to Kentucky in search of land. Marshall also began to speculate on his own once he got out of the army. As an officer in the Continental line, he was entitled to an allotment of 4,000 acres. As a lawyer for officers, many of whom were his former comrades-in-arms, he was in a position to deal in land warrants, which very quickly become items of speculation during the postwar land boom. Marshall was well placed to garner a sizeable piece of the action: to buy at a discount and sell at a profit, or to sell a part to pay for the rest. Judging from his dealings with Arthur Lee and James Monroe, he was not only successful but aggressive. As he confessed to Monroe regarding his various land dealings, "If I succeed I shall think myself a first rate speculator." He also assured his old friend "that you will not lose more."[43]

Marshall was also heavily involved in Kentucky land speculation with his father. The District of Kentucky was opened to speculators by the Virginia legislature in 1779, which set aside land as payment to members of the Virginia and Continental lines for military service. Sensing a boom in the making, Thomas Marshall—with the somewhat reluctant approval of Washington, it would seem—got a leave in 1780 from the Virginia artillery regiment he commanded to case out the best land. In the same year, he became surveyor of Fayette County, a position that gave him a leg up in the competition for choice land. In 1785 he moved his family permanently to Fayette County, where he quickly established himself, as he had years before in Fauquier County, as one of the leading citizens of the district as well as one of the big land speculators.

43. In grappling with Marshall's complex land dealings, I have relied on the meticulous scholarship of the editors of *The Papers of John Marshall*. See especially PJM, 1: 100–4; 2: 140–49. On his land business, see Marshall to Monroe, 12 December 1783, PJM, 1: 109–11; Marshall to Monroe, 17 April 1784, PJM, 1: 120–21; Marshall to Arthur Lee, 17 April 1784, PJM, 1: 118–19; Marshall to Monroe, 17 April 1784, PJM, 1: 120–21.

John Marshall was well placed to help his father. As a resident of Richmond, he was near the land office, where he could purchase treasury warrants for Kentucky land and continue to buy up military warrants. Marshall then sent the warrants to his father, who could locate them on specific tracts of good land, enter the title, and arrange for a survey, which by Virginia law was necessary for the completion of title. Herbert Johnson estimates that nearly 230,000 acres were entered to land located in Fayette and Bourbon Counties, and of these, some "201,815 acres were surveyed for John Marshall and registered in the survey books of the Land Office." Some 41,000 acres were entered in Marshall's name alone, a figure that rises to 152,229 if one counts his assignees.[44]

Marshall's involvement in Kentucky land speculation marks him as a forward-looking investor who liked the prospects of the new age—and on that account also liked the economic stability the new Constitution promised. Much more directly relevant to his pro-Constitutional position in 1788, and to his Contract Clause rulings as chief justice later, was his growing interest in the Northern Neck lands of Thomas, Lord Fairfax who died in 1781, leaving his estate to his nephew Denny Martin (Fairfax), who resided in England. Marshall did not purchase the Fairfax lands until 1793 (some 215,000 acres purchased jointly with his brother James Markham Marshall and brother-in-law Rawleigh Colston). In 1786, however, as lawyer-in-residence representing the Fairfax interests, Marshall defended the legality of the proprietary grant, which was being challenged by private parties claiming under a Virginia order of council dating from the 1730s. In *Hite v. Fairfax* (1786), the Court of Appeals ruled against the particular claims asserted by Marshall's clients, but more importantly it affirmed the general validity of the Fairfax proprietary grant—the point Marshall emphasized in his argument and the one that laid the legal foundation on which his own title would rest.[45]

Marshall had no way of knowing that *Hite* would be the opening scrimmage of a legal war that would last some thirty years and that in its final stage would pit the state of Virginia (its legislature and its Court of Appeals) against

44. For Herbert Johnson's discussion of Marshall's Kentucky land dealings, see PJM, 1: 100–4. The Kentucky context is treated in Patricia Watlington, *The Partisan Spirit: Kentucky Politics, 1779–1792* (New York, 1972).

45. For the background to *Hite v. Fairfax*, see Editorial Note, PJM, 1: 150–53; for Marshall's argument, PJM, 1: 153–64. The fullest treatment of the Hite litigation and its indirect connection to *Martin v. Hunter's Lessee* is found in John A. Treon, "*Martin v. Hunter's Lessee*: A Case History" (Ph.D. diss., University of Virginia, 1970).

the Supreme Court of John Marshall. He must have known—what in fact had been true since the original royal grant in the 1630s—that Virginia, first as a colony and then as a state, was at odds with the vast proprietary claims in the Northern Neck. Once he studied the Constitution itself, he must also have realized—as a lawyer for the Fairfax estate and as a potential speculator in Fairfax lands—that supreme national law favoring property rights and the sanctity of contracts, which was enforceable against recalcitrant states by a separate national system of courts, might protect the holders under the Fairfax grant against Virginia's increasingly aggressive confiscatory policies. This is not to say that personal interest—real and anticipated—automatically made Marshall a nationalist, but only that economic self-interest and dedication to public service were inextricably connected. The first he displayed as an ambitious, upwardly mobile, professional lawyer with business connections and a passion for land speculation; the second by serving first in the army, then in the state legislature.[46]

Marshall entered the House of Delegates as representative from Fauquier County in May 1782, slightly more than two years after his discharge from the army and two after his admission to practice (also in Fauquier County). He was twenty-six years old. The fact that he was able to win election with no serious opposition and with no prior experience in public life is a measure of his father's status, his own military reputation, and his own large ambition. In truth, his first term in the legislature reveals little else but ambition and hubris. He was immediately appointed to several committees, the most important of which were the Committee for Courts of Justice and a special committee to reorganize the state militia. Whatever influence he had on these committees was negligible, however, because after only two months' service he was appointed to the Council of State. His appointment to an office reserved for seasoned statesmen was clearly due to family influence: that of his future father-in-law, state treasurer Jaquelin Ambler, and probably that of his father as well. Influence peddling among the elite was common practice in Virginia, but young Marshall's sudden elevation was resented even among those such as Edmund Pendleton, who liked Marshall and recognized his ability. "Young Mr. Marshall is elected a Councillor," Pendleton opined to James Madison. "He is clever, but I think too young for that department, which he should rather have

---

46. On the inseparability of economics and politics in constitution making, see Forrest McDonald, *We the People: The Economic Origins of the Constitution* (Chicago, 1958), the first volume of his masterful trilogy on the Constitution.

earned as a retirement and reward by 10 or 12 years hard service in the Assembly." A harsh assessment from one of Virginia's most astute jurists (and the one after whom Marshall modeled his own chief justiceship). Informal pressure from the likes of Pendleton may have caused Marshall to reckon the costs of social promotion, but what finally prompted his resignation was the determination by the General Court that members of the council could not argue cases before the state courts. He resigned on April 1, 1784. Duly humbled, he "made a small excursion" back to Fauquier County to see whether the voters might be willing to return him to the House of Delegates, from which he had resigned to serve on the council. They obliged him with a second term in 1784.[47]

Since Marshall twice went out of his way to get into the legislature, one might assume that he thought well of it. In fact he did not. Disenchantment set in almost immediately. Why is not entirely clear. Certainly the legislative agenda in the 1780s stood in sharp contrast to the glory days of the pre-Revolutionary House of Burgesses, when Virginia patriots laid claim to those constitutional rights Marshall fought for in the war. Possibly a soldier's prejudice against the feckless wartime legislature lingered to poison his opinion. Maybe it was the contrast he saw between the decisiveness of Washington's wartime leadership and the legislative way of doing things. In any case, legislative *democracy* was not precisely the source of his sudden disaffection—for the simple reason that the House of Burgesses had not yet been democratized. The committee structure, which had permitted the colonial elite to dominate the House of Burgesses, was still pretty much in place, and the idea, if not reality, of noblesse oblige was far from dead. In fact, a significant number of the old guard remained in positions of authority both inside the legislature and out. As Marshall saw it, the dead hand of tradition, especially as embodied in county government, was a large part of the problem.

The other part was the Virginia Constitution of 1776, which in a burst of democratic idealism made the legislature the dominant branch of state government. A constitutionally supreme legislature linked to the local power structure through the county system of representation was not up to the challenge of the new age. To make matters worse, counties congealed into regional align-

47. Beveridge, *Life of John Marshall*, 1: 204–5 (citing the *Journal of the House of Delegates*, October Session, 1782), treats Marshall's appointment to the council. Edmund Pendleton to Madison, 25 November 1782, David John Mays, ed., *The Letters and Papers of Edmund Pendleton, 1734–1803* (Charlottesville, Va., 1967), 2: 429.

ments—Tidewater, Southside, Northern Neck, and the western counties, which were further divided into the Shenandoah Valley and the District of Kentucky. With localism and regionalism in the saddle, it was all but impossible to get the legislature to act with the energy and broad (read national) vision Marshall expected. And the more legislators behaved as modern political brokers— which they had to do to get anything done—the less they resembled his wartime model of statesmen. It didn't help, either, that many of the new legislators, especially those from the western counties, were rough hewn, ill spoken, and often poorly prepared for the chore at hand. One contemporary observer described the House of Delegates in Marshall's time as a scene of confusion bordering on chaos, a place where legislators talked more about "horse races, runaway Negroes, yesterday's play" than about affairs of state.[48]

Marshall may have felt the need to distance himself somewhat from these men since he was not only young and inexperienced but also slightly rough hewn himself. But his main concern, like that of Madison and other critics of the legislature, had to do not with manners of the legislators but the substance of the laws they passed—or neglected to pass. Writing to an army friend in February 1783 after having served in the legislature only a couple of months, he was hard pressed to defend legislative policy. Virginia sought to "oppose successfully our British enemies & to establish on the firm base of certainty the independence of America," he explained to William Pierce. Well and good. "But in the attainment of this object an attention to a variety of little interests & passions produces such a distracted contrariety of measures that tis sometimes difficult to determine whether some other end is not nearer the hearts of those who guide our Counsels." Marshall was willing to concede that Virginia had more virtue "than our neighbors will give us credit for," but he doubted whether it had enough to do the job. What Virginia needed, as he put it to James Monroe, was "wisdom," which is to be found in "men whose virtue & abilities have secured the esteem & good opinion of their country." Writing to another friend, Leven Powell, after the "long session," Marshall noted that "not a single bill of Public importance" had been passed. Again he blamed "Gentlemen of character" who "cannot dismiss their private animosities, but will bring them in the Assembly." When the legislature defeated the effort to reform the court system in 1784, he was even more pointed in his criti-

48. See Jackson Main, "Sections and Politics in Virginia, 1781–1787," *William and Mary Quarterly,* 3d ser., 12 (January 1955): 96–112 on the divisions in the Virginia legislature. See also Dabney, *Richmond,* 36.

cism. As he complained to Charles Simms, the problem lay with "The County Court lawyers," who "are suspicious that they do not possess abilities or knowledge sufficient to enable them to stand before judges of law," and with the justices of the peace, who "will not assent to anything which may diminish their ideal dignity & put into the hands of others a power which they will not exercise themselves." The only thing worse than localism was localism sinewed with self-serving ignorance.[49]

Marshall saw nothing during the remainder of the decade to change his harsh early assessment. Yet there were some things worthy of praise. Virginia's justly famous bill for establishing religious freedom, passed in 1786, comes to mind. Also the state made a serious effort to retire the Revolutionary War debt—this in the midst of a major economic depression, which came with the collapse of the international tobacco market. Instead of seeing Virginia as gradually making its way out of the inevitable political and economic dislocations of the postwar period, however, Marshall saw only legislative ineptitude. Nor was he alone. Even Jefferson, whose theory of government led him to favor state legislative government as the most reliable depository of authority compatible with liberty, was critical. Washington, who was disposed to think the worst from his war experience, did exactly that. Above all, it was James Madison, who served both in Congress and the Virginia House of Delegates in the 1780s, who pointed out the deficiencies of state governments under the Articles of Confederation. His "Vices of the Political System of the United States," the basis of the Virginia Plan and his nationalist strategy at the Philadelphia Convention in 1787, was primarily a critique of the deficiencies of state government, most particularly that of Virginia, which he knew firsthand.[50]

Marshall left nothing faintly comparable to the "Vices," only scattered references to various legislative battles in Virginia in the period leading to the ratifying convention. Nonetheless, he agreed with Madison that structural deficiencies and institutionalized localism, along with general legislative incompetence, doomed measures designed to strengthen the central government. To be sure, Virginia did cede its claims to western lands—an act essential to the ratification of the Articles of Confederation. The Virginia legislature also ap-

49. Marshall to William Pierce, 12 February 1783, PJM, 1: 95. Marshall to Monroe, 3 January 1784, PJM, 1: 114. Marshall to Leven Powell, 9 December 1783, PJM, 1: 109. Marshall to Charles Simms, 16 June 1784, PJM, 1: 124.

50. Madison's growing disillusion with the Articles government in the 1780s is treated with precision in Lance Banning, *The Sacred Fire of Liberty: James Madison and the Founding of the Federal Republic* (Ithaca, N.Y., 1995), chs. 1 and 2.

proved sending delegates to the Annapolis Convention in 1786, which in turn led to the calling of the federal convention in 1787. On the other hand, Virginia opposed efforts to make the Articles into a viable government by creating a national impost and enlarging the commerce powers of the Confederation Congress. The state also opposed all efforts to alter Article 13 of the Articles of Confederation, which made amendments contingent on unanimity, a provision that made reasonable change next to impossible. Marshall was not on hand to debate these crucial measures, but the point was clear to him: a weak national government based on state sovereignty permitted Virginia to pursue its own version of self-interest. What the state did with its sovereign power was at odds with both Marshall's wartime nationalism and his professional and private interests.[51]

Nowhere was this more clear, or the consequences more far-reaching, than in the state's repudiation of pre–Revolutionary War debts owed by Virginia planters to British and Scottish merchants. It may seem paradoxical that Marshall faulted his state on the British debt issue since he profited handsomely as a lawyer defending Virginia debtors. The debt issue, however, was connected to the general issue of contractual obligation, and not just between Virginians and Englishmen but among Virginians themselves. Inextricably connected to debt was taxation, the same issue that brought on the Revolution. And the debt-money-tax issue went to the heart of the debate between the localists and nationalists—from the Revolution through the struggle over the ratification of the Constitution and beyond.

The debate in Virginia on these questions was searching and passionate because there was truth on both sides. For Virginians to pay back prewar debts to British citizens appeared to many to negate the Revolution itself by rewarding the British enemy at the expense of state citizens, who were already suffering from economic dislocation and specie shortage. Not to repay the debts, however, by reneging on promises made in the Treaty of Paris, which ended the war, would seriously undermine the credibility of the American Congress and jeopardize economic relations with other nations. For the state to countenance the violation of private contracts in one area, moreover, would surely weaken them all around—a vital point since Virginians were enmeshed in creditor-debtor ties with each other, with citizens of other states, with their own state, and with the Articles of Confederation government as well.

51. Norman K. Risjord, *Chesapeake Politics, 1781–1800* (New York, 1978); Alan Schaffer, "Virginia's 'Critical Period,'" in *The Old Dominion: Essays for Thomas Perkins Abernethy,* ed. Darrett B. Rutman (Charlottesville, Va., 1964).

Given the broad ramifications, it is not surprising that the divisions over the British debt question in Virginia prefigured divisions over the ratification of Constitution. Opponents to the payment of the debt noticed two things about the proposed Constitution that led them to oppose it, too. First, Article 6 validated "all debts contracted . . . before the adoption of this Constitution" and made treaties the supreme law of the land binding on states. Second, Article 1, Section 10, prohibited states from passing laws that impaired the obligation of contract. Crèvecoeur, who followed the preconvention debate over the Constitution in Virginia closely, summed up contemporary wisdom on the matter when he noted "that the greatest obstacle to the adoption of the new Constitution in Virginia, are debts & dignity; in effect, one can see that those who owe much look to put off the Establisht. of a Govt. that promises to all the most Impartial Justice—as for dignity, say those who know Virginia better than I, there are a great many People who fear to see their personal Importance eclipsed, by the brilliance of a truly Federal & Energetic Govt." More than a few people on the eve of the convention, including John Marshall, thought Patrick Henry was the unfortunate embodiment of Crèvecoeur's generalization.[52]

The "dignity and debt" issue, which turned some Virginians into states' rightists, confirmed Marshall's wartime nationalism. "Dignity," the fear of being "eclipsed," as Crèvecoeur quaintly put it, was assuredly no problem for the highly successful young lawyer. As for the debt issue, it led Marshall to favor a "truly Federal & Energetic Govt." rather than fear it. He was a professional lawyer, an economic progressive, and a serious land speculator, and on all counts he wanted legal stability, contractual sanctity, and the payment of honest debts, even if taxation was part of the bargain. Regarding these matters, there was much in Virginia to make him uneasy. The transition from colony to state, as Rhys Isaac has recounted, set in motion a vast transformation that touched every aspect of life. The Revolution also produced a massive disruption of traditional markets, raised profound questions about the status of English law in Virginia courts after independence, and exacerbated the perennial shortage of specie.[53]

52. E. James Ferguson, *The Power of the Purse: A History of American Public Finance, 1776–1790* (Chapel Hill, N.C., 1961); Crèvecoeur to William Short, 1 April 1788, VRD, 2: 636.

53. Marshall addressed the British debt issue in his letter to Augustine Davis, 13 November 1793, printed as a letter from Gracchus in the *(Richmond) Virginia Gazette and General Advertiser*, PJM, 2: 231–38. For Marshall and the British debt question, I have relied on Charles F. Hobson, "The Recovery of British Debts in the Federal Circuit Courts of Virginia, 1790 to 1793," *Virginia Magazine of History and Biography* 92 (April 1984): 176–200; Rhys Isaac, *The Transformation of Virginia, 1740–1790* (Chapel Hill, N.C., 1982).

In this environment, tax and debt collection was all but impossible; economic and governmental stability was a dream of the future. As Marshall put it to James Monroe in 1784, "There is not one shilling in the Treasury & the keeper of it could not borrow one on the faith of the government." When Patrick Henry showed up at the spring 1784 session of the House of Delegates "chargd high with postponement of the collection of taxes," as Marshall wrote to Monroe, it was a signal that political factions in Virginia in the 1780s would fall out along economic lines. The ensuing debate found Marshall on the side of the creditors and the Constitution—not because he hated debtors (of which he was one), but because he wanted a government that would guarantee stability, protect property rights, and secure the principles of contract law on which those rights rested. Like so many other "nationalists" of the period, Alexander Hamilton being the notable exception, Marshall's support of the new Constitution (the real meaning of which could only be imagined) was determined to a substantial degree by the concrete notion of what it would do to check state legislative excess. What he also learned from the 1780s was that law administered by a trained bench and bar provided more reliable rules to live and work by than statutes passed by legislators given to demagoguery and factious disputation.[54]

Marshall's belief that lawyers and judges could and should actually govern, and the connection of this notion with judicial review, will be developed later. But it should be noted here that Marshall's experience in the 1780s laid the foundation. The defining issue was judicial reform. Like other forward-looking professional lawyers, he was convinced that economic progress in Virginia depended on an efficient court system, manned by trained lawyers and judges grounded in scientific law. To this end, he supported a series of legislative bills designed to upgrade the judicial system. The first of these, put forth by James Madison in 1784, was designed to rein the authority of the county courts, which were the institutional embodiment of local culture and power. Marshall practiced only briefly in the Fauquier County Court, but it was long enough to convince him that the idiosyncratic law administered there by untrained justices of peace was not adequate to the economic needs of Virginians, especially those of an entrepreneurial bent. He was also convinced that local justices of the peace were instrumental in defeating attempts on the part of British citizens

54. Marshall to Monroe, 24 February, 15 May 1784, PJM, 1: 116–17, 123. On the debt question in Virginia politics in the 1780s, see Jackson Main, *Political Parties before the Revolution* (Chapel Hill, N.C.), especially ch. 9.

to collect pre–Revolutionary War debts owed by Virginia merchants and plant-ers: "Those Magistrates who are tenacious of authority will not assent to any thing which may diminish their ideal dignity & put into the hands of others a power which they will not exercise themselves." Opposed also were the "County Court lawyers," Marshall said, who "are suspicious that they do not possess abilities or knowledge sufficient to enable them to stand before judges of law." It was "the County Court establishment," as he called it, that was "de-termined against every Measure which may expedite & facilitate the business of recovering debts & compelling a strict compliance with contracts." The same group also defeated another reform bill drafted by Marshall in December 1786, presumably for the same reasons. It was also in 1786 that the Court of Appeals ruled against Marshall and his clients in *Hite v. Fairfax,* essentially up-holding the Virginia sequestration act of 1777, and obliterating the title of Lord Fairfax and the titles of the purchasers who claimed under it, one of whom was soon to be John Marshall.[55]

Neither the defeat of judicial reform by the entrenched forces of local inter-est nor the setback in *Hite* suddenly turned Marshall against Virginia's legal system. He was a part of that system for nearly two decades and for most of that period was one of its shining stars. Virginia lawyers and judges were among his closest friends, and almost everything he learned about the law, he learned in Virginia. What *Hite* did suggest, however, and what three decades of litigation on Marshall's Fairfax claims would later confirm, was that even Virginia's best and brightest lawyers and judges operating in the highest courts of the state might prefer state and local priorities to contractual sanctity and other legal principles suitable to the emerging national and international mar-kets. He was intrigued by the new market possibilities not simply because he was a nationalist, but rather because Virginia's participation in that market would, in his opinion, be in its own best interest. When local justices of the peace made up law to suit their own interests, when Virginia's legislature pur-sued policies that loosened the bonds of contractual obligation that threatened the property rights of creditors, it hurt Virginians most of all. Marshall was a Virginian before he was a nationalist, and his intuitive economic calculus re-garding the new Constitution was based on Virginia experience. Among the

55. On the judicial reform movement in Virginia, with references to John Marshall in the 1780s, see Roeber, *Faithful Magistrates,* 192–202. Marshall to Charles Simms, 16 June 1784, PJM, 1: 124; also Marshall to James Monroe, 2 December 1784, PJM, 1: 131; Marshall's legisla-tive bill, 25 December 1786, PJM, 1: 193–201. The *Hite v. Fairfax* litigation is summarized in PJM, 1: 150–53. For Marshall's argument, see PJM, 1: 153–64.

most important lessons he learned—witness his speech on the federal judiciary at the Virginia ratifying convention and his extensive practice in the federal courts in the 1790s—was that the system of federal courts provided by the new Constitution offered solutions to problems Virginians could not or would not solve in their own judicial system. In regard to the courts and much else, Marshall considered the new Constitution to be in the best interest of Virginia. Indeed, as Forrest McDonald has demonstrated, it was the struggle to define *state* self-interest—whether it could best be served in or out of the new Union—that drove the various ratification debates. Virginia's was no exception.[56]

For Marshall, this struggle, as it took shape in the 1780s, came down to the bedrock issue of law and social order. Two events, one general and international in origin and the other specifically domestic, gave substance to his fears in this regard. Both centered on the perennial issues of debt, taxes, and contractual sanctity. The general factor was the near total collapse of tobacco prices in 1785, an event precipitated by Robert Morris's unsuccessful effort to corner the international market. Deprived of their major source of revenue and plagued with a chronic shortage of specie, Virginia planters and businessmen reneged on their private debts. Since debtors in Virginia were also creditors, this unleashed a contagion of default. Faced with popular resistance to debt collection, the kind that was soon to erupt in Massachusetts and Pennsylvania, the legislature considered various measures of debt relief, including commutation laws (one of which Marshall actually voted for), stay laws, and paper money (a policy heretofore opposed by all segments of Virginia society). The fear that such populist measures might pass was greatly increased when the legislature postponed the payment of British debts by temporarily closing state courts to British creditors and, as Marshall suspected, by failing to restructure the antiquated county court system, which was a haven for planter debtors, run by planter justices. The depth of the crisis and the inadequacy of public response, as James Madison reported to Jefferson in December 1787, had alienated not only "the body of sober & steady people" but the "lower order" as well. Looking at the widespread indebtedness and growing resistance to taxes, the Reverend Matthew Maury said he was certain that "we are on the Eve of a Revolution."[57]

56. Forrest McDonald, *E Pluribus Unum: The Formation of the American Republic 1776–1790* (Boston, 1965).

57. Madison to Jefferson, 9 December 1787, VRD, 1: 227–28; Maury to James Maury, 10 December 1787, ibid., 228.

What turned the debt crisis in Virginia into a law-and-order crisis for Marshall was the news of Shays's Rebellion in Massachusetts. He did not see, as historians have, the property-owning, law-abiding, republican nature of the protest. Projected against the growing economic crisis in Virginia, he saw instead a debt-driven populist uprising against private property, lawyers, and judges. "Massachusetts is rent into two equal factions," he explained to James Wilkinson on January 5, 1787, "and an appeal I fear has by this time been made to the God of battles." Marshall was admittedly uncertain of the details about the exact "motives and views of the insurgents" or of the outcome of the struggle, but he was sure that the events would "deeply affect the happiness and reputation of the United States." The conservative principles of the American Revolution were in danger in Massachusetts, as they were in Virginia: The "violent, I fear bloody, dissentions in a state I had thought inferior in wisdom and virtue to no one in the union," plus "the strong tendency which the politics of many eminent characters among ourselves have to promote private and public dishonesty cast a deep shade over that bright prospect which the revolution in America and the establishment of our free governments had opened to the votaries of liberty throughout the globe." His deepest fear was that "another revolution" would repudiate the true Revolution and prove once and for all a most "degrading" truth: "that man is incapable of governing himself."[58]

The complex issues of the 1780s in Virginia and the nation had, it would seem, been reduced to a question of governance, which in turn was linked inseparably to considerations of economic policy. Henry would sing the praises of Virginia, and Federalists and Anti-Federalists alike would speak the language of republicanism. The fact remains, however, that constitution making was really inseparable from matters of social class, economics, personality, ambition, and self-perception. Putting all these together helps explain Marshall's defense of the new Constitution. He entered the Richmond convention as a Harringtonian and a Lockean—and it didn't matter whether he had actually studied James Harrington's *The Common-wealth of Oceana* or Locke's *Second Treatise of Government*. He was a Harringtonian because he was a man with a stake in society who was fast coming to believe that only those with property should govern. He was a Lockean because he believed that liberty and property went hand in hand, that the purpose of government and responsibility of legal institutions was to secure property against the vagaries of man in a state of nature. As Marshall saw it, Virginia under the Articles of Confedera-

58. Marshall to Wilkinson, 5 January 1787, PJM, 1: 199–201.

tion had begun to resemble just such a state. This did not mean that he ceased to be a Virginian. Rather he believed that state interest, as well as his own, could best be served by supporting a strengthened national union. If that union would keep Virginia localists from destroying property rights and jeopardizing his own economic dreams, so much the better. At Richmond, Marshall would fight vigorously for a truly national government, because he loved the nation he helped to create and because more government at the national level would mean property-respecting, law-abiding government at the state level. Energetic government run by the wise and good would favor a talented, ambitious young lawyer who aspired to a good life for himself and his family in the city and state he loved—which in 1788 is where he planned to stay.

Ratifying the Constitution: Securing the Revolution

A copy of the newly drafted Constitution reached Virginia in September 1787, eight months before the scheduled ratifying convention. Its much-anticipated arrival set in motion one of the most important and intellectually remarkable debates in American history—important because the success of a national union depended on Virginia's joining, arresting because of the debate's intensity, scope, and sophistication. The debate began early as opponents and champions of the Constitution took to the hustings in anticipation of the popular election of delegates scheduled for spring 1788. Newspapers sprang up overnight, ten in the period from September 1787 to June 1788, and disappeared almost as quickly. Political oratory, heretofore the domain of the elite, took on an egalitarian cast as Patrick Henry showed the way. Indeed, Henry's preconvention act was one hard *not* to follow. Even crusty George Mason was forced to shift deferential gears. When Mason's Northern Neck constituency repudiated the great man's Anti-Federalism, it was clear that deference no longer controlled automatically, that the new concept of popular sovereignty was more than a mere political talking point for the old elite. Invigorated with a new relevance, also, was ancient history and republican theory. Even the British constitution made its appearance in the debates. These ideas, or rather, conflicting versions of them, focused on questions of liberty and power, on human nature, and also on the meaning of the Revolution and the lessons of the Articles of Confederation.

Behind this elevated political discourse lurked an old-fashioned question: What was best for Virginia? Delegates to the Richmond convention—

established leaders such as Edmund Pendleton, Edmund Randolph, George Mason, and Patrick Henry, as well as aspirants such as James Monroe and John Marshall—appreciated the stakes. Rely on the "spirit of America," exhorted Randolph; honor the "genius of Virginia," demanded Henry. Seize the day and save the Revolution, all agreed. June 1788 was Virginia's "Machiavellian moment," a watershed time of sorting, sifting, and resolution, when a people considered the past in order to shape their collective destiny. It was also an ideal moment for an aspiring statesman such as Marshall to make his debut: to be there at the creation, to stand up and be counted, and to learn something in the process.[59]

At the completion of the convention, Madison ranked Marshall fifth in overall influence, a remarkable ranking in light of the competition. Perhaps it was a bit of a surprise as well—at least it was to Hugh Grigsby, who described him as "a tall young man, slovenly dressed in loose summer apparel" who was "convivial almost to excess." Despite Marshall's appearance and his youth, however, he was remarkably well prepared for the important role he was assigned to play by Madison, who was obviously not among those deceived. Marshall was not a great orator as was Henry. Nor was he an accomplished student of classical and recent history as was Madison. Marshall did subscribe to the Virginia Constitutional Society in 1785, organized by Madison to study constitutional issues, but there is no evidence he attended any meetings. Marshall also had access to *The Federalist* essays, which began to appear in local newspapers in September 1787 and which were available in printed volumes in time to influence the debates. More important still, he had practical experience. He was a seasoned and confident trial lawyer with well-honed adversarial skills. He also knew the main casts of characters on both sides in the forthcoming debate and understood their strengths and weaknesses. Fellow Federalist Henry Light-Horse Harry Lee was an army comrade. James Monroe, who joined the ranks of the Anti-Federalists in the debates, was not only a fellow soldier but a boyhood friend from Campbelltown Academy days. As a fellow lawyer, Marshall had taken the measure of Patrick Henry, against whom he would be pitted at the convention. And so it went. Slovenly he may have been, but in the small circle of Virginia, Marshall was known and liked by all, a fact to which Grigsby also attested.[60]

59. See Introduction, VRD, 1: xxiii–xxxix. J. G. A. Pocock, *The Machiavellian Moment: Florentine Political Thought and the Atlantic Republican Tradition* (Princeton, N.J., 1975). The phrase "spirit of America" appears several times in Randolph's speech of 4 June 1788, VRD, 2: 931–41.

60. See "Virginia Constitutional Society Subscription Paper," in PJM, 1: 140–42. Grigsby is quoted, ibid., 252 n. 8.

One final point: Unlike the half dozen or so delegates who waffled in uncertainty, and were targeted for conversion by both sides, Marshall was identified in preconvention polls as "strongly federal." He knew exactly where he stood. The constitutional lessons he learned as a soldier had been confirmed by his experience as a legislator, and those lessons were also congenial to his personal interests and ambition. He did not come to the convention to be convinced. He came with his mind made up and fully determined to lead the charge for the Constitution if asked to do so.[61]

In fact, Marshall struck a blow for ratification even before he was asked. During the final weeks of the fall 1787 session of the state legislature, while delegates were choosing sides over the Constitution, Patrick Henry moved to make the call to the ratifying convention contingent on the acceptance of a second national convention to be charged with amending the work of the first. Marshall immediately saw the dangers inherent in such a concession. Astute politician that he was, Marshall also understood that a frontal assault on Virginia's great patriot at this point, even if successful, would strengthen Henry's hand at the convention. Accordingly, "with his usual perspicuity," as the contemporary newspaper account put it, Marshall cited arguments on both sides of the question before supporting George Nicholas, who believed that the people should not be prejudiced against the Constitution before the convention met. Marshall's resolution that the convention should be called and "the new Constitution should be laid before them for their free and ample discussion" was accepted as a compromise. It was an important early victory for the forces of ratification, and an indication as well that Marshall was destined to be a Federalist "of first influence," providing he could get elected to the convention. His opponent was William Foushee, sheriff of Henrico County and a perfect "Henryite," as Edmund Randolph called him. Marshall won by a vote of 198 to 187, thanks to the strong Federalist showing in Richmond and to his personal popularity among friends and army veterans. The closeness of the election indicated that he had his work cut out for him at the convention.[62]

What that work would be was settled in part by James Madison and other Federalist leaders, who knew from preconvention polling what had to be done and planned accordingly. Judging from the fact that Marshall prepared his

61. Marshall's purchase of volume 1 of *The Federalist* is recorded in his Account Book, PJM, 1: 409. Marshall is listed among the preconvention leaders on the Federalist side by William Short in his letter to Thomas Lee Shippen, 31 May 1788, VRD, 2: 895.

62. For the legislative debate over calling the convention see VRD 1: 110–120. Robarge's "John Marshall and His Times," 152–53, has a very concise discussion of the election, including the Randolph quote.

speeches before delivering them, it is possible he was in on the planning. In any case, he played to his strengths and to the vulnerabilities of the Anti-Federalists. Contrary to prevailing scholarship, the latter were as well organized as the Federalists, at least in Virginia. The Anti-Federalists' strategy operated at several levels. Sometimes their maneuvers seemed entirely tactical—as when Mason persuaded the convention to debate the Constitution clause by clause, a rule that in fact helped the Federalists and was increasingly ignored by the Anti-Federalists, or when Henry attacked the legitimacy of the Philadelphia Convention, a line of argument he quickly abandoned once he made his point. It was mainly Henry who set the tone, supplied the inspirational rhetoric, and led the main assault, though Mason, as the author of the Virginia Declaration of Rights and a dissenting member of the Philadelphia Convention, was also well placed to speak authoritatively about the consolidationist and rights-threatening nature of the Constitution. Reputable statesmen on one side, it was clear, were supposed to neutralize their counterparts on the other. Federalists and Anti-Federalists alike were also careful to call on a younger generation of leaders, especially those with military credentials. Captain Marshall fit the bill perfectly for the Federalists, as did his friend James Monroe for the Anti-Federalists.[63]

Together Henry and Mason stated the Anti-Federalists' position: that the Revolution was about liberty not national unity, and that liberty lay mainly with the republican institutions of the states, where the legitimate voice of the sovereign people could be most clearly heard. The central problem, they insisted, was not the Articles of Confederation, which was presented as a model arrangement, but the proposed Constitution, which "squints toward monarchy" and which was "calculated to annihilate totally the State Governments." The allocation of power to the new national government, they insisted, was analogous to the power claimed by the British government before the Revolution. To substantiate this charge, they declaimed about human nature: how "the natural lust of power so inherent in Man" made men untrustworthy in matters of government. Even more than the Federalists, it would seem, they drew on classical history to illumine their view of republicanism. Somewhat ironically, in light of the anti-English motif in Anti-Federalism, there were also numerous references to the beauties of the English constitution, so many in fact that the Federalists demanded a moratorium on historical references. Along-

---

63. On the Anti-Federalists, see VRD, 2: 823–24; for Henry's retreat, VRD, 2: 917. On Marshall's role see the Editorial Note, "The Virginia Ratifying Convention," PJM, 1: 252–55.

side the high-flown eulogies to "the genius of Virginia" and the "goddess of Liberty" was a searching criticism of the operative features of the proposed national government. Only one major issue, that of slavery, was not debated openly, though securing the institution was very much connected to Anti-Federalist suspicions of national majority rule. When Henry declaimed in one of his numerous asides, which did not make it into the records of the debates, *"They'll free your niggers!"* the delegates knew whereof he spoke. Other major, and some not-so-major, issues were aired fully. Several full days were given over to arguments against granting Congress control over scheduling elections and settling disputed elections. The dangers of standing armies were detailed at length, usually in contrast to the virtues of the state militia. Questions calculated to appeal to wavering delegates received special attention. One such, dear to the hearts of delegates from the District of Kentucky, was whether a distant national government controlled by northern interests might not bargain away the navigation rights to the Mississippi, as ambassador John Jay had been willing to do in his treaty negotiations with Spain in the 1780s.[64]

As could have been predicted, the debt question and the related question of federal taxing power called forth some of the most heated rhetoric. Power was what the Federalists wanted most for the national government and what the Anti-Federalists most feared—thus the latter's sustained attacks against the executive (incipient monarchy they charged) and against separation of powers (a too-feeble protection against tyranny). Significantly for Marshall, they also assailed the newly proposed federal judiciary, which would, they charged, bring supreme federal law to bear directly on individuals. With federal law enforced by federal courts came the power to collect debts and enforce contracts, this without the protective shield of state authority. Finally there was the passionate and prophetic assault on the principle of implied powers, which seemed to be built into the Constitution—not just in Article 1, Section 8, but also in Article 2 (on executive power) and Article 3 (on the federal judiciary). In their argument against the central government, the Anti-Federalists turned for support to the radical Whig tradition of the eighteenth century and the great debate that led up to the Declaration of Independence. The Federalists focused on recent history: on what had happened under the Articles of Confederation as

64. Henry's speech of 5 June, VRD, 2: especially 962–63. The superb cumulative index to the VRD is an indispensable guide to the various subjects discussed during the convention. Henry's aside on slavery is discussed in Hugh Blair Grigsby, *The History of the Virginia Federal Convention of 1788* (1890; reprint, New York, 1969), 157 n. 142.

America struggled to win the War for Independence and defend national rights in a hostile world.

In countering Anti-Federalist arguments, Virginia Federalists, one senses, chose to not say what they really thought (but what they did express privately): that Henry, brilliant and formidable though he was, was also a bit of a windbag who was not above using demagoguery to protect the debtor interests of his Southside constituency; that Mason was driven by a combination of gout, pride, and sour grapes (he being one of the three Framers who voted against the Constitution at Philadelphia). There was also the feeling among Federalists, Marshall included, that many Anti-Federalists opposed the Constitution because they feared for their own careers.[65]

Whatever the Federalists expressed and intimated in private, they generally kept to the high road in public, projecting moderation, common sense, patriotism, a faith in man and institutions, and a hope for the future. Edmund Pendleton called forth "the spirit of America" that "carried us through the war"—several times. Governor Edmund Randolph assailed the incompetence of the Virginia legislature and the debility of the Articles government. Pleading in the name of "experience and history" and common sense, he urged the convention to accept the Constitution, even with its imperfections, as the only hope of national union. Where Henry spoke of the "genius of Virginia," six times in one speech, Randolph, like Pendleton, called on "American spirit," and "American pride." Madison weighed in, too, on the side of Enlightenment rationality. His measured speeches combined his mastery of the Constitution itself with arguments from philosophy, more Hobbesian than Lockean; from "experience and practise"; and from the recent history of the Articles of Confederation, whose "vices" he had previously dissected. When Henry and others asserted "that Government is no more than a choice among evils," Federalists countered just as passionately that government was a necessary good; that it could be constructed so as to preserve liberty; that it was necessary to protect property, secure the payment of debt, and avoid social disorder of the kind that threatened Massachusetts during Shays's Rebellion. When the Anti-Federalists summoned feelings of fear and mistrust, the Federalists stood firm in the tradition of Virginia deferential politics, which was built on trust and responsibility. Where Henry put "Liberty over Union," Federalists argued that union and lib-

---

65. Newspaper accounts and the private letters bearing on the convention are collected in a marvelous feat of scholarship by the editors of the VRD and presented at relevant places in the three volumes on Virginia.

erty were inseparable and that both required a government with energy and power.[66]

At thirty-three, Marshall did not rank with the established statesmen who set the tone and strategy of debate. Indeed, his easy conviviality, casual summer attire, and frontier accent seemed to locate him closer to the delegates from the District of Kentucky than to the likes of Edmund Pendleton, who arrived in a fancy phaeton, attired in silk and powdered wig as befit a statesman of the old school. During twenty-five days of debate, Marshall made only three relatively short speeches. Judging from the substance and targets of his remarks, however, he had been assigned an important role to play. He would later complain that his speeches had been badly mutilated in the reporting, but several things were unmistakably clear. He was supremely confident and bold and able enough to challenge Henry and Mason head-on. He was a formidable debater, with a penchant for logical textual analysis. And despite his reputation as easy-going and convivial, he could, when it served his purpose, be cutting, sarcastic, and angry. Theory and philosophy he left to others.

Marshall staked out his general constitutional position in his maiden speech of June 10, in answer to Patrick Henry. Henry was the undisputed leader of the Anti-Federalist cause and, as such, was the cannon to be spiked. He had opened the convention for the Anti-Federalists with an all-out attack on the Constitution; on June 9, the assault turned into a full-scale jeremiad. Marshall made no attempt to disguise his contempt for what he heard, and he was un-daunted by the great orator's reputation as the champion of American liberty. Indeed, Marshall's first move, in good lawyerly style, was to call attention to Henry's unliberty-loving support of the act of attainder passed by the House of Delegates in 1776 against Josiah Philips, alleged to be the leader of a band of outlaws responsible for terrorizing frontier settlements. Marshall did not defend Philips, who was apparently guilty, but rather criticized the legislature for punishing him without a trial. If this was an example of Henry's state-sponsored liberty and democracy, then Marshall wanted nothing to do with it. "We, Sir, idolize Democracy," he said sarcastically before he went on to say what he really liked, which was "a well regulated Democracy" (a phrase he used twice in five minutes) in which government was held by law to "a strict observance of justice and public faith." The point was self-evident: if a govern-ment could take a man's life without the benefit of the law, it could also take

66. The tone of the debate is apparent throughout, but see in order of the quotes: VRD, 2: 946, 971–76, 990–91, 1035, 947, 986, 1001.

his property. Law and order, and property, as Marshall and the Federalists saw it, was what the Constitution was all about.[67]

After this unsubtle ad hominem jab, Marshall challenged Henry point by point. One issue vitally important to Virginians residing in the District of Kentucky was free commerce on the Mississippi River and open access to the port of New Orleans. Whereas Henry, in the untrusting mode of Anti-Federalism, argued that officials of the new government would fail to defend the rights of westerners, Marshall argued that only a powerful national government was adequate to the job. He also addressed Henry's demand that ratification be made contingent on prior amendments, arguing that subsequent ones would be impossible. Marshall was quick to point out the flaw in logic. "If he was right, does not his own argument prove, that in his own conception, previous amendments cannot be had; for, Sir, if subsequent amendments cannot be obtained, shall we get amendments before we ratify?" The main point, however, was not logic but motive. What Marshall assumed was that Henry's strategy in 1788 was the same as it had been in the House of Delegates in 1787: namely, to insist on amendments as a condition for ratification, then to introduce such debilitating ones that they would fail and the Constitution fail along with them. Whether Marshall believed the rumor, widely circulated during the convention, that Henry wanted to defeat national union in order to create a southern confederacy with himself at its head, we don't know. But there is little doubt that Marshall's barbed allusion to "the decided enemies of the Union," was aimed at the great patriot himself. From the tone of his speech, Marshall's objective, one might reasonably infer, was to discredit not just Henry's ideas but the man himself. It was hazardous duty to say the least. And one suspects, though it can't be verified, that Marshall was chosen because his record as a soldier permitted him to criticize the self-appointed interpreter of Revolutionary truth. Certainly, Marshall's common sense and lawyerly style played well against Henry's bombastic delivery and his sonorous generalities.[68]

In answering Henry, Marshall first sounded the main themes of his own constitutional philosophy: the need for an energetic government run by an experienced elite for the benefit, and with the support and trust, of those who elected them. The question was not whether power was good in the abstract, but rather, "*Is the power necessary—and is it guarded?*" History, "the great

67. Ibid., 1116–17. The *Philips* case is discussed in Dumas Malone, *Jefferson the Virginian* (Boston, 1948), 292–93.

68. VRD, 2: 1117.

volume of human nature," speaks to the former; the Constitution to the latter. And history for Marshall, as for the Federalists generally, was not mainly the history of ancient Greece and Rome, nor was it the constitutional history of England, which Henry constantly cited. Marshall was not unmindful of the relevance of ancient history, but he was more interested in lessons of the recent past. He cited the "late disturbances" in Holland to prove that "the want of proper powers," and "the consequent deranged and relaxed administration" could lead to internal violence and foreign conquest. Closer at hand was the weak-kneed Articles of Confederation. Here he spoke passionately, indeed angrily, from his wartime experience—exactly the kind that Henry could *not* call on. "We are told," he said, referring to the latter's celebration of the Articles as the best government in the world, "that the Confederation carried us through the war." Nonsense. "Had not the enthusiasm of liberty inspired us with unanimity, that system would never have carried us through it." Moreover, the war "would have been much sooner terminated had that Government been possessed of due energy." The problem was simple: "The Confederation has nominal powers, but no means to carry them into effect." The solution was as plain as the problem: create a general government with power adequate to protect American interests in time of war and further them in time of peace—"to protect the United States, and to promote the general welfare."[69]

In Marshall's discourse on power—the word appears more than a dozen times in his short speech—he pointed to threats from a hostile world: the threat of Spain to the right of free navigation on the Mississippi, of the Tripolitan pirates to American commerce in the Mediterranean, and of the "powers of Europe" who hated and feared the fledgling Republic. Only a strong national government could defend the rights of American citizens in such a hostile world. No less important was the need to contain the forces of social upheaval at home. Taxes had to be collected "without a civil war." State debts had to be honored. Because of its own weakness and because it gives the states free reign, the Confederation government "takes away the incitements to industry, by rendering property insecure and unprotected." In contrast, the Constitution would create an environment favorable to individual enterprise.[70]

Here Marshall's argument blended self-interest, what historians have called liberalism, with public good, republicanism in the current lexicon. For him, the two concepts were not only intertwined but complementary: "The interest of

69. Ibid., 1119–20.
70. Ibid., 1123, 1126, 1121, 1123, in order of quotes.

the community is blended and inseparably connected with that of the individual. When he promotes his own, he promotes that of the community. When we consult the common good, we consult our own." With Madison, Marshall agreed that man's selfish nature made energetic and powerful national government necessary; with Hamilton he agreed that the objective of government was to energize economic individualism, which, as Adam Smith reasoned, would in turn strengthen the nation. The role of national government was not to regulate economic individualism but to encourage it by protecting private property, guaranteeing stability and encouraging the growth of markets. There is no evidence that he worried, as did Madison in *Federalist* 10, that competition among humans of unequal ability and property would result in factions that would threaten republican values. Madison thought the problem would be solved by enlarging the size of the Union; Marshall believed that the size of the Union was what necessitated power at the center in the first place. On this point, as on others, Marshall preferred Hamilton's views over Madison's. With both men he agreed that properly arranged institutions of government—a *written* constitution, separation of powers, and judicial review by the Supreme Court—constituted adequate barriers against the abuse of power by those who governed.[71]

And what about the people themselves in his scheme of government? With the Federalists he agreed that the sovereign people, and only they, could make or unmake constitutions. But could they also govern? Later Marshall would have doubts, and perhaps he already had them. But he was not foolish enough, as was Hamilton in 1800, to denigrate the people's capacity to govern—then ask for their vote. Accordingly, he expressed his faith in self-government. Or rather, he believed that those of the people who could vote were wise enough to elect their betters, then have enough sense to let them rule. This was his argument in defense of the Philadelphia Convention against Henry's charge that the Framers had usurped power. It was the same theory of representation Marshall used to defend the generous grant of power to Congress. Common sense tells us, he insisted, that "if you repose no confidence in delegates, because there is a possibility of their abusing it, you can have no Government; for the power of doing good, is inseparable from that of doing some evil." He reminded those who feared national government that national leaders would be chosen in free elections and that the states themselves were represented in the political branches of national government. Henry and company counted on

71. Ibid., 1123–24.

fear and distrust to preserve liberty and harkened back to the English constitution for comfort. Marshall looked forward to national institutions created by wise and inspired men and manned by proven leaders—the kind who once governed Virginia and stepped forth to lead the Revolution. Like Madison in *The Federalist* 51, he trusted the leaders of the new government with power, not just because of institutional guarantees against tyranny, but because the best and wisest would gravitate to the national government.[72]

Marshall's first address was his most general. In his following appearance, June 16th on the militia question, and in his final speech, June 20th on the federal judiciary, he applied the general principles he had previously adumbrated to the specific issue at hand. The style and tone of these speeches, though somewhat more muted, continued to be adversarial, which is to say, Marshall discredited his opponent's argument by ad hominem innuendo, feigned astonishment, and a high level of intolerance for sloppy reasoning and logical inconsistencies, which he had a lawyer's gift for spotting. Both speeches incorporated Federalist theory that the Constitution and the institutions of government created by it derived their authority from the sovereign people. Both reiterated his demand for a national government armed with real power and based on trust in the representative institutions, especially that of Congress.

Marshall's brief speech of June 16 about the militia, the shortest of his three speeches, addressed a curious argument put forth by Henry and William Grayson. They contended that the power given to Congress to call forth and regulate the militia—in Article 1, Section 8—totally obliterated states' "constructive implied power" in this area, thereby destroying their power to suppress insurrections. Marshall did not challenge the general theory regarding the virtues of the militia, that it was the republican alternative to standing armies. His position, firmly rooted in military experience and backed by no less an authority than Washington himself, was simply that short-term state militia units, which were reluctant to fight outside state borders, made strategic planning impossible. In times of national emergency, Congress needed the authority "to call forth the resources of all to protect all." Further, it did not follow that because Congress was authorized to do this by the Constitution that the states had surrendered permanent control over their own militia units.[73]

Nor was it the case that state authority could be established only by resorting to the tortured notion of a "constructive implied power." Using an axiom

72. Ibid., 1118–20.
73. VRD, 3: 1308.

of construction that would become his hallmark in federalism cases before the Supreme Court, Marshall contended instead that "each government," state and national, "derived its powers from the people; and each was to act according to the powers given it." The rule is this: "When power is given to the General Legislature, if it was in the State Legislatures before, both shall exercise it; unless there be an incompatibility in the exercise by one, to that; by the other; or negative words precluding the State Governments from it." In the case of the militias, there were no such incompatibilities and no negative words. "To me it appears then unquestionable, that the State Governments can call forth the militia, in case the Constitution should be adopted, in the same manner as they could have done, before its adoption." The states were free to use their militia "when they find it necessary"—as in cases of slave insurrection, which was probably the contingency that troubled Henry and Mason. In twelve years, during the Gabriel slave uprising in Richmond, Virginia would call out its militia to do just that. As a general in the state militia, John Marshall would be there.[74]

Marshall's speech on the militia is a window on his early thinking about federalism, and what he thought differs considerably from his reputation as a consolidating nationalist. In this area, as in others, he believed that state and national governments, armed with concurrent power, would actually cooperate to further the common good. In contrast were Henry and Grayson, who argued that congressional power to govern and call out the militia might be used to "form an Aristocratic Government." Marshall treated their argument as conspiratorial fantasy rooted in an unnatural fear and distrust. "When the Government is drawn from the people . . . and depending on the people for its continuance," he said, "oppressive measures will not be attempted, as they will certainly draw on their authors the resentment of those on whom they depend." If the people cannot be trusted to rule directly, he seemed to be saying, they can be trusted to judge those who do. In a curious manner, the young conservative statesman trusted the people because, in the deferential political culture he knew, they trusted the likes of him.[75]

Marshall spoke on the militia question as a soldier; he spoke about the federal judiciary as a Virginia lawyer. His impressive command of state legal process was a great advantage, because the Anti-Federalists claimed that the proposed federal judiciary would "annihilate" the business of the state courts.

74. Ibid., 1306–7.
75. Ibid., 1307–8.

When Mason, Henry, and company preached doom, Marshall spoke with authority about state dockets "crouded with suits." When they objected that the new Constitution did not specify the right to challenge jurors, or guarantee that jurors would be chosen from the vicinage, Marshall countered with the fact that neither did Virginia's constitution—nor did the English constitution, which Anti-Federalists persisted in citing as authority. Why, he argued, should federal jury trials be guaranteed in all cases when Virginia's constitution and state bill of rights did not do so? "The Legislature of Virginia does not give a trial by jury where it is not necessary. But gives it wherever it is thought expedient. The Federal Legislature will do so too, as it is formed on the same principles."[76]

The line of argument here is both clever and profound. He disarmed his adversaries by telling them what historical scholarship has shown to be true: that the federal government under the Constitution embodied many of the principles of existing state governments, that it was fashioned from native American materials, that it would be for the most part made up of Americans duly elected by the same people who elected state and local magistrates. Officials of the national government deserved trust and respect no less than those of Virginia. In short, why always think the worst? Article 3 gave Congress the authority to establish a system of lower federal courts. Why assume they would abuse this authority? How could Mason, Marshall asked, raise the specter of a federal judiciary that would drag Virginians to a distant capital, where they would be treated as foreigners, and at the same time object to the power given Congress to create lower federal courts within the reach of the people of each state? He was even more contemptuous of Mason's oft-expressed fear that "the Federal Sheriff," armed with the authority of supreme federal law and the compliance of the federal courts, "will go into a poor man's house, and beat him, or abuse his family." "Does any Gentleman believe this?" Marshall queried in a tone of voice that is easy to imagine. "Is it necessary that the officers will commit a trespass on the property or persons of those with whom they are to transact business? Will such great insults on the people of this country be allowable?" To ask the question was to answer it and, of course, to tag one of the Anti-Federalist mainstays as a man given to hysteria.[77]

This interchange with Mason takes us to the heart of the controversy and to the philosophical assumptions on which Marshall's constitutionalism rested.

76. Ibid., 1431–32, 1434–39.
77. Ibid., 1430–33.

Mason, like Henry and the Virginia Anti-Federalists in general, assumed the worst: that men would abuse power; that national power would inevitably destroy the states; that federal and state governments at best were destined to be in a perpetual state of conflict. Where Mason was motivated by fear and paranoia, Marshall relied on faith and trust. As he saw it, there was no reason to assume that national officials, who were elected by the people, were bent on evil; nor was there reason to doubt that local institutions and local courts could stand on their own against occasional abuses of authority. And there was, he insisted, nothing in the Constitution to keep them from doing just that. What Marshall adumbrated here, in his exchange with Mason over the extent of federal judicial power, was a view of federalism that operated on the basis of power sharing and mutual respect between state and nation. In the great sweep of American history, cooperation has been the norm. Marshall's mature constitutional view of federalism was designed to make this possible.[78]

It is also worthy of note that Marshall, the incipient conservative, had not entirely given up his early faith in the people, as he recalled having done. Even with his doubts, Marshall demonstrated more faith in popular, representative government than Anti-Federalists such as Mason and Henry, who presented themselves as the champions of the people. He hammered the point home when he returned to the question of whether Congress could be safely trusted with the power vested in it by Article 3 to create a system of lower federal courts. "Why not leave it to Congress?" he asked. "Will it enlarge their powers? Is it necessary for them wantonly to infringe your rights? Have you anything to apprehend, when they can in no case abuse their power without rendering themselves hateful to the people at large? When this is the case," and here he fell back on Virginia's own tradition of deferential leadership, "something may be left to the Legislature freely chosen by ourselves, from among ourselves, who are to share the burdens imposed upon the community, and who can be changed at our pleasure. Where power may be trusted, and there is no motive to abuse it, it seems to me to be as well to leave it undetermined, as to fix it in the Constitution." What he inferred here is what he later made

78. This functional view of federalism is developed in the first two volumes of Leonard D. White's pioneering four-volume administrative history: *The Federalists: A Study in Administrative History* (New York, 1948); *The Jeffersonians: A Study in Administrative History* (New York, 1951).

explicit in *McCulloch v. Maryland* (1819): that the Constitution was not and ought not be a code of laws. What he also learned to appreciate in 1788, and what became a staple of his jurisprudence, was the simple but profound fact that the Constitution was a *written* document that declared itself to be the supreme law of the land.[79]

This is to highlight the obvious: that the war over interpretation, which consumed so much of Marshall's life, and the life of the Supreme Court, began at the Virginia ratifying convention. What the future chief justice said about the Judiciary Article therefore is of special interest—not because his interpretations and predictions proved correct, but because we see him like everyone else peering through a glass darkly. For example, concerning federal jurisdiction over "disputes between a State, and the citizens of another State," he denied with assurance "that a State will be called at the bar of the Federal Court." Five years later Marshall was summoned to appear in *Chisholm v. Georgia* (1793), and he peremptorily refused to do so. On the other hand, Marshall was correct in asserting that suits in federal courts involving citizens of different states would be governed not by the law of the forum, as Mason fearfully predicted, but by the law of the state where the contract was made. In assessing the power of the federal judiciary stemming from its jurisdiction "in all cases arising under the Constitution and the laws of the United States," Marshall was partly right, partly wrong, and perhaps deliberately obtuse. He was correct in reminding Anti-Federalists that the power of Congress to pass federal laws was limited, a fact that automatically limited the interpretive domain of the federal courts. In the same reassuring vein, he observed that Congress cannot "make laws affecting the mode of transferring property, or contracts, or claims between the citizens of the same State." He did not see, or at any rate did not mention, the possibility that federal courts operating through diversity jurisdiction over suits between citizens of different states might make inroads into the domain of state contract law, which in fact they did. Even on the matter of Article 1, Section 10—which prohibited states from printing paper money and passing laws impairing the obligation of contracts—he downplayed the possibility of a standoff between the federal and state judiciaries. Obviously he had no foreknowledge of Section 25 of the Judiciary Act of September 1789, which would sharpen the conflict between state and federal courts by permitting the

79. VRD, 3: 1433.

Supreme Court of the United States to reverse or affirm state court decisions that held against a right claimed under a federal law.[80]

Given the Federalists' strategy of minimizing the nationalizing potential of the Constitution, it is impossible to say for sure whether Marshall said what he really believed regarding Article 3. Clearly he was far from omniscient. What he did see and appreciate, however—what the Anti-Federalists' arguments compelled him to acknowledge—was that the Constitution created a new body of supreme law, which the federal courts were obliged to bring to bear directly on the citizens of the states. This was a truly radical proposition. And what was true of the Contract Clause (Article 1, Section 10) was also true of the treaty-making authority granted to the president and the Senate. While the authority of Congress to legislate was limited, and thus indirectly the power of the federal courts under federal questions jurisdiction, the power of the national government to establish national law through the treaty power was not. Treaty law, even if it had domestic implications, would be binding on the states and their citizens and enforceable against them in federal courts. For the states' rights–minded Anti-Federalists—who were thinking of the provisions in the 1783 Treaty of Paris, which put national authority behind the payment of British debts—the treaty power in the Constitution, like implied powers, was a Trojan horse. For Marshall, the treaty power was an attribute of sovereignty. He had no way of knowing in 1788 that the Supreme Court over which he presided would use the treaties of 1783 and 1795 to confirm his title to the Fairfax lands by invalidating Virginia's sequestration act of 1777. What he must surely have understood was that the Constitution, treaty-making power included, would create an environment where business would thrive, because debts were secure and property safe.[81]

To argue that Marshall was commercial minded, is not to accuse him of being part of a capitalist conspiracy, any more than Henry was part of an agrarian conspiracy. Still, Marshall's personal interests influenced the way he perceived the public good. In fact, the connection between the two surfaced in an embarrassing way at the convention. The issue, raised by George Mason, concerned quitrents and the Fairfax lands in the Northern Neck. The delegates were well aware of the ongoing struggle between the state and the owners of

80. For Marshall on the danger of states being brought before the Supreme Court and on the jurisdiction of federal courts in general under the proposed constitution, ibid., 1433–36. *Chisholm v. Georgia,* 2 Dallas 419.

81. *Fairfax's Devisee v. Hunter's Lessee,* 7 Cranch, 603 (1813). For Anti-Federalist's criticism of treaty power, see VRD, 1: 44–45; VRD, 2: 806–7; VRD, 3: 1211–12.

the Fairfax lands. As George Nicholas observed caustically, "There are gentle-men who have come by large possessions, that it is not easy to account for." The collection of quitrents on those possessions was the specific point in dis-pute, and it was a highly fraught symbolic issue. Under English law, a quitrent was a rent paid by tenants of a freehold, discharging them of any other rent. To Northern Neck tenants who were required to pay this nominal rent, the tax, in addition to being a much-hated vestige of British authority, was simply a gouge. After Lord Fairfax's death in 1781, the Virginia House of Delegates passed an act sequestering all the quitrents due from the holders of those lands until the question of title was settled. The following year the legislature passed another act directing the quitrents to be paid to the legal representative of the Fairfax estate, that is to say, to John Marshall.[82]

Mason's attack was unmistakably ad hominem, and so was that of the ten-ants themselves, who referred to the Marshalls derisively as "lords" of the land. More important, however, Mason argued passionately that the federal courts under the new Constitution would override state confiscation of North-ern Neck land and validate the rights of speculators at the expense of the set-tlers who claimed under state law. Marshall wove and dodged as best he could, arguing—what after the adverse decision of the Court of Appeals to his clients in *Hite v. Fairfax* he already had some reason to doubt—that the whole matter of quitrents and title would be settled fairly and equitably by "our State Courts." Then realizing that the new Constitution would give federal courts a say in the matter, he included them in his formula. "If we can expect a fair decision any where," he asked rhetorically, "may we not expect justice to be done by the Judges of both the Federal and State Governments? . . . If a law be executed tyrannically in Virginia, to what can you trust? To your Judiciary. What security have you for justice? Their independence. Will it not be so in the Federal Court?" Both federal and state judges, and by extension the lawyers who argued before them, it would seem, were destined to be the special guard-ians of republican justice. The projected cooperation of state and federal courts was another dimension of his embryonic theory of cooperative federalism.[83]

Which brings us, as it brought him, to the question of judicial review—the power of the federal courts to void acts of Congress that violate the Constitu-tion and to do the same to state laws passed in violation of the Constitution,

---

82. For Mason's argument about the federal courts and the Northern Neck lands, see VRD, 3: 1407–9.

83. Marshall responded to Mason on June 20 in his speech on the judiciary, ibid., 1436.

treaties, and federal statutes. The *general* concept of judicial review, that legislative acts might be held answerable to higher law by the courts, was not new to the delegates and certainly not to Virginia lawyers. American patriots, interested in undermining the authority of Parliament before the Revolution, resorted to the idea of higher law and found some solace in Sir Edward Coke's holding in Dr. Bohnams's case (1610) that the common law trumped even an act of Parliament. The colonial practice, wherein colonial statutes in conflict with the common law might be disallowed by the privy council, was also a precedent of sorts. More directly relevant were examples from the postindependence period, in which state courts moved tentatively toward disallowing state statutes in conflict with state constitutions. One case, indeed the first one, from Virginia, which Virginia lawyers surely must have known, though it was not officially reported until much later, was *Commonwealth v. Caton* (1782). Most important were the relevant articles in the Constitution itself: Article 3, which gave federal courts jurisdiction over federal law, and Article 6, which made the Constitution, treaties, and federal statutes the supreme law of the land. If delegates did not see how these articles implied some form of judicial review, they had only to read Hamilton's *Federalist* 78 or, on the Anti-Federalist side, Robert Yates's "Letters of Brutus," the most compelling contemporary analysis of how the terms of the Constitution lead unavoidably to judicial review.[84]

The point is not that Marshall studied all of these general and specific precedents for judicial review or that he glimpsed the future meaning of the doctrine, rather that judicial review *as a general constitutional idea* was in the air in 1788. Given the remarkable growth of legislative government in both England and America in the late eighteenth century, the idea of judicial review was relevant as never before. Its existence was acknowledged by Federalists, who liked it but for obvious reasons minimized its nationalizing potential, and by Anti-Federalists, who disliked it because they saw that potential all too clearly. Marshall was one of the delegates who got the point, and he addressed the issue in

---

84. Jack M. Sosin, *Aristocracy of the Long Robe: The Origins of Judicial Review in America* (Westport, Conn., 1989), is especially good on the English background of judicial review. Learned discussions of the background of judicial review are found in Sylvia Snowiss, *Judicial Review and the Law of the Constitution* (New Haven, Conn., 1990), and Robert Lowry Clinton, *Marbury v. Madison and Judicial Review* (Lawrence, Kans., 1989). *Commonwealth v. Caton* is discussed in Mays, *Letters and Papers of Edmund Pendleton*, 2: 190–202. Yates's "Letters of Brutus" are conveniently excerpted in Alpheus T. Mason, ed., *The States Rights Debate: Antifederalism and the Constitution* (Englewood Cliffs, N.J., 1964), 104–10.

his June 20 speech on the federal judiciary. What he liked most about judicial review, judging from what we have seen of his experience in the 1780s, was that it could be applied against the states, a point explicitly made in Article 6. What he emphasized in his speech, however—to appease the Anti-Federalists' fear of national government and to disguise his disillusionment with state government—was that judicial review could work to limit the power of Congress. "If they [Congress] were to make a law not warranted by any of the powers enumerated," he declared in language that echoed Hamilton's *Federalist* 78, "it would be considered by the Judges as an infringement of the Constitution which they are to guard:—They would not consider such a law as coming under their jurisdiction.—They would declare it void."[85]

Marshall did not say whether the Court's decision in such a case would be binding on Congress, or only on the parties in the case; or what the Court would do if Congress ignored its decision or if the president refused to enforce it. These fundamental issues were not addressed by Marshall or anyone else in 1788. In fact, Marshall would not address them fully in *Marbury v. Madison* (1803), which leaves us to consider what he added to the idea of judicial review in that opinion that Federalist and Anti-Federalist theorists, lawyers, and judges had not already considered.

His June 20 speech on the judiciary was his last of the convention, which wound up its work a week later. The vote on ratification, conditioned on a promise for amendments but not for a second convention, was eighty-nine for, seventy-nine against, two absent. It was a decisive victory for the nationalists, for without Virginia in it, the Union might well have died aborning, especially since New York might have followed suit. It was also a personal triumph for young Marshall. In an age when great men spoke and others listened, he had spoken with force, and if we believe Madison, he ranked fifth among convention worthies in terms of his contributions. His position as a Virginia statesman was secure and so was the promise of a future in the national government, should he choose to have one. Marshall had also staked out the general constitutional position he would bring to the political battles of the 1790s and ulti-

---

85. PJM, 1: 277. On growth of legislative government in England, see David Lieberman, *The Province of Legislation Determined: Legal Theory in Eighteenth-Century Britain* (New York, 1989). Gordon Wood's Holmes Devise Lecture, "The Origins of Judicial Review Revisited, Or How the Marshall Court Made More Out of Less," 9 October 1998 at Washington and Lee School of Law, builds on Lieberman to explore the political context of judicial review in the early Republic. Wood's speech is printed in *Washington and Lee Law Review* 56 (summer 1999): 787–809.

mately to the Supreme Court. There were, of course, many puzzling ambiguities. He was a nationalist, but what that meant in an age in which culture was still local was far from clear. His position on political democracy was also ambiguous. There is no doubt that the 1780s had diminished Marshall's faith in popular government. At the convention, however, he championed representative government at the national level, leaving it to the Anti-Federalists to question the capacity of the people to govern. If he showed his colors as a law-and-order conservative, he also demonstrated faith that the American people, with the help of well-constructed institutions, could control their collective destiny.

Patrick Henry glimpsed the complex truth of the matter when he observed that the Constitution Marshall supported "is a revolution as radical as that which separated us from Great Britain." Henry was right: creating a nation where there was none and superimposing it on a predominantly local culture was a radical thing to do. By this reckoning, Marshall the common-law, law-and-order conservative was also a radical. Six years of fighting and six more of governing and lawyering taught him a constitutional version of the American Revolution. In his view, this law-abiding, property-protecting Revolution would make further revolution unnecessary. On the other hand, Marshall's conservative view of the Revolution led him to support a Constitution that promised and promoted a radical transformation of society. And herein lay the Anti-Federalists' objections to ratification—and Marshall's objections to the Anti-Federalists. Whereas Henry and company believed that the Constitution repudiated the Revolution, Marshall believed the Constitution secured it. In the 1790s, when revolution swept France and Europe and social upheaval and political democracy unsettled America, these contending versions of the American Revolution would assume a new relevance. In defending his version of the Revolution in this turbulent decade, Marshall would fashion a constitutional-political philosophy that would govern his life's work on the Supreme Court.[86]

86. For Henry on the Constitution, see VRD, 2: 951.

CHAPTER TWO

Judicial Statesman *in the* Making: *Law and Politics in the 1790s*

There is no part of my Life that I look back upon with more pleasure, than the short time I spent with you. And it is the pride of my life that I have given this nation a Chief Justice equal to Coke or Hale, Holt or Mansfield.

—*John Adams to John Marshall, August 17, 1825*

His counsels were always the counsels of moderation, fortified and tried by the results of an enlightened experience.

—*Joseph Story on Marshall*

SOMETIME IN OCTOBER 1800, President John Adams learned that Chief Justice Oliver Ellsworth planned to resign because of ill health. Adams first offered the position to John Jay, who had served in the position from 1789 to 1795 and who on that account would be acceptable to the sitting justices and to the badly divided Federalists in the Senate. Jay refused, citing the weakness of the Court, whereupon Adams considered William Cushing, more it would appear for political than juridical reasons. Marshall, who as secretary of state no doubt had Adams's ear, favored William Paterson over either man. What Marshall apparently did not know was that Adams had decided to go outside the Court—so that he would not be denied the appointment due to the pending Federalist judicial bill, which reduced the size of the Court from six to five beginning with the next vacancy. To Marshall's great surprise, and the surprise of most everyone else, the president chose him. The exchange, as he recounted it many years later, went like this: "Who shall I nominate now?" asked Adams. Marshall suggested Paterson again and got a decided no. Then Adams said, "I believe I must nominate you." That apparently was pretty much the end of it. "Pleased as well as surprised," Marshall "bowed in silence" and left. It was a supremely republican moment. Adams said little and Marshall less. Nevertheless, both men understood that the mantle of Federalism had passed, from a past president to a future chief justice and from one generation to the next. The facts spoke for themselves. Not only had Jefferson beaten Adams in the November 1800 election, but the Democratic-Republicans, as the new party was called, had captured both the Senate and the House. Adams's unspoken assumption was that Federalist principles and the future of the Republic itself now rested on the Supreme Court and its new chief justice.[1]

Marshall and Adams saw the 1790s as a time of crisis, and scholars have begun to explore what they intuited: that the decade was a truly formative period in American political and constitutional development. Translating the words of the Constitution into practice, it would appear, was an act of creativity hardly less impressive or disputatious than framing the document in the first place. The necessities of governing, rather than quieting disagreements over the Constitution, only escalated the debate. When Secretary of the Treasury Hamilton announced his political/economic program, and only then, was it really clear what the Constitution meant. And it was decidedly not what James Madison had in mind when he framed the document or what Virginia statesmen had in mind when they ratified it.

More troubling still, as Americans tried to locate themselves in a hostile world where England and France struggled for commercial and ideological dominance, the debate over foreign policy exacerbated divisions over domestic policy. Taking their cue from Edmund Burke, Federalists viewed the social disruption at home, notably the Whiskey and Fries Rebellions and the rise of Democratic Societies, as inseparable from the Jacobeanism of the French Revolution. Not to be outdone in paranoia, the emerging party of Madison and Jefferson perceived the Federalists as a beachhead of English corruption, which the American Revolution was fought to destroy. During that great event, Americans had united to create a nation. Now they divided over what *kind* of nation they had created. By the end of the decade, the divisions had coalesced

---

1. John Stokes Adams, ed., *An Autobiographical Sketch by John Marshall* (Ann Arbor, Mich., 1937), 29–30. On the appointment, see Kathryn Turner [Preyer], "The Appointment of Chief Justice Marshall," *William and Mary Quarterly*, 3d ser., 17 (April 1960): 143–63.

into embryonic political parties, the kind the Constitution was supposed to make unnecessary and the size of the Union impossible. The one quality Federalists and Jeffersonian Republicans lacked, the essence of mature parties, was the willingness to compromise. The lines of cultural division they drew in the sand bided ill for the young Republic.[2]

Marshall was both a witness to and participant in the turbulent 1790s. Not only did he serve as a state legislator, but he quickly became the recognized leader of Virginia Federalists. His success in defending the domestic and foreign policies of Washington (and later Adams), in turn opened opportunities at the national level. Indeed, in the course of the decade, Marshall turned down jobs as attorney general of the United States, minister to France, and associate justice of the Supreme Court. Only reluctantly and at Washington's special urging did he run for Congress in 1799. Before that he served with Elbridge Gerry and C. C. Pinckney on the XYZ mission to France, where he got an unparalleled opportunity to compare revolutions. After serving a short term in the House of Representatives, and immediately before his appointment to the Supreme Court, Marshall served as secretary of state under Adams. Throughout the entire period, though less so after his return from the French mission in 1797, Marshall continued to practice law in Virginia. Indeed, as legislator, diplomat, and cabinet officer, he never ceased thinking as a lawyer—or comparing the way lawyers and judges governed to the devious ways of party politicians.

Wherever he turned in the 1790s, Marshall encountered the same perplexing questions: Could the radical social/economic forces abroad in the land be harnessed to the public good and harmonized with the principles of the Revolution as he understood them? Could the sovereign people, newly organized into political parties, be contained within the confines of deferential political culture? Could liberty rooted in a pervasive localism be accommodated to the national institutions created by the Constitution?

What he also came to realize as he grappled for answers was that political

2. The now standard work on the 1790s is Stanley Elkins and Eric McKitrick, *The Age of Federalism* (New York, 1993). More thematically focused is James Roger Sharp, *American Politics in the Early Republic: The New Nation in Crisis* (New Haven, Conn., 1993). John Howe's essay "Republican Thought and the Political Violence of the 1790s," *American Quarterly* 19 (summer 1967): 147–65, is still valuable. The rise of political parties is treated in Noble Cunningham Jr., *The Jeffersonian Republicans: The Formation of Party Organization, 1789–1801* (Chapel Hill, N.C., 1957); and Richard Hofstadter, *The Idea of a Party System: The Rise of a Legitimate Opposition in the United States, 1780–1840* (Berkeley, Calif., 1969).

questions had become constitutional ones and that the Constitution itself had become the focal point of party division. The question being debated, moreover, was not just what the Constitution meant, but *who was in charge of the process of interpretation*. Marshall himself would answer that question, at least in part, in *Marbury v. Madison*. But what he said in that case was a distillation of lessons learned in the 1790s about the possibilities of law and the limitations of politics. As a common lawyer in Virginia, where lawyering was governing, he came increasingly to see the judicial interpretation of the Constitution as the only alternative to a politicized Constitution. One may not agree with the line Marshall attempted to draw between law and politics, but there is no doubt that the distinction between the two was fundamental to his doctrine of judicial review and to his conception of the Supreme Court as uniquely essential to republican government.

Virginia Lawyer, the Science of Law, and the Art of Governance

Writing in 1803 as a "British Spy" traveling through America, William Wirt, a young Virginia lawyer on the eve of a distinguished legal career, pondered the decline of Virginia in the councils of the nation. The root cause, he concluded, was the gradual disappearance in Virginia of the great statesmen of the Revolution. To reverse the decline, he pinned his hopes on the two rising stars, James Monroe and John Marshall, and on the redeeming qualities of literary eloquence. It did not matter to Wirt's argument that the former school friends and Revolutionary comrades were now of different political persuasions. What counted was that both men, like Wirt himself, were lawyers and as such were equipped to play the role of redeemers. Wirt seems to have intuited what Tocqueville would later make explicit: that lawyers in America, by virtue of their monopoly on the legal process constituted a "party" that "acts upon the country imperceptibly, [and] finally fashions it to suit its own purposes." Wirt understood that law was the language of power and those who mastered it were in a position to mediate disputes between individuals and shape policy for their communities, their states, and their nation. In the republican scheme of things, lawyers were an integral part of the scheme of self-government.[3]

3. William Wirt, *The Letters of the British Spy* (1803; reprint, Chapel Hill, N.C., 1970), letter 5, 171–85. Alexis de Tocqueville, *Democracy in America*, ed. Phillips Bradley (New York, 1959), 1: 288–90.

Virginia's legal culture, caught as it was in the throes of republican reform, was uniquely constituted to drive this lesson home to Marshall. Behind the reforms of this period—the creation of a new state constitution in 1776; the adoption of a bill of rights and a statute of religious freedom; and the effort inspired by Jefferson, Pendleton, and Wythe in 1779 to reform Virginia statute law—was a profound proposition: that law can be deliberately fashioned by a people to suit its needs and its genius. While Marshall was too young to have been involved in these early reforms, he got the message nonetheless. Especially suitable to his practical temperament and more relevant to his life was the effort to modernize the state court system and, at the same time, professionalize the practice of law.

The main target of this reform movement was the county court system. Peopled by lay judges elected co-optively from the local gentry, these institutions symbolized the Old Dominion's standing order. Few of the justices of the peace who sat on the courts were lawyers, and the law they dispensed was rough-hewn, idiosyncratic, and for those reasons increasingly inadequate to the economic needs of Virginia's business and planter interests. Reformers attempted to solve the problem by establishing four new state courts. The General Court, the main common-law forum of original jurisdiction and the intermediate appellate court hearing appeals from the county courts, was made up of five judges. Reformers also established a separate Chancery Court, made up of three judges, reduced later to one; a Court of Admiralty; and finally, as the state's final appellate court, the Court of Appeals. Originally composed of judges from all the other superior courts, the Court of Appeals was later made a separate court composed of five judges elected by both houses of the legislature. It had authority to hear appeals from all the other courts, subject only to limitation based on the money at issue in the case. The judges who sat on these courts and the lawyers who practiced before them, unlike those at the county court level, would be trained in the law.[4]

Two other changes, supported by Marshall, completed the picture of institutional modernization. One was the passage in 1788 of a district court bill, which, in order to provide an alternate forum to the county courts, divided the single General Court into eighteen districts, each with its own judges. The

---

4. For late eighteenth-century Virginia legal culture, see A. G. Roeber, *Faithful Magistrates and Republican Lawyers: Creators of Virginia Legal Culture, 1680–1810* (Chapel Hill, N.C., 1981). David J. Mays, *Edmund Pendleton, 1721–1803: A Biography*, 2 vols. (Cambridge, Mass., 1952), is a magnificent study of Virginia law in action during this period. PJM, vol. 5, *Selected Law Cases, 1784–1800*, is the basic source on Marshall's legal practice.

other change, which came with the ratification of the federal Constitution and the passage of the Judiciary Act of 1789, was the appearance in Virginia of a federal district court, limited in this period largely to admiralty and maritime matters, and a federal circuit court. To the modern eye, the division of jurisdiction between federal and state courts provided by this act was a reasonable compromise. Anti-Federalists at the Virginia ratifying convention, and Jeffersonian Republicans in the 1790s, were not pacified. For Anti-Federalists, the new courts were dangerous intruders, ones that inevitably diminished state judicial authority by providing alternate legal forums for the settlement of disputes. They were right, especially regarding the new federal circuit court, which was authorized to hear cases in which the state was a party and cases in which the Constitution, federal statutes, or treaties were called into question. Most importantly, the federal circuit courts had jurisdiction in suits between citizens of different states. It did not relieve Anti-Federalist fears, either, that the circuit court, manned by a district judge and two U.S. Supreme Court justices on circuit (one after 1793), was located in Richmond and conveniently held two yearly sessions, in the spring and in the fall. For Virginia localists, federal justice, and the federal authority that came with it, was *too* readily available. For Marshall, the new federal courts made justice more accessible and opened new opportunities for the best lawyers.[5]

The arrangement of federal and state courts in Virginia defined the parameters of Marshall's legal world. Conveniently for him, Richmond was its epicenter. Both federal courts held their sessions there. So did the Virginia Court of Appeals, the state's highest court; the High Court of Chancery, which in Virginia was a separate court with its own bar; and also the state Court of Admiralty. Richmond in a sense was a lawyer's town, where professional prowess was a mark of distinction. The lawyers who gravitated there were Virginia's best and brightest, and most of them, like Marshall, belonged to Virginia's ruling class as well. Tightening the professional bonds more was the fact that the lawyers who practiced before the various courts frequently went on to serve as judges on them. George Wythe, who presided over the Court of Chancery dur-

---

5. Roeber, *Faithful Magistrates*, passim; and for a lucid summary, "The Court System of Post-Revolutionary Virginia," and Introduction, PJM, 5: xxviii–xxxiii. Charles Warren, "New Light on the History of the Federal Judiciary Act of 1789," *Harvard Law Review* 37 (1923): 49–132, discusses the compromise between nationalism and states' rights in the act of 1789. The conflict between state and federal courts in Richmond is discussed in Stephen B. Presser, *The Original Misunderstanding: The English, the Americans, and the Dialectic of Federalist Jurisprudence* (Durham, N.C., 1991), especially chs. 8 and 9.

ing these years, had taught many of the lawyers who argued before him, including Marshall. St. George Tucker, who as federal district court judge would sit with Marshall on circuit, was on the General Court during Marshall's years of practice. Edmund Pendleton, first as lawyer and later as senior judge on the Court of Appeals, had a profound influence on all those who associated with him, which included Marshall. The reformed district court system also facilitated the relationships among lawyers, since established practitioners farmed out their business before the General Court to beginning lawyers practicing in outlying districts, reserving appeals to themselves. Marshall followed this practice. Among the many noteworthy lawyers and judges whose lives would intersect with his were Patrick Henry, whose partisan opposition turned to friendship and love; Spencer Roane, Marshall's ablest and most caustic critic; Littleton Tazewell, who was a critic without being caustic; and William Wirt, a Jeffersonian who was also an early and influential admirer of Marshall and who as attorney general of the United States would present grist for Marshall's great nationalist opinions. Also among Marshall's friends and rivals at the bar were John Wickham, Edmund Randolph, John Taylor of Caroline County, and Bushrod Washington.[6]

The Richmond Bar was deeply rooted in the life of the community, understanding its business needs and, as shall be seen shortly, sharing its deepest secrets. The city's lawyers were also highly competitive and conscious of degrees of eminence and rank won in honest adversarial combat. Some of these lawyerly jousts were highly personal, as was the long and bitter rivalry between the scholarly Wythe on the Court of Chancery and the more practical-minded Pendleton, leading judge on the Court of Appeals. On the whole, however, camaraderie prevailed, rooted as it was in shared social values and the "taught tradition of the common law." Virginia lawmakers put their own impress on that tradition. Significantly, and ironically, their most audacious act of creation was to adapt the English legal inheritance to chattel slavery. Or to be more precise, they made chattels out of slaves in order to make English rules of property applicable to the plantation-slave economy. In any case, Virginia lawyers had to know the common law and Virginia modifications of it. Those, like Marshall, who practiced extensively in Richmond's federal district and circuit

---

6. On Richmond's legal community, Roeber, *Faithful Magistrates,* especially ch. 5. Marshall's practice and the Virginia court system is summarized in PJM, 5: Introduction, xxiii–lx, and in the editorial notes throughout. Mays, *Pendleton: A Biography,* ch. 7, contains a spirited description of Marshall and his contemporaries at the bar.

courts also had to master federal law. Binding the entire system together, supplying both its intellectual premises and its institutional framework, was the common law, which survived the Revolution remarkably intact. In both state and federal courts, the common-law, case-controversy process prevailed, thanks in large part to the federal Process Acts of the early 1790s, which made the procedural rules of state courts applicable to federal practice. The ancient practice of writ pleading, though modified and streamlined, still prevailed in Virginia common-law courts as well, although judges rarely nonsuited cases because of technical errors in filing. Nearly all of Marshall's common-law cases, as the editors of *The Papers of John Marshall* have established, were either debt cases or cases brought to recover damages for personal injury. These cases proceeded by formal causes of action referred to as writs. The writs Marshall commonly pleaded were "debt," where the specific amount due was generally acknowledged by contract under seal; "assumpsit," for contractual obligations not under seal; and "trespass on the case" or just "case," which was applicable to a wide range of personal injuries such as libel, slander, and nuisance. Even special pleading, the most intricate and demanding aspect of traditional common-law practice, was still in use.[7]

What Marshall concluded about law from this highly structured way of doing business can only be surmised, since he did not theorize about the matter. Indeed writ pleading discouraged theorizing. Pleading writs also tended to support the idea, prevalent in Blackstone and the continental jurists as well, that the law administered in the courts preexisted as something to be discovered and not created: a body of time-tested, perhaps even God-given, legal principles embodied in judicial decisions over time and rooted in time beyond memory in custom.

On the surface, then, Marshall's legal practice was highly formal, but it was also highly practical and down to earth. Mastering the formal writs was only the first step. After that, the challenge was not to change the law or to speculate about it, but to fit the facts presented by the client into standard legal pigeonholes. To make the system work, lawyers had to master the business of their

7. Common-law procedure in Virginia during Marshall's practice is discussed in PJM, 5: xxxiii–li. William E. Nelson, *Americanization of the Common Law: The Impact of Legal Change on Massachusetts Society, 1760–1830* (Cambridge, Mass., 1975), discusses the shift away from writ pleading in another jurisdiction. On Virginia slave law, see Thomas D. Morris, *Southern Slavery and the Law, 1619–1860* (Chapel Hill, N.C., 1996), and Philip J. Schwarz, *Slave Laws in Virginia* (Athens, Ga., 1996). On the Process Acts, see Julius Goebel Jr., *Antecedents and Beginnings to 1801* (New York, 1971), 509–35.

clients, whether it concerned a contract between planters and Scottish factors doing business in the international tobacco market or was a contested will among family members over land and slaves. The second feature of Virginia practice in Marshall's time was pleading in open court. Modern litigators pleading simply to either guilt or innocence locate the determinative issues of both fact and law in open-ended and ongoing arguments during the course of the trial. In late eighteenth-century Virginia, the give and take, if not entirely prefabricated, was carefully channeled into well-worn legal categories. As long as the factual environment remained fairly constant, the writ system of meshing law with fact continued to work. Marshall's legal world, then, was one where continuity and change were held in delicate balance, where practicality and serviceability held sway over theorizing.

His talents fit the demands of this professional world to a T. Indeed, the fit was so snug that historians have been tempted to believe Marshall when he said in 1818 that he was "destined for the bar from infancy." At the very least, Virginia culture, as refracted through his father, pointed him in that direction at an early age. Thomas Marshall put a copy of Blackstone in his son's hands in 1772, because he knew what was common wisdom among the planter elite: that law was the open sesame to power and possibly even republican fame. It helped, too, that legal education was easy to acquire, the more so because of the chaotic nature of the profession during the Revolution. A bit of Blackstone before the war, three months with George Wythe at William and Mary in 1780, and a few months of reading later got John Marshall in the door. More surprising still, this minimalist legal education served him remarkably well. In a legal system that was still deeply English, a study of Blackstone's *Commentaries* was indeed a practical introduction for a working lawyer, not least because every other lawyer in Virginia started the same way. In addition to being a law dictionary and encyclopedia, Blackstone served book-starved American lawyers as a guide to substantive legal principles, conveniently backed by English cases ready for citation. Blackstone's focus on the law of real property made the *Commentaries* especially relative to Virginia, as did the mixture of legal science and natural law he made the foundation of his jurisprudence. If Marshall concluded from Blackstone that law was a "scientific" body of time-tested rules and principles, he joined hundreds of other American lawyers of his age.[8]

8. Marshall to Joseph Delaplaine, 22 March 1818, PJM, 8: 187. On the unique attraction of American lawyers to Blackstone's *Commentaries,* see Daniel J. Boorstin, *The Mysterious Science of the Law: An Essay on Blackstone's Commentaries* (Boston, 1958).

George Wythe's law course at William and Mary built on the foundation Blackstone laid by mixing learning with practical application. For example, Marshall's participation in moot court exercises and mock legislatures—the heart of Wythe's program—was immensely useful in a legal culture that relied on oral debate both in the courtroom and the halls of the legislature. Wythe was also familiar with leading decisions of Virginia's courts, which were not yet printed, and no doubt drew on them for his lectures. He also introduced his students to the legislative process, knowing that many of them would serve in the Virginia House of Delegates. Marshall participated in the mock legislatures, and we know from his commonplace book that he studied the Virginia Acts of Assembly (1769). No practicing lawyer could ignore the work of the House of Delegates, if for no other reason than the fact that statutes were the chief means of adjusting English common law to Virginia circumstances. In fact, Marshall spent as much time or more during the early years of his practice in the House of Delegates as he did in the courtroom.[9]

Judging from the numerous citations in Marshall's legal arguments, his introduction to formal treatise literature under Wythe was also extremely relevant. It is impossible to ascertain the full range of his reading, though we do know, thanks to the scholarship of Hamilton Bryson, that the range of available legal literature in Virginia was surprisingly large. Marshall's commonplace book, compiled during his study with Wythe indicates that he spent considerable time studying Matthew Bacon's *New Abridgement of the Law,* the standard encyclopedia of English law for that age. Equally important were Hugo Grotius and above all Emmerich de Vattel. These jurists dealt primarily with the emerging law of nations, or international law, a subject especially useful to Marshall in the early decades of his tenure as chief justice, when the American involvement in the struggle between France and England made international law a staple of adjudication. Like Blackstone's *Commentaries,* the continental jurists conveyed the impression that law was a moral enterprise where rational principle could be made to prevail in the affairs of nations. Without knowing it, the young men who grew up in Revolutionary Virginia, who read law with George Wythe, shared in the Enlightenment belief that human rationality might control human destiny. It was Wythe's assumption,

9. See Alonzo Thomas Dill, *George Wythe: Teacher of Liberty* (Williamsburg, Va., 1979). For Marshall's "Law Notes," with an editorial introduction, see PJM, 1: 37–87. Mays, *Pendleton: A Biography* contains useful information on Wythe as well as on the practice of law in Virginia in this period. Also W. Hamilton Bryson, *Legal Education in Virginia, 1779–1979: A Biographical Approach* (Charlottesville, Va., 1982), Introduction and essay on Wythe, 749–55.

and his students' as well, that they were destined to play a role in this great enterprise—indeed, that it was their republican duty to do so.[10]

Marshall shared the republican approach to lawyering, and the fact no doubt contributed to his success. Other things helped, too, one being friends in high places. One such was Edmund Randolph, who took the newly minted lawyer in as a junior partner. Only two years older than Marshall, Randolph was an ideal conduit into the elite ranks of Virginia lawyers. He came from a distinguished line of Virginia jurists that started with his grandfather, Sir John Randolph, who had been one of the select group of Virginia lawyers who studied in the Inns of Court. Following in the footsteps of his father, under whom he studied, and his uncle Peyton Randolph (both studied law at the Middle Temple), Edmund Randolph became Virginia's first attorney general under the new state constitution of 1776. He had a lucrative practice, was a gifted teacher, and also was one of the official examiners for admission to the bar. He was a lawyer who knew what Virginia lawyers needed to know.[11]

Working alongside Randolph, Marshall learned on the job. And because the courts were closed to regular business from 1781 to 1784, there was ample time to do so. Among the staples of his continuing legal education during these years were newly available treatises on law and equity and reports of English cases in both. Increasingly, these were supplemented by the reports of Virginia appellate courts and by state statute law. The availability of these important Virginia legal materials, it should be noted, did not alter the basic common-law structure. The challenge was to meld native materials with continental treatise literature into that structure. Marshall's mastery of the process is clear from the fact that Randolph transferred his extensive practice to him when Randolph became governor in 1786.[12]

If one counts Marshall's three years with Randolph as a sort of apprenticeship, it is clear that Marshall's legal education, far from being deficient, as was once thought, was one key to his success. Personal popularity also counted heavily in his favor, since Richmond lawyers and judges were closely connected and mutually dependent. And since the profession was still the domain, if not the birthright, of a privileged elite, it helped business to be a family friend of

10. On legal literature in colonial Virginia, consult W. Hamilton Bryson, *Census of Law Books in Colonial Virginia* (Charlottesville, Va., 1978).

11. PJM, 5: lii–liii. For Randolph, see *Dictionary of American Biography* (New York, 1953), 15: 353–55.

12. Charles F. Hobson describes Marshall's early practice and friendship with Randolph in PJM, 5: lii–liii.

George Washington; a blood relative, however distant, of the founder of the Randolph line; and a son-in-law of state treasurer and first-family patriarch Jaquelin Ambler. With connections such as these, it is not surprising that Marshall's practice included a goodly number of Virginia's first families, partisan divisions notwithstanding. The military associations that propelled him into political office also augmented his early practice. A burgeoning case load, the importance of his clients, and even the fact that he represented plaintiffs in a disproportional number of cases, all point to the same conclusion: that by the early 1790s, Marshall was Virginia's "can do" lawyer, the man to retain when the stakes were high and the legal terrain rough.[13]

If personality and social connections aided his rise, what kept him on top was a genius for making law work for his clients. This quality is easier to document than to explain. One thing was clear: he did not succeed by emulating his mentor George Wythe, who loved legal learning for its own sake, Latin quotations as well, and who as chancellor never ceased being the professor. This is not to say, as was once said, that Marshall was deficient in black-letter learning. The main point, however, was not how many authorities he could cite but that he knew which ones were relevant to the case at hand. Marshall was a working lawyer, whose knowledge of the law was working knowledge at the ready. What he knew transported him from point A to point C efficiently, convincingly, and better than almost anyone around. On this, friend and foe agreed. Francis Gilmore, who had crossed swords with him many times over the years, noted that Marshall's mind "is not very richly stored with knowledge," but "is so creative, so well organized by nature, or disciplined by early education, and constant habits of systematick thinking, that he embraces every subject with the clearness and facility of one prepared by previous study to comprehend and explain it." Even Thomas Jefferson, who very early on disliked and distrusted Marshall, reputedly found his ability to persuade dangerously hard to resist. If you granted Marshall the toehold of a premise, Jefferson is reputed to have complained, then all was lost: "Why, if he were to ask me whether it were daylight or not, I'd reply, 'Sir, I don't know, I can't tell.'"[14]

13. My account of Marshall's practice draws heavily on Hobson's Introduction and editorial notes in PJM, 5.

14. Gilmore is quoted in Albert J. Beveridge, *The Life of John Marshall* (Boston, New York, 1916–1919), 2: 178. Rutherford B. Hayes heard the anecdote in Joseph Story's lecture at Harvard Law School and recorded it in his diary, 20 September 1843, *Diary and Letters of Rutherford Birchard Hayes*, ed. Charles R. Williams (Columbus, Ohio, 1922–1926), 1: 116. Story repeated the substance of the anecdote in his eulogy of Marshall. William W. Story, ed., *The Miscellaneous Writings of Joseph Story* (Boston, 1852), 686.

Perhaps William Wirt, whose arguments would one day impress Chief Justice Marshall, best captured the unique blend of law learning and logic, style, and personality that accounted for Marshall's effectiveness in the courtroom. His success, Wirt tells us, was not physical appearance, which verged on eccentricity. Nor was it rhetorical sophistication or dramatic delivery. Marshall's voice, as Wirt described it, was "dry, and hard; his attitude, in his most effective orations, was often extremely awkward; as it was not unusual for him to stand with his left foot in advance, while all his gesture proceeded from his right arm, and consisted mainly in a vehement, perpendicular swing of it, from about the elevation of his head, to the bar, behind which he was accustomed to stand." Yet for all Marshall's inelegance, Wirt concluded that he "deserves to be considered as one of the most eloquent men in the world; if eloquence may be said to consist in the power of seizing the attention with irresistible force, and never permitting it to elude the grasp, until the hearer has received the conviction which the speaker intends." Marshall's "one original, almost supernatural, faculty," Wirt continued, was "the faculty of developing a subject by a single glance of his mind, and detecting at once, the very point on which every controversy depends"—this "as easy as vision" itself. As did Jefferson, Wirt detected in Marshall the wily intellect of a superb lawyer: "In a bad cause his art consisted in laying his premises so remotely from the point directly in debate, or else in terms so general and so specious, that the hearer, seeing no consequence which could be drawn from them, was just as willing to admit them as not; but his premises once admitted, the demonstration, however distant, followed as certainly, as congenially, as inevitably, as any demonstration of Euclid."[15]

That Marshall preferred clarity of argument to copious citations and idle displays of learning was a point strongly in his favor given the nature of Virginia practice. Not coincidentally, it was also the style of Judge Edmund Pendleton, after whom Marshall modeled himself. The common-sense common law Marshall argued and Pendleton handed down worked well for Virginians. Indeed, in its own way, Virginia law was no less functional and policy driven than the "instrumentalist" legal culture generated later by rapid industrialization in the middle and northern states. The chief difference was that Virginia lawmakers did not have to transform the basic precepts of common law to make it work. Rather than a vision of what law should be, Marshall had an intimate understanding of the social/economic interests of Virginians, from the

---

15. Wirt, *Letters of the British Spy,* 179–80.

businessmen in Richmond and Norfolk, who were interested in expanding manufacturing and commerce and who hoped to integrate Virginia into the growing national and international market, to the agrarian, slaveholding planters, who still dominated Virginia's political and economic life and who were trying to adjust to a world where tobacco was no longer profitable and cotton was not yet king. Those who mediated conflict among these interests—who maintained rules for the exchange of goods, who settled disputes over inheritance—were the governors of Virginia no less than elected officials. John Marshall belonged to this group. Indeed, he possessed all the attributes of Tocqueville's American legal aristocracy—forty years before the Frenchman articulated the concept. Marshall's mastery of law's mysteries set him apart from his clients, yet he belonged to their social class. They turned to him with trust because he understood what they wanted and delivered what they needed.

Not surprisingly, the cases Marshall tried trace the contours of Virginia's social/economic landscape. In the first place, he practiced almost exclusively at the state appellate level and after 1790 in the federal circuit court in Richmond. Because of jurisdictional cutoffs and because the appeal process itself was expensive, most of his cases involved considerable amounts of money. Prominent merchants and planters appear frequently among his clients. Among the most prominent was Robert Morris of Pennsylvania, one of the richest and most aggressive entrepreneurs of his age. As a constitutional nationalist, Morris no doubt liked Marshall's Federalist politics. It helped, too, that John Marshall's brother James Markham Marshall married Morris's daughter and was the front man for many of Morris's speculative ventures in land. Above all, Morris was an astute businessman, who channeled his Virginia business to Marshall because he was the best money could hire. Since he was a professional lawyer who lived on professional earnings, money counted for Marshall, too, and after his purchase of the Fairfax lands in 1793, it counted a lot more. That simple fact accounts for much concerning Marshall's practice of law: why he gravitated to appellate courts, why he latched on to the British debt cases as a professional staple, and why he stayed away from criminal cases, which were notoriously fee poor. Like other leading Virginia lawyers of his time, he was not often retained by ordinary folk.[16]

Marshall's high-profile cases from the 1790s bear witness to his stature in the profession and his connection with Virginia's social elite. More to the

16. For an overview of Marshall's professional life, see Hobson's Introduction and editorial notes in PJM, 5.

point, however, they illustrate his role as republican lawyer. Especially revealing in this regard are *Bracken v. College of William and Mary* (1790), *Commonwealth v. Randolph* (1793), and *Ware v. Hylton* (1796). In the first case, Marshall helped resolve a policy dispute between the faculty and board of governors of Virginia's leading educational institution. The second, one of Marshall's few criminal cases, dealt with charges of infanticide brought against a member of one of Virginia's leading families, one to which Marshall himself belonged. In *Ware,* he was retained in what amounted to a class-action suit, designed to shield Virginia planters and merchants from their pre-Revolution debts to British merchants. Though radically different in subject matter, all three cases converge on the fact that Virginia lawyers in general, and Marshall in particular, were deeply involved in the process of community rule making and conflict resolution.[17]

Bracken concerned the governance of the College of William and Mary. In it, the visitors, the governing body under the original charter, were pitted against the faculty for control of educational policy at the institution. The case was set in motion in 1779 when the visitors introduced reforms designed to improve the quality of education and bring the school into the republican age. One thing they did was abolish the grammar school, which had been attached to the college and which had the responsibility of preparing students for admission by upgrading their skills in the classical languages. In the process, the visitors also eliminated the faculty member in charge of the school. In defense of its authority, and of the property right of the professor to his position, the faculty claimed that the act of the visitors was *ultra vires,* that it exceeded the powers granted the visitors by the charter. When negotiations between the parties failed, the faculty retained John Taylor of Caroline County and turned to the courts to settle the matter. Marshall was retained by the visitors in 1787 and argued the first of two cases regarding the college before the Court of Appeals in 1790.

The case turned on the meaning of the ambiguously worded language of the charter, which authorized the board of visitors to pass regulations for the governance of the college in "all Business of great Weight and Consequence especially if the President and Masters cannot agree." The charter also granted the

17. *Bracken* is discussed by editors Charles T. Cullen and Herbert A. Johnson in PJM, 2: 67–72; for Marshall's argument in the Court of Appeals, ibid., 72–81. The Randolph case, heard before the Cumberland County Court, is analyzed in PJM, 2: 161–68; *Ware v. Hylton,* 3 Dallas 199, is discussed in PJM, 3: 4–7. Marshall's argument appears at ibid., 7–14.

president and faculty "ordinary Authority" in the administration of the school. Taylor contended that the changes in the structure and curriculum introduced by the board of visitors in 1779 exceeded its powers under the charter and in doing so infringed on the traditional prerogatives of the faculty. Accordingly, he asked the court to issue a mandamus, directed to the visitors and prohibiting them from firing the Reverend John Bracken and from implementing other structural reforms they had ordered.[18]

Marshall responded astutely. Rather than dispute the ambiguities of charter language, the inconclusiveness of which invited a political resolution of the dispute, he argued a strictly legal point: that by law the college was "a private eleemosynary institution." The distinction was between corporate aggregates that are "for public government" and those that are "for private charity." In the latter, authority belongs to the founder-benefactor and to whomsoever he vested power to govern in perpetuity, in this case, the visitors. Taylor's contention that Bracken had a vested right in his job, claimed Marshall, ignored the rule governing charitable corporations: that the donor can "annex such conditions as his own will or caprice may dictate." Marshall also mobilized authority to prove that the eleemosynary nature of William and Mary had not been altered by the fact that the colony and state of Virginia had given it public support. In support of these general and other more subtle points, Marshall expounded on Lord Holt's famous opinion in *Philips v. Bury* (1694), and cited *King v. Bishop of Ely* (1756) and *King v. Chancellor, Masters, and Scholars of the University of Cambridge* (1681), among other English cases. References to Blackstone's *Commentaries* figured throughout to bolster Marshall's argument that the powers of the board of visitors followed from the private nature of the corporation.[19]

Marshall impressed the judges, who ruled unanimously for the visitors and for reform. His effort was remarkable in several respects, not the least of which is the fact that his argument prefigured in several important respects his famous opinion three decades later in *Dartmouth College v. Woodward* (1819), which also turned on the distinction between public and private corporations. *Bracken* also bears the distinctive stamp of Marshall's advocacy: an ability to combine "reason" and "authority," as the court acknowledged; a knack for bringing complex matters into sharp conceptual focus (into three main ques-

18. PJM, 2: 69–70.
19. Ibid. 75. Marshall's citations from English case law are found in the editorial footnotes to his argument, ibid., 74–81.

tions); and his preference for plain English over arcane law terminology. The fact that Marshall drew freely on arguments prepared by St. George Tucker in the trial phase of the case, as well as those of Edmund Randolph, also illustrates the cooperative, and elite, nature of the Virginia Bar at this time. That Marshall handled the final phase of such an important case after only six years of practice is clear evidence of his high professional standing. That his argument carried the day also illustrates the point stressed here: that private lawyers were active participants in public lawmaking. To put it another way, the telling point in *Bracken* was not the doctrine that colleges were private eleemosynary institutions but rather that the political dispute regarding the nature and form of higher education in Virginia was settled by judges and by lawyers like Marshall. Tocqueville was on to something when he observed that the bench and bar in America "form the only enlightened class whom the people do not mistrust."[20]

Evidence that Marshall was a trusted mediator of class interests is conspicuous in all facets of his practice, but nowhere more dramatically than in *Commonwealth v. Randolph,* heard on April 29, 1793, before the magistrates of the Cumberland County Court. The circumstances leading up to the case and, indeed, the resolution of the case itself are far from clear, except for one thing: that genteel society in Virginia was obsessed and bewildered by the enormity of the crime allegedly committed by two of their own. The accusation, circulated first as rumor and then as a charge, not to be confused with an indictment, in formal proceedings before the justices of the peace of the Cumberland County Court, was that Richard Randolph had impregnated his sixteen-year-old sister-in-law, Nancy Randolph, then assisted her in killing the baby by either aborting the fetus or murdering the newborn infant. In the plain language of the court, Richard Randolph "stands committed and charged with feloniously murdering a child said to be born of Nancy Randolph."[21]

What we know about this case itself—called by one authority "Virginia's most famous eighteen-century criminal proceeding"—comes entirely from Marshall's "Notes of Evidence," which were copied in the hand of John Randolph of Roanoke, who then expanded on the matter in his correspondence. Confusion abounds. There is no clear proof, for example, as to who actually brought the case. As the editors of *The Papers of John Marshall* point out, however, it is probable that Randolph himself, in consultation with his stepfa-

---

20. Tocqueville, *Democracy in America,* 1: 289.
21. Cumberland County Court Order Book, quoted in PJM, 2: 164 n. 7.

ther, St. George Tucker, and possibly with Marshall, brought the case as a way of stifling the increasingly vicious rumors. The proceedings of the court appear to have been highly informal, despite the fact that the magistrates were in effect sitting in the capacity of a grand jury in a capital felony case. Their ruling that Randolph was not guilty as charged and did not have to stand trial did not put the matter to rest. In fact, the evidence presented, according to Marshall's summary of it, seems clearly to have been enough to warrant indictment. By making the testimony public, moreover, the hearing may in fact have fueled rather than quelled the conflagration. In the unsettled aftermath of the hearing, Richard Randolph died and Nancy Randolph fled the state in disgrace. She became governess for the children of Gouverneur Morris in New York, then his wife.[22]

The entire episode lends itself more to melodrama, or perhaps a play by Tennessee Williams, than legal analysis. It does, however, throw light on Marshall's lawyering. He took notes on the testimony presented to the court by the witnesses, most of whom were relatives of Nancy Randolph and the accused. From these notes he fashioned, perhaps on the spot, what would appear to be a contingency brief in defense of Nancy should the case proceed to trial. Then he broke down the testimony into five questions, following which he sketched out, as Wirt said he was wont to do, a strategy designed to circumvent the damaging testimony, which most of it was. Or as Marshall euphemistically put it, he worked out a way of framing the questions so they might be examined "without favor or prejudice." In response to each piece of evidence against the accused—Richard and Nancy's reputedly unusual public displays of affection, Nancy's obvious "appearance of pregnancy," the application of "a medicine to produce an abortion," her strange behavior, and her refusal to be seen unclothed by family members or to be examined by Mrs. Page for evidence of pregnancy—Marshall fashioned a plausible interpretation for the court's ears.[23]

Whether his stratagems would have rescued Richard and Nancy from the severity of the law, we don't know; the case was never tried. The fact that it wasn't tells us something about the class-based system of communal justice

22. PJM, 2: 168, for quote about trial. "Marshall's Notes of Evidence," appear at ibid., 168–78; the excellent editorial treatment of the hearing at ibid., 161–68. For John Randolph's ruminations and relevant letters concerning the episode, see William C. Bruce, *John Randolph of Roanoke, 1773–1833* (1922; reprint, New York, 1970), 2: 272–98.

23. See Marshall's "Notes of Evidence," PJM, 2: 168–78, and also Editorial Note, ibid., 161–68.

and Marshall's place in it. In the confident, authoritative tone of his undelivered defense, he spoke the soothing words of a community leader, which is why he was retained in the first place. He also spoke as a man of moderation and good sense, who had seen a good deal of life and who refused to stand in judgment and urged others to do the same. His final words were: "The friends of Miss Randolph cannot deny, that there is some foundation on which suspicion may build: nor can it be denied by her enemies but that every circumstances may be accounted for, without imputing guilt to her. In this Situation Candor will not condemn or exclude from society, a person who may be only unfortunate." Fifteen years later, his friend Gouverneur Morris asked his opinion of Nancy Randolph, with whom Morris was contemplating marriage. Marshall again refused to pass judgment on "this unfortunate lady," who, whatever she did, was not a criminal but rather "the victim of a concurrence of unfortunate circumstances." Here and elsewhere, in his personal life as in his jurisprudence, Marshall started with human nature as he found it, life as it was and not as he wished it to be. His counsel was to live and let live.[24]

As a lawyer, his job was to facilitate community life—by mediating disputes and by supplying the rules by which Virginians lived and worked. This was true not only in leading cases such as *Bracken* and *Randolph* but in the run-of-the-docket cases that constituted the staple of his practice. His daily business was the business of Virginians, and it was often complex fare. Sometimes he argued in equity, sometimes in law. Sometimes he elected to argue in Virginia courts, where law and equity were administered in separate courts, and sometimes in federal courts. Presumably, he mediated out-of-court settlements when circumstances permitted it, though there is little documentation to prove it. Sometimes he litigated to facilitate a settlement; other times he litigated to judgment and execution. In every instance, he was, as part of the judicial system of Virginia, the nexus between the authority of the state and its individuals. And in the ordinary course of lawyering, Marshall unavoidably confronted the republican dilemma: how to balance the interests of the community as embodied in law with the liberty of individuals who wanted to harness law (backed by the authority of the state) to their own interests.

In an age before legal specialization, Marshall was of necessity a general practitioner. He moved easily between state and federal courts, which in many instances were governed by similar rules of procedure. He also practiced both law and equity—the latter before his old teacher George Wythe, who after

24. PJM, 2: 178, for quote; Marshall to Morris, 12 December 1809, PJM, 7: 220–21.

1788 was the sole chancery judge in Virginia, the former before Edmund Pendleton, the leading judge of the Virginia Court of Appeals. Given its centrality to Virginia justice, Marshall had to master equity and readily did so. Judging from *Barrett v. Floyd* (1790), however, he preferred the common law. *Barrett* was a prize case, decided first in the Court of Admiralty, then in the county court, the High Court of Chancery, and from thence to the Court of Appeals, where Marshall argued against the jurisdiction of the Court of Chancery on the ground that the common law could and indeed had provided a remedy. If the Court of Chancery "may interpose in this case," he warned, "there is no point of law which may not be carried into it." He further warned: Just because the judgment of the county court was contrary to the law as expounded by the Court of Admiralty, "does by no means admit the cognizance of a court of equity. Juries, under the direction of a court of law, judge upon the justice, as well as law of a case; and it would erect a Court of Chancery into still more than a Court of Appeals, if their verdicts might be set aside for injustice." What Marshall feared, if one might read between the lines, was that equity courts might, in their pursuit of pure justice, interfere with the regular administration of well-established common-law principles governing property and contract. Marshall loved and admired Chancellor Wythe, no doubt, but when push came to shove, he did not hesitate to choose the common law, and Edmund Pendleton, as the surest guarantee of liberty and property.[25]

Marshall's prejudice against equity expressed in *Barrett* was no doubt sincere, and not unusual among common lawyers on both sides of the Atlantic. But lest we take him too literally, it should be noted that his antiequity musings in that case also served the interests of his client by playing to the prejudices of Pendleton, whose rivalry with Wythe Marshall fully understood and exploited. In any case, Marshall, whatever his prejudices, willingly turned to equity because it was uniquely suited to Virginia's land-based, family-oriented, socially hierarchical society. Conflict in these areas generally involved fiduciary relationships, which were the speciality of equity jurisprudence. In contrast to the common law, for example, there were no juries. Not surprisingly, this was the source of much criticism, but it meant, among other things, that courts of equity could render judgment for one party or the other, or if justice required, for both. Wythe's Court of Chancery, like all equity courts, could also gather evi-

---

25. Such appeals made up "a large proportion" of his reported cases before that court. PJM, 5: 465. Also see ibid., 483–85. The Wythe-Pendleton rivalry is treated in Mays, *Pendleton: A Biography*, 1: 226–32; 2: 290–96. Also see Editorial Note on *Barrett v. Floyd*, PJM, 5: 479–82.

dence in writing from any party who might throw light on the dispute. On the positive side, its evidentiary procedures were flexible, comprehensive, and non-confrontational; on the downside, witnesses could not be cross-examined in open court, the much-cherished method of common-law courts. Through the injunction, equity could also prevent injustice from being done, whereas the common law could act only after the fact. Injunctive relief could also prevent costly and time-consuming litigation. So, too, could the unique equitable practice of interpleading, which required multiple plaintiffs suing the same defendant in the same court for the same thing to settle the priority of their claims in pretrial pleadings.[26]

Marshall may well have preferred the masculine sternness of the common law (a sexual association common to the age), but a substantial percentage of his cases fell on the equity side. Three of these illustrate his mastery of the subject, as well as the remarkable applicability of equity principles in post-Revolution Virginia—and not just to "women, children and lunatics," as the common lawyers loved to put it, but to merchants, planters, and businessmen. Witness the prolonged litigation in *Morris v. Alexander & Company,* where Marshall represented the famous financier of the Revolution (and one of the biggest plungers of the period). The case involving two business partners and two contracts was a perfect subject for equity adjudication. One contract was between the firm of Alexander and Company, in which Morris was a partner, and the Farmers-General of France. The other was between Morris and a French businessman, in which Morris agreed to deliver twenty thousand hogsheads of tobacco annually, beginning in 1785. The collapse of the international market in tobacco in the mid-1780s doomed both ventures and left Morris, who had borrowed heavily to jump-start the venture, vastly overextended. To cut his losses, Morris sued his former partner William Alexander in Wythe's Chancery Court, accusing him of mismanaging funds. The importance of the litigation was dramatized when Morris moved to Virginia to oversee the litigation, which lasted from 1788 to 1801 and involved five separate decisions in both the High Court of Chancery and the Court of Appeals. During this prolonged litigation, Marshall established himself as Morris's man in Virginia—the beginning of the long-term business association between Morris and the Marshall family.[27]

---

26. On the nature and advantages of equity, see Joseph Story, "Chancery Jurisdiction," reprinted in Story, *Miscellaneous Writings* 148–79. For equity in Virginia and Marshall's equity practice in particular, see Hobson's Editorial Note, PJM, 5: 53–61.

27. PJM, 5: 93–116. Hobson's Editorial Note, ibid., 93–97, puts the complex litigation in context; I have drawn on his account for my summary.

Morris put the case in motion with his letter to Marshall of June 16, 1788, setting forth the complex details of his failed venture in tobacco. On the basis of this information, Marshall presented a bill of equity in midsummer of 1788 and at the same time began to gather the written depositions equity procedure allowed. In the meantime, his bill was cross-billed by Alexander's lawyers. Marshall answered them in November 1789 and amended his bill in March 1792. Cross-billing in the case resumed in 1796 and was not completed until 1798. By this time, Marshall had essentially withdrawn from the case as a result of having undertaken the XYZ mission to France in 1797. Victory came for Morris in 1801, but it was not in time to rescue his crumbling financial empire or to keep him out of debtors prison. For Marshall, the results were more beneficial. He had garnered some handsome fees, mastered the operations of the international market, and prepared himself in the kind of commercial litigation he would face as chief justice of the Supreme Court, which position he occupied when the case was finally settled. The whole process does not appear to have been very glorious. He had not forged any new equitable doctrines, or modified old ones either, and in the end he could not save Morris from his economic hubris. Still Marshall had played an indispensable role in mediating economic conflict, in greasing the gears of the market with his legal strategy and arguments, and in keeping Morris afloat for five years. Morris did end up in debtors prison, only to be released by the Bankruptcy Act of 1800—an act Congressman Marshall was instrumental in getting passed.[28]

In the *Morris* case, Marshall was in touch with the world of international commerce. The equity case of *Shermer v. Shermer's Executors* (1794) located him at the very center of Virginia's unique economic world—which is to say it was an inheritance case involving land and slaves, which in the Old Dominion meant social status and political power. In *Shermer,* Marshall pitted his skills, as he did a number of times, against John Taylor of Caroline County. In the 1820s, Taylor would produce three massive tomes of constitutional theory in three years, all designed to demolish Chief Justice Marshall's constitutional nationalism. In the 1790s, the two men were friendly and respectful rivals. In *Shermer,* they joined issue over the construction of a will that impinged on the family structure and economic interests of many people over many years. The story, reconstructed by Charles Hobson, has a familiar Virginia ring. It went back to 1742, when an impoverished younger son of English gentry by the

---

28. PJM, 5: 94–95. Marshall's role in getting the bankruptcy bill through the House is treated in PJM, 4: 34.

name of John Shermer married a rich widow and in the process acquired a handsome estate in land and slaves (decidedly a Virginia thing to do). When Shermer died in 1775, his estate, valued at more than £11,000, included 2,600 acres, and 120 slaves, plus livestock and personal property. This impressive estate he willed to his wife for life; upon her death it was to be divided equally between whomever would designate as her heir(s) and his brother.[29]

The main problem, which generated a raft of other problems, was that Mrs. Shermer died shortly after, without a will designating her heir(s). This was a bad break for Richard Shermer, the brother, and his nephew and heir, William Shermer, since the case remained in the Virginia courts until 1802, when it was finally taken by William Shermer to the board of commissioners established to settle American debts to British citizens. It was a good break for John Marshall, who filed the first bill for Richard Shermer in 1787, for a handsome fee of £28, and who represented his nephew and heir in all the subsequent litigation—first and successfully before Wythe's Chancery Court in 1792 and then in Pendleton's Court of Appeals in 1794, where Marshall also prevailed. Along the way, he collected some additional fees, blundered embarrassingly by misfiling the case, and finally demonstrated that he could match equity knowledge with the best of them. The dispute was settled peacefully if belatedly. At the end, Marshall and the other lawyers were a bit richer and William Shermer a lot older and not much better off—this despite eleven transatlantic trips to America from England and a fee bill for nearly three decades of litigation. Again, with the compliance of their lawyers, some good people in Virginia had escaped their English creditors. Virginia law, or equity in this case, in the hands of a skilled lawyer, it would seem, could be marvelously instrumental without being innovative at all.

Wayles's Executors v. Randolph et al. (1795–1799), the last of Marshall's three equity cases to be considered, reveals something of both his law practice and his lawyering skills. As in *Shermer* and *Morris*, considerable money was on the line—some £30,000 sterling, according to Thomas Jefferson. Like the infanticide hearing in the *Commonwealth v. Randolph* case, leading families of Virginia were involved: Here the Randolphs faced off against Thomas Jefferson, whose wife, Martha, was one of Wayles's executors. Richard Randolph was born to the purple but died on the verge of bankruptcy thanks to the erratic fluctuations of the European market and, equally, his own mismanage-

29. Editorial Note, PJM, 5: 72–75. Documents relating to the case appear at ibid., 75–92.

ment and extravagance. To escape his debt to the English firm of Farell and Jones, Randolph willed the bulk of his estate in land and slaves to his four sons, the defendants in the suit. The plaintiffs sued in equity to set aside the will and apply the estate toward the payment of his debt. The interest of the plaintiffs, which nicely illustrates the fragile family-based interdependency of Virginia's economic system, stemmed from the fact that Richard Randolph, the father of the defendants, and John Wayles, the father of the plaintiffs, had jointly contracted with an English company engaged in the slave trade to take a consignment of 280 slaves transported from Africa. Farell and Jones, who had served as sureties for the transaction, joined with Wayles's executors to have the deeds to Randolph's sons set aside and the proceeds of the estate employed to satisfy his debts. Wayles's executors sued to break the Randolph will, which, if allowed, would have left them solely liable for a bond executed by Randolph to the captain of the slaver for which their father served as surety.[30]

Marshall joined with four other well-known lawyers to represent the Randolph interests in a series of cases before the High Court of Chancery and finally in 1799, before the Court of Appeals. The litigation was exceedingly complicated. Marshall's job was to separate the wheat from the chaff, to focus on those facts that defined the issue, then mobilize both law and equity on the points of dispute. Business acuity, legal learning, common sense, and the ability to juggle fact and principle, dodge weakness, and build on strength all went into his successful argument before the Court of Appeals in 1799. This case, now called *Richard Randolph v. Wayles's Executors et al.* was an appeal from Wythe's High Court of Chancery, which had ruled in favor of Wayles's executors, holding that the heirs of Richard Randolph (his son Richard Randolph to be specific) were liable in their inheritance to Wayles's executors. Additionally, Wythe ordered that the land inherited be sold toward the satisfaction of the executors' demand. Wayles's executors, in short, were given the same remedy against the son of Richard Randolph as Captain Bivens would have had against Richard Randolph the father for the nonpayment of his bond. Randolph appealed Wythe's decree to the Court of Appeals, where it was heard in 1797. Marshall, absent in France when Wythe's decree was issued, had one last chance to rescue his client from the debts he had inherited from his father, which Wythe now ruled must be paid.

Marshall's argument in the final appeal was impressive. He had mastered the intricacies of the facts and detected the weakness of his opponent, who as

---

30. PJM, 5: 117–60, for Editorial Note and the documents in the case.

it turns out was George Hay (who ten years down the line would appear before Marshall as lawyer for the government in the Burr treason trial). The executors of Wayles were not specialty creditors as the equity court had presumed and as Hay continued to argue, declared Marshall. Nor was the case one "of marshalling assets," as Hay claimed. Marshall then took a few subtle jabs at the court of equity, which was a smart thing to do since he was asking Pendleton's court to reverse Wythe's equity decree. (Wythe's court asserted "a principle invented for the sake of affecting justice," Marshall averred, when it should have refused "an act when injustice would follow from it.") He then proceeded to analogize the suit "to the case of old incumbrances in the doctrine of mortgages," citing John Powell's *Treatise upon the Law of Mortgages* to make his point. The lien on his clients' lands placed there by the decree in equity was also untenable at law, and here Marshall expounded learnedly on the statutory writ of elegit as set forth in the Statute of Westminster II, 13, and Edward I, c. 18, as modified by statute in Virginia. After this foray into ancient law, he moved back to current policy considerations, demonstrating why it would be unworkable to burden land with the encumbrances of ancient debt imposed by county courts, the records of which were unrecoverable. The legislature of Virginia, he reasoned, "by the record laws meant to favour and secure purchasers; and therefore the court ought not, by mere construction and implication, to raise up an inference, entirely contrary to the spirit and intent of those laws."[31]

Before he was finished, Marshall had drawn on axioms of statutory construction to prove his point about Virginia's lien laws; compared Virginia and English law on the subject, citing numerous cases to prove his point; explored the details of the Randolph business dealings by reference to letters put in evidence during the equity proceedings; and cited Elizabethan statutes and English equity decisions, along with principles gleaned from Bacon's *New Abridgement of the Law* and a variety of other English sources. It was an impressive example of legal learning in action, and it impressed Edmund Pendleton and his colleagues, who voted unanimously to reverse Wythe (yet again), upholding the deed of Richard Randolph to his son.[32]

If knowledge in action is the highest form of knowledge, *Wayles's Executors v. Randolph et al.* ought to remove once and for all the notion that

31. PJM, 5: 148–56. Marshall's argument is explicated in editorial footnotes, ibid., 156–58.
32. PJM, 5: 152. The footnotes to Marshall's argument contain full titles of works cited by Marshall, ibid., 156–58.

Marshall was deficient in legal learning. The case also illustrates the social foundation of Virginia's legal elite. When Marshall represented the Randolphs, he was in fact representing his own family line. The Wayles's executors were only slightly less prominent, and the fact that one of them, Martha, was the wife of Thomas Jefferson makes the point, and not incidentally adds to the list of reasons why the future president of the United States came to detest the future chief justice. The case also called into action a conspicuous segment of Virginia's elite legal community—a segment that included not only lawyers on both sides of the case but the Court of Appeals itself. Indeed, when the case was appealed from Wythe's High Court of Chancery to that court, three of the five sitting judges recused themselves because of their interest in the outcome of the case, forcing the legislature to appoint a special court. Why the judges recused themselves was not specified, but some combination of family ties and economic interest was no doubt the reason. The point is that law, lawyers, judges, and Virginia's ruling classes were part of a single social organism, which to a large extent rested on law. The foundation of that organism was land, and the value of that land depended on racial slavery. What might be obscured in *Wayles's Executors v. Randolph et al.* by talk of bonds, contracts, liens, and learned discourse about scire facias and *terretenants* and the like is that the whole case was set in motion by a contract to buy 280 human beings to work the plantations that permitted Virginia planters to live well and expound on the virtues of liberty and freedom.[33]

As a lawyer in a society where slaveholding was pervasive, Marshall could not entirely avoid the question of slavery and freedom, especially since Virginians in the 1790s were openly debating the issue. Marshall did not engage in that debate, but as a small slaveholder, his actions spoke louder than words. Professionally, he had no qualms: he seems simply to have accepted whatever cases came to him, and the harsh realities of the institution of slavery along with them. In some cases he helped his slaveholding clients hold on to their slaves. In others he argued for slaves who sued for their freedom, as they could do under Virginia law in this period. The most revealing of these cases was *Pleasants v. Pleasants* (1799), which involved the efforts of Quaker slaveholder John Pleasants to free his slaves. Virginia law did not allow private manumissions at the time Pleasants executed his will. In the post-Revolutionary surge

33. On the matter of recusements, see PJM, 5: 148 n. 5. Edmund Morgan explores the relation of slavery and freedom talk in his *American Slavery, American Freedom: The Ordeal of Colonial Virginia* (New York, 1975).

of republican idealism, however, he had reason to think that such a law would be passed. In this expectation, he devised his slaves to his heirs with the proviso that they would be freed when Virginia law made it possible, which it did in 1782. The suit originated when some of the heirs attempted to overturn the will. Robert Pleasants, who was the executor of his father's estate, brought suit to secure enforcement and retained Marshall to get the job done. The case began in the Court of Chancery, where Chancellor Wythe issued a sweeping decree ordering immediate emancipation of some 400 slaves, and ended in the Court of Appeals, where the scope of Wythe's ruling for freedom was severely restricted.[34]

Marshall argued the case on the side of liberty, and though he lost, his argument might appear to forecast later participation in the American Colonization Society and his own last will and testament, which offered manumission to his personal slave. His involvement in several other freedom suits during this period, though less dramatic than *Pleasants,* appears to substantiate that conclusion. Lawyer's arguments, like judge's opinions, however, are not always reliable statements of personal belief. In any case, the question is not whether Marshall was opposed to slavery but rather how deeply he was opposed to it. At the very least, it should be noted that his argument in *Pleasants* was narrowly legal and devoid of the kind of antislavery sentiment that was current in post-Revolutionary Virginia. That sentiment was real—witness Wythe's sweeping decree in *Pleasants,* or Richard Randolph's manumission of his 250 slaves, or St. George Tucker's idealistic essay favoring manumission in 1796. There is no compelling evidence that Marshall shared it very passionately. Not only did he not go on public record against slavery at this time, he seems not to have pondered the moral problem in private either. What he observed daily as a lawyer was that slavery insinuated itself into every aspect of Virginia society and Virginia law. Slaves as the chief source of agrarian labor were inseparable from land, the key to its ultimate use value. They were bought and sold and willed like other pieces of chattel property—witness *Wayles v. Randolph;* indeed, witness Marshall's own slave transactions. Slaves were used regularly to secure legal transactions and legal disputes over contract and bonds; all forms of indebtedness generally involved slaves either directly or indirectly. As a citizen, Marshall could with some effort have avoided the institution; as a lawyer in Virginia, he had no choice but to be deeply implicated in the administration of slave law. He accepted the burden without reservation or complaint

34. PJM, 5: Editorial Note, 541–44.

just as, when chief justice, he would find a secure place for human bondage in his constitutional jurisprudence.[35]

In slavery cases, Marshall took the law where his Virginia clients wanted it to go. He did the same in the so-called British debt cases, and nowhere, perhaps, was the pragmatic, community-serving aspect of his practice more apparent. These cases were initiated by British and Scottish businessmen, or other parties associated with them, who sought repayment, with interest of pre-Revolutionary debts owed by Virginia planters and merchants. The English and Scottish mercantile firms involved made the international market work for Virginians in the late colonial period: by extending credit to planters and merchants and by taking their products on consignment for sale in England and Europe. Bad weather, lean crops, and a radical fluctuation of tobacco prices in the world market, joined with a tendency of Virginians to live beyond their means, drove many merchants and planters deeply into debt. To what extent their desire to escape the burden of this indebtedness was a cause of the Revolution is a point of scholarly disputation. But there is no doubt that anti-British sentiment, intensified by memories of the fighting and by postwar economic dislocation constituted powerful reasons for not paying the debts. It mattered little that Article 4 of the Treaty of Paris of 1783 stipulated that creditors on both sides of the Atlantic should meet no impediment to the collection of their debts, which should be paid in sterling. Opposition to Article 4 was particularly strong in Virginia—because her debt was large and the specie supply short and because Virginians still sought compensation for slaves freed by the British during the Revolution. Additionally Virginians believed that the British, who in defiance of the treaty had not yet evacuated posts in the Northwest Territory were responsible for stirring up Indian raids on the Virginia frontier. To avoid paying, Virginians closed their courts to British creditors, as noted, and supported the political faction led by Patrick Henry, which opposed the Constitu-

35. The inseparability of slavery, economics, and law is clarified in Judith Schafer, *Slavery, the Civil Law, and the Supreme Court of Louisiana* (Baton Rouge, 1994); Morris, *Southern Slavery and the Law.* Also see Thomas D. Russell, "South Carolina's Largest Auctioneering Firm," *Chicago Kent Law Review,* 68 (1993): 1241–82. On the changing status of slavery in post-Revolution Virginia, see Robert McColley, *Slavery and Jeffersonian Virginia,* 2d ed. (Urbana, Ill., 1973); Gerald W. Mullin, *Flight and Rebellion: Slave Resistance in Eighteenth-Century Virginia* (New York, 1972). The dispute among historians on the extent of antislavery sentiment in post-Revolutionary Virginia is discussed in Douglas R. Egerton, *Gabriel's Rebellion: The Virginia Slave Conspiracies of 1800 and 1802* (Chapel Hill, N.C., 1993), 192 n. 46.

tion, Article 6 of which promised that the debts would be repaid.[36] With the opening of federal courts under the new Constitution in 1790, British creditors, hoping to avoid state judges and juries, resumed their efforts to recover. When they did, the creditors found a formidable opponent in Marshall, who emerged as the chief lawyer for Virginia debtors. With somewhere between $10 million and $15 million at stake, not to mention the impact payment in sterling would have had on Virginia's struggling economy, it is understandable why state debtors retained the best legal talent available. Why Marshall so willingly represented them is not so clear given the fact he hated the economic policies of Henry's antidebt coalition in the 1780s and championed the Constitution, which favored creditors and explicitly prohibited states from violating private contracts. Why did he represent them, indeed, since his purchase of the Fairfax lands in the Northern Neck in 1793 rested on a general respect for contractual sanctity on the part of Virginia, which his lawyering for debtors required him to circumvent? And why did he litigate to circumvent the debt provisions of the Treaty of Paris of 1783, whereas he worked to get a special provision inserted in the Jay Treaty of 1795 protecting his interests in the Northern Neck lands from state confiscation?[37]

Part of the explanation lay simply in the fact that Marshall was part of a new breed: a professional lawyer who made his living by practicing law. As such, he went where the business was without reference to ideology or politics or, as in the debt cases, even his own economic self-interest. There was another, more important reason for his involvement, however, and it had to do with the relation between lawyering and community interest. The debt cases concerned the economic well-being of the entire state. And Marshall's clients, by and large, were substantial planters and merchants, whose business interests were part of a statewide web of debtor-creditor relations. Payment of debts in specie, and with interest as British creditors demanded would constitute a serious drain on an economy already made fragile by the collapse of the tobacco market. To put it plainly, forced collection almost certainly would bring wide-

36. For the debt question in Virginia politics in the 1780s, see Jackson Main, *Political Parties before the Revolution* (Chapel Hill, N.C., 1973), ch. 9; and in the 1790s, Richard Beeman, *The Old Dominion and the New Nation, 1788–1801* (Lexington, Ky., 1972), 123–25, and passim. Documents public and private relating to the debt issue are found in the three volumes of VRD. On the Indian problem in Virginia, see Beeman, *Old Dominion,* 99–103.

37. On Marshall's effort to get a guarantee of title to the Fairfax lands in the treaty, see PJM, 2: 144–45.

spread economic dislocation, if not a total collapse, of the state's economy. In a state riddled with debt, the health of the commonwealth may well have depended on default. In working to facilitate nonpayment, which was the end result of his efforts, Marshall could be seen, and probably saw himself, as representing the interests of the community at large. That may help explain why his unpopular Federalist politics and controversial land speculation, which pitted him against his own state, did not destroy his personal and professional reputation among his Virginia neighbors.[38]

The expert on Marshall's debt litigation estimates that he argued no fewer than one hundred debt cases in the 1790s, primarily in the federal circuit court sitting in Richmond and almost always on the side of defendant debtors. Most of these cases were not dramatic, either in regard to the clients involved or the legal doctrines relied on. Since profits depended on processing large numbers of cases efficiently, Marshall printed standard forms for processing the cases and developed standardized pleas to justify nonpayment. He pleaded both equity and law as the case demanded. His skill in the former has been noted, and he was equally, indeed supremely, at home in the common law, where he pleaded according to Virginia's modified writ system, as was the common practice. His arguments bristle with learned citations to English case law and English statutes, ancient and modern. He special pleaded, too, as in the British debt case of *Jones v. Walker* (1787), where he sparred brilliantly with opposing counsel before losing on the merits. English law, it would appear, was alive and well in Virginia. Indeed, observing Marshall in action, one wonders why, having so recently fought the English, he turned so readily to them in his practice of law. The reason may be in part that he was using English law to repudiate English debts, just as colonists used English law to defend American rights. In any case, it is clear that his lifelong admiration of English culture was very much rooted in his practice of law.[39]

Marshall's major debt case, the only case he argued before the United States Supreme Court, was *Ware v. Hylton. Ware* was the final phase of litigation that began as *Jones v. Walker,* which he argued in the federal circuit court in November 1791. By the time the Court decided that case, Jones had died, but the

---

38. See especially Charles F. Hobson, "The Recovery of British Debts in the Federal Circuit Courts of Virginia, 1790–1793," *The Virginia Magazine of History and Biography* 92 (April 1984): 175–200. Also his Editorial Note in PJM, 5: 259–63. Antidebt politics in the 1790s are treated in Beeman, *Old Dominion,* 122–25.

39. On pleading in Virginia, see PJM, 5: Introduction, xl–xliii. Documents in *Jones v. Walker,* along with the Editorial Note, are found in ibid., 264–94.

case was revived in the name of his administrator and argued at the May 1793 term of the U.S. Circuit Court sitting in Richmond. From there, it was appealed to the Supreme Court. At issue in both *Jones v. Walker* and the circuit trial of *Ware* was a bond for nearly £1,500, executed by Daniel Hylton, a Virginia import merchant, to the Bristol firm of Farell and Jones in 1774. By the terms of the Virginia sequestration act of 1777, debts owed to British citizens could be discharged in depreciated paper currency paid into the state loan office. Pursuant to that act, Hylton paid £933 inflated currency, or £15 sterling. Continuing the suit brought by Jones in 1790, Ware sued for the difference in real money, resting his case mainly on the controversial Article 4 of the Treaty of Paris of 1783, which promised to remove impediments to the collection of pre-Revolutionary debts, such as those erected by the Virginia sequestration act. The economic issues at stake were immense. So were the constitutional ones, since Virginia debtors rallied behind state sovereignty against the force of federal treaty law made supreme by the new Constitution. The fact that British creditors chose to sue Virginia citizens in federal court further acerbated states' rights sentiment, and appeared to validate Anti-Federalist arguments against federal courts made during the Virginia ratifying debates.[40]

The significance of the case is clear from the stature of the lawyers retained by the debtor interests of Virginia. Marshall, who argued against Henry in the ratification debates on both the debt issue and the matter of the federal courts, now argued with him and with James Innes, attorney general of Virginia, as well as Alexander Campbell. Marshall followed Henry's opening on May 23, 1793, in what appears to have been a carefully orchestrated defense effort. Judging from the reconstructed notes of Marshall's argument, his job was somehow to escape the main vulnerabilities of the debtors—which were, first, the manifest unfairness of allowing Hylton's £15 payment to satisfy a £1,500 debt; second, the debilitating impact that would come if Virginia's sequestration statute of 1777 could escape the operation of Article 4 of a federal treaty. His approach was to avoid the constitutional issue and rest his case wherever possible on international law. This he did by citing "Modern Books as well as ancient"—a broad category that included Vattel, Grotius, Jean-Jacques Burlamaqui, and Samuel Puffendorf. Blackstone was there, too, along with abundant citations to English cases and American Supreme Court decisions. As for Virginia's sequestration law of 1777, it was enacted before the ratification of

---

40. *Ware v. Hylton,* 3 Dallas 199. For Marshall's circuit argument in *Ware,* consult PJM, 5: 300–13.

the Constitution and thus fell within the rights a sovereign and independent nation could claim in time of war, likewise the statute of 1782, which closed the door to British creditors in Virginia courts. To circumvent what appeared to be the clear meaning of Article 4 of the treaty, Marshall put forth two main arguments, the first being that the treaty did not operate retrospectively. The second was that the words of Article 4 concerning the payment of debts did not operate "on payments—but *on general claims*"—a distinction he maintained by reference to international law. Regarding the Article 4 argument of opposing counsel, the best Marshall could do was to remind the justices that Great Britain, by failing to evacuate the Northwest posts, had not lived up to its treaty obligations either.[41]

Marshall prevailed in the circuit court, perhaps because his catchall argument included something for everyone, including an argument diminishing the reach of federal treaties, which he clearly did not believe himself. At the Supreme Court level, however, where he argued on appeal in 1796, using his same argument, he failed to carry a single justice. To be sure, Justice Chase, who wrote the leading opinion, found much to praise in Marshall's argument, so much, in fact, it appeared after reading the first few pages of the official report of the case as if he had actually won. Ironically, it was the states' rights portion of Marshall's argument that Chase liked the most, and that Marshall personally liked not at all: namely, that Virginia was, as its constitution of 1776 declared, a sovereign and independent state. If this were true, the sequestration act of 1777 was constitutional and, in addition, obligatory on the federal courts. Except, that is to say, for Article 4 of the Treaty of Paris of 1783. On this point Chase annihilated Marshall's ex post facto argument and his esoteric linguistic manipulation of Article 4. Instead, Chase settled on a commonsense reading of the text by which the English creditor was entitled to recover his prewar debt in full, regardless of the act of 1777 and Hylton's payment into the loan office under its authority.[42]

Marshall appears to have lost his biggest case. But did he? Did he really want to establish the validity of the sequestration act of 1777, which would have put a constitutional foundation under Virginia's anticontractual policies, which he strongly opposed? Did he really want to win the Court over to his states' rights argument in the process? The truth is, Chase delivered an opinion that would have gratified Marshall in 1788, one that Chief Justice Marshall

41. Marshall's argument as recorded in Justice Iredell's notes, PJM, 5: 305.
42. Chase's opinion at 3 Dallas 220–46. All five justices wrote opinions.

would have been proud to have written. More important and less speculative were the indirect consequences of Marshall's efforts in *Hylton,* indeed, in all of the British debt cases. What Marshall and other lawyers for Virginia debtors succeeded in doing in these cases was to postpone the collection of debts, sometimes for years or long enough, in any case, for witnesses to disappear and plaintiffs to exhaust their patience and their money. After *Hylton,* many British creditors simply gave up on the courts and turned for partial satisfaction to the Special Claims Commission established by Congress, a commission that came in the wake of *Ware* and, to some extent, as a result of it. In the meantime, Virginia specie that might have gone to repay honest debts was available to fund needed economic development at the state level, which Marshall enthusiastically supported. Not least, the Supreme Court had affirmed a nationalist interpretation of the Constitution that underwrote sound credit and contractual responsibility, a position Marshall passionately endorsed as essential to national interest, as well as his own.[43]

Several aspects of *Ware* make it one of Marshall's most revealing arguments, one being that he was, in making law serve his clients regardless of his personal interests, behaving like the professional lawyer he was. His view of the matter, one might reasonably infer, was not that each lawyer was obliged to argue on the side of virtue and truth, but that virtue and truth, or some reasonable approximation thereof, would emerge if lawyers did their best with what they had to work with. With a bit of stretch, this view was compatible with republicanism. It was also tinged with more than a bit of policy-minded instrumentalism. By helping Virginians escape their British creditors, Marshall not only gave his countrymen a new economic lease on life but made foreign merchants bear the cost.

The instrumentalist law Marshall helped administer as a Virginia lawyer, one hastens to add, was not the transformative jurisprudence scholars have discovered in the nineteenth century, when policy-conscious judges and lawyers transformed the common law itself by making it serve the radicalizing forces of a growing market economy. Rather, the law Marshall practiced was traditional and instrumentalist at the same time. It was deeply indebted to the common law for both method and doctrine. It was also instrumentalist as the common law had in fact always been, whether in nineteenth-century Massachusetts or eighteenth-century England, which is to say that Virginia law, with

43. On *Ware v. Hylton* and the claims commission, see Goebel, *Antecedents and Beginnings,* 748–56.

the help of lawyers like Marshall, adjusted itself readily to the dominant economic forces of Virginia society. Practicing law was, or could be, a form of governance. Well before he became chief justice, Marshall came to believe that lawyers and judges, no less than legislators, could be statesmen. Just how essential judicial statesmanship was, he learned in the 1790s, when he saw new-fangled political democracy in operation in Virginia. In this experience lay buried the roots of *Marbury v. Madison*.[44]

A Washington-Adams Federalist in Jeffersonian Virginia

Of all the strands that make up the rich tapestry of Chief Justice Marshall's constitutional jurisprudence, none was more important than the distinction he drew between law and politics. Whether he actually succeeded in maintaining that distinction is a point of dispute (among scholars as among contemporaries) between those who see Marshall's protestations of legality as a cover for result-oriented, politically-motivated decisions and those who believed what he believed: that the Court's word was law, not politics. However one resolves the dispute, it seems beyond question that the 1790s were crucial in shaping Marshall's ideas about the relationship of law and politics. The interaction of two fundamental developments were of especial importance in this regard. One was the unplanned and unexpected emergence of political parties. First in point of time and sophistication was the Democratic (Jeffersonian) Republican Party, then in response, the Federalists, under Presidents George Washington and John Adams. These were not modern parties. In fact, they were created by men who uniformly denounced party. But their appearance, even in their chrysalis stage, significantly altered the way public business was conducted. Jefferson's victory in 1800, based as it was on party organization, indicated that party government was there to stay, which was why Marshall and Adams feared for the future.[45]

The second development to shape Marshall's thinking in the 1790s was the progressively intensifying debate over the Constitution. Whether one calls it the constitutionalization of politics or the politicalization of the Constitution,

44. Morton J. Horwitz, *The Transformation of American Law, 1780–1860* (Cambridge, Mass., 1977).

45. Party development in the 1790s is treated generally in Hofstadter, *Idea of a Party System*; and more specifically in Cunningham, *Jeffersonian Republicans*.

the bottom line was the same: namely, that the great policy questions of the decade were translated into questions of constitutional interpretation and argued out in the language of constitutional law. Such was the debate over Hamilton's Bank of the United States, over the Jay Treaty, and finally over the Alien and Sedition Acts, which in turn called forth the Virginia and Kentucky Resolutions (which in turn called forth *Marbury v. Madison*). What Jefferson and Madison said in the resolutions—what Marshall heard with alarm—was that the Constitution was a contract created by sovereign states and that disputes over its meaning should be settled by those states and not the Supreme Court. Some historians have downplayed the resolutions, arguing that they were meant only to be a platform for the upcoming presidential election and not a full-blown theory of states' rights constitutionalism. Marshall would have found no comfort in that argument. He feared the resolutions precisely because they made constitutional interpretation a matter of party orthodoxy, thus fusing the two most frightening developments of the decade: the idea of state sovereignty and the rise of political parties. If disputes over constitutional interpretation should be settled by state legislatures in control of party politicians, then all would be lost. He had not yet fully formulated his theory, set forth in *Marbury,* that constitutional questions of a legal nature were the exclusive prerogative of the Supreme Court. In assessing the constitutional crisis of the late 1790s, however, he could not help but contrast the interpretive methods of the common law and common lawyers with those of state legislatures driven by partisan goals. Virginia was his model, and what he learned there took him one large step closer to the doctrine of judicial review.[46]

The circumstances that drew Marshall into the vortex politics unfolded in ways he did not fully or instantly comprehend. One thing he did perceive, however, was the existence in Virginia of an influential phalanx of politicians who were opposed to the Constitution as it was ratified and who were determined to produce structural changes in it that would reduce its nationalist thrust and elevate the role of the states. This group demanded a second convention as a condition of ratification. Roughly the same faction—operating on the radical premise that the worst is the best—also opposed the ratification of the newly proposed federal Bill of Rights in Virginia, even though they appeared to champion it, hoping that failure would generate a movement for a fundamen-

46. On the constitutional history of the Virginia and Kentucky Resolutions, see James M. Smith, *Freedom's Fetters: The Alien and Sedition Laws and American Civil Liberties* (Ithaca, N.Y., 1956).

tal restructuring of the Constitution. Some like Patrick Henry, John Taylor, and possibly even Jefferson himself, carried opposition to ratification directly into the first decade of the new government. There were also those who had supported the Constitution but who reneged when Hamilton put a consolidationist spin on it. Among those nationalists who disagreed with Hamilton's version of nationalism was Madison himself. And it was Madison, and later Jefferson, who organized a political party based on democracy and the doctrine of states' rights.[47]

What called the new party into being were a series of developments in domestic and foreign policy perceived to be inimical to Virginia's interests. First came the nationalist financial policies of Hamilton, which included the assumption of state debts, the creation of a national bank, and a protective tariff. To agrarian-minded Virginians, these measures looked ever so much like the policies of Great Britain that brought on the Revolution. Washington's foreign policy fortified this impression. Anglophobic Virginians saw the president's proclamation of neutrality in 1793 and the Jay Treaty of 1795 as pro-English policies designed to subvert not only the French Revolution but the American one as well. In this new age, the old ideological division between court and country, which shaped pre-Revolutionary politics, again seemed relevant. Conspiracy was in the air as men and measures were brought to judgment. To Federalists, Jefferson was a raging Jacobin; to Democratic-Republicans, Hamilton was Walpole, or maybe even Caesar, and "Honest John Adams" was a closet monarchist. Even Washington, who preached against parties, was accused of being partisan—by the partisans of Virginia no less. In the cold-war climate of the 1790s, political opposition was treason, and events such as the Whiskey Rebellion, the Genêt affair, and the Fries Rebellion became battles over republican civilization.[48]

Marshall apparently had no glimmer of the political violence the decade would generate. Like most Americans, he assumed that the ratification of the Constitution would usher in a new age of harmony in which old disputes would be irrelevant and political parties unnecessary. Even after the onset of political violence, he was determined not to interrupt his profitable law practice and contented social life with political wrangling, a point he made several

47. On Madison, see Drew McCoy, *The Last of the Fathers: James Madison and the Republican Legacy* (New York, 1989), and Lance Banning, *The Sacred Fire of Liberty: James Madison and the Founding of the Federal Republic* (Ithaca, N.Y., 1995).

48. Sharp, *American Politics* is especially good on the deep political rifts of the 1790s. The most comprehensive account of the age is Elkins and McKitrick, *Age of Federalism*.

times in his autobiographical recollections of the period. What changed his mind was the realization that the Constitution was still not secure and that the forces opposed to ratification were fighting the same war over interpretation. What first alerted him to the ongoing effort to put an Anti-Federalist stamp on the Constitution was the debate over the ratification of the Bill of Rights in Virginia. Even more to the point was Patrick Henry's resolution of November 3, 1790, which declared assumption to be "repugnant to the Constitution, as it goes to the exercise of power not expressly granted to the General Government." Following the spirit of Henry's resolution, a special committee of the house issued *The Address of the General Assembly of the Commonwealth of Virginia to the United States in Congress Assembled.* Framed in the memorialist tradition in which colonies had petitioned Parliament before the Revolution, the address was the first of Virginia's many states' rights manifestos. It set forth in nonnegotiable language the interests of agrarian slaveholding society, conflated Federalist financial policy with English tyranny, and concluded with a theory of states' rights constitutionalism that looked back to the Articles of Confederation, forward to the Virginia and Kentucky Resolutions, and beyond them to Calhoun's nullification theory. By a few votes only did Virginia's upper house draw back from making the address official. But as Richard Beeman put it, the statement reverberated throughout the 1790s as "a practical guidebook for anyone wishing to attack the federal government in the future."[49]

Marshall was a member of the Virginia House of Delegates when Henry issued his states' rights manifesto and in fact may have returned for the specific purpose of combating it. Not only did Marshall speak out against Henry, but he spoke in favor of Hamilton's nationalizing policies and the constitutional foundation on which they rested. Contesting Virginia's revered revolutionary statesmen and defending its political nemeses was costly. For his efforts, Marshall recalled, he was resented by "the great political party that led Virginia," "attacked with virulence in the papers and was so far honored in Virginia as to be associated with Alexander Hamilton, at least so far as to be termed his instrument."[50]

Marshall was also Virginia's most stalwart defender of Washington's foreign policy and ultimately of Washington himself. Foreign policy as the defining political issue of the early Republic began with the radicalization and

---

49. Adams, *Autobiographical Sketch by John Marshall,* 13, for the quote. On constitutional politics in Virginia and the debate over Henry's resolution, see Beeman, *Old Dominion,* 78–81.

50. Adams, *Autobiographical Sketch by John Marshall,* 14.

internationalization of the French Revolution in 1793—developments that soon pitted Great Britain and revolutionary France in an all-out fight for political, economic, and ideological supremacy of the cis-Atlantic world. The twin pillars of Washington's foreign policy in this hostile world were neutrality, which he proclaimed in April 1793, and increased commercial ties with Great Britain, which he achieved in the Jay Treaty of 1795. Both policies, while tinctured with ideology, were grounded on some hardheaded realism. Neutrality rested on the military and naval weakness of the United States, as well as the assumption, which events would soon prove correct, that neither France nor Great Britain were concerned about American rights. The Jay Treaty, which promised to secure pre-Revolutionary debts of American citizens with English merchants (which it did not do) in return for English withdrawal from the Northwest posts (which it did do), rested on the ground that a quid pro quo, with the added possibility of resumed trade on a new basis of equality, was a fair bargain. For the emerging Democratic-Republicans of Virginia, neutrality was a violation of the 1778 Franco-American Alliance, which had helped secure an American victory in Revolution. The Jay Treaty was the final confirmation of the Democratic-Republicans' worst fears: that Washington had sold out to Hamilton and the northern commercial interests, who had a secret preference for monarchy and a willingness to subject American interests to English commercial and ideological dominance.

Marshall joined in this highly ideological and sharply polarized debate when he rose to defend Washington's foreign policy at a proadministration rally in Richmond on August 17, 1793. The immediate occasion of the meeting was the triumphant trip through Virginia of Edmond-Charles Genêt, the new French minister to America. Genêt represented the new French Republic that had just deposed (and was about to behead) its king. His mission was to enlist American support for France's war for liberty, equality, and fraternity against Great Britain and the Old-World champions of monarchy and tyranny. Idealistic, naive, brash, and ignorant, and encouraged in these qualities by his initial popularity with the American public and the democratic press, Citizen Genêt proceeded blithely to ignore Washington's policy of neutrality by enlisting Americans in a privateering war against British shipping. When Washington, with remarkable restraint, attempted to restrain the young diplomat's impetuosity, Genêt responded by appealing over the president's head to Congress and finally to the American people themselves. Along the way, he analogized Washington's neutrality proclamation to a royal edict, supplied his own interpretation of relevant treaty law, and rendered his personal interpretation of the international law of neutrals, about which he knew nothing.[51]

Genêt's excesses, and the fact that he stayed on in America to marry into Hudson River aristocracy, invite a seriocomic interpretation of his actions. John Marshall, who incidentally was the first historian to interpret the affair, was not in the least amused by Genêt's one-man assault on Washington's neutrality policy. To make his point, Marshall organized a proadministration rally in Richmond on August 17, 1793. The meeting was presided over, at Marshall's urging, by George Wythe, who imparted dignity and moderation to the proceedings. The proadministration resolutions, which Marshall wrote and which were subsequently published in the *(Richmond) Virginia Gazette and General Advertiser* (August 21, 1793), were anything but moderate, however. Framed in Manichaean dichotomies, the resolutions depicted Washington and neutrality as blessed with "the eye of cool and temperate reason" and "the good genius of America." In the democratic camp was "any wicked citizen . . . who, disregarding his own duty, and the happiness of the United States, in violation of the law of the land and the wish of the people, shall dare to gratify his paltry passions at the risk of his country's welfare, perhaps its existence." Marshall was equally harsh as a historian, describing Genêt's style as "lofty" and "offensive" and full of "extravagant pretensions" and "indiscreet arrogance." The only thing more contemptible than Genêt himself, as historian Marshall saw it, were the Democratic Societies, the popular press, and the emerging Democratic-Republican Party, whose members hooted Genêt on. Above all, and behind all, there was Secretary of State Jefferson, the only cabinet member who refused to back Washington's forceful response to Genêt.[52]

Marshall's participation in the Richmond rally was not without some serious contradictions, not the least being that he blasted his opponents for organizing the masses while he was doing precisely that himself—and with conspicuous success. Nor was everyone convinced by his protestations of disinterested republicanism. One perceptive critic was James Madison, who opined to Jefferson that personal interest played a considerable role "in the active character he [Marshall] is assuming." Especially troubling to Madison was

51. Elkins and McKitrick, *Age of Federalism,* ch. 8.

52. PJM, 2: 196–200, for copies of the address and resolutions. John Marshall, *The Life of George Washington,* 2d ed., revised and corrected (Philadelphia, 1832), 2: 262. Marshall's fullest statement on the Genêt episode came in his letter to Augustin Davis, 20 November 1793, which was printed in the *(Richmond) Virginia Gazette, and General Advertiser,* 20 November 1793, PJM, 2: 238–47.

Marshall's dependence on Hamilton's new national bank, "or people connected with it," for the procurement of funds for Marshall's purchase of the Fairfax estate, which deal was concluded in 1793.[53]

While Marshall was losing ground with Madison and Jefferson, he gained where it most counted, with Washington himself. The president took personal notice of Marshall's efforts on his behalf and responded publicly and gratefully to Marshall's address in the *(Richmond) Virginia Gazette and General Advertiser,* September 11, 1793. The Richmond rally, along with Washington's special notice of his contributions, marked Marshall as the leader of the Virginia Federalists. It was in this capacity that he stepped forward again to defend the Jay Treaty of 1795, which turned out to be one of the central political and constitutional catalysts of the decade. Jay, who was a sitting chief justice at the time, was dispatched to England to settle outstanding disputes, old and new, between the two countries. Given America's obvious lack of coercive bargaining power, he probably did as good a job of resolving them as could have been expected. But Virginia opponents thought otherwise. They ignored the fact that the British did evacuate the Northwest posts as required by the treaty, thus reducing the Indian problem on Virginia's northwest frontier. Opponents conveniently forgot that Virginians continued to resist the payment of British debts in defiance of the treaty. They did not consider that the controversial Article 12 of the treaty, containing concessions to Great Britain in the West Indies trade, was never ratified at all. What they did see was that the Jay Treaty was manna from Philadelphia: a brush to tar Washington as an Anglophile and a rallying cry for conjuring the lost spirit of the American Revolution. As Marshall was quick to observe, opponents also attacked the treaty on constitutional grounds: arguing that the Senate had exceeded its constitutional powers in ratifying the treaty and that the treaty itself infringed on the commerce power given Congress in Article 1, Section 8. Constitutional federalism was also corrupted, as Virginia states' rightists saw it, by the fact that states were taxed, in effect without representation to pay for the treaty's implementation. Separation of power became an issue, too, when Democratic-Republican opponents in the House of Representatives, having lost their fight to force Washington to disclose the details of negotiations, attempted to defeat the treaty by withholding implementation money. By the time the constitutional debate

53. Madison to Jefferson, 2 September 1793, Madison Papers, Library of Congress, cited in PJM, 2: 198 n. 6.

shifted to the Virginia House of Delegates in 1795, it abounded in high-flown rhetoric about slavery and freedom, liberty against power.[54]

Again, Marshall had not intended to get involved. Not only had he withdrawn his name as a candidate for the 1795 election to the House of Delegates, but he had come out publicly in support of "an intimate friend," who, as Marshall remembered, was running against "an infuriated politician who thought every resistance to France subserviency to Britain." When Marshall went to vote, however, he was accosted by a supporter who insisted on opening a poll for him. Marshall left thinking he had dissuaded the man from doing so, only to be informed that evening that he had been elected. We in turn are left to ponder the fact that Marshall was clearly cut out for elective politics—and entirely disinclined to play the game. What he did was to assume the leadership of the Federalists of Virginia, while denying that he was a party man. Given the fact that Virginia Federalists never really emerged as a party, Marshall was telling the truth. It is probably true as well that his antipathy to party organization hurried the marginalization and final demise of Virginia Federalists in the 1790s.[55]

Marshall's spirited defense of Washington's policies, and of Washington himself, in 1795 and 1796 was his last major political effort at the state level. The battle in the fall session of the state legislature began when the antiadministration forces moved a resolution approving the negative vote of Virginia's two senators against the Jay Treaty. The gauntlet was thrown down. Marshall and a small band of Federalists answered the challenge with a counterresolution denying the authority of the Virginia house to pass judgment on the treaty on the ground that the treaty was federal law. When the critics defeated that counterresolution, they moved on to dispute the constitutionality of the treaty itself, arguing essentially that the treaty-making power usurped the authority of both Congress and (surprisingly) the federal courts as well. Marshall again denied the legislature's authority to debate federal constitutional questions, particularly since the commercial provisions of the treaty were being debated by the U.S. House of Representatives. His defeat on this point must have reminded him of what was becoming all too clear: Federalism in Virginia was essentially a rearguard action doomed to defeat. He may also have sensed that

54. Washington's response is noted in PJM, 2: 198 n. 8.

55. Adams, *Autobiographical Sketch by John Marshall*, 15. I have relied on Beeman's account of the debate in Virginia over the Jay Treaty in *Old Dominion*, 144–51.

his defeat was a victory for those who argued that state legislatures had a role to play in constitutional interpretation.[56]

In any case, Marshall stepped forward again in the spring of 1796, and again the issue concerned state legislative competence in matters of constitutional interpretation. The sparking argument, broached first by Virginia's representatives in Congress, was that the treaty-making authority, because it bypassed the House of Representatives entirely, was an unconstitutional and tyrannical aggrandizement of executive authority. Administration critics, behaving more and more like disciplined party members, demanded that the Virginia legislature rescue the country from galloping monarchism: first by demanding that Washington turn over executive documents relating to the negotiation of the treaty; second, by withholding money essential to the implementation of the treaty itself. While urging Congress to assert itself, Virginia Republicans took the message to the people themselves.

Marshall was compelled to do the same and explained his reasons for doing so to Hamilton. The strategy of the Richmond meeting, Marshall admitted, had been risky for those who believed, as both he and Hamilton did, that the "people" themselves ought not to be called into action regarding matters of state. "We coud not venture an expression of the public mind under the violent prejudices with which it had been impressed so long as a hope remained that the house of representatives might ultimately consult the interest or honor of the nation. But now when all hope of this has vanishd, it was deemed advisable to make the experiment however hazardous it might be." Under Marshall's direction, the Federalists did push through a resolution opening the meeting to nonfreeholders, a historic first in Virginia. Federalists also succeeded, thanks to Marshall's debating skills, in passing a resolution supporting the implementation of the treaty as the law of the land.[57]

Marshall was not so successful during the fall 1796 session of the Virginia House of Delegates, his final appearance in that body. This time, the issue, much to his distress, focused not only on the Jay Treaty and Washington's foreign policy but on the president himself. The specific question, which would have been inconceivable three years earlier, was whether the House should laud Washington's "wisdom" on his announced retirement or whether it

56. Beeman, *Old Dominion,* 144, cites Joseph Jones to Madison, 22 November 1795, Madison Papers.
57. Marshall to Hamilton, 25 April 1796, PJM, 3: 23–24. Also see Beeman, *Old Dominion,* 149.

should censure the great man by lukewarm praise. The debate, which, as Marshall recalled, covered the entire "course of the Administration" and called forth "all the strength and violence of party," ended with a rebuke for the Federalists and unmistakably for Washington himself. When the smoke of demagoguery had cleared, it was apparent that Virginia Federalism, even when championed by Virginia's greatest national hero, was doomed, not just as a party but even as an effective minority. As the leading scholar of 1790s Virginia politics noted, only Marshall himself seems to have escaped the powerful undertow of local culture and democratic politics. Virginians, it would seem, loved John Marshall, even while they hated his conservative nationalist ideas. They did not love him enough, however, to heed his parting jeremiad warning Virginians that in attacking Washington, they were repudiating their own best tradition.[58]

Even the bruising party battles of 1796 did not destroy Marshall's affection for his home state or his belief that one could be a Virginian and an American at the same time. Accident and necessity, however, drew him increasingly to affairs at the national level. Indeed, the more he was excluded by Jefferson, Madison, and the other leading Democratic-Republicans of his own state, the more attractive Marshall became to the Virginia Federalists, who hoped that his popularity might help resuscitate their waning fortunes. Federalist leaders in Philadelphia also took favorable notice, especially the president. Washington not only appreciated Marshall's effort on his behalf, but said so publicly. Even more to the point, on August 26, 1795, Washington offered Marshall the office of attorney general of the United States. Marshall declined for professional and financial reasons, the two were intertwined, but Washington's offer called further attention to Marshall's services and his ability. By Marshall's own account, his efforts were "spoken of in such extravagant terms as to prepare the federalists of Congress to receive me with marked attention and favour, the ensuing winter when I attended in Philadelphia to argue the cause respecting British debts before the Supreme Court of the United States." Among the Federalist leaders who welcomed Marshall, he listed "Mr. Cabot, Mr. Ames, & Mr. Dexter & Mr. Sedgewic, of Massachusetts, with Mr. Wadsworth of Connecticut and with Mr. King of New York."[59]

Shortly after Marshall's argument in *Ware v. Hylton* in February 1796, Washington again tried to lure him into public office, this time as a replace-

58. Adams, *Autobiographical Sketch by John Marshall*, 20.
59. Ibid., 19.

ment for James Monroe, who had been recalled as ambassador to France. The offer was testimony of Marshall's status both as a lawyer and a statesman. But for a second time, he chose to remain a lawyer in Richmond, a position, he said, "which appeared to me to be more independent and not less honorable than any other." It was "honorable" because he approached the practice of law not just as a way to make money, though it was that, but as a matter of public service. It was "independent" because he did not have to play the game of popular politics that had become de rigueur in the new age of party. The better Marshall played the game, it seemed, the less he liked it, and the more he feared its consequences for the Republic. What he also concluded, or was about to conclude, was that practicing law, as opposed to politics, was an alternate way of governing.[60]

An American in Paris: XYZ and the Story of Two Revolutions

The rapidity of Marshall's political ascendancy in the four years after his decision to retire from politics in 1796 may well be unmatched in American history. In June of 1797 he agreed to represent the United States in what became known as the XYZ mission to France. After a triumphal return, he was elected to the U.S. House of Representatives, where he almost immediately rose to a position of leadership as a spokesman for President Adams's moderate Federalism. Marshall's brief stint in Congress was followed immediately by his appointment as secretary of war and four days later, secretary of state. After only nine months in that office, Marshall was appointed chief justice. During this period he watched events unfold with unsettling rapidity. Against the background of the quasi–naval war with France, which threatened to turn into a real war, he witnessed the impressment crisis with England and the constitutional crisis over the Alien and Sedition Acts and the Virginia and Kentucky Resolutions. These events confirmed his fear that imported French radicalism, linked to democratic excess and the rise of political parties, threatened the survival of the Republic. He also concluded that liberty had to be tempered with law and order. Even before John Adams offered Marshall a seat on the Court, he had come to believe that the rule of law was essential to the continuation of the Republic and that the judges and lawyers had a special role to play in the process of salvation. In sum, Marshall's multifaceted national career in the late

60. Ibid., 21.

1790s was on-the-job training. Not only did he win himself a place on the Supreme Court for his services, but in the process he learned what he had to do once he got there.

In this process of self-education—one might even say, self-definition—the XYZ mission was uniquely important. The fact that Marshall was chosen to join C. C. Pinckney and Elbridge Gerry in the delicate negotiations with France was another feather in his cap, the more so because he had no diplomatic experience, and seasoned diplomacy was what was called for. Relations between the two republics and former revolutionary allies, already strained by Washington's neutrality policy and the Genêt affair, worsened with the Jay Treaty, which France interpreted as a repudiation of the Franco-American Alliance of 1778 and as a tacit alliance with its mortal enemy. At home, foreign relations not only crystallized divisions between the Federalists and the Democratic-Republicans, the evil Washington warned against in his Farewell Address, but created a threatening fissure in the Federalist Party as well, one John Adams inherited. The president was hard pressed from every angle. He wanted to preserve American neutrality, which meant placating both Great Britain and France, or at least not offending either, to the point of a war, which America was not prepared to fight. At the same time, he was pledged to defend American commerce and national honor, neither of which Great Britain or France had the slightest interest in recognizing. While grappling with these strategic problems, he had to fend off the extreme Frankophiles among the Jeffersonians and dodge the barbs of the radical pro-British wing of his own party, which under Hamilton's leadership secretly set out to destroy him. Adams needed someone who was principled, patriotic, and politically astute—a moderate, rational man of principle to confront hostility abroad and dampen the growing hysteria of domestic politics. The XYZ mission was Marshall's ordeal by fire.[61]

Adams's reasons for appointing Marshall are readily apparent. Not only was Marshall a personal favorite of Washington, he had distinguished himself as a stalwart defender of the policies Adams hoped to continue. In the hurly-burly of popular politics, moreover, he had more than held his own. In the process, he gained a reputation for moderation and good sense. Adams must have sensed also that Marshall added balance to the mission—a moderating influence between Elbridge Gerry, whose pro-French bias made him an easy

61. On the division among the Federalists, see Manning J. Dauer, *The Adams Federalists* (Baltimore, 1968), and Stephen G. Kurtz, *The Presidency of John Adams; The Collapse of Federalism, 1795–1800* (New York, 1961).

target for manipulation, and C. C. Pinckney, whose "romantic" sense of honor might prove to be yet another kind of disability in the negotiations. It helped, too, that Marshall was a Virginian.

Marshall was not surprised at his appointment and, judging by his quick acceptance, seems to have expected it. Still, in light of his family responsibilities and his determination to maintain his thriving legal practice, it was not an easy decision. He accepted finally, though he had turned down other impressive offers before, for personal as well as civic reasons. Among the former was the prospect of a quick infusion of cash, some $18,000 as it turned out, which he needed to make payments on the Fairfax land acquisition he and his brother and brother-in-law had concluded in 1793. The journey to Paris also gave John Marshall a chance to confer with his brother, who was in London working on other land deals for his debt-ridden father-in-law, Robert Morris. Incidentally, Talleyrand, the infamous French foreign minister with whom Marshall would match negotiating skills, was also an investor in American land—and as it turned out, a savvy one. Marshall himself was involved in land speculation business as attorney for Morris, who was connected peripherally with the XYZ negotiations. Like other men of his age, Marshall had no trouble mixing personal interest with public business. In any case, he thought that "the mission was temporary, and could not be of long duration." His plan, as he put it, was to "return after a short absence, to my profession, with no diminution of character, & I trusted, with no diminution of practise."[62]

A sense of civic duty also influenced Marshall to take on the French mission. The subject of foreign affairs and French policy in particular had, he recalled, "occupied a large portion of my thoughts." Like other Federalists, he displayed a strong preference for English cultural institutions, especially legal ones. As he did in the Jay Treaty debates, he also saw the practical advantages to America of reestablishing economic ties with England, provided, of course, that they could be achieved on an honorable basis. Whatever the case, the reactionary course of the French Revolution after the Reign of Terror in the summer of 1793 settled his mind. The military purge of moderates and the concentration of power in the hands of the militant radicals on the Directory in 1797, as Marshall noted later, "blasted every hope of an accommodation between the United States and France." Even before that, however, he had concluded that

62. On his acceptance, see PJM, 3: 80. On the Robert Morris connection, see William Stinchcombe, *The XYZ Affair* (Westport, Conn., 1980), 61, and ch. 4 n. 39. Also Adams, *Autobiographical Sketch by John Marshall,* 22.

"temperate firmness" was the order of the day. To resolve the outstanding problems with France would remove the threat from abroad and diminish social and political radicalism at home. And, as he confessed later, "the *eclat*" of pulling off such a coup was a stimulation to noble ambition. Little did Marshall suspect that the "*eclat*" would come not from the success of the mission but its noble failure, or that in failure, he would become a national hero.[63]

Marshall succeeded both personally and publicly as a result of the XYZ mission. His precise role, however, was not so clear—in part, perhaps, because Marshall himself, in the final volume of his Washington biography, wrote the first history of the mission. He also put his imprint on the historiography of the XYZ mission in his brilliant diplomatic dispatches from Paris to President Adams. In any case, the heroic interpretation of the mission that emerged at the time pitted Old-World tyranny and corruption against straight-shooting American republicanism, with Marshall as its ultimate embodiment. In this view, expounded at length by Albert J. Beveridge, Old-World evil was personified by the French foreign minister, Talleyrand, who denigrated American honor by keeping the ministers waiting, then insulted them further by demanding a monetary tribute before negotiations could begin. In the meantime, as Marshall himself was quick to note, French depredations against American neutral commerce continued unabated. The story ended when the ministers rejected the insulting offer and left with dignity and national honor intact—except for Gerry who stayed on under the mistaken assumption that his association with the pro-French party in America would make him successful where his Federalist colleagues had failed.[64]

Standard wisdom is that Marshall was the star of this show: the first to take Talleyrand's measure, the most unswerving champion of national honor, and in general, the canniest, the least ideological, the wisest of the three ministers, and the coolest under fire. While there is considerable truth in this heroic rendition, the whole truth is more complicated. In fact, Marshall's anti-French and pro-English bias may have tended to mislead him regarding Talleyrand's position. Of all the French negotiators, it turns out, Talleyrand was the most committed to a peaceful resolution of the dispute with the United States—not because he was sentimental about a sister republic but because, he saw cor-

63. Adams, *Autobiographical Sketch by John Marshall,* 22–23.
64. Stinchcombe, *XYZ Affair,* contains a full account. The documents and the extensive correspondence relating to Marshall and XYZ are printed, with editorial comment by Stinchcombe, in PJM, vol. 3.

rectly, that an American-British rapprochement, which failed negotiations might produce, would hurt France. Marshall also appears to have considered the French minister's delaying tactics, using Gerry as a front, of the same magnitude of evil as the demand for bribes, that is to say, as a deliberate effort to humiliate the United States. In fact, Talleyrand was stalling for time in order to fight off the more extreme and well-placed anti-American foes in the government of the Directory. Time did in fact create a more favorable climate for negotiation, which paid off in the second Adams mission to France and finally in the convention between the two countries in 1800. Thereafter, it was England more than France that held American rights and honor in contempt, until the War of 1812 set the matter straight.[65]

If the image of Marshall in the XYZ affair as all-wise and all-knowing is misleading, still the fact remains that he never lost sight of his charge, which was to secure neutral rights for American shipping and salvage some respect for the young Republic in an age hostile to republicanism. If he came with cultural baggage, he was quick to discard it when it was a hindrance. In diplomacy as in law, Marshall was a quick learner. His cultural bias against France did not blind him to English depredations. Nor did it blind him to an ugly fact of international politics: that either France or England, or both, would gladly crush America if it furthered their interests to do so. He also perceived correctly that France did not want a war that would unite the United States and Great Britain against it. Operating on this strategic premise, Marshall reasoned that the best policy for the United States was to negotiate forcefully from whatever strength it could muster. Assuming that France would avoid war at all costs, American negotiators could be forceful in their demand for respect. This assumption, plus the fact that Marshall misunderstood Talleyrand's true position, led him to do the right thing, which was to take umbrage when Talleyrand's messenger demanded a bribe and finally to leave with national honor and self-respect intact.

If Marshall dealt forcefully with Talleyrand and messieurs XYZ, he dealt sensitively and deftly with Gerry and Pinckney. This was an impressive display of leadership, one that bided well for the future. Gerry arrived late and brought with him an unyielding ideological preference for France that blinded him to the realities of negotiation. On top of that, he was self-righteous, suspicious of

65. Stinchcombe, *XYZ Affair*, contains the definitive account of Marshall's role in the negotiations.

his colleagues for political reasons, and generally brittle and arrogant. Increasingly Gerry operated on the destructive premise that only he could save the day for America. Marshall treated him with respect but understood early on that Gerry would be more a part of the problem than part of the solution. With Pinckney on the other hand, Marshall "worked together most cordially." The distinguished South Carolinian was two years younger than Marshall, and where Marshall was easygoing and convivial, his colleague tended to be formal and a bit stuffy. Marshall called him a gentleman "of high and even romantic honour." Both men were Federalists, both southerners and ardent patriots. While Marshall generally took the lead in forcing Talleyrand's hand, Pinckney was quick to agree. They also agreed that Gerry's faith in France's goodwill and his own ability were grievously misplaced. Marshall not only set the operative agenda for negotiations while in Paris, but he was the one who was mainly responsible for interpreting the mission to President Adams and, through him, to the American people. Those who read these remarkable state papers will not be surprised at the grand style and persuasive force of Marshall's opinions as chief justice.[66]

Marshall was not the first or the last American to represent his country in France. Jefferson had preceded him to Paris, and so had Marshall's friend James Monroe. Before any of them was Benjamin Franklin. Like Franklin, Marshall was quintessentially American and proud of it. Both men also fit easily, not to say enthusiastically, into Parisian culture, which during Marshall's stay was decidedly un-American and unrepublican. Marshall clearly enjoyed the attractions of the great city, one of which was Madame de Villette, in whose house he and Gerry roomed. Madame de Villette apparently lavished attention on Marshall, and there is, according to Marshall's most recent biographer, some evidence he responded with a bit too much enthusiasm. During his long stay in Paris, he wrote only one letter to Polly, who was struggling after the death of one child and two miscarriages. As it turned out, Marshall would have been better off not to have written that one, because Polly may well have read into it that the madame and John were more than friends. Whether this was true or not, believing it may have added to her already pre-

66. Adams, *Autobiographical Sketch by John Marshall*, 24, for quote. George A. Billias, *Elbridge Gerry, Founding Father and Republican Statesman* (New York, 1976), is the authoritative biography. Also see Stinchcombe, *XYZ Affair*, passim. Marshall's diplomatic dispatches are printed in PJM, vol. 3, as is the journal he kept while in Paris.

carious emotional state, and perhaps to Marshall's lifelong effort to reassure her of his undying love. There is no evidence to support the suspicion of some historians that Madame de Villette was an agent for Talleyrand.[67]

Fortunately, the public impact of Marshall's mission to France can be assessed with more certainty than the influence it had on his marriage. Word of the XYZ business had proceeded Marshall's return, primarily in the form of his dispatches to President Adams, which is to say that Marshall not only starred in the drama but wrote his own script. In both respects, the reviews were enthusiastic, despite some grumbling from the Republicans, as reported in his own words: "On my arrival in New York I found the whole country in a state of agitation on the subject of our mission. Our dispatches had been published and their effect on public opinion had fully equalled my anticipation." Anticipation, indeed. Marshall clearly understood when he wrote his reports that they would enter into the already volatile political discourse of the period. He was convinced before he left that American nationalism and patriotism needed a shot in the arm. Three months in France had only deepened this conviction. His firsthand view of revolutionary France—and the postrevolutionary world it had created—also cast a searing light on the nature of the American Revolution and the mission of the American Republic. From Paris, Marshall summed up the lesson of comparative history for his former comrade-at-arms Charles Lee. That France *"is not and never will be a republick is a truth which I* scarcely *dare* whisper *even to myself,"* he concluded. *"It is in America and America only that human liberty has found an asylum. Let our foreign factions banish her from the United States and this earth affords her no longer a place of refuge."*[68]

This was the message Marshall carried to the American people. Judging by his reception, the people were eager to receive it—and in some deep cultural sense needed to believe it. He disembarked in New York to the popular acclaim of ordinary folk, who lined the roads to cheer him as he journeyed south to Philadelphia and Richmond. Marshall, it appeared, had not only represented the United States to France but had in the process represented Americans to themselves. Not unlike Washington's Farewell Address in 1796, or the Monroe Doctrine in 1823, shining republican truth was painted against the dark back-

---

67. Jean Edward Smith's account of Marshall's mission to France, including Marshall's possible dalliance with the beautiful Madame de Villette, is especially informative, *John Marshall,* ch. 8. Also see Stinchcombe, *XYZ Affair,* 68.

68. Adams, *Autobiographical Sketch by John Marshall,* 24–25. Marshall to Charles Lee, Paris, 12 October 1797, PJM, 3: 251.

ground hues of Old-World tyranny and decadence. Where the French were du-plicitous, America, like Marshall, had been honest and forthright and courageous. Marshall's slogan, "millions for defense but not a penny for trib-ute" became a rallying cry for a young nation trying to define itself and deter-mined to stand tall before monarchies of the Old World. The XYZ mission made Marshall into a genuine American hero. It also taught him the difference between the French and American Revolutions—how one celebrated social up-heaval and the other secured social order. Not long after his return, he under-took to write a biography of George Washington that would embody that newfound wisdom.

A Passionate Moderate in the Age of "Political Violence"

If Marshall had trouble reentering the provincial life of Richmond after his stay in Europe's greatest city, he never let on. Nor did he evince any pressing desire to cash in his new notoriety for a place in the political arena. What he wanted to do was simply to continue where he left off—as a lawyer and as a family man with a lovely wife and a growing family in a city he loved. As he put it in his *Autobiographical Sketch,* he "returned to Richmond with a full determina-tion to devote myself entirely to my professional duties, and was not a little delighted to find that my prospects at the bar had sustained no material injury from my absence." When pressed by friends to run for Congress, Marshall was, as he said, "peremptory" in his refusal. Even the personal intervention of George Washington could not change his mind—at least for a few hours.

The great man was moved to intervene because he feared that party division over foreign policy might destroy the country. And events in Virginia culminat-ing in the states' rights resolutions passed by the legislature in late 1798 con-vinced him that a crisis was at hand. Accordingly, he summoned Marshall with "a pressing invitation" to spend "few days at Mt. Vernon." Present also was Washington's nephew (and Marshall's friend and future colleague on the Court) Bushrod Washington. The president, recalled Marshall, "urged us both very earnestly to come into Congress & Mr. Washington assented to his wishes. I resisted, on the ground of my situation, & the necessity of attending to my pecuniary affairs." Refusing to serve one's country in the time of its trou-bles was hardly the "republican" thing to do as Washington was quick to re-mind his young friend. Thirty-some years later Marshall could still recall vividly "the manner in which Washington treated his objection." Fortunately for his future career, Marshall heeded the general's admonition, though not before he had been offered a seat on the United States Supreme Court, which he declined. As it turned out, Bushrod Washington, who had been elected to Congress, withdrew before serving to accept the appointment on the Court that Marshall had turned down. Marshall in turn agreed to run for the House of Representatives for the Richmond district in the April 1799 election. As it turned out, that contest was not a temporary diversion from his law practice, but a decisive turning point in his career.[69]

The election was in many ways the culmination of a decade of constitutional politics in Virginia. It revolved around the debate over the Alien and Sedition Acts, passed by the Federalist majority in Congress on strict party, and largely sectional, lines in the summer of 1798. The act was part of a comprehensive plan, which included a bill to retaliate against French violations of American neutral rights on the high seas and another to establish a provisional army. The most controversial provision was Section 2 of the Sedition Act, which punished any criticism of the president or Congress by a fine of $2,000 and imprisonment of up to two years. Federalists argued, and scholars after them, that the act (Section 3) was really a liberalization of the common law of seditious libel since, unlike English law, it allowed truth as a defense and permitted juries to render general verdicts. The provision was largely negated, as Virginians were quick to point out, by the fact that cases involving the sedition law would be tried in federal courts by federally impaneled juries who would be instructed by Federalist judges. Fourteen indictments were brought, all against Republican critics of the Adams administration.[70]

For the Democratic-Republicans of Virginia, the Alien and Sedition Acts were both a curse and a blessing. They were a curse in that their enforcement over a long stretch of time would put the party out of business, which was what the Federalists intended. On the blessing side, the controversial measures, by putting the Federalists in the worst light, helped Republicans to recoup losses from the XYZ mission and the growing rift with France over American neutral rights. Virginia Republicans, with the Virginia and Kentucky Resolutions as their platform, now moved in for the kill. One of them was John Clopton, John Marshall's opponent in the 1799 congressional election in

69. For Marshall's account of the meeting, see Adams, *Autobiographical Sketch by John Marshall,* 25. On his refusal of a seat on the Supreme Court, see PJM, 3: 508.

70. Beeman's account of the congressional election in Virginia is especially useful, *Old Dominion,* ch. 7, as is the Editorial Note on Marshall's congressional election campaign in PJM, 3: 494–502.

Richmond. The election was seen by both parties as a test of strength on the most divisive constitutional issue of the day.

Marshall's opening gambit in the campaign—a sure sign of his willingness to engage in popular politics, which he professed to dislike—was to write himself a letter, send it to the *(Fredericksburg) Virginia Herald* under a pen name, and then answer it under his own. The "From a Freeholder" letter of October 2, 1798, consisted of five queries that essentially ran the gamut of Federalist foreign and domestic policies of the 1790s, ending with the recently passed "alien and sedition bills." In "To a Freeholder," Marshall answered his own questions in plain language plain people could understand. His first answer was a subtle but cutting attack on Republican states' rights radicalism. To make his point, he personalized the issue, proclaiming himself "an American, attached to the genuine principles of the constitution, as sanctioned by the will of the people, for their liberty, prosperity and happiness." For candidate Marshall, as for Chief Justice Marshall, the Constitution was "the rock of our political salvation, which has preserved us from misery, division and civil wars; and which will yet preserve us if we value it rightly and support it rightly."[71]

In addressing questions two and three, Marshall played the XYZ card, hoping no doubt to draw attention to his own popularity and away from the detested Alien and Sedition Acts. It was smart politics. He had just been feted as a hero in a rally in Alexandria, a fact that influenced his decision to enter the congressional race. In Richmond, too, he was the man of the hour. In the *(Richmond) Virginia Gazette and General Advertiser,* August 14, 1798, appeared an address "From the Citizens of Richmond," dated August 11, 1798, welcoming Marshall back "to this Land of Freedom, and into a country, which glories in your virtues and repays your generous exertions with thanks and approbation, the highest rewards to a virtuous mind." The address went on to predict that Marshall's "manly and dignified conduct" in Paris would inspire future generations "to defend national honor and dignity at all costs."[72]

On August 14, 1798, in the same newspaper, Marshall thanked the "Citizens of Richmond" for their tribute. His reply was a model of humility, as well as a powerful defense of Washington's and Adams's foreign policy. A wise policy of neutrality and military preparedness, plus three thousand miles of ocean granted by "a gracious providence," he promised, would save America from

71. The two letters are found in PJM, 3: 502–6; quote on 504.
72. Again I have drawn heavily on "Congressional Election Campaign," PJM, 3: 494–502, and Beeman, *Old Dominion,* especially ch. 7.

the invading forces of Old-World despotism. "We shall remain free," he promised, "if we do not deserve to be slaves." He never spoke of himself, except to thank his Richmond friends. In the process, he complimented them for their patriotism and Republican virtue. "I rejoice to find, though they know how to estimate, and therefore seek to avoid the horrors and dangers of war, yet they know also how to value the blessings of liberty and national independence: They know that peace would be purchased at too high a price by bending beneath a foreign yoke, and that peace so purchased could be but of short duration." Concerning the foreign yoke, in "To a Freeholder," dated September 20, 1798, he dwelled on the military ambition of France and its "hope of involving us in her wars as a dependent and subordinate nation." If the Republicans failed to see this, it was only because they "shut their eyes on the history and conduct of that nation."[73]

Marshall's final point dealt with the Alien and Sedition Acts, which he knew were destined to be the dominant issue in the upcoming meeting of the Virginia legislature and in the election campaign as well. Given Marshall's well-known constitutional nationalism, as well as his reputation for plainspokenness, one might have expected a forthright discussion of the acts. Instead he was marvelously equivocal. He confessed that he was "not an advocate for the alien and sedition bills: [and] had I been in congress when they passed, I should, unless my judgment could have been changed, certainly have opposed them." Still, he did "not think them fraught with all those mischiefs which many gentlemen ascribe to them. I should have opposed them, because I think them useless; and because they are calculated to create, unnecessarily, discontents and jealousies at a time when our very existence, as a nation, may depend on our union." Concerning any effort to repeal the acts before their date of expiration, Marshall was both the modern politician and the old-style leader who followed his own best judgment. If the repeal movement were still viable when he took office, he would "obey the voice of my constituents." But his personal opinion, freely given, was that the acts should simply be allowed to expire and should not be renewed.[74]

What Marshall did not say about the Alien and Sedition Acts is more revealing than what he did say. What he did *not* address was the underlying constitutional issue: whether Congress had exceeded its enumerated powers in passing the acts, especially the Sedition Act. More fundamental still was Marshall's

73. PJM, 3: 483, 505.
74. Ibid. 504–6.

failure to address the claim set forth in the Virginia and Kentucky Resolutions that the states, not the federal courts, should settle disputes over constitutional interpretation. In explaining why he dodged these questions, one must assume he understood what was obvious: that an outright defense of the Alien and Sedition Acts, or an outright repudiation of the Virginia and Kentucky Resolutions, would put him at odds with dominant sentiment in Virginia.

Just how much at odds he was, he discovered by watching the Virginia legislature in December 1798, when demagoguery and states' rights ideology was the order of the day. The session opened with an attempt by the Republicans to dislodge moderate Federalist John Wise from the speakership, which failed; it ended with the passage of the Virginia Resolutions, which succeeded too well. These resolutions embodied the essence of states' rights thinking in Virginia from the ratifying debates through the 1790s. They were written by Madison but amended at the last minute through the backstage efforts of Jefferson, who in this instance could not be restrained by his moderate friend. Madison's version condemned the Sedition Act as "a deliberate, palpable and dangerous exercise of power" not granted by the Constitution. It resolved that the states "are in duty bound to interpose" in resisting this abuse of power. Jefferson's more radical version went on to pronounce the Alien and Sedition Act "not law, but utterly void, and of no force or effect." As Richard Beeman noted, this was "not a mere statement of opinion but an explicit defiance of federal law." Jefferson's amended version failed after an intense debate between not only Federalists and Republicans, but between moderate Republicans and radicals, like John Taylor and others who wanted nothing less than a states' rights restructuring of the Constitution. While Republicans were skating rhetorically to the brink of disunion, Federalists were accusing the French, and by implication the pro-French Republican Party, of advocating a slave uprising. Rumors circulated that Virginia was gathering arms and men in case it should be necessary to resist the enforcement of the federal sedition law by military force. On the other extreme, it was rumored that the newly authorized army, presumably a defensive measure against French invasion, was really intended for Virginia. In this superheated atmosphere, the complex questions of the day were reduced by Federalists and Republicans alike to nonnegotiable issues of constitutional right and wrong.[75]

While the legislature was ranting and raving about constitutional truth,

75. See Harry Ammon and Adrienne Koch, "The Virginia and Kentucky Resolutions," *William and Mary Quarterly,* 3d ser., 5 (1948): 145–76. Beeman, *Old Dominion,* ch. 7; quote on 191.

Marshall and Clopton were waging a campaign of gentlemanly decorum. Indeed, most of what was said in the election campaign was said not by the participants themselves but by their supporters, who argued issues and character in local newspapers and pamphlets. At times, readers must have been hard pressed to distinguish the positions of the two candidates. Clopton, like Marshall, was a veteran of the Revolution and a lawyer from a good family who was well known and well liked in Richmond. Both men were political moderates who stood apart from the radical wings of their respective parties and apparently also from the more extreme political tactics of their campaign advisers. Clopton's two terms in Congress taught him to fear and distrust Federalists, but he had supported Washington's neutrality policy and continued to hope for a peaceful resolution of the dispute with France. He refused to believe that Virginia was about to be invaded by federal troops. Unlike Marshall, who admitted only that the Alien and Sedition Acts were unwise, Clopton believed the acts were unconstitutional, though here also, judging from his letter to John Allen of Richmond, Clopton was notably restrained in making the point. His most distinct advantages over Marshall were incumbency and the fact that the Republican Party, despite its setback in the XYZ affair, remained dominant in both Congress and the Virginia legislature, as well as among the people of Virginia at large. Marshall in turn could count on the spin-off from the XYZ affair, plus dependable support in Richmond, where he was unusually popular and where political moderation tended to be well received.[76]

Marshall won in April 1799 by a narrow margin of 108 votes. Several points are worth noting about the election, not the least of which was the transitional nature of the Virginia political culture in which it took place and the transitional political behavior, if you will, of Marshall himself. As Charles Syndor's study of Virginia political culture in eighteenth-century Virginia has made clear, the setting of the congressional race in 1799 was not on the surface appreciably different from that in which Washington ran for the House of Burgesses in the 1750s. Voting was still oral. Marshall and Clopton, seated behind their respective polls at the voting table, knew many of those who voted personally and often thanked them for their votes, and thanked them again by paying for liquor, which flowed as freely in 1799 as it had in 1757. Another vestige of deferential politics was the fact that the candidates stood back from the fray, leaving it to their supporters to sling the mud. The most vicious attack on Marshall, and one of the most revealing, came from John Thompson of Pe-

---

76. PJM, 3: "Congressional Election Campaign," 494–502.

tersburg (writing as Curtius), who spent much of his forty-page essay excoriating the Federalists as "hirelings of Great Britain" and Marshall as their servile "proselyte." Marshall's sincerity and integrity were also impugned and his excessive ambition condemned. What was most telling, however, was the criticism of his refusal to take a stand on the Alien and Sedition Acts. This barb was telling because it was true. Also interesting was Thompson's explanation for Marshall's equivocation: that, for all of his protestations to the contrary, Marshall was playing the party game.[77]

Was he? Or to frame the question in somewhat more general terms: Where did Marshall stand in the political culture of Virginia as it moved from the politics of deference to those of party, the transition period Ronald Formisano has aptly designated "deferential-participatory." Marshall took a firm stand—with one foot in each camp. He entered the popular arena reluctantly and with considerable trepidation. And in many ways, he continued to play by the gentlemanly rules of traditional politics. Thus, he refused to be drawn into the vortex of popular disputation, even when Curtius accused him of being an arrogant aristocrat for not doing so. To be sure, Marshall did not stop his friends from defending him against the likes of Curtius, which they willingly did. But even then, he abided by the old rules of fair play. Thus when he heard that Secretary of State Timothy Pickering was about to bring a charge of seditious libel against Clopton for criticizing President Adams, Marshall sent word through his brother-in-law Edward Carrington urging Pickering not to do so. On the other hand, counseling moderation was also good politics. Certainly a libel action under the hated Sedition Act brought by the highest of the High Federalists would have made an instant martyr of Clopton, thus proving what the Republicans claimed all along: that the Sedition Act was an instrument of party tyranny designed to silence Republican opposition.[78]

Marshall, it would appear, was both an instinctive politician and a member of the traditional elite—except on the constitutionality of the Sedition Act, where he was, as Thomson claimed, all finesse. Like a true politician, Marshall was neither out front nor on the record. Even after the passage of Madison's Virginia Resolution in December, which laid the cornerstone of southern states' rights constitutional theory, Marshall hung back. It was his friend Light-

77. Charles S. Syndor, *American Revolutionaries in the Making: Political Practices in Washington's Virginia* (New York, 1962); *Letters of Curtius* (Richmond, 1798), 10.

78. Ronald P. Formisano, "Deferential-Participant Politics: The Early Republic's Political Culture, 1789–1840," *American Political Science Review* 68 (1974): 473–87.

Horse Harry Lee who stepped forward to say what Marshall believed: that turning constitutional interpretation over to the states, as Madison's resolution argued, would destroy both the Constitution and the federal Union.[79]

The point is not to condemn Marshall for failing to speak out, but only to say that in not doing so, he embodied all the attributes of a transitional political figure. And a clever one he was. Marshall was a genuinely modest man with a large ambition, and he calculated his odds carefully. He refused to either condemn or defend the wisdom or the constitutionality of the Alien and Sedition Acts, which offended both Virginia Republicans and the High Federalists, both of whom condemned his middle course as cowardly equivocation. Marshall left it to Lee to expose the nihilism of the Virginia Resolution, too, when his own convictions called for candor. What Marshall did instead was to survey the political terrain, locate the voters he needed to win, and behave accordingly. Northern Federalists might not have liked what he did, or didn't do, but as Marshall knew, they didn't vote in Virginia. The radical Republicans he could also afford to offend because they would vote against him no matter what he did. The votes he needed, in addition to those of the Federalists, which he had sewn up, were those of the moderate Republicans of Henrico County. By projecting moderation, Marshall kept the moderates from defecting to Clopton, leaving his reputation as a Revolutionary hero and a man of principle and sound judgment to carry the day.[80]

What that reputation was and how important it proved to be is clear from Patrick Henry's remarkable letter of support, written to refute Thompson's charge that Marshall was a closet aristocrat who traded Virginia's well-being to advance his political career. The letter read:

Independently of the high gratification I felt from his public ministry, he ever stood high in my esteem as a private citizen. His temper and disposition were always pleasant, his talents and integrity unquestioned. These things were sufficient to place that gentleman far above any competitor in the district for Congress. But, when you add the particular information and insight which he had gained, and is able to communicate to our public councils, it is really astonishing that even blindness itself should

79. Marshall's position is analyzed carefully in "Congressional Election Campaign," as is that of his attackers and defenders, PJM, 3: 494–502.

80. Ibid., on the importance of Marshall's personal popularity in his electoral victory.

hesitate in the choice. . . . Tell Marshall I love him, because he felt and acted as a Republican, as an American.[81]

Henry was Virginia's grand old man of the Revolution, second only to Washington in popular esteem, and probably superior to him in that regard after the Jay Treaty. Marshall knew of Henry's feats of patriotism in the 1760s, just as Henry knew of Captain Marshall's commitment as a soldier of the Revolution. The two men served in the Virginia legislature in the 1780s and parted company over the issues of the day. It was young Marshall who was deputed by Madison to answer Henry in the Virginia ratifying convention. As lawyers, they had argued cases together and against one another. Henry had taken Marshall's measure—as a man, a lawyer, and a politician—for nearly two decades. What Henry said in his letter came from his respect for Washington and his fear that states' rights sentiment in Virginia had gone too far. What he said about Marshall came from experience and from the heart. Like another great Virginia states' rights man, John Randolph of Roanoke, Henry loved Marshall for his character, his decency, his integrity, and his patriotism. Like other Virginians, he saw the significance of the XYZ mission, where Marshall showed himself to be a man of peace who advocated military preparedness, an American who was able to teach the American people what it meant to be one. Henry loved Marshall for the lesson he taught, as would the American people.

Marshall bridged a transition in Virginia from political deference to political parties, and he took from both traditions. He was a statesman of the old school with all the makings of a modern politician. The fact that he hated parties made him even more attractive as a party candidate. He was not, as Henry's letter was designed to show, a member of the Virginia aristocracy, but he was a member of Virginia's born-to-rule ruling class. Marshall hated political demagoguery, yet he was highly adept at shaping public opinion, whether in his XYZ dispatches or his letters to and from himself in the campaign of 1798–1799. He had serious doubts about the political wisdom of ordinary people, especially under the influence of party. Yet he felt completely at home in their midst, and they in turn trusted him. On an issue as important as the repeal of the Alien and Sedition Acts, he even promised to follow their will. In two decades of public service at various levels, Marshall had never lost a popular election. If personality and character, instinct and sensitivity counted, he was a

81. Henry to Blair, 8 January 1799, in Moses Coit Tyler, *Patrick Henry* (Boston, 1887), 409–11, as quoted in PJM, 3: 500.

traditional politician who seemed destined for success in the party culture of the new age.

The only problem concerning his political future in Virginia, and it was all but insurmountable, was his unflinching commitment to a nationalist interpretation of the Constitution conjoined to his equally unyielding opposition to the radical states' rights pronouncements emanating from the state legislature. He didn't have to speak out on this subject in 1799 because people knew where he stood. On this great issue, Henry and Marshall came to agree—Henry in the last year of his life, Marshall on the eve of his judicial career. It was Washington who brought the two men together. He had pleaded with Henry to step forward and keep Virginians from destroying the Union they had been so instrumental in creating. For the same reason, Washington urged Marshall to run for Congress. All three men agreed that Enlightenment rationalism and the spirit of nationalism that had put the Old Dominion in the forefront of the Revolution and constitution making was giving way to a new kind of democratic romanticism, led by politicians laying claim to Virginia's history. The vestiges of Washington's version of republican nationalism, Madison's too as of 1787, were not yet dead in Virginia, but they were fading fast. To Marshall's discerning eye, the 1790s were beginning to resemble the 1780s. And who can say he was wrong?

The Political Origins of Judicial Review

A strange thing happened on John Marshall's way to the Supreme Court that threatened to keep him from getting there at all. When word of his nomination spread, a firestorm of protest broke out among leading Federalists, chief of whom were Fisher Ames, George Cabot, Theodore Sedgwick, and Rufus King from New England, and Robert Goodloe Harper from Maryland. Marshall's ability was not the issue. Several of the group had heard him argue *Ware v. Hylton* before the Supreme Court in 1796 and were greatly impressed. They were also admiring of his behavior in the XYZ mission or at least were willing to make effective political use of his dispatches. His talents were on display on the floor and behind the scenes during his short term in the House of Representatives in 1799, as was his support of Adams's moderate Federalism. This was a problem for the northern wing of the party. Northern Federalists wanted a war against France and a standing army to defeat a possible French invasion and, if the occasion arose, to deploy against domestic uprisings, such as the Whiskey Rebellion. John Adams not only opposed these things, but didn't mind saying so. In return, Adams's enemies, who had infiltrated his cabinet in order to undermine his policies, were determined to eliminate him as a candidate in the upcoming presidential election. This they succeeded in doing, with Hamilton in the vanguard, by a combination of intrigue and self-destructiveness unmatched in American political history.[82]

For the High Federalists, John Adams's support of John Marshall was reason enough to doubt Marshall's qualifications. What they wanted in a chief justice at the very least was ideological purity backed by an unqualified determination to save republicanism from the onslaught of the Jeffersonian Republicans. Marshall simply did not fit their bill for chief justice, any more than did Adams for the presidency. Marshall's easygoing nature, casual dress, and manners raised questions about his resoluteness. Worse yet was his demonstrated popularity with the very populace Federalist leaders expected him to keep in check. Troublesome also was his independence of mind. Like the president who appointed him, Marshall displayed a willingness to follow his own reasoning, even if it led him to deviate from party orthodoxy. Particularly distressing was his equivocal stand on the Alien and Sedition Acts, which were the touchstone of High Federalist policy as well as Federalists' main instrument for eliminating the Jeffersonian menace. A generous explanation was that Marshall's equivocation was the price paid for electoral success. But the Federalists, who feared the imminence of Armageddon, were not in an understanding mood. In Virginia, Marshall was accused of having sold out to Hamilton. At least one of his northern critics entertained the preposterous notion that Marshall was a secret convert to "Virginia theory." The only things equally damning in their eyes were that he had been a stalwart defender of Adams's administration and that he had the president's unwavering support.[83]

This deep bond between the two men is worth exploring for what it reveals about Marshall on the eve of his ascension to the Court. On the face of it, their friendship seems more than a bit improbable. Certainly their differences were conspicuous. John Adams, dubbed "His Rotundity" by his many critics, was short, dumpy, and bald; Marshall was tall, sinewy, and athletic and blessed with a thick head of hair. Marshall was never happier than when socializing. Good nature and good humor, much of it at his own expense, were his hall-

82. On the reaction of the High Federalists to Marshall, consult Turner [Preyer], "Appointment of Chief Justice Marshall," 156–63.

83. Ibid.

marks. Adams was restrained, especially among strangers, austere in his demeanor, and much inclined to solitude, introspection, and study. "Honest
John Adams" he was, but he was also a prickly curmudgeon, given to self-
righteousness and highly critical of those who didn't measure up to his own
high standards, which was pretty nearly everyone except his wife, Abigail.
Marshall was as unyielding as Adams in matters of principle, but in personal
matters, he was remarkably nonjudgmental and devoid of malice. We have
noted his unwillingness to join the crowd in condemning Nancy Randolph. He
also maintained a deep and active friendship with John Randolph of Roanoke,
who *did* condemn her and whose romantic states' rights ideology contradicted
Marshall's constitutional philosophy on nearly every point. Marshall even remained on good terms with the irascible and highly opinionated Timothy Pickering, who was one of Hamilton's cronies in Adams's cabinet attempting to
subvert the president and who in response to Jefferson's election talked openly
of New England secession. Even Pickering's pomposity and long-windedness
did not appear to rile the easygoing Marshall. There were many things about
American society that did rile him, as we shall see, and that would call him
into action. But except possibly for his cousin Thomas Jefferson and neighbor
Spencer Roane, Marshall was disinclined to personify evil. And unlike John
Adams, his habit was to accept things he could not change. Marshall the Virginia gentleman knew how to enjoy life, while Adams the New England Puritan was inclined to judge it.[84]

What brought these two very different men together, and what finally
brought Marshall to the Supreme Court, in addition to his availability and the
serendipitous unwillingness of Paterson and Jay to take the job, was a shared
view of the 1790s as a crisis in social order. Both men appreciated the constitutional nature of the American Revolution. Both feared the French Revolution
as speculation and metaphysics run amuck, a sure road to anarchy ending in
tyranny. With Washington, both men feared the fusion of French radicalism,
states' rights theory, and political democracy in the party of Thomas Jefferson.
Adams's goal, and Marshall's as congressman and secretary of state, was essentially to continue the policy of the Washington administration. Neutrality
and noninvolvement in the affairs of Europe that did not touch American inter-

84. As minister to France in 1798, Marshall maintained an active diplomatic correspondence
with Pickering, who was Adams's secretary of state. As a sample of their epistolary friendship in
later life, see Pickering to Marshall, 9 January, 10 March 1828; Marshall to Pickering, 28 March
1828, PJM, typescript.

ests was one cornerstone of the policy; the freedom to pursue commercial advantage, as in the Jay Treaty, another. Peace with both France and England, if it could be achieved honorably, was another policy goal. The domestic challenge was to preserve national unity created by the momentary idealism of the Revolution and institutionalized by the Constitution. Like General Washington, who realized that victory lay in keeping his army in the field, Marshall and Adams realized that with time, thinking constitutionally could turn into a national habit, providing that states' rights theorists didn't interpret it into oblivion. Adams and Marshall were moderate Federalists when moderation was under siege.[85]

Just how difficult it was to pursue moderation, and to support President Adams, Marshall discovered when he arrived at the nation's capital in December 1799. Like the American people, the Sixth Congress was rife with distrust and paranoia. Southern Federalists, who rallied to Adams for his strong stand in the XYZ affair, could not be counted on to support the nationalist program of the northern wing of the party. Commercial-minded Federalists in the north, on the other hand, wanted to exploit the affair further—as a possible first step to war and as an excuse for elimination of Republican political opposition once and for all, a goal they already had set out to achieve in the Alien and Sedition Acts. When Adams announced a second mission to France aimed at a peaceful settlement of outstanding disputes, Republicans set out to subvert the plan and to depose Adams as the Federalist candidate in the upcoming election. The Republicans, looking to the election of 1800, also renewed their assault on the Adams administration and on Adams personally. Ideological differences and electoral politics permeated every aspect of the Sixth Congress.

Marshall's instantaneous ascendancy in this highly politicized environment requires some explanation. Aside from sheer ability, which even Federalist critics acknowledged, he had several things going for him. One was his reputation among both Republicans and Federalists, as well as the people in general, for his role in the XYZ mission. Twenty years of legal experience and a reputation as the leading lawyer of Virginia also weighed in his favor, as did his experience in the Virginia ratifying convention and the state legislature. Lawmaking, after all, was his line of work. And even if politics wasn't, Marshall showed up in the new capital city as the recognized leader of a block of newly elected southern

85. Dauer, *Adams Federalists.* Adams, like Marshall, also distrusted abstract speculation, especially of the French variety. See Zoltán Haraszti, *John Adams and the Prophets of Progress* (Cambridge, Mass., 1952).

Federalists. It also helped that the Federalists, riding on the anti-French senti-ment generated by the XYZ affair, had regained control of the House. Espe-cially significant, given Marshall's political reputation in Virginia, was the election of a substantial bloc of Federalists from the southern states, where the party had been all but moribund. With a base of support in the South, a reputa-tion for moderation in the North, and general popularity among the rank and file, Marshall was the logical choice to defend Adams from the radicals in both parties. His objective was to rally a moderate centrist coalition from both par-ties around the principles of national unity.

Marshall's support of moderate Federalism was apparent in almost all of his actions in the Sixth Congress, beginning with his response to the president's address to Congress. The fact that Marshall was chosen by Sedgwick to write the response tells us that Marshall's reputation had preceded him to Philadel-phia. Judging from the language and substance of his speech, he aimed to sup-port Adams, without offending the High Federalists, and smite the Jeffersonians. His emphasis on law and order accomplished all those things and was heartfelt as well. No "portion of the American people," he said, "should permit themselves . . . to be seduced by the arts and misrepresentations of designing men into an open resistance of a law of the United States." It was a statement broad enough to include the recently suppressed Whiskey Rebel-lion and the radical proposition set forth by Jefferson in the Kentucky Resolu-tion, which openly counseled resistance to the Sedition Act. Marshall went on to promise that the Federalist majority would back the president in an effort to strengthen the federal judiciary, a point on which all Federalists agreed and one that led to the controversial Federal Judiciary Act of 1801.[86]

Marshall spent most of his short address on the subject of foreign pol-icy—at once the most pressing concern for Adams and the most threatening to party unity. To support Adams without antagonizing the High Federalists, Marshall set forth the foreign policy guidelines established by Washington and continued by Adams. He praised the president for appointing a second mission to France to do what the first was unable to accomplish. He expressed hope that outstanding grievances with Great Britain concerning the enforcement of the Jay Treaty could be accomplished by negotiation, a subtle way of reaf-firming the wisdom of the treaty, which tweaked the Republicans and united Federalists of all stripes. Regarding both France and Great Britain, he then promised what all good Federalists wanted to hear: that Congress would main-

86. Address, PJM, 4: 40.

tain American rights, peacefully if possible but by defensive military action if necessary. "Experience, the parent of wisdom, and the great instructor of nations," he noted, had established that "nothing short of the power of repelling aggressions will secure to our country a rational prospect of escaping the calamities of war or national degradation."[87]

Marshall's policy speech was a feather in his cap; and so was the fact that he was chosen to deliver the eulogy for George Washington, who died December 14, 1799. As the leading Virginia Federalist, it was appropriate that Marshall should have been selected and coincidental, too, in that he was about to embark on writing a massive biography of the general. Marshall's speech was a political coup, but the words of praise came from his heart. They were also, one senses, intended to cool partisan rancor and reaffirm the centrist tradition of moderate Federalism. Marshall's much-quoted words, that Washington was "first in war, first in peace, and first in the hearts of his country," would be remembered for ages to come, even though they originated from Marshall's friend Light-Horse Harry Lee.[88]

Marshall's eulogy was the beginning of a lifelong effort to unite a divided nation around its greatest leader. His pleas for moderation and party harmony, however, fell on deaf ears, even among the Federalists, who proceeded apace to squander their majority, split themselves further, and deliver the presidency to Thomas Jefferson. The ideologues in the party could not be dissuaded from pursuing a war with France, which they hoped would mean the death of the Democratic-Republicans. Adams's courageous decision to pursue a negotiated settlement instead ended all hope of party reconciliation and left Marshall stranded. He continued to be Adams's main defender in the House, however, and he also continued his own efforts to find common legislative ground on which his party could unite. One area in which Marshall played a crucial mediating role concerned federal bankruptcy legislation, an issue he would address prominently as chief justice. The bill under consideration in 1799, designed to encourage investment and stimulate entrepreneurial activity, provided for the discharge of insolvent debtors and the abolition of imprisonment for debt. It had failed passage in 1798 by a slim margin and appeared doomed again. Marshall saved the day by fighting successfully to restrict the scope of its operation and by requiring a jury trial to establish the fact of bankruptcy. Orthodox

87. Ibid., 43.
88. For his brief eulogy, see PJM, 4: 46–48; quote at 48. For Lee's role in drafting the resolutions, which Marshall introduced and from which the famous quote came, see ibid., 48 n. 4.

Hamiltonians such as Sedgwick were not pleased with the compromise, a "mischief" Sedgwick attributed to "Virginia theory." He also acknowledged that without Marshall's amendments, the bill would have failed. The bill, which operated prospectively, also abolished imprisonment for debt.[89]

Strengthening the federal judiciary, since it was the only hedge against Republican dominance, was the one subject on which the lame-duck Federalists could unite. As a leading member of the House committee appointed to revise the judiciary, Marshall played a role in framing the bill, which was finally passed as the Federal Judiciary Act of 1801. This bill did not add luster to his legislative career, though it is difficult to tell how much he was responsible for in its final version. Knowledgeable men in both parties recognized that some reform was necessary, but what finally emerged was unmistakably partisan. The act created sixteen new federal circuit judgeships, which Adams filled with loyal Federalists, one of whom was John Marshall's brother James Markham Marshall. By expanding the jurisdiction of the federal judiciary, at the expense of state courts, the measure added to the already firm conviction among Republicans that the federal courts were being redesigned to do the work of the Federalist Party. Republicans were confirmed in this impression by the provision of the final bill that reduced the number of Supreme Court justices from six to five, effective at the next vacancy—a provision that aimed to deprive Jefferson of an appointment to the Court that was expected to occur with the death or resignation of William Cushing. Such blatant partisanship guaranteed that Jefferson would declare open season on Marshall and his Court. Marshall, of course, did not know in 1799 that Jefferson would be president or that he would be chief justice. But Marshall did understand, and perhaps even fear, the highly partisan nature of the bill. He supported it anyhow—partly as a means of uniting the Federalists and partly because he believed that a strengthened federal judiciary was essential to preserve federal law. On this point, the Virginia and Kentucky Resolutions most surely came to Marshall's mind, since they proposed to take away the authority of the federal courts to interpret the Constitution and place it in the hands of state legislatures.[90]

89. Sedgwick to Rufus King, 11 May 1800, Charles R. King, ed., *The Life and Correspondence of Rufus King . . .* (New York, 1971), 3: 236–39. On the bankruptcy act, see Peter Coleman, *Debtors and Creditors in America: Insolvency, Imprisonment for Debt, and Bankruptcy, 1607–1900* (Madison, Wis., 1974), ch. 2; and Charles Warren, *Bankruptcy in United States History* (Cambridge, Mass., 1935). Also see Kathryn Turner [Preyer], "Federalist Policy and the Judiciary Act of 1801," *William and Mary Quarterly,* 3d ser., 22 (January 1965): 10, and PJM, 4: 34.

90. Turner [Preyer], "Federalist Policy and the Judiciary Act of 1801," remains the best study of that controversial act.

If Marshall hewed to the party line on the judicial bill, he deviated from it on the Disputed Election Bill, which Congress debated in the spring of 1800. The Federalist bill proposed to establish a joint congressional committee, presided over by the chief justice, to settle disputed electoral votes, especially those expected to come from Pennsylvania in favor of Jefferson in the upcoming presidential election. Marshall opposed the measure on both constitutional and practical political grounds and essentially defeated it by his amendment to reduce the findings of the committee to recommendations only. Contrary to what he said in 1799, Marshall also worked behind the scenes to secure the repeal of the Sedition Act, a show of independence from party that found him voting with the Republican opposition. Perhaps the most conclusive evidence of Marshall's independence from partisan excess was that party ideologues lumped him with John Adams.[91]

Nowhere was his loyalty to the president and his rational approach to matters of state more conspicuous than in Marshall's speech on the extradition of Jonathan Robbins, or Thomas Nash, as Marshall insisted on calling him. Robbins was charged with having taken part in a mutiny and murder aboard the British ship of war *Hermione* in 1797. When Robbins showed up in Charleston, South Carolina, on an American ship, he was identified as an Irish sailor, Thomas Nash, who had allegedly taken part in the mutiny and murder and possibly piracy, as well, depending on how the term was defined. British consul Benjamin Moode, who resided in Charleston, asked federal district judge Thomas Bee to extradite Robbins to Jamaica for trial under authority of Section 27 of the Jay Treaty. At the show cause hearing before Judge Bee, Robbins produced papers purporting to show he was not Nash but Jonathan Robbins, an American citizen born in Danbury, Connecticut. He also claimed in defense that he had been impressed aboard the British frigate and that he had not taken part in the mutiny and murder. On preliminary examination, Judge Bee appears to have determined that Robbins was indeed an American citizen, but the judge continued to detain him, waiting for further instructions from President Adams. After considering the documents in the case and the relevant question of American jurisdiction over crimes committed on the high seas, but apparently without regard for Bee's findings regarding Robbins's citizenship, Secre-

91. For Marshall's amendment to the Disputed Election Bill, passed by the Senate on 28 March 1800 and forwarded to the House for its consideration, see PJM, 4: 128–30; David Scott Robarge, "John Marshall and His Times: A Virginia Lawyer and Southern Federalist in the Early Republic, 1755–1801" (Ph.D. diss., Columbia University, 1995), 308–9. On Marshall and repeal of the Sedition Act, see PJM, 4: 37.

tary of State Timothy Pickering recommended extradition. Adams, who seems not to have studied the documents closely, was inclined to follow Pickering's advice but was uneasy about interfering with the judicial process. Accordingly, Pickering instructed Judge Bee to proceed with extradition, providing "such evidence of his criminality be produced as, by the laws of the United States or of South Carolina would justify such action." Technically at least, as one careful scholar noted, "The final decision in the case . . . was left fully in the hands of the judiciary." In the meantime, pressure was building in Charleston for a formal habeas corpus trial, which would consider fully all matters of fact and law. Especially relevant was the impact of Nash's alleged American citizenship and impressment on the extradition question. Without the benefit of formal proceedings and no doubt acting under the perceived pressure of Pickering's letter backed by the president's authority, Bee ordered Robbins up for extradition. The unfortunate young man was shipped to Jamaica, where he was tried by court-martial, convicted, executed, and his body hung in chains in August 1799.[92]

In ordinary times, the affair would have ended with Robbins's execution. But times were not ordinary, and the episode suddenly became a cause célèbre in the upcoming presidential election. The Republican press praised Robbins as a martyr to Republican liberty, an impressed American sailor who stood up for his freedom against British injustice only to be defeated by his own government, which denied him the most fundamental of procedural protections. The administration and the president were pilloried as inhumane, excessively pro-British, secretly monarchical, and tyrannically oppressive. Antiadminstration lawyers weighed in, too, challenging the legal reasoning of both the administration and Judge Bee. The case took on ominous political overtones early in 1800 when Edward Livingston introduced a bill on the floor of the House of Representatives censuring Adams for intruding unconstitutionally into the proceedings of the federal district court in South Carolina. For the first time in American history, Congress attempted to censure a sitting president. Adams's precipitate action and Bee's compliance, the charge was, denied Robbins access to a habeas corpus hearing and a trial by jury. To prove his case and to further

92. Larry D. Cress, "The Jonathan Robbins Incident: Extradition and the Separation of Powers in the Adams Administration," *Essex Institute Historical Collections* 111 (1975): 102–3, concluded that Adams and Pickering left the matter in Judge Bee's hands. I have relied on his article and on Ruth Wedgewood's comprehensive essay "The Revolutionary Martyrdom of Jonathan Robbins," *Yale Law Journal* 100 (November 1990): 229–368. Marshall's speech and related documents plus a concise discussion of the case appear in PJM, 4: 23–28, 83–109.

embarrass Adams, Livingston urged the House to demand access to executive documents related to the case. As with the dispute between Washington and the House of Representatives over the implementation of the Jay Treaty, the Robbins case turned into a full-blown constitutional shoot-out. The specific questions at issue, echoing the Jay Treaty debate, were whether the president was the sole power in foreign affairs or shared that authority with the House of Representatives and whether Section 27 of the Jay Treaty was self-executing, since Congress had not clarified the procedures associated with extradition. In addition, the case for the first time in American history demanded a clarification of the relation of executive authority and the federal judiciary.[93]

As the leader of the Adams Federalists in the House of Representatives, it was all but inevitable that Marshall would defend the president's action in the Robbins case. He did so first in an anonymous essay printed in the *Virginia Federalist* September 7, 1799—after his election to Congress but before taking his seat, and after Robbins had been executed. Marshall's only aim, he claimed, was to clarify the confusion produced by the politically motivated attacks on the president. His position was straightforward and lawyerly. The Jay Treaty, which Marshall discretely referred to as "the Treaty of Amity," clearly provided for extradition; the mode of executing the extradition process, even though it was not spelled out in Article 27, fell, as did all affairs between states, to the executive branch. The president had no choice but to act and in doing so "appears to have done no more than his duty." Marshall did not say whether Adams's determination (and Pickering's) of Robbins's guilt was correct, only that the president had the authority and the duty to decide the matter. Marshall was apparently not aware either of Bee's preliminary finding concerning Robbins's American citizenship. Nor did that issue seem to matter, since Marshall denied the federal courts any determinative role in the matter of extradition.[94]

Marshall's fullest statement on the matter came in his detailed and much-praised speech before the House on March 7, 1800. His timing was perfect, and no doubt carefully planned. The debate over Livingston's censure resolutions had rumbled on noisily and inconclusively for several weeks: The Republicans demanded papers; the president supplied them. Livingston and others accused Adams of subverting judicial independence by taking the case out of

93. See Cress, "Jonathan Robbins Incident," 112–13, and Wedgewood, "Revolutionary Martyrdom," 333–53.
94. PJM, 4: 23–28.

Judge Bee's hands. The jurisdictional question and associated questions of international law were batted about, as were the factual questions concerning Robbins's citizenship. On the latter question, Robbins's lawyers presented enough evidence at the show cause hearing to convince Bee that Robbins was an American citizen, though definitive proof was hard to come by. Even more difficult to prove, or disprove, was Robbins's claim that he had been impressed off an American vessel, though all agreed that the British had been and were still engaging in that nefarious practice. In all the confusion, perhaps only one thing was clear: a full trial and more time would have been required to determine the matter.

Marshall's answer to these confusing and unsettled legal and political questions boiled down to two main points. First, as to the role of the federal judiciary regarding the interpretation of treaties generally and of extradition in particular, Article 3 of the Constitution limited the authority of the federal courts exclusively to matters of law and equity, a delineation no doubt appreciated by the common lawyers in Congress. Second, regarding executive authority, relations among nations are by definition political in character and, as in the enforcement of the extradition provisions of Article 27 of an international treaty, are the exclusive domain of the president.

Both points added up to an expansive definition of presidential authority in matters of foreign affairs. As Marshall explained, the questions not only involved the president's power to negotiate treaties, but his constitutional duty to enforce their provisions. The request for extradition under a federal treaty in the Robbins case, he stated, "was in its nature a national demand made upon the nation." Not only was this a political question beyond judicial cognizance, it was one that belonged exclusively to the president. In Marshall's prescient words: "The President is the sole organ of the nation in its external relations, and its sole representative with foreign nations. . . . He possesses the whole executive power, he holds and directs the force of the nation." If force should be called for, it "is to be performed through him." "He is charged to execute the laws. A treaty is declared to be a law. He must then execute a treaty, where he and he alone possesses the means of executing it." Marshall further claimed that where "political discretion" is called for in foreign relations, it is the executive who must exercise it. This was what Adams did in the Robbins case, and this is what the Constitution allowed, or would allow once Marshall set forth his argument.[95]

95. For Marshall on executive power in foreign affairs, see especially ibid., 104–5.

Ironically in light of his reputation for judicial activism, Marshall went on to expound a constricted and even contradictory definition of federal judicial authority under Article 3 of the Constitution. The "judicial power of the United States," he emphasized, did *not* extend, as Livingston's resolutions said, "to *all questions* arising under the constitution, treaties and laws of the United States," but only "to all *cases in law and equity* arising under the constitution, laws and treaties of the United States." The difference encompassed the distinction between a strictly legal grant of power and a broadly political one. Marshall spelled it out emphatically: "By extending the judicial power to all *cases in law and equity,* the constitution had never been understood, to confer on that department, any political power whatever. To come within this description, a question must assume a legal form, for forensic litigation, and judicial decision. There must be parties to come into court, who can be reached by its process, and bound by its power; whose rights admit of ultimate decision by a tribunal to which they are bound to submit."[96]

As a statement of the case-and-controversy principle of Anglo-American law—that the court cannot act except when presented with a legitimate case—this statement is unexceptional. Marshall, however, went one large step farther, arguing that cases that have political implications cannot be heard at all. Since the Constitution is a political as well as a legal document, such an extreme version of what came to be known as the "political question doctrine" would seem to diminish significantly the federal judiciary's subject matter jurisdiction over constitutional questions. In his willingness to remove federal district judge Bee entirely from the extradition proceedings, Marshall also went beyond what was necessary to make his point. In fact, a fairly convincing case can be made, and was made at the time, that the preliminary hearings before Bee—wherein Robbins made a convincing prima facie case for his American citizenship, which the judge himself acknowledged—went to the very heart of the dispute. By the time Marshall spoke, Robbins had already been executed. But the fact remains that Marshall justified wresting the case from the district court before the essential question of citizenship could be settled by a habeas corpus trial. Had Nash/Robbins been able to establish his American citizenship, his extradition, even if the matter fell within the powers of the executive, would probably not have occurred.[97]

96. Ibid., 95–96.
97. Cress argues the possibility that Robbins was who he said he was, "Jonathan Robbins Incident," 116.

Should Marshall have taken a stand for a jury trial even at the expense of embarrassing the president? To have done so, though it might have been costly politically, made legal sense. In fact, Marshall had worked to amend the bankruptcy bill of 1800 to give the jury fact-finding authority. In the Robbins case, Marshall admitted that Congress might assign such authority to the federal courts. Still he chose not to advocate the necessity of doing so. Indeed, given the absence of any implementing language in Section 27, Marshall could as easily have given the courts a limited role in extradition cases as to argue that the matter was entirely political and exclusively executive. Certainly as an experienced lawyer he understood that courts and juries possessed time-honored procedures for discovering factual truth and upholding procedural guarantees against the abuse of power. One can only surmise that in favoring executive discretion, he had Adams and Washington in mind as models of disinterested and fair-minded statesmen, an assumption he was unwilling to extend to Jefferson. Marshall may well have sensed, too, that the chaos of the 1790s called for forceful and decisive executive leadership.[98]

Marshall's speech did not, as is sometimes claimed, put an end to the Robbins case as a political issue in the election of 1800. Republican newspapers continued to hammer Adams and Pickering for denying Robbins a trial by jury, especially when there were precedents for doing so. Marshall, on the other hand, came out a winner, although he did not escape censure. Jefferson zeroed in on Marshall's failure to consider the citizenship and impressment allegations and shot some holes in his jurisdictional argument as well. Marshall's defense of Adams was also noted unfavorably in the Republican press, though Adams and Pickering appear to have received the brunt of criticism. Federalist papers, on the other hand, uniformly praised his argument, and some, such as the *Salem (Massachusetts) Gazette,* reprinted his speech. American lawmakers took due notice as well, treating Marshall's argument almost as a judicial precedent, this before he became chief justice. The first such occasion was the trial of Thomas Cooper in the Philadelphia circuit court of Supreme Court Justice Samuel Chase in 1800. Cooper was charged under the Sedition Act of 1798 for his vicious attack on Adams, which included reference to Adams's handling of the Robbins extradition. In his charge to the jury, Chase cited Marshall's Robbins speech as law. Marshall was also relied on in framing the extradition provisions of the Webster-Ashburton Treaty of 1842. Congressman Marshall also made a cameo appearance in Justice Sutherland's expansive definition of

98. Ibid., 115.

executive authority in foreign affairs in *U.S. v. Curtiss Wright Export Corp.* (1936).[99]

The most immediate result of the Robbins speech was that it won Marshall the admiration and gratitude of John Adams. And there was much to admire. As with Marshall's arguments in the Virginia courts and before the Supreme Court in *Ware v. Hylton*, there was his conspicuous ability to harness relevant legal authorities to practical political and constitutional matters. One sees, too, the gift of persuasion of which Wirt spoke, the knack for explicating exceedingly complicated matters in a colloquial style that seemed to unfold with a natural and irresistible logic. The subjects about which Marshall spoke—the authority of a president, who was hated by Republicans and many in his own party as well, and the treaty rights of Great Britain, which was then treating American interests with supreme contempt—were politically explosive. Remarkably, however, there was no trace of political rancor or partisan vindictiveness in his long speech. In some almost mysterious way, his statesmanlike exposition of law seems to have quieted the turbulent mood of the Congress, at least for a brief moment.

It is tempting to think that Adams glimpsed in Marshall's Robbins speech the legal learning, the analytical sharpness, the tone of moderate rationality that would make Marshall a great chief justice. The first thing Adams did, however, was to nominate Marshall as secretary of war, then two days later, on May 9, 1800, name him secretary of state. For Adams, who had just purged his cabinet of the closet Hamiltonians, who were pushing for war with France, the appointment made sense. Marshall, who seems not to have been consulted, got word of the appointment on his way home for a much-needed rest after the stormy legislative session. Being a cabinet member was not something he aspired to, but the president needed immediate assistance. Marshall took the job out of a sense of duty and because he agreed with the foreign policy of the administration, which was now in jeopardy. In any case, he realized that his future as a Federalist politician in Republican Virginia was dim.

Marshall served as secretary of state less than nine months, counting the time he remained in office, at Jefferson's request, after he had been appointed chief justice. During this period, he undertook no new policy initiatives and left

99. The reaction to Marshall's speech is discussed in Wedgewood, "Revolutionary Martyrdom," 311–33; John Marshall, "Speech in the Case of Jonathan Robbins," in *American Eloquence: A Collection of Speeches and Addresses . . .* , ed. Frank Moore (New York, 1859), 2: 20–32. His speech is cited by the Supreme Court in *U.S. v. Curtiss Wright Export Corp.*, 299 US 304.

no appreciable mark on the office. Indeed, the office afforded him little opportunity to do so. Like other cabinet offices during this period, the Department
of State was a modest operation. Surviving papers and correspondence with
American ambassadors and consuls indicate that Marshall was a careful administrator, as well as a consistent supporter of the president's policies. Caution and moderation, mixed with a good sense of what the situation allowed,
were the hallmarks of his tenure. As an ardent champion of American national
honor, Marshall might have been expected to act forcefully against the Tripolitan pirates, who regularly threatened American ships in the Mediterranean. Instead he continued the policy of paying them off. More importantly, he
continued to support Adams's effort to settle outstanding grievances with both
France and England peacefully and with careful regard for national honor and
American neutral rights. Peace was Marshall's goal, but he never lost sight
of American sovereignty or American interest. Like Adams, he believed that
America could best be served by preserving the international rule of law. In a
world governed by fair and equitable rules and where peace prevailed, American resources and ingenuity would carry the day. As Marshall saw it, the role
of government and the function of law, in foreign as in domestic policy, was
to create a rational rule-governed environment that would facilitate individual
entrepreneurial creativity. All of this is to say that Marshall's respect for the
rule of law and the moderation, rationality, and good sense that he displayed
as secretary of state were precisely the qualities needed for the office of chief
justice.[100]

Marshall was nominated for that office on January 20, 1801, and after considerable backroom resistance among Federalists, he was confirmed by the Senate on January 27. Adams never explained why he chose Marshall or why he
was willing to defy the leaders of his own party to do so. But the reasons seem
readily apparent, starting with Marshall's record of personal loyalty. Equally
important was the ideological compatibility between the two men, a factor that
from the beginning had shaped presidential appointments to the Court. Beyond that, were Marshall's professional qualities essential to the office. John
Adams was a lawyer, even though he had not practiced for years, and he knew
legal talent when he saw it. With Marshall, there was much to see. His reputation at the Richmond Bar was widely appreciated and was vouched for by his
argument in *Ware v. Hylton,* even more so, perhaps, by his Robbins speech.

---

100. See Frances Howell Rudko, *John Marshall and International Law: Statesman and Chief
Justice* (New York, 1991), especially ch. 5.

Adams was even more directly familiar with Marshall's XYZ dispatches, which in their clarity of language and analysis bear the mark of a judicious, and judicial, mind.

The only remaining question was whether the easygoing Virginian had the grit and determination to stand up to the triumphant forces of Jeffersonian democracy. And here, even the ultras relented, or at least Theodore Sedgwick did when he conceded about Marshall that "there is not a man in the U.S. of better intentions and he had the confidence of all good men." Adams never had any doubt. What he saw from the beginning, and what might not be apparent to less discerning observers, was that Marshall's moderate style and his moderate version of Federalism, like Adams's, masked a passionate commitment to social order. Both men believed that the pervasive social chaos of the 1790s was a threat to the Constitution and the federal Union it created. Both men tended to blame the now triumphant political party led by Thomas Jefferson, perhaps even Jefferson himself. Both also sensed, and recent scholarship has confirmed, that the election of 1800 itself was a major step in the development of a permanent party system. Jefferson thought of the election as a democratic "revolution" that would put the Republic back on track after twelve years of Federalist misrule. For Adams and Marshall, Jefferson's election was indeed a revolution—one made in France that had to be stopped before it subverted the Constitution. Both men looked to the Supreme Court to get the job done.[101]

It was assumed by Adams when he appointed Marshall chief justice, and by Marshall when he accepted the office, that the Supreme Court would play a significant role in checking the rampant democracy represented by the victorious Democratic-Republican Party. What precisely Marshall thought the Court under his leadership could do, however, is not so clear. As a political realist, a constitutional lawyer, and a trenchant on-the-spot observer of public life, he surely appreciated the Court's political and institutional vulnerabilities to the political branches. He knew, too, that the Court had been and still was Federalist to the man and that its major decisions had followed the vested rights and nationalist priorities of the Federalist Party. When he observed Justice Chase preside over Callender's sedition trial in Richmond in 1798, Marshall gauged the depth of local opposition to national law. Perhaps he also recognized that most of the important constitutional issues of the first decade—the debate over

---

101. Sedgwick to Rufus King, 26 September 1800; King, *Life and Correspondence of Rufus King*, 3: 309. On Jefferson's French sympathies and how he was unfit to be president, see Marshall to Hamilton, 1 January, 1801, PJM, 6: 46–47.

Hamilton's Bank of the United States and the Jay Treaty, the Alien and Sedition Acts, not to mention the Judiciary Acts of 1789 and 1801—had been fought out in Congress, not the courts. Looking at the paucity of great cases in the Court's early history, the high turnover rate among justices, and the difficulty of getting qualified men to serve only confirmed Hamilton's assessment in *The Federalist* 78, that the Court was the weakest and "least dangerous" of the three branches. The real question was whether, as former Chief Justice John Jay predicted in 1801, the Court's disabilities were permanent.[102]

Marshall, for one, did not believe they were. In fact, to the discerning eye, the Court's potential was substantial, which is why Jefferson feared it. The general principle of judicial review was widely accepted. The Court, with the help of Congress to be sure, had implemented rules of procedure to guide its deliberations. Federal circuit courts, manned by the perambulating justices sitting with federal district judges, were a going concern, too, as Marshall well knew from his own extensive circuit practice. By the end of the decade, the justices had also decided a number of leading cases, such as *Ware v. Hylton,* where the Court used its power of review to nullify a state law in conflict with a federal treaty, and *Calder v. Bull* (1798), in which the Court exercised its interpretive powers to settle the meaning of the Ex Post Facto Clause of the Constitution. In *Hylton v. U.S.* (1796), the Court laid claim to its power to review acts of Congress and to disallow them if they violated the Constitution. More important still was the uncontested power of review over constitutional questions decided by state courts, which the Supreme Court claimed under Section 25 of the Judiciary Act of 1789. The point is not that the Court's powers were fully defined by the Jay and Ellsworth Courts, but rather that its authority to interpret the Constitution and check state legislative and judicial power had begun to take concrete form. This was no more or less than what the structure of the Constitution itself decreed, what the generous allocation of power in Article 3 of the Constitution established, and what was noticed by Federalists and Anti-Federalists alike at the time of ratification.[103]

---

102. Presser, *Original Misunderstanding,* ch. 9, treats Chase, Marshall, and the Callender trial.

103. *Ware v. Hylton,* 3 Dallas 199; *Calder v. Bull,* 3 Dallas 386; *Hylton v. U.S.,* 3 Dallas 171. On the institutional development of the Court in the 1790s, see Goebel, *Antecedents and Beginnings;* William R. Casto, *The Supreme Court in the Early Republic: The Chief Justiceships of John Jay and Oliver Ellsworth* (Columbia, S.C., 1995). The definitive documentary record of the early Court is Maeva Marcus et al., ed., *The Documentary History of the Supreme Court of the United States, 1789–1800,* 6 vols. to date (New York, 1985–).

As a lawyer who practiced extensively in the federal courts, Marshall witnessed the rise of the federal judiciary. It was not just that he acknowledged judicial review, which he did in 1788, but that he sensed its importance in the democratic polity that was taking shape in the 1790s. Several developments drove this lesson home. One was the distinction between law and politics, and connected to this was the distinction between adjudication and legislation in the republican scheme of government. Behind the distinction was the lesson Marshall learned as a common lawyer in Virginia: that adjudication was a form of governance, one that contrasted favorably with the legislation cranked out by state legislatures in control of party politicians. For Jefferson, the state legislatures were the safest depository of the people's newfound sovereign power; for Marshall, they embodied the worst features of the new democratic political order.

Indeed, it was precisely the state legislatures that Marshall knew best and feared the most—with Virginia's House of Delegates as a case in point. It was bad enough that it passed bad laws and too many of them, which it did in the 1780s and 1790s, as Marshall saw it. It was infinitely worse that the same legislature should declare itself the sole representative of the sovereign people with the right to settle constitutional disputes, which was the message of the Virginia and Kentucky Resolutions. By placing themselves over the Supreme Court as final interpreters of the Constitution, the legislatures of Virginia and Kentucky threw down a gauntlet Marshall was obliged to pick up. Everything he learned since the Revolution pointed to the necessity of curbing state legislative excess. The key to success, he also learned from the 1790s, was to make the Court into a legal institution. Doing so would permit him to fend off the Republican attack he knew was coming; it would also justify the broad interpretive powers that the Court had already begun to claim and that he no doubt hoped to expand. In the coming battle of Armageddon, the Court might just be the salvation of the Republic. In any case, as John Adams and his new chief justice well knew, it was the only show in town.

CHAPTER THREE

Marshall, Jefferson, *and the* Rise *of the* Supreme Court

> Nothing should be spared to eradicate this spirit of Marshallism.
> —*Jefferson on Marshall*

> The Morals of the Author of the letter to Mazzei cannot be pure.
> —*Marshall on Jefferson*

> Of the importance of the judiciary at all times, but more especially the present I am fully impressd & shall endeavor in the new office to which I am called not to disappoint my friends.
> —*Marshall on the Supreme Court*

T HE ELECTION OF 1800 has been seen as the great happening in American political history: The peaceful transfer of power from the Federalists to the Jeffersonian Republicans signified the legitimacy of political opposition, which was the sine qua non of the two-party system. With party government, so the argument goes, divisive ideology disappeared, and compromise and pragmatism became the touchstones of American public life.[1]

However much this keen insight from hindsight helps us understand American political history in its long sweep, it runs the danger of obscuring our understanding of the constitutional struggles of the early national period. Neither Federalists nor Jeffersonian Republicans thought of the transfer of power as

1. Richard Hofstadter, *The Idea of a Party System: The Rise of a Legitimate Opposition in the United States, 1780–1840* (Berkeley, Calif., 1969), especially ch. 4.

conclusive. Nor did they celebrate, even if they saw it, the implication of this shift for the rise of permanent political parties. As for the peaceful nature of the transfer to power, unless that means only the absence of a forceful attempt by the Federalists to displace the Republicans or separate from the Union, it has little meaning. In short, the passion and political violence of the last decade of the eighteenth century continued unabated during the first decade of the nineteenth century as Americans struggled to govern themselves under the new Constitution. The inchoate nature of that document, which meant that each decision was a precedent for the future, only added to the intensity of the political warfare. Political parties, which would someday mitigate the ideological conflicts among regions and interests, were themselves as much the source of deep division as they were instruments of peace and harmony.[2]

If the ideological passions of the 1790s continued into the first decade of the new century, so did the tendency of those passions to focus on the Constitution. What is remarkable is how much of this continuing battle over the Constitution was a struggle among Virginians. On one end of the ideological spectrum were the radical agrarians John Taylor of Caroline and John Randolph of Roanoke; next to them was Jefferson, and slightly to the right of him was Madison, who had abandoned his extreme nationalism after Hamilton showed him what it really meant. Other Virginia jurists, such as St. George Tucker, Spencer Roane, and William Wirt, also weighed in on the side of what came to be called "Virginia theory," which left Marshall to uphold the national constitutionalism that had been associated with Washington and Adams Federalism.

It was Jefferson and Marshall, however, who symbolized and personalized the competing constitutional persuasions of the age and brought them into explosive focus. Each had taken a stand on the great foreign and domestic issues of the 1790s; each had conflated those issues into a dispute over the meaning of the Constitution. When fate and ambition made Jefferson president and Marshall chief justice, the institutional stage was set for what is one of the most creative confrontations in American constitutional history. At stake was not just the position of the Supreme Court in American government but the place of law in republican culture. Neither of these great issues had been settled by

---

2. The two most recent studies of the 1790s do not address directly the problem of periodization, as is noted by James M. Banner Jr., in his review of Stanley Elkins and Eric McKitrick, *The Age of Federalism* (New York, 1993), and James Roger Sharp, *American Politics in the Early Republic: The New Nation in Crisis* (New Haven, Conn., 1993), in *William and Mary Quarterly* 52 (January 1995): 167–70.

the Constitution; both would be influenced significantly by the personalities of Jefferson and Marshall—and by their unrelenting mutual hatred. The success of Marshall's claim that the Court, not the executive, was the special guardian of the Constitution and the Republic cannot be understood without understanding the failure of the president to make good his counterclaim. Ironically, the chief justice could not have accomplished what he did for the Court without the implacable opposition and the strategic miscalculations of his old enemy. Biography and history were conjoined, then, along with accident and chance, to shape the great constitutional events of Marshall's first decade as chief justice. Those events—even the great case of *Marbury v. Madison*—did not stand alone, but assumed significance and can be fully understood only as separate acts in a single drama, or to use Holmes's military metaphor, as ongoing engagements in a single "campaign of history."[3]

A Grand Creative Hatred

Unfortunately for historians, there were no cameras to record the deliciously ironic moment on March 4, 1801, when the new chief justice administered the oath of office to the new president. With his hand on the Bible held by Marshall, Jefferson swore to uphold the Constitution Marshall was sure he was about to destroy. Whether the new president thought at this moment to rue his earlier wish that Marshall might be buried in the judiciary, is not known. What is known is that Jefferson had already concluded that the federal judiciary would have to be humbled and "the spirit of Marshallism" eradicated. Nor was it coincidental that Marshall turned his back to the president during the ceremony. Less then two months before the inauguration, Marshall wrote to Alexander Hamilton that Jefferson's "foreign [French] prejudices" and his personal quest for power made him "totally unfit" "for the chief magistracy of a nation which cannot indulge those prejudices without sustaining debt & permanent injury." Jefferson was not an "absolute terrorist," to be sure, but almost as bad; he was, as Marshall saw it, a "speculative theorist" who would soon "sap the fundamental principles of the government."[4]

---

3. Oliver Wendell Holmes Jr., "John Marshall: From the Bench, February 4, 1901," *Collected Legal Papers* (New York, 1920), 267.
4. Marshall to Hamilton, 1 January 1801, PJM, 6: 46; Marshall to C. C. Pinckney, 4 March 1801, ibid., 89–90.

Both men knew the gauntlet was down then, both believed the fate of the Republic was on the line, and both had translated the great ideological issues of the day into a struggle between judicial and executive authority, sinewed with unyielding personal aversion. Where the antipathy started, what nourished it over the years before 1800, is not precisely clear. So ingrained was it that one is tempted to argue that a chemical disaffinity was the source of the problem. Indeed, it is difficult to imagine John Marshall building a nest like Monticello, playing the fiddle at the soirees of royal governor Fauquier, or speculating about every idea under the sun. Nor can we readily see Jefferson joking about the pretty girls who followed the Revolutionary troops—even if he had been there to do so—or racing with the enlisted men at Valley Forge, betting the ponies or playing quoits at the Barbecue Club, or playing practical jokes at his own expense. No one, so far as we know, loved Jefferson for his laugh, as Joseph Story loved Marshall. Marshall was aristocratic in his politics and democratic in his behavior; Jefferson reversed the order. Marshall was content to practice law; Jefferson wanted to reform it—along with most everything else. As a quintessential common lawyer, Marshall moved comfortably in the experiential, nontheoretical gradualist world of incremental change. Jefferson was an Enlightenment thinker who believed that philosophic speculation was the key to civic redemption.[5]

Jefferson's French prejudices and Marshall's English ones clearly stood for more than differences over the Jay Treaty. Mixed in with irreconcilable differences in personality and philosophy was some plain old-fashioned contempt. Marshall knew that Jefferson had not fought in the Revolution and that as governor he had beaten an apparently ignominious retreat before British troops advancing on Richmond, never mind that a legislative investigation cleared him of dereliction of duty. He knew that while Jefferson championed legal reform in Virginia, he had also supported the bill of attainder against Josiah Philips in the legislature. He knew that Jefferson's organization of a party pledged to democracy worked to enhance Jefferson's personal power—and charged him with demagoguery, which in Virginia, as in ancient Rome, meant a defection from class. Perhaps Marshall guessed that it was Jefferson who egged on Minister Genêt to subvert Washington's neutrality policy, then left the naive Frenchman twisting in the breeze. In his letter to Philip Mazzei, which was made public in May 1797, Jefferson not only attacked the administration but

---

5. Story to Samuel P. P. Fay, 25 February 1808, in *Life and Letters of Joseph Story . . .* , ed. W. W. Story (London, England, 1851), 1: 167.

impugned the honor of Washington himself. That alone was sufficient to seal Marshall's animus. But on top of this, he saw Jefferson as the evil genius behind the rising states' rights movement, which Marshall sincerely believed threatened to destroy the Constitution and the federal Union.[6]

Both men were prepared to do battle. Marshall confessed to C. C. Pinckney that he was "very fully impressed" with "the importance of the judiciary" in the new age. He also promised "not to disappoint my friends" in regard to the Court's critical duties. Marshall wanted to energize the Court; Jefferson was determined to humble it. Nor was the president's hostility surprising given the fact that the federal judiciary under Washington and Adams had been exclusively Federalist. The Federalist justices had enlarged the Court's jurisdiction at the expense of state courts and had gone so far as to claim jurisdiction under federal criminal common law—a most unrepublican thing to do, as Jefferson and his supporters correctly pointed out. In other important areas, the Court's decisions throughout the 1790s followed Federalist policy preferences, for example, the protection of vested rights against state intrusion and the supremacy of federal statutes and treaties over state law. In fact, almost all of the great issues Marshall and his Court would confront, including that of judicial review, had been addressed, though not always settled, by the Court under Jay and Ellsworth. The justices had gone a great distance, too, with the help of the Judiciary Act of 1789 and the Process Acts of the same year (revised in 1792 and 1793), in establishing rules of procedure and working relationships with state judiciaries and lower federal courts.[7]

Marshall inherited a functioning Court, then, but one more politically exposed for the institutional strides it had made and more vulnerable still because it got openly entangled in the violent partisan politics of the 1790s—on the losing side no less. Quite simply, the Court was out of sync with the most far-reaching political development of that decade: the rise of political parties, which in turn rested on the radical notion that government belonged to the people. In an age when deference was increasingly under assault, the Court was conspicuously aristocratic. As critics pointed out, from the ratifying conven-

6. For a discussion of the Mazzei letter, see Merrill D. Peterson, *Thomas Jefferson and the New Nation* (New York, 1970), 570–72. Marshall printed the Jefferson letter and other related documents in *The Life of George Washington,* 2d ed., revised and corrected (Philadelphia, 1832), 2: Notes, 2–32. On Genêt, see Elkins and McKitrick, *Age of Federalism,* 341–54, especially 348.

7. Marshall to C. C. Pinckney, 4 March 1801, PJM, 6: 89. On the Court in the 1790s, see Charles Warren, *The Supreme Court in United States History,* new and rev. ed. (Boston, 1926), 1: chs. 1–3; Julius Goebel Jr., *Antecedents and Beginnings to 1801* (New York, 1971).

tions on, the justices, unlike all other officials, were not answerable to the popular electorate. They worked in secret and spoke in a language that was both arcane and distressingly Anglican in tone. When the Jeffersonian Democrats attacked the Federalists as pro-English, monarchical, consolidationist, and biased in favor of commercial New England, they could with some justification single out the Court under Jay and Ellsworth as the chief case in point. That Chief Justice Jay's aristocratic preferences were so conspicuous made their case even more compelling.[8]

Marshall knew that the Court would come under attack, and he also understood that the institution he inherited was weak. The justices had handed down important decisions, but they averaged barely more than one a year for the first decade—hardly enough to keep six grown men busy. And for all the institutional progress it had made in the 1790s, the Court was still not the center of constitutional action. Congress had staked out an imposing claim on constitutional interpretation, and so, even more threateningly, had the states. In the Callender trial in Richmond in 1800, Marshall witnessed firsthand the tenacity of local jurisprudence and the hostility to federal judges who challenged it. The decade before 1800, as well as the one after, was also replete with examples of successful state resistance to Court-imposed federal law. For example, Georgia threatened to use force to prevent the enforcement of *Chisholm v. Georgia,* just as Pennsylvania would do later in regard to *U.S. v. Peters* (1809). As the passage of the Eleventh Amendment in 1798 indicated, states could also use the amending process in Article 5 to overturn unpopular judicial decisions, in this case, *Chisholm.* The famous Virginia and Kentucky Resolutions of 1798, written by Madison and Jefferson, not only protested the unconstitutionality of the Alien and Sedition Acts but claimed that the states, not the Supreme Court, rightfully possessed the authority to strike down acts of Congress that violated the Constitution. Since the resolutions served as a plank in the election platform of the Democratic-Republican Party in 1800, and since that party now controlled the national government, Marshall had reason to expect the worst.[9]

8. On the Court in the 1790s, consult William R. Casto, *The Supreme Court in the Early Republic: The Chief Justiceships of John Jay and Oliver Ellsworth* (Columbia, S.C., 1995); the political involvement of the Jay and Ellsworth Courts is also documented in Warren, *Supreme Court,* 1: 1–168, passim. See also Sandra F. VanBurkleo, " 'Honour, Justice, and Interest': John Jay's Republican Politics and Statesmanship on the Federal Bench," *Journal of the Early Republic,* 4 (fall 1984): 239–74.

9. The standard account of the Alien and Sedition Acts is James M. Smith, *Freedom's Fetters: The Alien and Sedition Laws and American Civil Liberties* (Ithaca, N.Y., 1956). On the sedition

Whether Marshall had developed a strategy in advance for dealing with the attack he was sure would come, is not known. What is known is that he was not about to concede, as had former Chief Justice John Jay, that the weakness of the federal judiciary was a permanent condition. After consulting the history of the 1790s, he may have well decided even before assuming office that the wisest course was to extricate the Court from political activity and build on its strength as a legal institution. At any rate, that is what he did. Like General Washington, whose biography he was now writing, Marshall and the Court would have to avoid a frontal assault, strengthen their internal lines of communication, and capitalize on the enemy's mistakes. Just as Washington did at Valley Forge, he would somehow have to keep his army in the field. How he would do this and also manage to save the Constitution and the Republic, which he promised his friends and his party he would do, was not so clear.

Consolidating the Court; Taking Command: The Circuit Court Crisis of 1802

Jefferson's effort to eradicate the "spirit of Marshallism" and humble the Federalist Court began immediately. One of the first acts of the new president—the one that ended with *Marbury v. Madison*—was his decision not to deliver the stack of justice of the peace commissions for the District of Columbia that Secretary of State Madison found on his desk on March 5, commissions for offices created by the Federalist Party and filled by President Adams, literally at the last minute, with loyal Federalists. Then there was the almost certain impeachment of Justice Samuel Chase, whose fate was sealed by his contemptuous treatment while on circuit of Virginia lawyers and "Virginia theory" in the sedition trial of James Callender in 1800 and his anti-Jefferson harangue to the Baltimore grand jury in 1803. Of greater importance, however, was the repeal of the Federalist's Judiciary Act of 1801, which had replaced the act of 1789. Passed by the lame-duck Federalist Congress, the act abolished circuit riding; created sixteen new circuit judgeships, which were filled with loyal Federalists by John Adams; and significantly expanded the jurisdiction of the federal courts, largely at the expense of state judiciaries. Put forth as a genuine reform, the act struck the Jeffersonians as a crass, last-ditch attempt to resist the will of the sovereign people as expressed in the election of 1800. This was not an

trials in Virginia, see Stephen B. Presser, *The Original Misunderstanding: The English, the Americans, and the Dialectic of Federalist Jurisprudence* (Durham, N.C., 1991), chs. 8 and 9.

unreasonable conclusion given the fact that the act also reduced the size of the Court from six to five, effective at the next vacancy, so as to deprive President Jefferson of a chance to place a Republican on the Court.[10]

The Repeal Act of March 1802 might be seen as a victory for moderation, since it basically returned the federal courts to the arrangement established by the Judiciary Act of 1789. And so it was compared to the extreme alternatives put forth by anti-Court radicals. But the debate over repeal, orchestrated by Jefferson and reported widely in the political press of the day, was anything but moderate. Federal criminal common-law jurisdiction claimed by the Court in the 1790s was denounced as unrepublican. Federalist judicial bias was denounced and judicial indiscretions were condemned in the harshest terms. No one, least of all the justices of the Supreme Court, could attend to the anti-Court tirades of Republican orators and editors without at once sensing that American democracy was at fundamental odds with federal judicial power. The opening of the impeachment campaign against federal district judge John Pickering of New Hampshire, who had the misfortune of mixing alcoholism with his Federalist politics, drove home the same lesson. The administration's refusal to appear before the bar of the Court in *Marbury* was another slap in the face, as was Jefferson's order to administration witnesses not to testify in the case. One final insult came when Congress, after reinstituting the old circuit arrangements, passed a law that effectively adjourned the Court for fourteen months, from December 1801 to February 1803.[11]

Probably no one foresaw that the Repeal Act and the cancellation of the 1802 session would be the occasion for one of the most important victories in the history of the Court. But thanks to Marshall's deft leadership, it was. The dilemma posed by the Repeal Act, which the chief justice turned to the Court's advantage, concerned the question of whether the justices should ride circuit as required by the Judiciary Act of 1789 and reinstated by the Repeal Act. Not to do so, that is, behaving as if the Judiciary Act of 1801 were still in force,

10. Kathryn Turner [Preyer], "Federalist Policy and the Judiciary Act of 1801," *William and Mary Quarterly*, 3d ser., 22 (January 1965): 3–33; Richard Ellis, *The Jeffersonian Crisis: Courts and Politics in the Young Republic* (New York, 1971); George Lee Haskins and Herbert A. Johnson, *Foundations of Power: John Marshall, 1801–1815* (New York, 1981).

11. Warren, *Supreme Court*, 1: ch. 4, makes excellent use of newspapers. For Jefferson's assault on the judiciary and repeal of the Judiciary Act of 1801, consult Ellis, *Jeffersonian Crisis*, ch. 3, and Haskins and Johnson, *Foundations of Power*, ch. 5. The impeachment of Samuel Chase is treated in *Foundations of Power*, ch. 7; Ellis, *Jeffersonian Crisis*, ch. 5; Peter C. Hoffer and N. E. H. Hull, *Impeachment in America, 1635–1805* (New Haven, Conn., 1984), especially pt. 4.

would be to deny the constitutionality of the Repeal Act. The point here, pressed on Congress by a petition from eleven of the circuit judges whose appointments had been confirmed under the 1801 act, was that the elimination of circuit judgeships violated Article 3, Section 1, which provided life tenure during good behavior for federal judges.[12]

No one put the case for resistance more forcefully than did Justice Samuel Chase. Living up to his reputation as a "stormy petrel," he called for a showdown with the administration. In a long and powerfully reasoned letter to Marshall on April 24, 1802, he set forth reasons, chapter and verse, why the Repeal Act was unconstitutional and why the Court should void it on that ground. Chase's argument was as impressive as it was arrogant. He did profess a willingness to change his opinions "on being convinced that they are erroneous," but between the lines was an unmistakable, and for Chase a characteristic, sense of assuredness that admitted no doubt. Since he was willing to sink the ship for principle and go down with it, Chase was a force with which to reckon. Not only did the president of the United States and a majority in Congress want the Court's hide, but the Court was badly divided, with the most experienced justice urging a *Götterdammerung*. It complicated matters even further for Marshall that he was strongly inclined to agree with Chase's view that the Repeal Act of 1802 was unconstitutional.[13]

What began as a dilemma for the justices had turned into a crisis over Marshall's authority, and since everything was a precedent, over the internal operations of the Court. Internal divisions, as revealed to Marshall in the correspondence from the other justices during April 1802, and time constraints, the need to settle the matter before the circuit courts were scheduled to open for their spring term, limited options severely. Since the constitutionality of the Repeal Act was not directly before the Court, there could be no escape through seriatim opinions—the regular mode of doing business before 1801 and one particularly suitable to a divided Court.

Marshall and the Court were caught in a bind. If the justices performed circuit duties as required by the Repeal Act, they might avoid a direct confrontation with Congress, though that was far from certain. Such a course would also be a confession of weakness. That course of action, especially onerous to those

12. See especially the speech of Bayard, quoted in PJM, 6: 105 n. 4; Charles Grove Haines, *The Role of the Supreme Court in American Government and Politics, 1789–1835* (New York, 1960), 242, for the ongoing coverage of the episode in the *Philadelphia Aurora*.

13. Chase to Marshall, 24 April 1802, PJM, 6: 109–16. On the relationship between Marshall and Chase, see Presser, *Original Misunderstanding*, 161–69.

who thought the Repeal Act was unconstitutional, might in turn further divide and demoralize the justices. Marshall was on the spot: He could placate the resisters by entering the fray as an advocate of principle and constitutional purity and, as some insisted, "the intent of the framers." Given the disagreement among his colleagues, the confusion of the moment, and his own genius for argument, he might well have carried the day—and at the same time have stolen some legal thunder from Chase. Such a course, however, ran the risk of making him just one voice among many—an advocate, that is to say, rather than a leader. A defeat would cost him prestige; a victory would alienate those brethren who disagreed. A decision not to ride circuit would also complicate matters further, since it would almost certainly invite litigation from the displaced circuit judges, who would rightly infer that the Court had implicitly declared the Repeal Act unconstitutional. Victory for principle, since it meant defiance, finally would have pitted the Court directly against the Republican majority in Congress—just at the time when moderate Republicans were needed to hold back the radicals, who were considering even more extreme reprisals against the Court, including wholesale impeachments.

Marshall's choice was more difficult (and also revealing) because a strictly legal analysis of the Repeal Act led him to conclude that the justices should not ride circuit. As he explained to Oliver Wolcott Jr., one of those whose judgeship had been abolished by the Repeal Act, he did not doubt the authority of Congress to alter the nature of the lower appellate courts or establish rules governing their operation. He even conceded that some aspects of the Repeal Act, those that "involve no party or political questions," were necessary improvements. The portion of the Repeal Act that eliminated circuit judgeships was another matter, however. He put it bluntly to Justice William Paterson on April 6, 1802: "I confess I have some strong constitutional scruples. I cannot well perceive how the performance of circuit duty by the Judges of the supreme court can be supported." He repeated this position to Paterson on April 19, elaborating in greater detail his constitutional objections to riding circuit. In the same letter, he asked Paterson to write Justice Cushing about the matter.[14]

There is no reason to doubt the sincerity of Marshall's "strong constitutional scruples." No less than Chase, he wanted the Court to do its duty. On the other hand, he was not about to lead a frontal charge when the other side had all the heavy guns. Indeed, in the same letter to Paterson in which Marshall

14. Marshall to Oliver Wolcott Jr., 5 April 1802, PJM, 6: 104; Marshall to Paterson, 6 April 1802, ibid., 106; 11 April, ibid., 108–9.

stated his attachment to principle, he began subtly to advise a decorous retreat from a principled resolution. "This is a subject not to be lightly resolved on," he explained in reference to the problem of whether to ride circuit. "The consequences of refusing to carry the law into effect may be very serious. For myself personally I disregard them, & so I am persuaded does every other Gentleman on the bench when put in competition with what he thinks his duty, but the conviction of duty ought to be very strong before the measure is resolved on. The law having been once executed will detract very much in the public estimation from the merit or opinion of the sincerity of a determination, not now to act under it."[15]

In short, legal reasoning would have to be balanced by a consideration of the political impact that reasoning might have—on Congress and on the people at large. Political considerations, as it turned out, carried the day. The justices did agree to hold circuits as required by the Repeal Act of 1802. And in *Stuart v. Laird* the following year, they translated their pragmatism into a principle of constitutional interpretation by upholding the constitutionality of the Repeal Act. Since Marshall had sat on the case when it was tried in the circuit court, Paterson spoke for the Court. His opinion upheld the Repeal Act of 1802 by a broad construction of Article 3, Section 2, clause 2, which gave Congress power to structure the federal courts. In refuting argument of counsel that justices of the Court could not serve on circuit without "distinct commissions for that purpose," Paterson held "that practice, and acquiescence" in circuit riding "for a period of several years, commencing with the organization of the judicial system, affords an irresistible answer, and has indeed fixed the construction." The question of the circuits, which had occupied the attention of the justices and Congress for over a year, "is at rest, and ought not now be disturbed."[16]

The *Stuart* decision and the negotiations that preceded it were a vindication of Marshall's unique style of leadership. His common sense and nonconfrontational style of leadership reflected his personality. At the same time it was uniquely appropriate to the crisis at hand and to the institutional character of the early Court, which was both intimate and informal. Like other national officials, the justices left their families at home when they came to Washington City, as the new capital was called. They worked cheek-by-jowl in the cramped basement room of the Capitol's north wing, an architectural reflection of Jef-

15. Marshall to Paterson, 19 April 1802, PJM, 6: 109.
16. 1 Cranch 308 (1803).

ferson's view of the Court. They lived together in a boardinghouse, where they ate, slept, and mooted cases. Gentle persuasion, Marshall-style—his modesty, sensitivity to differences of opinion, a commitment to collective reasoning— was a perfect fit. And by setting himself up as a facilitator of a collective decision-making process, the chief justice invited his colleagues to think of themselves not as six isolated justices, which in the years before 1801 they had been, but as a single entity. Silently and without fanfare, the Court under Marshall's leadership had taken a giant step toward the abandonment of seriatim opinion writing. And by promising to abide by the collective judgment of the whole Court, the chief justice also, with an intuitive canniness, set himself up to be the logical spokesman for it.[17]

Just how important this newfound unity would be was about to be demonstrated in the case of *Marbury v. Madison,* which had been pending while the justices were grappling with the circuit court dilemma. The circuit court issue, as it turned out, was ideal preparation for the major battle in *Marbury.* The justices had been reminded in no uncertain terms of their political vulnerabilities. Indeed, the danger of confronting Congress over the circuit court bill was directly analogous to that in the mandamus case should the Court challenge the president directly. More to the point, deliberations over the circuit crisis revealed a willingness on the part of Marshall and his colleagues to make political calculations a part of the decision-making process itself. The Court spoke law in *Stuart,* which was decided six days after *Marbury* and which upheld the Repeal Act of 1802, in the process salvaging an enduring rule of constitutional construction. But behind the legal principle lay a carefully calculated strategy. The Court and its chief justice discovered the great truth that political calculation and judging, in the American constitutional system, could never be entirely separate. The final lesson, one Marshall applied brilliantly in *Marbury,* was that the Court could survive its political vulnerabilities most effectively by projecting itself as a legal institution.

Marbury v. Madison and the Rule-of-Law

Historians love a good mystery—which may well explain their continued fascination with the great case of *Marbury v. Madison.* All agree that the decision

---

17. See Warren, *Supreme Court,* 1: ch. 10, on the working conditions of the early Marshall Court; also Haskins and Johnson, *Foundations of Power,* pt. 1, ch. 1; pt. 2, ch. 1. James S. Young,

was one of the most influential in the Court's history, but the books and articles about motive and significance continue unabated, and if the recent group is any indication, the uncertainties regarding the decision have not yet been settled. Some view the decision as the definitive statement of judicial review sprung full blown from the head of Zeus. Others, emphasizing the eighteenth-century foundations of judicial review, note the *un*originality of the opinion. One leading constitutional scholar, implicitly depicting Marshall as both all-knowing and all-competent, views the decision as flat-out usurpation, echoing another great legal scholar writing in the early twentieth century who echoed contemporary critics of Marshall. Yet another historian, while not denying *Marbury*'s importance, argues that its reputation as *the* great moment did not come until the late nineteenth century. Still other interpretations suggest that Marshall's rendition of the Court's powers was not only inconclusive but quite conventional, that is to say, both unoriginal and nonusurping. Some see the opinion as a victory of law over politics, others as supremely political, which leads one to wonder whether it was not, like the Constitution itself, both at once. Like a great work of art, *Marbury* yields different meanings to different viewers at different times—which may be the true mark of greatness.[18]

The case of *Marbury v. Madison,* which Marshall turned into a *legal* victory for the Court, was born in *political* controversy. The Organic Act for the District of Columbia, passed by the lame-duck Federalist Congress on February 27, 1801, authorized the appointment of a number of justices of the peace for the governance of the district. Adams appointed forty-two, all good Federalists. One of the very last acts of the outgoing president, in fact, had been to sign the commissions and forward them to the office of the secretary of state,

---

The Washington Community, 1800–1828 (New York, 1966), though it does not deal with the Court per se, is very suggestive regarding the living arrangements and working condition in the new capital.

18. Recent works of note on judicial review include Christopher Wolfe, *The Rise of Modern Judicial Review: From Constitutional Interpretation to Judge-Made Law* (New York, 1986); Robert Lowry Clinton, *Marbury v. Madison and Judicial Review* (Lawrence, Kans., 1989); Sylvia Snowiss, *Judicial Review and the Law of the Constitution* (New Haven, Conn., 1990); and Jack M. Sosin, *Aristocracy of the Long Robe: The Origins of Judicial Review in America* (New York, 1989). Dean Alfange Jr., "*Marbury v. Madison* and Original Understanding of Judicial Review: In Defense of Traditional Wisdom," *Supreme Court Historical Review* (1994), is very useful in sorting through recent scholarly arguments about *Marbury*. On Marshall's leadership of the Court, Herbert A. Johnson, *The Chief Justiceship of John Marshall, 1801–1835* (Columbia, S.C., 1997) is outstanding.

where they were affixed with the seal of the United States. The problem was they had not yet been delivered, as Madison discovered when he assumed his duties as secretary of state on March 5. Jefferson viewed the plethora of Federalist justices of the peace as simply another example of Federalist perfidy, an especially painful one because of the part played by his old friend John Adams. He ordered Madison not to deliver the commissions. The Court was thrust into the political thicket when William Marbury and three others who had been appointed asked the Court for a writ of mandamus directed to Madison, ordering him to show cause why the commissions should not be delivered; supporting affidavits were presented to the Court at the December 1801 term. Due to repeal of the Judiciary Act of 1801 and the cancellation of the 1802 term of the Court by the Republican-controlled Congress, the case was not decided until February 1803. The intervening period permitted Marshall and his colleagues to ponder both the constitutional significance of the Repeal Act of 1802, which deprived newly appointed circuit judges of their offices, and the dangers of challenging executive authority head-on by issuing the mandamus.

Those who view Marshall's opinion as entirely political have contended the chief justice planned it that way. Such was not the case, although it is clear from the written affidavits the justices considered in 1801 and from Charles Lee's arguments before the Court in 1803 that Marshall and his brother James were involved from the beginning. Marshall's position was particularly complicated, if not compromising. After being confirmed as chief justice on January 27, 1801, he stayed on at Jefferson's request as acting secretary of state. It was in that capacity that he failed to deliver the commissions, which had been delivered to his office on March 4, all duly signed by President Adams and affixed with the seal of the United States, presumably by one of the clerks. Acting as a duly appointed circuit court judge under the act of 1801, James showed up at the office of the secretary of state on March 4 and picked up eleven commissions for the justices of the peace of Alexandria County in the District of Columbia, so, as he claimed, he could call on them to help maintain order in case of expected riots protesting Jefferson's election. According to his sworn affidavit, he returned several of the commissions on the same day, as he put it, because he was unable to carry all of them. Though he claimed to have signed for the commissions he picked up, no written evidence was presented in Court to validate the fact, nor did the clerks so testify. Since no lawyer for Madison appeared in the case, no challenge was made to James Marshall's testimony, which the Court appears to have accepted as evidence of the existence of the commissions.[19]

In the absence of an explanatory letter, it is impossible to say with certainty what, if anything, John Marshall was up to here. It makes a dramatic story to infer, as some accounts have done, that by not delivering the opinions, then bringing his brother in to verify their existence, John Marshall had planned the case from the beginning. That radical interpretation, which assumes the chief justice was all-knowing as well as unethical, is not credible on several counts. First, it should be remembered that Marshall continued as secretary of state until the last moment, not because of nefarious scheming, but because President Jefferson requested he do so. Another problem is that Marshall was not responsible for the last-minute delivery of the commissions to his office, unless he had persuaded honest John Adams to join the conspiracy. Beyond that, we have to assume Marshall had an opinion ready before the case appeared; that he knew Jefferson would not permit the delivery of the commissions, that William Marbury would go to the trouble to sue for them, and that Marbury would bring a case directly to the Supreme Court under Section 13 of the Judiciary Act of 1789. The chief justice would have also had to have known how Charles Lee, as Marbury's lawyer, would present the case and how his colleagues on the Court would respond.[20]

To say that Marshall did not initiate the litigation, however, is not to say he did not understand the political implications of it. Assuredly he did, and so did the president. In fact, it was Jefferson who made the first overt political moves in the case when he refused to deliver the commissions and insulted the Court by refusing to permit counsel to appear or executive witness to be heard. Certainly the Court's dilemma was readily visible: If it issued a mandamus, as Marbury requested, the president and secretary of state would delight in ignoring it, leaving the Court helpless and humbled; if it didn't, the justices would be damned by their own caution. An additional disability stemmed from the

---

19. 1 Cranch 138–54. For the conspiratorial view see John Garraty, "The Case of the Missing Commissions," in John Garraty, ed., *Quarrels that Have Shaped the Constitution* (New York, 1962), 1-14.

20. Perhaps the most reputable scholar to assume that Marshall manufactured the case was Edward S. Corwin, who concluded in his influential book, *The Doctrine of Judicial Review* (Princeton, N.J., 1914; reprint 1963), 9, that Marshall's opinion "bears many of the earmarks of a deliberate partisan *coup*." Jefferson and Marshall exchanged letters on the latter's position as acting secretary of state: Jefferson to Marshall, 2 March 1801, PJM, 6: 86–87; Marshall to Jefferson, 2 March 1801, PJM, 6: 86–87.

often-forgotten fact that in a case of original jurisdiction, the Court was a trial as well as an appellate court. Since no record came from a lower court, the facts had to be established, in this case, the existence of the commissions themselves. The record reveals not only that Madison did not deliver the requested commissions but that he refused applications for information from Charles Lee as to whether the commissions were signed and sealed, as indicated in Marbury's affidavits. He even declined to certify "the nomination of the applicants, and of the advice and consent of the Senate."[21]

Stonewalling by the administration continued when arguments resumed on February 4, 1803, by which time it was clear the witnesses were being directed by none other than the president himself. Arguing ex parte, Charles Lee struggled to get even the most basic facts of the case on record. "Reasonable information had been denied at the office of the department of state," he complained, and the Republican-controlled Senate had refused to cooperate, despite a "respectful memorial" to the Senate requesting that its secretary "give extracts from their executive journals respecting the nomination of the applicants to the senate, and of their advice and consent to the appointments." When Lee attempted to interrogate Department of State secretaries Jacob Wagner and Daniel Brent, who had been summoned as witnesses because they refused to supply affidavits concerning the disposition of the commissions, they declined, claiming either executive privilege or faulty memories. Jefferson's attorney general, Levi Lincoln, pleaded both executive privilege and the Fifth Amendment until Marshall cajoled him into testifying by noting that "the fact whether such commissions had been in the office or not, could not be a confidential fact," but one "which all the world have a right to know." When Lincoln testified the next day, however, he was unable to remember much except that there were several unspecified commissions for justice of the peace in the Department of State.[22]

It would appear that the case was dead on arrival, and indeed it would have been if not for the fortuitous appearance of that mysterious affidavit from James Marshall concerning the missing commissions. Did he really have reason to believe there would be riots in the District, his justification for picking up the commissions? If so, would a handful of justices of the peace have made much difference? In fact, did James Marshall pick up the commissions from the office of secretary of state at all? There was no record of his having done so. And why did he return some and not others?

21. 1 Cranch 138.
22. Ibid., 138–39, 140–46.

These questions were never answered because they were never asked, and they were never asked because Jefferson had not permitted counsel for Madison to appear. Though never stated explicitly, it appears that James Marshall's affidavit of convenience was read into the record, which permitted the case to go forward. We are left to ponder whether the chief justice may have bent the rules as a favor to his old friend Charles Lee from Virginia, who was arguing, somewhat desperately it would appear, for truth and justice. In any case, if Marshall let politics creep into the conduct of the trial, it was because Thomas Jefferson had introduced them there by denying the authority of the Court and obstructing the conduct of the trial. The president did that, it should be recalled, because the Federalist Party had set up the Court with its new chief justice to challenge him.

To say that political considerations permeated the case from beginning to end is perhaps to state the obvious. It is not so obvious—given the scholarly emphasis on that part of Marshall's opinion concerning judicial review of acts of Congress—that the case was primarily a contest between the Court and the executive, indeed, between Marshall and Jefferson. If one looks at the way in which circumstances framed the issues, the manner in which Lee presented them; if one reads the whole text of the reported case and all of Marshall's opinion and remembers that he consistently supported an expansive view of Congressional power, it is hard not to conclude that Marshall's lecture to Jefferson about the rule of law, far from being obiter dicta introduced to embarrass Jefferson, was central to his opinion. Moreover, the chief justice's rule-of-law lecture, though obviously political, was also profoundly legal and constitutional. Finally, noting the centrality of the Court-executive theme in *Marbury* may help explain what a simple reading of the opinion reveals: that Marshall did not, in setting forth the Court's right to declare acts of Congress unconstitutional, claim that its interpretation was binding on Congress, or that it transcended the case at hand, which in a strict precedential sense was limited to acts of Congress treating judicial matters, as was Section 13 of the Judiciary Act.[23]

Marshall did not expound fully and definitively on the Court's power to review acts of Congress, because his primary objective was not to restrain Congress, then or ever, but to rein in a rampaging president. To put it another way, the overriding issue in *Marbury*, of which judicial review was a part, was rule

23. For an excellent brief discussion of the context of *Marbury*, see Editorial Note, PJM, 6: 160–65, especially 162.

of law. How the modest case of *Marbury* came to be cast as a fundamental rule-of-law issue, and indeed how Marshall finally resolved that issue, can be seen by attending closely to the arguments of Charles Lee. Both in his preliminary effort to get the evidence on the record and his argument on the merits, Lee aimed to distinguish the political aspects of the case from the legal ones. He argued convincingly that the secretary of state's duties, and the president's, were both political and legal in nature. The political duties were personal and advisory and, as such, were not subject to public scrutiny, nor reachable by way of mandamus proceedings, that is to say, they were a matter of executive privilege and presidential control.

Lee also argued that the secretary of state was charged by statute with a wide range of record-keeping responsibilities, including the safekeeping in his office of all copies of records and papers authenticated under the great seal. These duties, said Lee, are "of a public nature" and are "uncontrollable by the president." Since these "public ministerial duties" were "enjoined upon the secretary of state by law," he was answerable to the Courts for nonperformance. "It is not consistent with the policy of our political institutions, or the manners of the citizens of the United States," Lee continued, in language that would clearly reach beyond Madison to the president himself, "that any ministerial officer, having public duties to perform, should be above the compulsion of the law, in the exercise of those duties." This argument was even more imperative, Lee insisted, because the duty enjoined by law bore on the vested rights of individuals—as it did in the case of William Marbury, whose office was vested by the commission Madison and Jefferson refused to deliver. To drive home this point, Lee turned to Sir William Blackstone's much-quoted axiom: "that every right, when withheld, must have a remedy, and every injury its proper redress."[24]

In Lee's masterful argument, the case, which started as a political confrontation between his Federalist client, the Federalist Supreme Court, and the Republican president, was transformed into a rule-of-law issue, and finally, as if to fortify the latter point, into a common-law rule and remedy. If the right turned on the writ, as it did in the common-law process under which the Court operated, then it followed that the right writ was a mandamus. Lee was on familiar ground when he turned to argue, with impressive learning, that a writ of mandamus, issuing from the Supreme Court, was the appropriate remedy: "It is a writ of a most extensively remedial nature, and issues in all cases where

24. Lee's argument at 1 Cranch 138–53; quotes at 141, 147.

the party has a right to have anything done, and has no other specific means of compelling its performance." It ordinarily issued from the Courts of the highest jurisdiction; it was well known as a remedy in enforcing private rights against public officials and where parties have specific legal rights but no other means of enforcement. Not only was it the writ of last resort in the most general sense, but it was given prominence in the Federal Judiciary Act of 1789, Section 13, where it is specified that the writ may be issued "in cases warranted by the principles and usages of law, to any courts appointed, or persons holding office, under the authority of the United States."[25]

If the mark of a good lawyer is to fashion his argument to the judge's liking, then Marshall's old friend was a great lawyer. Marshall thanked him for his able effort, as well he should have, since Lee handed him the makings of his opinion. With the help of Marshall's brother, Lee had gotten the facts on the record. Those facts, so loaded with political significance, had been elevated into a rule-of-law issue and then translated into common-law right and legal remedy, all of which permitted Marshall to talk law even when he was dealing with political business attending the law. Everything was in place then, except the Supreme Court's unequivocal right in the first place to hear the case under original jurisdiction as defined in Article 3 of the Constitution. On this point, Lee's argument was a masterpiece of obfuscation, which was also a break for Marshall, since responding to Lee's arguments about original jurisdiction gave him an opportunity to expound the Court's powers of judicial review.

Marshall's opinion, often depicted as freewheeling legal improvisation, in fact drew deeply from Lee's argument in regard to both structure and substance—this was true even though in the end Lee lost the case. After noting the "peculiar delicacy" of the case, "the novelty of its circumstances," and "the real difficulty attending the points which occur in it," the chief justice went directly to the first of his famous three questions: Did Marbury have "a right to the commission he demands?" Lee had already asked the question, and answered it as well, by noting at various points in his argument that the commissions were "made out," were "signed by President Adams," "were recorded," and had "the seal of the United States . . . affixed to them." Marshall, who had already tacitly agreed with Lee on this point by admitting the commissions into the record, now turned Lee's argument into an elementary civics lecture on the constitutional basis of the appointing process. His real objective, however, was to show that Marbury's office was vested when the president signed his com-

25. Quotes at 1 Cranch 147–48.

mission: "The signature is a warrant for affixing the great seal to the commission; and the great seal is only to be affixed to an instrument which is complete. It attests, by an act supposed to be of public notoriety, the verity of the presidential signature." Once signed, the "time for deliberation has then passed. He has decided." With his signature, the president's political discretion ended and the operation of law began.[26]

Here was the rule-of-law motif, which Marshall, again following Lee, then went on to join with the rights issue. If Marbury "has a right, and that right has been violated, do the laws of this country afford him a remedy?" Answering his own question, Marshall began his lecture to Jefferson with a general proposition that allowed no disagreement: "The very essence of civil liberty certainly consists in the right of every individual to claim the protection of the laws, whenever he receives an injury. One of the first duties of government is to afford that protection." Such was the wisdom of the common law, most emphatically if the right involved property and the ubiquitous Blackstone was quoted to make the point.[27]

As for the government of the new Republic, it is "emphatically termed a government of laws, and not of men." Then turning to the real issue: Does the law of the land control the president, or the secretary of state, after he has vested a right in Marbury's commission by signing it? Yes, and following Lee again, just as surely as if Marbury or anyone had legally purchased a piece of land only to be denied a patent to it by the secretary of state under order of the president. The right to a commissioned office, even if it was a minor position and lasted only five years, was as tangible as real property. Marshall went back again to the political aspect of appointment, as distinct from the legal obligation to deliver a bona fide commission, then went in for the kill: The first officer of the nation "cannot at his discretion sport away the vested rights of others." "[W]here a specific duty is assigned by law, and individual rights depend upon the performance of that duty, it seems equally clear that the individual who considers himself injured, has access to the laws of his country for a remedy." Such an examination is by its very nature judicial and falls within the province of the "judicial authority."[28]

The only remaining question, the one that brought Marshall and the Court to the edge of the political precipice, was whether Marbury was "entitled to

26. For Lee's three questions, ibid., 146. For Marshall, ibid., 154, 158, 160–62.
27. Ibid., 163.
28. Ibid., 163, 166, 167.

the remedy for which he applies." That is to say, was a writ of mandamus issuing from the Supreme Court to the secretary of state the proper remedy for the right Marbury had been denied and for which the law of the land promised a remedy? That question was in turn subdivided, still following the argument of Lee, into two more questions, which were based on the three Lee asked about the nature and appropriateness of the writ of mandamus and "the power of this court." Marshall addressed the first question about the general scope of the writ in the same broad way as had Lee, citing Mansfield and Blackstone to establish the sweeping remedial nature of the writ of mandamus. Could the secretary of state or any cabinet officer be the officer to whom the writ is directed? No, said Marshall emphatically, not if the officer was acting in his political capacity as "the mere organ of executive will." It was not the Court's business to "intrude into the cabinet, and to intermeddle with the prerogatives of the executive." The "province of the Court," as Marshall had already taken great pains to emphasize, was the rule of law as it involved the rights of individuals. So the answer followed inexorably that "if one of the heads of departments commits any illegal action, under colour of his office, by which an individual sustains an injury, it cannot be pretended that his office alone exempts him from being sued in the ordinary mode of proceeding, and being compelled to obey the judgment of the law." And in cases justified by law, the writ of mandamus can issue. "The doctrine [concerning the mandamus], therefore, now advanced, is by no means a novel one," added Marshall, and he cited precedents from the 1790s to make his point, precedents which, according to some scholars, he then proceeded to ignore. "This, then," Marshall concluded, "is a plain case for a mandamus, either to deliver the commission, or a copy of it from the record; and it only remains to be inquired, Whether it can issue from this court."[29]

Thus far, Marshall had focused his remarks on the manner in which law applied to the actions of the executive branch, for twenty pages of his twenty-six-page opinion to be exact. These matters were clearly not incidental, but just as clearly, Marshall wanted desperately to write about "this court" and structured his opinion so as to expound on its jurisdiction and its powers. Finally, Marshall got to expound on judicial review, which he was clearly hankering to do all along. In this regard, however, it needs to be remembered that he did not

29. Ibid., 146, 168–69, 170, 172–73. For a discussion of Marshall's cavalier disregard of these precedents, see Susan Low Bloch and Maeva Marcus, "John Marshall's Selective Use of History in *Marbury v. Madison*," *Wisconsin Law Review* (March–April 1986), 301–37.

gratuitously introduce the subject of judicial authority into the litigation. It was no secret the subject had been on Jefferson's political agenda since his election and even before. The Court's powers, or lack of them, had been earnestly debated in Congress for the better part of two years, as well as when Federalists and Jeffersonians debated the Judiciary Act of 1801 and its repeal. Most immediately, the whole question of judicial authority was woven into the fabric of the case by Jefferson himself. Given the circumstances, it is not surprising Lee framed his argument so as to emphasize the legal nature of the case and the Court's legal obligation to decide it. How better to secure Marbury's job, one might ask, than by equating it with the Court's authority to give it to him? That authority, in Lee's argument, came to hinge on Section 13 of the Judiciary Act of 1789, the crucial part of which authorized the Supreme Court to issue "writs of *mandamus*, in cases warranted by the principles and usages of law, to any courts appointed, or persons holding office, under the authority of the United States." Marshall declared this part of Section 13 unconstitutional on the ground that Congress had no authority to enlarge the original jurisdiction of the Court, since original jurisdiction, unlike appellate jurisdiction, which was specifically made subject to congressional authority, was specifically defined by the Constitution itself.[30]

Historians have argued that Marshall need not have found Section 13 unconstitutional: that a reasonable construction would have held that Section 13 did not enlarge the Court's original jurisdiction but simply defined remedies available, including the writ of mandamus, in cases where it had jurisdiction. The operative interpretive rule here, one to which Marshall subscribed, was that the Court would void an act of Congress only in the clearest of cases. The second criticism leveled by scholars against Marshall's opinion, which like the first speaks to its political character, was that of timing. If the Court had no power to act in Marbury's case, the argument goes, Marshall should have said so immediately and avoided the lecture to Jefferson and the extended essay on judicial review. The gravamen of these objections, taken singly and altogether, is that Marshall cynically manipulated the law to reach the political objective he already had in mind, which is what finally Jefferson himself came to believe.[31]

Given the circumstances surrounding the origins of the case, it would be

---

30. *U.S. Statutes at Large*, 1 (1789): 81; US Const, Art 3, § 2.
31. Jefferson to Madison, 25 May 1810, in *The Works of Thomas Jefferson*, ed. Paul L. Ford (New York, 1904–1905), 11: 141.

pointless to deny its political dimensions. Marshall acknowledged them both privately and in the opinion itself. It does not follow, however, that his legal reasoning was nothing but a cynical mask disguising a predetermined political objective. The opinion, like the Constitution itself, was both political *and* legal; no one, including the chief justice, knew for certain where and how the balance would be struck, where and how the familiar principles and methodology of the common law informed the written text of a constitution that was supreme law and supremely political as well. Nowhere was the problem more "delicate" and the legal doctrine more "novel," to use Marshall's words, than on the question of whether the ancient common-law writ of mandamus could, under the separation of powers principle of the Constitution, issue from the Court to the leading member of the president's cabinet. And nowhere was the confusion greater than on the elemental matter of jurisdiction: whether Marbury was entitled to sue in the Supreme Court under Section 2, paragraph 2, of Article 3, which provides for original jurisdiction in "all cases affecting Ambassadors, other public Ministers and Consuls, and those in which a State shall be Party." Nothing in the brief debates at Philadelphia explicated the meaning of "public Ministers," of whom presumably James Madison was one, and it would not have mattered, since those debates were not available to aid the justices in their interpretive chores. Common sense as well as contextual evidence, however, left little doubt that the phrase, along with "Ambassadors" and "Consuls," referred to representatives from foreign countries, who as a matter of respect and convenience were granted direct access to the high court. Such was the meaning employed in Hamilton's *Federalist* 44; in the Virginia ratifying debates, which Marshall attended; and in Vattel, which Marshall read and cited on exactly that point. Such, indeed, was the unmistakable meaning of the first part of Section 13 itself, where the term "other public ministers" is used in a context that makes its meaning clear. Marshall acknowledged precisely this meaning in his opinion in referring to the original jurisdiction clause as emanating from "the solicitude of the convention, respecting our peace with foreign powers."[32]

32. 1 Cranch 175. For an extensive discussion of this meaning of "cases affecting ambassadors, other public ministers, and consuls" and why original jurisdiction should apply, see Joseph Story, *Commentaries on the Constitution of the United States . . .* , 5th ed. (Boston, 1891), 2: 460–64. This was the position taken at the Virginia ratifying convention, as in the June 18 speech of Edmund Pendleton, and it was also referred to in numerous Supreme Court opinions. See David J. Mays, *Edmund Pendleton, 1721–1803: A Biography* (Cambridge, Mass., 1952) 2: 539. Marshall cited Vattel on that interpretation in *The Schooner Exchange v. McFaddon* (1812), reprinted in PJM, 7: 312.

By this widely understood definition of "public Minister" in Article 3, Marbury had no right to sue under original jurisdiction, and the Court had no authority to hear the case, which is exactly why Lee relied instead on Section 13 of the Judiciary Act of 1789, which authorizes the Court to issue writs of mandamus to "persons holding office, under the authority of the United States." It may be clear to scholars who criticize Marshall's opinion for unnecessarily voiding an act of Congress that Congress here meant simply that federal courts have the authority to issue writs of mandamus in cases where they had jurisdiction. But that was not the only interpretation of the words. More to the point, it was not Lee's interpretation. Not only did Lee argue for a literal meaning of the crucial phrase in Section 13, but he went on to the general point that "Congress is not restrained from conferring original jurisdiction in other cases than those mentioned in the constitution." This was not an unreasonable interpretation given the fact that the writ of mandamus in the English common-law system did in fact conflate remedy and jurisdiction—which, it should be emphasized, is precisely what Lee did when he made his case turn on that part of Section 13 that allowed the Court to issue the writ of mandamus to officers of the United States government. This "legislative construction of the constitution" he supported by citing three Supreme Court decisions from the 1790s.[33]

Given the clearly restrictive meaning of "public Minister" in Article 3, a meaning that would have doomed his case at the threshold, Lee did the best he could. More to the point, his argument was good enough to convince John Marshall. A more cynical interpretation, one that looked at *Marbury* as politics pure and simple, would be that Marshall only pretended to be convinced by Lee's argument that Section 13 had extended the original jurisdiction in order to declare that section unconstitutional and thus open the way for a reasoned justification of the Court's power to review acts of Congress. Marshall did what sitting judges trained in the common law generally do: expound and refute, if necessary, the arguments of counsel. This is what Marshall was famous for doing as a justice, it is what he said he was going to do in 1803, and it is basically what he did. Also, when accounting for the Court's position on Section 13, it is good to note that the interpretation contended for by Lee would have bestowed on the Court a sweeping power to police the political system, one that conceivably could have produced an avalanche of original jurisdiction litigation. The Court's position, in short, was remarkably sensible,

---

33. Section 13: U.S. Statutes, 1 (1789): 80–81; Lee's argument: 1 Cranch 148, citing *U.S. v. Judge Lawrence*, 3 Dallas 42; *U.S. v. Peters*, 3 Dallas 121; *U.S. v. Hopkins*, 2 Dallas 298.

and never did Marshall state it more plainly than in *Ex parte Bollmann* and *Ex parte Swartwout* (both 1807) when he said "that this court would not exercise original jurisdiction except so far as that jurisdiction was given by the constitution."[34]

The point is not that Marshall was blind to the political implications and consequences of his ruling, but only that he addressed the issue within a familiar legal framework, one that allowed him to believe sincerely that the Court was simply doing its constitutional duty. Such also was the case with his famous exposition of the doctrine of judicial review of acts of Congress:

> It is, emphatically, the province and duty of the judicial department, to say what the law is. Those who apply the rule to particular cases, must of necessity expound and interpret that rule. If two laws conflict with each other, the courts must decide on the operation of each.
>
> So, if a law be in opposition to the constitution; if both the law and the constitution apply to a particular case, so that the court must either decide that case, conformable to the law, disregarding the constitution; or conformable to the constitution, disregarding the law; the court must determine which of these conflicting rules governs the case: this is of the very essence of judicial duty. If then, the courts are to regard the constitution, and the constitution is superior to any ordinary act of the legislature, the constitution, and not such ordinary act, must govern the case to which they both apply.[35]

These, the most quoted and most disputed words from the Court's most famous opinion, were not in 1803 much noted at all—either by those who wanted a strong Court, including the justices themselves, or even by those predisposed to think the worst of the Court and the chief justice. The explanation may well be that judicial review as Marshall expounded it in *Marbury* was in fact not radical, not definitive (or perhaps not radical because it was not definitive), and not original.[36]

The *general* idea of judicial review, rooted in colonial and state experience as well as in the general idea of higher law, was well known to the statesmen of the founding generation. While the Constitution does not mention judicial

34. PJM, 6: 485.
35. 1 Cranch 177–78.
36. On the contemporary reception of *Marbury,* see Warren, *Supreme Court,* 1: ch. 5.

review in so many words, the architecture of the document, especially the juxtaposition of Articles 3 and 6, and the rule-of-law spirit that pervaded it pointed to some form of "judicial control," to use the words of Charles Beard. And though they disagreed sharply as to its wisdom, both Federalists (Hamilton's *Federalist* 78) and Anti-Federalists (Yates in the Brutus letters) agreed that judicial review was embodied in the new constitutional arrangement. As previously noted, Marshall had read Hamilton on judicial review, probably Brutus as well, and he had spoken presciently about judicial review at the Virginia ratifying convention. As a leading lawyer in Virginia, moreover, it may be assumed that he was familiar with the principle of judicial review as it operated in both the state courts, as in *Kamper v. Hawkins* (1793), and the federal courts, as in Hayburn's Case (1792), which he cited in his opinion, and *Hylton v. U.S.* He was a colleague of Samuel Chase, who was an early champion of judicial review and whose views on that matter had been expressed forcefully to Marshall less than a year before *Marbury* in regard to the circuit court crisis. Indeed, Marshall himself had alluded, indirectly but unmistakably, to judicial review in *U.S. v. Schooner Peggy* (1801), one of his first opinions.[37]

Not only was the idea of judicial review set forth in *Marbury* not original, but its application to the case at hand was limited by the circumstances that gave rise to it. It is true that *Marbury* was the first time an act of Congress had been voided *on constitutional grounds* and Marshall's reasoned justification combined with action put teeth in the doctrine that it never had before. But the voided act dealt exclusively with the federal courts, which in a strict sense of precedent limited the sweep of the decision. If Marshall intended that the Court's powers of review extend to nonjudicial matters as well, he never said so explicitly. Nor did he claim that Congress was bound by the Court's interpretation. Finally, he avoided entirely the question of enforcement: what would

---

37. Charles A. Beard, *The Supreme Court and the Constitution* (New York, 1912). On Beard in the context of the debate over judicial review, see Alan F. Westin's Introduction to *The Supreme Court and the Constitution* (Englewood Cliffs, N.J., 1962). Edward S. Corwin, *The "Higher Law" Background of American Constitutional Law* (Ithaca, N.Y., 1959), reprinted from his earlier articles in the *Harvard Law Review*. The Brutus letters can be found in Herbert J. Storing, ed., *The Complete Anti-Federalist* 7 vols. (Chicago, 1981), as can the "State house speech" of James Wilson of 4 October 1787. For a discussion of judicial review in *Kamper v. Hawkins,* see Charles T. Cullen, *St. George Tucker and Law in Virginia, 1772–1804* (New York, 1987), 85–89. For Marshall's speech of 2 June 1788 on the federal judiciary in the Virginia ratifying convention, see PJM, 1: 275–85. For judicial review in his *Schooner Peggy* opinion, see PJM, 6: 101–2. Chase to Marshall, 24 April 1802, PJM, 6: 109–16, especially 112.

happen, that is to say, if Congress chose to ignore the Court's decision or if the president refused to cooperate in its enforcement.

The Court's power of review as set forth in *Marbury* was limited, too, by the fact that it came into play only in an actual case. Judging by the way Marshall transcended the limits of the case by his aggressive approach to the jurisdiction question, it might be argued that this was no limitation at all. But compared to the comprehensive power of review the modern Court has acquired through the certiorari process, or to the plenary review provisions in Madison's proposed council of revision, it was a real limitation. The case-and-controversy nature of judicial review can also be seen, and was no doubt seen by contemporaries, in the common-law tone that permeated both Lee's argument and Marshall's opinion. In truth, without the language and methodology of the common law, neither would have had much to say or a way of saying it. Even the famous paragraph on judicial review in Marshall's peroration was borrowed from Blackstone's tenth rule of construction. It could, of course, be argued that Marshall tossed in Blackstone to disguise the political character of the decision. More likely, he was simply doing what he had done as a practicing lawyer for a quarter century at the Virginia bar.[38]

One thing he certainly did *not* do in *Marbury* was to put forth the Court as an adversary of Congress. Marshall spent his pre-Court career as an advocate of expanded legislative authority at the national level. To be sure, he sometimes had doubts about the wisdom of congressional action, for example, when his own party passed the Alien and Sedition Acts. And he had doubts about the constitutionality of the Repeal Act of 1802. Nor can there be any doubt he reserved for the Court the right to declare unconstitutional acts of Congress in violation of the Constitution. His general attitude, and that of his Court as well, however, was to give Congress the constitutional benefit of the doubt. What called southern states' rights theorists into action was not that he used the principle of judicial review set forth in *Marbury* to strike down acts of Congress, but that he didn't. Had he done so, say in *McCulloch v. Maryland,* when he had the chance, he would have secured himself a place in the pantheon of southern heroes and altered the course of antebellum history.[39]

38. For Marshall's use of Blackstone in *Marbury,* see Clinton, *Marbury v. Madison and Judicial Review,* 18–20. On Blackstone's influence, also see Wolfe, *Rise of Modern Judicial Review,* 18–19.

39. Marshall considered the Alien and Sedition Acts unwise and unnecessary, but there is considerable doubt whether he thought them unconstitutional. For a general discussion of his position, see "Congressional Election Campaign": Editorial Note in PJM, 3: 494–502.

All this is to say that the principle of judicial review of acts of Congress, as Marshall described it in *Marbury,* was not at odds with the limited government persuasion of the Jeffersonian Republican Party, which may explain why the Court was not humbled by Congress for its decision. Put simply, it was presidential power, not congressional authority, Marshall targeted. Judicial review, in this republican scheme of things, was inseparable from the rule of law, a necessary means to that end. *Marbury* was the natural culmination of a struggle for constitutional law and order that went back to the American Revolution, which Marshall considered a constitutional revolution; it went back to the 1780s, when the forces of constitutional law and order contended against states' rights localists; it went back to the 1790s, when the new Constitution and national Union were threatened by newly combined forces of states' rights, democracy, and political parties. The great danger to republican government was not Congress, not even executive power, which Marshall had defended when it was used by Washington and Adams. Instead, the pressing danger in 1803 came from Thomas Jefferson, who abused the power of his office to subvert the rule of law, which was the polestar of republican constitutional culture.

Was it really possible that the president of the United States did not understand the meaning of the written Constitution? Did he possibly think that he spoke for the sovereign people simply because he was elected in 1800? Marshall, for one, believed Jefferson thought so and believed, worse, that Jefferson and his party were misleading the American people into thinking they acted in their sovereign capacity simply by voting. What Jefferson needed to hear, and what the people needed to know, was some good old-fashioned Federalist constitutional wisdom. This, along with the argument for judicial review, is what they got in *Marbury.* The genius of that opinion was not originality, nor was it the exposition of Federalist constitutional theory, in which it was perfectly orthodox. Rather it was the melding of the two in an opinion that was law, delivered in the name of the whole Court and in the authoritative voice of a genuine hero of the Revolution.

In *Marbury,* then, the chief justice spoke for the newly unified Court to the American people themselves. It was a lesson in republican civics, concerning the relation of the sovereign people to the written Constitution, to the Supreme Court, and finally to the supreme law of the land. Marshall began with a question that was "deeply interesting" to America: "whether an act, repugnant to the constitution, can become the law of the land," and from thence, to the theory that answered the question. "Happily," he continued, the question was not complicated, provided one recognized the "long and well established principle" of popular sovereignty: "That the people have an original right to establish, for their future government, such principles, as, in their opinion, shall most conduce to their own happiness, is the basis on which the whole American fabric has been erected." The fundamental principle Marshall referred to here, the one established first in the struggle over the Constitution of 1780 in Massachusetts and confirmed on a grand scale at Philadelphia in 1787 and in the subsequent state ratifying conventions, was that only the people, acting in specially called constitutional conventions, could create a written constitution that limited and defined government and was "permanent" and supreme over ordinary law. In other words, the people speaking in their sovereign capacity in organic convention limited the people speaking through their elected representatives, equally so when they voted for Jefferson in 1800. For emphasis, he repeated the theme he and others had sounded in the Virginia ratifying convention in 1788: that it was to guarantee "that those limits may not be mistaken, or forgotten" that "the constitution is written."[40]

Marshall set forth these principles as if they were incontestable. And on one level they were, not because he or anyone else said so, though many had, but because Americans of the Revolutionary War period, in creating their governments, had acted on them. The same certitude was meant also to apply to the corollary principle of judicial review. To reach this high ground, Marshall inched from one logical premise to another. Having established that written constitutions formed the "fundamental and paramount law of the nation," it followed inexorably "that an act of the legislature, repugnant to the constitution, is void." This was "one of the fundamental principles of our society," and it led unavoidably to judicial review. Marshall put the question so that there was but one answer: "If an act of the legislature, repugnant to the constitution, is void, does it, notwithstanding its invalidity, bind the courts, and oblige them to give it effect?" To say so would be "an absurdity too gross to be insisted on."[41]

Following the chief justice's logic, the Court had no choice but to void laws in conflict with the Constitution, not because the Court was a supremely wise political institution, but because it was a court of law whose "province and

---

40. 1 Cranch 176. Gordon S. Wood discusses the Federalist innovations regarding popular sovereignty in *The Creation of the American Republic, 1776–1787* (Chapel Hill, N.C., 1969), 532–43.

41. 1 Cranch 177.

duty" was, in the course of judicial proceedings, "to say what the law is." Common sense, logic, and Federalist theory comported exactly with Blackstone's tenth rule, which Marshall now quoted. For the Court to measure acts of the legislature, even if it claimed to speak for the sovereign people, or acts of a president, who appeared to identify himself with the sovereign people, was the "very essence of judicial duty." When the Court did its duty, it did so because the sovereign people in their Constitution so commanded. Without the sovereign people, there would be no Constitution; without the Constitution, there would be no judicial review; without judicial review, the written Constitution, America's "greatest improvement on political institutions," would be reduced to mere nullity.[42]

Marshall's compelling words remind one of his reputation as a great persuader. Indeed, so persuasive is his reasoning, so appropriate to the task at hand is his language, that it is easy to forget that in 1803 the Court's future was still highly uncertain. The role of the Court in the process of constitutional government, even when it was supported by the logic and eloquence of John Marshall, could not carry the day in the face of judicial incompetence or ineptitude. And with the Jeffersonians in power, there was little margin for error. Of immediate concern was the mounting campaign of impeachment against the Court, and not far down the road was the Burr treason trial, which would again pit the chief justice against the president and where again the issue would be the rule of law. Unless the Court could survive these challenges, the authority claimed in *Marbury* would wither on the vine.

Shoot-Out in Richmond: The Burr Treason Trial

Looking back at the first decade of the nineteenth century, one might well puzzle over the failure of the president and the chief justice to declare a truce and get on with the business of governing. After all, both men loved their country, had served it with distinction, and had watched it weather the growth pangs of early youth. Even their seemingly contradictory positions revealed ample grounds for mutual accommodation: For all of his talk about "revolution" in 1800, the president had maintained remarkable continuity with previous Federalist policies. The public debt was being scaled down to be sure, and downsizing the navy was in the offing, but Hamilton's Bank of the United States was

42. Ibid., 177–78.

still in place, along with the administrative structure created by the Federalists for the operation of the new government. Jefferson, who had been critical of Washington and Adams for their excessive use of executive power, had himself proven to be equally energetic. His acquisition of the Louisiana Territory in 1803 not only illustrated his bold executive leadership but rested on precisely the same doctrine of implied powers the Federalists had championed and the Democratic-Republicans had condemned. And this is not to mention the Embargo of 1807, which called the national government into the lives of American people more intrusively than anything Washington or Adams had done—in the name of law and order no less.[43]

Marshall, who liked energetic national government, who believed firmly in implied powers, who liked forceful presidents, and who feared for law and order, might have assumed that the obligations of leadership had imparted wisdom to his cousin. For his part, Jefferson might have seen the Federalists, who had retreated into states' rights, as no longer threatening. Even Marshall's opinion in *Marbury* could be seen in a favorable light, since it employed judicial review and the written Constitution to limit the power of Congress, which was the major goal of Jefferson's party after the Virginia and Kentucky Resolutions.

Rather than abating, however, the differences separating Jefferson and Marshall after 1803 became ever more personal and more sweeping in their ideological implications. At the core of their continuing dispute lay the unexplored terrain of republican law itself, where it belonged in the scheme of popular government and who should say what it meant. The Constitution, rather than settling the matter, had, since ratification, become the focus of the debate. Since it institutionalized the sovereignty of the people, a point emphasized by the Federalists themselves, it could be seen as the most radical and transformative act of the American Revolution. While proclaiming the ultimate power of the people, the Constitution as supreme law had put limits on them, particularly as they operated at the state and local level.

The struggle between politics and law, then—between the political and legal branches of the government—was built into the constitutional fabric. Thanks in no small part to *Marbury,* that struggle centered on the Supreme Court, for the reason that Jefferson and key members of his party believed, and what the twentieth-century Legal Realists thought they discovered, that judges actually

43. On the nationalism in Jeffersonian policies, see Richard Hofstadter, "Thomas Jefferson: The Aristocrat As Democrat," in his *The American Political Tradition* (New York, 1948).

made law when they interpreted it. Well before Tocqueville, they saw judges and lawyers, especially as they became more professional, as a high-toned, antirepublican aristocracy, determined to undermine the people and their elected representatives. Judges did their work in secret, talked a language that ordinary citizens could not understand, and at the federal level were not only distant from the people but not answerable to them through popular election. For Jefferson's party, which believed in the self-sufficiency of ordinary citizens and the primacy of the legislative branch as the direct voice of the people, and which believed that local government is the most compatible with freedom and that the "best government is the one which governs least," this knowledge was troublesome in the extreme.[44]

Marshall went out of his way to establish the democratic credentials of the Court in *Marbury,* but compared to the growing egalitarian ethos of the age, that decision and the Court that handed it down seemed seriously at odds with the main course of American history. Unfortunately, Justice Samuel Chase made that lesson all too obvious to the Jeffersonians in Congress, who impeached him in 1805. Chase was indicted by the House for his blatantly anti-Jefferson harangue to the Baltimore grand jury in 1803 and for misconduct in the treason trial of John Fries and in the seditious libel trials of James Callender and Thomas Cooper. The Callender and Cooper trials were especially telling because they proved what Republicans had been saying all along about federal law and federal judges: that federal law operating directly on citizens of the states through the federal courts was a transforming thing. Both men had been indicted under the hated Sedition Act of 1798, which was now being enforced in Virginia, in the state capital no less, by a federal circuit court presided over by a judge who seemed determined to play the part of a model tyrant. Not only was Chase contemptuous of Virginia lawyers, who were themselves prideful and arrogant, but he challenged the authority of the jury, which according to Republican political theory was the embodiment of local knowledge and accordingly the last bastion of defense against the tyranny of central authority. Chase's circuit ruling that the jury had no authority to stand in judgment on the constitutionality of the Sedition Act demolished that assumption. When lawyers insisted on arguing the point, he cut them off peremptorily and ulti-

44. The debate over the repeal of Judiciary Act of 1801 is particularly revealing. Also see Ellis, *Jeffersonian Crisis;* Warren, *Supreme Court,* 1: ch. 4; and Turner [Preyer], "Federalist Policy and the Judiciary Act of 1801," 15–22. Also relevant is Maxwell Bloomfield, *American Lawyers in a Changing Society, 1776–1876* (Cambridge, Mass., 1976), especially ch. 2.

mately forced them to withdraw from the case—or at least gave them an excuse for leaving. Particularly questionable in the Callender trial was Chase's unwillingness to permit the testimony of John Taylor of Caroline County. Taylor, the chief witness for the defense, was prepared to testify to the truth of Callender's charge that Adams had in fact harmed the interests of his country, which according to prevailing law was a defense against the charge of seditious libel. Justice Chase insulted both Taylor and the jury by prohibiting Taylor's testimony on the ground that it would mislead the jury into thinking that he had refuted the entire charge against Callender.[45]

Scholarly concern about the impeachment trial has tended to focus on the irascible character of Chase himself and whether his intemperate and biased conduct as a trial judge and his attack on Jefferson constituted impeachable "high crimes and misdemeanors." Chase's impeachment, however, did not concern Chase alone. Jefferson understood, as did Marshall, that the Court was on the line, that the impeachment vote was a referendum on *Marbury.* As John Randolph of Roanoke, who managed the impeachment proceedings in the House of Representatives, put it, "There is no cure short of extirpation. Attorneys and judges do not decide the fate of empires." Jefferson's anti-Court point man William Branch Giles, was even more explicit: "If the Judges of the Supreme Court should dare, as they had done, to declare an Act of Congress unconstitutional, or to send a mandamus to the Secretary of State, as they had done, it was the undoubted right of the House of Representatives to impeach them, and of the Senate to remove them, for giving such opinions, however honest or sincere they may have been in entertaining them." John Quincy Adams saw the implications of such sweeping language when he concluded that the attack on Chase was but the opening campaign in a war against the entire Marshall Court.[46]

Marshall got the message and saw the problem. "I have just received the articles of impeachment against Judge Chase," he wrote to his brother James, April 1, 1804. "They are sufficient to alarm the friends of a pure & of course an independent judiciary, if among those who rule our land there be any of that description." The problem was twofold: first, that Chase could be and had

45. Presser, *Original Misunderstanding*, 134–36. Also see F. Thornton Miller, *Juries and Judges versus the Law: Virginia's Provincial Legal Perspective, 1783–1828* (Charlottesville, Va., 1994).

46. J. Q. Adams, *Diary*, I, entry of 21 December 1804, and Adams, *Writings*, 3: letters of 8, 14 March 1805, as cited in Warren, *Supreme Court*, 1: 294. Haskins and Johnson, *Foundations of Power*, 215–45, treats the Chase impeachment.

been arrogant, imperious and intemperate, all the things Marshall was trying to not be; second, that Chase had most offended those who held the most power. One must infer that Marshall carefully calculated the political odds. Privately he supported and encouraged Chase, promising to gather information in Richmond that might be useful in Chase's defense and tendering his opinion that Chase's ruling on the inadmissibility of Taylor's testimony was not an impeachable offense, though Marshall thought it was the wrong legal call. Privately he thought the whole thing was a Jeffersonian conspiracy against truth and justice. As a witness at the impeachment proceedings, however, he was all but silent. There was no ringing defense of the independent judiciary, nothing in defense of his friend. Apparently the chief justice thought discretion was the better part of valor, at least when the other side operated from strength. Judging by Chase's acquittal, it was sound, if not heroic, strategy. [47]

Chase's acquittal was a personal victory for Marshall and a telling defeat for Jefferson. Chase was chastened, to be sure, and the justices were taught to mind their judicial manners. But *Marbury* had weathered the storm. Whether Marshall's reasoning in that opinion actually persuaded moderate Republicans in the Senate that the Court was essential to republican liberty, we can't tell. At the least he convinced them it was not a threat. It seems clear, too, that Marshall's less than sweeping statement of judicial review was all the traffic history would bear. Any more would probably have sunk the judicial bark on its maiden voyage. As for the president, he learned to his disgust that impeachment was "a mere scarecrow of a thing," a "farce not to be tried again."[48]

By raising the ante so high, Jefferson had added luster to Marshall's victory. His own defeat at Marshall's hands, the second in three years, may well have prompted him to try again, and events were already taking place that would give him the chance. The face-off, one of the most important and dramatic state trials in American history, originated in the boundless ambition of Aaron Burr and the strange and tragic course of his political career. Like Marshall and Jefferson, Burr belonged to that elite group of privileged young men who seemed destined to govern the young Republic. His family pedigree was impeccable; he fought bravely in the Revolution; he was a brilliant, well-trained, and highly successful lawyer, one of the few New York lawyers who could hold his own against Alexander Hamilton. He was an audacious, if somewhat unscru-

47. Marshall to Chase, 23 January 1805, PJM, 6: 347–48; Marshall's "Testimony in the Trial of Samuel Chase," ibid., 350–57.

48. Jefferson to Spencer Roane, 6 September 1819, *Works of Jefferson*, 12: 135–40.

pulous, entrepreneur, and contemporaries attested to his charisma and leadership abilities, as did his rapid ascent in the ranks of New York Republicans. As chief strategist for that party in the election of 1800, he won second place on the ticket with Jefferson.[49]

That coup put him in direct line of succession to the presidency, which in turn brought his fall from grace. Burr's fatal mistake was his failure to make it clear in the disputed election with Jefferson in 1800 that he would not accept the presidency. His unwillingness to withdraw invited some Federalist strategists to surreptitiously put him forth as an alternative to Jefferson. Burr never openly negotiated with them, but Jefferson, who already harbored doubts about Burr's reliability, concluded he was a viper in the nest and vowed to destroy him. Cast out by the Republican organization and ultimately repudiated by the Federalists, who acted on the advice of Hamilton, the golden boy was suddenly transformed into a political pariah. The fatal dual at Weehawken in July 1804, where he wreaked vengeance on Hamilton, left Burr a social outcast as well and a fugitive from justice, under indictment in New York for murder.

Cornered and forestalled in the civilized East, like many of his contemporaries, he traveled west to redeem his fortune and his reputation. Rather than glory, his adventures there brought him before John Marshall's circuit court in Richmond, where he stood indicted for treason against the United States for having planned to separate the Southwest from the Union. What Burr and the small band of adventurers who followed him actually did to call down the wrath of Jefferson still remains shrouded in mystery. But this much is clear: He toured the West in 1805 to assess, and stir, interest in a filibustering expedition against Spanish possessions in the Southwest, possibly Mexico itself. Furthermore, he approached British minister to the United States Anthony Merry in an effort, unsuccessful as it turned out, to raise money to support the expedition against Spanish territory, the supposition being that what hurt Spain would help England. Burr talked expansively about his plans, which gave some credence to the charges against him; he also talked openly to numerous people, including Andrew Jackson, which was not the behavior of a man engaged in high treason.[50]

Brash talk and tall tales were the idiom of the American West, as that aristo-

---

49. Of the several biographies of Burr, I have found Milton Lomask, *Aaron Burr,* 2 vols. (New York, 1979, 1982), to be the most useful. The election of 1800 is treated in Hofstadter, *Idea of a Party System,* ch. 4.

50. Lomask, *Burr,* 2: chs. 1–7, on the background to the conspiracy.

cratic easterner Aaron Burr perfectly understood, and so was an inveterate hatred of Spain, whose presence in West Florida, if not North America, was increasingly looked upon as an unnatural barrier to America's continental destiny. A war with Spain, which some wanted and many expected, would have legitimized Burr's plans, perhaps even made him a hero. In case there were no war and no chance for military glory, Burr negotiated the purchase of a tract of land on the Washita River, which could be settled by those young men desperate or romantic enough to join him. Whatever was intended, the undisputed fact was that Burr, along with a young Irish nobleman named Harmon Blennerhassett, did "procure an assemblage" of men and furnish them with provisions and arms. In December 1807, this motley band, which numbered fewer than a hundred, departed from Blennerhassett's Island in the Ohio River, bound for some place in the Southwest to do something or other. Aaron Burr, who dreamed up the scheme, who did the procuring, and who never paid any of the bills, fortunately and perhaps deliberately was not there when the men gathered or when they departed, though he did join the flotilla later. As to what Burr had in mind, it may be exactly what the convoluted and voluminous records show: a vague set of contingency plans, laced with a large dose of desperation-tinged romanticism, all calculated to benefit Aaron Burr. Neither before nor after the events on Blennerhassett's Island did he show the slightest concern for the well-being of the young men he enlisted or for hapless Harmon Blennerhassett, who risked his fortune and lost it all. The man John Marshall rescued in the name of law from the clutches of a determined president was, whatever else, an arrogant, spoiled, self-centered scoundrel. Whether he was a threat to the Republic and deserved to hang as a traitor, as Jefferson thought, was another matter.

Why President Jefferson reached that grim conclusion is unclear. He registered doubts about Burr's character as early as 1796, as did others who knew him, including Washington. After the disputed election of 1800, Jefferson's misgivings turned to hate. On the other hand, the president was well aware of, and favorably disposed to, Burr's early recruiting activities in the West, probably because they would strengthen his hand in negotiating with the Spanish about West Florida. At any rate, Jefferson showed no concern even when in November 1806 federal district attorney Joseph Hamilton Daveiss issued a compulsory process for Burr's arrest on the ground that he was engaged in a treasonable plot to dismember the federal Union. Daveiss and his compatriot Humphrey Marshall, both of whom were married to sisters of the chief justice, were Federalists who admired Hamilton and thus hated Burr. They also wanted to embarrass Jefferson, which probably explains why the president did not take seriously their accusations against Burr. In the meantime, Burr appeared voluntarily in the company of his attorney Henry Clay and was totally exonerated by the grand jury of the charges against him. Daveiss's second effort to indict Burr two weeks later in the same court also failed to convince the assembled grand jury. Neither case produced a single witness to support the charge of treason; neither deterred Burr, who proceeded blithely on his way after declaring both to his lawyer and to the court that he was totally innocent of "any measure to promote a dissolution of the Union, or a separation of any one or more States from the residue." Burr also insisted to Clay that his views "are well understood by the administration and seen by it with complacency."[51]

That complacency ended on October 21, 1806, when the president received two letters from General James Wilkinson, commandant of the American army and the man in immediate control of New Orleans and the southwest frontier. The covering letter warned of the imminent threat to New Orleans from an invading force of eight thousand to ten thousand men led by Burr. The other, the infamous cipher letter, was a copy of a letter Wilkinson claimed was written by Burr that recounted, supposedly in Burr's own words, his plan to attack New Orleans as the first step in his treasonable effort to separate the Southwest from the federal Union and set himself up as ruler of a new empire. Written in July, this incriminating letter was delivered to Wilkinson by Erick Bollmann, a German doctor caught up in the romance of the western adventure, and Samuel Swartwout, an aristocratic New Yorker who later distinguished himself by stealing several hundred thousand dollars from the New York Port Authority.

Why Wilkinson waited until October to inform the president of the plot he had known about since July was not immediately clear. Why a letter purportedly from Burr spelling out his treasonable intentions should have been delivered to Wilkinson was also an interesting question. Jefferson did not press for answers. Instead, on November 27, 1806, acting mainly on the basis of Wilkinson's letters, he formally declared the existence of a conspiracy and ordered the arrest of the conspirators—or, if you believe Burr's defense lawyer Luther Martin, "let slip the dogs of war, the hell-hounds of persecution" against an inno-

51. David L. Chandler, *The Jefferson Conspiracies: A President's Role in the Assassination of Meriwether Lewis* (New York, 1994) is suggestive on the Jefferson-Burr relationship. Also Albert J. Beveridge, *The Life of John Marshall* (Boston, New York, 1916–1919), 3: 315–19; Mary-Jo Kline, *Political Correspondence and Public Papers of Aaron Burr* (Princeton, N.J., 1983), 2: 978. Burr to Clay, 1 December 1806, as quoted in Beveridge, *Life of John Marshall,* 3: 318.

cent man. In the meantime, Wilkinson declared martial law, set himself up as the military ruler of New Orleans, and threw Bollmann and Swartwout into jail without a formal charge over the objection of the presiding territorial judge. Orders were also dispatched by Wilkinson to arrest Burr. Fearing for his life, apparently with some justification, the former vice-president surrendered in February and was taken under guard to Richmond to await formal arraignment before Marshall's circuit court, which convened on March 30, 1807.[52]

Thanks to the abundance of trial records and extensive newspaper coverage, the trial affords a unique view of Marshall as a trial judge (the circuit court was sitting as a trial court). The combination of legal and political issues were designed to put the chief justice to the test, especially in light of the rule-of-law promises he had made in *Marbury*. At stake was the life of Aaron Burr, since the punishment for treason was set by statute as death by hanging. The fate of Burr's accomplices Bollmann and Swartwout added further to the pressure on Marshall. Connected with the rights of the accused, was the great question concerning the meaning of treason in Article 3, Section 3 of the Constitution, which provided: first, that "Treason against the United States, shall consist only in levying war against them, or in adhering to their enemies, giving them aid and comfort"; second, that "No person shall be convicted of treason unless on the testimony of two witnesses to the same overt act, or on confession in open court." A broad construction of that section, following the English doctrine of constructive treason, i.e., that in treason all are principles, would snag Burr but would also run the risk of politicizing treason in America, as had happened in England. A strict construction of this section would put American treason law on a liberal path, but at the risk of allowing Burr to go free. What made the question doubly difficult was that Thomas Jefferson was determined to prosecute Burr even if it meant resorting to English doctrine, which he hated and which his own party had renounced. Jefferson's personal involvement in the case meant that the president and the chief justice would square off yet again over the meaning of republican law.[53]

Jefferson set the stage for his encounter with Marshall in Richmond by taking a uniquely personal stake in the case. His first act of commitment was to rely on, possibly even believe, Wilkinson's letters concerning Burr's guilt. To

---

52. David Robertson, ed., *Reports of the Trials of Colonel Aaron Burr* (1808; reprint, New York, 1969), 1: 128. Leonard Levy, *Jefferson and Civil Liberties: The Darker Side* (Cambridge, Mass., 1963), ch. 4.

53. Bradley Chapin, *The American Law of Treason: Revolutionary and Early National Origins* (Seattle, Wash., 1964).

be fair, the president did not know what historians now know when he issued his all-points bulletin in November 1806, namely, that Wilkinson had been in the secret employment of Spain since 1787 and that he had constantly used his official positions in the army as a springboard for various ventures of his own in the Southwest, some identical to the one that landed Burr in jail. In point of fact, Wilkinson was a principal in the very conspiracy he accused Burr of having masterminded. Burr's biographer dates the conspiracy and the copartnership of Burr and Wilkinson from April 24, 1804, when the two met in Washington to map their plans for money and glory. Moreover, careful historical detective work has shown that the general's letters to Jefferson were patent attempts on Wilkinson's part to distance himself from a failing venture—a risky one, too, since Burr had already been charged with treason in the federal district court. Moreover, the famous cipher letter, the main evidence against Burr and the grounds for indicting Bollmann and Swartwout, who delivered it to Wilkinson, was not written by Burr but by Jonathan Dayton, a confidant of Burr. The purpose of the letter, ironically, was to reinforce Wilkinson's faltering commitment to the project. The copy of the letter (the original was never found) sent to Jefferson was obviously doctored by Wilkinson to hide his own involvement.[54]

Jefferson ought not be blamed for what he had no way of knowing, but he did know what others knew, that Wilkinson was a shady character with a reputation for dishonesty and fast dealing. It was rumored as early as the 1790s that he was a secret agent of Spain. All that might have caused the president to ponder the wisdom of trusting Wilkinson's letters, especially considering that Burr had been already acquitted in a court of law for the very charge brought against him in the letters. One can only guess why Jefferson did not wonder why it took Wilkinson two months to inform him of the cipher letter, which warned of the impending fall of the Republic. Even with these cavils, Jefferson's decision of November 1806 to move against the conspiracy with dispatch might be justified in light of the constant talk of dismemberment, secession, and filibustering that plagued the early Republic. Federalists, including the chief justice, as well as Jeffersonian Republicans were willing to believe the worst of their adversaries.

Whether Burr's initial arrest was justified or not, it was what happened afterward that defined the legal conflict between Marshall and Jefferson and ele-

54. Lomask, *Burr*, 2: 23. Kline, *Political Correspondence*, 2: 973–90. Also Lomask, *Burr*, 2: ch. 6.

vated it into a rule-of-law drama of the first order. Relying on the Wilkinson letters to arrest Burr was one thing; using them as evidence for a treason charge without exploring their accuracy or the credibility of Wilkinson was another. The president made no attempt to look into, or curb, the reign of military rule instigated by Wilkinson in New Orleans, which defied rule of law on numerous counts. Even after the general had been exposed at Richmond as a fool and a liar, the president continued to support and even praise him. More questionable and more to the point, the president pursued Burr with a relentless and personal passion that bordered on obsession. Indeed, while Burr awaited arraignment in Richmond, Jefferson, on January 22, 1807, sent a special message to Congress, which was printed in the newspapers and widely circulated, describing the conspiracy and declaring before Congress and the entire nation that Burr was guilty of treason, this before the grand jury had been convened to consider the evidence against him.[55]

As a forecast of what was to come in Richmond, the president also intervened personally in the case of Bollmann and Swartwout. In order to avoid any slipup, they had been dispatched separately, each with an identical letter, the one allegedly written by Burr, to Wilkinson, urging him to stay with the venture, which meant incidentally that it was full of incriminating big talk and assurances of success. Wilkinson, who had already decided to avoid trouble, at first befriended the messengers, pumped the German for more information about Burr, then charged them with treason, clamped them in irons, and hustled them off to Washington under military guard in defiance of a writ of habeas corpus issued for their release by the territorial judge. While they were being held in confinement in the capital, Jefferson hand-carried the Wilkinson letters to the federal attorney for the District of Columbia and insisted that he issue a bench warrant for their incarceration on charges of treason. The Jeffersonian Republicans on the circuit court, over an eloquent dissent by Federalist William Cranch, ruled two to one to commit the men without bail. As in *Marbury* and the impeachment of Chase, Jefferson had put his own authority, and his own view of law, on the line. He must have known, too, since Burr awaited trial in Marshall's court, that this would bring him face to face with his old adversary.[56]

Marshall's first direct involvement came in *Ex parte Bollmann* and *Ex parte Swartwout,* an appeal from the circuit court's decision to incarcerate the two

55. Levy, *Jefferson and Civil Liberties,* 70.
56. Warren, *Supreme Court,* 1: 301–8.

men on the charge of treason. Two politically explosive questions arose concerning the imprisonment of Bollmann and Swartwout. The first was a technical question as to the competence of the Court to issue the writ of habeas corpus, as requested by Bollmann's and Swartwout's lawyers; the second, on the merits, was whether there was sufficient evidence against them to justify incarceration for treason. Marshall addressed the question of the Court's authority to issue the writ, provided for in Section 14 of the Judiciary Act of 1789, on February 13, 1807. The issue was particularly sensitive because Jefferson pressured Congress, while the case was pending, to repeal Section 14. The Senate, where William Branch Giles led the charge, voted for repeal; the House refused to do so by a resounding vote, thanks in part to the defection of John Randolph. The fiery Virginian confessed to being struck with "consternation" that the accused had been seized by "the strong hand of military power, while the other twin member of the civil arm (all the while no doubt unconscious of the outrage) is ready to receive him."[57]

The failure of the Republicans to emasculate habeas corpus jurisdiction opened the door for Marshall's opinion on the Court's jurisdiction under Section 14. The key words of his opinion read: "That all the before mentioned courts of the United States shall have power to issue writs of *scire facias, Habeas Corpus,* and all other writs, not specially provided for by statute, which may be necessary for the exercise of their respective jurisdictions and agreeable to the principles and usages of law." Often ignored as mere technical overkill, his broad reading of the statute set forth a fundamental rule of construction, that "the true sense of the words is to be determined by the nature of the provision and by the context" rather than a "strict grammatical construction."[58]

The chief justice also addressed, though indirectly, the federal criminal common-law issue, which had surfaced as a key part of the Republican attack on the Court during the debate over the Repeal Act. The meaning of constitutional and statutory language must, he insisted, be determined by reference to the common law, following which he expounded the various types of writs embraced by the generic phrase *habeas corpus.* The key point was that the Court's jurisdiction "must be given by written law." A technical argument, perhaps an

---

57. *Ex parte Bollmann,* 4 Cranch 100; *Ex parte Swartwout,* 1 Cranch 101. The federal circuit court decision *U.S. v. Bollmann,* 24 Fed. Cas. 1189 (C.C.D.C. 1807) (No. 14,622) is discussed in Haskins and Johnson, *Foundations of Power,* 255–56. Also Warren, *Supreme Court,* 1: 302–3. John Randolph to Joseph H. Nicholson, 5 February 1807, Nicholson Papers MSS as quoted in Warren, *Supreme Court,* 1: 305 n. 1.

58. PJM, 6: 480–81.

obiter dictum as well, that simple statement moved the Court out of the direct line of Republican fire and forecast its final repudiation of nonstatutory criminal jurisdiction for federal courts in *U.S. v. Coolidge* (1816). Keen strategist that he was, Marshall had determined that the Court should not fight on losing ground.[59]

Marshall's second opinion, which dealt with Bollmann's and Swartwout's confinement on the charge of "treason in levying war against the U.S." shaped, if it did not actually determine, the course of the pending Burr trial in Richmond. The chief justice opened by stating the general principles on which the case would turn, this being a clarification of Article 3, Section 2, clause 1, which held that treason "shall consist only in levying war against them [the United States], or in adhering to their enemies, giving them aid and comfort." Then he distinguished treason from the conspiracy to commit treason. To constitute treason, he ruled, "war must be actually levied against the U. States." Conspiring to levy war may be a "flagitious" crime, but it "is not treason." Indeed, even the "actual enlistment of men to serve against the government does not amount to levying war."[60]

Addressing the specific case before the Court, Marshall went on to say that "a design to overturn the government of the U.S. in New Orleans by force, would have been unquestionably a design which if carried into execution would have been treason, and the assemblage of a body of men for the purpose of carrying it into execution, would amount to levying of war against the U.S." Exactly how much "force" was necessary to constitute "execution" was not clearly delineated, though Marshall quoted approvingly Chase's holding in the Fries treason trial that "any force connected with the intention, will constitute the crime of levying war." On the crucial matter of intention, Marshall went on to rule that the evidence introduced to prove that was insufficient. Particular attention was given to the problems surrounding James Wilkinson's affidavit presented to the circuit court, "which purports to be as near the substance of the letter from Colonel Burr to General Wilkinson as the latter could interpret it." This document—the one delivered by Jefferson to the federal prosecutor and the mainstay of the government's case against all of those indicted for treason, including Burr—was found insufficient to justify commitment. Over

59. Ibid., 480. *U.S. v. Coolidge,* 1 Wheaton 415. See Haskins and Johnson, *Foundations of Power,* 633–46, on the debate over federal common law of crimes. Also Andrew Lenner, "A Tale of Two Constitutions: Nationalism in the Federalist Era" (M.A. thesis, University of Virginia, 1993).

60. PJM, 6: 488.

strong presidential objection, both prisoners were released on bail to be tried later, not for treason, but for high misdemeanor.[61]

Marshall had come away the winner in the first round. Bollmann and Swartwout were out on bail on a lesser charge. And much to Jefferson's consternation, Wilkinson's affidavit, the main evidence against Burr and all of those indicted for treason, had been significantly discredited. With Jefferson's unwitting help, Marshall had turned his disagreement with the president into a rule-of-law issue, which played to the institutional strengths of the judicial branch. In addition, he managed to slip in a *Marbury*-like lecture aimed at Jefferson. Referring clearly to Jefferson's personal intervention in the case, he warned the president about the dangers of crying treason. The "punishment in such cases," he declared, "should be ordained by general laws formed upon deliberation, under the influence of no resentments, and without knowing on whom they were to operate, than that it should be inflicted under the influence of those passions which the occasion seldom fails to excite, and which a flexible definition of the crime, or a construction which would render it flexible, might bring into operation."[62]

The president would now be playing on the chief justice's turf and according to his rules, which Marshall now made synonymous with the rule of law itself. As in *Marbury,* Jefferson was cast in the role of a law defier, if not a vengeful tyrant. All had gone well for Marshall, except for one inadvertent concession to the prosecution and the president, now one and the same. In the second *Bollmann* opinion, whether deliberately or inadvertently under the pressure of time and events, the chief justice appeared to invite indictments under the English doctrine of constructive treason: in treason, all are principles. Immediately after he had distinguished treason from the conspiracy to commit treason, Marshall went on to say, "It is not the intention of the court to say that no individual can be guilty of this crime who has not appeared in arms against his country. On the contrary, if war be actually levied, that is, if a body of men be actually assembled for the purpose of effecting by force, a treasonable purpose, all those who perform any part, however minute or however remote from the scene of action, and who are actually leagued in the general conspiracy, are to be considered as traitors."[63]

Reasoning from this statement about constructive treason in the *Bollmann*

61. Ibid., 489–91.
62. Lomask, *Burr,* 2: 203–8; PJM, 6: 489.
63. PJM, 6: 488.

opinion, the government in the subsequent trial at Richmond decided, not unreasonably, to indict Burr for treason, even though he was not present on Blennerhassett's Island where the levying of war took place, if it did take place. This proved to be a fatal miscalculation, for Marshall repudiated the English doctrine at Richmond. Some scholars argue that this change of definition was proof that Marshall manipulated the law for political ends, while accusing Jefferson of doing exactly that. Not surprisingly, Jefferson saw it precisely this way. A more generous view is that Marshall's repudiation of constructive treason in Richmond was a clarification of the *Bollmann* opinion, not a repudiation of it. In any case, what was only an embarrassment for Marshall was a disaster for the prosecution, which found itself saddled with a formal charge it was not prepared to prove. In more ways than one, then, the stage was set for the Richmond trial even before the hearings began.[64]

The various phases of the trial in Richmond lasted from late March to mid-September 1807: There was the probable cause hearing held in Richmond's Eagle Tavern on March 30 and 31; the grand jury proceedings lasted from May 22, the opening day of the spring circuit, until the last week of June, when the grand jury returned indictments of treason and misdemeanor, to which Burr pleaded innocent; the trial, including jury selection, lasted from mid-August until September 1, when the jury returned a verdict of not guilty on the charge of treason. The final stages of the trial, which occurred during late September and concluded mid-October, centered on the government's halfhearted efforts to prosecute Burr for a misdemeanor, i.e., his planned military expedition against Spain, and for treason and misdemeanor, based on his joining the flotilla after it had departed Blennerhassett's Island. The government did not pursue these charges even though, on October 20, Marshall ordered Burr to stand trial in Ohio for misdemeanor. Although Burr was not exactly vindicated, he was a free man. He lived the remainder of his long life just, but not too far, beyond the pale of respectability, using his immense talent to do what he had always done so well: look out for Aaron Burr. His treason trial—or to be more precise, what John Marshall made of it—turned out to be Burr's most constructive legacy.[65]

Historians rightly celebrate Marshall's clarification of treason doctrine at Richmond, a definition that repudiated the English doctrine of constructive treason and thus helped put treason beyond the reach of vindictive politicians.

64. Chapin, *American Law of Treason*, 109–11.
65. Editorial Note, PJM, 7: 4–5, with abundant thanks.

Seen as a victory of law over politics, the Burr trial is a fitting climax to Marshall's decade-long battle with Jefferson to make constitutional interpretation the business of lawyers and judges, not politicians. Marshall's victory in Burr, however, cannot be understood simply as a matter of constitutional doctrine. As in *Marbury*, the chief justice made his way to constitutional truth, with a small *t*, only in the course of a long and arduous trial. Though he sat with federal district judge Cyrus Griffin, Marshall was the presiding judge, the man on the spot. During three grueling months, he handed down no fewer than fifteen distinct opinions, which fortunately he wrote, on a variety of procedural, evidentiary, and doctrinal matters, not counting numerous and largely undocumented rulings from the bench aimed to move the trial along, preserve order, and keep the lawyers in line. In these small matters, as well as in the large doctrinal ones, justice was served; it was also on display. It would not be too much to say in this regard that the promises made in *Marbury* about due process and rule of law now came due.[66]

Marshall understood this fact fully and appreciated the circumstances that made it so. As he put it to his colleague William Cushing when the trial was well under way, "It has been my fate to be engaged in the trial of a person whose case presents many real intrinsic difficulties which are infinitely multiplied by extrinsic circumstances." The real intrinsic difficulties, as Marshall went on to note, had to do specifically with the constitutional meaning of treason. The words seemed plain enough, but the informing context was anything but clear. Treason "shall consist only in levying war" against the United States, but what does "levying war" mean? Does the phrase mean planning for war? Does the nation have to wait until the first blood is shed before it can move? Even more to the point, are those who plan treason but are not there to carry it forward in war also traitors? Even English experience, on which the Founders relied, was confused, and the developments in the American states compounded the difficulty. When Marshall hovered uncertainly between constructive treason in *Bollmann* and the repudiation of it in Burr, he reflected exactly this state of confusion.[67]

The "extrinsic circumstances," if anything, were more daunting than the legal ones, and not the least of these was the fact that the trial had turned into a public spectacle. Newspaper coverage was extensive, even national in scope,

66. PJM, 7: 11.
67. Marshall to Cushing, 29 June 1807, PJM, 7: 60. Chapin, *American Law of Treason*, ch. 3, discusses developments in treason law at the state level.

and highly politicized, which is to say Marshall's every move was reported and scrutinized. Hundreds of onlookers, who like their English forebears considered treason trials as public entertainment, thronged into Richmond to catch a glimpse of the famous and infamous characters involved. When again could ordinary folk see a former vice-president on trial for his life—one who had laid low the great Hamilton to boot? So numerous was the crowd that Marshall adjourned the hearings to the Virginia House of Delegates, where galleries were packed for the duration.[68]

Watching the great lawyers in action was also a treat for the spectators, but a constant tribulation for Marshall since egos on both sides had constantly to be reined in. The chief prosecutor, if one does not count the president, was federal attorney George Hay, who as it turned out, somewhat to his distress, was Jefferson's contact man. Attorney General Caesar Rodney and Virginia Lieutenant Governor Alexander McRae also appeared for the prosecution. Most impressive of all for his eloquence and legal acumen, as well as his delicate ego, was young William Wirt, the same who had gone public in praise of Marshall's genius. On Burr's seven-member defense team, the most notable member was Burr himself, who seems to have called many of the strategic shots. The defense also included Marshall's longtime friend, Charles Lee of *Marbury* fame and Edmund Pendleton, with whom and against whom Marshall had crossed swords in Virginia for many years. For brilliance and sheer eloquence, perhaps none matched John Wickham, another of Marshall's professional acquaintances from Richmond. Finally, there was the "Federalist bull dog," Luther Martin. Having recently saved Chase from the impeachment ax, he now hoped to save Burr from the gallows—and pillory the president when he got the chance. His presence all but guaranteed sport for the crowd and trouble for Marshall, who had to keep the old lawyer from saying the things about Jefferson that Marshall himself believed to be true.[69]

Other distractions, too, threatened to turn the trial into a circus. Burr's wife and daughter were there and could be seen making their way to and from the Court; even Burr himself was free to move about until indicted by the grand jury, which in an age when deference still counted might well have been an attempt to shape prevailing opinion and thus jury deliberations. The government

68. The pro-Jefferson *Richmond Enquirer* provided the most extensive coverage of the case, and its accounts were widely circulated. Warren, *Supreme Court,* makes admirable use of newspaper coverage in this as in other cases. Beveridge, *Life of John Marshall,* 3: 372–73, is excellent on the general coverage of the trial.

69. The best source on the lawyers is Robertson, *Reports of the Trials of Colonel Aaron Burr.*

had assembled more than a hundred witnesses, many of whom were celebrities and all of whom were prepared to testify about something or other they had heard Burr say or seen him do in his meanderings through the West. Among those who preached Burr's innocence and condemned Jefferson's persecuting tactics were Andrew Jackson and Winfield Scott. Thanks no doubt to the pro-Republican *Richmond Enquirer,* the sentiment against Burr, and Marshall as well, ran strong. The grand jury that indicted Burr was chaired by none other than John Randolph, who had been Jefferson's Speaker of the House of Representatives and manager of the Chase impeachment trial, and included William Branch Giles, one of Marshall's most outspoken critics. Randolph, fresh from his failure to convict Chase, arrived in Richmond a stalwart Jeffersonian whose goal was to see that judges did not rule empires; he left Richmond with serious doubts about Jefferson and a growing respect for the chief justice, which would blossom into a deep and ideology-defying personal friendship. Topping the list of public figures, and easily the most flamboyant and controversial of them, was archaccuser and chief government witness James Wilkinson, who added to the drama by keeping the court waiting for weeks for his arrival. His fantastic military outfit, of his own design, was almost as outrageous as his testimony, which was so tinctured with lies and contradictions that it nearly got him indicted for treason.[70]

Perhaps the most compelling of the "extrinsic difficulties" shaping the trial, though perhaps not the most visible, was the ongoing struggle between Marshall, who literally had the home-court advantage, and Jefferson, who held the highest political cards. Jefferson was not there in person, but his presence was decidedly felt. The press, which was highly partisan and overwhelmingly Republican, pressed Jefferson's case against Burr at every turn. Jefferson pressed it, too. The president had already announced Burr's guilt to Congress and the nation. He had personally intervened in the Bollmann and Swartwout case. In the Burr trial, as the numerous letters to George Hay attest, the president took personal command of the prosecution. Marshall did not know the full extent of the president's involvement, nor did the public or the press, but it was no secret that *U.S. v. Burr* (1807) was also Jefferson versus Marshall. It was also clear that pronouncements on legal doctrine, no matter how inspiring, would carry little weight unless the trial that gave rise to them was conducted fairly

70. Haskins and Johnson, *Foundations of Power,* 267.

and with scrupulous attention to due process. As in *Marbury,* the line between law and politics, while real, was almost imperceptible.[71]

The trial record indicates Marshall conducted a fair trial; it is also clear he exercised considerable discretion as trial judge and in ways that offended Jefferson and embarrassed the prosecution. One such judgment came in the probable cause hearing, when Marshall was asked to commit Burr for a grand jury inquiry on two counts: a misdemeanor, "for setting on foot and providing the means for an expedition against the territories of a nation at peace with the U.S.," and high treason against the United States. After discoursing in the mode of Blackstone on the lower level of proof required in a probable cause hearing, Marshall ruled to commit Burr only on the charge of misdemeanor. The ruling permitted Burr to go free on bond, which Marshall set at a figure Burr readily raised. Freeing the accused to enjoy the hospitality of Richmond, which he did with style, appeared to signal Marshall's view of the case, particularly when several days later Marshall appeared at a party where Burr was also a guest. Given the politicized atmosphere of Richmond, it was a blunder so blatantly insensitive one is tempted to credit the argument that Marshall did not know beforehand Burr was going to be present. The fact that Marshall left early and did not converse with the defendant did not keep the administration from assailing Marshall's partiality. And it probably didn't help matters that Marshall had managed to lecture Jefferson, yet again, about treason "being employed as the instrument of those malignant and vindictive passions which may rage in the bosoms of contending parties struggling for power."[72]

Marshall's April 1 ruling on evidence and standards of proof, a ruling that would haunt the prosecution in days to come, also drew political fire. Marshall had already established evidentiary standards for treason in *Bollmann,* standards by which he found Wilkinson's affidavit insufficient as grounds on which to commit Bollmann and Swartwout on the charge of treason. For Marshall to have ruled differently in Richmond would not have merely reversed the decision of the whole Court but would have hopelessly confused the evidentiary rules on which the trial would proceed. Accordingly, he went out of his way to clarify the meaning of the *Bollmann* holding as it applied to the Richmond

71. According to one count, Hay "wrote more than fifty letters to Jefferson" during the trial, "and received almost as many from him." Paul S. Clarkson and R. Samuel Jett, *Luther Martin of Maryland* (Baltimore, 1970), 246 n. 3.

72. PJM, 7: 13; ibid., 16–17.

trial. "I should feel much difficulty in departing from the decision then made," he declared, "unless this case could be clearly distinguished from it." If there were some misunderstanding about the earlier opinion concerning the definition of treason and matters of proof, it would have to be clarified. If war were actually levied (since no actual hostilities took place, Marshall was referring to the events on Blennerhassett's Island), there would have to be at least two witnesses to the overt act: "The assembling of forces to levy war is a visible transaction, and numbers must witness it. It is therefore capable of proof; and when time to collect this proof has been given, it ought to be adduced or suspicion becomes a ground too weak to stand upon." How, he asked pointedly, could the prosecution allege that "an armed body of 7,000 men," the figure given in Wilkinson's letter to Jefferson, had been assembled by Burr, when after several months not a single witness to the act had been produced?[73]

It was a tough question, asked, as the trial record suggests, with considerable exasperation, so that the prosecution may well have wondered whether the playing field was really level. On the other hand, had the prosecution listened carefully, or had a vindictive president not been directing traffic, it might have settled for a lesser charge, which Marshall's reasoning invited it to do. Instead of reconsidering the charge, Jefferson on the advice of William Giles, who was present when Marshall ruled on evidence, intervened more aggressively to mobilize witnesses against Burr. One of the most egregious tactics employed concerned Erick Bollmann, who had been persuaded to inform against Burr by Jefferson, with the promise that his statement would not be used. Jefferson broke the promise in Richmond, though he did agree to a pardon, since Bollmann's testimony impugned not just Burr but Bollmann as well.[74]

These behind-the-scene efforts to manipulate the legal process were not known to the crowd and could only have been suspected, if that, by Marshall and the defense lawyers. Occasionally, however, the political hatred burst forth for all to see and in ways that threatened to engulf the entire trial. Such was the case on Tuesday, June 9, when Burr, acting as his own lawyer, rose to request the Court to issue a subpoena duces tecum to the president, ordering him to deliver the "letter and other papers which he had received from Mr. Wilkinson, under date of 21st of October." The letter was the cipher letter; the papers were "certain orders of the army and navy which were issued respecting me," orders Burr averred were intended "to destroy my person and my property."[75]

73. Ibid., 18–20.
74. Levy, *Jefferson and Civil Liberties,* 72–73.
75. Robertson, *Reports of the Trials of Colonel Aaron Burr,* 1: 113–14.

Burr's request for the Wilkinson letter ignited the political explosives that were tied inseparably to the legal issues, put there, one has to agree with Burr, by the president himself. Burr emphasized that it was on the basis of Wilkinson's letter that the president declared him a traitor in a special message to Congress. The letter had also, as Burr cleverly noted, "already appeared to the court, in the course of different examinations, that the government had attempted to infer certain intentions on my part, from certain transactions." Indeed, the grand jury proceedings showed that the government's witnesses were simply being asked to validate what Wilkinson claimed in his letter to Jefferson had happened, and what the president had said Wilkinson said that Burr said.[76]

Homing in on the Wilkinson letter was brilliant strategy, but the request for a subpoena duces tecum to the president to obtain it put Marshall on the hot seat. The fact he actually issued the subpoena seems to confirm that he was out to embarrass Jefferson. The president and his supporters saw it that way, and some historians have as well. Marshall did point out by way of partial justification, however, that the issuance of the subpoena was customary in Virginia, providing the "materiality" of the evidence requested was clear and "no great inconvenience" to the recipient of the writ was involved. Marshall must have known that a sitting president would refuse to appear in person, and indeed Burr made it clear that he did not "demand the presence of the executive officers at this place. All that I want, are certain papers." Since Burr didn't want Jefferson to appear and Marshall knew that he would not, why issue the subpoena at all? That was the very question Burr asked Marshall. "The reason is," replied Marshall, "that in case of a refusal to send the papers, the officer himself may be present to show cause. This subpoena is issued only where fears of this sort are entertained." The reply appears a bit feeble, but it should be recalled that Marshall remembered *Marbury,* where the president had deliberately withheld papers from the Court. *Marbury* indeed came up and was cited by McRae for the government as a precedent for *not* subpoenaing the president. But with a man's life on the line, perhaps a bit of pressure was in order. If the whole episode called attention to Jefferson's contempt for the legal process and the authority of the Court, it could hardly have displeased the chief justice.[77]

Whether Marshall's own subtly conveyed opinion of the president signaled

76. Ibid., 114.

77. 3 August 1807, ibid., 363; ibid., 116; ibid., 133; Robertson, *Reports of the Trials of Colonel Aaron Burr,* 2: 521, 524.

the defense is hard to say. But judging from "some warm desultory conversation at the bar," his statement appears to have unleashed a torrent of anti-Jefferson abuse from Luther Martin. Having recently defended Chase for haranguing Jefferson, Martin went on to do a bit of haranguing of his own. Is the president some "kind of sovereign?" he asked. By what right does he proclaim publicly that Burr is guilty beyond doubt? "He has assumed to himself the knowledge of the Supreme Being himself, and pretended to search the heart of my highly respected friend. . . . He has let slip the dogs of war, the hellhounds of persecution, to hunt down my friend." "And would this president of the United States, who has raised all this absurd clamour, pretend to keep back the papers which are wanted for this trial, where life itself is at stake?" How could he? "He is no more than a servant of the people." Not only did the defense have a right to subpoena the papers in question, Martin insisted, "but if the president were here himself, the court would have a right to demand, whether in confidential conversations general Wilkinson had not given very different statements from those which he might here produce." That prompted William Wirt to wonder if it was relevant for Martin to speak so fervidly of his personal friendship with Burr or to exhibit him "as a persecuted patriot: a Russell or a Sidney!" and ask what the defense expected to get from "these perpetual philippics against the government."[78]

A fair question it was, and it led Wirt to ask another especially relevant for the historian: Did the Court, Marshall, that is to say, "feel political prejudices which will supply the place of argument and innocence on the part of the prisoner?" The truth is Marshall did *feel* those prejudices. Though impossible to prove, it is more than a guess that Marshall secretly enjoyed hearing Martin censure Jefferson's law-defying behavior. It is a logical inference to be drawn from the record, too, that Marshall's "fear" about Jefferson, expressed at the outset of the debate about the subpoena, invited Martin's attack on the president. Canny trial that lawyer he was, Martin knew what the traffic would bear. Marshall's failure to call the old bulldog off the political scent did him no credit.[79]

To say that Marshall did not entirely escape the political contagion surrounding the Burr trial, however, is not to say what needs to be said: that his main concern and greatest accomplishment was to move American constitutional law toward a nonpolitical definition of treason and to assure Aaron Burr

---

78. Robertson, *Reports of the Trial of Colonel Aaron Burr,* 1: 126–30, 133.
79. Ibid., 144.

a fair trial according to prevailing legal standards. Nowhere is Marshall's genuine concern about the law, "intrinsic difficulties" of the case as he put it, more evident than in his letter of June 29, 1807, to Justice William Cushing (and apparently to other brethren as well). Following the practice developed in the debate over the circuits in 1802, the chief justice expressed his "earnest wish to consult with all my brethren of the bench on the various intricate points that occur," in part because he was not himself clear on the law but mainly because "a contrariety of opinion ought not to prevail in the different circuits."[80]

Among the unsettled questions Marshall had not decided was "whether a Grand Jury ought to require two witnesses to the same overt act to justify their finding a true bill on an indictment for treason." In the trial before the petit jury, scheduled to begin on the first Monday in August, he anticipated "many points of difficulty . . . which cannot be foreseen & on which I must decide according to the best lights I possess." Among problems sure to occur and on which "I most anxiously desire the aid of all the Judges," was that of constructive treason, the doctrine he and the Court appeared to have embraced in *Bollmann*. How far, he wondered, might the English doctrine be "carried in the United States." And how did it apply, if at all, to the assemblage on Blennerhassett's Island? Other questions concerned evidence: How far could "declarations or confessions of one person be given in evidence against another?" and "Is there a distinction between written & verbal declarations?" An even more vexing question concerned "whether an overt act of treason committed out of the district & consequently not laid in the indictment, can be given in evidence." In struggling with this question, Marshall turned for guidance to English statutes and common-law practice, but he was also aware that the American federal system presented unique problems and might even permit the accused, "notwithstanding the constitution," be twice put in jeopardy for the same offence.[81]

What the chief justice was *not* doing here is as important as what he was doing. He was not preoccupied with politics, except to admit that they made a difficult job even more so. He did not complain about the intense and often critical newspaper coverage, though it created problems regarding jury selection. There were no remarks about the long-windedness of prosecutor Hay. He said nothing about the predictable explosiveness of Luther Martin, the rhetorical excess of William Wirt, or the tendency of both sides to plunge headlong

80. PJM, 7: 60–62; the same letter was sent to Bushrod Washington.
81. Ibid., 60–61.

into arguments irrelevant to the issues at hand. Instead he was struggling, humbly at that, with the complex legal matters before him. He knew that reasoning about treason began with English authorities, but he also knew those authorities were not uniformly understood in America or controlling of a written constitution. A written constitution had altered America's constitutional universe—without clearly mapping its coordinates. As a constitutional judge, he would have to further clarify the doctrine of constructive treason he had broached in *Bollmann;* as a trial judge, he would have to clarify for the jury, for the lawyers, and for subsequent courts the relationship between that doctrine and the murky facts of the case at hand.

Clarification of these matters and others associated with keeping the trial on track came in a series of rulings, ten in all, Marshall made after the resumption of the trial on August 3. Sometimes things did not go smoothly, or even clearly. On August 11, for example, one finds the judge beating a hasty and disorderly retreat from his ruling the previous day on jury challenges for cause. On August 10, the prosecution had objected to a question asked of a prospective juror by Burr's lawyer about whether the juror "had formed and expressed an opinion about the guilt of Colonel Burr." Hay objected to the question's vagueness, contending that if such a challenge were permitted by the court, "there could not be a jury selected in the state of Virginia." Unhappily he cited in support of his argument a ruling by Justice Chase in the Callender trial of 1800 in which the justice had refused to disqualify a juror who admitted to have formed an opinion on *part* of the evidence against the accused. Marshall accepted the analogy to Chase's ruling, forgetting no doubt that it was one of the grounds on which Chase had been impeached, and ruled for the prosecution.

Marshall seems to have remembered the next day. After a brilliant exchange among counsel over standards of jury selection, Marshall clarified his ruling of August 10 and his understanding of the *Callender* precedent, which he admitted candidly had been wrong. His new opinion, which cited a wide array of authorities intermingled with common-sense observations, extended the benefit of doubt to Burr, which was proper since his life was on the line. Eating crow on *Callender* was also wise given the political baggage that came with that case. It was smart, too: That the best lawyer in the room could gracefully admit he was wrong may have helped subdue legal tempers on both sides. On the other hand, the fact that Marshall was tempted in the first place strengthened the impression that he was truly above the fray, which he was. And not least, the logjam of jury selection had been broken. August 11 was a good day's work for a trial judge.[82]

If August 11 was a good day, August 31 was a momentous one—the moment of truth when Marshall was forced to clarify the constitutional meaning of treason and relate doctrine to evidence and both to the facts of the case. The problem facing him, the same that had plagued the prosecution from the beginning and that had been argued off and on directly and indirectly throughout the trial, stemmed from the fact admitted by both sides that Burr had not been present when the men assembled on Blennerhassett's Island or when they set off downriver. The question, the one he asked Cushing's advice on, was about whether the definition of treason in the Constitution meant to embrace the English doctrine of constructive treason. Marshall's *Bollmann* opinion seemed to say it did; and the prosecution, as Hay's argument on August 17 indicated, framed its indictment on that reading. Marshall now abandoned that reading of *Bollmann*, which, he argued, had to be considered "with a view to the case in which it was delivered." Whether he was deserting *Bollmann* or simply clarifying it is not clear.[83]

What became clear was that the Constitution did not adopt the "the whole doctrine of the English books on the subject of accessories to treason." Treason consisted solely in actually "levying war" against one's country or aiding and abetting the enemies of the country in time of war. Marshall was willing to define "levying of war" broadly. A "rebel army vowing hostility to the sovereign power" and fronting the government did levy war, even if no shots were fired. The same would be true even "without the usual implements of war." But this broad construction of "levying war" did not, as Marshall hastened to point out, endorse constructive treason. "Without saying that the assemblage must be in force or in warlike form, they express themselves so as to show that this idea was never discarded, and they use terms which cannot be otherwise satisfied." Planning treason without a show of violence and force was conspiracy to commit treason and, while punishable by law, was distinct from treason. With Burr in mind, Marshall continued, "The advising certainly, and perhaps the procuring, is more in the nature of a conspiracy to levy war than of the

82. Marshall's rulings of August 10 and 11 are found in ibid., 63–70; also Robertson, *Reports of the Trials of Colonel Aaron Burr*, 1: 366–421.

83. PJM, 7: 75. Hay's opening statement, Monday 17 August, in Robertson, *Reports of the Trials of Colonel Aaron Burr*, 1: 435–40, especially at 436. Hay cited English statute and case law, too, but his most conclusive argument rested on Marshall's opinion in *Bollmann*, PJM, 7: 87. Marshall did somewhat discredit the decision by noting the divisions on the Court, PJM, 7: 79.

actual levying of war. According to the opinion, it is not enough to be leagued in the conspiracy, and that war be levied, but it is also necessary to perform a part; that part is the act of levying war."[84]

After canvassing English and American authorities on the matter of levying war, Marshall went on to observe, almost as an afterthought, that the formal indictment must indicate specifically and in what particulars the defendant had in fact levied war and concluded that "it would seem to follow irresistibly, that the charge must be proved as laid." What appeared to be a mere technical ruling, however, was the pivot on which the whole case turned, and on which Burr was set free. Burr was indicted for treason specifically for events that took place on Blennerhassett's Island, when it was clear, and agreed upon by all parties, that he was not present when those events transpired.[85]

Burr and his lawyers pounced on that fact. On August 17, after the jury had been selected and shortly after the prosecution witnesses had begun to testify, Burr objected that the witnesses were being interrogated about events extraneous to those on Blennerhassett's Island. Such corroborative testimony, Burr and his lawyers argued, was inadmissible until the *"open deed of war"* mentioned in the formal indictment had been proved. Since the Constitution required two witnesses to the overt act, since the act itself was hardly warlike, and since, even assuming it was warlike, any such witnesses to it would have had to be principals themselves in the act of treason, the difficulty in placing Burr at the scene of the crime was immediately apparent, as it had been throughout the trial. The chief witnesses for the prosecution simply could not come through. Wilkinson was discredited from the start, and in any case he was not a witness to any overt act. Bollmann had more to offer and was in fact promised a pardon by Jefferson if he would testify, but having been deceived once already, he refused. William Eaton, a military hero and early confidant of Burr, was willing to testify against him, but his deposition was easily rebutted because it appeared to be motivated by his desire to escape complicity. None of the other witnesses, while they could speculate about Burr's character, his role in procuring men, or his alleged intent, could connect him to the specific act for which he had been indicted.[86]

Marshall's definition, or redefinition, of treason, his exposition of the mean-

84. Ibid., 80–81, 89, 92–93, 109.

85. Ibid., 97.

86. Robertson, *Reports of the Trials of Colonel Aaron Burr*, 1: 452, 459. Lomask, *Burr*, 2: 109–11, 263–641, 273–74 on Eaton.

ing of "levying war," and his strict insistence on the two-witness rule had clearly put the prosecution on the ropes. The knockout blow came on August 31 when he applied his general rules of evidence to the case at hand. Responding to a motion from Burr, Marshall ruled that no further testimony would be heard unless it bore on the events that transpired on Blennerhassett's Island, where the alleged "levying of war" took place. Left stranded were the dozens of prosecution witnesses, who were prepared to testify about everything about Burr except what counted. On the evidence presented and witnesses heard, the jury had little choice but to acquit Burr on the charge of treason, which it did on September 1 in a report delivered by jury foreman Edward Carrington, who incidentally was John Marshall's brother-in-law. For practical purposes, the long ordeal was over.

The case ended as it had begun, amidst charges that the chief justice had politicized the legal process and the countercharge that Jefferson had done the same. Marshall's decisive ruling of August 31 on further witnesses brought the dispute between the two men into precise focus. The ideological differences came down to a dispute over the respective roles of the judge and jury in republican law. What the chief justice had done on August 31 when he restricted proof to the specific events on Blennerhassett's Island, or so it appeared to Jefferson and his supporters, was to substitute his own judgment about the guilt or innocence of the defendant for that of the jury. The republican alternative was to let twelve honest men hear *all* the evidence and then, without the interference of the judge, let them sort it out as to reliability and relevance, specifically, let them hear all there was to hear about Aaron Burr before deciding whether he was a traitor to the republic and republicanism. In this view, the jury, perhaps even more than the electorate, was the sovereign people speaking and the people's best shield against overweening state power. To say that Marshall subverted this sacred institution was to lump him with Samuel Chase and analogize Burr's trial to the jury-bashing circuit trials of Fries, Callender, and Cooper.

Before analogizing Marshall to Chase, however, it ought to be recalled that the chief justice, if he intervened at all, did so *against* the force of the state mobilized by a president bent on conviction. Marshall cherished the jury as a uniquely republican institution designed to protect the liberties of the citizen. But as a practicing lawyer, he understood that juries were subject to political manipulation and amenable to prevailing prejudices and passions. Liberty worked best when it was under law. To have permitted the Burr jury to render a verdict on evidence beyond the charge—or to expect it to return an unbiased verdict of guilt or innocence on the specific charge of treason after being bombarded with falsified evidence and speculative testimony about matters of personal character beyond the compass of the indictment—would have been to expect a superhuman feat from ordinary mortals. In short, Marshall was a hard-nosed realist about human nature; he was also an idealist regarding the process by which law might aid human beings in rational deliberation. His concept of judging was deeply rooted in his notion of the common law itself, which was part and parcel of his view of republican leadership. And this was the legacy of a couple of centuries of English law and a quarter century of lawyering in Virginia.

In any case, it was not Marshall who doomed the prosecution's case in Richmond. As trial judge, he did take charge of the trial. He made errors, but he also corrected them, and in sharp contrast to his colleague Chase, he was never imperious or overbearing. Both sides did finally have their day in court, or to be more exact, their three months. What really sank the government's case was not Marshall's prejudgment, but Jefferson's relentless and law-defying pursuit of Burr. In his insatiable ambition, his contempt for the general good, Burr was, as Jefferson believed, a mocker of republican values. But that did not make him a traitor by the definition and standards of proof set forth in the Constitution that Marshall was pledged to uphold. If Marshall was quick to judge the case, it was because that fact was clear almost from the outset. Put plainly, the president's case against Burr was doomed by the impenetrable factual uncertainty surrounding the objective of the expedition itself, by the indisputable fact Burr was not present when the levying of war allegedly took place, by the fact that the levying of war was most *unwarlike,* and by the total unbelievability of the prosecution's chief witness and the president's chief informant, James Wilkinson. No one knows, of course, what Burr would have done if he had reached New Orleans, or what he would have done if he had discovered, when he got there, a disposition on the part of the Southwest to go its own way apart from the Union. Jefferson, perhaps because he trusted republican citizens so fully, was not willing to extend the benefit of the doubt to so unrepublican a scoundrel as Burr. Marshall was no great admirer of Burr, especially after he killed Hamilton, whom Marshall did admire, but he believed that even scoundrels were entitled to the law's presumption of innocence. It was probably fortunate for Jefferson's reputation as America's champion of human rights that Marshall spared Aaron Burr from the gallows.

The First Decade Goes to Marshall and the Court

The first decade of the nineteenth century was unique in the history of the Court, unique in the way small matters took on large ideological meaning, in the interconnectedness of great constitutional moments, and in the way those moments were defined by the ever-deepening enmity between the president and the chief justice. In this sense, *Livingston v. Jefferson* (1811) was a fitting conclusion to the first ten years. The case involved a dispute over the ownership of the Batture Sainte Marie, an alluvial deposit (*batture*) left by the Mississippi River in the New Orleans suburb of Sainte Marie. Such deposits were recognized as communal property by French law. The common folk of the city, without knowing much about law, assumed the *batture* belonged to them. They were overruled in 1807 when the disputed land was privatized by a decision of the Superior Court of the Orleans Territory, which ruled on the basis of Spanish law. Legal title went to one Jean Gravier, who then sold it to Edward Livingston, Gravier's lawyer in the suit. Citizens of New Orleans, now backed by the city's municipal government, continued to claim the *batture,* however, and in their ongoing struggle with Livingston, persuaded Jefferson to intervene on their behalf. On the advice of Attorney General Caesar Rodney, and acting under the putative authority of an 1807 congressional act against public squatters, Jefferson ordered the U.S. marshal to evict Livingston. When his personal appeal to the president was turned down, Livingston brought suit against Jefferson, who was now a private citizen, claiming damages of $100,000. Livingston chose the Richmond venue partly for technical jurisdictional reasons—and almost certainly because he knew of Marshall's feelings toward Jefferson. As it turned out, he was right about the hatred and wrong about the jurisdiction.[87]

Why Jefferson refused to consider Livingston's legal claims, why he refused to submit them to arbitration as Livingston requested, is not clear. His correspondence suggests he was sincerely motivated by a concern for the citizens of New Orleans, who had continued to resist the decision of the Superior Court privatizing the *batture.* He may have been out to get Livingston, too, who had

87. *Livingston v. Jefferson,* 15 Fed. Cas. 660 (C.C.D.Va.). The case is discussed at length in Beveridge, *Life of John Marshall,* 4: 100–16. George Dargo's *Law in the New Republic: Private Law and the Public Estate* (New York, 1983) has been particularly useful for its concise analysis and because it includes nearly all of the relevant correspondence and documents related to the case.

been an important figure in New York's Democratic-Republican Party but who had not supported Jefferson against Burr in 1800 with sufficient enthusiasm. Livingston was also the lawyer who resisted the tyrannical rule of James Wilkinson in New Orleans by suing out a writ of habeas corpus for Bollmann and Swartwout. For whatever reasons, Jefferson decided against Livingston's claims and, as in the Burr case, used his influence to shape the outcome of the debate in Congress. His effort to influence the litigation at Richmond was even more extraordinary. Private citizen Jefferson now urged his friend President Madison to fill the seat on the Federal District Court for Virginia, vacated by Cyrus Griffin, with someone who would resist the influence of Marshall and who would be favorable to Jefferson's claim in the pending litigation. John Tyler was the man, and he did the job. Jefferson also attempted, unsuccessfully as it turned out, to influence Madison's appointment to the Supreme Court, anticipating that the case might find its way there on appeal.[88]

In the trial at Richmond both the personal and ideological differences between the chief justice and the president came into play. Marshall saw the case as another example—like *Marbury,* the Chase impeachment, the trial of Burr, the embargo, and the Louisiana Purchase—of Jefferson taking the law into his own hands. Jefferson, on the other hand, firmly believed "Marshall's character" had "induced" Livingston to sue in the first place. "His twistification of the law in the case of Marbury, in that of Burr, & the late Yazoo case," he complained to Madison, "shew how dexterously he can reconcile law to his personal biases: and nobody seems to doubt that he is prepared to decide that Livingston's right to the batture is unquestionable, and that I am bound to pay for it with my private fortune." In a letter to John Tyler, whom Madison appointed to sit with Marshall on circuit, Jefferson charged the chief justice with prostituting the law "to party passions," and making it into "nothing more than an ambiguous text, to be explained by his sophistry into any meaning which may subserve his personal malice." Jefferson won the case in Richmond on a technical point of jurisdiction but only after Marshall took the extraordinary liberty of lecturing him yet once again on the rule of law.[89]

Rule of law was indeed the issue, as it had been in every one of their disputes during the first decade of the nineteenth century. Jefferson believed that the

---

88. Jefferson to William Branch Giles, 12 November 1810; Jefferson to Madison, 25 May 1810; Jefferson to John Tyler, 26 May 1810; Jefferson to George Hay, 1 August 1810; Jefferson to Albert Gallatin, 27 September 1810; Jefferson to Madison, 15 October 1810. Relevant portions of these letters are included in Dargo, *Law in the New Republic.*

89. 15 *Fed. Cas.* 8, 411, 663–65.

American people, freed by the Revolution from the shackles of the Old World, were destined to produce a new social order. He organized a new party to give the people a voice, and he believed they had spoken in 1800. As he saw it, his election was a second revolution to reaffirm the values of the first, a mandate from the American people to reclaim the republican ground that had been captured by Federalist aristocrats and monarchists. When he acted to withhold William Marbury's ill-gotten office, to impeach Justice Chase for blatant partisanship, to hang Burr as a traitor to republicanism, to keep Edward Livingston from expropriating the property of the working folk of New Orleans, he did so in the name of the American people. The same personalization of popular power also characterized Jefferson's role in the acquisition of Louisiana and the Embargo of 1807, all of which pushed executive authority to the limits of the Constitution or beyond. Critics in his own party reminded him that this tremendous exercise of national authority was at odds with the states' rights platform on which he was elected. But he was firm in his belief that American history and the American people were on his side. And it was this possibility that troubled Marshall. Jefferson and his party have brought "evil times," he complained to C. C. Pinckney in 1808 as another electoral defeat loomed. "Indeed my dear Sir I never have known a time which I beleived [*sic*] to be more perilous than the present. The internal changes which have been already made & those further changes which are contemplated by a party always hostile to our constitution & which has for some time ruled our country despotically, must give serious alarm to every attentive & intelligent observer."[90]

This is a surprisingly grim assessment, especially coming from a man who had championed an energetic national government for a quarter of a century and who only recently argued brilliantly for an expansive view of presidential power. Would he have opposed Jefferson's policies if they had been executed by Adams, one wonders? Would he have dared lecture Washington on rule of law? These are frivolous questions, except that they make the point that Marshall could not separate the man from his actions. Style aside, what distressed Marshall most was that Jefferson as president took the law in his own hands and then strengthened his hand by organizing political parties and working through them to control Congress. When the president and his party challenged the Supreme Court to do something about it, Marshall fought back. What he had to do, given the political lay of the land, was to convince the American people that the Court, for all of its elitist characteristics,

90. Marshall to Pinckney, 21 September 1808, PJM, 7: 182–83.

somehow spoke for them; that it was uniquely qualified to stand guard over the Constitution.

Looking at the key episodes of the first decade, it seems clear Marshall was remarkably successful in making this point. This is not to say the Court's victories were final or that they convinced everyone. Court-bashing and Marshall-hating continued and, with Jefferson's blessing, reached new heights during the 1820s. Still the victories of the first decade were impressive, especially when one considers the weakened condition of the Court in 1800 and its persistent institutional vulnerabilities. Marshall had outmaneuvered Jefferson in the Burr treason trial and in the process had laid the foundation for modern American treason law. *Marbury,* though not conclusive, was still a telling victory for the Court and a desperately needed one. Federalist constitutional theory had been brought directly to bear on the Court's powers for the first time in history, and the theory had been implemented by the Court's decision to void an act of Congress on constitutional grounds—another first. In *Fletcher v. Peck* (1810), the Court struck down an act of a state on constitutional grounds, also for the first time. Most significantly, since it was essential to the exercise of the newly claimed powers of review, the chief justice had persuaded his brethren to speak in a single voice. During this early period, that voice was almost always John Marshall's.[91]

In the short period of ten years, Marshall staked out a large claim of power for the Court and himself as chief justice. Evidence suggests that his claims were widely accepted not just among Federalists but among moderate Republicans. This centrist coalition defeated root-and-branch judicial reform in 1802. And when push came to shove in the impeachment trial of Chase, which was a referendum on the claim to judicial authority staked out in *Marbury,* moderates in both parties rallied to the Court's defense. Jefferson's prosecutorial excess lost him some support in the Burr trial as well, even among stalwart anti-Court men such as John Randolph of Roanoke. Most indicative of the Court's newly won legitimacy—and it signaled the beginning of a new period of cooperation between the executive and the Court—was the action of President James Madison. That the greatest living authority on the Constitution, who was also Jefferson's most trusted adviser and the author of the Virginia Resolution of 1798, should support the Supreme Court against the states was a remarkable shift. But this is precisely what happened when Madison supported

---

91. Robert G. Seddig, "John Marshall and the Origins of Supreme Court Leadership," *University of Pittsburgh Law Review* 36 (summer 1975) 36: 785–833.

the Court's sweeping assertion of jurisdiction in *U.S. v. Peters*, which had been challenged head-on by the Pennsylvania legislature acting on the authority of the Eleventh Amendment and in the spirit of the Virginia and Kentucky Resolutions. With the threat of impeachment gone, with moderates in Congress and the new president on its side, the Court's claim to interpretive authority seemed on solid ground at last.[92]

When mere survival would have been an accomplishment, how was it the Court under Marshall was able to consolidate its power—how, indeed, since it was an aristocratic institution in an increasingly democratic polity? Certainly there was nothing in the Constitution to suggest that judges would be the special guardians of the Constitution. Indeed, judging from the 1790s, the center of constitutional action was Congress, not the Court. Congress, no less than the Court, was organizing itself to do business: witness the growth of parties as instruments to mobilize legislative majorities, standing committees as a means of ordering legislative business, the adoption of parliamentary rules of order to structure debate, and the growing power of the Speaker. More important still was initial dominance of Congress in constitutional matters: in setting up the other departments of government, including the judiciary; in creating the Bill of Rights; in debating and resolving the great question of implied powers, as it did in chartering Hamilton's Bank of the United States; and in defining First Amendment freedoms, as it did when it passed the Alien and Sedition Acts. Indeed, since the people were sovereign and since Congress was most directly answerable to them, one might think its voice would resonate in constitutional matters.

Fortunately for Marshall and the Court, Congress did not realize its potential in this area. It would continue to debate constitutional issues, of course, and as long as the Jeffersonians were in control, it would continue to be a vociferous critic of the Court. But the institutional fact of the matter was that it could not, even with its more efficient organization, speak in a single, authoritative voice about the Constitution. In addition, congressional claims to interpretive authority were diminished by President Jefferson, who regularly took constitutional matters in his own hands—as in the acquisition of Louisiana, without the benefit of amendment; and as in the passage of the Embargo of 1807, which despite its constitutional significance was rammed through a compliant Congress in three days. Even the impeachment proceedings against Jus-

92. *U.S. v. Peters*, 5 Cranch 115.

tice Chase, where the constitutional action was located explicitly in Congress, were orchestrated by the president.

Despite his forceful display of constitutional authority, Jefferson did not make a compelling case that constitutional interpretation belonged to the executive. What he demonstrated instead was a tendency to take law into his own hands. Protecting individual rights, in the Anglo-American legal tradition, was the special province of the judiciary. To challenge those rights in Marshall's Court was to invite defeat. In short, Jefferson gave Marshall the perfect opportunity to do what Congress had not been able to do, namely, to set forth and demonstrate the Court's unique institutional qualifications to interpret the Constitution. In the context of the times, Marshall's argument was well-nigh unanswerable. Building on Federalist constitutional theory, and the plain architecture of the Constitution itself, he established the fact that the Court had the same relation to the sovereign people as did the political branches. The *sovereign* people speak only in organic convention, and when they spoke in 1787, they created the Supreme Court and defined its status and duties. Emanating from the sovereign people, the Court had democratic credentials no less impeccable than those of the elective branches. In an age when the people were laying claim to the sovereignty promised them by the Framers, it was prudent for the Court to make its peace with them. Not only was the Court allowed to speak about the Constitution by the people themselves, it had an institutional character that suited it to the responsibility. Making the Court small, freeing it from constant electoral pressure by providing life tenure did not, of course, guarantee that its deliberations would be free of bias or politics. Compared to either of the political branches, however, it was an oasis of rational discourse.

Seen from the angle of comparative institutional history, Marshall succeeded in identifying the Court with the Constitution and, indeed, with the republican tradition of governance. He did so not just because of his command of Federalist constitutional theory, or his dazzling legal mind, or his irresistible personality, or his reputation as a Revolutionary hero, but also because he shared the common-law tradition with the other members of the Court and with many members of the political branches regardless of party affiliation. Personal biases did not disappear automatically from the Court's deliberations on this account, or from Marshall's either. But they were filtered through an elaborate process of thinking and structured argumentation, which was the end product of several centuries of Anglo-American experience. It was not just a matter of judicial review, but rather the entire institutional and intellectual apparatus of judicial deliberation that was relevant. Imperfect though it was, the Court was a unique deliberative forum, one remarkably useful to the American people as they entered the new century. By casting itself as a legal institution, by fusing common and constitutional law, the early Marshall Court began to produce a coherent body of rules for Americans to live by not only in the few celebrated cases but, hardly less important, in the innumerable small ones as well. Except for the Court's success in doing so, the claim to power in *Marbury* would have been a hollow victory.

In defining the Court as a branch of government on a par with Congress and the executive, Marshall drew on the Constitution itself and the formidable labors of the justices in the 1790s. By the same token, it is impossible to imagine the Court's emergence without him at its helm. He persuaded six justices to act as one Court, and more than anyone, he defined the unified Court as a *legal* institution. In the process, the office of chief justice, which was not in high repute in the 1790s, took on new authority. Not only did he preside authoritatively over the Court's legal deliberations, he guided it through the troubled political waters of the first decade with remarkable political savvy. He believed, as did others of his age, in the science of law, but he also understood the Court's political vulnerabilities. For the Court to do its legal duty, it had to overcome the opposition of a popular and powerful president. Marshall protected the Court's political flanks by settling for less in *Marbury* when more would have been dangerous; by speaking in the even tones of rationality in *Burr,* even when he was seething with contempt. Where the president came off as impetuous, vindictive, and self-righteous, Marshall was patient, methodical, and disarmingly modest, especially when pushing hardest for the Court's powers. He was not a political judge in the ordinary sense of the word, but he was a judge who realized that building on the Court's legal character was wise politics. He sensed also, as did Washington in the Revolution, that being outnumbered can be turned to advantage. Paradoxical it may seem, but Marshall probably could not have unified the Court or enhanced the powers of the chief justice, without Jefferson's unrelenting enmity.

CHAPTER FOUR

Republican Judge *as* Lockean Liberal

According to the stern principles laid down for their government, the impru-
dent and idle could not be protected by the legislature from the consequences
of their own indiscretion; but should be restrained from involving themselves
in difficulties, by the conviction that a rigid compliance with contracts would
be enforced.

—*John Marshall, Life of George Washington*

We may say that the movement of the progressive societies has hitherto been
a movement *from Status to Contract.*

—*Sir Henry Maine, Ancient Law*

W HEN LOOKING FOR the essence of Marshall's jurisprudence, it
is tempting to focus on *Marbury v. Madison* and the doctrine of judicial review—with considerable justification. After all, the rise of the Court as an institution is one of the great themes of Marshall's tenure and probably his most
lasting claim to fame. The opinion itself invites reification, too, as it soars
nobly above the mundane issues that gave rise to it. The possibility that judging
might be influenced by personal experience was obscured by Marshall's Olympian language and by the compelling distinction he drew between law and politics. By his reckoning, judges were saved from personal bias in judging because
they abided by stare decisis in administering firmly established principles of
law. In this common-law scheme of things, judicial review applied to the Constitution was a uniquely republican corrective for the maladies associated with
the political branches of a republican government. As we have seen, Marshall's

message during his first decade as chief justice, dramatically stated in *Marbury* and reaffirmed in the Burr treason trial (1807), was that the Court was a *legal* institution, that judicial review was synonymous with the rule of law, that scientific law kept judging objective.

However, one opinion—or two, assuming Marshall salvaged justice from the murky politics of the Burr treason trial—even a great one like *Marbury,* does not a republican judge make. The republican model of impartial judging was subjected to a more revealing test in cases dealing with economic disputes growing out of the ordinary business of American life. In fact, most of what the justices did, both on circuit and in Washington, had to do with property and some form of economic activity. These cases came to the Court via Section 25 of the Federal Judiciary Act, as appeals from state decisions, or under diversity jurisdiction, when citizens of one state sued citizens of another. Such cases almost always employed common-law reasoning and principles, the kind Marshall and his fellow justices had practiced as lawyers. Even the Marshall Court's great law-shaping constitutional decisions, not excluding *Marbury,* originated in economic conflict, where private lawyers representing private interests argued points of public law, almost always without the benefit of government counsel. The line between public and private law in early national jurisprudence was plainly imprecise. So was the distinction between private entrepreneurial activity and public welfare, at least in the economically-grounded, common-law-infused constitutional jurisprudence of the new chief justice.

Nowhere were economic policy-making implications of the Court's responsibilities, or the influence of the common law on them more conspicuous than in those cases arising under the Contract Clause of the Constitution (Article 1, Section 10). Inserted at the last minute with little informing debate, at least in Madison's *Notes of the Debates in the Federal Convention,* Section 10, in addition to prohibiting states from passing ex post facto laws and emitting bills of credit, prohibited them from "passing laws impairing the obligation of contracts." One of the signal accomplishments of the Marshall Court was to give precise meaning to these words—and to spell out their implications for the location of power between state and nation. Marshall led the way in *Fletcher v. Peck* and *Dartmouth College v. Woodward,* both of which rank among his most influential opinions. His lone constitutional dissent in *Ogden v. Saunders* (1827) was also a Contract Clause opinion, one of his most revealing. With Marshall in the vanguard, the Court's Contract Clause decisions forged what Edward S. Corwin called "the basic doctrine of American constitutional law," the Lockean assumption that law should protect private property in the name of liberty. For Marshall, as for the age, property and liberty were eternally bonded, and both were connected to contractual freedom. When Marshall used the Contract Clause of the Constitution to restrain states from interfering with public and private contracts, he did so in the name of the Framers, who attempted, as did Marshall himself, to strengthen the Union by harnessing the energies of creative entrepreneurs. All this is to argue that Marshall's Contract Clause opinions take us to the heart of his constitutional federalism and to the unarticulated economic premises, and personal experience, on which it rested.[1]

Huidekoper's Lessee v. Douglass (1805) and the Problem of Disinterested Judging

For scholars seeking to understand Marshall's constitutional-economic philosophy, *Fletcher v. Peck* has been the defining case. As the Court's leading Contract Clause decision, it is, of course, central to the story. But *Fletcher* was preceded, and in important respects prefigured, by Marshall's opinion in *Huidekoper's Lessee*. This was not a Contract Clause decision or even a constitutional one, but rather dealt with a long-forgotten Pennsylvania statute governing the disposition of public land. It is interesting and revealing for several reasons. First, Marshall's opinion for the Court shaped economic policy, and defied state legislative authority and Jeffersonian philosophy to do so. The issues raised, moreover, were similar to those in Virginia that pitted Marshall the land speculator against the state legislature. This, plus the fact that Marshall's brother was connected to the *Huidekoper* case through his father-in-law, Robert Morris, invites us to evaluate the central axiom of Marshall's judi-

1. Edward S. Corwin, "The Basic Doctrine of American Constitutional Law," *Michigan Law Review* (February 1914), reprinted in *American Constitutional History: Essays by Edward S. Corwin,* eds. Alpheus T. Mason and Gerald Garvey (New York, 1964), 25–45; Benjamin F. Wright Jr., *The Contract Clause of the Constitution* (Cambridge, Mass., 1938). For a comprehensive legal analysis of the Marshall Court's contract decisions, see George Lee Haskins and Herbert A. Johnson, *Foundations of Power: John Marshall, 1801–1815* (New York, 1981), 336–543, 594–600; and especially G. Edward White, *The Marshall Court and Cultural Change, 1815–1835* (New York, 1988), ch. 9. The standard account of *Fletcher* is in C. Peter Magrath, *Yazoo: Law and Politics in the New Republic; The Case of Fletcher v. Peck* (Providence, R.I., 1966). For some keen insights on the Contract Clause and Federalism, see Steven R. Boyd, "The Contract Clause and the Evolution of American Federalism, 1789–1815," *William and Mary Quarterly,* 3d ser., 44 (1987): 529–48.

cial philosophy: that judges had a special place in the republican scheme of government because scientific law guaranteed "disinterested" judging.[2]

Huidekoper grew out of a struggle between large land speculators and settlers in 1783, when as a result of the Revolution, Pennsylvania gained control over several million acres of land located in its northwest counties. The disposition of this land was influenced by several factors, the first being that Indians had not yet been forced out. Only with Anthony Wayne's defeat of the Indians at the Battle of Fallen Timbers, which paved the way for the Treaty of Grenville in 1795, was the territory finally safe for settlement. Before that, however, both individual settlers and large speculators had begun to move in. The settlers who braved the terror of Indian attacks to settle the land hoped to be rewarded with legal title, a reasonable hope given Pennsylvania's stated need to populate the frontier as a protection against Indian incursions. At the same time, large absentee speculators, hoping to buy cheap and sell dear, were called to action by the vision of bonanza profits. The speculators also promised to encourage settlement. But primarily what they offered the state, in addition to sweetheart deals with state officials, was the quick sale of large chunks of land, which, even at giveaway prices, would replenish Pennsylvania's much-depleted state treasury.[3]

The situation pitted speculators against settlers. The extent to which state land policy favored one or the other in the years leading up to *Huidekoper's Lessee* depended on the faction or party in power. Indeed, disagreements over land policy helped define party alignments. As defenders of state sovereignty and popular democracy, with a stronghold in the western part of the state, the Democratic-Republicans of Pennsylvania tended to favor small holders and actual settlers. Federalists championed the large investors associated with consolidated wealth, who were located mainly in Philadelphia. When Federalists lost control at the local and state level to the Democratic-Republicans, they turned to the federal courts, which brings us to the chief justice and *Huidekoper's Lessee*.

The specific issue before the Court was the interpretation of the Pennsylvania statute of April 1792, which aimed to bring order out of the competition

2. 3 Cranch 1; *Huidekoper's Lessee* is treated in Haskins and Johnson, *Foundations of Power,* 317–22; 590–96.

3. For the complicated background facts, see the arguments of counsel in the case at 3 Cranch 1–65. On land speculation in the region, see Elizabeth K. Henderson, "The Northwestern Lands of Pennsylvania, 1790–1812," *Pennsylvania Magazine of History and Biography* 60 (April 1936): 131–60.

between speculators and settlers on the contested northwest frontier. Judging from the wording of the statute, it tended to favor actual settlers rather than large speculators, a policy bias of Pennsylvania law from the days of William Penn up through the state's first land law of 1784. In this vein, the initiating motion to the legislation, made by Thomas Ryerson of Washington County, was "to revise, amend or alter the present established modes of disposing of the vacant lands of this common wealth, and to digest a general system for that purpose, upon principles more adopted to the convenience of the poor and actual settler, than those continued in the present laws relative to the land office." To this end, the price of land was substantially lowered and holdings were limited to no more than 400 acres. Special provisions extending payments over ten years were made for those who could not make the initial payment.[4]

Also working to the advantage of the actual settlers and against absentee investors were the settlement requirements, which permeated the various sections of the act, most particularly paragraph 9, which read: "That no warrant or survey, to be issued or made in pursuance of this act . . . shall vest any title in or to the lands therein mentioned, unless the grantee has, prior to the date of such warrant, made or caused to be made, or shall, within the space of two years next after the date of the same, make, or cause to be made, an actual settlement thereon, by clearing, fencing and cultivating, at least two acres of every hundred acres contained in one survey, erecting thereon a messuage for the habitation of man, and residing, or causing a family to reside thereon, for the space of five years next following his first settling of the same." In case of default regarding the settlement precondition, the state reserved the right "to issue new warrants to other *actual* settlers for the said lands."[5]

Because the statute was democratic, even populist, in tone, it appeared to be the property of the Democratic-Republicans, the party that viewed state legislatures as the voice of the sovereign people. It was no accident that Albert Gallatin, the rising star of that party in Pennsylvania, should have stated the settlers' case. It was in the interest of the commonwealth, he said, to encourage "the poorer class of people . . . to become freeholders." At a minimal cost, this class would be "able to live comfortably . . . , dependent only on their industry and exertions." With a little help from the legislature, the Jeffersonian yeoman would bring republican civilization to the West, and not incidentally provide a

4. Quote from 1792 statute and its political context in Henderson, "Northwestern Lands," 131–36.
5. 3 Cranch 5. Author's emphasis.

buffer against hostile Indians. The fact that legislators from eastern Pennsylvania, who spoke for large land speculators, objected to the special treatment given poor settlers, whom they branded as lawless frontiersmen, only seemed to make the democratic cast of the bill more evident.[6]

If the Act of 1792 was victory for the small claimants who would actually settle, clear, and improve the land and fight the Indians, who were fighting for *their* land, it was an inconclusive one. The large speculators in Pennsylvania were well represented in the state legislature, not to mention the Pennsylvania land office, and the act set a place for them at the table. Indeed, the two principles in the bill that might have seriously restricted speculators were both qualified, in the first place by the ambiguous wording of the statute and in the second by the history of the controversy, which was used to inform the wording. One important issue concerned the 400-acre limit imposed on individual land warrants, a provision that seemed designed to favor actual settlers. It was, however, a well-understood practice in Pennsylvania that large investors might circumvent this restriction by making out warrants in the name of individuals who would make only a cursory effort to fulfill the settlement requirement, after which the investors surveyed the land and went on to claim title. The Holland Company and its subsidiary, the Population Land Company, plaintiffs in *Huidekoper's Lessee,* used this practice to gain title to large tracts of land, for which they paid $500,000 into the state treasury. Among the most prominent of those who took out warrants under fictitious names were Robert Morris and Supreme Court Justice James Wilson.[7]

A more serious obstacle for the speculators was the stipulation that warrant holders establish actual residence and begin clearing, fencing, and cultivating the land in the space of five years following entry. This requirement seems clearly designed to aid the actual settlers, but unfortunately for them as it turned out, the statute contained a vaguely worded exemption from the settlement requirement, one made necessary by the fact that the land opened for sale had not yet been relinquished by the Indians. In order to permit the sales of land to begin immediately, it was provided in paragraph 9 "that *if any such actual settler, or any grantee, in any such original or succeeding warrant, shall, by force of arms of the enemies of the United States, be prevented from making such actual settlement, or be driven therefrom, and shall persist in his endeavors to make such actual settlement as aforesaid, then, in either case, he and his*

6. Gallatin quoted in Henderson, "Northwestern Lands," 135.

7. Ibid., 138–39.

heirs shall be entitled to have and to hold the said lands, in the same manner as if the actual settlement had been made and continued." Whether this vaguely worded section had been deliberately inserted in the statute as a sop to the large land speculators or whether they simply turned the vague language to their advantage is not clear from the legislative journal. It is clear, however, that the exception to settlement provision in paragraph 9 became the main item of legal and political contention between settlers and large speculators in the 1790s. It was also the major issue before the Marshall Court in *Huidekoper's Lessee.*[8]

The main plaintiff in the case was the Holland Land Company, which was a conglomerate of earlier companies and individuals who had invested heavily in northwestern Pennsylvania lands beginning with the passage of the Act of 1792. The warrants issued to the company, or to those individuals who sold their warrants to the company, were not surveyed or actually settled as required by law because of the ongoing struggle with the Indians. With General Wayne's victory over the Indians at the Battle of Fallen Timbers and the Treaty of Grenville in 1795, however, large numbers of actual settlers quickly moved into the region and began clearing land and erecting houses preparatory to taking out land warrants; many settled on the unsettled land claimed by the company.

For a decade preceding the Court's decision in *Huidekoper's Lessee,* and for another three decades thereafter, settlers and the absentee speculators battled over contested claims in both the courts and the legislature. Various efforts to resolve the conflict were tried, but all of them crashed on the rocks of politics. Only with the consolidation of Republican control of the state government, including the Pennsylvania Supreme Court after 1799, did the state align itself fully with the settlers. When the court ruled against the company in 1801, it sued under diversity of citizenship in the federal circuit court. A division of opinion on the second circuit between Justice Bushrod Washington, who ruled for the settlers, and district judge Richard Peters sent the case to the Supreme Court, where Marshall confronted it in 1805.[9]

The questions certified to be decided focused, as had the legal-political debate at the state level, on the meaning of that part of paragraph 9 of the Act of

8. Ibid., 138; 3 Cranch 5–6.
9. Henderson, "Northwestern Lands," 145, who cites 4 Dallas 170, and *Opinions of the Judges on the Claim of the Holland Company* (Lancaster, 1802).

1792, which provided "that if any such actual settler, or any grantee . . . shall, by force of arms of the enemies of the United States, be prevented from making such actual settlement, or be driven therefrom, and shall persist in his endeavors to make such actual settlement . . . then, in either case, he and his heirs shall be entitled to have and to hold the said lands." The company had purchased land warrants for half a million acres in August 1793, but allegedly had been prevented from settling the land because of Indian hostilities. By 1796, by which time the Indians had been driven out, actual settlers had occupied much of the land claimed by the company. Lawyers for the settlers claimed that the company had forfeited claim to title by failing to settle the disputed land once it could have done so safely. The company admitted that actual settlement had not taken place. But drawing on the ambiguous wording of paragraph 9, it claimed to have satisfied the settlement requirement by persisting to do so over two years. The question was whether Section 9 excused actual settlement as a precondition for taking title or whether it had merely postponed that obligation, in which case the company would be hard pressed to oust the settlers as it attempted to do in *Huidekoper's Lessee.*[10]

The legal and policy issues in the case made it especially revealing. On one side were the plain people who had invested their labor and sometimes their lives; on the other the company, which stood to lose as much as half its investment, money which, as its lawyers were careful to point out, the state had been more than glad to take. Coming as it did during the 1805 term of the Court when the impeachment ax hung over Justice Chase, the case was also politically volatile. A decision for the land speculators would appear to validate the Jeffersonian contention that the Court was a bastion of Federalist aristocracy. States rights was an issue, too, since the authority of the state legislatures to establish public land policy was at issue, an authority widely conceded to belong exclusively to the states. Since the state supreme court had already interpreted state law in favor of the small holder, and the state legislature, a reversal by the Supreme Court would raise explosive jurisdictional issues. This was especially so after the highly controversial Federalist Judiciary Act of 1801, which had given the federal courts jurisdiction over public land cases previously decided by state courts. Whether the Supreme Court acting under diversity jurisdiction could accomplish indirectly what that much-hated, now

10. Paragraph 9, Act for the Sale of the Vacant Lands, Section 9, 73, as quoted in Haskins and Johnson, *Foundations of Power,* 318.

defunct, law had attempted to do directly was a loaded question Marshall could not dodge.[11]

If the political status of the Court was an issue, so was Marshall's reputation as an impartial judge. As a large speculator himself and as an active partner in the Marshall family land syndicate, the chief justice had felt the abuse leveled at the Holland speculators. Indeed, at the time he was pondering the issues in *Huidekoper's Lessee,* his own title to Northern Neck land was being contested in the state courts of Virginia on the ground that state judicial interpretation of state land law was definitive and ought not to be the subject of federal judicial review. On top of this problem was the fact, well appreciated by his enemies, that the moving spirit in the Holland Land Company was Robert Morris, Marshall's former client, personal friend, and confidant, and the father-in-law of his brother James, who was also a member of the Marshall family land syndicate. The precise extent to which Marshall's brother's investments in land were bound with those of Morris will probably never be known, but James Markham Marshall was deeply involved on both sides of the Atlantic in trying to rescue the Morris investment portfolio from impending collapse and his father-in-law from debtors prison. Also relevant to the chief justice's deliberations was the fact that Morris and his supporters had gained control of the Pennsylvania land office, so much so that the 1792 act could be seen as an effort to take land policy from grasping aristocrats and return it to the people.[12]

Marshall ruled for the speculators and against the settlers. It was a highly controversial decision and not only because it overruled a state judicial interpretation of a state statute. For example, Marshall seems to have disregarded Section 34 of the Judiciary Act of 1789, which required the Supreme Court to follow state decisions in matters of local law, especially that concerning real property. Nor did he follow the Court's own oft-stated rules of statutory construction derived from the common law, the kind he called on in *Marbury.* Several such rules appeared applicable to his construction of Section 9 of the 1792 statute. Lawyers on both sides of the question, both at the state and Supreme Court levels, admitted that the section was ambiguously worded, as did Su-

11. Kathryn Turner [Preyer], "Federalist Policy and the Judiciary Act of 1801," *William and Mary Quarterly,* 3d ser., 22 (January 1965): 15–22. Also Haskins and Johnson, *Foundations of Power,* 107–35.

12. Shaw Livermore, *Early American Land Companies: Their Influence on Corporate Development* (New York, 1939); Barbara Ann Chernow, *Robert Morris, Land Speculator, 1790–1801* (New York, 1978).

preme Court justices on circuit. In such cases, intent was ordinarily discovered by reference to the whole statute: to its legislative history, to its context, and to its preamble. If the "spirit of the Constitution" might be gleaned from such common-sense rules of interpretation, which Marshall believed to be the case, why not the spirit of state statutes?[13]

Indeed, if the 1792 act had a "spirit," it was one that favored the settlers. Such was the thrust of the preamble; such was the implication drawn from the supportive references throughout the bill to the actual settlers. And such was the interpretation adopted by the Pennsylvania Supreme Court. It was also the construction placed on the act in the circuit opinion of Justice Bushrod Washington, whose judgment and good sense were often relied on by his close friend John Marshall. The main policy objective of the legislation, as interpreted by these various authorities, was to place actual settlers on the land regardless of whether they took it directly from the state or indirectly through the company.[14]

In ruling for the Holland Company, Marshall not only ignored these authorities but made no effort to discover the intent of the statute by customary means. Rather his assumption, following the arguments of counsel for the company, was that the confusion in the language of the statute was due to legislative incompetence and could only be corrected by rewriting the statute. Remarkably, and explicitly, this is what his opinion did. "The law requiring two repugnant and incompatible things," he declared in an unmistakably derogatory tone, "is incapable of receiving a literal construction, and must sustain some change of language to be rendered intelligible." Admittedly, he said, the changes introduced by the Court "ought to be as small as possible, and with a view to the sense of the legislature, as manifested by themselves." Rather than make the attempt himself, however, he relied on the Holland Land Company lawyers, whose interpretation "appears to be most reasonable, and to comport best with the general language of the section, and with the nature of the subject." The linguistic analysis, which Marshall derived from the sophisticated argument of Edward Tilghman for the plaintiff, boiled down to a simple point: that by persisting in the *desire* to settle the land instead of actually settling it, the company satisfied the settlement requirement imposed by the 1792 law. To

13. Section 34 of the Judiciary Act of 1789, which governs diversity cases, stipulates that the Court should be guided by the laws of the state in this area. Even Joseph Story, whose interpretation of that section was aggressively nationalist, singled out the law of real property as "state laws strictly local" and thus not subject to federal judicial construction. See R. Kent Newmyer, *Supreme Court Justice Joseph Story: Statesman of the Old Republic* (Chapel Hill, N.C., 1985), 334.

14. *Huidekoper v. Burrus*, 12 Fed. Cas. No. 6,848, C.C.D.Pa. (1804), 840–45.

put it another way, the law would be interpreted one way for the actual settler, whose warrant depended on his occupancy or his actual attempt to occupy the land, and another for the speculators, who purchased the warrant with hard cash and claimed to have persisted in their desire to settle the land without having actually done so.[15]

As Marshall put it, "The two cases are, the actual settler, who has been driven from his settlement, and the warrantee, who has been prevented from making a settlement, but has persisted in his endeavors to make one. It is perfectly clear, that in each case, the provision substitutes something for the settlement to be made within two years from the date of the warrant, and for the residence to continue five years from the commencement of the settlement, both of which were required in the enacting clause. What is that something? The proviso answers, that in the case of an 'actual settler,' it is his being 'driven from his settlement by force of arms of the enemies of the United States,' and in case of his being a grantee or a warrantee, not having settled, it is 'persisting in his endeavors to make such actual settlement.' In neither case, is residence, or persisting in his endeavors at residence, required." In other words, warrant holders who persisted for two years in trying to settle did not have to take up residence later when it was possible. The settlers got possession for having actually settled and cleared the land, built a dwelling on it, endured the hardships of frontier life, and made what payments the legislature saw fit to exact; the company got clear title to the land for having simply paid in full for the warrant. In short, the law followed the money.[16]

Huidekoper's Lessee was an extraordinary opinion for what it attempted, and failed, to do; for the interpretive rules *not* employed; and for the qualifying light it throws on the theory of disinterested judging. It was one thing for the Court to criticize the statute for its obscurity, quite another to rewrite it to judicial, and Holland Land Company, specifications and admit to having done so. What seems to have prompted Marshall in this bold course of action was his stated conviction that the case was really a contract case in which the company purchased land from the state. Once money changed hands, the matter was settled. The interpretation of the 1792 statute contended for by the settlers in effect confiscated the property rights of the speculators. As Marshall summed it up: "All those principles of equity, and fair dealing, which constitute the basis of judicial proceedings, require that courts should lean against such a construc-

15. 3 Cranch 66.
16. 3 Cranch 68–69.

tion." When he rewrote the statute of 1792, and overruled the state court decision in the process, he effectively accomplished this objective.[17]

It was the Court's effort to rationalize the rules of the land market in *Huidekoper's Lessee* that connects the opinion with *Fletcher* and the entire line of Contract Clause cases that followed in its wake. The problem was that judicially imposed rules for the land market, however rational, ran headlong into the rights of state government to make policy governing state land. The Pennsylvania law of 1792, which Marshall and the Court contemptuously rewrote, was an effort to make policy along democratic lines, a point that becomes clear when the Pennsylvania statute is compared to Marshall's interpretation of it. As legislator and judge, Marshall gave the benefit of the doubt to land speculators; Pennsylvania gave it to the ordinary settler. Marshall justified his preference by "principles of equity and fair dealing," in short by the common law's unyielding preference for contractual sanctity and absolute property rights. What he tended to discount, and what the Jeffersonian Democrats realized in Pennsylvania and elsewhere, was that post-Revolution America could have been different. Given the millions of acres of public land, there was no reason why aristocratic land speculators like Robert Morris, operating on eighteenth-century English patterns of patronage and drawing on well-placed connections in state and national government, should engross the public domain at the expense of ordinary settlers, who actually settled and farmed the land.

Marshall's opinion in *Huidekoper's Lessee* did not settle the matter. For three decades or more after the decision, the struggle between the company and the settlers continued. Pennsylvania vigorously protested the opinion as well and worked to introduce an amendment that would have withdrawn similar state-based land cases from the jurisdiction of the federal courts. More immediately, the state simply resisted the enforcement of the decision, thus contributing to the growing tradition of resistance to Supreme Court decisions, which would culminate in the massive anti-Court movement of the 1820s. What would surface in that movement, among other things, was a direct assault on Marshall's theory of disinterested republican judging. That issue was especially conspicuous in *Huidekoper's Lessee*. It is difficult to separate Marshall's aggressive opinion for the speculators from the fact that he was a speculator, and this is not to mention the even more direct connection between the Morris and Marshall families. It was not that *Huidekoper's Lessee* put money in his pocket, but rather that the speculative interests so prominent in that case were

17. 3 Cranch 71.

those with which he resonated. No doubt he believed sincerely in the "principles of equity, and of fair dealing, which constitute the basis of judicial proceedings," for which he vouched in his opinion. Clearly in his Contract Clause decisions, he believed passionately in the Lockean doctrine of possessive individualism rooted in contract. It seems not to have bothered him that these principles as they actually operated in the world carried special benefits for those, like Morris, who had lots of property and political clout. Possibly the mask of principled law worked to disguise its economic and social preferences—not just to the world at large but to the lawmakers themselves.

Fletcher v. Peck and the Privatization of Constitutional Law

Huidekoper's Lessee was important more for what it revealed about judging than what it established as law. As a case of state statutory interpretation, it was limited by the factual environment that gave rise to it, not to mention the peculiarities of Pennsylvania political history. Not so with *Fletcher v. Peck,* where Marshall established the doctrinal starting point for a series of decisions in which the scope and meaning of the Contract Clause were ever more broadly construed to protect private and corporate property from state regulation. As such it provided the constitutional, positive law foundation for the ancient doctrine of vested rights, which was embedded in several centuries of common law. *Fletcher* and its progeny did not destroy the tradition of state involvement in the economy; nor did it prohibit all efforts by the states to regulate private property—witness the rise of state eminent domain law during this period and Story's concurrence in *Dartmouth College v. Woodward,* which permitted states to impose explicit regulations in corporate charters. Nevertheless, *Fletcher* was a formidable obstacle to state interference with private property and remained so until it was modified by the "public trust doctrine," introduced by Justice Stephen Field in *Illinois Central Railroad Co. v. Illinois* (1892) and, until it was overtaken entirely by the realities of the Great Depression, in *Home Building and Loan Association v. Blaisdell* (1934).[18]

In addition to being one of Marshall's most influential opinions, *Fletcher*

18. 290 US 398 (1934). On *Illinois Central Railroad Co. v. Illinois,* see 146 US 387. In the context of late nineteenth-century constitutional history, see Charles McCurdy, "Justice Field and the Jurisprudence of Government-Business Regulations," reprinted in *American Law and the Constitutional Order: Historical Perspectives,* eds. Lawrence M. Friedman and Harry N. Scheiber (Cambridge, Mass., 1978), especially p. 258.

was also one of his most controversial. As in *Huidekoper's Lessee,* the Yazoo case, as it was called, pitted large land speculators against the state legislature, so that the issues involved were again ones in which Marshall was personally interested, and ones in which personal interest may have subtly intruded into his opinion. Two additional factors add some credence to that possibility. One was the fact that the Court proceeded to hear the case despite clear evidence that it was collusive or "feigned" since both parties wanted the same outcome. The other was the fact that Marshall's interpretation appeared to depart from the generally understood meaning of the Contract Clause, namely that it applied only to contracts between individuals and not to those in which the state was a party. Put simply the questions are these: Did Marshall play free and easy with the Framers' intent in order to rationalize and privatize the land market, and was he was moved to do so by his long-running war with Virginia over his investment in the Fairfax lands?

The case originated in a sale by Georgia of some 35 million acres, roughly the combined acreage of the present states of Alabama and Mississippi, to four land companies, for a penny and a half per acre. State land sales to private parties was common practice, and sweetheart deals between speculators and state officials were not that unusual. What made the Yazoo case unique was the amount of land at stake and the magnitude and brazenness of corruption involved. Shortly after the act of sale, it was discovered that all of the legislators who had voted for it, save one unsung hero, had been bribed by the speculators. Among those implicated in the fraud were two United States senators; two congressmen; three judges, including James Wilson of the United States Supreme Court; and a territorial governor, not to mention a number of other prominent businessmen and politicians. Robert Morris was also a key player and so, indirectly, was his son-in-law James Marshall. A political campaign waged in the name of republicanism against land speculators and political corruption led to a purified legislature in 1796, which promptly repealed the act of the previous legislature. In the meantime, land acquired under the 1795 act had been sold to third parties, the most important of which was the Boston-based New England Mississippi Land Company, which included leading political figures of both parties. It was the effort of the New England Mississippi Land Company speculators to validate their title to the Yazoo lands in the federal courts that led finally to Marshall's far-reaching opinion in 1810.[19]

19. *Fletcher v. Peck,* 6 Cranch 87. For extensive discussion of the case see Magrath, *Yazoo,* and also Haskins and Johnson, *Foundations of Power,* 336–54.

In the fourteen years of political maneuvering preceding the Court's decision in 1810, the distinction between law and politics had all but been obliterated, precisely the distinction, that is to say, on which Marshall rested the authority of the Court. Yazoo was a political issue on both the state and national levels. The question was politicized at the national level, even before the Georgia Repeal Act, when President Washington, noting the impact of the sale on Indian relations, asked the Senate to investigate its legality. On the state level, Yazoo corruption and states' rights became the rallying cry of a victorious Democratic-Republican Party, led by James Jackson, who resigned from the Senate to lead the anti-Yazoo forces. The issue tended to break down along party lines. But moderates in both parties hoped for a political compromise, in part because powerful interests in both had purchased lands from the original Yazoo speculators and in part because the Democratic-Republicans wanted to build a party organization in Federalist New England where pro-Yazoo sentiment was strong. Despite impassioned opposition from John Randolph and his followers, who made the Yazoo deal the subject of a jeremiad on the decline of republicanism, a political compromise was worked out in which Congress acquired title to the disputed lands in 1798. Georgia was given $1,250,000 to relinquish its claims, and Congress agreed to set aside 5 million acres to satisfy investors, whose claims were finally settled by a federal commission in 1814.[20]

Fletcher v. Peck was the centerpiece in a legal stratagem designed by the speculators in the New England Mississippi Land Company to strengthen their case before the federal claims commissioners. The company, which was centered in Boston but included leading politicians in both parties, purchased 11 million acres of Yazoo land at ten cents per acre from the Georgia Mississippi Land Company, one of four companies that purchased from the state. The sale returned 650 percent on the original investment. With windfall profits on the line and purchase money of $1,138,000 in jeopardy, both companies had ample reason to impugn the legality of the Georgia Rescinding Act of 1796, which stood in the way of clear title. In fact, the ink was barely dry on that act when Alexander Hamilton and Robert Goodloe Harper, an investor in and lawyer for the original land companies, fixed on the strategy that would bring the case into the federal courts. They argued that the state law authorizing the sale was a contract and that the Rescinding Act violated the Contract Clause of the Constitution, which prohibited states from passing laws impairing the obligation of contracts. This bold idea had its difficulties, however, the first

---

20. Magrath deals with the political settlement of the Yazoo claims in *Yazoo*, ch. 2.

being the uncertain meaning of the Contract Clause itself: whether it was intended to reach public contracts in which the state was a party or only private ones between individuals. If the former were intended, then the federal judiciary would confront state legislative authority head-on. Needless to say, a decision by the Court overturning an act of the sovereign people of Georgia on a matter of state law would be perceived as political. Exacerbating this problem was the Court's ruling in *Chisholm v. Georgia* that Georgia could be sued in federal courts by private citizens, who it turned out were Yazoo speculators. The Eleventh Amendment, passed in 1798, reversed the Court on this point, but the memory still rankled Georgians and would continue to do so well into the next century.[21]

The litigation, which brought the conflict before Georgia and the Marshall Court to a head, and which circumvented the Eleventh Amendment bar against private suits against states, originated on June 1, 1803, in the federal circuit court sitting in Boston. The plaintiff was Robert Fletcher from New Hampshire, who had purchased 15,000 acres of Yazoo lands from John Peck of Massachusetts, a speculator associated with the New England Mississippi Land Company. Arguing that the Georgia Rescinding Act of 1796 had invalidated the deed of sale to these lands, Peck sued Fletcher for breach of warranty of title, that is, for selling land he did not own. Historians have confirmed what contemporaries suspected and what is clear on the face of it: the case was a collusive one. Fletcher and Peck were not truly adversaries, since both wanted a decision that would validate title by declaring the Georgia Rescinding Act unconstitutional. Whether this was a serious obstacle for the Court is not clear, though Justice Johnson was concerned enough to mention it in his opinion. Obviously Marshall was not troubled, and he probably persuaded Johnson to drop his objections. But the collusive nature of the case worked to undercut Marshall's contention that the Court and its chief justice were above politics.[22]

Collusive though it was, the litigation strategy in *Fletcher* was adroit, because a suit between individuals brought under diversity of citizenship jurisdiction permitted the lawyers to argue the constitutionality of the Georgia Rescinding Act without presuming to sue the state. By casting the issue in terms of breach of warranty of title, the pleadings permitted lawyers, and Marshall as

21. Ibid., 15, on the percent of profit; Ibid., 20, for a discussion of Robert Goodloe Harper's *The Case of the Georgia Sales on the Mississippi Considered . . .* (1814).

22. On the matter of collusion, see Magrath, *Yazoo*, 54, and Haskins and Johnson, *Foundations of Power*, 343–45. Some scholars suspect Marshall may have persuaded Johnson to go along despite Johnson's misgivings about the feigned nature of the case. PJM, Editorial Note, 7: 227.

well, to speak law, not politics, a point of special importance given the obvious political implications of the case. Seeking a decision by the Supreme Court to leverage a favorable decision from the commission appointed to settle the dispute was wise, too, given the fact that the political branches were controlled by the Jeffersonian Democrats, the party most inclined to defend state authority and question the republican values of greedy land speculators.

Fletcher was deeply politicized by the time it reached the Court. It originated as an economic issue, and in fifteen years—in state legislatures, in Congress, in party councils, in pamphlets, in newspapers, in the personal correspondence of men from all sections—it came to subsume and reflect the great political issues of the age: republicanism, since the question of morality in government was on the line; and Federalism, since the struggle pitted state legislatures, which claimed in the name of republican principles to speak for the sovereign people, against the Court, which claimed to do the same. When the lawyers entered the picture, which they did almost immediately, they brought with them a strategy fashioned to make law serve the political and economic objectives of their clients. It would appear law and politics had become inseparably entwined.

In *Marbury,* Marshall asserted that law and politics *were* separable; now in *Fletcher* he had to demonstrate the truth of his assertion. This he did by turning a public-policy issue into a question for the common law. In speaking the language of covenant, of breach of deed, he took for granted or possibly even deliberately obscured what had to be proven: that the case turned on "a private contract between two individuals," which a court of law could resolve. As he put it, "The question was, in its nature, a question of title" to be governed by "those rules of property which are common to all citizens of the United States." Moreover, those same common-law rules of private property also controlled the Georgia legislature, or so Marshall and his brethren ruled. The state statute of 1795 under which the speculators held title, as the justices saw it, was tantamount to a private contract between individuals. The Rescinding Act of 1796 was an unconstitutional impairment of that contract.[23]

But how was it, one might ask, as lawyers for Georgia *did* ask, that a state statute passed to correct massive fraud could by the wave of a judicial wand be reduced to the status of a private contract between individuals? Was not Georgia a state with sovereign powers? Did not the representatives of the sov-

23. 6 Cranch 133–34. The editors of *The Papers of John Marshall* noted that pleadings were lawyer's law. PJM, 7: 229.

ereign people of a state have the power to repeal a law that gave away the public lands of the state in clear violation of all the tenets of republican government? Marshall acknowledged the questions without answering them. Georgia *was* a sovereign state. It *was* a universally recognized principle "as a matter of general legislation" that "one legislature cannot abridge the powers of a succeeding legislature." And fraud *was* a problem. "That corruption should find its way into the governments of our infant republics and contaminate the very sources of legislation, or that impure motives should contribute to the passage of a law or the formation of a legislative contract, are circumstances most deeply to be deplored." The chief justice even conceded, though discreetly, that courts would ordinarily "set aside a conveyance obtained by fraud, and the fraud be clearly proved," providing the conveyance was between the original parties.[24]

All of these concessions came to nothing, however, because the contract Marshall chose to make dispositive, and here he followed the pleadings of Fletcher's lawyers, was between Fletcher and Peck. By his reckoning, both men were innocent third parties, purchasers in good faith who had no knowledge of the Rescinding Act of 1796. "If the original transaction was infected with fraud, these purchasers did not participate in it, and had no notice of it. They were innocent. Yet the legislature of Georgia has involved them in the fate of the first parties to the transaction, and, if the [rescinding] act be valid, has annihilated their rights also."[25]

Marshall and the Court, it should be noted, had no way of knowing for certain whether Fletcher and Peck were really innocent third parties, that is to say, whether they contracted without knowing that Georgia had rescinded the 1795 act *or was about to do so.* This key question should have been argued by Luther Martin for Fletcher, and for Georgia. In fact, Martin, despite his reputation for astuteness, never presented a single substantive point of law for the Court's edification; indeed, he was so drunk Marshall had to adjourn the Court until he sobered up. In any case, given the anti-Yazoo political agitation that preceded the Georgia elections of 1796, there is considerable reason to doubt whether Fletcher could really have been ignorant of the repeal movement. Moreover, even as the 1795 act of sale was being debated in the legislature, a strong principled opposition to it, led by William Crawford among others, was taking shape. One thing was clear: if the speculators were aware

24. 6 Cranch 135, 130, 133.
25. Ibid., 132.

of the repeal, then a transaction under innocent-third-party guise would be a logical first step in circumventing it. The fact that the case was collusive only adds to this likelihood. The New England Mississippi Land Company, of which Peck was a member, was after all a well-oiled special interest group composed of sophisticated lawyers, seasoned politicians, and land speculators. With millions of acres of land and hundreds of thousands of dollars on the line, "innocent" hardly seems the appropriate adjective to describe them.[26]

Nevertheless, the innocent-third-party argument was a vital part of Marshall's opinion both legally and rhetorically. Legally, as noted, it permitted the case to be pleaded, and decided, as a private contract between two individuals, thus circumventing the Eleventh Amendment bar. He derived considerable rhetorical advantage, as well, by emphasizing the innocent-party argument, since it shifted attention away from the Rescinding Act, which was seen by many in Georgia and elsewhere as an act taken to redeem republican justice and honest government from the corrupting influence of land jobbers. But sanctity of contract and property rights were also republican matters. By focusing on them instead of the fraud perpetrated by the speculators, Marshall shifted the antirepublican onus from greedy and corrupt speculators to the legislature of Georgia, perhaps even to the people of Georgia themselves. Marshall protested that he did not intend "to speak with disrespect of the legislature of Georgia or of its acts," but he did so unrelentingly throughout his opinion. "The legislature of Georgia was a party to this transaction," he declared in reference to the destruction of the property rights conveyed in the private contract between Fletcher and Peck, "and for a party to pronounce its own deed invalid, whatever cause may be assigned for its invalidity, must be considered as a mere act of power which must find its vindication in a train of reasoning not often heard in the courts of justice." And again he said: "If the legislature felt itself absolved from those rules of property which are common to all the citizens of the United States, and from those principles of equity which are acknowledged in all our courts, its act is to be supported by its power alone, and the same power may divest any other individual of his lands, if it shall be the will of the legislature so to exert it." In speaking of the new national government in 1788, Marshall praised power to the heavens; when Georgia's legislature exercised it in pursuit of community justice in 1796, it was an act from hell.[27]

26. Magrath discusses *Fletcher* as interest-group litigation in *Yazoo*, ch. 3, and comments on Martin's drunkenness at 68–69.

27. 6 Cranch 134, 132, 134, in order of quotes.

Marshall's analysis had subtly transformed the issue of republican morality into a question of individual rights, as guaranteed by law, versus the naked legislative power of the state. It boiled down, as it had in *Marbury* and Burr and before that in the Robbins case, to a question of law as distinct from, and superior to, politics. The problem of corruption, Marshall conceded, was real, but legislative immorality was not "examinable in a court of justice." In what manner, he went on to argue, could a court measure corruption? "Must it be direct corruption, or would interest or undue influence of any kind be sufficient? Must the vitiating cause operate on a majority, or on what number of members?" For the Court to answer these questions, "to enter into an inquiry respecting the corruption of the sovereign power of a state," would not only be impossible to perform, but it "would be indecent, in the extreme." Corruption was a matter of politics between the people of Georgia and their elected representatives. Here, the chief justice ignored the fact that the elected representatives of Georgia had acted: they had thrown the corrupt legislators out in 1796 and had repudiated a contract that originated in bribery and corruption. In any case, as he saw it, the validity of that political act "does not appear to the court" in the pleadings presented. Forget that the pleadings were collusive and that the Court might have chosen not to attend to them. The question they presented concerned not whether the sovereign authority of the state included the power to repudiate corruption, but whether the state could void a public grant to a private land company that operated to void a private contract between Fletcher and Peck. By the lawyers' arguments and Marshall's reasoning, this was a legal question on which the Court and the law were more than ready to act.[28]

By making the question an exclusively legal one, Marshall was well on his way to the conclusion he no doubt wanted to reach, which was that Georgia's grant of land in 1795, however fraudulent, was a contract that was impaired by the Rescinding Act of 1796 in violation of Article 1, Section 10. To reach that conclusion, however, he had to demonstrate that the constitutional prohibition against impairment applied to contracts in which the state was a party as well as to those between private parties. To establish this proposition, or circumvent the problem, he turned to private contract law for a working definition, a strategy that imparted a common-law tone to the entire opinion. Working creatively from Blackstone's definition of executory and executed contracts, the chief justice reasoned that "the contract between Georgia and

28. Ibid., 130–31.

the purchasers was executed by the grant. . . . A grant, in its own nature, amounts to an extinguishment of the right of the grantor, and implies a contract not to reassert that right." And since "a grant is a contract executed, the obligation of which still continues, and since the constitution used the general term contract, without distinguishing between those which are executory and those which are executed, it must be construed to comprehend the latter as well as the former." Having collapsed the meaning of public and private contracts, Marshall was now ready to interpret the Contract Clause in Article 1, Section 10. He put the question this way: "If, under a fair construction of the constitution, grants are comprehended under the term contracts, is a grant from the state excluded from the operation of the provision? Is the clause to be considered as inhibiting the state from impairing the obligation of contracts between two individuals, but as excluding from that inhibition contracts made with itself."[29]

By obliterating the distinction between public and private contracts, Marshall got to the central question: Could the state exempt itself from the operation of the great principle of contractual sanctity, which was demanded of all citizens and which was guaranteed by the Constitution itself? To ask the question was to answer it. And with his answer subtly implanted in the mind of the reader, Marshall then turned to a favorite topic, what the Constitution and the Founding Fathers thought about the nature and limits of state sovereignty: "Whatever respect might have been felt for the state sovereignties, it is not to be disguised that the Framers of the constitution viewed, with some apprehension, the violent acts which might grow out of the feelings of the moment; and that the people of the United States, in adopting that instrument, have manifested a determination to shield themselves and their property from the effects of those sudden and strong passions to which men are exposed. The restrictions on the legislative power of the states are obviously founded in this sentiment; and the constitution of the United States contains what may be deemed a bill of rights for the people of each state."[30]

This seemingly harmless rhetoric embodied several ideas crucial to Marshall's argument. One such was the standard Federalist argument that the Constitution itself was a charter of rights for the citizens of every state. And among the rights guaranteed, none was more important than the right to be secure in one's property. This position Marshall supported by reference to the "senti-

29. Ibid., 137.
30. Ibid., 137–38.

ment" of the time, which was put forth as a rule of construction when the words of the document were unclear. Having shown that the meaning of words can be understood by reference to history, Marshall, as he had in *Huidekoper's Lessee* with such devastating effect, then turned to the words themselves and to yet another axiom of construction: that the primary meaning of the Constitution derives from the words of the text and, as a corollary, that the meaning of words and phrases are derived from common sense and the general architecture of the document of which they are a part. Meaning emanates from syntax. He started with the concept, already set forth, that constitutions, including the one of 1787, are limiting devices. Then he proceeded to the "sentiment" of the preconvention period, which singled out states as the special target for limitation; then to Article 1, Section 10, which, in all three of its sections, specifies no fewer than fourteen things prohibited to the states. Then he moved to the prohibition against the impairment of contracts, which, for purposes of analysis, Marshall yoked to the prohibition against bills of attainders and ex post facto laws, which directly precede the Contract Clause in the text. If the express purpose of these two prohibitions was to protect "the lives and fortunes of individuals" from the power of state legislatures, asked Marshall, "what motive then for implying in words which import a general prohibition to impair the obligation of contracts, an exception in favor of the right to impair the obligation of those contracts into which the state may enter?" Still more pointedly he said, "The legislature is then prohibited from passing a law by which a man's estate or any part of it shall be seized for a crime which was not declared, by some previous law, to render him liable to that punishment. Why, then, should violence be done to the natural meaning of words for the purpose of leaving to the legislature the power of seizing for public use, the estate of an individual in the form of a law annulling the title by which he holds that estate? ... This rescinding act would have the effect of an *ex post facto* law. It forfeits the estate of Fletcher for a crime not committed by himself, but by those from whom he purchased. This cannot be effected in the form of an *ex post facto* law or bill of attainder; why, then, is it allowable in the form of a law annulling the original grant?"[31]

Of course, it wasn't allowable. "It is, then," declared the chief justice, "the unanimous opinion of the court that ... Georgia was restrained, either by general principles which are common to our free institutions, or by the particular provisions of the constitution of the U. States, from passing a law whereby the

31. Ibid., 138–39.

estate of the plaintiff . . . could be constitutionally and legally impaired and rendered null and void." Every justice agreed. The only cavil came from Johnson, whose separate concurrence ignored Marshall's Contract Clause interpretation and voided the Rescinding Act as a violation of natural law "on the reason and nature of things: a principle which will impose laws even on the Deity."[32]

Authorities agree that *Fletcher* was "one of the leading decisions of American constitutional law." On a practical level, it was an unqualified victory for the land speculators, putting a constitutional foundation under what Beveridge described as "the greatest real estate deal in history." *Fletcher* did not immediately put money directly in speculators' pockets, but it did greatly strengthen the claims they were making for congressional compensation, claims settled favorably for the speculators in 1814. *Fletcher* also occasioned the first instance of the Court striking down a state act as being in violation of the Constitution; to quote Beveridge again, the opinion was "one of the earliest and strongest judicial assertions of the supremacy of Nationalism over Localism." It was also the first definitive reading of the Contract Clause of the Constitution, one that, according to Peter Magrath, "provided the first great constitutional mechanism for protecting vested property rights." Whether the opinion drew on the culture of contract that was already well entrenched or whether it created that culture shall be considered shortly. But this much seems clear: by giving the sanctity of contract the sanction of supreme law, the opinion, especially as the principle expanded from land grants to corporate charters, operated to create a stable, reliable environment for all sorts of commercial negotiations in which the state was a party.[33]

By adapting the Constitution to the needs of market capitalism, Marshall put the Court on the winning side of American history. But was his opinion good law; or, to recast the question, was he guided by objective legal principles, as he claimed, or by political considerations (his well-known hatred of state legislatures) and personal interest (his equally well-known involvement in land speculation)? One contemporary who had serious doubts about both the wisdom of Marshall's opinion and its objectivity was Justice William Johnson. It might be argued that Johnson was not a trustworthy critic, since he had been appointed in 1804 by Jefferson for the specific purpose of countering Mar-

32. Ibid., 139–43.

33. Albert J. Beveridge quoted on the real estate deal in *The Life of John Marshall* (Boston, New York, 1916–1919) 3: 551; second quote on 556. Magrath, *Yazoo*, 101.

shall's growing influence on the Court. The South Carolinian, however, was remarkably independent, as Jefferson discovered when the new justice challenged the wide-ranging executive discretion Jefferson claimed in regard to the Embargo of 1807. Johnson also disappointed Jefferson by favoring the appellate powers of the Court and the implied powers of Congress as much as did the chief justice. Indeed, shortly after his appointment, Johnson supported Marshall's rule-of-law position in *Marbury* and *Burr.* In *Fletcher,* however, he not only parted company with the chief justice, but raised serious questions about his objectivity.[34]

Johnson's concurrence in *Fletcher* overturned the Georgia Rescinding Act by reference to natural law rather than to the Contract Clause. Indeed, by referring to property as so much a part of an individual's rights as "to become intimately blended with his existence, as essentially so as the blood that circulates through his system," Johnson's opinion might appear lacking in substance. Taken seriously and in its entirety, however, his concurrence is a biting and realistic critique of Marshall's opinion, starting with the fact that the case was collusive. Johnson not only made that fact a point of record, which invited other critics to do the same, but intimated that he had been pressured by the chief justice to go along with the majority against his will, which was another familiar Jeffersonian criticism of Marshall. As Johnson put it, "I have been very unwilling to proceed to the decisions of this cause at all. It appears to me to be strong evidence, upon the face of it, of being a mere feigned case. It is our duty to decide on the rights, but not on the speculations of parties. My confidence, however, in the respectable gentlemen who have been engaged for the parties, has induced me to abandon my scruples, in the belief they would never consent to impose a mere feigned case upon this court." Johnson's statement is important, not only because it suggests that he might have felt considerable pressure from his Federalist colleagues on the Court, including the chief justice, but because it tells us that the pleadings, which were loaded against the state and in favor of privatizating the Contract Clause, were feigned and need not have been decided at all. If political considerations call law into action, can law be above politics?[35]

Johnson's main point, however, indeed the main reason for his concurring

34. On Johnson's jurisprudence and his independence, see Donald G. Morgan, *Justice William Johnson, The First Dissenter: The Career and Constitutional Philosophy of a Jeffersonian Judge* (Columbia, S.C., 1954).

35. 6 Cranch 143, 147, 148.

234 / John Marshall *and the* Heroic Age *of the* Supreme Court

opinion, was to challenge Marshall's legal reasoning about the Contract Clause. As he put it regarding his concurrence: "I have thrown out these ideas, that I may have it distinctly understood, that my opinion . . . is not founded on the provision in the constitution of the United States, relative to laws impairing the obligation of contracts." Where Marshall was concerned with the property rights of speculators, Johnson was concerned with the impact of the decision on the legitimate authority of state government to speak for the public interest, "a subject of the greatest delicacy and much difficulty." Rather than expanding on the natural-law premise, which he reasonably might have been expected to do, he started from a positivist, republican premise, that "the states and the United States are continually legislating on the subject of contracts, prescribing the mode of authentication, the time within which suits shall be prosecuted for them, in many cases, affecting existing contracts by the laws which they pass, and declaring them to cease or lose their effect for want of compliance, in the parties, with such statutory provisions. All these acts appear to be within the most correct limits of legislative power, and most beneficially exercise, and certainly could not have been intended to be affected by this constitutional provision." Marshall's interpretation, in other words, said Johnson, "is going very far beyond the obvious and necessary import of the words, and would operate to restrict the states in the exercise of that right which every community must exercise, of possessing itself of the property of the individual, and which perhaps amounts to nothing more than a power to oblige him to sell and convey, when the public necessities require it."[36]

Johnson's opinion, which drew on anti-Yazoo sentiment going back to the Georgia rescinding of 1796, puts Marshall's opinion in critical perspective. What Marshall did in *Fletcher,* which is precisely what he tried to do in the *Batture* opinion in the same year and what the Court would succeed in doing over the next twenty years, was to privatize public law and in the process shorten the reach of state sovereignty. A grant, so the train of his inferential logic went, was a contract within the meaning of Article 1, Section 10; the state was for purposes of interpreting the "contract" to be considered as nothing but a private party to a private contract. Even the principles of private law and equity, which voided contracts originating in fraud, were rendered largely inoperative because of the third-party argument, that is to say, the equitable defense of nonpayment good for original parties did not apply to future contracts resting on the original one. Gone for practical purposes, as the preface to the

36. Ibid., 144–45.

rescinding legislation emphasized, was the ability of the people of Georgia and their representatives to correct massive corruption—even if they were willing to compensate truly innocent investors for losses on their investments, though not for anticipated profits, which the Rescinding Act of 1796 did.[37]

Johnson's concurrence, along with the obvious political aspects of the case, raises the question of whether Marshall really believed that he and the majority had risen above politics. Or, had they found law, not made it? It is tempting to say no. Indeed, given that the decision in *Fletcher* was congenial to Marshall's personal interest as a land speculator, it is possible to fashion a plausible conspiratorial interpretation in which the chief justice cynically used the law as a cover for a blatantly self-interested, policy-making political decision. The determination of his motivation in that case, and in other related cases, however, is not so simple. That personal experience and personal interest influenced Marshall, there can be little doubt. Whether the connection was consciously conspiratorial is doubtful, unless by conspiracy we mean the manner in which the common law, the Constitution, and capitalism were symbiotically connected. As a member of Virginia's elite, Marshall grew up in a society built on private property, especially real property. He spent his professional life making law serve those who had property and wanted to get more or keep what they had. The Framers were of like mind. They may not have had public contracts specifically in mind when they wrote the Contract Clause, but as Jennifer Nedelsky and others have shown, they most assuredly had private property in mind when they wrote the Constitution. Experience under the Articles government taught them, as it had Marshall, that democratic state legislatures armed with unlimited powers posed a serious threat to property rights. Marshall may have stretched the constitutional language of Article 1, Section 10, to reach public contracts, but he did so in the "spirit of the Constitution," as he often put it. That spirit was as much "liberal" as it was republican. If he took considerable interpretive liberties, he did so on the way to a decision that comported closely to the general, if not the explicit, intent of the Framers. For him, as for them, private property and liberty were inseparable, and both were guaranteed by the common-law doctrine of contract, which now became a part of the Constitution. In a manner of speaking, public law had been privatized.[38]

37. On the privatization movement in early national American law, see George Dargo, *Law in the New Republic: Private Law and the Public Estate* (New York, 1983).

38. Jennifer Nedelsky, *Private Property and the Limits of American Constitutionalism: The Madisonian Framework and Its Legacy* (Chicago, 1990).

John Marshall, Market Capitalism, and the Legacy of Fletcher v. Peck

Great legal opinions have a way of transcending the factual circumstances from which they arose, and *Fletcher* is a case in point. However tinged with politics, it immediately assumed the status of unquestioned legal precedent. Even a cursory glance at Shepard's citation system, which traces the citation history of the Court's decisions in federal and state courts, reveals the long shadow cast by *Fletcher*. Over the years, the decision was cited thousands of times by federal and state courts and by judges of all persuasions. There was much to cite. Sometimes it was Marshall's definition of *ex post facto*, or his brief obiter dictum on Indian land titles, or even his statement about judicial restraint and the inappropriateness of judicial inquiry into legislative motive. But mainly, the decision was employed to shield private property from state regulation. Indeed, until the rise of the substantive interpretation of the Fourteenth Amendment in the late nineteenth century, the Contract Clause as construed by Marshall was the primary constitutional bulwark against state economic regulation. Extrapolating from his Contract Clause decisions and from *Marbury*, which they proceeded to take out of context, late nineteenth-century conservative champions of laissez-faire enlisted Marshall in their cause.[39]

The assumption that Marshall's jurisprudence applied automatically to the world of legal formalism was highly anachronistic to say the least. Nevertheless, it seems clear that his opinion in *Fletcher* fit readily into the emerging market culture, which relied on contractual freedom and dependability to liberate economic individualism. As much was clear in the case of *New Jersey v. Wilson* (1812), the first in a series of major Contract Clause decisions curbing state legislative power. The facts of the *Wilson* case went back to an agreement in 1758 between commissioners representing the colony of New Jersey and the Delaware Indians, wherein the Indians agreed to surrender all claims to a vast body of land in return for certain other lands within the colony granted to them in perpetuity. In an act passed in 1758, the colonial legislature accepted the terms of this mutual cession of land and, apparently as an inducement to the Indians to do the same, provided that the lands newly granted to the Indians "shall not hereafter be subject to any tax, any law usage or custom to the contrary thereof, in any wise notwithstanding." In 1801 the Indians requested

39. Magrath traces the impact of *Fletcher* on American constitutional law in *Yazoo*, ch. 7. Also see Wright, *Contract Clause*.

the right to sell their New Jersey lands so they could join other members of the tribe living in New York. Permission to sell was granted by statute in December 1801, and in 1803 the lands were sold to the plaintiffs George Painter and others. When the state legislature repealed the tax exemption section of the 1758 act in 1804 and assessed the new owners for taxes, the owners sued in the state courts, arguing that the tax exemption provisions, as part of the legislative grant of 1758, constituted a contract the state was prohibited from repealing by Article 1, Section 10, as interpreted in *Fletcher.* The New Jersey Supreme Court of Judicature, which heard the case in 1807, was not persuaded and ruled for the state, whereupon the plaintiffs brought the case to the Supreme Court under Section 25, which meant the Court was restricted to the federal question, that is, to the applicability of the Contract Clause à la *Fletcher.*[40]

Marshall reduced the facts of the case to a simple self-answering proposition/question: *Fletcher,* "decided in this Court on solemn argument and much deliberation," established that the Contract Clause of the Constitution "extends to contracts to which a state is a party," so that the "question then is narrowed to the inquiry whether in the case stated, a contract existed? and whether that contract is violated by the act of 1804?" His answer, which closely followed the plaintiff's argument at the state level and which was supported by a unanimous Court, came in two short paragraphs that vault deftly across the difficulties to what is presented as a self-evident conclusion: that "every requisite to the formation of a contract is found in the proceedings between the then colony of New Jersey and the Indians." "A proposition . . . is made, the terms stipulated, the consideration agreed upon." The Indians, then, executed their deed of cession and the assembly executed its side of the bargain in the act of 1758. Not a single reference is made to the New Jersey act of 1803, which repealed the tax exemption provisions of the 1758 statute and which the Court voided. Could a colonial legislature, operating in the legal context of the British Empire, pass a law that would forever diminish the state of New Jersey's power to tax? Could a provision of the Constitution of 1787 concerning contracts be applied retrospectively to uphold such an intrusion into the sovereign powers of a state? Was it really unarguable that the tax exemption extended to the Indians went with the land, when it was clearly passed to deal specifically with the Indians? This was an especially relevant question since, by the Court's ruling, the plaintiffs came to hold public land on privileged terms not applicable to other buyers, thus violating the functional justi-

40. 7 Cranch 165; facts recounted, ibid., 164–66.

fication for judicial intervention in the first place, which was to make land law uniform.[41]

Marshall's failure to address all or any of these questions throws some interesting light on his use of *Fletcher* as a controlling precedent. That decision, rather than being the starting point of the traditional common-law mode of reasoning, the kind Marshall used with great effectiveness when he wanted to, now became an excuse for not reasoning at all. Perhaps the reason for not reasoning was that *Fletcher* was not fully applicable, at least if one adhered to the basic rule of stare decisis, that doctrine cannot be separated from the facts that gave rise to it. Looking closely at the facts, comparing those in *Fletcher* with those in *Wilson*, might well lead one to question Marshall's easy assumption that the former decision was so obviously controlling. What did seem to be controlling, or at least constant, instead, was a general disposition on his part to bend common-law methodology to create uniform, property-protecting rules for the land market.

The need to settle land titles on regular principles was especially urgent during the early nineteenth century, when Americans in ever-increasing numbers poured into new territories and newly admitted western states. So it is not surprising that monitoring land law was an important function of the Marshall Court both before and after *Fletcher*. While that case was central, it should be noted that the lower federal courts, along with the state judiciaries, played an important role in shaping land law, especially in the western states. Moreover, only a small number of the Court's land-law decisions were constitutional in nature. One careful scholar noted that in the years between 1815 and 1825, the Court decided no fewer than eighty-three cases based on the common-law action of ejectment, which was the common-law method of settling title disputes. These cases, coming under diversity and Section 25 jurisdiction, "constituted 21.2% of the High Court's total caseload in these eleven years, or 30.6% of its non-maritime business." Most of these cases, along with the key constitutional questions, emanated from Kentucky, Tennessee, and Ohio, which states were among the first recipients of the vast wave of Americans flooding into the new West. Kentucky was the source of particular difficulty for the Court, and for Marshall personally, because of the separation agreement of 1792 between that state and Virginia, which aimed to secure the holdings of Virginia specula-

41. Ibid., 166–67.

tors in the new state. Among those speculators were the chief justice, his father, and other members of his family.[42]

Marshall's impact on this emerging body of American land law was critical, although it is hard to delineate precisely given the collective nature of the Court's deliberations and its reliance on state and lower federal court decisions and arguments of lawyers. He did not speak for the Court in such cases as *Terrett v. Taylor* (1815) and *Green v. Biddle* (1821, 1823), two leading land cases in the decade after 1815. He also recused himself from the Virginia case of *Fairfax Devisee v. Hunter's Lessee* (1818), in which he had a direct conflict of interest, and in the famous case of *Martin v. Hunter's Lessee* (1816), which grew out of the *Fairfax* case. He did, however, speak for the Court in many of the private law cases that came before the Court during his tenure, including several in which his or family interests were directly involved. Though not dramatic, these run-of-the-docket cases settled disputes over tens of thousands of acres and in the process brought a semblance of legal order out of the political rivalries that ordinarily settled frontier land disputes.[43]

In treating these mundane but essential matters, the justices followed the policy preferences of *Fletcher, Huidekoper's Lessee,* and *Wilson.* This is to say, they rationalized land law to serve the needs of large speculators and in the process curbed the power of state legislatures to shape public land policy, even while conceding their right to do so. Running through these decisions was a consistent disregard of equity and a preference for the harsher doctrines of the common law. *Fletcher* set the tone and the agenda, reminding us again of the intellectual symbiosis between public and private law. Two cases dealing with state law and public land policy during this formative period illustrate the expansive nature of private contract doctrine. Neither was a Marshall opinion, but both built on his vested-rights rendition of the Contract Clause in the Yazoo case. The first was *Terrett v. Taylor,* which involved a tract of land purchased from a private party by the Episcopal Church in 1770, whose title was then indirectly sanctioned by three subsequent state statutes: the first in 1776, which, according to Story's opinion, "completely confirmed and established the rights of the church to all its lands and other property"; another in 1784,

---

42. Sandra VanBurkleo, "'An Independence Beggarly and Barren': Kentucky Land Politics, Depression, and the Case of *Green v. Biddle*," MS, 60; see appendices, tables 2 and 4.

43. For a scholarly analysis of Marshall's personal involvement in Kentucky land cases, see Mary K. Tachau, *Federal Courts in the Early Republic: Kentucky, 1789–1816* (Princeton, N.J., 1978), especially 184–99.

which made the minister and vestry of a corporation capable of holding and using in perpetuity all glebe lands and other church property; and a third in 1788, which gave the trustees of each parish the right "to take care of and manage" church property. The question turned on the legality of the acts of 1798 and 1801, the first of which repealed the previous statutes as violations of the separation of church and state provided for in the Virginia constitution of 1776 and the second of which authorized the overseers of the poor in the parish, now a part of the District of Columbia, to sell church lands and "appropriate the proceeds to the use of the poor of the parish."[44]

One insightful analysis of *Terrett* concluded that the case was "absurdly easy to decide," first, because it plainly took property from one party and gave it to another in violation of agreed upon first principles and, second, because it was a state regulation of property within the District of Columbia, which was, according to the Constitution, the exclusive domain of Congress. Story, as was his wont, made simple matters complex. In voiding the state statutes, he and the majority stood on the "great and fundamental principle of a republican government, the right of the citizens to the free enjoyment of their property legally acquired," and "on the principles of natural justice, upon the fundamental laws of every free government, upon the spirit and the letter of the Constitution of the United States, and upon the decisions of the most respectable judicial tribunals." Though unspecified, "the letter of the Constitution" was clearly Article 1, Section 10, perhaps the Taking Clause as well, even though it applied only to Congress. The "decisions of the most respectable judicial tribunals" meant the Supreme Court in *Fletcher*. The problem was the plain fact that none of the state acts voided even remotely resembled a contract within the meaning of Article 1, Section 10. Judging by Story's opinion, the Contract Clause was well on its way to becoming an all-purpose instrument for protecting private property from state regulation, even when no contract was involved.[45]

The most telling and politically explosive example of the expansive nature of Marshall's contract doctrine in the area of land law was *Green v. Biddle*, which generated not just one controversial decision but two, the first in 1821, written by Story, and the second in 1823, written by Bushrod Washington. The

---

44. VanBurkleo, "'Independence Beggarly and Barren,'" 72–80. *Terrett v. Taylor,* 9 Cranch 43.

45. I am indebted to G. Edward White's careful analysis of *Terrett* in his *Marshall Court,* 608–11. *Terrett* at 9 Cranch 50–52.

issue in both decisions concerned the constitutionality of the Kentucky claimant statutes of 1797 and 1812, and that question in turn hinged on the meaning of the agreement between Virginia and Kentucky at the time of the latter's separation in 1789. The latter agreement provided that land titles in the new state of Kentucky should be settled according to Virginia law, a provision inserted to guarantee the holdings of Virginia speculators who had invested in Kentucky land before Kentucky became a state. Title disputes, already a hazard of life in the region, quickly grew to avalanche proportions when new immigrants to Kentucky settled, either knowingly or unknowingly, on land held in absentia by Virginia speculators. The Kentucky acts of 1797 and 1812 attempted to bring some order and equity to the ensuing tangle of conflicting claims. The first of these statutes provided "that the occupant of land, from which he is evicted by better title, shall, in all cases, be excused from the payment of rents and profits accrued prior to actual notice of the adverse title, provided his possession in its inception was peaceable, and he shows a plain and connected title, in law or equity, deduced from some record." More favorable still to Kentucky occupants was the 1812 act, which, drawing on the equity side of the law, provided "that the peaceable occupant of land, who supposes it to belong to him in virtue of some legal or equitable title founded on a record, shall be paid by the successful claimant for his improvements." Claimants under Virginia title could, of course, escape the obligation to pay for improvements by simply selling the land for the going rate minus the value of the improvements made on it by the occupant, which value was to be determined by a state-appointed commission.[46]

The Court's decisions constituted a devastating two-pronged attack on the Kentucky laws in question, with Story extrapolating boldly from *Fletcher* while Washington relied more on the common-law reasoning characteristic of the Court's other decisions on state land law. Story's interpretation of the separation agreement of 1789 and the Kentucky laws of 1798 and 1812 is hard to refute. The first, he said, was meant to secure the undiminished rights and interests of purchasers of land in Kentucky as determined "exclusively" by the laws of Virginia. The claimant laws just as clearly diminished the rights the 1789 agreement aimed to secure by forcing the holder to "pay for improvements which he has not authorized," or failing to do that, sell at the price "fixed by others." Here was a clear case of taking without compensation— which might well have been decided under the Taking Clause of Article 5—a

46. 8 Wheaton 4–7.

resolution that would have forced Kentucky to compensate Virginia holders who were forced to pay occupants to clear their titles to sell at a loss. Story might also have voided the Kentucky laws as violating the federal statute of 1792, which recognized the admission of Kentucky as a state and presumably put the imprint of superiority under Article 6 on the agreement of 1789. Instead, he voided the Kentucky laws on the ground that they violated the separation agreement of 1789, which he held to be a contract within the meaning of Article 1, Section 10. That he resorted to highly dubious Contract Clause reasoning over the more obvious constitutional solution makes the point that contract thinking derivative from private law had insinuated its way into constitutional discourse as the chief protector of property rights.[47]

The fact that Justice Washington, in the second *Green* decision, went out of his way to repudiate equity in favor of the common law makes the point even stronger. Obviously, he was not persuaded by Henry Clay, who pressured the Court for a second argument in the case and who then argued as a friend of the court for the claimants and Kentucky. Clay made several telling points, the first being that Story's Contract Clause argument was fundamentally flawed, because there was no evidence the Framers intended to make agreements between states into contracts within the meaning of Article 1, Section 10, and, more conclusively, because the 1789 agreement between Virginia and Kentucky was itself unconstitutional since it had never been agreed to by Congress as required by Article 1, Section 10, paragraph 2, of the Constitution.[48]

There was also, Clay reminded the justices, "the true theory of our government" to consider, namely "that of perfect equality among the members of the Union." For Kentucky to surrender control over its territory to Virginia, an "indisputable" ingredient of its sovereignty as even Story agreed, or for it to concede to the Supreme Court, "foreign interpreters" as Clay put it, the right to override the courts and the legislature of Kentucky concerning its land policy would violate this fundamental theory (shades of *Huidekoper's Lessee*). That the Court might violate state sovereignty using a tenuous reading of the Contract Clause, which ignored Article 1, Section 10, paragraph 2, in short, was incomprehensible. So Clay argued, and it is hard not to agree with him on this point and on his final observation about the relationship of law and poli-

---

47. Story, ibid., 16–18. See White, *Marshall Court*, 642–48, for a superb analysis of the opinions in *Green*.

48. 8 Wheaton 40–42. For Clay's role in *Green* and for a lucid analysis of the complexities of that case in general, see Maurice G. Baxter, *Henry Clay the Lawyer* (Lexington, Ky., 2000), ch. 3.

tics: "This court is not a mere court of justice, applying ordinary laws. It is a political tribunal, and may look to political considerations and consequences."[49]

Clay's simple proposition, coming as it did from a friendly critic and fellow nationalist, was a direct challenge to the basic premise of Marshall's Contract Clause jurisprudence: that reliance on the common law made politics go away. Justice Washington was not persuaded. His opinion for the majority in the second *Green* decision reaffirmed Story's position in the first by an extended reference to common-law doctrine. Kentucky was not persuaded by the Court. State resistance to the opinion, plus a change in the membership of the Court, resulted in a partial circumvention of *Green* in *Hawkins v. Barney's Lessee* (1831), which applied Kentucky's statute of limitations to occupants whose titles had not been contested for seven years. With South Carolina and Georgia joining Kentucky in open defiance, that year was a bad one for the Court and for the chief justice.[50]

To acknowledge the mounting resistance to the Marshall Court's decisions did not, however, signal the demise of *Fletcher*. The principles of contractual sanctity and rule stability established in that case, along with the corollary principle that the Court would not inquire into legislative motive, continued as controlling precedent. Nowhere was the impact of the latter rule more apparent, or its consequences more problematic, than in a series of land decisions involving the disposition of millions of acres of land acquired by treaty throughout the antebellum period. Typical of these cases and precedent-making in themselves were *U.S. v. Arredono* (1832) and *U.S. v. Clarke* (1834), both of which involved title to land acquired under the Adams-Onís Treaty of 1819. Under that treaty, the United States agreed to recognize land grants made by the king of Spain prior to January 24, 1818. While ratification was pending, however, a spate of hastily manufactured and fraudulent grants were made to American venture capitalists by Spanish officials. To validate their precarious titles, these speculators turned to the federal courts, which, following *Fletcher*, refused to look into the fraudulent origins of transactions. As Marshall put it for the Court in *Clarke*, "He who would controvert a grant executed by the lawful authority, takes upon himself the burden of showing . . .

49. 8 Wheaton 42, 45, 57, for Clay's argument.

50. For Washington's opinion in *Green*, see 8 Wheaton, 69–94. Johnson's opinion in *Hawkins v. Barney's Lessee*, 5 Peters 457, held that Kentucky's statute of limitations applied to Kentucky claimants whose title had gone uncontested for seven years. See Baxter, *Henry Clay*, 46.

that the transaction is tainted with fraud." Armed with this presumption of legality, speculators made good their claims to millions of acres of public land.[51]

In assessing Marshall's opinion in *Fletcher v. Peck,* one needs to consider that the Contract Clause of the Constitution called into action was designed by the Framers to protect property from state action. He was not tailoring law out of whole cloth. Even so, it is striking how much interpretive latitude he carved out for himself, while denying he was doing so. Discretion in *Fletcher,* as in *Huidekoper's Lessee,* came in his interpretation and prioritization of the facts; creativity in the protean generality of his opinions. In *Fletcher* he assumed without proving, and against strong inferential evidence that the plaintiffs were innocent third parties. Thus the case of a public contract between the original speculators and the state is turned into a private contract amenable to common-law adjudication, outside the prohibition of the Eleventh Amendment. Freed from its origins in political corruption, his doctrinal pronouncement, framed both in terms of positive constitutional law and natural law, emerged newborn in the immaculate guise of constitutional truth. Because Marshall framed the principle in unqualified general terms, it could be, and was, applied to circumstances neither he nor the Framers could have foreseen. One common characteristic in these unforeseen applications—at least in those such as *New Jersey v. Wilson, Green v. Biddle,* or *Arredono*—was that common-law principles of contract grafted onto the Constitution worked to the advantage of large land speculators, leaving ordinary settlers to take the hindmost. There were critics off the Court, lawyers Albert Gallatin and Henry Clay and the settlers of Kentucky, and on it, Justice William Johnson and, later, Justice Peter Daniel, who saw the truth of the matter and objected. Marshall saw the truth, but he saw it through the sympathetic eyes of a large land speculator. Naturally, he did not object to what he saw, or to what he could also reasonably extrapolate from the intent of the Framers.

Dartmouth College v. Woodward, the Corporation Question, and the Limits of Omniscient Judging

Of all the progeny generated by *Fletcher,* none had a greater impact on American history than *Dartmouth College v. Woodward,* an impact felt first in the

---

51. *U.S. v. Arrendono,* 6 Peters 691; *U.S. v. Clarke,* 8 Peters 436, 452–53.

field of private higher education, then in the development of the American business corporation. As the author of the majority opinion in both cases, Marshall put the Court and the Constitution on the cutting edge of radical change. Whether, or to what degree, he understood what he had wrought is another question, an important one, too, since the answer will help locate him in the rapidly shifting culture of the early Republic. A close look at his legal reasoning in the college case suggests that he was much less innovative then is generally thought and considerably less omniscient as well.

In its early stages, the college case did not appear to have great lawmaking potential. Probably no one, including Marshall, could have prophesied that it would play a key role in the rise of the American business corporation, or that the corporation would be the main vehicle for the industrial revolution in America. At issue was the constitutionality of an act passed in 1816 by the Republican-controlled New Hampshire legislature, which attempted to transform tiny Dartmouth College, a bastion of Federalist orthodoxy, into Dartmouth University. Several laws were passed to effect this change, but the main one altered the mode of governance provided for in the college's original charter, granted by authority of the British Crown in 1769. The new law increased the size of the board of trustees from twelve to twenty-one and provided that the new members would be appointed by the Republican governor. When the Republican-controlled majority on the newly constituted board attempted to take control of the college, they were met at the threshold by the old trustees, who hired Jeremiah Smith, Jeremiah Mason, and Daniel Webster, the best lawyers in New England, to defend their rights under the old charter. This they did by bringing a common-law action of trover against Woodward, who as secretary and treasurer represented the university, for recovery of the records, corporate seal, and other property, which they claimed as the rightful governing authority of the college.[52]

Arguments before the New Hampshire Superior Court blended constitutional and private law. Lawyers for the college argued that the New Hampshire law that altered the 1769 charter violated both the New Hampshire constitution and the Contract Clause of the U.S. Constitution. Counsel for both parties also focused on the legal status of the corporation: whether it was public, in

52. See *Dartmouth College v. Woodward*, 4 Wheaton 518. For a comprehensive legal analysis of the opinion in the context of the Court's other Contract Clause decisions, consult White, *Marshall Court*, ch. 9, especially 612–28. A full discussion of the case is found in Francis N. Stites, *Private Interest and Public Gain: The Dartmouth College Case, 1819* (Amherst, Mass., 1972).

which case the legislature could more readily claim the right to alter its charter, or private, in which case the presumption was against the state regulatory authority. Chief Justice William Richardson, writing for a unanimous court, apparently had no trouble accepting the argument that the Contract Clause of the Constitution applied to corporations, but it did so only if the purpose of the corporation was to further the property interests of private individuals. Since Dartmouth College had been created to educate and Christianize Indians, it was by definition a public corporation and, as such, subject to legislative control. The New Hampshire court's holding that the Contract Clause in Article 1, Section 10, did not apply was brought to the Supreme Court on a writ of error, argued in 1818, and decided early in the 1819 term. Marshall wrote for the majority, Story and Washington delivered separate concurring opinions, and Gabriel Duvall entered a silent dissent.[53]

The chief justice's opinion vindicated the college on every point. First, Dartmouth was not a public university as the court below had ruled but a private charitable institution, which meant that the state had no more authority to regulate it than it did any other type of private property. To put the matter in contractual terms, which is what Marshall did, the charter, since it created a private corporation, not a public one, was a private contract even though the state was a party. As a private contract, it came easily within the meaning of the Contract Clause of Article 1, Section 10. Accordingly, the New Hampshire act of 1816 was unconstitutional. Dartmouth College was rescued from the brink. Private institutions of education chartered by the state now rested on a secure constitutional foundation. Their multiplication after 1819 speaks to the formative cultural impact of the decision. Also benefiting from the Court's decision were thousands of state-chartered private voluntary associations, which became a hallmark feature of American culture in the century following the American Revolution. Among these, none was more important, or more revolutionary in its consequences, than the business corporation.

The business corporation was the unique creation of American lawmakers during the late eighteenth and early nineteenth centuries, made by the state legislatures that chartered corporations, the state courts that created a body of decisional law for their internal governance, and the Supreme Court that defined the institution by establishing its relationship to the states. What these lawmaking institutions discovered was that the corporate form, used in En-

---

53. Actually the configuration was more complicated, for which see White, *Marshall Court,* 621–23.

gland and the colonies to organize charitable and public institutions, could be refashioned to suit the special needs of American entrepreneurs. New production technology, especially in textiles, required large capital investment. In a country where the government did not regularly finance production ventures and where private resources of individuals were inadequate to the need, broad-based stock ownership made imminent sense, especially when it was accompanied by centralized management, a key feature of the corporate form. Armed with immortality by its charter, unlike the earlier joint-stock companies organized for a single venture, and limited liability, provided gradually during this period by legislative enactment, the corporation was an increasingly attractive investment vehicle for entrepreneurs, provided the investment could be secured against state regulation.[54]

This was exactly what the college decision did, and it is no accident the decade immediately following 1819 witnessed a virtual revolution in business incorporation. Already in 1819, there were fifty business corporations—corporations, that is to say, engaged in transportation, the production of goods, or the extraction of minerals from the ground—for every private educational corporation such as Dartmouth College. By 1830, according to the leading scholar on the subject, New England alone had almost nineteen hundred business corporations, of which nearly six hundred were related to manufacturing or mining. For the remainder of the nineteenth century, the college decision was a potent legal and ideological weapon for corporations who sought to defeat regulation and establish the ideological primacy of laissez-faire capitalism. In the process, the business corporation came to be seen as just another enterprising individual, the personification in law of the individual stockholders who composed it. As such, it was made the beneficiary of the Anglo-American legal tradition, which equated property rights with individual liberty. In America, unlike England, the corporation became both the instrument and the chief cultural symbol of economic modernization.[55]

54. The standard work remains E. Merrick Dodd, *American Business Corporations until 1860, with Special Reference to Massachusetts* (Cambridge, Mass., 1954). Also relevant are Oscar and Mary Flug Handlin, "Origins of the American Business Corporation," *Journal of Economic History* 5 (May 1945): 1–23; and G. S. Callender, "The Early Transportation and Banking Enterprises of the States in Relation to the Growth of Corporations," *Quarterly Journal of Economics* 17 (November 1902): 111–62.

55. Dodd, *American Business Corporations,* 11. For a discussion of the policy impact of the college decision, see Louis Hartz, *Economic Policy and Democratic Thought: Pennsylvania, 1776–1860* (Cambridge, Mass., 1948), passim, but especially 243–53.

Whether Marshall planned it this way is unknown. A circumstantial case can be made that he did so plan it, and that he disguised his modernizing agenda in the language of eighteenth-century legal science. In fact, he appears to admit as much in his opinion when he notes that corporation charters were not in the contemplation of those who framed the Contract Clause in Article 1, Section 10. In his words, "It is more than possible that the preservation of the rights of this description was not particularly in view of the framers of the constitution when the clause under consideration was introduced into that instrument." Despite this admission, he went on to rule that corporate charters were contracts within the meaning of the Contract Clause. For him to expound a bold new doctrine in doubtful cases, especially when he professed to believe that judicial review was not appropriate in such, invites a search for a hidden agenda. Adding further to the impression that he was up to something was his protestation that he wasn't; that the "magnitude" and "delicacy" of the question required that the Court should proceed with "cautious circumspection" and that "in no doubtful case" would it "pronounce a legislative act to the contrary to the constitution."[56]

Having made assurances that nothing much was happening, Marshall made things happen in a rapid succession of seemingly innocent statements that in fact embodied the substance of the decision. First, came the rhetorical pronouncement that "it can require no argument to prove that the circumstances of this case constitute a contract." Then came the key question of whether the corporate charter was a contract protected by the Constitution from the act(s) of New Hampshire's legislature. That question was followed by a generalization, whose "correctness . . . cannot be controverted": that the protection of contracts respecting private property was very much on the mind of those who framed the Constitution. Building on this assumption, Marshall went on to observe, "The parties in the case differ less on general principle, less on the true construction of the constitution in the abstract, than on the application of those principles to this case, and on the true construction of the charter of 1769." The charter question, whether the charter of Dartmouth College created a public or a private corporation, was then treated as a matter of common law. When readers learned that the common law established the private nature of Dartmouth College, just as it settled the private nature of William and Mary in Marshall's argument in *Bracken v. College of William and Mary* in 1790,

56. 4 Wheaton 644, 625.

they were prepared to accept on faith the chief justice's unproved holding that corporate charters were contracts within the meaning of the Contract Clause.[57]

Given the transformative impact of the decision and Marshall's bold rhetorical strategy, it is tempting to see him as an omniscient statesman who saw the modernizing impact of the business corporation and a manipulative genius who felt free to shape law to the desired result. A closer look, however, suggests he was neither. Sometimes people, including judges, actually believe what they say. Judging from what Marshall actually said in his long argument, the issue on his mind was not the future of the business corporation in America but the status of a private educational institution in the backcountry of New England. Nor did the politics of the dispute flag his attention or play to his Federalist bias. The dispute originated not as a struggle between the Republican legislature and the Federalist college—not between good guys and bad, that is to say—but as a decade-long struggle between Eleazar Wheelock, the founder's son, and a faction of the board of trustees. Republican governor William Plumer, champion of the new university, moreover, was not a raging Jacobin but a decent, fair-minded ex-Federalist turned moderate, property-loving, civic-minded Republican.[58]

Nor was it Marshall who first perceived the case in terms of the private contract law but rather the old trustees themselves in their battle against the new state-sponsored university. And it was Daniel Webster, more than the parties themselves, who politicized the case, because as New England's leading Federalist, with ambitions for political glory, he needed to bash the emerging Republican Party of New Hampshire. It was Jeremiah Mason and Jeremiah Smith and Webster, lawyers for the trustees and the old college, who translated the private-contract thinking of their clients into a Contract Clause question. Even here, as both Judge Richardson's opinion and Marshall's for the Court indicate, the determinative question was not a constitutional one but a factual one susceptible to a common-law interpretation, that is, whether the college corporation was public or private. When Marshall applied traditional common-law reasoning to settle the matter, he was not aiming to disguise the doctrinal constitutional innovations he was about to make but instead was doing what he had done since he began the practice of law in the 1780s and what *every other* American lawyer of the age regularly did: reasoning by common-law analogy

57. Ibid., 627, 629.

58. Stites, *Private Interest and Public Gain* is excellent on the background of the case. Also see Lynn W. Turner, *William Plumer of New Hampshire, 1759–1850* (Chapel Hill, N.C., 1962).

and using common-law definitions and principles to interpret the words of the Constitution.

The serendipitous way in which the case gathered doctrinal steam as it rolled along is also incompatible with the idea that it was a doctrinal coup masterminded by a wily chief justice. Even if Marshall saw fully the doctrine-making potential of the facts, and there is no sign he did, he had less to do with the original definition of the issues than the lawyers for the old college, the state judges, and perhaps even the old trustees themselves. They defined the questions and to some extent provided the answers that guided Marshall's reasoning. Nor is it clear that he, or they, grasped the radical potential of his opinion in terms of the business corporation. He did say that "the law of this case is the law of all," but he was clearly speaking of the law of charitable institutions. Justice Washington, like Marshall, also dwelt on the law of private charities in his concurrence, referring especially to the famous English case of *Philips v. Bury.* Washington went on to say explicitly what Marshall only suggested: that "it will be proper clearly to mark the distinction between the different kinds of lay aggregate corporations, in order to prevent any implied decision by this court of any other case than the one immediately before it." Only Story in his concurrence appeared to have looked beyond the case at hand to business corporations, which is not surprising since his own state of Massachusetts and his friends the Jacksons, the Cabots, and the Lowells were leading the way in business incorporation. Even then, Story made specific reference only to banking corporations, though as the president of two, he surely understood the predominantly private character they had come to have in the course of the early nineteenth century.[59]

Marshall's approach to corporations and corporate contracts was far from prescient. In his long opinion there is no discussion of the corporation as a new form of property whose public significance and power might require regulation by the state. Indeed, there is no hint that the corporate form might be applied to private productive enterprise. The question was not about whether the power to create a corporation implied the power to regulate it, or whether it should be regulated in the public interest, but rather whether the state could take away private rights vested by contract, or charter, without the agreement of both parties. Corporate rights, moreover, were conceived only in terms of

59. Washington at 4 Wheaton 659. On Story's concurrence and the business corporation, see R. Kent Newmyer, "Justice Joseph Story's Doctrine of 'Public and Private Corporations' and the Rise of the American Business Corporation," *DePaul Law Review* 25 (summer 1976): 825–41.

corporate property, and corporate property was defined in terms of the property rights of individual corporate members.

This static, one might say premodern, approach to corporate property in *Dartmouth College* was forecast in *Bank of the United States v. Deveaux* (1809), where the question was about whether a corporation could sue in the federal courts. No provision was made for such suits in the Judiciary Act of 1789, but Marshall upheld jurisdiction anyway, reasoning that the rights of individual stockholders to sue could be transferred to the corporate entity. Since the stockholders of the bank were citizens of Pennsylvania, the corporation could sue under diversity of citizenship in the federal courts. *Deveaux* was abandoned as unworkable in 1844 in *Louisville, Cincinnati, and Charleston Railroad v. Letson* (1844) when the Court ruled that for jurisdictional purposes the corporation was a citizen of the state in which it was incorporated. What remained, however, and what was the key to Marshall's approach in *Dartmouth College,* was the working assumption that the legal rights of corporations could be defined by the individual rights of the stockholders. It followed that the property of corporations was entitled to the same legal protection as the private property of individuals, even though the corporation was created by the state and might have a public function.[60]

By Marshall's reasoning in the college case, then, the right to govern, granted in the old charter—like the right to office in *Marbury* or the right to sue in *Deveaux*—was simply a matter of property vested by contract. To emphasize the point, he noted further that the right to govern included the right of the trustees, if they saw fit, to give themselves teaching jobs for real money. Having established that the charter had bestowed property rights on the trustees, it was an easy, indeed nearly unnoticed leap to conclude that it was a contract within the meaning of the Contract Clause of the Constitution. There was no doubt in Marshall's mind that the Contract Clause "must be understood as intended to guard against a power of at least doubtful utility, the abuse of which had been extensively felt; and to restrain the legislature in future from violating the right to property." If any authority for the interpretation was needed, he found it in the history of the states under the Articles of Confederation. The law according to Marshall was that corporate property was identical to private property, that the legal character of the corporation might be inferred from the rights belonging to individual stockholders. All of this he stated

---

60. *Bank of the United States v. Deveaux,* 5 Cranch 61; *Louisville, Cincinnati, and Charleston Railway Co. v. Letson,* 2 Howard 497.

before he got to the main point, the Court's holding, assumed but not proved, that a corporate charter was a contract within the meaning of the Contract Clause of the Constitution.[61]

Given the conceptual improvisation in Marshall's opinion, and the fact that it was cited so often to support corporate development throughout the nineteenth century, it is tempting to conclude that Marshall was a modernizer par excellence: that he read the future and brought the law into harmony with it. A close consideration of his reasoning, however, reminds us that even the wisest of men sometimes create what they know not. This does not deny the role Marshall's opinion played in nineteenth-century economic development, but only insists that his reasoning and his vision were deeply anchored in the traditional common-law world he knew firsthand in Virginia. He concentrated on the law governing eleemosynary corporations and the vested-rights doctrines that went with it, not because he was trying to disguise his doctrinal innovations, but because he believed that the old law he cited so copiously was controlling.

To put it another way, his reasoning in *Dartmouth College* did not advance appreciably over his argument in *Bracken v. The College of William and Mary* in 1790. It was Joseph Story, not Marshall, who put a modern spin on these ancient ideas and in doing so made them serviceable to the new American business corporation. What Story said in his concurring opinion, and what Marshall only touched on, was that the public or private character of a corporation is determined not by its *function* but by its *foundation*. If the foundation, the capital, is private, according to Story, then so is the corporation. Private corporations, even though they were chartered by the state and even though they might be connected with the welfare of the public, were immune from state regulation unless the state explicitly reserved the right to do so in the charter. Those who founded Dartmouth College with private donations were protected from state regulations and state taking by the Contract Clause of the Constitution. So were the bold capitalists and friends of Story who created the new textile corporations of the Merrimack Valley in the 1820s.[62]

This is not to argue that Marshall did not advance the doctrine of *Fletcher*, that grants were contracts, in *Dartmouth College*, where he held that corporate charters were contracts. He did so, however, not as a self-conscious innovator, or a sly modernizer, but as a traditional judge applying old principles to

---

61. 4 Wheaton 628–29.
62. Newmyer, "Story's Doctrine of 'Public and Private Corporations.'"

new problems, which is what common-law judges always did. When he brought the Contract Clause of the Constitution to bear on corporate charters, he did so cautiously via a familiar process of extrapolation from private law. Indeed, the constitutional breakthrough in *Dartmouth College* seems to have been driven by private-law reasoning, thus blurring the distinction between public and private contracts that has figured so much in scholarly criticism of his opinion. Once he conceived of corporate property as private property, it was but a small leap to see corporate charters as analogous to private contracts. Once he saw charters as private contracts, it was no leap at all to conclude that corporate charters were contracts within the meaning of Article 1, Section 10. When Marshall claimed he was following the intent of the Framers—another manifestation of his traditionalism—he told it as he saw it, and the way it really was. Included in the "intent of the framers," moreover, was not just their view of the Contract Clause as an omnibus protector of private property but, as Jefferson Powell has shown, also their assumption that the common-law hermeneutical tradition would guide constitutional interpretation when the text of the document was not clear. And this fusion of private and public, of the common law with the Constitution, comes through strongly in *Dartmouth College v. Woodward*, as it did in all of Marshall's Contract Clause decisions and nearly, if not all, of his great constitutional opinions. Marshall worked in this tradition, thought in it, because it was the only one he knew, and because the Framers intended it that way.[63]

Ogden v. Saunders: John Marshall, John Locke, and the Culture of Contract

Judging from his major Contract Clause opinions, Marshall believed that the old law was suitable to the new age, and indeed it was. He was also concerned with practical results *and* principled law, just as he looked optimistically to the future without taking his mind off the past. He would also have been mystified by the tendency of some recent scholars to separate liberal capitalism and republican morality. He saw no disjunction between the two. In his mind, republicanism in law boils down to principled adjudication, which was what capitalists needed. More pointedly still, businessmen operating in the national

---

63. H. Jefferson Powell, "The Original Understanding of Original Intent," *Harvard Law Review* 98 (March 1985): 885–948, reprinted in *Interpreting the Constitution: The Debate over Original Intent*, ed. Jack N. Rakove (Boston, 1990).

market needed protection from the intrusion of state legislatures. With the growth of the national market, regularity and uniformity came to depend on judicial enforcement of the Contract Clause. Principled law was also practical law.[64]

But what if principled adjudication were not so obviously practical? What if some of the hoary axioms of the old law were irrelevant to the needs of American entrepreneurs doing business in the emerging and highly volatile market economy? What if contract principles applied absolutely were impractical in this new age or even antidevelopmental? Or, to be more specific, what if in response to the radical economic fluctuations and business cycles of the new age, state legislatures were called upon to soften the harshness of unregulated competition? What if they did so in the name of both republican law and economic progress?

Marshall confronted these questions and answered them in *Ogden v. Saunders* (1827), his first and only dissent in a constitutional case. Though Justices Story and Duvall signed on to his dissent, he spoke for himself and with uncharacteristic passion. When forced to choose between the expedient demands of the new commercial age and the legal principles of the old, even when pressured by his best friend on the Court to bend a little, he stuck with the old law, which he rendered in the uncompromising language of John Locke.[65]

Ogden involved the constitutionality of the New York bankruptcy statute of 1801. It was a law that fit the new economic age and the democratic one as well. Unlike English bankruptcy statutes, and most American colonial ones, it was not limited to a select class of merchants but rather was broad-based both in terms of its coverage and its operation. Upon the surrender and disposition of all assets, it freed the insolvent debtor from all future obligations. Those entrepreneurs who crashed in the new economic age, the argument went, were victims not of their own bad judgment—or extravagance or improvidence—but of impersonal market forces over which they had no control. If they had no control, they bore no responsibility. The sooner they were absolved of debt and brought back into the mainstream of capitalist endeavor, so the argument went, the better for them and for the country as a whole. The only problem

64. For the recent debate among historians on liberalism and republicanism in the early Republic, I have found the following very useful: Daniel T. Rodgers, "Republicanism: The Career of a Concept," *American Historical Review* 97 (June 1992): 11–38; Michael Merrill, "Putting 'Capitalism' in Its Place: A Review of Recent Literature," *William and Mary Quarterly* 52 (April 1995): 315–26.

65. *Ogden v. Saunders,* 12 Wheaton 213.

was that bringing them back with a clean slate meant that their creditors were forced to pay the price of their rehabilitation. Legally, it was a matter of private contract law. Constitutionally, the question asked whether and to what extent state bankruptcy laws could modify the substance of private contracts. Economically, it was a question of who should pay the costs of economic modernization.[66]

The Court, with Marshall speaking for the majority, had confronted some of these questions in *Sturges v. Crowninshield* (1819). The state insolvency law at issue in that case, unlike that in *Ogden,* operated retrospectively, that is, applied to contracts made before as well as after the passage of the act. In striking down the state law as unconstitutional, the justices agreed that states had concurrent power in the field of bankruptcy in the absence of federal bankruptcy legislation. Beyond this, however, confusion abounded, as Justice Johnson made abundantly clear in his concurring opinion in *Ogden.* Some justices voided the New York law as a violation of the ex post facto provision of Article 1, Section 10, conveniently forgetting that the Court had ruled in *Calder v. Bull* that the Ex Post Facto Clause applied only to criminal matters. Others appeared to make a distinction between contracts passed before the passage of the law, which were unconstitutional, and those passed afterward, which were not. Marshall's majority opinion also emphasized the distinction between state laws affecting the *remedy* of the contract, which he accepted, and those affecting its substance, which he didn't. All of this is to say that Marshall's opinion was a political compromise among the justices that settled the case but not the law.[67]

This compromise unraveled in 1827 when the Court addressed the yet unanswered question of whether a state law that affected future contracts only but that also altered the substance of the contract was a violation of the Contract Clause. Several arguments were advanced by counsel in favor of the constitutionality of such laws: that the grant to Congress to pass uniform bankruptcy law in Article 1, Section 10, was not exclusive; that states and colonies had a history of passing such legislation; and that no objection was made

---

66. For a general history of bankruptcy legislation in this period, see Peter J. Coleman, *Debtors and Creditors in America: Insolvency, Imprisonment for Debt, and Bankruptcy, 1607–1900* (Madison, Wis., 1974). Also useful is Charles Warren, *Bankruptcy in United States History* (Cambridge, Mass., 1935). White, *Marshall Court,* 648–58, contains a detailed legal analysis of the *Ogden* decision.

67. For Johnson's recollections of the divided Court in *Sturges,* see *Ogden v. Saunders,* 12 Wheaton 272–73.

to their doing so in the several conventions that ratified the Constitution. The most compelling point, however, the one put forth by Bushrod Washington in his opinion, was that because the law preceded the contract, the law became a part of the contract. Those individuals who contracted after the passage of the insolvency act, the argument went, were presumed to have known about the state law and, accordingly, accepted its provisions *as part of the contract.* Overall, the issue was whether the Court's interpretation of the Contract Clause would recognize the authority of state legislatures to accommodate the realities of the new age of democratic capitalism.

There was no opinion of the Court, but Justice Washington's opinion, supported by Trimble, Johnson, and Thompson, made several points, none of which pleased the chief justice. All agreed that *Sturges* had not settled the constitutional issue, and Johnson went so far as to define that decision as a compromise, an embarrassing fact directly at odds with Marshall's view of the Court as a legal institution dispensing authoritative and objective law. Following counsel for New York, the majority justices, some explicitly, others implicitly, agreed that the new law was needed for the new age. Well before the general acceptance of legal positivism in England or America, those justices rested the new law on a positivist foundation, namely that law was not God-given but man-made; that its authority did not rest on morality but on the force of the state. Counsel for the defendant in *Ogden* put the matter bluntly, declaring that "the contract was what the parties understood it to be, and they understood it as the law declared it to be," or "the legal obligation is that which the law imposes." As he stated even more pointedly, "There is nothing of mere human institution (and it is with this that the constitution deals) which binds to the performance of any contract, except the laws under which the contract is made, and the remedies provided by them to enforce its execution."[68]

Much to Marshall's distress, his colleagues accepted the argument, which had been anticipated by Johnson's concurrence in *Fletcher.* In their surprisingly modern view, the principles of contract law as applied to the field of bankruptcy legislation were not matters settled by natural law. Nor were they matters embodied in the common law or even in the Constitution. As Washington and his colleagues saw it, bankruptcy was simply a matter of economic policy to be decided by the people through their legislatures. The universal moral-law argument, Washington conceded sarcastically, might "create the obligation of a contract made upon some desert spot, where no municipal law exists," but

---

68. The lawyers arguments on positivism appear at 12 Wheaton 234–35.

the United States in 1787 was not such a place, and the Framers could not be assumed to have had universal moral law in mind when they framed Article 1, Section 10. Moreover, he added, the states would not have agreed to a Constitution that contained such a blanket repudiation of their sovereign powers. Perhaps, Washington conceded, "this common law of nations, which has been mentioned may form in part of the obligation of a contract," but "I must unhesitatingly insist, that this law is to be taken in strict subordination to the municipal laws of the land where the contract is made, or is to be executed. The former can be satisfied by nothing short of performance; the latter may affect and control the validity, construction, evidence, remedy, performance and discharge of the contract. The former is the common law of all civilized nations, and each of them; the latter is the peculiar law of each, and is paramount to the former whenever they come in collision with each other."[69]

Marshall never appeared more passionately sure of himself than in *Ogden*. But in truth, the case presented him with a genuine interpretive dilemma. His position on contractual sanctity was clear, but so was his entrepreneurial bias and his sensitivity to the realities of the market economy. As a commercial-minded judge and an experienced entrepreneur himself, he must then have listened with care to counsel when it emphasized the needs of the business community regarding bankruptcy legislation. Surely he attended sympathetically to the argument that bankruptcy legislation was familiar both to England and its North American colonies; that it was also common among the states without being constitutionally challenged. Here the majority confronted him with his own rule of construction, announced authoritatively in *McCulloch,* that interpretation in doubtful cases should be informed by practice. On top of these factors, Marshall had to be aware of the Court's political vulnerabilities to the powerful states' rights anti-Court movement set in motion by *McCulloch,* forces he accommodated in his Commerce Clause opinions and in those involving state banking corporations, slavery, and the slave trade as well.

Even on the subject of state bankruptcy legislation, if one takes *Sturges* to be a political compromise, Marshall appeared to be a practical-minded, flexible judge, who preferred institutional harmony over doctrinal purity. Such is also the impression conveyed by his letter to Bushrod Washington concerning *Golden v. Prince* (1814), a case Washington encountered on circuit in Pennsylvania and about which he queried his friend. In replying, Marshall acknowledged he had not thought deeply about the issue. He did recognize as a matter

69. Ibid., 258–59.

of history, however, that bankruptcy laws "exist in commercial countries where credit is in its most flourishing state, & were I believe common in the commercial states of the Union at the adoption of the constitution." He was not aware that they "excited any complaints or were considered as impairing credit in the states in which they were in operation." Nor was he prepared to object to such laws on the ground that the grant to Congress to pass uniform bankruptcy laws automatically excluded the states, which would have meant that the states that had bankruptcy laws at the time of the ratification would continue to have them, while others would be prohibited from passing them. Most interesting, since it was precisely the question the Court confronted in *Ogden,* was the impact of the Contract Clause on state bankruptcy laws operating prospectively. He doubted that such laws impaired the obligation of contract, at least when applied only to citizens of the state that passed the law. He admitted more doubt concerning a prospective law of a general nature, though he admitted that "the biass [*sic*] of my mind at the moment is rather in favor of the validity of the law though I acknowledge I feel very great doubts whether I shall retain that opinion."[70]

It is not clear what caused him to remove these doubts between 1814 and 1827. And why was his dissent so uncompromising and uncharacteristically ideological? Believing so passionately in unifying the Court and suppressing dissent, why would he dissent so passionately? And why advertise the Court's internal divisions during its time of troubles? The answers are not clear. Perhaps it is simply that constitutional doctrine requires a gestation time. Maybe it was the general resurgence of states' rights in the 1820s or the contagion of bankruptcies in the wake of the 1819 panic that raised the possibility that debt repudiation might become an accepted feature of capitalism. In any case, Marshall's doubt was gone in *Ogden,* along with any tolerance for state bankruptcy laws and seemingly little for the benighted position of his colleagues. It was a fight to the finish. Like the lawyer he never ceased being, Marshall went straight for the jugular. The "single question," plain and simple, asked "whether the act of the state of New York is consistent with, or repugnant to, the constitution of the United States." If this was a "delicate" question, he did not acknowledge the fact; there were no professed "sentiments of profound and respectful reverence" for the state legislature whose handiwork was on the line. Instead, Marshall indelicately said, "If it be right that the power of preserving the constitution from legislative infraction, should reside anywhere, it

70. Marshall to Washington, 19 April 1814, PJM, 8: 34–35.

cannot be wrong, it must be right, that those whom the delicate and important duty is conferred should perform it according to their best judgment."[71]

He was also impatient with the majority's overwrought disquisition on the rules of interpretation, which was a bit like the pot calling the kettle black. For him the answer was as plain as the question: "The intention of the instrument must prevail"; "this intention must be collected from its words"; those "words are to be understood in that sense in which they are generally used by those for whom the instrument was intended"; and "its provisions are neither to be restricted into insignificance, nor extended to objects not comprehended in them, nor contemplated by its framers." Nor was there anything between the New York act in question and the words of the Constitution to be construed. Neither *Sturges* nor any of the other cases cited in the opinions of the majority, said Marshall, "comprehended" the question of prospective contracts; "it is, consequently, open for discussion."[72]

Since intent of the Framers was controlling and the text of the document was the key to intent, Marshall turned immediately to the words of Article 1, Section 10, and particularly to the Contract Clause. The significant interpretive point about this paragraph, he argued, is the fact that it treats absolute prohibitions on state action, whereas paragraphs 2 and 3 of Article 1, Section 10, treat state acts that are permitted with congressional approval. States could not enter into treaties, could not coin or print paper money; nor could they impair obligations of contracts. The absolute interdiction on the former informed the latter, which fact prompted Marshall to look for some evidence to modify such a conclusion. This further permitted him to move from the words in question to the larger meaning of intent. And here he sounded a familiar theme: "When we consider the nature of our Union; that it is intended to make us, in a great measure, one people, as to commercial objects; that, so far as respects the inter-communication of individuals, the lines of separation between states are, in many respects, obliterated; it would not be a matter of surprise, if, on the delicate subject of contracts once formed the interference of state legislation should be greatly abridged, or entirely forbidden." His point here was not that general intent should determine the meaning of particular words, only that it should serve as an interpretive guideline. As he put it, "In the nature of the provision, then, there seems to be nothing which ought to influence our construction of the words; and in making that construction, the whole clause,

71. 12 Wheaton 332.
72. Ibid., 332–33.

which consists of a single sentence, is to be taken together, and the intention is to be collected from the whole."[73]

Marshall identified another point to be drawn from the words in question, one that linked his other Contract Clause opinions and much else in his jurisprudence to the case at hand and one that settled the fate of the New York law in question. Looking at the whole of Section 10 of Article 1, again he noted that paragraphs 2 and 3, which prohibited the states from such things as regulating imports, keeping troops or ships of war, or entering into agreements with foreign powers, dealt with political matters and treated the "exercise of sovereignty." Paragraph 1, however, treated only the "rights of individuals," those involving criminal law and those dealing with civil law. It was an important distinction, since it permitted him to conclude that those portions of paragraph 1 that dealt with criminal matters were precisely those that applied only to laws that operated retrospectively.[74]

He was now poised to interpret that part of paragraph 1 that dealt with civil matters where ex post facto did not govern, that is, to the Contract Clause as it applied to prospective contracts. Here he confronted the central point in Washington's opinion, the one on which the majority united, that the New York insolvency law, since it was on the books and presumably known by the contracting parties, had implicitly become a part of the contract. Judging from his letter to Bushrod Washington regarding *Golden v. Prince,* Marshall appears to have once been intrigued with this line of reasoning. Now the hidden assumptions of such a contention, as well as the "enormity of the result," struck him as abhorrent and entirely destructive of a key feature of the Constitution, one designed by "the good and the wise" for "securing the prosperity and harmony of our citizens." That key feature of the Constitution was to guarantee the integrity of the contracts made between rational, moral, responsible individuals. A decision of the Court upholding prospective state bankruptcy law would be tantamount to permitting state legislatures to intrude into this sacred domain of individual contract making. His point was simple: Contracts should be regulated not by politicians in state legislatures but by "acts of free agents," that is, the rational and moral individuals who bound themselves legally to the terms of the agreement.[75]

73. Ibid., 334.

74. Ibid., 334–35.

75. Marshall to Washington, PJM, 8: 35; note that Washington used the principle to settle *Golden v. Prince.* 12 Wheaton 339–43. "Free agent" quote at 12 Wheaton 354.

Marshall's statement is a testament to his faith in the efficacy of contractual individualism, part of the ethos of the new age, which celebrated free will and enlarged the domain of individual action through contract as the key to progress. This did not mean he was in harmony with the egalitarian spirit of the day. When he confronted the issue at the Virginia constitutional convention of 1829, he had deep misgivings about the democratization of American politics. Even in the area of contract law, he was somewhat less egalitarian than it might appear, since he understood and accepted the fact that contractual freedom did not extend to slaves, Native Americans, and women. Simply put, contract as the basic instrument of American individualism worked best for those who understood the system, who had a stake in society, the Americans who had property to bargain with and contract about. To understand the limited applicability of the contract culture is to appreciate how it was that a conservative such as Marshall, who distrusted the masses and feared the egalitarian tendencies of the age, could champion the idea of contract with its liberal economic implications. But there was a republican dimension to his position as well. Call it morality, duty, or honor, Marshall believed those individuals who shared the benefits of the contract culture were also fully responsible for the contracts they made. And it was the duty of the law to make them so. As he put it in *Ogden*, "Contracts are framed with the expectation that they will be literally performed." This was, of course, a widely shared view among leading jurists and intellectuals of the age such as Blackstone, William Paley, Story, Kent, and Gulian Verplanck and among merchants as well, such as the Rockdale, Pennsylvania, textile manufacturer who, when asked for his contractual promise, pointed to his loins to seal the bargain. It was also the view that was subtly giving way to the realities of a market economy, as when "consideration" ceased to be required evidence of the good-faith intentions of contracting parties, or when damages awarded by courts for nonperformance replaced the doctrine of specific performance.[76]

State bankruptcy legislation that altered the substance of the contract, like that at issue in *Ogden*, was but another example of the pressure on law to accommodate the market revolution. Marshall's view was that law should control the revolution. The judge famous for moderation was not in a moderating mood. He conceded, as anyone who lived though the panic of 1819 would

---

76. Ibid., 343. The moral concept of contract is discussed in Newmyer, *Justice Joseph Story*, 150–52. For the subtle shift in contract doctrine during the antebellum period, see Morton J. Horwitz, *The Transformation of American Law, 1780–1860* (Cambridge, Mass., 1977), ch. 6.

have had to, that bankruptcy was a reality of economic life. He conceded concurrent power to states to pass bankruptcy legislation, as long as it affected the remedy and not the substance of the contract. He was not willing, however, to concede that bankruptcy was the norm of American economic life to which the law had to bend. Insolvency, as he put it, was "a casualty which is possible, but is never expected," and "it would be entirely contrary to reason, to consider it as a part of the contract." But this is precisely what his brethren had done, and to make it worse they grounded their action on the relativistic theory of legal positivism.[77]

Marshall countered the legal positivism and moral relativism of his brethren with an unadulterated dose of moral truth from the heart—and from John Locke's *Second Treatise*. The fundamental error in the majority's position was to assume "that it is not the stipulation an individual makes which binds him, but some declaration of the supreme power of a state to which he belongs, that he shall perform what he has undertaken to perform." Against this notion, Marshall pressed "the idea of a pre-existing obligation on every man to do what he has promised on consideration to do." As he put it in another place, "If, on tracing the right to contract, and the obligations created by contract, to their source, we find them to exist anterior to, and independent of society, we may reasonably conclude, that those original and pre-existing principles are, like many other natural rights, brought with man into society; and, although they may be controlled, are not given by human legislation."[78]

This reference to natural rights in the manner of John Locke was not in itself remarkable. Such arguments, introduced originally in the struggle with Great Britain and culminating in Jefferson's Declaration of Independence, remained common parlance well into the nineteenth century, especially among lawyers and judges. What is striking about judicial references to natural law, however, especially those of the Supreme Court, was that they rarely, if ever, stood alone in disposing of the legal questions at issue but rather were harnessed to specific constitutional provisions and most specifically to the Contract Clause in Article 1, Section 10. Marshall had employed this mix of natural and positive law himself in *Fletcher v. Peck*. Now in his *Ogden* dissent, he made natural law the primary determinant. Not only did he read the Contract Clause through Lockean spectacles, but he appeared to take Locke's state-of-nature version of natural law literally, which most likely Locke did not do. So un-Marshallian was Marshall's reasoning that it deserves to be quoted at length:

77. 12 Wheaton 343.
78. Ibid., 344–45.

In the rudest state of nature, a man governs himself, and labours for his own purposes. That which he acquires is his own, at least while in his possession, and he may transfer it to another. This transfer passes his right to that other. Hence the right to barter. One man may have acquired more skins than are necessary for his protection from the cold; another more food than is necessary for his immediate use. They agree each to supply the wants of the other from his surplus. Is this contract without obligation? If one of them, having received and eaten the food he needed, refuses to deliver the skin, may not the other rightfully compel him to deliver it? Or, two persons agree to unite their strength and skill to hunt together for their mutual advantage, engaging to divide the animal they shall master. Can one of them rightfully take the whole? or, should he attempt it, may not the other force him to a division? If the answer to these questions must affirm the duty of keeping faith between these parties, and the right to enforce it if violated, the answer admits the obligation of contracts, because, upon that obligation depends the right to enforce them. Superior strength may give the power, but cannot give the right. The rightfulness of coercion must depend on the pre-existing obligation to do that for which compulsion is used. It is no objection to the principle, that the injured party may be the weakest. In society, the wrong-doer may be too powerful for the law. He may deride its coercive power, yet his contacts are obligatory; and if society acquire power of coercion, that power will be applied without previously enacting that his contract is obligatory.[79]

Marshall's reliance on Lockean natural-law reasoning appears at first glance to be at odds with much in his jurisprudence as it is commonly understood. In *McCulloch,* for example, he seems to be the flexible judge who wants a flexible Constitution, one capable of adapting itself to the "various *crises* of human affairs." In *Ogden,* he is stubbornly unyielding. In contrast to the practical-minded common-law judge so often celebrated, he is an ideological one. His insistence on an extratextual interpretation of the Contract Clause stands in sharp contrast also to his emphasis, going back to the ratification debates in Virginia, on the *written* Constitution and to his first rule of constitutional construction: the words of the document count most in determining its meaning. Indeed, the words of the Contract Clause as he had usually interpre-

79. Ibid., 345–46.

ted them were perfectly adequate to the disposition of *Ogden*. Bringing Locke's natural-law injunction to bear on the bankruptcy issue, on the other hand, introduced an anomaly in that the Constitution specifically authorized Congress to pass bankruptcy laws. Since Article 1, Section 10, applied only to the states, the only constitutional restriction on Congress was that its bankruptcy laws be "uniform." Does this mean then that Marshall would have held federal law to natural-law standards? If not, why? In working to achieve the passage of the short-lived Federal Bankruptcy Act of 1800, he showed no inclination to do so.

Anomalies and unanswered questions aside, the fact remains that Marshall's dissent was consistent with the basic tenets of his jurisprudence: undying distrust of state legislative government and unqualified respect for the rights of private property. Indeed, his dissent casts some new interpretive light on both concepts. First, concerning property rights, property for him was not a static concept, not simply a parcel of land, a ship at sea, an investment in slaves, but was at once more dynamic and more philosophical. That is why he found John Locke so congenial. What he resonated to was what C. B. Macpherson identifies in Locke's philosophy as "possessive individualism." In Marshall's law, as in Locke's philosophy, the emphasis was on individual freedom and individual property *in action*. Property was not merely the right of the individual to *keep* what he had, the essence of "practical conservatism"as Clinton Rossiter defines it, but his natural inclination and his right as an individual to use his individual talents to acquire property and to deploy it creatively as he saw fit and to enjoy its fruits without hindrance. Contract was the energizing mechanism. When the American patriots eliminated the king in fashioning their republic, they destroyed the cement of hierarchical, patronage-dominated class society. Pledging themselves to freedom and equality, even if those concepts did not apply across the board, meant that Americans needed a new way of relating to one another. Given the egalitarian radicalism of the American Revolution, contract may well have been the only way available. Sir Henry Maine was right: The rise of contract was inversely related to the prevalence of social status.[80]

As a contract jurist, then, Marshall operated on the premise, fortified by his personal experience as a land speculator, that republicanism and economic liberalism were mutually supportive. Contract was the connecting link. Not only

80. C. B. Macpherson, *The Political Theory of Possessive Individualism: Hobbes to Locke* (Oxford, England, 1962); Maine, *Ancient Law*, 141.

did contract law liberate individual economic energy, it harnessed that energy to the collective prosperity and well-being of society. Nowhere did Marshall theorize about these things, but according to his reading of the Constitution as revealed in his opinions, the duty of the Court was to preserve the integrity of the contracting process; it mattered not whether the interference to it came from state governments that broke their own contracts, as in *Fletcher*, or from irresponsible individuals who reneged on their promises fairly made and then called on the state to bail them out, as in *Ogden*. Call it honor, as the business community regularly did, or morality, as jurists like Blackstone, Story, and Kent and philosophers like Hobbes, Locke, and Vattel did; contract was a concept that comported both with the free-will, individualistic culture of the antebellum United States and also with the ideal of republican citizenship. For Marshall, possessive individualism and republican community were inseparable. As he put it during the ratification struggle in Virginia, in language Adam Smith would have approved, "There is no exclusive personal stock of interest. The interest of the community is blended and inseparably connected with that of the individual. When he promotes his own, he promotes that of the community. When we consult the common good, we consult our own."[81]

Like other American conservatives of his age, Marshall had no complaint against rapid, even transformative, change as long as it could be controlled, which brings the discussion back to his contract opinions and his dissent in *Ogden*. What can be seen, somewhat surprisingly in light of his reputed contributions to the growth of the nation-state, is a strong streak of antistatism. It was not only that he abhorred states' rights constitutionalism. What he feared just as much as *theories* about the nature of the Union was state legislative meddling with contracts, either by passing laws that undercut contracts between individuals or by reneging on its own. The duty of government was not to tell the people what to do, not to regulate what they did, but to help them do what they wanted to do—and to keep them honest in what they did. If the Court facilitated and energized individualism by making contracts work, it could also keep the system moral, and republican, by holding contracting individuals, states included, to their promises. This is precisely what it failed to do in *Ogden*. Rather than preserving the integrity of the contracting process, as Marshall thought the Constitution mandated, his colleagues corrupted it;

81. Marshall speech of 10 June, VRD, 2: 1124. Matthew H. Kramer, *John Locke and the Origins of Private Property: Philosophical Explorations of Individualism, Community, and Equality* (Cambridge, Mass., 1997), explores the community aspects of Locke's individualism.

rather than prohibiting the states from interfering with the sanctity of private contracts, the Court permitted them to become a party to those contracts and justified that intervention by the theory of legal positivism, which threatened the very idea of unchanging moral and legal principles. Having put forth the Court as the ultimate guardian of republican values in a liberal age, Marshall was devastated that his brethren failed to do their duty, and that he failed to convince them that they should.

Thomas Marshall
The Library of Virginia

Mary Keith Marshall
The Library of Virginia

John Marshall at age forty-three, from a miniature painted in Paris, c.1797
The Library of Virginia

Mary ("Polly") Marshall, 1799, crayon on silk
Collection of the Museum of Early Southern Decorative Arts, Winston-Salem, North Carolina

Home of John Marshall at Richmond, Virginia, from 1783 to 1835
Library of Congress

William Cushing, associate justice of the Supreme Court, 1789–1810, portrait attributed to James Sharples, c. 1795–1800
Independence National Historic Park

Samuel Chase, associate justice of the Supreme Court, 1796–1811, engraving after a portrait by John Wesley Jarvis
Library of Congress

William Paterson, associate justice of the Supreme Court, pastel portrait attributed to James Sharples, c. 1800–1804
Collection of the Supreme Court of the United States

Alfred Moore, associate justice of the Supreme Court, 1799–1804
Library of Congress

Bushrod Washington, associate justice of the Supreme Court,
1798–1829, etching by Albert Rosenthal, 1891
Library of Congress

William Wirt delivers a speech at the trial of Aaron Burr. Chief Justice Marshall presides. From a painting by C. W. Jeffreys.
©*Bettman/Corbis*

William Johnson, associate justice of the Supreme Court,
1804–1834, c. 1820s, artist unknown
Library of Congress

Thomas Todd, associate justice of the
Supreme Court, 1807–1826
Library of Congress

Gabriel Duvall, associate justice of the
Supreme Court, 1811–1835
Library of Congress

Joseph Story, associate justice of the Supreme Court, 1811–1845, engraving from a painting by Chester Harding, c. 1815
Library of Congress

Henry Brockholst Livingston, associate justice of the Supreme Court, 1806–1823, etching by Albert Rosenthal, 1891
Library of Congress

William Pinkney, engraving from a painting attributed to Chapperl, c. 1811
Library of Congress

Daniel Webster, engraving by James B. Longacre
Library of Congress

William Wirt, attorney general of the United States, from a portrait by Charles B. King
Library of Congress

John Randolph of Roanoke, by Gilbert Stuart, c. 1804, Andrew W. Mellon Collection
Photograph ©Board of Trustees, National Gallery of Art, Washington, D.C.

John Taylor of Caroline, oil portrait attributed to William J. Hubbard
The Library of Virginia

John Marshall, chief justice of the Supreme Court, 1801–1835, oil attributed to John Blennerhassett Martin, c. 1834
Collection of the Supreme Court of the United States

Smith Thompson, associate justice of the Supreme Court, 1823–1843, etching by Albert Rosenthal, 1889
Library of Congress

Henry Baldwin, associate justice of the Supreme Court, 1830–1844, etching by Max Rosenthal, 1890
Library of Congress

John McLean, associate justice of the Supreme Court, 1829–1861, from Thomas Sully's 1831 portrait
Library of Congress

CHAPTER FIVE

Constitutional Law *for a* New Nation

America has chosen to be, in many respects, and to many purposes, a nation; and for all these purposes, her government is complete; to these objects, it is competent.

—*Chief Justice Marshall, Cohens v. Virginia*

In a word, the Constitution became a substitute for any deeper kind of national identity. American nationalism is distinct because, for nearly its first century, it was narrowly and peculiarly constitutional. People knew that without the Constitution there would be no America.

—*John Murrin, "A Roof without Walls"*

A MERICAN NATIONALISM was Marshall's one and only great conception," wrote Albert Beveridge, "and the fostering of it the purpose of his life." Indeed, there is hardly an aspect of Marshall's long public life that did not bear on that subject. His most telling contributions, however, came in the brief period of euphoric nationalism generated by the War of 1812. It is ironic that this war-spawned nationalism should have called Marshall into action, for he was convinced that the second war with England was unnecessary and unwise. In fact, the War of 1812 hardly seemed the occasion for a resurgence of nationalism at all, since it was fought for ends that had been largely achieved by diplomacy, concluded by a treaty that settled nothing that was unsettled, and was devoid of military glory except for a battle won after the war ended. Rather than uniting the American people, fighting the war widened the schism between northern and southern states, which had appeared in the

1790s. New England's opposition to "Mr. Madison's war" was so bitter that some of its leaders even flirted with secession. Thoughtful Americans, among them John Marshall, had no reason to take constitutional union for granted.[1]

Given the sectionalism generated by the war, it was surprising and ironic that the Treaty of Ghent (1814), which ended the war, should have generated so much nationalist sentiment. For the first time in national history, Americans were simultaneously at peace with Europe and with themselves. France, beaten and weak, was no threat. Britain, also exhausted, was already calculating the advantages of free trade, a policy that would bind it economically to the United States and permit the reassertion of common cultural ties that had been in abeyance since the Revolution. Separatist tendencies and partisan feelings, the monopoly of no one section or party, seemed to dissipate as the Federalist Party, suffering under the burden of the Hartford Convention, disappeared from the national scene. The diverse economic energies of the agrarian South, increasingly committed to growing cotton, and the commercial north, now the center of a revolution in textile production, appeared to be building blocks of a self-sustaining national economy rather than a cause of disunity.[2]

In short, the time was propitious for a new generation of statesmen to create national institutions that would capture the unique potential of the moment. Madison spoke to and for these statesmen in his Seventh Annual Message, December 5, 1815, when he declared there is no country "where nature invites more the art of man to complete her own work for his accommodation and benefit." Congressional nationalists were so enthusiastic about the president's list of national projects that they ignored his cautionary note concerning "any defect of constitutional authority," namely, that it "can be supplied in a mode which the Constitution itself has providently pointed out," that is to say, by formal amendment. Anxious to complete the work of nature, Congress responded with proposals for a national bank, a protective tariff, and federally sponsored internal improvements, appropriately called the American System.

1. Albert J. Beveridge, *The Life of John Marshall* (Boston, New York, 1916–1919), 4: 1. On the fragile, experimental nature of the new Constitution, see Paul C. Nagel, *One Nation Indivisible: The Union in American Thought, 1776–1861* (New York, 1964).

2. James M. Banner Jr.'s *To the Hartford Convention: The Federalists and the Origins of Party Politics in Massachusetts, 1789–1815* (New York, 1970) remains the standard work on the Hartford Convention. Concerning the ongoing impact of the convention, see Harlow W. Sheidley, *Sectional Nationalism: Massachusetts Conservative Leaders and the Transformation of America, 1815–1836* (Boston, 1998), especially 17–19. On post–War of 1812 nationalism: George Dangerfield, *The Awakening of American Nationalism, 1815–1828* (New York, 1965).

Other "American" projects—national scientific expeditions, a national university, a national military academy to train officers for a standing army—waited in the wings.[3]

Marshall's dream of American greatness and the realities of American history appear to have converged. Clearly he was positioned to help history along. His Court had recovered from the Chase impeachment and was wiser and stronger for it. Its working procedures were in place, and Marshall's credentials as first among equals were amply validated. The Court also enjoyed a period of unparalleled stability. Indeed, after Madison's appointment of Joseph Story and Gabriel Duvall in 1811, there were no changes in personnel for a dozen years. After *Marbury* and *Martin v. Hunter's Lessee* and the preceding fifteen years of successful adjudication, its interpretive powers also appeared to be firmly established. The Marshall Court was ready to go to work.

And there was great work to be done. Most in need of resolution was the issue of congressional power—its scope and limitations; its relation to state sovereignty and to the well-established tradition of state governance. On this issue, the Court had not yet spoken. When it did, it was Chief Justice Marshall who laid down the law. In *McCulloch v. Maryland,* he set forth the doctrine of implied powers: that Congress was not limited by a strict enumeration of powers in Article 1, Section 8, but could by way of the Necessary and Proper Clause in that article choose the means necessary to implement the powers specifically granted to it. Marshall closed the circle of doctrinal nationalism five years later in *Gibbons v. Ogden* (1824) with an expansive definition of congressional power over interstate commerce and with the corollary principle that the enumerated powers, while limiting what Congress could do, were virtually unlimited in the power they granted.

Marshall's opinions in *McCulloch* and *Gibbons* were the twin pillars of constitutional nationalism—and the foundation of his lasting fame. Subsequently, whenever the Supreme Court underwrote an expansion of national authority—as it did tentatively in the late nineteenth and early twentieth centuries and more decisively after 1937, when it validated the New Deal welfare, regulatory state—it cited his opinions for authority. In doing so, the New Deal Court inadvertently joined nationalist historians such as Beveridge in validating contemporary critics of Marshall, including Jefferson, John Taylor of Caroline, and Spencer Roane of the Virginia Court of Appeals. What Beveridge and

3. For Madison's remarks, see James D. Richardson, comp., *A Compilation of the Messages and Papers of the Presidents, 1789–1897* (Washington, D.C., 1896–1899), 1: 567–68.

Jefferson appear to have agreed on was that the chief justice had run rough-shod over his compliant colleagues and turned the Court into a personal instrument, which he then used to consolidate national power and reduce the states to impotency. Friend and foe alike, the New Deal Court as well, made Marshall a nation-building hero of mythical proportions.[4]

All myths contain some element of truth, and the Marshall myth was no exception. But his constitutional nationalism is easier to celebrate than it is to understand. To further understanding, several corrective factors need to be remembered, starting with the fact that the Marshall Court was not monolithic, even in the golden age of nationalism. Marshall's voice was a powerful one on that Court, and his leadership was often decisive, but he did not dominate the Court as contemporary critics and some historians claimed. Nor did Marshall and his colleagues rewrite constitutional history or control it. The Court's nationalist decisions, themselves often the product of collective deliberation and even compromise, were often resisted outright, undone, or watered down by subsequent political developments. Even, indeed especially, the great nationalist decision in *McCulloch* was not what it seemed. It figured significantly in the growth of the nation-state in the modern period, to be sure, but its meaning was altered significantly by Jackson's election in 1828 and the emergence of the states' rights Court of Chief Justice Roger Taney. Rather than settling the matter definitively, *McCulloch* produced a states' rights, anti-Court reaction that diminished its authority during the remainder of the antebellum period.

In assessing Marshall's constitutional nationalism, and hopefully avoiding the pitfall of anachronism, it needs to be recalled that the nation-state with its vast interventionist and regulatory bureaucracy was more than a century in the future. Local culture remained dominant throughout Marshall's life and for much of the nineteenth century and early twentieth century as well. To be sure, Marshall's constitutional nationalism did draw on post–War of 1812 nationalism, but the nationalist sentiments of that period were short-lived. Like the Framers, Marshall worked from a vision of what the new nation might become; but he never lost sight of what it actually was, which is to say he never underestimated the tenacity of local culture. Indeed, the nationalist doctrines he formulated during the golden age were deeply influenced by his fear that aggressive localism, organized politically under the states' rights banner, would subvert the Constitution and plunge the Republic back into the milieu of the Articles of Confederation period, when states ruled and chaos prevailed. In this

4. *McCulloch v. Maryland,* 4 Wheaton 316; *Gibbons v. Ogden,* 9 Wheaton 1.

respect, Marshall thought of himself and his Court as working to consolidate and legitimate the work of the Philadelphia Convention. The intent of the Framers was not just an interpretive rule of the Court but, as the chief justice saw it, was the essence of its being.

Viewed in perspective, Marshall's constitutional nationalism was much closer to the eighteenth century than to the twentieth, which fact qualifies him as a bone fide conservative. In many ways he remained an eighteenth-century man who simply believed that eighteenth-century values were relevant to the new age. As a constitutional nationalist and nation builder, however, he stood for change, indeed was on the cutting edge of it. This was also true of his dynamic conception of property and his passionate commitment to economic individualism. The problem, addressed in this chapter, is to clarify the symbiotic relationship between this individualism, with its antiregulatory bias, and his constitutional nationalism, which has historically been the source of governmental regulatory authority.[5]

The resolution of this paradox, and the key to the contextual meaning of Marshall's nationalism, is that his great nationalist opinions, in *McCulloch, Gibbons,* and *Dartmouth College,* aimed to create not a nation-*state* but a national market, an arena in which goods and credit moved without hindrance across state lines. Such a market, if the Court could fashion one from the raw material of the Constitution and the pressing needs of a new class of entrepreneurs, would provide an arena where enterprising individuals operating according to common-law principles of contract could put their creative energies to work for themselves and for their country. Contractual freedom, and contractual responsibility, guaranteed by the rule of law was the thread that united Marshall's multifaceted jurisprudence, including his approach to international law. His goal, in short, was to liberate not regulate, to create an environment where property was free to realize its productive potential and where individual property owners were free to rise or fall on their own merits.[6]

Marshall's effort to create a national market did not, as his states' rights critics charged, make him a consolidationist out to destroy the states. Indeed, when states acted to promote entrepreneurial activity, as they did judicially in

5. For an excellent discussion of the lasting influence of the eighteenth-century ideas on Marshall, see William E. Nelson, "The Eighteenth-Century Background of John Marshall's Constitutional Jurisprudence," *Michigan Law Review* 76 (May 1978): 893–960.

6. See Charles Sellers, *The Market Revolution: Jacksonian America, 1815–1846* (New York, 1991), and his critics Melvyn Stokes and Stephen Conway, eds., *The Market Revolution in America: Social, Political, and Religious Expressions, 1800–1880* (Charlottesville, Va., 1996).

the regular administration of common law and statutorily in the construction of canals and the improvement of river transportation, he was a states' rightist himself, as evidenced by his active support of internal improvements in Virginia. His constitutional nationalism, to put it another way, was designed to accomplish two things. The first was to give Congress the power to facilitate economic development, as in the creation of a national bank. The second was to prevent states under control of popular politicians from interfering with property rights, contractual sanctity, and/or federal efforts to facilitate their operation. Marshall's goal was balanced federalism, not national consolidation. In pursuing that goal, he did what constitutional logicians such as Calhoun and John Taylor, not to mention Jean Bodin, refused to do: he divided sovereignty, the power to govern, between state and nation. His aim was to make the nation supreme and secure in its rights and the states safe and sovereign in theirs, including the right to hold slaves. By unleashing the entrepreneurial energies of the American people, he hoped to neutralize states' rights thinking and bind the diverse regions in a Union of perceived self-interest. That done, the young nation could enter the family of nations on equal terms and face a hostile world without fear.

A Nation among Nations: International Law and National Identity

Nations, especially new ones, hammer out their identities in opposition to other nations. It is therefore important to note that the first two decades of Marshall's tenure on the Court were the last two decades of the century-long struggle between France and England for military, commercial, and ideological dominance of the cis-Atlantic world. In the context of this hegemonic conflict, the United States struggled to establish its status as a full member in the family of nations. France and England could have cared less, especially when their own survival was on the line. Nor did it help in this nation-defining endeavor that the United States had no army or navy, that its national boundaries were as yet undefined, that its institutions were inchoate and untested. Worse still, the nation was divided against itself, between Federalists, who wanted to put an English spin on American policy and culture, and Jeffersonian Republicans, who looked for support and inspiration to revolutionary France. Indeed, at no time in American history, not even during the cold war, were foreign affairs and domestic developments so intertwined as in the three decades from the

Treaty of Paris in 1783, which ended the first American Revolution, to the Treaty of Ghent in 1814, which ended the second.[7]

Marshall confronted this hostile world during much of his life, as a young soldier, as Federalist politician, as envoy to France, as secretary of state, and finally as chief justice. His experience drove home three lessons that greatly influenced his work as a nation builder. The first was a deep prejudice against revolutionary France, which nation he associated with the forces of anarchy and social disorder in the American body politic. The second was an abiding affinity for English institutions, and for Edmund Burke's philosophical justification of them. The third, more profound, lesson was that the United States, to survive in a hostile world, should prepare itself to resist *both* France and England, since both held American rights hostage to their self-interest. This was the harsh lesson that led him to fight England during the Revolution and support the Constitution in 1788, and to oppose revolutionary France and support Washington's neutrality policy in the 1790s. As secretary of state under Adams, he operated on the premise that national honor, national self-interest, and national preparedness went hand in hand. It was also the point of departure for his work on the Supreme Court in the field of international law.

International law, a staple of Marshall's early years as chief justice, is a logical starting point in evaluating his nationalist jurisprudence. In this area, in contrast to many others shared with state judiciaries, the Constitution made the Supreme Court the final undisputed tribunal for the settlement of disputes. Inevitably the conflict between England and France from 1801 until the Treaty of Ghent in 1814 and beyond presented the justices a wide array of international law questions. Out of the "quasi-war" with France in 1796–1798, came cases arising from the violation of federal statutes interdicting commerce with France and French possessions in the West Indies. Neutral rights was another pressing issue before the Court during the years leading to the War of 1812. These complicated questions were complicated further by federal statutes starting with the Embargo Act of 1807 and its numerous amendments, by the various versions of the Non-Intercourse Act of 1809, and by the several measures enacted to prohibit trading with the enemy during the War of 1812. Constantly

7. Bradford Perkins, *The First Rapprochement: England and the United States, 1795–1805* (Philadelphia, 1955); J. C. A. Stagg, *Mr. Madison's War: Politics, Diplomacy, and Warfare in the Early American Republic, 1783–1830* (Princeton, N.J., 1983); Roger H. Brown, *The Republic in Peril: 1812* (New York, 1964); Stephen Watts, *The Republic Reborn: War and the Making of Liberal America, 1790–1820* (Baltimore, 1987).

shifting national policy goals throughout the period added further to the Court's interpretive woes, as did a raft of poorly drawn federal statutes.[8]

During this hazardous period of international politics and war, the Marshall Court laid the foundation of a coherent body of international law suitable to the needs of the young Republic. According to Marshall, international law was the law of nations, and his definition of it said much about the kind of law he fashioned. "That law," as he explained it to Talleyrand during the XYZ negotiations, "forms, independent of compact, a rule of action by which the Sovereignties of the civilized world consent to be governed. It prescribes what one nation may do without giving just cause of war, and what of consequence another may and ought to permit without being considered as having sacrificed its honour, its dignity or its independence." The process of bringing the United States into this international system of law was an act of national self-definition. Under Marshall's leadership as chief justice, the United States made its debut as a champion of international law and order. To champion law in a world at war was a moral thing to do and a republican one as well. It was also a realistic policy that accommodated America's weakness, its lack of military and naval strength, and played to America's strength, its growing commercial prowess. Marshall's international law and municipal jurisprudence was, then, part of a single policy designed to expand the operation of the free market and liberate the energy of American businessmen.[9]

The materials for forging a body of such law were readily available. Most important, the justices had at their disposal a body of international law from the seventeenth and eighteenth centuries fashioned by the continental publicists to govern the nation-states of Europe. Unlike Story, and some state judges in maritime jurisdictions such as New York and Pennsylvania, Marshall neither had nor claimed to have a commanding knowledge of Grotius, Puffendorf, Bynkershoek, or Vattel, to name the most frequently cited of these jurists. Indeed on many matters of international law, he graciously deferred to his ambitious and scholarly colleague from Massachusetts. On the other hand, he had a working knowledge of the leading authorities from his brief study with George Wythe at William and Mary and from his private practice in Virginia. Emmer-

---

8. Marshall's contributions to international law are treated in Benjamin Munn Ziegler, *The International Law of John Marshall: A Study of First Principles* (Chapel Hill, N.C., 1939); also see the authoritative analysis in George Lee Haskins and Herbert A. Johnson, *Foundations of Power: John Marshall, 1801–1815* (New York, 1981), especially pt. 2, ch. 5, and G. Edward White, *The Marshall Court and Cultural Change, 1815–1835* (New York, 1988), ch. 13.

9. Memorandum from the Envoys to Talleyrand, PJM, 3: 338.

ich Vattel, the eighteenth-century Swiss jurist, continued to be a favorite with Marshall, perhaps because as Peter and Nicholas Onuf suggest, Vattel "was a man of liberal tendencies who saw no reason why liberalism and republicanism could not be reconciled in law and state craft." More important perhaps, Vattel, like Marshall, started his reasoning in international law from the premise that nations were sovereign, that they could be counted on to pursue self-interest, and, accordingly, that their adherence to the rule of law depended on whether it was in the national interest to do so. Cornelius van Bynkershoek was also cited frequently by Marshall, perhaps because both men reasoned from a positivist premise. English jurists, such as Lord Stowell, were also cited by Marshall and his colleagues, though sometimes as the foil to, rather than the source of, American law, as in the case of *The Nereide*.[10]

In international law no less than in the common law, Marshall acknowledged the importance of tradition. Or as he put it in *Dunlop & Co. v. Ball* (1804), it is "best to adhere to old decisions." But the challenge was not simply to apply old rules, of which there were few, nor was it to create new ones. Rather it was to choose the most appropriate rules from a wide array of often conflicting sources and apply them creatively to settle individual disputes on an equitable basis compatible with American sovereign power and national interest. For the most part, it was on-the-job training for Marshall and his colleagues. What made him a formidable voice in this collective endeavor were those same qualities that made him a good lawyer. Occasionally he spoke in the "grand style," most notably in *The Schooner Exchange v. McFaddon*. But in the run-of-the-docket cases, his was only one voice among several, and more than once he found himself on the losing side. What he did *not* lose in the midst of this lawyerly give-and-take was his authority as leader of the Court. As chief justice, he was responsible for maintaining a rational environment for debate, where the diverse talents of his colleagues could be utilized and where complex and unsettled legal questions could be disputed openly, fairly, and free of the partisan rancor that characterized foreign-policy debates in the political branches. In harnessing the justices to the legal work at hand, he succeeded admirably.[11]

10. Emmerich de Vattel, *The Law of Nations; or, the Principles of the Law of Nature . . .*, trans. Charles G. Fenwick, introduction by Albert De Lapradelle (Washington, 1916). Peter Onuf and Nicholas Onuf, *Federal Union, Modern World: The Law of Nations in an Age of Revolutions, 1776–1814* (Madison, Wis., 1993), 17. Ziegler, *International Law of Marshall*, ch. 1, treats Marshall's general view of international law.

11. 2 Cranch 185, as quoted in Haskins and Johnson, *Foundations of Power*, 548.

What guided him through the maze of complex and often controversial cases was a conviction that American national interest could best be served in a world governed by legal rules fairly and impartially administered. As he put it to Court reporter Henry Wheaton, who was on his way to becoming America's leading scholar in international law, the law of nations is "a law which contributes more to the happiness of the human race, than all the statues which ever came from the hands of the sculptor, or all the paintings that were ever placed on canvass." Marshall believed this law should rule, but he also understood that legal principles, however elegant, did not always govern the affairs of nations. Since power, corruption, and greed often determined the affairs of nations, as it did those of individuals, it followed that the United States should be prepared to fight if called on to do so. Indeed, there was a martial motif in Marshall's life and law, one that late-nineteenth-century expansionists such as Beveridge resonated with. Having fought to create a nation, Marshall was willing to fight to defend it. At the same time, he was reluctant to beat the drums of war, as Americans of both parties were fond of doing in the frustrating decade leading to the War of 1812. He was also strongly opposed to the second war with England, believing that it was brought on by the duplicity of France and naivete of the Madison administration. So strong were his feelings that he was even considered by some to be the logical peace candidate for the Federalist Party in the election of 1812.[12]

Mainly Marshall aimed to avoid war by being prepared to fight one, as can be noted in his spirited defense of the regular army, compared to the militia, at the Virginia ratifying convention. Even more to the point was his speech in defense of the standing army in January 1801. The debate in Congress was prompted by the motion on January 1, 1801, by John Nicholas of Virginia to repeal the Federalist army bills of 1798 and 1799, which had enlarged the army in anticipation of a possible French invasion. Virginia states' rightists opposed the bill as an unnecessary expense and because some of them feared a national army controlled by Federalists was a threat to Virginia. Nicholas's resolutions were particularly controversial in light of the fact that the Adams administration was negotiating with France in an effort to end the undeclared war that had been going on since the failure of the XYZ mission. Marshall's

12. Marshall to Wheaton, 24 March 1821, PJM, 9: 147–48. On the war policy, see Marshall to Robert Smith, 27 July 1812, PJM, 7: 337–39. For Marshall as a possible peace candidate, PJM, 7: 340 n. 4, citing James H. Broussard, *The Southern Federalists, 1800–1816* (Baton Rouge, 1978), 139–46.

speech, printed in the *Philadelphia Aurora* of January 17, was imperfectly recorded, but his disgust with the feeble arguments of his Virginia opponents is abundantly clear. As he saw it, France, and by extension other countries as well, would respect America only if it were prepared to defend its interests by force as well as words. As for the argument that preparedness cost too much, it was beyond contempt. "Suppose," he said, "this had been the language of '75—Suppose at the commencement of our revolution, a gentleman had risen on the floor of congress, to compare our revenues with our expenses—what would have been the result of the calculation? . . . If vast exertions were then made to acquire independence, will not the same exertions be now made to maintain it? The question now is—whether self-government and national liberty be worth the money which must be expended to preserve them." Marshall asked the question as a soldier of the Revolution and the hero of XYZ; the majority of the House answered by defeating the Nicholas resolution.[13]

Marshall's realpolitik approach to international relations was no doubt conditioned by his experience negotiating with Talleyrand. It wasn't just France that troubled him but human passion and greed as it was reflected in the affairs of nations. He took the hard line on military preparedness because he had lived sixty years of his life in an age of war or threat of war and because America was notoriously unprepared to do battle on land or on sea. For the very same reasons, and with the same concern for national self-interest, he worked for the peaceful resolution of disputes between nations by recourse to international law. Making law fashioned by foreign jurists to fit the European state system of the seventeenth and eighteenth centuries suitable to the nineteenth-century United States was a new line of work for Marshall. Fortunately, there was also considerable intellectual overlap between national and international law, so that experience in one area was readily transferable to the other. Textual interpretation was obviously a staple feature of both systems, for example, and constitutional cases involving international law were still constitutional cases to be settled by familiar interpretive methods. Common-law thinking was regularly, and probably unavoidably, employed in international law cases, too, as can be witnessed in the Court's tendency, following Vattel, to consider treaties between nationals as analogous to contracts between individuals. Indeed, in Marshall's international law opinions lies buried a subtle but certain Lockean (common-law) subtext: Legal disputes between nations almost always involved the clash, if not directly of great sovereign powers themselves, then of

13. For Marshall's speech, see PJM, 4: 53–58, quote at 56.

individuals who, as surrogates for their respective nations, aggressively pursued their own property interests. Questions of competing sovereignties were never far from the surface in such cases, but Marshall privileged individual rights and private property where possible. Above all, he rarely overlooked the benefits to national prosperity and world peace of expansive commerce operating in the international market governed by rational and dependable legal rules. Not surprisingly, Marshall's rendition of international law greatly resembled the law-abiding, rule-conscious, liberal-republican contours of his municipal jurisprudence.[14]

Indeed, Marshall assumed that international law was part of municipal jurisprudence and, following the Constitution, that the rules of international law, written and unwritten, were applicable in the settlement of disputes in the federal courts, a point made explicit in *The Nereide* (1815). He was also concerned that judicial interpretation of those rules be consistent—witness, for example, the rules of construction he set forth in *Murray v. Charming Betsy* (1804), *The Nereide,* or his circuit opinion in *The Brig Wilson v. U.S.* (1820). Nowhere was Marshall's effort to promulgate a principled, coherent, and policy-wise international law, or the difficulty of doing so, more apparent than in *The Schooner Exchange.* The case originated as a libel brought by Greetham and McFaddon, both of Maryland, in the U.S. District Court for Pennsylvania against the schooner *Exchange,* which the libelants claimed as their property. The ship had been taken by a French warship in 1810 and confiscated by the French government under the Rambouillet Decree of March 23, 1810, which, in retaliation to the Non-Intercourse Act of March 1, 1809, declared open season on all American ships entering French ports. The following year, the *Exchange,* now renamed the *Balaou,* was commissioned as a French ship of war. The ship was sailing under a French captain and crew when it entered the port of Philadelphia for emergency repairs. When the legal niceties of their libel were stripped away, what the former owners, as citizens of the United States, wanted was for the federal court, speaking for the United States government, to give them back what France and the accidents of international war had unjustly taken. Both American sovereignty and the property rights of Americans were on the line.[15]

14. Robert K. Faulkner notes the Lockean individualism (via Vattel) in Marshall's international law in *The Jurisprudence of John Marshall* (Princeton, N.J., 1968), 6.

15. *Murray v. Charming Betsy,* 2 Cranch 64; *The Nereide,* 9 Cranch 388; *The Brig Wilson v. U.S.,* US Cir. Ct. Va., reprinted in PJM, 9: 31–40. *The Schooner Exchange v. McFaddon,* 7 Cranch 116–35. See Beveridge, *Life of John Marshall,* 4: 121, for praise of *McFaddon.* Also see Haskins

For Marshall, who cherished both and who also saw Napoleonic France as a threat to civilization, the issue was indeed "delicate," the more so because there was no certain law governing the case. Alexander Dallas and William Pinkney, lawyers for the plaintiff, thought differently and cited Bynkershoek and Lord Stowell authoritatively, a bit arrogantly as well, to prove their point. Marshall was not persuaded by their display of learning. As he put it, in exploring this "unbeaten path," there were "few, if any aids from precedents or written law." This meant, and here he spoke like a common lawyer, that the justices would have "to rely much on general principles, and on a train of reasoning founded on cases in some degree analogous to this." This also meant that the Court had considerable leeway to do what it wanted, which meant it would in the volatile political climate on the eve of the War of 1812 be blamed for what it did.[16]

Given the creative options available and Marshall's personal biases, it is remarkable that he handed down an opinion that could be, and was, construed by a hostile press as a victory for Napoleonic France and that, at the same time, refused to summon American sovereignty to protect the property rights of American citizens. The legal reasoning that carried him to this unpopular conclusion reveals both his independence of mind and the way he balanced American sovereignty and the international rule of law. He started by conceding what had to be conceded: the sovereign power of a nation over its own territory was undisputed. "All exceptions" to that principle, "therefore, to the full and complete power of a nation within its own territories, must be traced to the consent of the nation itself." And why should the new American nation, jealous of its newly won independence, surrender a portion of its sovereignty? Why in this case, would it grant immunity from a just suit against a public armed vessel of another sovereign power in derogation of the property rights of American citizens? His answer was that American adherence to accepted principles of international law, even if they had to be ascertained by creative analytical reasoning, was in the long run national interest. "The world being composed of distinct sovereignties, possessing equal rights and equal independence, whose mutual benefit is promoted by intercourse with each other, and by an interchange of those good offices which humanity dictates and its wants

---

and Johnson, *Foundations of Power,* quoting Judge Dumbald, who probably quoted Beveridge, 531. Charles Warren, *The Supreme Court in United States History,* new and rev. ed. (Boston, 1926), 1: 425–26, described the opinion as "one of the great fundamental decisions in international law."

16. PJM, 7: 307.

require, all sovereigns have consented to a relaxation in practice, in cases under certain peculiar circumstances, of that absolute and complete jurisdiction within their respective territories which sovereignty confers." Put simply, the sovereign people, through the Constitution, made the law of nations the law of the land. The duty of the Supreme Court, it followed, was to determine what the law of nations was and in what cases and under what circumstances it applied. International law was not something common lawyers such as Marshall knew from practice; the method of doing it was.[17]

What Marshall did in *McFaddon* regarding international law was what he did in *Marbury* regarding constitutional law: He pledged himself and the Court to rule by principle and not by whim or political expediency. His efforts in behalf of principled adjudication are the more notable because of the admittedly broad discretion allowed to judges in matters of international law and because he was not the undisputed expert in the field. District judges such as Richard Peters of the eastern district of Pennsylvania and John Davis of the federal district court in Boston, whose opinions the Court often reviewed, were at least Marshall's equal in areas of commercial international law. On the Supreme Court, Justices William Johnson, Bushrod Washington, and even John Cushing until his death in 1810, felt comfortable in challenging him. He could parse cases and mobilize legal authorities with the ablest of them, to be sure, as *McFaddon* attests. But his bent was to draw freely on the labors of federal district judges, the talented Supreme Court bar, and the expertise of his colleagues. Marshall was especially deferential to Joseph Story, whose scholarly disposition and experience in the practice of maritime law made him an instant authority. The two men would part company on important matters including wartime executive authority and international law governing neutral rights. But by deferring to Story, the chief justice harnessed the young scholar's impressive expertise to the work of the Court, just as he drew freely on the legal arguments of Dallas, Thomas Emmet, Pinkney, Wirt, and Webster in fashioning his own opinions. Marshall's goal was not to dominate his colleagues, as his critics charged, but to maintain an atmosphere of free and open debate wherein each could contribute to the collective enterprise according to his talents.[18]

17. *The Schooner Exchange v. McFaddon,* 7 Cranch 135–36.

18. On the Marshall-Story collaboration, see R. Kent Newmyer, *Supreme Court Justice Joseph Story: Statesman of the Old Republic* (Chapel Hill, N.C., 1985) generally; on the creative tension between them in the field of international law and the resulting atmosphere of intellectual freedom and creative endeavor, ibid., ch. 3.

Operating collectively, the Marshall Court gradually built up a body of case law that located the United States in the world community and defined the rights and duties of American citizens in the international arena. Much of its work—notably in those cases arising under the embargo laws and, after the repeal of the embargo, under the various non-intercourse acts passed by Congress—was run-of-the-mill statutory construction. It was important work. Large amounts of property were often involved, not to mention the livelihood of entire communities. Moreover, the statutes in question, particularly those involving the Embargo Act of 1807 and its amendments, not only involved an unparalleled intrusion of federal power into local affairs but also were often loosely and vaguely drawn. At stake was rule of law itself. Especially was this the case in New England, where the violation of wartime restrictions on the trading-with-the-enemy laws was considered a patriotic act.[19]

On the whole, the Supreme Court, the lower federal courts as well, upheld the broad exercise of national sovereignty in foreign affairs, adhering to the principle laid down in *The Schooner Exchange* that nations have sovereign control in foreign policy matters in their own territory. In adjudicating international law questions, the party affiliation and ideological preferences of the justices rarely appear. It was district judge John Davis of Massachusetts, for example, who upheld the authority of Congress to pass the Embargo Act, the only decision on the constitutionality of that controversial law and one that ran directly counter to Davis's Federalist politics and those of his section. It was William Johnson, appointed to the Court by President Jefferson in 1804, who spoke out most vigorously against the excessively broad discretionary powers of enforcement granted to the executive branch by the 1809 amendment to the Embargo Act, an amendment pushed by Jefferson himself. Story's strenuous efforts on the first circuit to enforce trading-with-the-enemy laws were taken in the face of opposition from his New England friends and supporters.[20]

Marshall went along with the foreign policies pursued by Jefferson and Madison not because he always agreed with them but because he believed that the Constitution granted broad powers to the executive in matters of foreign policy. While conceding power to the national executive, however, he also in-

19. Haskins and Johnson, *Foundations of Power,* pt. 2, ch. 2.

20. Ibid; Newmyer, *Justice Joseph Story,* ch. 3; Warren, *Supreme Court,* 1: ch. 7; Donald G. Morgan, *Justice William Johnson, The First Dissenter: The Career and Constitutional Philosophy of a Jeffersonian Judge* (Columbia, S.C., 1954), chs. 4 and 5.

sisted that it be exercised within the bounds of law, thus his opinion in the war-time prize case of *Brown v. U.S.* (1814). The issue was whether a quantity of British timber floating in a tidal creek automatically and without the benefit of special legislative act became subject to confiscation as enemy property with the declaration of war. Brown, who purchased from British owners after the outbreak of war but before confiscation, argued the negative. The case was particularly interesting because it pitted the rights of private property against governmental authority in time of war and because it involved the doctrine of implied powers Marshall was soon to announce in *McCulloch v. Maryland.* In *Brown,* however, it was not Marshall but Story, in dissent, who contended that the president, "as an incident of the office," had the wide discretionary power to prosecute the war effort without statutory authorization.[21]

Marshall disagreed. In speaking for the majority, he reiterated the principles that run through his and the Court's international law decisions: first, that the power of the sovereign state was plenary within its jurisdiction, second, that it had to be exercised according to "the modern law of nations in its modern state of purity and refinement." There was no doubt, he continued, that "war gives to the sovereign full right to take the persons and confiscate the property of the enemy wherever found." And when the sovereign acts, the "judicial department must give effect to its will." At the same time, "the humane and wise policy of modern times"—the rule of law, that is—requires the sovereign to speak in clear and unequivocal terms when exercising power. Congress had the undisputed right to authorize the confiscation of enemy property but had passed no law specifically saying so at the time of the confiscation. The war-time powers of the president alone were not sufficient to the chore. "The universal practice of forbearing to seize and confiscate debts and credits, the principles universally received, that the right to them revives on the restoration of peace, would seem to prove that war is not an absolute confiscation of this property, but simply confers the right of confiscation. Between debts contracted under the faith of laws, and property acquired in the course of trade, on the faith of the same laws, reason draws no distinction."[22]

Marshall's view that national sovereignty in foreign affairs was simultaneously plenary and law-abiding, as well as his solicitude for private property,

21. *Brown v. U.S.,* 8 Cranch 110; for a discussion of the case, see Haskins and Johnson, *Foundations of Power,* 543–45; Newmyer, *Justice Joseph Story,* 94–95; Story quote at 8 Cranch 128–29, 149.

22. *Brown v. U.S.,* 8 Cranch 122–24; also see Ziegler, *International Law of Marshall,* 48–50.

can also be seen in his approach to the treaty power in Article 2, Section 2, of the Constitution, which authorizes the president to make treaties with the advice and consent of the Senate. Marshall lived in an age of treaties, many of which touched his life directly. The Treaty of Paris of 1763 ended the Seven Years' War and helped bring on the American Revolution, in which he fought; the 1778 treaty of military alliance with France contributed to American independence, which was recognized by the Treaty of Paris of 1783. The Jay Treaty of 1795 was a signal event in the emerging party system of the 1790s. As a Federalist politician, Marshall defended it against Jeffersonian critics; in the XYZ mission, he tried to justify it to Talleyrand. Marshall's duties as secretary of state were circumscribed by international treaty law. As he put it in one of his XYZ dispatches, "The right to form these treaties has been so universally asserted & admitted, that it seems to be the inseparable attribute of sovereignty, to be questioned only by those, who question the right of a nation to govern itself, and to be ceded only by those, who are prepared to cede their independence."[23]

As chief justice, Marshall consistently supported a broad construction of the treaty-making provisions of the Constitution. He and his colleagues confronted the issue several times and on subjects as varied as the "cession of territory, the descent and tenure of property, the confiscation of debts, and extradition," not to mention questions of war and peace, commerce, and relations with Native Americans. Following Vattel, Marshall assumed treaty obligations made in these various areas were moral obligations no less binding than were contracts between private individuals. Never did he challenge the federal treaty power or curtail its constitutional reach. And in one notable instance, that of *American Insurance Co. v. Canter* (1828), he expanded that authority by necessary implication to include the right of the sovereign to acquire and govern new territory by treaty. Marshall also adhered to the principle he set forth in his speech on Jonathan Robbins, that the president was "the sole organ of the nation in its external relations" and that the Court would not interfere. The most he could do as chief justice he did, which was announce to the world in his opinions that the new American Republic planned to enter the family of nations armed with all the attributes of a sovereign nation and with a republican law-abiding spirit as well.[24]

23. Ziegler, *International Law of Marshall,* ch. 13, on Marshall and treaties is excellent. For Marshall quote, see his memorandum to Talleyrand, 17 January 1798, PJM, 3: 360.

24. Again, see Ziegler, *International Law of Marshall,* ch. 13, especially 330 and 335; also *U.S. v. Schooner Peggy,* 1 Cranch 110; *American Insurance Co. v. Canter,* 1 Peters 511.

In this scheme of things there was no contradiction between national sovereignty and international rule of law, since by definition sovereign states could bind themselves internationally. It followed logically that sovereign nations could *not* bind third parties, nor could they bind themselves by implication or by reference to generalized notions of universal moral principle. Marshall made both points forcefully, indeed painfully clear in the slave trading case of *The Antelope* (1825). The case is relevant here for two reasons: first, because it confirms Marshall's recognition of national sovereignty, and national self-interest, as the foundation of international law; second, because it shows the strong element of legal positivism that infused his juridical thinking. The legal question emanating from the immensely complicated factual environment in the case was about whether the international slave trade was prohibited by international law. In the circuit case of *U.S. v. La Jeune Eugenie* (1822), Story contended that it was, arguing that the slave trade was outlawed by the great principles of "Christian duty, the dictates of natural religion, the obligations of good faith and morality, and the eternal maxims of social justice." He also addressed the positivist argument, contending that the positive laws against the slave trade passed individually by France, Great Britain, and the United States, plus joint action limiting the trade, taken at Vienna, Aix-la-Chapelle, and London, added up to a positivist mandate against the trade, enforceable in American courts as a rule of international law. Marshall's *Antelope* opinion for the majority rejected Story's argument on both points, holding that there was no law of nations, Christian or otherwise, prohibiting the international slave trade and that none could be cobbled together by implication. Nations could agree collectively to ban the "abhorrent" and "unnatural" traffic, as he called it, but they would have to do so explicitly by convention or multinational treaty action before their action had the force of international law.[25]

The Court's restraint in *The Antelope* might be seen as a calculated concession to southern states' rightists, who were out to trim the Court's sails. As chief justice, Marshall was also obliged to consider the passionate divisions among the justices, a point he made in his opinion. But his reluctance to create international law by judicial mandate also stemmed from his general conviction, stated as far back as his Robbins speech, that the Court would defer to the executive branch in foreign affairs, particularly to the executive's treaty-making authority granted in Article 2, Section 2, paragraph 2. Judging from

---

25. *The Antelope*, 10 Wheaton 66 at 115–16; *U.S. v. La Jeune Eugenie*, 26 Fed. Cas. 832 (No. 15, 551) (C.C.D.Mass.); also Newmyer, *Justice Joseph Story*, 347–50.

Marshall's spirited defense of Washington in the Jay Treaty conflict, he firmly believed politics ought to stop at the water's edge. Judging from his opinion in the *American Insurance Co. v. Cantor,* he also believed separation of powers ought not to obstruct America's effort to deal with foreign states. The specific question in that case, the foreign policy counterpart to the implied powers question in *McCulloch,* asked whether the national government could acquire territory by treaty when the power to do so was nowhere specifically granted by the Constitution. The general issue was whether and to what degree the treaty power was itself limited by the Constitution. Speaking for the Court, Marshall deferred to executive authority and presidential discretion. The unspoken assumption, with Washington and Adams as models no doubt, was that presidents ought to be trusted to use judgment and good sense. At the same time Marshall indicated, by implication, that the treaty-making power, like congressional authority, was subject to constitutional limitations. His Court never ruled on that.[26]

By far the most controversial cases involving treaties were those in conflict with state laws, and/or with individual rights claimed under them. The issue made its appearance first at the Virginia ratifying convention, where Anti-Federalists opposed Article 2 on the ground that treaty making was an aristocratic threat to democratic states' rights. And so it appeared to be in *Ware v. Hylton.* Marshall argued for the Virginia debtors and states' rights in that case, but he did so as his client's lawyer, not by conviction. For him, the broad authority of the nation to bind itself and its citizens by treaty was an essential attribute of national sovereignty, a point he made forcefully during the Jay Treaty debates and more forcefully still to Talleyrand in 1798. Marshall's conflict with Virginia over title to the Fairfax lands also depended to a considerable degree on the supremacy of federal treaties over state law and was, in fact, settled on that ground in *Fairfax's Devisee v. Hunter's Lessee* and *Martin v. Hunter's Lessee.* Virginia's response to those decisions was the opening salvo in a major assault on the Court in the 1820s and early 1830s, but for Marshall the decisions vindicated both the Court's appellate power and the supremacy of federal treaty law over states' statutes and judicial decisions. Those decisions also struck a blow for freedom of contract and the rights of private property, including Marshall's land in the Northern Neck.[27]

26. *American Insurance Co. v. Canter,* 1 Peters 511.
27. *Fairfax's Devisee v. Hunter's Lessee,* 7 Cranch 603; *Martin v. Hunter's Lessee,* 1 Wheaton 304.

Concern for property rights also figured in his opinions on neutral rights. The challenge here was to balance national sovereignty with national self-interest, which was bound up in a world order secured by principles of international law. Of all the areas of international law the Court confronted, neutral rights was the most obviously political. Indeed, Marshall himself entered active politics as a defender of Washington's neutrality policy in 1793. It was a policy, as he put it in his biography of Washington, to which the American government "inflexibly adhered, and to which much of the national prosperity is to be ascribed." Marshall adhered to it himself as envoy to France in the XYZ mission, as John Adams's secretary of state, and finally as chief justice. As chief justice, however, he found the problems of implementation to be highly complicated. Not only did party divisions over foreign policy threaten to invade the Court, but the law governing neutral rights was the least well developed of all the fields of international law. As a leading scholar on the subject notes, it had "not advanced much beyond a recognition of the fact that such a doctrine did exist." One problem was that neutral rights were generally beyond the reach of treaty or municipal law, which meant that the Court could not fall back on the tradition of strict statutory interpretation. Nor was there a body of American precedents to follow, especially since English case law was biased toward Great Britain. Even the great treatise writers of the seventeenth and eighteenth century on the law of nations had failed to develop a fully coherent set of guiding principles. And even when principles could be ascertained, gaining respect for them was difficult when France and England violated them with impunity.[28]

Neutral rights cases presented the justices with a wide range of issues, the most important being the nature of blockade, the rights of belligerents to interdict neutral trade with other belligerents; the definition of contraband and neutral goods; and the adjudication of prize, which raised a series of questions concerning the nature and reach of municipal law. The Court's answers to these questions are impossible to summarize briefly. But what comes through in nearly all is the adherence to the principle Marshall laid down in *The Schooner Exchange*: that the safest course for the Court and the best policy for America was to avoid politics and follow so far as they could be ascertained the established principles of international law.

Perhaps no case better illustrates Marshall's commitment to this principle,

---

28. Marshall's *Life of Washington,* 5: 408, is quoted by Ziegler, *International Law of Marshall,* 182. Ziegler discusses Marshall's position on neutral rights, ibid., ch. 9.

and the difficulty of maintaining it on a divided Court, than *The Nereide.* The issue was neutral rights, and the question, as he put it, asked whether "the conduct of Manuel Pinto . . . had impressed a hostile character on his property . . . laden on board of the Nereide," thus making it subject to capture and condemnation as lawful prize. Pinto was a citizen of Argentina, a neutral power in the war between the United States and Great Britain. In 1813, he chartered the armed merchant ship *Nereide,* belonging to British subjects, for a voyage from London to Buenos Aires and back. The charter party expressly stipulated that the ship sail under the protection of a British convoy. On the first leg of the voyage, the vessel was accidentally separated from the convoy, and while attempting to return, the ship was taken captive by an American privateer and taken to New York, where Pinto's property, along with the British property aboard, was condemned as lawful prize. The condemnation was upheld by federal district judge William Van Ness in a decision Story thought "unanswerable." Pinto appealed to the circuit court, where a pro forma division sent the case to the Supreme Court for decision in 1815.[29]

The case put Marshall and the Court to the test. It had been argued brilliantly on both sides, as Marshall noted, and with plenty of diversionary material thrown in to appeal to the justices, or to throw them off track. References to Vattel, Bynkershoek, and other authorities were scattered generously throughout arguments of counsel. There were copious references on the side of the captors to Sir William Scott, England's most distinguished admiralty lawyer and one whom Marshall greatly respected. Inferential reasoning from American treaties was cited to clarify, or obscure, the issue. American property was on the line, since a decision against Pinto would put money in the hands of American privateers. Equally important were the policy questions at stake. An expansive definition of neutral rights had been a consistent element of American policy, which is not surprising since the United States had taken advantage of the war between France and England to corner a lion's share of the international carrying trade. Commercial New England, hard hit by the wartime cessation of trade, looked to the future when neutral rights would support its reemergence as a major force in international trade. As Story forcefully reminded the majority in his dissent, however, the United States was a belligerent in the war with England. Looking forward to the day when the American navy rather than England's might rule the waves, Story insisted on an expansive view of belligerent rights. To support his position, he cited Van Ness's district

29. *The Nereide,* 9 Cranch 388. See Newmyer, *Justice Joseph Story,* 95.

court opinion approvingly, but mainly he relied on Lord Stowell and other English authorities to bolster his position. Marshall, who generally deferred to Story on questions of admiralty and maritime law, no doubt listened attentively, the more so since, like Story, he advocated military and naval preparedness.[30]

Deciding *The Nereide* put Marshall and his brethren to work doing what they did best and most often, which was not making law wholesale but building incrementally through analogy, extrapolation, and matching principle to fact. In this respect, doing international law was not that different from doing the common law. Marshall was no expert in neutral rights, but he was a quick learner and a keen listener with a genius for separating the wheat from the chaff. After lengthy and impressive oral arguments from both sides and a spirited debate among the sharply divided justices, he came out for an expansive interpretation of neutral rights that won over a majority of his colleagues. His opinion was rendered with great authority, even though he wasn't one, and with a friendly combative zest that still jumps out of the dry and dusty reports. In two pages, he dismantled the outer defenses of Pinkney and Hoffman, who contended that Pinto failed to prove his neutral character and that the treaty with Spain, along with the general principles of reciprocity, settled the matter in favor of condemnation. Sorting through the relevant testimony and trial documentation carefully, Marshall rejected their arguments without hesitation. He was equally dismissive of Dallas's contention that by explicitly accepting the well-known principle "that neutral bottoms make neutral goods" in the treaty of 1795, Spain and the United States had by necessary construction accepted the principle "that enemy bottoms shall communicate the hostile character to the cargo." The latter notion, declared Marshall, was not an accepted principle of international law and, if admitted as such, would significantly diminish the generally accepted body of neutral rights. True to his general respect for national sovereignty in international law, he conceded that sovereign nations might pledge themselves to such a rule by treaty, but they would have to do so "by express compact." After examining the relevant treaties with the trained eye of a former secretary of state, he concluded that no such express stipulation existed. Left undiluted was the traditional principle that neutral ships make neutral goods.[31]

These questions, Marshall said in a gentle rebuke to learned counsel, "have

30. Newmyer, *Justice Joseph Story*, 95–97.
31. 9 Cranch 418 for quote.

been found on examination to be simple and clear" once they had been "stripped of the imposing garb in which they have been presented to the court." Not so was the remaining question of balancing belligerent and neutral rights. It was agreed that neutrals could ship their goods on belligerent vessels, and Marshall cited both Vattel and Bynkershoek to nail down the point. But it was also an agreed principle that neutrals who did so could not behave so as to identify themselves with the belligerents without subjecting their goods to confiscation. Whether Pinto had done so was the real issue, and it was an extremely difficult one because the facts were contested and because the line between neutral rights and neutral obligations was "not so distinctly marked as to be clearly discernible." Indeed, he continued, "It is impossible to declare in favor of either, without hearing, from the other, objections which it is difficult to answer and arguments which it is not easy to refute. . . ." All the Court could do was "avail itself of all the aid which has been furnished by the bar," give the "subject a patient investigation," then decide, knowing that the result was "not completely satisfactory, even to ourselves."[32]

Following his own admonition, Marshall threaded his way painstakingly through conflicting arguments, coming down finally on the side of Pinto and neutral rights. Yes, he conceded, the *Nereide* was a belligerent vessel; yes, it was armed; yes, it resisted capture. But no, these facts did not alter the neutral status of Pinto's goods, because evidence proved to the Court's satisfaction that Pinto was not instrumental in arming it. Resistance was a more serious matter, since Pinto was aboard the vessel. But all available evidence—the charter party, the letters of instruction from the owner to the master—indicated that he had no real control over the vessel except in lading his own goods. The facts worked for Pinto, but the difficulties with the principle remained. As Story pointed out in his dissent, citing Lord Stowell, if neutrals could ship their goods on armed belligerent vessels that resisted capture, how could belligerents exercise their right of search, which was essential if they were to prohibit the shipment of contraband, their acknowledged right.[33]

Marshall was correct, then, as Story's argument demonstrated, that the law drew no clearly discernible line between the rights of neutrals and the rights of belligerents. That fact did not keep the chief justice from doing what sitting judges are required to do which is to settle the case with the materials at hand in the short time allotted. In this case, as in most others, judging required not

32. Ibid., 423, 425.
33. Ibid., 427–28.

the creation of new principles but the application of old and often imperfect ones to a unique body of facts. The relevant facts in *The Nereide* were, as Marshall noted in a backhanded compliment to Pinkney, whom Marshall had just put in his place, not so easy to discern either. "With a pencil dipped in the most vivid colors," he said, most likely with a sparkle in his eye, "and guided by the hand of a master, a splendid portrait has been drawn exhibiting this vessel and her freighter as forming a single figure, composed of the most discordant materials of peace and war. So exquisite was the skill of the artist, so dazzling the garb in which the figure was presented, that it required the exercise of that cold investigating faculty which ought always to belong to those who sit on this bench, to discover its only imperfection; its want of resemblance." In truth, the "Nereide has not that centaur-like appearance which has been ascribed to her. She does not rove over the oceans hurling the thunders of war while sheltered by the olive branch of peace." The less dramatic truth was that Pinto was a merchant plying his trade as best he could in a world at war, and he got Marshall's sympathy for precisely that reason. Marshall knew, of course, that nations often resort to war in the pursuit of self-interest, but he also believed that war ought to be the exception and peaceful commerce the rule. When judgment and discretion allowed, as they did here, he put law on the side of private property and neutral rights even when it meant parting company with Lord Stowell, whose decisions he respected, and Joseph Story, who was emerging as his most useful ally on the Court.[34]

Marshall was the most modest of men, but secretly he must have savored winning a hard-fought intellectual duel with his young friend; clearly he relished taking the brilliant and arrogant Pinkney down a peg or two. Still for all this, *The Nereide* was not truly a great opinion. Marshall did not set forth any new principles in international law, and neither, by his own admission, did he succeed entirely in clarifying conflicting authorities on the point in question. In this respect, *The Nereide* was a representative decision, for the Marshall Court, even when it was united and even when the chief justice spoke for the majority, did not settle American international law once and for all. The justices did, however, work case by case to lay the foundation and in the process did establish the Court's undisputed authority to adjudicate international law for the new nation. Marshall was central to the process. In the individual give-and-take among the justices, he was formidable; in the collective enterprise, as chief justice, he was indispensable. In cases such as *McFaddon,* he pledged the Court

34. Ibid., 430.

to principled international law. As leader of the Court, he guaranteed an arena where rational discourse could take place. Cases such as *The Nereide,* present a glimpse of what this meant, as justices and lawyers worked together with spirit, zest, ability, and a sense of camaraderie even when they disagreed. By virtue of its ongoing, undramatic contributions, the Supreme Court under Marshall's leadership was quietly becoming the representative institution of republican government.

McCulloch v. Maryland: National Union via National Market

The year 1819 was "the great term" of the Marshall Court and the high point as well of Marshall's career as chief justice. In little more than a month, he delivered three memorable opinions for the Court. *Sturges v. Crowninshield* addressed state bankruptcy legislation for the first, though not the final, time. *Dartmouth College v. Woodward* curtailed state regulatory power over state-chartered corporations, greatly facilitating the growth of private institutions of higher learning and the development of the American business corporation. The greatest of Marshall's 1819 opinions, perhaps the most masterful of his long career, was *McCulloch v. Maryland.* Here for a unanimous Court, he upheld the constitutionality of the second Bank of the United States, arguably the single most extensive *private* monopoly in American history. In the process, he set forth two fundamental doctrines, one of which at least has become constitutional orthodoxy: First and least understood was the doctrine of dual or balanced federalism, which demarcated the line between states' rights and federal authority; second and more famous was the doctrine of implied powers, which, in addition to upholding the Bank of the United States, was nothing less than a universal touchstone to constitutional interpretation. Like the mandamus opinion, *McCulloch* was a transcendent opinion that guaranteed Marshall a place of continued relevance in American history and law.

It is also the opinion that locates Marshall most fully in his own age. The second Bank of the United States, to begin, was the centerpiece in America's post–War of 1812 nation-building impulse—the institutional foundation of Henry Clay's American System, which included federally sponsored internal improvements and a tariff to protect and encourage American manufacturing. The new bank, continuing in the tradition of the old one, was also the source of ongoing agitation between political parties, or, more accurately, among political factions. Touching law, economics, politics, nationalism, and federalism,

it related those issues to the history of the early Republic in ways that resonated personally with Marshall. From the Revolution forward, monetary issues had been at the heart of American nationalism and nation building—and
at the center of constitutional disputation. The nationalists of the 1780s, the
same who spearheaded the call for the convention that framed the Constitution, were closely connected to Robert Morris, whose Bank of North America
was instrumental in financing the American Revolution. In the 1790s, Hamilton's Bank of the United States, along with other aspects of his legislative program, was designed to rally the financial interests of the country to the
nationalist cause. Debate over the Bank's constitutionality was the first significant constitutional debate in American history after ratification, one incidentally that took place not in the federal courts but in Congress. The memoranda
on the bank's constitutionality from Secretary of State Jefferson and Secretary
of Treasury Hamilton, requested by Washington, setting forth the strict and
broad construction of the Constitution, respectively, defined the debate over
implied powers that shaped politics and law from the 1790s to the Civil War.
Finally, it was the dispute over the bank during the presidency of Andrew Jackson and the last years of the Marshall Court that consolidated the victory of
the Jacksonian Democrats and, indeed, precipitated a debate over the nature
of American society itself.[35]

Marshall had not been an idle bystander during these nation-defining debates over banking and monetary policy. He was after all Robert Morris's chief
legal representative in Virginia, arguing the great financier's cases in both state
and federal courts. With his brother's marriage to Morris's daughter, John
Marshall became a member of the family, so to speak. His relationship with
Hamilton was even more formative and productive. Whether the two men met
during the Revolution is not clear, but Marshall knew him indirectly as a fellow officer as well as a confidant of Washington. He armed himself with Hamilton's nationalist essays in the Federalist papers in preparation for the Virginia
ratifying convention. He publicly supported Hamilton's policies in the 1790s
and paid the price for it in states' rights Richmond. Marshall also drew freely
on the New Yorker in several of his celebrated opinions—on *The Federalist*
78 in *Marbury;* on Hamilton's legal advice to the Mississippi Land Company,

---

35. Though it is partial to Biddle and the bank, Bray Hammond's *Banks and Politics in
America, from the Revolution to the Civil War* (Princeton, N.J., 1957) remains the standard ac-
count. On the symbolic force of the Bank of the United States in American politics, see Marvin
Meyers, *The Jacksonian Persuasion: Politics and Belief* (New York, 1960), ch. 5.

published as a pamphlet in 1799 in *Fletcher v. Peck;* and most notably, and liberally, on Hamilton's Bank of the United States memorandum to Washington in 1791 in *McCulloch.* In the latter case, the ideas, indeed the careers, of the two men united on the proposition that national union and market capitalism were reverse sides of the same coin, which was precisely what troubled Jefferson and the states' rights agrarian theorists of Virginia.[36]

McCulloch v. Maryland originated, as did the second Bank of the United States itself, in the tumultuous years following the War of 1812, referred to euphemistically, and misleadingly, as the "era of good feelings." Chartered by Congress in a moment of national exuberance in 1816, the bank was modeled after Hamilton's bank, whose charter had been allowed to lapse on the eve of the war with England, exactly at the time it was most needed. Wartime experience without a central banking agency, as well as postwar nationalism, accounted for the new bank. Like the old one, it was a mixed public/private corporation, capitalized at $35 million, one-fifth of which was to be subscribed by the government and four-fifths by private stock subscriptions. Governance followed capital investment, which meant that five members of the governing board, appointed by the U.S. president, represented the government while twenty, chosen by the stockholders, represented private investors. Presiding over the institution, which was located in Philadelphia with branches in eighteen major cities, was a corporate president, who was appointed by and held office at the pleasure of the board. The bank's function, like its governing board, was both public and private. Though it was called the Bank of the United States, it was controlled by private stockholders, who expected and got a handsome profit on their investment. As a private, profit-making monopoly, it was in competition with state banks. The bank was also the exclusive depository of public monies, on which it could issue its own circulating notes. In return for this privilege, the bank was obliged by its charter to loan money to the federal government in anticipation of taxes. Most important, it was a regulatory agency, controlling the value not just of its own notes but of those issued by state banks, of which there were more than two hundred in 1819. By accumulating the notes of any given bank, as Nicholas Biddle would later testify, and presenting them for redemption, the Bank of the United States could frighten state banks into maintaining adequate specie reserves. Sound banking

36. Samuel J. Konefsky, *John Marshall and Alexander Hamilton: Architects of the Constitution* (New York, 1964) is a vivid and scholarly reconstruction of the Marshall-Hamilton relationship; see especially 122–23 on *Fletcher.*

practices enforced by the Bank of the United States, the assumption went, would guarantee a national circulating currency that was uniform and reliable, that is to say, redeemable any place in the country at or near the face value. For commercial and manufacturing interests looking to the creation of a national market, it was an objective much to be desired; the fact that the public power bestowed by the charter on the bank was controlled by private interests was equally pleasing.[37]

Unfortunately, operation of the bank during its first three years did not correspond to the theory. Rather than regulating state banks, as the charter contemplated, the Bank of the United States, under the management of William Jones, competed with them in providing easy credit for the land boom, especially in the South and West. To save itself when the inevitable collapse began in 1818, the bank called in loans to state banks, which brought them down in unprecedented numbers. Blaming the bank for their troubles and for the depression that followed, the states, especially in the South and West, moved against the bank. The degree of opposition varied considerably, from moderate in Virginia, where leading state bankers were closely connected to the Richmond branch of the national bank, to radical in Ohio, which passed a law outlawing the bank and which later engaged in outright defiance of the Court's decision upholding the institution. Whether radical or moderate, state opponents to the bank complained that it was essentially a private monopoly, privileged by its connection with the national government; that it worked to the special advantage of the commercial North; and that it was dominated by an undemocratic and unrepublican aristocratic elite, which included a dangerously large number of foreign, largely English, stockholders.

Circumstances surrounding the origins of the case in Maryland gave considerable credence to these criticisms. The litigation began in 1818 when William McCulloch, cashier of the Baltimore branch, was sued in Baltimore County Court for issuing notes without having paid the state tax. A decision for the state was immediately appealed to the Maryland Court of Appeals, which issued a peremptory ruling for the state, which was immediately taken on a writ of error to the Supreme Court, where it was argued for nine days beginning on February 22, 1819. The expeditious course of the appeal, plus the fact that Marshall handed down his polished opinion less than a week after the closing

---

37. The regulatory aspects of the Bank of the United States are emphasized in Hammond, *Banks and Politics,* while numerous critics of the institution, contemporary as well as modern, have noted the conflict between the public and private character of the institution.

of arguments, led one scholar to wonder whether he had written all or part of the opinion before he heard the arguments of counsel. In any case, it was common knowledge at the time and the source of much criticism that the case was arranged, which explains why it came forth so expeditiously. It is even plausible to argue that the state and the bank not only wanted a decision but that they wanted the same result, the one Marshall provided when he upheld the constitutionality of the Bank of the United States and the unconstitutionality of the state tax on it. Maryland, and Baltimore especially, located at the commercial crossroads between North and South, was the most commercial of the states that legislated against the bank. The state party in power was closely connected to the commercial sector, which was in turn deeply enmeshed in the operations of the Baltimore branch—which was about to go under due to the mismanagement, if not criminal behavior, of McCulloch and other local bank officials. To settle the constitutional question before the collapse of the Baltimore branch, which might well have threatened the bank itself, was therefore imperative. Settling the matter quickly would also work to disarm the more violent opposition to the bank gathering in states such as Ohio. The gravamen of all this, as critics saw it, was that the Bank of the United States with the crème de la crème of the federal bar on its side threatened to make the Court an instrument of its evil designs on American democracy and states' rights. The stage was set for a case one newspaper called "great" even before arguments of counsel had been heard.[38]

That the case was so fully loaded with political and economic significance may well explain why Marshall, following the lead of the bank's lawyers, cast his opinion so conspicuously in the neutral language of constitutional law. Critics were not silenced, but it was a magisterial performance nonetheless, one that displayed Marshall's "grand style" at its grandest and his mature understanding of judicial review as well. If Jefferson was right that Marshall's hallmark was to build his arguments on an uncontestable proposition that, if accepted, would lead inexorably to the conclusion he wanted to reach, then *McCulloch* was a case in point. The foundational proposition was that the Constitution was created by the American people and was intended to govern a great nation. "The government of the Union," Marshall declared in language

---

38. Richard Ellis, "The Maryland Origins of *McCulloch v. Maryland* (1819)," paper delivered at the annual meeting of the Organization of American Historians, Washington, D.C., March 1995. For an authoritative discussion of the legal issues in the case, see White, *Marshall Court,* especially 541–52.

that Lincoln, with a few changes, would immortalize, "is emphatically and truly, a government of the people. In form and in substance it emanates from them. Its powers are granted by them, and are to be exercised directly on them, and for their benefit." If the sovereign people created the Constitution, he argued, then "we must never forget," that "it is a constitution we are expounding." That great document was not a legal code encumbered with a "prolixity" of details that "could scarcely be embraced by the human mind" and that "would probably never be understood by the public." "Its nature, therefore, required that only its great outlines should be marked, its important object designated," leaving "the minor ingredients which compose those objects [to] be deduced from the nature of the objects themselves." For Marshall, this was the guiding interpretive principle of American constitutional law, and it came from the "nature of the instrument" itself. But it was also set forth explicitly in Article 1, Section 8, clause 18, which declared that Congress, in addition to the enumerated powers, shall have the further authority "to make all laws which shall be necessary for carrying into execution of the foregoing powers, and all other powers vested by this constitution, in the government of the United States, or in any department thereof."[39]

Having set forth the rule, grounding it in the nature as well as the language of the Constitution, Marshall then applied it to the question at hand: In the absence of an enumerated power specifically authorizing it to do so, could Congress charter a national bank? What, in short, was the meaning of "necessary and proper"? Logic, hermeneutics, and Hamiltonian constitutional theory shaped his answer, along with twenty years of precedent. In fact, the arguments presented by counsel regarding "necessary and proper" in 1819 were mainly those presented by Jefferson and Hamilton in 1791 in their memoranda to Washington on the constitutionality of the first Bank of the United States. Marshall quickly homed in on the weakest part of the Jeffersonian argument, asserted by counsel for Maryland, namely, that the Necessary and Proper Clause, "though in terms a grant of power," was really intended to restrict "the general right, which might otherwise be implied, of selecting means for executing the enumerated powers." To deprive Congress of the right to choose laws for the execution of its granted powers would be to take away the power to govern, a power that, to put it plainly, any self-respecting national government must have. To grant discretion in the choice of means was not, he hastened to add, a grant of unlimited power to Congress. "We admit, as all must admit, that the

39. *McCulloch v. Maryland,* 4 Wheaton 404–5, 407.

powers of the government are limited, and that its limits are not to be tran-scended. But we think the sound construction of the constitution must allow to the national legislature that discretion, with respect to the means by which the power it confers are to be carried into execution, which will enable that body to perform the high duties assigned to it, in the manner most beneficial to the people." With the help of Pinkney's argument, which borrowed Hamilton's words, the rule was this: "Let the end be legitimate, let it be within the scope of the constitution, and all means which are appropriate, which are plainly adapted to that end, which are not prohibited, but consist with the letter and spirit of the constitution, are constitutional." The end was Congress's enumer-ated power to regulate the currency; the bank was the means to this end, and it was not prohibited by or violative of the spirit of the Constitution. These memorable words were supported by two very practical facts: first, that Con-gress had chartered a national bank not once but twice and both times after extensive debate; and second, that businessmen in all parts of the country had relied on the bank's notes and both parties had accepted it as a practical fact of national economic life.[40]

Marshall's position thus far was highly *un*original. Indeed, as the actions of Congress in 1791 and 1816, the general acquiescence of the American people, and the unanimity of the justices in *McCulloch* indicate, the constitutionality of the bank appears to have been a foregone conclusion. Not so the second question in the case: Could a state tax the Bank of the United States, which Marshall had described as an instrumentality of the national government? In treating this states' rights issue, Marshall picked up the ideological gauntlet thrown down by counsel for Maryland. For them, the issue boiled down to a question of sovereignty, which, following the Anti-Federalists and the Virginia and Kentucky Resolutions, they insisted belonged to the separate states as par-ties to the Constitution. Translated into a rule of constitutional interpretation, this meant that in disputed cases over federal authority, the benefit of the doubt should go to the states.

Marshall fully understood the provenance of the argument, that it went back to the Anti-Federalists at the time of ratification, back to the Virginia and Kentucky Resolutions, back to Thomas Jefferson. As was his wont, he coun-tered with a proposition he assumed was beyond dispute: "This great principle is, that the constitution and the laws made in pursuance thereof, are supreme; that they control the constitution and the laws of the respective states, and can-

40. Ibid., 421.

not be controlled by them." From this, he said, "are deduced as corollaries: 1st. that a power to create implies a power to preserve. 2nd. that a power to destroy, if wielded by a different hand, is hostile to, and incompatible with these powers to create and to preserve. 3d. that where the repugnancy exists, that authority which is supreme must control, not yield to that over which it is supreme." In applying these axioms to the case at hand, Marshall never inquired as to the actual effect the Maryland tax had on the bank, perhaps because the tax of $15,000 was not really a threat to the bank's operations. In any case, the "degree" of permissible taxation, Marshall said, was a "perplexing enquiry . . . unfit for the judicial department." Instead he explored the sovereignty-taxation issue as it impinged on the structure of constitutional federalism. The "original right of taxation," he conceded, "was essential to the very existence of government." This power resides in the states, "and may be legitimately exercised on the objects to which it is applicable, to the utmost extent to which the government may chuse to carry it." The only restraint, "the only security against the abuse of this power, is found in the structure of the government itself," that is, the federal system under the Constitution. The rule here is that in imposing a tax, the state legislature may tax only its own constituents, and by the same principle is prohibited from taxing citizens of other states and citizens of the United States.[41]

Put simply, his point was that the legislature of Maryland could not tax the Bank of the United States because the bank was created by Congress, which represented all the people of all the states. It all boiled down, said Marshall, to "the magic word *confidence*," which he then proceeded to illustrate by way of hypothetical questions and answers. "Would the people of any one state trust those of another with a power to controul the most insignificant operation of their state government? We know they would not. Why then should we suppose that the people of any one state should be willing to trust those of another with a power to controul the operations of a government to which they have confided their most important and valuable interests?" The government of the United States represents all the people. It follows that "the Legislature of the Union alone, therefore, can be trusted by the people with the power of controuling measures which concern all, in the confidence that it will not be abused."[42]

To allow the citizens of Maryland through their state legislature to tax an

41. Ibid., 426, 428.
42. Ibid., 431.

instrumentality of Congress would, then, permit them to infringe on the rights of the American people. To drive home the point, Marshall then recast his principle in language suitable to its importance: "That the power to tax involved the power to destroy; that the power to destroy may defeat and render useless the power to create; that there is a plain repugnance in conferring on one government a power to controul the constitutional measures of another, which other, with respect to those very measures, is declared to be supreme over that which exerts the controul, are propositions not to be denied." Except they were being denied in Maryland, Ohio, and other states working to destroy the bank, and most of all in Virginia, "where the spirit of malignancy never sleeps." "The question is, in truth, a question of supremacy; and if the right of the states to tax the means employed by the general government be conceded, the declaration that the constitution, and the laws made in pursuance thereof, shall be the supreme law of the land, is empty and unmeaning declamation." Here Marshall said what he truly believed, and what history shows to have been true: The Union was in danger from the states and from a persistent cultural localism, not the other way around.[43]

Judging from the violent reaction, Marshall's statement on the dangers of states' rights was right on the mark. His opinion, however, was also a self-fulfilling prophecy in that it set in motion a broad-based states' rights movement, which turned into a no-holds-barred debate over the nature of the Court, the Constitution, and the federal Union. The full impact of this anti-Court movement on Marshall as chief justice will be considered in the following chapter. But it needs to be mentioned here because of *Osborn v. Bank of the United States* (1824), which began as an attack on *McCulloch* and ended in a frontal challenge to the jurisdiction of the Court. The case involved Ohio, which, like other states in the South and West, had been particularly hard hit by bank failures in the panic of 1819. Like Maryland, the state blamed the Bank of the United States for its woes and levied a tax of $50,000 on each branch; the same law authorized the state auditor, one Ralph Osborn, to collect the tax by forcible entry if necessary into the building housing the bank. In defiance of the Court's decision in *McCulloch* and a federal injunction issued by the federal circuit court at the request of the bank's attorneys, the state demanded that the bank pay the tax and dispatched state officials to collect it. In retaliation, the bank sued the state officials involved for damages and got yet another injunction from the federal circuit court ordering the officials to return

43. Ibid., 431, 433.

the money they had taken in defiance of the first injunction. The second injunction was also ignored by the state treasurer, whereupon an attachment for contempt was issued against him and he was jailed. Armed with an order of the circuit court, federal officials now forcefully recovered $98,000 from the state treasury. The Ohio legislature countered by attacking Marshall's opinion and the subsequent decrees issued by the circuit court to enforce it. Finally in January 1821, the state outlawed the bank itself, justifying the act by reference to the Virginia and Kentucky Resolutions and the Eleventh Amendment, which barred individuals from suing states in federal courts. Ohio also contended that the bank was subject to state taxation because it was a private profit-making institution controlled by private investors, which was pretty much the truth of the matter. Indeed, had Marshall confronted this fact in *McCulloch,* had he looked more to facts and less to doctrine, the landscape of antebellum constitutional history would have been substantially altered.[44]

As it was, he could not ignore the direct challenge to the Court's authority emanating from Ohio, especially since Georgia was also mounting a case to justify its all-out resistance to *McCulloch.* By requesting that the arguments in the Georgia case be folded into those in *Osborn v. Bank of the United States,* Marshall gave himself the opportunity to address the full range of jurisdictional and substantive issues raised by the mounting state resistance to *McCulloch.* His lengthy opinion, probably "prewritten" according to G. Edward White, not only reaffirmed the correctness of *McCulloch,* but went beyond that decision to argue that judicial power of the Court must be "co-extensive with the legislative power." In creating the Bank of the United States as "an instrument of the government," Congress of necessity had to guarantee access to the federal courts, where it could sue and be sued. Thus for the second time, Marshall employed the implied powers reasoning in behalf of the bank. In *McCulloch,* he introduced the doctrine to validate the congressional charter. Now in *Osborn,* as William Johnson pointed out in his dissent, Marshall expanded the Court's jurisdiction again by necessary implication, reasoning that what Congress created, the Court must be allowed to protect against state action, even if it meant seriously narrowing of the Eleventh Amendment bar against suits against the states. By providing the Court the jurisdictional wherewithal to de-

44. White, *Marshall Court,* 524–35, provides an excellent legal analysis of the decision. Quote from *Western Herald and Steubenville Gazette,* 20 March 1819, is found in Warren, *Supreme Court,* 1: 527. Warren's account recounts the deep-rooted opposition to the bank and the Marshall Court in Ohio.

fend the bank, Marshall closed the circle of argument begun in *McCulloch*. By identifying the Court with the bank, he also appeared to validate the allegation of many states' rights critics that his Court was part of a Hamilton-like capitalist conspiracy designed to subvert the interests of the agrarian slaveholding South, the liberty of the people, and the power of the states.[45]

There is no direct evidence that Marshall was part of any conspiracy, capitalist or otherwise, in *McCulloch*. Certainly he went out of his way to talk law rather than economics, and when he talked law, he did so in the name of the American people. Nevertheless, the economic, policy-making implications of his opinion are conspicuous, especially when *McCulloch* is viewed along with *Sturges* and *Dartmouth College,* the other leading decisions of the 1819 term. All three, each in its own way, were attuned to the perceived needs of an emerging class of entrepreneurs—manufacturers, merchants, businessmen, and bankers—all of whom were interested in doing business across state lines. This new class was harnessing new forms of business organization to the new technology to produce a revolution in production and transportation, which has aptly been called "the market revolution." Judged by the policy consequences of the decisions rather than by Marshall's objective legal language, the Court does appear to have sided with the national commercial wing of the National Republican Party in implementing what came to be known as Henry Clay's American System, a plan whereby Congress would promote economic growth by means of a national bank, federally sponsored internal improvements, and a protective tariff.[46]

Marshall was careful not to allude to Henry Clay or the American System or to any other political agenda, but the fact remains he put a constitutional foundation under the second Bank of the United States, the objective of which was to establish a uniform system of national currency and credit. Indirectly, his doctrine of implied powers also permitted Congress to institute a system of federal internal improvements, though it never did so. In *McCulloch*, he spoke explicitly about the need to integrate economically the "vast republic," which, thanks to the Adams-Onís Treaty of 1819, now extended "from the St. Croix to the Gulph of Mexico, from the Atlantic to the Pacific." Marshall legitimated the Court's interpretation of implied powers by reference to original intent,

---

45. White, *Marshall Court,* 526–27.

46. Sellers explores the growth of a national market and its impact on American culture in his *Market Revolution*. On the importance of market in the late eighteenth- and early nineteenth-century United States, consult James Willard Hurst, *Law and Markets in United States History: Different Modes of Bargaining among Interests* (Madison, Wis., 1982), ch. 1, especially 10–22.

and by gathering intent from the expansive grant of powers to Congress in Article 1, Section 8: A "government, entrusted with such ample power, on the due execution of which the happiness and prosperity of the nation so vitally depends, must also be entrusted with the ample means for their execution. The power being given, it is the interest of the nation to facilitate its execution." Behind the words of the text, which Marshall parsed with unusual skill, was the spirit of the times and the challenge facing Americans as they set out in the years after 1815 to conquer the continent.

Facilitate is what the Court aimed to do, but pronouncements about nationalism, even when couched in Marshall's manly rhetoric, did not and could not create a nation. Anyhow, inspiring rhetoric was Jefferson's specialty. All Marshall and his brethren could do, and what they tried to do in *McCulloch*, was to help Congress help the people help themselves build a nation. Patriotism, love of country, and the recollection of national heroes and great moments went to make up John Marshall's America. But his nation, like that of the Founders, also relied on the efforts of an enterprising people working collectively. A national market—integrated by an efficient system of roads and canals and later railroads, guarded from the invasion of foreign goods by protective tariffs, and enhanced by a uniform currency and a national system of credit— encouraged them to do so. If the American people could forge an "economic e pluribus unum," they might just put a solid foundation and walls under the constitutional roof the Framers left suspended in the thin air of patriotism and historic memory. Marshall was among the first to appreciate that the time to do so was running short. Back in 1788 his friend Edmund Randolph urged him to "seize the moment," and this is precisely what Marshall attempted to do in 1819 and again in 1824. More than Hamilton and perhaps more than the Framers themselves, he was positioned to make ideas count. Creativity was not his forte; creative application was.

Steamboats, Gibbons v. Ogden, and the Completion of a National Market

Marshall used the phrase "economic e pluribus unum" in his *Gibbons* opinion. Apparently he appropriated the phrase from Daniel Webster's argument in the case, but what most inspired him to use it was the steamboat. Steam navigation was not new in 1824. Its possibilities had been demonstrated conclusively as early as the 1780s, when boats designed by Connecticut inventor John Fitch plied upriver from Delaware to Trenton, New Jersey. Members of the Constitutional Convention meeting in Philadelphia even turned out on one occasion to see the Fitch steamboat in action. Perhaps they grasped the connection between Fitch's invention and the creation of a national transportation system, but that possibility was immediately put on hold by the development of competing state monopolies in steam navigation. Among the most conspicuous was that created by the New York law of 1787 giving Fitch and his associates the exclusive right of navigation on state waters for a period of fourteen years. Personal problems culminating in Fitch's suicide prevented the monopoly from ever being used; and in 1798, Robert Livingston, former chancellor of the New York Court of Appeals and scion of one of New York's most prominent Republican families, laid claim to the monopoly on the ground that it had not been implemented. In the period between 1798 and 1811, Livingston, using his extensive network of family and political connections, kept his monopoly rights intact. In the meantime, he formed a partnership with Robert Fulton, whose steamboat the *Clermont* proved in 1807 beyond all doubt the practicability, if not the profitability, of the not-so-new invention. In 1811, the New York legislature granted the new partnership the exclusive right to navigate on New York waters, including the Hudson River, and on coastal waters between New York and New Jersey. No doubt to forestall opposition to this law, it was further stipulated that any vessel that violated the monopoly was subject to confiscation, with no provision for court costs or damages if the challenge were upheld by the courts. That provision notwithstanding, attempts to break the monopoly began immediately.[47]

Gibbons v. Ogden was the final act in the long, complex effort of rival steamboat companies to break the Livingston-Fulton monopoly, which was as aggressive in its tactics as it was out of touch with the needs of the new age. One problem that haunted the monopoly was the fact that Fulton had no substantial claim to originality, which, if it belonged to anyone, belonged to John Fitch. Livingston addressed the problem by buying out Fitch and by taking out a federal patent. When the patent line of defense collapsed, as it did in the federal circuit court in 1811, the monopoly sought to buy out competitors or to persuade them to take out licenses under the authority of the monopoly. When that and all else failed, the monopoly sought injunctive relief on the basis of the New York law of 1811, which it defended as a legitimate effort on the part of the state to promote commerce. After a long and complicated battle, begin-

47. Maurice G. Baxter, *The Steamboat Monopoly: Gibbons v. Ogden, 1824* (New York, 1972) is excellent on the complex background facts in the case.

ning in the New York Court of Chancery, the state Court of Errors in 1820 not surprisingly sustained the monopoly. Speaking for the Court of Errors, James Kent relied heavily on his own opinion as chancellor in *Livingston v. Van Ingen* (1812). His main point in sustaining the monopoly was the concurrent power doctrine, which he got from Hamilton's *Federalist* 32. He conceded that state laws in the area of interstate commerce that conflicted directly with federal statutes would have to give way; until that time, however, the state could continue to legislate in the area, as in fact it had done on numerous occasions. Significantly, Kent refused to accept the arguments put forward by Thomas Gibbons that the Federal Coastal Licensing Act of 1793 was in direct conflict with the New York statute of 1811.[48]

Kent's authority notwithstanding, his court's decision in 1820 did not settle the matter—in part because it was extremely difficult to enforce and also because it had no binding force outside the state. Efforts on the part of the Livingston-Fulton interests to get monopoly grants from other states failed everywhere except in New Orleans, where Edward Livingston, as Robert Livingston's lawyer, was able to persuade the territorial legislature to grant monopoly privileges to Livingston and Fulton. In the meantime, efforts to enforce the New York monopoly in coastal waters outside New York brought retaliation from other states, which, not without considerable irony, set up monopolistic counterclaims. This was the situation in 1821 when Gibbons appealed Kent's ruling, which Gibbons continued to defy, to the Supreme Court. Law defiance, state retaliation, and recrimination: The 1820s were beginning to look like the 1780s all over again. So at least John Marshall thought.

The "great steamboat case," as one of the lawyers called it, gave the chief justice a chance to make that point decisively. It also presented him with the opportunity to clarify the Commerce Clause of the Constitution, the power given to Congress in Article 1, Section 8, "to regulate commerce with foreign nations, and among the several States, and with the Indian tribes." This grant of power had been inserted in the Constitution by the Framers to correct a debilitating weakness in the Articles of Confederation, one that allowed the states to wage turf wars over trade and commerce, which in turn threatened to destroy the precarious union of states. The Commerce Clause went to the very heart of federalism, which is no doubt why the Framers made no attempt to clarify its precise meaning. In now undertaking that delicate job, the Court was

48. Ibid., ch. 1; *Livingston v. Van Ingen*, 9 Johnson 507, about which, see White, *Marshall Court*, 570–71.

presented with several specific questions. First, and most obvious, what was the meaning of the key words "commerce," "regulate," and "among"? Further, was the grant to Congress exclusive and self-executing, that is to say, did the mere grant of power automatically prohibit states from passing laws touching on interstate commerce? Alternately, was the power to regulate commerce concurrent, that is, could the states pass laws that regulated interstate commerce until Congress acted? And how much of a conflict between the two would there have to be before the state acts gave way to federal supremacy, assuming they would? Finally, who was to decide the questions? Did the Court, whose decisions in *McCulloch* and *Cohens v. Virginia* (1821) were already under assault as acts of judicial usurpation, have the final authority to interpret the Constitution and police the operation of the federal system? With that power, if it existed, came the additional power to influence public policy. Behind the doctrinal arguments and questions about judicial authority was the bedrock question of whether in the critical area of steamboat transportation there should be a national system of transportation or as many competing systems as there were states. Rephrased to recognize the intersection of doctrine and the consequences of doctrine, the question was about whether the Framers intended to create a national market.

Marshall had not explicitly addressed that question either on or off the bench, but his position could hardly have been more clear had he done so. His thinking about the matter, like that of the Framers, began with an acute awareness of the need for improving regional and interregional transportation and commerce. This was the purpose of the famous Annapolis Convention of 1786, which led to the Philadelphia Convention. One of the pressing issues at the Virginia ratifying convention concerned the opening of the Mississippi River to the commerce of the western country. The same concern involved George Washington in the Potomac project, designed to connect Virginia to the Ohio country via canals and rivers, and Marshall himself in the project to connect the James and Kanawha Rivers in 1812. Practically speaking, there was no real separation between state-based internal improvements and those that might be sponsored by Congress, a point even the Jacksonians appreciated, as is now known.

All of this is to say that Chief Justice Marshall, like many other Americans, had national commerce on his mind in the heady days of nationalism after 1815. Like the rest of the nation, he had listened to the debate over the constitutionality of the Bonus Bill of 1816, which set aside money from the sale of public land for federally sponsored internal improvements. Without a doubt, he pondered the significance of Madison's veto of the bill on the ground that a constitutional amendment was necessary before Congress could act. Indeed, it seems obvious that the doctrine of broad construction set forth in *McCulloch* was as much a response to Madison's strict construction views in the Bonus Bill veto as it was to arguments of counsel—witness Marshall's reference to the "vast republic" that needed to be bound together. Marshall made that point again in 1824: In the opening paragraph of his *History of the Colonies,* the original first volume of his five-volume biography of Washington, he referred to "the extent of this vast Republic," which was "two million square miles" and growing exponentially "in arts, arms, and in power."[49]

The notion of power figured prominently in his *Gibbons* opinion, as it had in his speech on the Constitution at the Virginia ratifying convention. And well it might figure, considering the states' rights challenge to the national government set in motion by *McCulloch.* Marshall understood the complex issues surrounding the case, the doctrinal questions that impinged on both national and state sovereignty, as well as the urgent need for a system of internal improvements to counteract the centrifugal forces of demography and states' rights ideology. Counsel on both sides—Daniel Webster and William Wirt against the monopoly and for national market as well as Thomas Oakley and Thomas Emmet for the monopoly and for state sovereignty—pressed their case with learning and conviction. Webster, fresh from his dazzling victories in *Dartmouth College* and *McCulloch,* was especially persuasive. Indeed, much has been said, especially by Webster himself, about the similarities between his argument and Marshall's opinion. While the resemblances are readily apparent, it must not be forgotten that Webster, clever lawyer that he was, also told Marshall what he already believed and wanted a chance to say. Marshall, clever lawyer that *he* was, did not need to be told how to deal with the states' rights theory. In any case, the able arguments of counsel on both sides presented Marshall with a wide range of options, the only problem being, as he noted, that both sides cited "with great earnestness" the same Constitution, the same legislative history, and the same judicial decisions to make their case.[50]

---

49. John Marshall, *A History of the Colonies Planted by the English on the Continent of North America* (Philadelphia, 1824), 10. He then went on to acknowledge the exponential advances "in arts, in arms, and in power" made by the nation after 1816. Ibid., 12. Marshall's *History of the Colonies* appeared originally as the first volume of his five-volume biography of Washington.

50. See Maurice G. Baxter, *Daniel Webster and the Supreme Court* (Amherst, Mass., 1996). G. Edward White discusses Webster as a lawyer, along with other leaders of the Supreme Court bar during Marshall's tenure, in *Marshall Court,* ch. 4.

Oakley and Emmet, for the monopoly, wasted no time getting to the heart of the matter, which for them was state sovereignty. There was nothing there Marshall had not heard before: in 1788 at the ratifying convention in Richmond; in the Virginia and Kentucky Resolutions ten years later; or in the arguments of counsel in *Martin v. Hunter's Lessee, McCulloch,* and *Cohens.* Oakley tapped into this ongoing discourse, declaring that the states were sovereign before the Constitution, made so by "their own act in the declaration of independence" and by New York's constitution, which vested "supreme legislative power" in the state legislature. Citing Marshall's opinion in *McCulloch* and Story's in *Houston v. Moore* (1820), Oakley went on, assuredly to the consternation of both men, to conclude that since "the constitution of the United States is one of limited and expressly delegated powers" it "must, therefore, be construed strictly, as regards the powers expressly granted, and the objects to which those powers are applied."

Applying this states' rights rule of thumb to the case at hand, Emmet argued for a narrow definition of commerce, which did not include steamboats, and for a generous view of state power over the subject. He conceded that a state law over interstate commerce, in direct conflict with a federal law on the same subject, would be invalid, a conflict that rarely occurred since Congress rarely legislated in the area. Except for that unlikely situation and for specific prohibitions against state regulations over interstate commerce in the Constitution, state power must be viewed as coextensive with the subject itself. What Emmet wanted, in short, was nothing less than constitutional and judicial recognition of state power over interstate commerce. In support of this unhinging position, he cited the Tenth Amendment, which reserved for the states, and the people, those powers not granted to Congress; "the nature of government"; and three decades of state legislation touching interstate commerce. The latter point could not be easily ignored by Marshall in light of the wide array of state legislation designed to promote commerce, which Marshall himself supported, and in light of his rule of construction, announced in *McCulloch,* that settled practice settles doctrine.[51]

Webster's interpretation of the commerce power rested on a firm conviction, which just happened to correspond to the policy interests of commercial New England, whose support he would need in any presidential bid. His point was simple: The Framers of the Constitution intended to create a single economic unit, an "economic e pluribus unum," as he put it, or a national market,

---

51. *Gibbons v. Ogden,* 9 Wheaton 33–34; Emmet's argument at ibid., 79–159.

as it would be put today. To this end, one senses, Webster really wanted to argue that the power to regulate interstate commerce given to Congress automatically excluded the states from the field. He resisted the temptation, perhaps out of deference to Chancellor Kent's position, maybe because he was unwilling to challenge the authority of *The Federalist* 22 head on, or most likely, because he did not want to supply more fuel to the states' rights juggernaut. He therefore conceded that states could, as they had done, legislate on state matters that touched on interstate commerce. However, such legislation, he insisted, rested on police power, the inherent authority all states possessed to legislate on the health, welfare, and morals of their inhabitants, not a concurrent power over interstate commerce. He reluctantly conceded some such power to the states, but quickly returned to an interpretation of congressional authority that all but excluded the states. "From the very nature of the case," he declared emphatically, congressional power "must be exclusive; that is, the higher branches of commercial regulation must be exclusively committed to a single hand." Monopolies such as the one created by New York were automatically prohibited under this interpretation—*with or without their being in direct conflict with a federal statute.* To weight the case further in favor of a national market, he concluded, extravagantly and without citation, that the silence of Congress regarding a field of commerce signified a claim of exclusive control over it. If states' rights theory gave the benefit of the doubt to states, Webster's nationalism eliminated all doubt whatsoever.[52]

The lawyers gave Marshall a rich palette from which to paint. He gave back a great painting highlighted by bold strokes, but with subtle shading as well, and, like all great art, subject to more than one interpretation. He began modestly with a polite bow to the learning of the judges of New York, whose opinion he was about to overturn. Then he said what Webster invited him to say, and what he had said with masterly thoroughness three years previously in *Cohens,* that it was the "province of this court" to review the constitutionality of the New York monopoly of 1811 and the New York decisions upholding it. He could only promise that the judges would do so with "that understanding which Providence has bestowed upon them" and "with that independence which the people of the United States expect from this department of the government."[53]

52. Webster at ibid., 13–14. Also consult Baxter's analysis of Webster's argument in *Steamboat Monopoly,* 39–42.
53. 9 Wheaton 186–87.

That promised, he moved abruptly to the contention of counsel for Aaron Ogden and New York that the Constitution mandated a strict interpretation of the Commerce Clause and of the enumerated powers in Article 1, Section 8, generally. Why, Marshall asked, should "powers expressly granted by the people to their government" be strictly construed? And why, he asked, referring to *McCulloch* but not citing it, did the Founders specifically include the Necessary and Proper Clause at the end of the enumerated powers if they intended a narrow construction of them? Indeed, he continued, "what do gentlemen mean, by a strict construction?" "If they contend for that narrow construction which, in support of some theory not to be found in the constitution, would deny to the government those powers which the words of the grant, as usually understood, import, and which are consistent with the general views and objects of the instrument—for that narrow construction, which would cripple the government, and render it unequal to the objects for which it is declared to be instituted, and to which the powers given, as fairly understood, render it competent—then we cannot perceive the propriety of this strict construction, nor adopt it as the rule by which the constitution is to be expounded."[54]

Clearly, Marshall had nothing but contempt for the theory underlying the Virginia and Kentucky Resolutions and the Bonus Bill, the "theory not to be found in the constitution." What he proposed instead, what he claimed the Framers of 1787 intended, what he had argued passionately for in 1788, was a Constitution that armed the agents of the "American people" with real "power." The grant of power to Congress over interstate commerce, he said, "is an investment of power for the general advantage, in the hands of agents selected for that purpose; which power can never be exercised by the people themselves, but must be placed in the hands of agents, or lie dormant. We know of no rule for construing the extent of such powers, other than is given by the language of the instrument which confers them, taken in connection with the purposes for which they were conferred."[55]

Here was the interpretive touchstone that caught Felix Frankfurter's attention, another of those self-verifying premises that led inexorably to an irresistible conclusion. Linguistic analysis, interpretive logic, common sense, and the policy considerations involved in the creation of a national market and a national system of transportation helped the medicine go down. Overall, informing all, was Marshall's sense of history: the struggles of the 1780s, the creation

54. Ibid., 188.
55. Ibid., 189.

of a new Constitution, and the struggles with states' rights theory that underlay the party battles of the early Republic. But first and foremost in his rule book of constitutional hermeneutics was the primacy of the written word: "As men, whose intentions require no concealment, generally employ the words which most directly and aptly express the ideas they intend to convey the enlightened patriots who framed our constitution, and the people who adopted it, must be understood to have employed words in their natural sense, and to have intended what they said."[56]

So what, he asked, was the intended meaning of the words in the disputed clause, starting with "commerce itself?" Surely, he insisted, it was not the confining definition urged on the Court by counsel for Ogden, which would have limited commerce to "traffic, to buying and selling, or the interchange of commodities." Marshall preferred instead Webster's definition of commerce as "intercourse." Expanding on that, he declared that commerce was "intercourse between nations, and parts of nations, in all its branches, and is regulated by prescribing rules for carrying on that intercourse." Such a definition easily embraced "navigation," read steamboats, and much else, too, as the subsequent history of the Commerce Clause proves. This then was the meaning of commerce intended by the Framers, "understood" by "all America" and sanctioned by years of usage—as in the numerous regulations of American shipping, including the Embargo Act of 1807, which he reminded his readers was put forward by the same states' rights party that now argued strict construction.[57]

Marshall then applied his broad definition of "commerce" to inform the other key words in the Commerce Clause, since "it must carry the same meaning throughout the sentence, and remain a unit, unless there be some plain intelligible cause which alters it." First, he dealt with the phrase "among the several states," and within that phrase, the operative word *among*: "The word 'among' means intermingled with. . . . Commerce among the states, cannot stop at the external boundary line of each state, but may be introduced into the interior." He hurried to explain that the regulatory power of Congress did not reach "the completely internal commerce of the state," which "may be considered as reserved for the state itself." But if the subject matter in question involved more than one state or several, he said, then the matter belonged to Congress. And this included commerce, now defined to include steamboats,

56. Ibid., 188.
57. Ibid., 189–90; 191–94.

taking place via "the deep streams which penetrate our country in every direction" and passing "through the interior of almost every state in the Union." The unavoidable conclusion was that "the power of congress . . . whatever it may be, must be exercised within the territorial jurisdiction of the several states."[58]

"What is this power?" he now inquired. What is "the rule by which commerce is to be governed?" These simple questions came so abruptly, were so off-handedly stated, that they appear at first glance to be merely another effort at definition. Marshall's answers, in fact, put a permanent constitutional foundation under the legislative authority of the national government. At issue was not just the meaning of the Commerce Clause and the fate of interstate steamboat traffic but the meaning of all of the powers granted by enumeration to Congress in Article 1, Section 8. His concise ruling bristled with authority and confidence and left no ground for doubt or compromise, or so it seemed: "This power [over commerce], like all others vested in congress, is complete in itself, may be exercised to its utmost extent, and acknowledges no limitations, other than are prescribed in the constitution. . . . If, as has always been understood, the sovereignty of congress, though limited to specified objects, is plenary as to those objects, the power over commerce with foreign nations, and among the several states, is vested in congress as absolutely as it would be in a single government."[59]

Marshall presented this sweeping statement of plenary congressional authority as one of those enduring constitutional principles the Court was bound to uphold. And it appeared to settle the matter of state authority over interstate commerce once and for all by eliminating it entirely, which was Webster's position. Having stated the principle, however, Marshall drew back from the exclusivist implications it contained, turning instead to the issue of concurrent power. His first point, again following Webster, was to refute the states' rights interpretation. He paid particular attention to the contention that the concurrent power of states over interstate commerce was the same as it was in regard to taxation, the subject Hamilton used in *The Federalist* 32 to illustrate his version of concurrent power. The power given to Congress to levy and collect taxes did not detract from the power of the state to tax, said Marshall, because the taxes in each case were raised for different purposes: Congress taxes for national purposes; states tax for state purposes. "There is no analogy, then,

58. Ibid., 194–96.
59. Ibid., 196–97.

between the power of taxation and the power of regulating commerce," he stated, nor to state inspection laws, even though they had "a remote and considerable influence on commerce." These laws, he said, along with quarantine laws, "health laws of every description," plus laws regulating the "internal commerce of a state," fell within the bounds of state authority not surrendered to the general government. But, he argued, they did not prove a version of concurrent power that gave the states a constitutional right to regulate interstate commerce; neither did the power of states to import slaves before 1808 or the right of the states to regulate the conduct of pilots operating out of state port cities.[60]

After repudiating the expansive version of concurrent power doctrine urged by Emmet and Oakley, Marshall returned to Webster's exclusivist argument "that, as the word 'to regulate' implied in its nature, full power over the thing to be regulated, it excludes, necessarily, the action of all others that would perform the same operation on the same thing." Marshall was sorely tempted, noting that "there is great force in this argument, and the court is not satisfied that it has been refuted." But he also conceded that just because the point wasn't refuted, didn't mean that it was proved. In any case, Marshall left the matter unresolved and went on to settle the case on the ground that the New York law granting the monopoly was in direct conflict with the Coastal Licensing Act passed by Congress in 1793, under which Gibbons purported to sail. What Marshall did *not* do was attempt to prove that there really was a conflict between the two laws. No less an authority than Chancellor Kent, for one, found no such conflict, and he had a point.[61]

As any good common lawyer would attest, defining facts is often as determinative as proclaiming doctrine, and infinitely more permissible, and Marshall had a habit of glossing over complex factual problems that stood in the way of doctrinal clarity. This is what he did in *Fletcher v. Peck* when he refused to consider the actual nature of legislative corruption that might have justified the state's Repeal Act of 1796, which he declared unconstitutional. Such was the case also in *McCulloch* when he declined to consider whether the Maryland tax was really a life-threatening burden on the bank. In *Gibbons*, he did not want doctrine to be confused by facts, or as he put it, the result was "nearly self-evident." His voice here was the voice of the highest appellate court of the land, a point he had established three years before in *Cohens v. Virginia*. To

60. Ibid., 199–209.
61. Ibid., 209.

guide lower courts and to educate the citizens of the Republic, the justices needed to speak plainly and forcefully, all the more so because there were "powerful and ingenious minds" who "by a course of well-digested, but refined and metaphysical reasoning" were trying "to explain away the constitution of our country, and leave it, a magnificent structure, indeed, to look at, but totally unfit for use." Confronted with ever more refined and articulate states' rights theory—metaphysical speculation in Marshall's book—the duty of the Court was to return to "safe and fundamental principles."[62]

Gibbons was a remarkable opinion, however, not just for what it said and what it settled but what it left unsaid and unsettled. Settled for all time, it would appear, was the spacious definition of "commerce" and the other key words in the Commerce Clause. Indisputably, the power of Congress over interstate commerce, now construed for the first time, was supreme in its operation on state laws that collided with it. Even counsel for Ogden admitted as much, and so most emphatically did Kent's opinion in *Van Ingen,* on which the counsel relied. Marshall's aggressive application of the doctrine, in assuming there was a *real* conflict between the Coastal Licensing Act and the state monopoly, also served to strengthen the doctrine and extend its application. A little collision, it would appear, could go a long way, and looking at the Court's use of *Gibbons* over the decades, it *did* go a long way. Not only did Marshall's definition of commerce power encompass the twentieth-century revolution in commerce and transportation, without the benefit of constitutional amendment, but it was a chief source of federal authority vis-a-vis the states and the American people. Taken in conjunction with the implied powers doctrine in the Bank of the United States case, *Gibbons* created a plenteous constitutional reservoir of national power. For future Courts looking to uphold the constitutionality of expanded national government, the two opinions provided a formidable one-two combination punch. If one didn't get the nationalizing job done, the other one would. This is not to say the modern corporate, welfare, regulatory state depended on *Gibbons* and *McCulloch,* or that it would not have come without them. But the fact remains that each of those opinions was cited literally thousands of times by federal and state courts, generally to extend the scope of federal power.

In light of the use to which *Gibbons* was put, one might assume Marshall's rendition of the Commerce Clause was unqualifiedly nationalist. Such was not the case. Indeed, despite his authoritative tone, his doctrinal pronouncements

62. Ibid., 221–22.

were far from definitive. First, by settling the case as a straight-out Article 6 conflict between state and federal law, he risked making some of his more nationalistic pronouncements obiter dictum. Moreover, these pronouncements were not all that monolithic to start with. Considerable effort, for example, was devoted to refuting the extreme version of the concurrent commerce power doctrine, without finally doing so. Marshall praised Webster's exclusivist argument and declared that it had not been refuted, but he did not use it to settle the case or adopt it as a rule of construction for future cases. Webster contended that the power over interstate commerce "in its higher forms" belonged automatically to Congress. Marshall, on the other hand, declared that only congressional acts dealing with more states than one fell into the exclusivist category. Since exclusivism itself was not positively endorsed, the doctrinal reach of that watered-down position was considerably shortened. Marshall also referred fleetingly to the police power doctrine that states possess innate power, regardless of constitutional limitations, to legislate regarding the health, welfare, and morals of their citizens. But he also left that concept in limbo.

The indeterminacy of *Gibbons* was no doubt a reflection of differences of opinions among the justices themselves. But there was a historical and an institutional explanation as well, and both speak to Marshall's astuteness. As a master stylist, he understood that rhetoric should match the moment. He knew instinctively that words could educate and inspire. But he did not assume that nationalist pronouncements, however eloquent, would by themselves make a nation. Judging by the nuances of his opinion, he knew that indeterminacy had its uses, which is to say he pushed nationalism only as far as the moment allowed but no further. National-minded justices in the future would find plenty to build on, to be sure. But there was also ample enough play in the doctrinal joints so the American people and future Courts could navigate the treacherous waters of federalism. If exclusivism was to remain a doctrine waiting to be born, so was the embryonic concept of state police power. The notion of concurrent power, neither advocated nor foreclosed by Marshall, also proved to be an invaluable implement of adjustment. One might even argue that the chief justice, with the help of Webster, adumbrated the functional rule of thumb developed for concurrent power cases by the Taney Court in *Cooley v. Board of Wardens* (1852): that commerce essentially local belonged to the states, and that commercial matters requiring uniformity by nature belonged exclusively to Congress. *Gibbons* was not cited in that case to support this new doctrine of select exclusiveness, to be sure, but neither did the nationalism of *Gibbons* have to be repudiated.[63]

Above all, *Gibbons,* like *Marbury* and unlike *McCulloch,* put the Court on the side of nationalism without calling forth retaliation from states' rights extremists. Even though Marshall's opinion bristled with national sentiment and with even greater nationalizing potential, it was widely accepted by the states, this in the midst of the greatest Court-bashing rampage in American history. The explanation is that Marshall's states' rights critics, good Jeffersonian Republicans who were then turning into good Jacksonian Democrats, were as opposed to monopolies as he was. In the meantime, the steamboats began to move freely on American waters between New York and New Jersey. One year after the opinion, they made their way up the Hudson River, then up the Mississippi and the Ohio. Close in the wake of the steamboat, came the railroad. With the help of the Framers and the lawmaking arguments of Daniel Webster, who spoke for the law-shaping demands of an emerging commercial class, Marshall and his colleagues helped launch a "transportation revolution" that helped the American people build a nation on the solid foundation of individual and sectional economic self-interest. To put it another way, his nationalism in *Gibbons,* as in *McCulloch,* was the facilitating kind. Doctrinal purity was not as important as practical result. In the context of his own age, the result was not to create a modern nation-state, but rather to prevent the states from interfering with the collective nation-making enterprise of the American people. It was a notion comporting exactly with his faith in possessive individualism and the culture of contract.

The Marshall Plan for America

In evaluating Marshall's judicial accomplishments, it is tempting to follow the lead of lawyers and judges who in the course of arguing and judging focus on specific cases and airtight doctrine. Not only do legal professionals live in a world bound by doctrine and case law, they have developed an ingenious system for making both instantly available. The citator system not only makes it

---

63. On law and language, see James Boyd White, *When Words Lose Their Meaning: Constitutions and Reconstitutions of Language, Character, and Community* (Chicago, 1984), especially ch. 9, which contains an insightful analysis of Marshall's opinion in *McCulloch. Cooley v. Board of Wardens,* 12 Howard 299, about which see R. Kent Newmyer, *The Supreme Court under Marshall and Taney* (New York, 1968), 105–7.

possible to think and work in the world of past cases but makes it hard to avoid. Marshall, of course, did not live to see the development of the West Law System, but he too worked in the realm of doctrine as developed in cases. As he made clear in *Marbury,* the Court's doctrinal pronouncements were statements, sometimes state papers, about "the principles and theory of our government."[64]

But doctrine does not stand alone as the measure of Marshall's nationalist jurisprudence, nor do opinions by themselves and separately, however great they might be. To say that Marshall had a genius for salvaging doctrines from the contingency of individual cases, of course, is to proclaim what is obvious. Judging from the nationalist opinions just studied, however, he also understood that half a nationalist loaf was better than none, which is to say he was willing to let doctrinal inconsistencies stand unresolved as the price paid for winning majority support on the Court. What is also clear, looking at the same cases, is that their *practical* results were remarkably consistent. Result-oriented jurisprudence, one might say, is where doctrine meets the road, where law intersects with history. For Marshall, the point of convergence, the place where doctrine in one area of law relates to doctrine in another to reveal his vision of American nationalism, was the national market: the political, economic, and legal system that permitted and encouraged interstate commercial activity.

For Marshall the lawyer and the judge, the concept of a national market—indeed, of market in general—was a practical matter. Nowhere did he theorize about *the* market, nor apparently did he read Adam Smith, who did theorize about it. Marshall came of age during the debate over the British Empire in North America, however, which in no small part was a debate over who controlled trade, commerce, and markets and to what end. As a state legislator in the 1780s, he witnessed a continuation of the same debate in an American setting with American players. As a Virginia lawyer attending the interests of clients engaged in international trade, he learned the importance of law to market capitalism. As a champion of the new Constitution in 1788 and as a supporter of Hamilton's economic policies in the 1790s, he clearly understood and approved of the economic aspects of the new Constitution—that it was designed to strengthen federal union by facilitating national economic activity. If the Constitution was implicated in the "market revolution" that took place in the

64. *Marbury v. Madison,* 1 Cranch 178.

early Republic, so from the beginning was John Marshall. And so was Chief Justice Marshall.[65]

As chief justice, Marshall was ideally placed to implement the broad "commercial minded" goals of the Framers and the growing needs of American entrepreneurs doing business across state lines. The business community needed economically informed rules, administered uniformly and operating on individuals without regard for state boundaries and local idiosyncrasies. Even more than Congress, the federal courts were in a position to supply such rules, both in national and international law. In the adversarial system based on common-law methodology inherited from England, individuals could call the courts into action. As the final appellate court in the structure of federal courts, the Supreme Court could in turn call on the collective authority of the nation to settle individual economic disputes. During Marshall's tenure, almost every case, excepting those dealing with the judicial process itself, treated economic disputes. Even cases dealing with the Court's jurisdiction—*Marbury, Martin v. Hunter's Lessee, Cohens,* and the great admiralty case of *De Lovio v. Boit* (1815) come readily to mind—were fraught with market-related consequences. Nearly every one of Marshall's great constitutional opinions, most notably *Fletcher, McCulloch, Dartmouth College,* and *Gibbons,* facilitated market development. The federal circuit courts in Marshall's time were also directly involved in the economic life of the people by virtue of the fact that they had jurisdiction over suits between citizens of different states. Marshall's circuit, consisting only of Virginia and North Carolina, was less on the cutting edge of economic development than was Story's New England circuit, but no less than Story, Marshall understood the market-enhancing potential of uniform circuit law.[66]

Market considerations, then, permeate almost every aspect of Marshall's

65. For the growth of a national market and a national economy and the role of the Constitution in the process, I have found the following general works especially insightful: Curtis Nettels, *The Emergence of a National Economy, 1775–1815* (New York, 1965); and Forrest McDonald, *We the People: The Economic Origins of the Constitution* (Chicago, 1958), which points out that politics and economics and law were really inseparable in the framing of the Constitution; also Jennifer Nedelsky, *Private Property and the Limits of American Constitutionalism: The Madisonian Framework and Its Legacy* (Chicago, 1990).

66. Sellers discusses the market-enhancing nature of Marshall and his Court in *Market Revolution,* especially 56–58, 84–90. On the commercial impact of federal circuit courts, see R. Kent Newmyer, "Justice Joseph Story on Circuit and a Neglected Phase of American Legal History," *American Journal of Legal History* 14 (April 1970): 112–35.

work on the Court, connecting the various aspects of his labors into a jurisprudential whole. Decisions in international law were no less a part of this integrated system than were those in constitutional law. Rule of law in the international setting had to be established without the aid of a written supreme law governing individual nation-states. But the rule of law was Marshall's object just the same, and the law he attempted to establish whenever possible respected private property and expanded the ability of individual entrepreneurs, whether American shippers or foreign merchants such as Manuel Pinto, to make their Lockean way in a world at war. His numerous Contract Clause opinions also fit the market scenario. In cases involving land transactions especially—in *Fletcher v. Peck* most conspicuously but also in *Huidekoper's Lessee, New Jersey v. Wilson,* and later *Johnson v. McIntosh* (1823)—he was guided, if not driven, by a concern for market regularity.[67]

Marshall's efforts to facilitate national economic activity climaxed in the remarkable triad of decisions in 1819 and ended with *Gibbons* in 1824. The correspondence between Marshall's plan for national unity and Henry Clay's American System, not to mention the national vision of newly elected president John Quincy Adams, was not coincidental. The Court's constitutional nationalism was a two-edged sword, and it cut both ways for economic unity: by prohibiting states from interfering with the national market, as in *Sturges* and *Gibbons,* and by giving Congress the power to promote the same, as in *McCulloch.* Even *Dartmouth College* fit the market scenario, readying the American business corporation to do business on a national scale. What these national decisions of the Marshall Court did *not* do, however, was create a modern nation-state, with its extensive regulatory apparatus. No one, least of all Marshall, expected Congress to *regulate* the national economy; indeed, the first modern regulatory statute did not come until three years after his death in 1838, when Congress passed modest safety laws regulating steam boilers on steamboats plying interstate waters. The federal income tax did not come until the Civil War, and even then it was temporary, thanks to the nullifying decision of the Supreme Court in *Pollack v. Farmers, Loan and Trust Co.* in 1895. What Marshall wanted was more modest—and more within the limited nationalist notions of the age. He believed in a national bank, advocated by Hamilton in 1791; in a tariff designed to protect fledgling American manufacturers, also advocated by Hamilton; and in federally sponsored internal improvements, the kind first advocated by Albert Gallatin in 1809. What he wanted the national

---

67. *Johnson v. McIntosh* is treated at length in ch. 7.

government to do, in short—what his Court empowered Congress to do—was facilitate individual economic activity. He wanted government to unleash the creative energy of Americans, not regulate it.[68]

Marshall's federalism was the federalism of the Framers—of Madison in his nation period, of Hamilton, Washington, John and John Quincy Adams. Accordingly, Marshall was dismayed by the small-government philosophy of the Jacksonian politicians, distressed that they put *McCulloch* and the doctrine of implied powers on the shelf. Even more depressing was the growth of outright state resistance to national authority. Marshall's distrust of state legislative government began in the 1780s, and it became more intense with the emergence of formal constitutional theories to justify state power and a political party to implement it. Every one of his opinions strengthening the authority of Congress explicitly curtailed state power, especially the state power to interfere with the operation of a national market. In *McCulloch,* his version of "necessary and proper" worked to prohibit the power of the states to tax the national bank and other instrumentalities of the national government. The practical thrust of *Gibbons,* when the dust of doctrinal speculation about exclusivism and concurrent commerce powers settled, was that an obscure act of Congress could foreclose state interference with interstate commerce. The Dartmouth College decision restricted state regulatory authority over corporations, even though they were chartered by the states. Again in *Sturges,* and in Marshall's dissent in *Ogden v. Saunders,* it was state regulatory power that went down.

For Marshall, as for the Framers, state legislative excess was a constant threat to the national Union; curbing that excess was the central theme of his constitutional jurisprudence. It does not follow, however, that he wanted a consolidated union that would eliminate state sovereignty entirely. Still, the pervasive antistate nature of his opinions again led to the question of what *kind* of nation informed his constitutional law. The market-oriented, liberal nature of that law is a telling clue because it resolves the key paradox: how Marshall the champion of contract liberalism with its antiregulatory implications could at the same time fashion a body of constitutional doctrine so readily adaptable to the needs of the post-1937 corporate welfare state in which bureaucratic regulation was endemic. The resolution of the paradox is

---

68. *Pollack v. Farmers' Loan and Trust Co.,* 158 US 601. Leonard D. White notes the paucity of federal regulation in the early Republic in his *Jeffersonians: A Study in Administrative History* (New York, 1951), 22–27. "An Act to provide for the better security of the lives of passengers on board of vessels propelled in whole or in part by steam" was passed 7 July 1838. *Public Statutes at Large of the United States,* Richard Peters, ed. (Boston, 1860), 5: 304–6.

simple: he did not visualize the modern regulatory nation-state at all, the one often sanctioned by the modern Court citing his opinions. One hastens to add that Marshall did not shy away from a nation armed with the sovereign power to govern. Power was a constant theme of his politics and his law. From the outset of his career to its end, he wanted a nation that could do what all nations had to do: defend the territorial integrity of the country from internal as well as external threat and expand that national territory peacefully by the treaty power broadly conceived. A real navy, not Jefferson's gunboats, a standing army, and a state militia subject to national control in times of national emergency were essentials, too, in a world hostile to republicanism. Marshall the old soldier believed that America should be prepared to fight a war, that military preparedness was necessary in a world full of tigers. He also believed that peace was better than war and that commerce and trade were antidotes to it. International law would curb the aggression of nations by unleashing the civilizing force of international trade. In the same way, market-oriented constitutional law would curb the excesses of states' rights at home and unleash the unifying forces of national commerce.

This said, it must be emphasized that Marshall did not believe that judicial decisions alone, or acts of Congress either, would create a nation. Rather, nation building was the business of the American people. In this respect, his Contract Clause decisions, and the idea of possessive individualism they manifest, are as much a clue to his nationalism as are *McCulloch* and *Gibbons,* the decisions usually cited to make the point. Marshall assumed the American people were like him; that they wanted to make their own deals, rely on their own talents, pursue their own happiness. Long before James Willard Hurst made the point, Marshall realized that law was no substitute for individual creativity; indeed, it depended on it. Without John Marshall and the Marshall family land syndicate, there would have been no *Martin v. Hunter's Lessee.* Without the inventive genius of Fitch, the entrepreneurial energies of Fulton and Livingston, the competitive instincts of Gibbons, the bold tactics of Cornelius Vanderbilt, who piloted Gibbons's ships in successful defiance of the New York monopoly, Marshall and the Court would have not been called into action in *Gibbons.* Well before Tocqueville wrote about it, the American people were already on the move. If Congress would give them a helping hand, if the states would stop interfering, they would fashion a nation with their own hands. Just as Americans from different states fought side by side in the Revolution to create a nation, they could work side by side to preserve and strengthen it.[69]

69. James Willard Hurst, citing Roscoe Pound, makes the point about the limits of law in *Law and Social Order in the United States* (Ithaca, N.Y., 1977), 46–47.

This was John Marshall's agenda for America. The problem was that it would take time to complete, and time was running out. Just as Americans were finally united against the outside world, just as they were beginning to reap the advantages of the revolution in transportation and production, they were caught up in a sectional conflict that threatened to turn into a civil war. And thanks to its market-oriented nationalism, the Court and the chief justice were in the eye of the storm. As in the last decade of the eighteenth century and the first of the nineteenth, Marshall the Virginia nationalist found himself pitted against his own state and his old nemesis, Thomas Jefferson. How he turned the Court's decade of troubles into an occasion for expounding its republican character and the full meaning of its powers, shall now be seen.

CHAPTER SIX

Embattled Chief

The Judiciary of the United States is the subtle corps of sappers and miners constantly working underground to undermine the foundations of our confederated fabric. They are construing our constitution from a coordination of a general and special government to a general and supreme one alone.

—Jefferson on the Marshall Court

A deep design to convert our government into a meer league of States has taken strong hold of a powerful & violent party in Virginia. The attack upon the judiciary is in fact an attack upon the union. The judicial department is well understood to be that through which the government may be attacked most successfully, because it is without patronage, & of course without power, and it is equally well understood that every subtraction from its jurisdiction is a vital wound to the government itself. The attack upon it therefore is a marked battery aimed at the government itself. The whole attack, if not originating with Mr. Jefferson, is obviously approved & guided by him. It is therefore formidable in other states as well as in this; & it behoves the friends of the union to be more on the alert than they have been.

—Marshall on Jefferson

*T*HE TEN YEARS from the end of the 1819 term of the Court to the inauguration of Andrew Jackson in 1829 was a determinative period in the history of the Supreme Court and in the career of John Marshall. To understand why this was so, it is necessary to locate the Court and its chief justice in this transformative period. The 1820s was a watershed not just in American constitutional law but in American history, simultaneously the end of the colonial period and the beginning of a new egalitarian age. Old ways and new existed side by side in a state of uneasy tension and often open contradiction. The glue holding traditional society together was coming unstuck. Gone with the Treaty of Ghent was the foreign policy struggle between England and France that had defined early national politics. Questions concerning tariffs, banks, corporations, and internal improvements—all talismans of the new market culture— quickly emerged and just as quickly divided Americans along regional and class lines. Unparalleled economic and territorial expansion generated both optimism and massive anxiety. While many Americans joined in the entrepreneurial orgy, many others were hopelessly marginalized. African American slaves made the market work for southern planters and, for their efforts, were increasingly treated like chattel. Journeymen workers, separated from their tools and their economic independence by market forces, abandoned their hopes of being players in the republican nation and turned to labor unions and workingmen's parties. The gap between rich and poor continued to widen despite the talk of equality. Even those who profited from the new commercial ethos needed assurance that they would not surrender the virtue of the simpler republican world.[1]

In short, accelerating market capitalism made the 1820s a truly anxious and volatile age. Without France or England to hate, Americans blamed one another for their troubles. Divisions between northern and southern states, which had been submerged in the constitutional compromise, surfaced as a debate over the nature of republican civilization. The result was trouble for the Marshall Court, whose decisions unavoidably impinged on the great economic and political issues of the day. Two interconnected developments were especially threatening. One was the emergence of a new virulent form of states' rights in the southern states. Until the 1820s, states' rights thinking, and acting, had not been the monopoly of any section; thereafter it moved south, becoming more radical as it went. Before J. C. Calhoun and South Carolina took charge, it was Virginia that led the way. As in the 1790s, Marshall found himself at war with the leading politicians of his own state over the role of the Court, the meaning of the Constitution, and indeed over the future of the Republic itself.

The emergence of the Jacksonian Democrats in the 1820s, and with that the permanent establishment of a two-party system in America, also boded ill for Marshall and the Court. The Court under Marshall claimed to be above party politics; the Democratic Party, fashioned by Martin Van Buren, celebrated them for the first time in American history. The Court pledged itself to principled adjudication; the new party system prided itself on coalition building, compromise, and accommodation. Worse still, the Jacksonians, who championed the new concept of party and who won the election in 1828 on the basis of a coalition forged by Van Buren between Virginia and New York, adopted

1. Charles Sellers, *The Market Revolution: Jacksonian America, 1815–1846* (New York, 1991). On labor, see Sean Wilentz, *Chants Democratic: New York City and the Rise of the American Working Class, 1788–1850* (New York, 1984).

the states' rights, anti-Court position previously articulated by Jefferson and his followers. The political contagion Marshall feared when he administered the presidential oath to Jefferson in 1801, and which he hoped would disappear after the War of 1812, had now resurfaced. It was a time of reckoning for his interpretation of the Constitution and his conception of the Court, a struggle for the preservation and the definition of constitutional union. Marshall responded accordingly to his numerous critics, first in a series of remarkable newspaper articles defending his opinion in *McCulloch* against attacks made in the *Richmond Enquirer;* then in *Cohens v. Virginia,* which reaffirmed the Court's right to decide such cases under Section 25. In response to Virginia critics, who accused him of being a consolidationist, he explicated, on and off the Court, a theory of divided sovereignty that preserved the authority of the national government and guaranteed abundant rights to the states. The heart of the matter was a theory of union, set forth in *Cohens v. Virginia,* that made the Supreme Court—armed with final appellate jurisdiction and guided by the doctrine of original intent—the institutional embodiment and chief guardian of republican truth.

Jackson's victory in 1828, the implementation thereafter of militant states' rights in South Carolina, and the emergence of a vocal states' rights element on the Supreme Court itself convinced Marshall that he had been defeated on all fronts. There was much truth in his perception. The period that began so auspiciously for his interpretation of the Constitution and his view of the Court as a republican institution turned from bad to worse. Rather than settling constitutional meaning once and for all, as he had hoped to do, his great nationalist opinions had called into action a southern states' rights movement that dominated politics from the 1820s to the Civil War. It also became apparent that the Supreme Court, *Cohens* to the contrary notwithstanding, did *not* have the final word on the Constitution. Constitutional history on the ground indicated, instead, that judicial review would be an ongoing struggle with the other branches of the government, with the states, and even with the American people in a complicated symbiotic give-and-take. In the course of defending the Court as an institution and the Constitution as he saw it, Marshall closed the circle of his jurisprudence and clarified its true meaning. Indeed, only in his great opinions from this period did the full meaning of *Marbury* become apparent. By grappling with his enemies so brilliantly, he also assured for himself a position of unchallenged preeminence in American history—even as his vision of the old Republic went down in flames.

Virginia Nationalist

John Marshall was sixty-four years old in 1819 and had accumulated eighteen years of service in the nation's highest judicial office. While the Court was never without its critics during these years, it had, thanks in no small part to his leadership, weathered the storm and consolidated its institutional status. Decisions such as *Martin v. Hunter's Lessee* generated opposition, and there was even outright, and sometimes successful, state resistance to the Court's decisions. Opposition to individual decisions, to be expected in a system where one side had to lose, had not, however, turned into a concerted attack on the Court. For one thing, political parties, themselves in a highly amorphous transitional state after the disappearance of the Federalists in 1816, were in no position to make the Court a political issue. And without the organizing force of party, Congress could not mount forceful opposition to the justices even if inclined to do so. Most important, the executive branch—on which the Court depended and to which it was most vulnerable—was occupied by moderate Democratic-Republicans James Madison and James Monroe. Madison believed that disputed constitutional interpretation on major issues should be settled by constitutional amendment, not judicial decision—a position he made clear in his veto of the federal internal improvements provisions of the Bonus Bill in 1816. But he did not seek to undermine the general appellate authority of the Court. One of the first acts of his presidency was to back Marshall's decision in *U.S. v. Peters* in the face of threats from the Pennsylvania legislature. Madison did not always agree with Marshall's "latitudinary mode of expounding the Constitution," as he put it to Spencer Roane regarding the decision in *McCulloch v. Maryland,* but he refused to join the public assault on Marshall. President Monroe was ideologically opposed to much of Marshall's judicial nationalism, but his opposition was tempered by a friendship that went back to school days at Campbelltown Academy and by a devotion to national union rooted in shared combat experience during the Revolution. He had neither the occasion nor the inclination to take on the Court or the chief justice. In any case, post–War of 1812 nationalism favored reconciliation and invited old enemies to bury the ideological hatchet. Virginia states' rights radicals such as John Randolph of Roanoke and John Taylor of Caroline did not give up the cause, but until *McCulloch* gave them a new lease on life, they were held at arms length by the moderate Republicans of the Richmond Junto, who ran the state. Even after that highly unpopular decision, the chief justice remained a popular and revered figure in states' rights Richmond.[2]

Marshall's status as a hometown hero reminds us of a central fact of his life, and his law, that he was not only an American but a Virginian. He lived in Virginia all his life and loved his friends and neighbors as much as they loved him. He knew as much about his state as did Thomas Jefferson, if not about the flora and fauna, then about the ordinary people who lived and worked there. Marshall's judicial responsibilities, especially his circuit duties, involved him deeply in the affairs of his state. Those duties also permitted him to be a full-time Virginian, except for the two months or so spent in Washington during the yearly session of the Court. His yearly retreat to the Blue Ridge also renewed his attachment to native ground. Oak Hill, the 1,700-acre estate Thomas Marshall purchased in 1773, was the family place. Marshall inherited the house and land from his father on the latter's death in 1803 and bequeathed it in turn to his son Thomas. During John Marshall's life, it was the summer gathering place for the Marshall clan. For Marshall, "the west country," as he longingly called it in many of his letters to his wife, was an escape from the burdens of office and the hothouse atmosphere and climate of the capital city. If time and a sense of place and continuity counted, then the Fauquier country helped make Marshall an Old Dominion man.[3]

"Dusty" Richmond, too, left a deep impress on Marshall and he on it. He literally grew up with the city and over time became a local institution. Hearth, home, and family were central to his life, the more so because of Polly's fragile health. Marshall, ever attentive, picked up the slack whenever he could, and domestic slaves—several over the years, including Robin Spurlock, who was Marshall's personal manservant in his old age—greatly eased the daily burdens of life. Marshall appears to have been a patriarchal figure whose authority rested on love and affection. Though his daughter Mary was a favorite, he was close to all his children, an attachment that was deepened by the death of four

2. *U.S. v. Peters*, 5 Cranch 115, is discussed in George Lee Haskins and Herbert A. Johnson, *Foundations of Power: John Marshall, 1801–1815* (New York, 1981), 326–31. Madison's letters to Roane are reprinted in Marvin Meyers, ed., *The Mind of the Founder: Sources of the Political Thought of James Madison* (Indianapolis, 1973), 456–69, quote on 458.

3. For the 1773 deed of sale, see Irwin S. Rhodes, *The Papers of John Marshall, A Descriptive Calendar* (Norman, Okla., 1969), 1: 6. For more on Oak Hill, consult Albert J. Beveridge, *The Life of John Marshall* (Boston, New York, 1916–1919), 4: 55–56. Frances Norton Mason, *My Dearest Polly: Letters of Chief Justice John Marshall to His Wife, with Their Background, Political and Domestic, 1779–1831* (Richmond, Va., 1961).

of them over the years. He was especially concerned that all four of his sons have the college education he did not have. Despite his connections with William and Mary, or perhaps because of them, he chose to send his sons out of state. Thomas, the eldest, graduated from Princeton in 1803 and returned to Richmond, where he followed his father into the legal profession. Second son Jaquelin studied medicine fitfully, pondered about trying the ministry, but did not pursue either profession. Both John Jr. and Edward went to Harvard, though neither graduated. John Jr. was expelled in 1815 for drinking and carousing, "immoral & dissolute conduct." After serving an apprenticeship with a Philadelphia merchant, which position his father procured for him, he settled in Richmond. Edward also departed Cambridge abruptly, leaving in his wake a failed love affair with the daughter of Story's friend and brother-in-law Samuel Fay, and leaving his father to make amends to Judge Fay. All of the boys settled in Virginia, where, thanks to their father's generosity and prudent land speculations, they inherited comfortable estates and, presumably, the cultural values that went with them. Thomas, who resembled his father most closely, was elected to the Virginia Assembly in 1814 and again in 1817; he served continuously from 1827 until his untimely death in 1835. He also joined his father as delegate from Fauquier County to the Virginia constitutional convention of 1829–1830.[4]

Marshall's closeness to his children and grandchildren, of which there were thirty-six by 1831, reminds us that Virginia was his home and Richmond his point of reference, even after it became the intellectual nerve center of states' rights ideology. He served on the Richmond Hustings Court and briefly as city recorder; he represented Richmond in the ratifying convention in 1788, in the state assembly, and later as a delegate to the state constitutional convention in 1829. When the legislature wanted to explore internal improvements in 1812, it chose Marshall to lead the commission and write the report. He was also an officer in the state militia, answering proudly to the name of "General Marshall." While Richmonders may not have liked his nationalism, by all accounts they liked having a national statesmen as a neighbor, especially since he carried

4. Building on Marshall's letters to his wife, Marshall's domestic life is reconstructed by Mason, *My Dearest Polly.* Marshall's occasional letters to his children, reprinted in PJM, are revealing. Marshall's effort to get his son Edward into Harvard is recounted in Marshall to Story, 1 June 1823, and Story to Marshall, 22 June 1823, 2 July 1823, PJM, 9: 323, 327. On Marshall's efforts to smooth the troubled waters of Edward's love affair, see Marshall to Samuel Fay, 15 October 1826, PJM, 10: 309–11. Marshall refers to "my son John's extravagence" and "indiscretion" in his letter to Philip Slaughter, 22 September 1827, PJM, typescript.

the office so gracefully. They also respected him as the presiding judge on the federal circuit court, which met twice a year in Richmond and which served as an important forum for the resolution of state economic disputes. Marshall was also deeply engaged as a private citizen. He was a lay leader of the city's Episcopal church, though apparently he did not take communion as a matter of principle. He was an active Mason in his early years, though he gradually lost interest, dropping out entirely in the 1820s. Among the other state and local institutions with which he was associated were the Potomac River Company; the James River Canal Company; the [Richmond] Fellowship Fire Company; the Virginia Agricultural Society, of which he was president; the Virginia branch of the American Colonization Society, of which he was also president; and the College of William and Mary, as a member of the board of trustees. In times of crisis, as during the days of panic following Gabriel's Rebellion in 1802 or after the tragic theater fire in Richmond in December 1811, he was there to lead and comfort. His name even appeared on a list of subscribers to a fund for the relief of former president Thomas Jefferson.[5]

Marshall was deeply involved in Richmond's rich and varied social life. His and Polly's table was graced by high spirits, good food, and fine wine from a plentifully stocked cellar. In addition, Marshall was a popular favorite in several local men's clubs, starting with the informal association of young lawyers and politicos who roomed at Formicola's Tavern in the 1780s. He frequented the local race track and was a member of the Jockey Club and the Barbecue Club. The latter was a self-selective society, whose members included the bankers, businessmen, planters, and other professionals, in general, the movers and shakers of the place, without distinction to party. Mint julep was the official drink, which appears to have suited Marshall well, and when members gathered for the annual banquet, he was often at the head of the table and always at the center of the talk and laughter. He was also a favorite at the Quoit Club, where he was not only a formidable competitor but also the chief judge of disputed points. One bit of apocryphal humor has the chief justice down on his knees measuring a disputed throw, using a straw for a ruler. In this jurisdiction, it would appear, his decisions were unchallenged.

Over the years, there developed an impressive body of anecdotes about Marshall in Richmond, most of which are found without attribution in Frances

---

5. Marshall's social involvement can be reconstructed by consulting the index to the several volumes of the PJM, as well as that of Mason's *Dearest Polly* and Beveridge's *Life of John Marshall*. Also useful is the extensive index in Rhodes, *Papers of John Marshall*.

Norton Mason's *Dearest Polly.* A rich vein of self-deprecating, Lincoln-like humor runs through all of them. One of the most frequently repeated has the sloppily dressed chief justice at the local market being offered a quarter by an unwitting stranger to carry a turkey home; he took the job and presumably the quarter, too. Another vignette depicts the long-legged chief on the back of a short-legged mule bound north out of Richmond for his Chickahominy farm, supposedly with his finger in a jug of something that wasn't water. Whether there was a turkey, or a mule, or a jug is not known, but the fact that there were stories says something about Marshall's status as a local legend. It is known from scattered references in his correspondence that he did have a "farm" (once, he called it a "plantation") on the Chickahominy River. Whether farm or plantation, it was part of a down-home experience, which gave him the opportunity to compare notes with friends and neighbors about new techniques of fertilization, crop rotation, and new seed and no doubt to complain about the weather and the perennial uncertainties of farming. Marshall could also speak with some familiarity about slavery. Domestic slaves played an important role in the daily life of the Marshall family, and slaves, some of whom he rented, also appear to have worked Marshall's various farms. Everything suggests he was a humane master, but the harsh fact remains that he bought, sold, owned, and rented slaves, used them as collateral to secure legal transactions, and willed them to his children. In this, as in so many other ways, Marshall the nationalist was a Virginian.[6]

What else could he have been? Virginia was where he was born and reared, lived and died, and where his ancestors and his children and theirs put down roots. It was where he studied law and learned about America. Virginia shaped his character, his personality, and inimitable style, as Jean Edward Smith's excellent biography shows. But did it also shape his constitutional jurisprudence? Did it matter that Marshall was Virginia-born and -bred when he fashioned his constitutional position on federalism, when he set out to balance the rights and interests of the states, Virginia included, against those of the nation? Virginia's radical states' rightists in effect said it didn't. Focusing especially on *McCulloch* and *Cohens,* they accused him of using the Court to crush Virginia

---

6. It is impossible to say exactly how many domestic slaves Marshall owned during his life; the number at any given period seems to have varied. According to the Richmond tax list of 1785, he owned two slaves; the tax list of 1788 mentions six tithable slaves. In 1830 the census listed one male slave between fifty-five and one hundred years of age, Robin Spurlock most likely. Rhodes, *Papers of John Marshall,* 1: 38, 70; 2: 201, 253, 348. In his index entry under "Slaves," Rhodes listed six Marshall slaves by name. Ibid., 2: 566.

and prostrate its interests at the feet of the northern commercial aristocracy that allegedly controlled the national government. This was the view Jefferson privately urged on his friends, the same that Spencer Roane and John Taylor of Caroline articulated publicly and interminably. This was the view of Marshall finally circulated as orthodoxy by the Richmond Junto and the *Richmond Enquirer,* which spoke for it. The same notion of Marshall as the national consolidationist par excellence also crept into the admiring work of Albert Beveridge, then into the numerous accounts of authors who drew on Beveridge's *Marshall* for their facts and interpretation.

Several questions are begged, however, the first being whether Virginians outside the elite circle of states' rights radicals and romantic agrarians agreed with this view of Marshall. Did Virginia legislators suppose they had a viper in their nest when they designated Marshall to head the committee exploring state internal improvements in 1812? Did they see consolidating evil in the brilliant report he wrote urging the Old Dominion to integrate its river system and tie into the growing national transportation system? What about those Virginians in Richmond and across the state who continued to celebrate him as a local boy made great? And what about those who elected him to the Virginia constitutional convention of 1829, against his inclination and over his objections? Didn't they understand that he was a Virginian, and didn't they count on him to support the conservative folkways of the Old Dominion, including slavery, when push came to shove?

To ask the questions is to answer them. Seeing Marshall in the Virginia context, taking note of his deep attachment to Virginia and its people and their deep affection for him, helps take measure of the man. Not so obviously it also provides an essential perspective on the great struggle of the 1820s over the Court and the Constitution. Marshall's intellectual face-off with Jefferson, Roane, Taylor, Randolph, and others was not just a struggle to define the nature of the federal Union, though it was certainly that. It was also a fight among Virginians for the heart and soul of the Old Dominion. By depicting Marshall as a manipulative judge and unrelenting consolidationist, Marshall's critics aimed not only to discredit him personally but to stamp out the tradition of Virginia nationalism that went back to the Revolution, to Washington, and to the ratification of the Constitution in 1788. Against them, Marshall proposed not a consolidationist jurisprudence but a federal system that left states a large body of rights, including the right to own slaves and control them. His defeat not only isolated him painfully from the state he loved but advanced the Old Dominion a large step farther along the road to Appomattox.[7]

McCulloch v. Maryland and "the sleeping spirit of Virginia."

Why Marshall's opinion in *McCulloch* should have set in motion "the whole antifederal spirit of Virginia," as he called it, or how his critics succeeded in discrediting the Court and isolating him from Virginia and Virginia from the nation, is not immediately clear. A national bank, as he carefully pointed out in his opinion, was not a new institution to Virginia or the nation; nor were the constitutional arguments in its favor new or original. The first Bank of the United States, which resembled its successor in every major respect, had been in existence for twenty years before its charter was allowed to expire in 1811. Washington had carefully considered the constitutional question and so had the First Congress, which passed the charter. Even though it was thoroughly Hamiltonian and despite the opposition to it from the agrarian wing of his own party, President Jefferson left the bank in place when he took office in 1801. For ten more years, he and Madison continued to draw on its services for the benefit of the nation. Four years without the bank during the War of 1812 spoke eloquently as to the value of those services. When the charter for the second Bank of the United States was introduced in 1816, it had the support of President Madison, who signed the bill into law, and moderates in both political camps, including John C. Calhoun, who led the pro-bank forces in the Senate. The combined votes of senators and representative in the nine southern and western states in favor of the bank was forty-five to twenty-six. Virginia was the only state whose representatives in Congress voted against the bank, but even there, the vote was eleven against and ten for, the latter reckoning no doubt that a branch would be located in Richmond. Among those who attacked Marshall for his opinion in *McCulloch,* as he suggested to Bushrod

7. For a general account of the intellectual struggles going on in early national Virginia, see Norman K. Risjord, *The Old Republicans: Southern Conservatism in the Age of Jefferson* (New York, 1965). Robert Dawidoff, *The Education of John Randolph* (New York, 1976), captures the romantic, atavistic tone of one leading Virginia states' rightist. Also see Robert E. Shalhope, *John Taylor of Caroline: Pastoral Republican* (Columbia, S.C., 1980). The standard account of southern sectionalism is Charles S. Syndor, *Development of Southern Sectionalism, 1819–1848* (Baton Rouge, 1948).

Washington, were many prominent Bank of the United States stockholders. Wilson Cary Nichols, president of the Richmond branch, was also a member of the Richmond Junto.[8]

Given the long history of the national bank, its support among moderates in both parties, and its integration into the financial and political community of Richmond and Virginia, it is not surprising that Marshall was caught off balance by the vehemence of the attack on his opinion and on him personally. Indeed, he concluded that it was not the bank that awakened the "sleeping spirit," or even the doctrine of implied powers in his opinion. Instead, it was his forceful repudiation of the states' rights theory set forth by counsel for Maryland, who rested their case on the assumption that the Constitution was nothing but a contract between sovereign states and ought, in doubtful areas, to be interpreted so as to privilege state sovereignty. The bank case may have involved Maryland, but the theory put forth by Jones, Martin, and Hopkinson for that state belonged to Virginia and traced its lineage back to the Virginia and Kentucky Resolutions. Marshall saw the connection immediately and correctly assumed that Jefferson, stirred by pride of authorship, was also stirring the states' rights pot behind the scenes. "If the principles which have been advanced on this occasion were to prevail," he wrote to Story, "the constitution would be converted into the old confederation."[9]

But why was the tone so apocalyptic on both sides? After all, states' rights theorizing had been around a long time, so had the Bank of the United States if one counts Hamilton's first Bank of the United States, and so had Jefferson's vendetta against Marshall. So what happened in 1819 and immediately thereafter to give such doomsday meaning to old ideas and old enmities? One thing was a rapid acceleration of market-oriented capitalism as reflected in the panic of 1819 and the onset of business cycles in American history. The second Bank of the United States was also a conspicuous feature, if not the key symbol, of the new economic age. Marshall was right to observe that Virginians were am-

8. Marshall used the phrase "sleeping spirit of Virginia" in his letter to Joseph Story, 24 March 1819, PJM, 8: 280. For the Marshall quote, see his letter to Story, 28 April 1819, ibid., 309. See Charles D. Lowery, *James Barbour, a Jeffersonian Republican* (University, Ala., 1984), 80–81, on the makeup of the Junto and the banking interests of some of its key members. For a breakdown of the charter vote, see Bray Hammond, *Banks and Politics in America, from the Revolution to the Civil War* (Princeton, N.J., 1957), 240. Marshall to Bushrod Washington, 27 March 1819, PJM, 8: 281.

9. Marshall to Joseph Story, 27 May 1819, PJM, 8: 314. For Marshall's harsh assessment of Jefferson, see his letter to Story, 13 July 1821, PJM, 9: 178–79.

biguous, not to say hypocritical, regarding the bank. Opposition to Hamilton's bank had been a tenet of Virginia Republicanism from the 1790s on. Even so, the effort of Virginia Republicans to create an alternate state banking system had been plagued with practical and ideological problems. In Marshall's opinion, the Bank of Virginia, controlled by the Richmond Junto, was a weak financial institution, which was no doubt why many Virginians, including Marshall, preferred the Richmond branch of the national bank. But the disparity between the two banks was precisely the point, since it seemed to illustrate the power of the Bank of the United States to destroy state financial institutions. And opponents had a point. When the second Bank of the United States called in loans to state banks, which it had improvidently made, to cover its own debts, which it had improvidently incurred, a default of banking institutions swept like wildfire across the southern and western states. If the "violent party" in Virginia wanted to dramatize the dangers of market capitalism, if it needed an excuse for a direct attack on Marshall and the Court, then the second Bank of the United States under the mismanagement of William Jones was a gift from on high.[10]

Marshall correctly assessed the provenance of Virginia's attack on the bank, but he underestimated the importance of the doctrine of implied powers as a bone of contention. Fear of implied powers had been a key feature of states' rights arguments in Virginia going back to the ratification debates in 1788. And it did not help matters that the dispositive paragraph in *McCulloch* on the subject came word for word from Hamilton. Circumstances in 1819 and the years immediately following made the doctrine even more threatening than it had been when Jefferson and Hamilton fought it out in their famous memoranda on the bank in 1791. Not only did Marshall side with Hamilton on the constitutionality of the bank, his doctrine of implied powers also overrode Madison's constitutional objections to federal internal improvements as set forth in his veto of the Bonus Bill in 1816. Madison favored such legislation, but believed that it required a constitutional amendment. Marshall's implied powers doctrine made an amendment unnecessary, a point that became abundantly clear when in an obiter dictum he referred to the need for federal improvements to bind the territories acquired in the Adams-Onís Treaty of 1819. Madison would ultimately reconcile himself to Marshall's view of judicial review, but other Virginians did not. As they saw it, *McCulloch* substituted the

10. For the peculiar noncapitalist qualities of southern banking, see Bertram Wyatt-Brown, *Southern Honor: Ethics and Behavior in the Old South* (New York, 1982), 183–84.

interpretive authority of the Court for the amending power of the states acting as constitutionally designated agents in the amending process. It was precisely the latter that John C. Calhoun's theory of nullification was designed to guarantee.[11]

Lurking in the background of *McCulloch* as inciting factors in the attack on Marshall were two other issues, one unspoken but specific in nature and omnipresent in states' rights thinking, the other general and historical in character. The specific issue was slavery, which came to be connected to Marshall's doctrine of implied powers by the debates in 1820 and 1821 about Missouri's entry into the Union as a slave state. Strangely little was said explicitly about the slavery issue in the initial attack on *McCulloch,* but the connection was there to see—and after the abortive Denmark Vesey slave uprising in Charleston, South Carolina, in 1822, impossible to ignore. The danger posed to agrarian slavery from *McCulloch* lay in the combination of an implied powers doctrine and the growth of a northern majority in Congress. If Congress could exceed the enumerated powers via the Necessary and Proper Clause, if the northern free-state interests could muster a majority in Congress, then they might threaten slavery in the states where it existed or, as they attempted to do in the Missouri debates, abolish it by statute in the new territories. The point is not that Virginians perceived an immediate threat to the "peculiar institution" but rather that Marshall's opinion invited them to think comprehensively about where they stood in the economic revolution gathering steam across the land. Virginians, heretofore noted for their moderation and their nationalism, now listened with new respect to the voices of extremism: to publicists such as John Taylor of Caroline and professors such as Nathaniel ("Beverley") and Henry St. George Tucker, all touting the Articles of Confederation as the model constitution; and to the mesmerizing oratory of John Randolph, who declared that the Constitution was worth but "a fig" and who asked his fellow Virginians to calculate "the value of union."[12]

Virginia, as Marshall understood, had come to an historic crossroad. Like other states of the seaboard south, it faced an economic dilemma of major pro-

---

11. On Madison's opposition to *McCulloch,* as well as his final reconciliation with Marshall and judicial review, see Drew McCoy, *The Last of the Fathers: James Madison and the Republican Legacy* (New York, 1989), 68–70.

12. For Randolph's biting critique of the new age's culture, north and south, see William C. Bruce, *John Randolph of Roanoke, 1773–1833* (1922; reprint, New York, 1970). A large portion of volume 1 is devoted to Randolph's long career in Congress; the quote from the *Annals of Congress* appears at 1: 492.

portions and with that a political and ideological one. The overarching question was about whether or to what degree the dominant agrarian-planter, slaveholding interests of the state could benefit by participating in the growing market economy, which the Marshall Court promoted. Fear of the present, uncertainty about the future, and talk of decline were familiar to Virginians—consider Wirt's lament as early as 1803 in his *Letters of the British Spy,* witness John Randolph's wistful longing for the cultural ways of Old England and Old Virginia. More to the point, perhaps, was Jefferson's effort to manufacture an Anglo-Saxon constitutional tradition against which to measure the "honeyed Mansfieldism" of Marshall and Story with its modernizing subtext. Still, one might have expected that declining cotton prices, soil exhaustion, and the prohibitive cost of maintaining a workforce based on plantation slavery would have inclined Virginians to retool, regroup, and embrace market capitalism, economic specialization, and liberal individualism. In fact, this is exactly what Marshall wanted to do, what planters in the Northern Neck were inclined to do, and what the democratic denizens of tramontane Virginia finally did. What the Old Dominion conservatives did instead was to dig in their heels—against change, against the encroaching national market, against the future, and against John Marshall and his view of the Court and the Constitution.[13]

McCulloch was their cause célèbre. On his return home from the Court's session in 1819, he heard rumors that a newspaper assault on his opinion was being mounted, that it was to be branded as *"damnably heretical,"* as he put it to Story. The attack was even more vehement, comprehensive, and long-lasting than he feared. Beginning on March 30 and running through June 22, there appeared a series of anti-Court, anti-Marshall essays in the *Richmond Enquirer,* two by William Brockenbrough, writing as "Amphictyon," and four by Spencer Roane, writing as "Hampden." The intellectual cudgel was soon picked up by John Taylor of Caroline County, Virginia's premier theorist who produced three books in three years to exorcize the nationalist heresy introduced by Marshall's opinion. Abel Upshur weighed in later with yet another tome. Before that, the Virginia legislature got in the act with resolutions condemning both the ideas and audacity of *McCulloch.* John Randolph of Roanoke added some of his most impassioned oratory to the cause. In time, both of St. George Tucker's sons—Henry St. George at the University of Virginia

---

13. Jefferson's discussion of the ancient Saxon constitution and his opposition to Mansfield is treated in David N. Mayer, *The Constitutional Thought of Thomas Jefferson* (Charlottesville, Va., 1994), ch. 1.

and Beverley at William and Mary—attempted to refute Marshall's nationalist position in their lectures, articles, and books. The "great Lama of the mountains" also descended from Olympus to join the fray, as Marshall noted bitterly to Story. Jefferson did not openly engage Marshall, and no doubt the attack would have occurred without him. But as Roane noted, the ex-president was the spiritual godfather of states' rights. Jefferson proudly assumed the role, spurring others, including Roane, to action and in general putting his imprimatur on the attack. Marshall paid his archantagonist a backhanded compliment by assuming that he was responsible for spreading Virginia theory to other states.[14]

Marshall did not foresee the specific course of antebellum history, but experience taught him to read history in a tragic light. He agreed with Jefferson, who heard a "fire bell in the night,"and his old friend Adams, who predicted that the heated oratory of Virginia radicals was but "the title page to a great and tragic volume." Marshall viewed the crisis of the 1820s not only as someone who thought of himself as an American but as someone who loved Virginia and who believed that nationalism and state interests were inseparably connected, not mutually exclusive. He also believed that *McCulloch* provided for precisely that symbiotic connection between national and state power. It was to prove this point and to show that the charges of consolidationism leveled against him were both false and dangerous that he decided to answer Brockenbrough and Roane. Marshall knew the risk of going public, something he had deliberately avoided following the impeachment of Chase in 1805. He surely appreciated the contradictions of doing so in light of his effort to cast the Court as a legal institution and to leave politics to the political branches and the politicians. What called him to the barricades in 1819 was his realization that the Court was already at the center of a political storm and his fear that the states' rights conflagration in Virginia might spread to other states. It was the ratification struggle all over again, the 1790s, and the first campaign against Jefferson. If Virginia would do right, it might save itself and regain a

14. Scholars are indebted to Gerald Gunther, ed., for discovering and reclaiming the text of these remarkable essays and for his insightful introduction to them in *John Marshall's Defense of McCulloch v. Maryland* (Stanford, Calif., 1969). The treatises of Taylor, Upshur, and Henry St. George Tucker are discussed in Elizabeth K. Bauer, *Commentaries on the Constitution, 1790–1860* (New York, 1952), especially ch. 5. For an outstanding analysis of Roane-Marshall debate, see Samuel R. Olken, "John Marshall and Spencer Roane: An Historical Analysis of Their Conflict over U.S. Supreme Court Appellate Jurisdiction," *Journal of Supreme Court History* (1990), 125–41; Marshall to Story, 18 September 1821, PJM, 9: 183.

position of honor in the councils of the nation that it once had. So Marshall took up his pen and entered the political fray to defend the Constitution and the Court. Neither would survive in the way he hoped, but his efforts left an indelible mark on the American constitutional tradition and on the Supreme Court as an institution.

Defending McCulloch: Balancing National Sovereignty and States' Rights

The assault began on March 23 when the *Richmond Enquirer* published the text of Marshall's opinion in *McCulloch*. Accompanying the opinion was a proclamation by Thomas Ritchie, editor of the *Enquirer*, leader of the Richmond Junto, and son-in-law of Roane, praising the Virginia and Kentucky Resolutions and demanding that Marshall's heretical departure from them "be controverted and exposed." A week later Ritchie put his editorial imprimatur on the first of two essays by William Brockenbrough, also a member of the Junto. These were followed, starting June 11 and ending June 22, by Roane's four essays, which were much attended to because he was the leading judge on the Virginia Court of Appeals. Marshall answered Brockenbrough with two "A Friend to the Union" essays, which appeared in the *Philadelphia Union*. By publishing in Philadelphia, Marshall no doubt hoped to preserve his anonymity, but the essays were so badly mangled in the printing that he instructed Justice Bushrod Washington, who was his accomplice in the venture, to place them in the *Gazette* and *Alexandria Daily Advertiser*, where they appeared with Marshall's corrections. Marshall answered Roane in nine essays written under the nom de plume, "A Friend of the Constitution," which appeared in the *Gazette* from June 30 to July 15.[15]

Marshall's essays responded directly to the charges against him, but they also stand as a coherent and carefully structured statement on the nature and location of power in the federal system. Brockenbrough and Roane, though perfectly united in their distaste for *McCulloch*, did not synchronize their efforts nearly as well, which gave Marshall a leg up. Amphictyon's first essay was short, hesitant in tone and highly derivative, quoting verbatim and at length from the Virginia and Kentucky Resolutions. Brockenbrough's second

15. On the background of the Marshall-Roane confrontation, see the editorial note, PJM, 8: 282–87. Gunther, *Marshall's Defense*, Introduction, discusses Marshall's effort, using the good offices of Bushrod Washington, to get his essays accurately printed.

338 / John Marshall *and the* Heroic Age *of the* Supreme Court

essay, perhaps in response to Marshall's heated reply, focused on the specifics of implied powers. It was decidedly more hard-hitting, but it did not soar. Roane's essays, however, took the argument to another level, in more ways than one. They were highly personal in tone and laced throughout with irony and sarcasm; they were also learned in the law, brilliantly argued, and comprehensive. The focus was on *McCulloch* and the doctrine of implied powers, but Roane drew freely on Anti-Federalist arguments made first in the Virginia ratifying debates, especially those of his father-in-law, Patrick Henry. Like Brockenbrough, he drew freely on the Virginia and Kentucky Resolutions and on Madison's Virginia Report of 1799, which was a brilliant restatement of the Virginia Resolutions of the previous year. Roane quietly cast aside Madison's subtle qualifications, however, and opted for absolute state sovereignty. With independence from England, his argument went, sovereignty, itself indivisible, devolved on each of the new states. The Constitution of 1787, which was ratified by state conventions, was a contract created by sovereign people in the sovereign states who were parties to the contract. The purpose of the Constitution, and the very essence of constitutionalism itself, was to *limit* the national government, not to strengthen and empower it, as Marshall contended in *McCulloch.* If the states were truly sovereign, if the Constitution was a mere contract among states rather than the creation of the entire American people speaking collectively, then all doubtful cases of interpretation went automatically to the states and against the national government. By this standard—and it was the gravamen of Roane's entire argument—Marshall's grant of discretionary power via the Necessary and Proper Clause was blatant usurpation.

The chief justice gave as good as he got, which is to say he came out swinging, responding first to Brockenbrough's essays of March 30 and April 2. Amphictyon's first and second essays contained more assertion than argument, but they did define the issues and establish the ironic and sarcastic tone of the entire debate. Brockenbrough referred to Marshall as a judge "of the most profound legal attainments" and admitted that his opinion was "very able." Nevertheless, there were problems. One was that Marshall's opinion was far too sweeping, and another was that his compliant colleagues uncritically followed him. Moreover, the chief justice, for all of his claims at impartiality, was blinded by Federalist politics and Hamiltonian values. For these reasons, the Court's decision was "not more binding or obligatory than the opinion of any other six intelligent members of the community." As for the true view of the Court's power of review, Brockenbrough cited Roane's opinion for the Virginia Court of Appeals in *Hunter v. Martin* (1815), which repudiated the

Court's appellate jurisdiction under Section 25. For the true view of the Constitution, he quoted at length from the third resolution of Madison's 1799 report. He concluded by addressing the dangerous policy consequences of *McCulloch*, not just in regard to the bank but also to internal improvements, education, the promotion of agriculture, poor relief, and religion. On all counts, he concluded, Marshall's enlarged "construction is inadmissible."[16]

Marshall's first essay (April 24), while it began to address the substantive issues of judicial authority and implied powers, made a special effort to disarm his critics by exposing the hyperbolic nature of their charge and the cynicism of their motives. He targeted not only Amphictyon but Ritchie and the whole states' rights party of Virginia. Here, he repeated in public what he had written in private: that the attack on *McCulloch* had little to do with the Bank of the United States, which "had become law, without exciting a single murmur"; rather it was merely the occasion "for once more agitating the publick mind, and reviving those unfounded jealousies by whose blind aid ambition climbs the ladder of power." The Court was attacked because it couldn't answer back; the purpose of the assault was simply to bring the justices into disrepute, to distort the way the Court did business, which was collective in nature, not the monopoly of one man.[17]

On top of that, Marshall claimed, Amphictyon and Hampden deliberately distorted what the Court had said: "It cannot escape any attentive observer that Amphictyon's strictures on the opinion of the supreme court, are founded on a total and obvious perversion of the plain meaning of that opinion, as well as on a misconstruction of the constitution." Besides, it was not the Court's decision that changed the Constitution, but critics who introduced states' rights theories from the 1790s to make their case. If Marshall's critics branded him as a consolidationist, he branded them as radical ideologues who wanted to undo the Constitution and return the country to the chaos of the 1780s, in short, who wanted to redirect the entire course of American constitutional history. As he put it: The "principles maintained by the counsel for the state of Maryland, and by Amphictyon, would essentially change the Constitution, render the government of the Union incompetent to the objects for which it was instituted, and place all its powers under the control of the state legislatures. It would, in a great measure, reinstate the old confederation." Whether, given the radical transforming nature of the Constitution itself, Marshall was

16. *Hunter v. Martin*, 4 Munford 1; Gunther, *Marshall's Defense*, 74–75.
17. Ibid., 78.

entitled to stake out the conservative ground here, to brand his opponents as radicals, is perhaps an open question. On one point, however, he was correct: that his states' rights critics looked to the Articles of Confederation, not the Constitution, as the true republican constitution.[18]

The Marshall-Brockenbrough exchange cast the debate as a mix of history, law, and ideology. Just as clearly, it was a confrontation of personalities and a war of reputations—and thus, as was the habit in Virginia, a matter of honor. This was more so when the chief justice of the United States took up his pen to refute and discredit the leading judge on the Virginia Court of Appeals, whose Hampden essays picked up where Amphictyon left off. Spencer Roane, "the great judge," as Marshall sarcastically called him, was a formidable combatant. From his position on Virginia's highest court, he spoke with special authority. In addition, though Roane was not actively engaged in Junto politics, he had been intimately connected with the states' rights movement in Virginia for more than two decades. Almost certainly he was consulted about the plan to diminish Marshall's influence. Like Brockenbrough, Roane conceded rhetorically that the Supreme Court "is a tribunal of great and commanding authority" and that, admittedly, the chief justice is a judge of "great abilities." Nevertheless, he said, the Court's opinions must not be received from on high as "the law and the prophets," nor should Marshall's opinion "be canonized." Stripped of false politeness and phony compliments, Roane's position was simply that Marshall was dead wrong and had to be brought down. Roane wanted the people of Virginia and the members of the General Assembly, who were scheduled to meet at the end of the year, to "hear him for his cause." That famous phrase, coming from the Henry speech that launched the Revolution in Virginia in 1765, said it all. It was the Revolution all over again; Roane was Patrick Henry stepping forth to defend liberty from the evils of consolidating and corrupting power. The cause was the "Rights of 'The States,' and of 'The People.'" The text to be explicated was the Tenth Amendment, which saved to the states all powers not delegated to the national government.[19]

Roane's four essays were orchestrated for maximum impact. They appeared at regular three- or four-day intervals over the period from June 11 to 22, giving readers a chance to digest and discuss the complex issues. Though skillfully interconnected and even repetitious, not unwise given the complexities of the argument, each essay fit into the overall argument: The first threw down the

---

18. Ibid., 99–100.
19. Ibid., 105–6, for a discussion of the first Hampden essay.

gauntlet in general terms and set the tone of the debate; the second bore down on the *general* constitutional theory of implied powers; the third focused sharply on Marshall's opinion, taking his argument up point by point. The final piece attacked the jurisdiction of the Court itself and, by necessary implication, Marshall's entire concept of judicial review. Roane's rhetorical strategy throughout was to submerge his own voice in the collective wisdom of Virginia. The issue was tyranny, "the proneness of all men to extend and abuse their power." The evil was not England as it had been in the decade before the Revolution but "our federal rulers," whose deliberate aim was to "obliterate the state governments, forever, from our political system." The problem was "a renegado congress"—which had adopted "the outrageous doctrine of Pickering, Lloyd, or Sheffey!"—and "the parasites of a government gigantic in itself" who were "turn-coats and apostates."[20]

Chief among those "turn-coats" and traitors to liberty, according to Roane, were the chief justice and his colleagues, who by "a judicial *coup de main*" in *McCulloch* gave "a *general* letter of attorney to the future legislators of the union." That opinion, by the man who "eulogized" Hamilton and supported his consolidationist philosophy, was "the '*Alpha* and *Omega,* the beginning and the *end,* the first and the last—of federal usurpations.'" Roane appointed himself to arouse the people of Virginia, who, he said, "are sunk in apathy," "sodden in the *luxuries* of banking," who have given in to "a money-loving, funding, stock-jobbing spirit," who "are almost prepared to sell our liberties for a 'mess of pottage.'" The problem, it would appear, was not that market capitalism was failing but that it was succeeding too well. To awaken Virginians from their prosperity-induced "torpor," Roane presumed to speak for "our forefathers, of glorious and revolutionary memory," for Mason and Henry and Jefferson. His goal was "liberty." His "Magna Charta," his "political bible," was Madison's "celebrated report to the legislature of Virginia, in the year 1799." Virginia wisdom, illuminated by the common law, at least as it was practiced in his court, would reveal Marshall's tyrannous usurpation. Of necessity, Marshall would be exposed for the traitor he was—by his next-door neighbor no less.[21]

Historians and mythmakers, who are sometimes one and the same, agree that Marshall was an even-tempered, moderate, superbly rational man who brought those personal qualities to his job as chief justice. And so he did. As a

20. Ibid., 108, 107, 109, 112.
21. Ibid., 110, 112, 113.

Friend of the Union, and Friend of the Constitution, however, he was not speaking for the Court but for himself. He could take off the judicial gloves and did just that, lashing back at his critics as "certain restless politicians of Virginia"—a party of "skilful engineers" who set out to destroy the Court because it lacked "power" and "patronage" and was "without the legitimate means of ingratiating itself with the people." Nor was that the worst of their sins. Attacking the Court, Marshall charged, was really their way of destroying the Union itself and the Constitution that bound it together. Here he spoke passionately of the "zealous and persevering hostility" of Virginia states' rightists going back to the ratification debates themselves, of their effort "to reinstate that miserable confederation, whose incompetency to the preservation of our union" was so abundantly demonstrated by "the short interval between the treaty of Paris and the meeting of the general convention at Philadelphia." This, then, was the glorious tradition of Virginia that Hampden with his "ranting declamation" and "rash impeachment" of the Court sought to resuscitate.[22]

This was not the easygoing, fun-loving John Marshall Richmonders knew and loved. What they thought of his transformation into a fighting polemicist can only be surmised, but it was clear to all that he put his reputation on the line, bet his character, so to speak, against that of his adversaries. If the congenial, kindly, neighborly Marshall was *that* agitated, the message said, then there must be good reason. Marshall spoke from passionate conviction but also from a strength that was a special blend of textual analysis and doctrinal exegesis, all fashioned into a sustained argument that seemed plain as day and above mere partisan bickering. The main point to be refuted was Roane's contention that *McCulloch*—its historical foundation, its doctrine, its rules of interpretation, as well as its practical consequences—was consolidationist and that it would literally obliterate the states. Marshall answered each element in Roane's charge but not before charging him with deliberately misrepresenting what the Court actually said. Judicial opinions, Marshall observed, especially "great constitutional questions," often "depend on a course of intricate and abstruse reasoning, which it requires no inconsiderable degree of mental exertion to comprehend, and which may, of course, be grossly misrepresented," which by Marshall's reckoning was precisely what Hampden had done—beginning with his allegation that the Court had gone outside the record to decide the case.[23]

22. Ibid., 155, 156.
23. Ibid., 156, 159.

Marshall, hurt by the accusation, rose to the defense of his colleagues. "Their construction may be erroneous," he conceded, and may certainly be "open to argument." But the notion that the decision was an act of judicial usurpation, he said, "exists only in the imagination of Hampden" and "can impose on no intelligent man." Marshall was probably sincere in his outrage, but Roane's claim that the cause was improperly before the Court ought not to be dismissed as mere malice. At the very least, it needs to be recognized that the origins of the case were much more complex and murky than Marshall admitted or the formal record revealed. Indeed, as Richard Ellis has shown, there was a strong element of collusion in the bank case. In fact, the governor of Maryland mentioned publicly that the decision by the Maryland Court of Appeals "was there had by consent" so that it could be carried to the Supreme Court for final decision. Noticeably, too, there was no real opposition to the decision in Maryland, even though it went against the state—most probably because the major economic players favored the bank. Justified or not, Marshall's high dudgeon served a rhetorical purpose. The point of the first exchange was that Roane was playing games with the reader, whom Marshall either explicitly or implicitly described as the model republican citizen. By distorting the words and the work of the Court, Marshall argued, Roane was counting on emotion and fear rather than rational argument, which was a decidedly unrepublican thing to do. Read the opinion yourselves, Marshall admonished his readers, which, he noted sarcastically, was more than Roane had done.[24]

Having neutralized "the bitter invectives which compose the first number of Hampden," and perhaps having even turned them to his own favor, Marshall then proceeded "to a less irksome task": the examination of his argument, beginning with the assertion that "the constitution conveyed only a limited grant of powers to the general government, and reserved the residuary powers of the government to the states and to the people." The advantage of dealing with this principle of limited national sovereignty was that Marshall agreed with it—in fact begged leave "to add to the numerous respectable authorities quoted by Hampden in support of it." Among the authoritative sources Marshall threw back at Roane was his own argument in *McCulloch*: "The government

24. Marshall quote, ibid., 159. Richard Ellis, "The Maryland Origins of *McCulloch v. Maryland* (1819)," paper delivered at the annual meeting of the Organization of American Historians, Washington, D.C., March 1995. Governor Charles Ridgely's speech quoted on 7–8 appears in the (Annapolis) *Maryland Gazette and Political Intelligencer,* 17 December 1818.

[of the United States] is acknowledged by all to be one of enumerated powers. The principle that it can exercise only the powers granted to it, would seem too apparent to have required to be enforced by all those arguments which its enlightened friends, while it was depending before the people, found it necessary to urge. That principle is now universally admitted."[25]

What Marshall had done here was what common lawyers often did in pleading when they demurred, that is, they admitted to the truth of what their adversary charged but denied the legal consequences presumed to flow from it. Hampden's "incontrovertible" propositions, "if admitted to be true, so far from demonstrating the error of that opinion [*McCulloch*], do not even draw it into question. They may be all true, and yet every principle laid down in the opinion be perfectly correct." Marshall's tactics here were effective rhetorically and substantively. Rhetorically speaking, he permitted Virginia readers to agree with much that Roane said about states' rights, which they probably were inclined to do anyhow, while backing off from the union-busting, Constitution-destroying implications of his position.[26]

More to the point, however, by arguing that the national government was limited by the Constitution and that states' rights were constitutionally protected, Marshall was arguing what he sincerely believed and what he set forth as law in his Bank of the United States opinion. For him, as for the Framers, there was a fundamental distinction between sovereignty as the ultimate foundation of the government and sovereignty as the actual power to govern. The former was indivisible and rested with the American people; the latter was divisible and had in fact been divided by the Constitution between the states and the federal government. Here, then, was Marshall's theory of divided sovereignty. It was, as he admitted, not easy to understand. This was especially so when he added his final corollary. What Marshall expected his republican readers to understand was that the powers given to the national government were not only limited, because they were divided, but that they were also supreme. Compared to Roane's simple, monolithic theory of state supremacy, Marshall's principle of divided sovereignty was subtle and complex. It rested, to paraphrase a line from Holmes, not on logic but rather on common sense and historical experience. What the practical-minded Framers recognized in 1787 was that any constitution that attempted to obliterate state government in an age when local government was all that people knew would be doomed

25. Gunther, *Marshall's Defense*, 161–62.
26. Ibid., 161.

from the start. What Marshall assumed he was doing was reaffirming the wisdom of the Framers. But in the 1820s, wisdom was one thing, security another. For Virginians, surrounded as they were by uncertainty and beleaguered by anxiety, complexity was a hard sell. Marshall had experience and the intent of the Framers on his side; Roane had logic and the deep insecurity of Virginians.

In defending *McCulloch*'s doctrine of divided sovereignty against Roane's passionate doctrinal assault, Marshall fell back, as he had done in *Marbury* and would soon do in *Cohens v. Virginia,* on Federalist constitutional theory, on "American principles," as he called them. In that scheme of government, sovereign authority in the Republic belonged to the American people, who could speak only, and who had spoken, in a written Constitution, the supreme law of the land. In that Constitution, the actual power to govern, which was distinct from the question of ultimate sovereignty, was divided between the states and the nation. In his first response to Roane, Marshall put the matter in plain language ordinary citizens could understand: "In fact, the government of the union, as well as those of the states, is created by the people, who administer it for their own good. . . . The constitution has defined the powers of the government, and has established that division of power which its framers, and the American people, believed to be most conducive to the public happiness and to public liberty." Marshall wanted a dual federalism, one that balanced the rights of the states with those of the national government. "The equipoise thus established is as much disturbed by taking weights out of the scale containing the powers of the [central] government, as by putting weights into it. His hand is unfit to hold the state balance who occupied himself entirely in giving a preponderance to one of the scales." Marshall's last point was a simple but compelling one in terms of the debate: it was not the national government but the states that were claiming absolute authority. Roane and his colleagues in the Junto were the radical purists, not Marshall and the Court.[27]

The next phase of the debate shifted from general constitutional theory to the interpretation of the Necessary and Proper Clause. Here the exchange quickly devolved into a battle of uncommonly able common lawyers over common-law hermeneutics. Roane cited Vattel to prove his point "that the limited grant to congress of certain enumerated powers, only carried with it such additional powers as were fairly incidental to them; or in other words, were necessary and proper for their execution." Marshall admitted the point, saying that it was in fact what *McCulloch* said, but disputed Roane's use of Vattel, who, according

27. Ibid., 159–60.

to Marshall, really said something entirely different. For lawyer Marshall, "the only principle that can be extracted from Vattel, and safely laid down as a general independent rule is, that parts are to be understood according to the intention of the parties, and shall be construed liberally, or restrictively, as may best promote the objects for which they were made."[28]

Roane responded with heavy artillery, citing the formidable Lord Coke to prove that the word "necessary" in the Necessary and Proper Clause meant nothing. Marshall objected this time on two grounds. The first was that Roane didn't know his Coke, almost a indictable offense in Richmond legal circles. Marshall's second and more revealing objection was that law did not always supply a "technical rule applicable to every case, which enjoins us to interpret arguments in a more restricted sense than their words import." Marshall was subtly working his way from the common law to common sense, arguing that both were the same. The common-law, common-sense view was that "the nature of the instrument, the words that are employed, the object to be effected, are all to be taken into consideration, and have their due weight." Interpretation, in other words, was subject to "that paramount law of reason, which pervades and regulates all human systems." The Constitution was not controlled by ordinary common law, however much the spirit and principles of that law may have insinuated itself into the document. What Roane had done, Marshall went on to explain, was to take those narrowly focused principles of the common law applying to contracts between individuals and make them the touchstone of the constipated constitutional interpretation he wanted.[29]

In *McCulloch*, Marshall urged the people to remember "that it was a constitution we are interpreting." In answering Roane, he expounded on those now famous words, with Edmund Burke to guide him. What he said goes to the heart of his constitutional philosophy:

> It [the Constitution] is not a contract between enemies seeking each other's destruction, and anxious to insert every particular, lest a watchful adversary should take advantage of the omission.—Nor is it a case where implications in favor of one man impair the vested rights of another. Nor is it a contract for a single object, everything relating to which, might be recollected and inserted. It is the act of a people, creating a government, without which they cannot exist as a people. The powers of this govern-

28. Ibid., 162, 166.
29. Ibid., 168–70.

ment are conferred for their own benefit, are essential to their own prosperity, and are to be exercised for their good, by persons chosen for that purpose by themselves. . . . It is intended to be a general system for all future times, to be adapted by those who administer it, to all future occasions that may come within its own view. From its nature, such an instrument can describe only the great objects it is intended to accomplish, and state in general terms, the specific powers which are deemed necessary to those objects.[30]

Here was the single most telling statement in his debate with Hampden, one that all Virginians, lawyers or not, could comprehend. Marshall put his reputation as a lawyer, as a Virginian, and as a statesman of the Revolution on the line for America. Roane did the same. Arguing from the Federalist papers, common law, history, and whatever was available, Roane insisted that *McCulloch* had transformed the Necessary and Proper Clause into a grant of additional power to Congress, whereas that clause, if it was not merely "tautologous and redundant" verbiage, was meant to delimit congressional power and reaffirm the limiting nature of constitutional government. Marshall responded point by point, with what seemed at times mind-numbing detail. Whether he argued from the common law, the Federalist papers, or Hamilton's memorandum to Washington in 1791, he fell back on one fundamental axiom: that the Necessary and Proper Clause as the Court interpreted it in *McCulloch* did not grant Congress additional powers and, therefore, did not destroy the concept of a national government of enumerated powers. The one and only thing it did was grant Congress the legislative means necessary to effect the specific powers granted to it by Article 1, Section 8, which was the same range of discretion Congress would have had if the clause had not been inserted. This was all, Marshall claimed, he said and meant to say. When Roane claimed otherwise, Marshall argued, he "misstates either directly or by insinuation" what the Court ruled.

The plain sense of the matter, put "without fear of contradiction," was this:

that the general principles maintained by the supreme court are, that the constitution may be construed as if the clause which has been so much discussed, had been entirely omitted. That the powers of Congress are expressed in terms which, without aid, enable and require the legislature

30. Ibid., 170–71.

to execute them, and of course, to take the means for their execution. That the choice of these means devolved on the legislature, whose right, and whose duty it is, to adopt those which are most advantageous to the people, provided they be within the limits of the constitution. Their constitutionality depends on their being the natural, direct, and appropriate means, or the known and usual means, for the execution of a given power.

This did not mean the Constitution was a blank check to Congress as Roane claimed and as some historians have assumed Marshall meant. "In no single instance does the court admit the unlimited power of congress to adopt any means whatever, and thus to pass the limits prescribed by the constitution." If it did so, if "congress under the pretext of executing its powers, pass laws for the accomplishment of objects, not entrusted to the government, it would become the painful duty of this tribunal, should a case requiring such a decision come before it, to say that such an act was not the law of the land." Marshall's point was telling: Judicial review, which the states' rights forces were attacking, was the quintessential instrument of limited government they liked.[31]

Marshall would return to defend the Court's powers of review again in his final essay—and more forcefully in *Cohens v. Virginia*—but before he did so, he circled back, in essays 6 and 7, to the central theme of divided sovereignty, and to Hampden's oft-repeated charge that *McCulloch* made the Constitution into "a consolidated, and not a federal government," that the states would be annihilated in the process. To make his point yet again and for a final time that *McCulloch* did no such thing, Marshall quoted no fewer than twelve specific instances from the text of the opinion that acknowledged the constitutional foundation of states' rights. For good measure, he zeroed in on state taxing power, which was at issue in *McCulloch:* "That the power of taxation is one of vital importance; that it is retained by the states; that it is not abridged by the grant of a similar power to the government of the union; that it is to be concurrently exercised by the two governments; are truths which have never been denied."[32]

"Two governments"—the nation and the states—was Marshall's mantra, and to reach states' rights doubters in Virginia, he cited one of their own. Now

31. Ibid., 186–87.
32. Ibid., 192–93.

it was not just Marshall against Roane, but James Madison, too, who said in *Federalist* 39 that the Constitution "is neither a national, nor a federal constitution; but a composition of both." Then Marshall turned back to Federalist constitutional theory and Hampden's charge that the only "people" in the constitutional formula of the Republic were people of the states. Contrary to Hampden, the Court, like the old Federalists, recognized the bedrock idea that "the people were divided into distinct societies" called states. But this fact did not mean that the "people of the United States" had not collective existence. Did Hampden deny they did? Marshall asked. "Have we no national existence? We were charged by the late emperor of France with having no national character," said Marshall drawing on his cachet from the XYZ mission, "but not even he denied our theoretical or constitutional existence. If congress declares war, are we not at war as a nation? Are not war and peace national acts? Are not all measures of the government national measures? The United States is a nation; but a nation composed of states in many, though not in all respects, sovereign. The people of these states are also the people of the United States. The two characters, so far from being incompatible with each other, are identified. This is the language of the constitution." And this is what *McCulloch* proclaimed, what the American people in their sovereign capacity mandated at the time of ratification.[33]

Marshall's final statement on divided sovereignty, presented in essay number 7, was a refutation of Roane's states' rights ratification theory. Like the Anti-Federalists before him and John C. Calhoun afterward, Roane rested his case for state sovereignty on the fact that ratification took place in specially called state conventions whose members were elected by the people of each state. From that, he deduced that the Constitution was simply a contract created by sovereign states as the primary contracting parties; the national government was nothing but "an alliance, or a league" of sovereign states. As a creature of the states, the Constitution ought to be construed so as to favor them, that is to say, the benefit of the doubt in such cases as presented in *McCulloch* should go automatically to states, who should be the final judges of the constitutionality of congressional acts.[34]

Marshall's response was simple and sensible. Ratification took place at the state level, not because the states were sovereign, but because that was the only practical and convenient way to proceed since the American people could not

33. Ibid., 194–95.
34. Ibid., 198.

ratify en masse. Or to put it another way, it was the representatives of the whole American people meeting in various states who decided the issue of ratification. Beyond that, Federalist constitutional theory applied: If the sovereign people wanted to divide governmental powers between the national government and the states, they had the ultimate authority to do so. If they wanted to make the government of the nation supreme within its sphere of action, they could do that, too. And that, according to Marshall's climactic argument, is precisely what they did: "I will premise that the constitution of the United States is not an alliance, or a league, between independent sovereigns; nor a compact between the government of the union, and those of the states; but is itself a government, created for the nation by the whole American people, acting by convention assembled in and for their respective states." Moreover, he continued, "the government of the union, 'within its sphere of action,' is 'supreme'; and, although its laws should be in direct opposition to the instruction of every state legislature in the union, they are 'the supreme law of the land, any thing in the constitution or laws of any states to the contrary notwithstanding.'"[35]

By connecting the words of the Constitution—the Supremacy Clause in Article 6—with the framing, Marshall rested his case finally on the experience of history and the wisdom of the Founders, which were one and the same. The Articles of Confederation, which Virginia theorists were pushing as the essence of constitutional wisdom, Marshall saw as "that awful and instructive period in our history." The weakness of the Confederation government led to "national disorder, poverty, and insignificance." The choice, said Marshall, quoting Hamilton's *Federalist* 15, was to transform the Articles "into an effective government, or to fall to pieces from the weight of its constituent parts, & the weakness of its cement. . . . The wisdom and patriotism of our country chose the former. Let us not blindly and inconsiderately replunge into the difficulties from which that wisdom and that patriotism have extricated us."[36]

Marshall's final Friend of the Constitution essay appeared on July 15, 1819, leaving future Americans to ponder the consequences and historical significance of his debate with Roane and Brockenbrough. Certainly the dialogue was remarkable in annals of American constitutional history—for the fact that the leading judicial officers of a state and the nation were involved, for the passion and asperity of the exchange, for the conspicuous brilliance and learning on both sides. Marshall's genius for argument is also on display, as is the pas-

35. Ibid., 202.
36. Ibid., 199–200.

sionate side of his personality, a side not often seen. His writing of eleven brilliant essays in less than four pressure-filled months should also remove doubts that Marshall could have turned out some of his great opinions so quickly without the help of others. (Speculation here centered on *Gibbons* and a possible Marshall-Story collaboration.)[37]

What comes through most profoundly, however—in his final essay and indeed in all his essays—is that Marshall spoke as a Burkean conservative, or as much of one as American circumstances allowed. He was repelled by reductionist abstractions as well as abstract idealism, even when it was couched, as was much of southern constitutionalism, in terms of a mythical past. He worked from the "given," accepted the world as it was, relished "the disorder of experience," to borrow a phrase from Charles Rosen. This included the federal system created by the Founders. The doctrine of divided sovereignty, which Marshall set forth in *McCulloch* and tried to explain to Virginians in 1819, was grounded in the complex structure of state-federal relations in the early Republic. It is fashionable, of course, to emphasize the great moments of conflict between state and nation in this system, and there were many. But as Leonard White showed many years ago, one of the truly great accomplishments of the early Republic was to work out, both institutionally and in practice, a system of state-national cooperation that touched almost all areas of government—including public finance, tax collection, and exports and imports—and that included a working relationship between federal and state judiciaries, as outlined by Article 3 of the Constitution, the Judiciary Act of 1789, and the federal Process Acts of the 1790s. Even Congress, whose authority was so much the issue in *McCulloch,* was inseparable from the states. The federal electorate, to start with, was keyed to state election laws. State legislatures elected federal senators who were expected to represent state interests. House delegations did the same. Senators and representatives also roomed together in Washington, consolidating even further their state and regional outlook. Even justices of the Supreme Court in the age of circuit riding were expected to be conversant with the interests of their own states and sections.[38]

---

37. The *New York Commercial Advertiser,* 24 February 1824, reported that Marshall had fallen and dislocated his shoulder, which was true, but noted that Story was "now engaged in completing" Marshall's opinion in *Gibbons.* Charles Warren, *The Supreme Court in United States History,* new and rev. ed. (Boston, 1926), 1: 608.

38. Rosen uses the phrase in "The Romantic Generation," *New Yorker,* 3 February 1997, 74. Especially relevant is the first volume of White's monumental four-volume administrative history, *The Federalists: A Study in Administrative History* (New York, 1948). On the boardinghouse phenomenon, consult James S. Young, *The Washington Community, 1800–1828* (New York, 1966).

Marshall's theory of divided sovereignty rested on this kind of experiential reality, a view of constitutional federalism built not just on peaceful coexistence of the state and national government but on mutual cooperation and respect. Banking was a case in point. Judged by the hostile standoff between state banks and the national bank in 1819, wherein flagrant mismanagement of the Bank of the United States contributed to equally flagrant mismanagement of state banks, the story was not pretty to be sure. But state banks had grown and prospered for twenty years under the supervising management of the first Bank of the United States, and they would do so again after 1823, when the bank, under the presidency of Nicholas Biddle, once again operated on sound principles of management. State banks and the Bank of the United States could peacefully and profitably coexist and indeed had done so in Virginia. The Richmond branch of the second Bank of the United States was not only managed by Virginians but, if Marshall is to be believed, by members of the Virginia state banking establishment. *McCulloch* was not designed to destroy state banks, then, but to keep states, or, as Marshall would have said, state politicians, from destroying the national bank. State-federal cooperative banking was not a tidy arrangement, but it had worked well for a long time and could again. This was Marshall's assumption and that of most states as well, including Maryland.[39]

What was true regarding state banking was true as well regarding the vast apparatus of state mercantilism that existed in the early Republic. State law touched the lives of Americans much more extensively than did federal law, and this included, as scholars have shown, an extensive body of economic legislation, both promotive and regulatory. Marshall's decision in *McCulloch,* despite the hue and cry raised by Virginia, left this vast area of state power largely untouched, including state regulation of slavery. What the states could not do, according to Marshall's constitutional jurisprudence, was destroy the still shaky structure of national government nor defeat the intention of national laws passed by a government in which they were abundantly represented—as states. *McCulloch* did not mandate a national bank, as, for example, the modern Court mandated one-man-one-vote in *Baker v. Carr* (1962), but only authorized Congress to create one if it decided to do so. To put it another way, Marshall, in the spirit of deferential government, trusted the freely elected representatives of the people to do the right thing; his Virginia opponents denied them the opportunity.[40]

39. See Hammond, *Banks and Politics;* also Thomas P. Govan, *Nicholas Biddle, Nationalist and Public Banker, 1786–1844* (Chicago, 1959).

40. On the vast domain of state economic activity in antebellum United States, see Oscar and Mary Flug Handlin, *Commonwealth: A Study of the Role of Government in the American Economy: Massachusetts, 1774–1861* (New York, 1947); and Louis Hartz, *Economic Policy and Democratic Thought: Pennsylvania, 1776–1860* (Cambridge, Mass., 1948).

Indeed, trust was the fundamental point on which Marshall and Roane parted company. Marshall saw both judicial and congressional power in terms of eighteenth-century deference, where the officials of government were expected to govern because they were presumed to be honest and able. The problem was that the American people, whom he trusted to elect men they trusted, were themselves not in a trusting mood. The more they felt the transformative consequences of the market revolution, the more distrustful they became, and the more they liked the reductionist solutions offered by demagogic politicians. Marshall's moderate nationalism and his moderate conservatism gradually yielded the high ground to the radical states' rights and radical conservatism of John Randolph, John Taylor, and John C. Calhoun. History, which Marshall hoped to control with institutions, was out of control. In a decade and a half, the Bank of the United States he upheld in 1819 would be dead, the victim of Jackson's wrath, Nicholas Biddle's political incompetence, and laissez-faire-minded state capitalists' ambitions. Marshall's doctrine of implied powers, along with other aspects of his moderate nationalism, would be shelved or modified by the Jacksonian Court of Roger Taney. Rather than strengthen the federal Union, *McCulloch*, despite Marshall's valiant effort to explain and defend it, set in motion the forces that would weaken nationalism and ultimately force the nation to defend itself on the field of battle. Ironically, the only thing that survived the conflict set in motion by *McCulloch* was the Court's power of judicial review. It is to that unlikely victory that one must turn to complete the story of Marshall's running war with his own state and with nineteenth-century history.

Defending (and Defining) Judicial Review

On September 1, 1831, John C. Calhoun wrote Virgil Maxcy concerning the Marshall Court: "The question is in truth between the people & the Supreme Court. We contend, that the great conservative principle of our system is in the people of the States, as parties to the Constitutional compact, and our opponents that it is in the Supreme Court. This is the sum total of the whole difference." Calhoun wrote while South Carolina was putting his theory of nullification to the test; while his colleague Senator Hayne was defending his theory of the Constitution as a contract against Daniel Webster in the soon-to-be-famous Webster-Hayne debate. In the course of a decade of constitutional wrangling over *McCulloch*, the Court and the chief justice found themselves in the eye of the storm. Invariably, policy questions turned into constitutional issues that pitted states against the nation and coalesced states into regional alignments. The final question was not just about what the Constitution said concerning the location of power in the federal system but about how constitutional disputes should be resolved. Calhoun's theory of nullification, building on the Virginia and Kentucky Resolutions, put the states at the center of the interpretive process. To Marshall fell the chore of defending—indeed, of defining—the Court's role as the chief interpreter of the Constitution, which brings the discussion back to *McCulloch*—this time with a focus not on the powers of Congress but on the position of the Court in American government.[41]

McCulloch is not generally seen as a major judicial review case, but it was, providing judicial review is seen in the proper light. Judicial review—the authority of the Court to void acts of states in conflict with the Constitution and federal laws and treaties, or to strike down acts of Congress in conflict with the Constitution and in the process to say what the Constitution means—was not the creation of any great moment or single case, not even the famous case of *Marbury v. Madison*. Rather, the authority of the Court as the chief expounder of the Constitution grew incrementally, starting with the Constitution itself and developing simultaneously, and often in response to, the changing configuration of Congress and the executive. In this long period of gestation, *McCulloch,* as critics of the case were quick to observe, occupied a pivotal position. Several reasons account for its centrality, starting with the theory of divided sovereignty Marshall developed in that case and also with his emphasis on the Constitution as a body of general principles rather than a code of law. By refusing to locate sovereignty with finality, as states' rights theorists did, Marshall made judicial review part of an ongoing process of interpretation. To put it another way, since there was no bright line separating state and national power, since general constitutional principles would have to be applied case by case to "changing crises of the American people," judicial interpretation was built into the constitutional process. Marshall wisely did not expand on the point, but he promised in no uncertain terms that the Court would preside impartially over the process, even if it meant holding acts of Congress unconstitutional.[42]

Judging by the way Marshall resolved the uncertainty in *McCulloch,* again as his critics perceived, judicial review unavoidably turned into constitutional

41. Galloway, Maxcy, Marko Papers, Library of Congress, Washington, D.C.

42. For the developmental nature of judicial review, see Christopher Wolfe, *The Rise of Modern Judicial Review: From Constitutional Interpretation to Judge-Made Law* (New York, 1986).

exposition: a *reasoned justification* for saying yes or no to requests of power from Congress, or the states, that drew on textual interpretation, history, and policy. Constitutional *exposition* was Marshall's hallmark, "the grand style" of opinion writing as Karl Llewellyn would later call it, which was more of a state paper than a judicial opinion in the ordinary sense of the word. Expounding, rather than simply settling disputes, signaled the emergence of the Court as an educational institution no less impressive than the president's bully pulpit—and considerably more impressive in Marshall's case since no fewer than five different presidents came and went during the course of his tenure. Adding to the Court's authority was the simple fact that what it said carried with it not just the force of words but the force of law, assuming the president backed it up with the power of the state.[43]

All this appeared to make the Court into a sitting constitutional convention, and *McCulloch* was the classic case in point. Marshall did in *McCulloch* what he only adumbrated in *Marbury*. Judicial review was applied to acts of Congress and not just those dealing with the judiciary as in the mandamus case. In one opinion, Marshall managed to tell Congress what it could do and with equal force tell the states what they could not do. Since the case came up under Section 25, it also involved the exercise of final appellate authority over the decisions of the state supreme courts. Building on early cases of review as it did, Marshall's opinion looked like a carefully planned conspiracy to aggrandize the Supreme Court at the expense of its interpretive rivals: Congress, state legislatures, and state courts.

Virginia critics of Marshall's opinion were quick to focus on its expansive implications for judicial review. Had Marshall used that power to strike down the act of Congress, there would have been no complaints, and antebellum history might have been considerably different. Rather, both Congress and the Court strengthened their power, and since both were agents of the national government, it seemed like a double-barreled conspiracy against the states. Marshall emerged as the chief conspirator, the evil genius who went out of his way and beyond his authority, to reach the decision in the first place, then bamboozled his colleagues into going along with the usurpation. This was Jeffer-

43. For a succinct analysis of Marshall's style of opinion writing, see G. Edward White, *The American Judicial Tradition: Profiles of Leading American Judges*, expanded ed. (New York, 1988), ch. 1. Also suggestive is James Boyd White, *When Words Lose Their Meaning: Constitutions and Reconstitutions of Language, Character, and Community* (Chicago, 1984), ch. 9. For an interesting essay on Marshall's style of opinion writing, see Lewis Henry La Rue, "How Not to Imitate John Marshall," *Washington and Lee Law Review* 56 (summer 1999): 819–39.

son's position, and it was also Roane's and Brockenbrough's, both of whom, with Jefferson's encouragement, set out to humble Marshall and the Court.

The public assault on the judicial review dimension of *McCulloch* began with the first Amphictyon essay, when Brockenbrough condemned the justices for not writing opinions seriatim, a tradition he claimed was of special importance "on this great constitutional question, affecting very much the rights of the several states composing our confederacy," and especially since the decision "abrogated the law of one state, and is supposed to have formed a rule for the future conduct of other states." Brockenbrough followed Jefferson on this point and again when he accused Marshall of traveling "out of the record to decide a point not necessarily growing out of it." Brockenbrough also preached the constitutional gospel according to the third resolution of Madison's 1799 Virginia Report, which assailed the power of the Court to rule with finality on questions regarding the powers of the states as "parties to the Constitutional compact."[44]

Roane continued the direct assault against the Court in his first essay, arguing not just that Marshall's interpretation of the Constitution was wrong but that he lacked authority to interpret it. As Roane saw it, Marshall's whole opinion was "a judicial *coup de main*." The justices "have gone out of the record," he claimed, but by not attending to the Tenth Amendment, they had completely misread "necessary and proper," indeed, had "expunged those words from the constitution." Great as it may be, Roane concluded, "the power of the Court does not extend to everything; it is not great enough to *change* the constitution." Not only did the opinion expand the powers of Congress to legislate for the people "in all cases whatsoever," it expanded the authority of the Court to rule in all cases whatsoever, even those involving the powers of the sovereign states.[45]

In Hampden 4, Roane returned again to the theme of judicial usurpation, this time picking up on Brockenbrough's earlier reference to Madison's "celebrated report of 1799." Madison's point there was that the Court's powers, whatever they might be, could not "be raised above the authority of the sovereign parties to the constitution," that is, the states. Such an authority "would annul the authority delegating it, and its concurrence in usurpation, might subvert, forever, that constitution which all were interested to preserve." To support this principle further, Roane turned to his own opinion in the case of

44. Gunther, *Marshall's Defense*, 54, 63–64, 55.
45. Ibid., 110–12.

Hunter v. Fairfax, in which the Virginia Court of Appeals denied the Supreme Court's appellate authority over state decisions under Section 25 of the Judiciary Act of 1798. Since state judiciaries had concurrent jurisdiction with federal courts to try federal questions, this would make the states the final judges of the constitutionality of their own acts. Roane also cited the Pennsylvania case *Commonwealth v. Cobbett* (1799) on this point and quoted extensively from the resolution of the Pennsylvania legislature instructing its representatives in Congress to oppose the recharter of the first Bank of the United States in 1811. This resolution declared that the Constitution "*to all* intents and purposes" was "a treaty among sovereign states." The "general government, by this treaty, was *not* constituted the *exclusive* or final judge of the powers it was to exercise; for if it were so to judge, then *its judgment,* and not the constitution, would be the measure of its authority." The Supreme Court, Roane argued, in effect had claimed "the right . . . to change the government: to convert a federal into a consolidated government. The supreme court is also pleased to say, that this important right and duty has been devolved upon it by the *constitution.*" But nowhere, he said, is that power of judicial review stated in the Constitution. And the constitution "could not give it, without violating a great principle; and we certainly cannot supply by *implication,* that which the convention dared not to express." The Constitution gave the Court the power to decide cases between states, Roane conceded, but contended that "it has not given to it a jurisdiction over its own controversies, with a state or states." To have done so would have made the Court, and thus the national government, the final judge in its own case.[46]

Roane had cut to the heart of his dispute with Marshall, and had also exposed the chink in his constitutional armor. If, as Marshall declared, sovereignty was divided between the states and the national government, if there was no bright line, if federalism cases had to be settled as they came up in constantly changing circumstances, then whoever had the power to settle the disputes had the ultimate power in the system. Roane opted for state power. But there were questions and problems on both sides. For starters, how, by what method, and according to what procedures were the states to proceed in resolving disputes over federalism? And how could there be one Constitution if each state got to say what it means? Could a theory of states' rights, which claimed to be rooted in the Constitution, be taken seriously if it ended up destroying the Constitution? Marshall's position was not without its own difficulties.

46. Ibid., 149–53; *Hunter v. Martin,* 4 Munford 1; *Commonwealth v. Cobbett,* 3 Dallas 342.

How, for example, could he lodge the power to interpret the Constitution in the Court, which of all branches of the government, state or federal, was farthest removed from the people admitted to be sovereign? How, on a practical level, could the Court gain the trust of the states, or of sister branches for that matter? What happened to law if states resisted the decisions of the Court? Who would correct the justices if they erred? Did the Court have some special institutional qualities that minimized the mistakes of its members, that eliminated personal bias or self-interest?

Marshall's main effort to answer Roane and to clarify and justify the true meaning of judicial review came in *Cohens v. Virginia.* But he opened his defense in the debate over *McCulloch.* In his first "A Friend to the Union" essay, he confronted Brockenbrough's charge that the justices had abandoned seriatim opinions and surrendered to the dominance of the chief justice. "The opinion is delivered," Marshall said in reference to *McCulloch,* "not in the name of the chief justice, but in the name of the whole court," and this applied to the reasoned justification of the opinion as well as its conclusion. Moreover, he said, the author of the Court's opinion "never speaks in the singular number, or in his own person, but as the mere organ of the court. In the presence of all the judges, and in their names he advances certain propositions as their propositions, and certain reasoning as their reasoning." Then Marshall asked Amphictyon and his readers "whether the judges of the Supreme Court, men of high and respectable character, . . . sit by in silence, while great constitutional principles of which they disapproved, were advanced in their name, and as their principles." Rather, he claimed, "the opinion which is to be delivered as the opinion of the court, is previously submitted to the consideration of all the judges; and, if any part of the reasoning be disapproved, it must be so modified as to receive the approbation of all, before it can be delivered as the opinion of all." Judges could join the majority opinion for their own reasons; they could dissent if they wanted, but one way or another, and here the Court differed fundamentally from Congress, each of the judges accepted responsibility for the Court's decision. Moreover, since "their decisions are reported, and are in the possession of the publick," each opened his thinking to public scrutiny. The Court might look aristocratic, as critics maintained, but in the final analysis it was more open and responsible than its rivals. Or so Marshall argued.[47]

In addressing Brockenbrough's charge that *McCulloch* was entirely obiter, Marshall replied that his discussion about the nature of the Union was in direct

47. Gunther, *Marshall's Defense,* 80–81.

response to arguments of counsel. As to the allegedly unavoidable national bias in the Court opinions regarding federalism, Marshall only alluded to what he spelled out elsewhere: that the Court was bound by, and kept honest by, the intent of the Framers. Marshall's final effort to discredit Amphictyon, delivered in "A Friend to the Union" 2, was a subtle jab at Brockenbrough for rousing the people against the Court, which was merely doing its constitutional duty, and for assailing the Court because it "is less popular, and therefore more vulnerable" than the other branches of government. Neither argument carried much water in post-*McCulloch* Virginia, but Marshall made a point dear to his heart: that the whole assault on the Court was a cowardly affair perpetrated by a new class of·weak-kneed and ambitious politicians, who were turning their backs on Virginia's history.[48]

Marshall amplified this line of defense in his first response to Roane on June 30, 1819. Here he repeated his Hamiltonian argument about the Court's institutional vulnerability to popular prejudice. Not only was it "without power, without patronage, without the legitimate means of ingratiating itself with the people," he said, but its work, by its "intricate and abstruse" nature was hard to understand and could easily "be grossly misrepresented." To attack the Court while attacking its decisions, was, in short, all but irresistible to Virginia states' rightists, especially since to attack the Court was to assail "the very existence of the [national] government." It was this point—that the very existence of the Constitution depended on the Court's powers of judicial review—that Marshall would make his main line of defense against Spencer Roane in *Cohens*.[49]

The Roane-Marshall exchange over the nature of the Supreme Court in *McCulloch* was a warm-up for the main bout. It was punch and counterpunch with no knockout blows on either side. Roane depicted the Court as a special engine of oppression. Marshall responded that the Court was adhering "to those American principles" set forth in the Constitution, which imposed on it "the duty, of preserving the constitution as the permanent law of the land." Roane claimed that the Court had traveled outside the record to do its dirty work. Marshall, referring to the obligatory jurisdiction imposed on the Court by Article 3 of the Constitution and the Judiciary Act of 1789, denied that it "had thrust itself into the controversy between the United States and the state of Maryland" or that it had "unnecessarily volunteered its services." And so it

48. Ibid., 81–85, 104.
49. Ibid., 156.

went, the exchange becoming more heated and more personal as it went along.[50]

Perhaps the most important, and prophetic, exchange took place over the Court's jurisdiction in cases involving the rights of states, a bitterly contested point that went back to *Martin v. Hunter's Lessee* and beyond. Marshall delivered a couple of sharp ad hominem jabs in answering Roane, but mainly he took the high ground of Federalist constitutional theory. Roane's mistake, according to Marshall, was that he assumed that the Supreme Court was a creature of the national government, when it was in reality the creation of the written Constitution, which emanated from the American people in solemn convention. The Court was not a "partial, local tribunal," presumably like the Virginia Court of Appeals on which Roane served, but a tribunal "erected by the people of the United States" for "the decision of all national questions." It was true, he granted, that the Virginia Court of Appeals denied this authority in *Hunter v. Martin*, with Roane speaking. But it was also true that this was "the only example furnished by any court in the union of a sentiment favorable to that 'hydra in government, from which,' says the Federalist, 'nothing but contradiction and confusion can proceed.'" Marshall's main point, however, was that *Hunter v. Martin* "was reversed by the unanimous decision of the Supreme Court in *Martin v. Hunter's Lessee,* which has not been disapproved by any other state courts even though they had many opportunities to do so." Indeed, he said, "in every instance, except that of Hunter and Fairfax, the judgment of reversal has been acquiesced in, and the jurisdiction of the [supreme] court has been recognized." Marshall clearly delighted in putting the matter in the most personal way: "If the most unequivocal indications of the public sentiment may be trusted, it is not hazarding much to say, that, out of Virginia, there is probably not a single judge, nor a single lawyer of eminence, who does not dissent from the principles laid down by the court of appeals in Hunter and Fairfax."[51]

Thus did the debate, which began over the scope of congressional powers under the Necessary and Proper Clause, turn into a struggle between lawyers, indeed, between judges and between courts. The personal, political, and professional rivalry between Marshall and Roane is also deeply rooted in Virginia history and is instructive on that count. Both men were descended from elite Virginia families; both consolidated their social and economic standing by

---

50. Ibid., 158.
51. Ibid., 159, 205–6; *Hunter v. Martin,* 4 Munford 25–54.

marrying into the first-family network. Both served in the Virginia House of Delegates in the 1780s, though on opposite sides of that decade's political divisions, and both served on the governor's council. Roane's legal education was more formal than Marshall's, but both men studied law with George Wythe at William and Mary. Probably they knew one another, since Roane graduated in 1780 and Marshall attended the Wythe lectures in the summer of that year. Both men studied the same books, entered the legal profession in the 1780s, shared the basic assumptions of Virginia legal culture. The difference was that Roane never cut his ties with that culture and Marshall did, not by repudiating it but by applying what Virginia taught him to the governance of the nation.

From the 1780s onward, Roane identified with "the genius of Virginia," as his future father-in-law put it at the Virginia ratifying convention. As a supporter of the states' rights party in the 1790s, Roane found himself in opposition to Marshall on almost all the great issues of that passionate decade, not just political issues but legal ones, too. Roane and Marshall first crossed swords as lawyers in the 1780s, but the legal rivalry that climaxed in *Cohens* began in earnest when Roane became a state judge—first on the General Court, the primary trial-level court in Virginia, then, until his death in 1822, as a member of the Virginia Court of Appeals. As a state judge, Roane's opposition to Marshall was both personal and institutional. As a member of the state judiciary, he ruled consistently against the Marshall syndicate in the protracted Fairfax litigation, a fact Marshall noted with asperity. Roane was a member of the Virginia Court of Appeals that voted to uphold the Virginia Statute of Escheats of 1777 that finally defeated the claims of the syndicate at the state level. When the Supreme Court reversed that decision on a Section 25 writ of error in *Fairfax's Devisee v. Hunter's Lessee,* Roane's court retaliated in *Hunter v. Martin,* which denied the Court jurisdiction to review state court decisions under Section 25. That opinion in turn generated *Martin v. Hunter's Lessee,* in which Story, for a unanimous Supreme Court and with the enthusiastic approval of Marshall, reaffirmed the appellate jurisdiction of the Supreme Court over state courts under Section 25, even in cases involving state common law.[52]

52. On Virginia's conflict with the Supreme Court and Marshall in the Fairfax land litigation, see Charles F. Hobson's Editorial Note, PJM, 8: 108–21; G. Edward White, *The Marshall Court and Cultural Change, 1815–1835* (New York, 1988), 165–73. The long history of the Fairfax litigation is traced at length in John A. Treon, "*Martin v. Hunter's Lessee:* A Case History" (Ph.D. diss., University of Virginia, 1970). For an excellent brief treatment of Roane and Virginia legal culture, see Timothy S. Huebner, *The Southern Judicial Tradition: States Judges and Sectional Distinctiveness, 1790–1890* (Athens, Ga., 1999), ch. 1.

Inseparable from the long personal and professional rivalry between the two men was the institutional rivalry between the courts, on which both served with distinction—the Virginia Court of Appeals and the Supreme Court of the United States. Ironically, the Virginia court was among the first in the nation to claim the power of judicial review. Marshall was familiar with those cases, admired the judges who handed down the opinions, and used both the men and the opinions as models. Roane employed the same tradition to strengthen the Court of Appeals, not only in his opinions but in his effort to persuade his colleagues to abandon seriatim opinions. By the time Roane challenged Marshall over *McCulloch,* he was the dominant voice on the Virginia high court and the leading spokesman for Virginia's legal community. Their confrontation in *Cohens v. Virginia* was the climactic struggle between two of Virginia's sharpest legal minds and between two rival constitutional traditions, both deeply rooted in Virginia history.[53]

The dispute over Section 25 jurisdiction in *Cohens* was perfectly calculated to join the issue between the two courts and the two judges. It was also an issue central to antebellum history. Section 25 of the Judiciary Act of 1789 allowed the Supreme Court to "reverse or affirm" decisions from the highest state courts on federal questions where rights claimed under the Constitution, federal law, or treaties, were denied. Since federal questions were routinely heard in state courts, the right of review provided by Section 25 was absolutely essential—unless it was desired that each state, via the interpretations of its own courts, should have its own version of the Constitution. If Section 25 was necessary for a unitary Constitution, it was also, in its wording and operation, unavoidably demeaning to state courts, judges, and lawyers. The writ of error itself, in its ancient common-law lineage, was a writ issued by a superior to an inferior court for the purposes of correcting errors of law made at the lower level. Customarily drawn by the party appealing the state decisions, the writ could be activated by the approval of a single Supreme Court justice, and once issued, it demanded peremptorily that the state court supply all the appropriate records of the decision in question. In effect, one justice could call the highest court of the state before the bar of the Supreme Court to defend itself. It was by means of Section 25 jurisdiction that the Marshall Court set itself up to overturn both state statutes and state court decisions interpreting them. Among those cases were *Fletcher v. Peck, Fairfax's Devisee v. Hunter's Lessee,*

53. Roane's influence on the Virginia Court of Appeals is treated in Huebner, *Southern Judicial Tradition,* ch. 1.

Martin v. Hunter's Lessee, and *Dartmouth College v. Woodward.* In fact, most of the Court's contract decisions arrived via Section 25. So did *Gibbons v. Ogden* and the controversial bankruptcy cases of *Sturges v. Crowninshield* and *Ogden v. Saunders.* And so would the Cherokee Indian cases in the 1830s.

McCulloch also was a Section 25 case, which allowed Roane to challenge *Martin v. Hunter's Lessee* yet again, something he was obviously hankering to do. Marshall, it should be noted, was involved in the *Martin v. Hunter's Lessee* controversy even though he had formally recused himself from the case. Since he was the dominant figure on the Court and was also close to Story, who wrote the opinion, it is not unreasonable to assume that Marshall had consulted with him and perhaps, given the intimate living arrangements of the Court, other justices as well. Story boasted that the chief justice "approved every word of the opinion," which has led some scholars to speculate that Marshall may have helped write it. What is beyond dispute is that Marshall went to unusual lengths, perhaps even unethical ones, to bring the case forward. He did not sign the petition for the issuance of the writ of error as he would ordinarily have done had he not recused himself. He did, however, as G. Edward White has shown, draft the petition itself. Perhaps, as White suggests, Marshall, having recused himself, did this as a private citizen who was a party to the case. Or perhaps the embryonic ethical traditions of recusement at this time permitted him to do so. But clearly, he pushed to the limit, and probably beyond, to bring the ruling of the Virginia Court of Appeals before his own Court. Virginia did not recognize the Court's power to issue the writ in *Martin v. Hunter's Lessee* and, indeed, never acknowledged having received it. Thus were the seeds sown that produced such bitter fruit in *Cohens v. Virginia.*[54]

The peculiar factual environment and legal issues of *Cohens* added fuel to the fire. On one level, the case involved a clash between congressional and state statute law, not identical to that in *McCulloch* but close enough to raise southern hackles. On the federal side was the congressional statute of 1802 that organized the District of Columbia into "a body politic and corporate" and authorized the sale of lottery tickets to effect "any public improvements in the city." On the state side was the Virginia act of 1820 that criminalized the sale of all lottery tickets in the state except those authorized by the state legislature. The jurisdictional phase of the case, which quickly overshadowed the conflict between federal and state statute law, began when the Cohen brothers, citizens

54. White, *Marshall Court,* 164–73.

of Virginia and agents for the D.C. lottery, were convicted and fined one hundred dollars in the Norfolk Borough Court for selling national lottery tickets in defiance of the Virginia law. Upon being denied appeal to the superior court—"inasmuch as cases of this sort are not subject to revision by any other courts of the commonwealth"—lawyers for the brothers requested a writ of error from the Supreme Court reviewing the borough court decision. The writ was issued, accompanied, as was customary in such cases, by notice to the governor and attorney general of Virginia, summoning the state to defend itself before the bar of the Supreme Court.[55]

The significance of the case was clear from the outset, so much so that some, contemporaries and historians alike, believed the case was contrived to give Marshall another shot at Roane and company. A leading scholar of the Marshall Court concludes that there is no convincing evidence establishing the feigned nature of the litigation. Nevertheless, the appearance of a joint letter in the nationalist *Niles' Weekly Register* by five leading members of the Supreme Court bar in favor of the Cohen brothers, published only one day after the brothers petitioned for a writ of error, raised unanswered questions. Shortly after these national-minded lawyers pounced on the case, states' rightists responded in the *Richmond Enquirer* with their own account. Their essays attacked Marshall and the Court for its nationalizing doctrines and restated old arguments about state sovereignty and the compact nature of the Constitution. But what really concerned them was the Court's appellate authority under Section 25, which they vehemently rejected. This was the main thrust of Roane's editorials, and it was the position taken by the Virginia legislature, which instructed counsel for Virginia to argue only the jurisdictional question. By the time the Court decided the case, the newspaper war had spread to the Washington papers and beyond. Whether the case was feigned or not really didn't matter, since both sides, still in battle formation after *McCulloch,* were anxious for a final showdown. The American people awaited the outcome.[56]

Whether they fully understood Marshall's complex opinion, however, is doubtful, though on one level it was as straightforward as it was unoriginal. The main points decided were these: that Section 25 of the Judiciary Act was constitutional, which was hardly surprising after *Martin v. Hunter's Lessee,*

55. 6 Wheaton 285, 290. White, *Marshall Court,* 507, quoting the *Richmond Enquirer.*
56. For a full and scholarly account of the Cohens case, consult White, *Marshall Court,* 504–24. Also see Warren, *Supreme Court,* 1: ch. 13. On Roane's charge that the case was "feigned," see Marshall to Henry Wheaton, 2 June 1821, PJM, 9: 150.

and additionally, that it applied to this case, regardless of the Eleventh Amendment, which Virginia argued protected the state from being hauled before the Supreme Court by private citizens, and despite the fact that the case came directly to the Supreme Court from the Norfolk Borough Court rather than from the highest court in the state as the literal reading of Section 25 requires. The significance of the opinion was in the details of Marshall's argument and in his memorable language. *Cohens* was one of Marshall's most eloquent and quotable opinions. In some ways, it was also the most tedious and tendentious, which is not surprising since it was Marshall's definitive answer to Roane and Virginia states' rights lawyers on the Court's appellate authority.[57]

Except for Marshall's determination to answer them conclusively, the case might have been resolved quietly. Certainly there was plenty of room for maneuvering and ample reason to downplay the conflict between Virginia and Congress and between Virginia and the Court. There is even some doubt as to whether a federal question was involved at all, which is necessary to activate Section 25. For example, the congressional act of 1802, under which the Cohens claimed the right to sell lottery tickets in Virginia, was clearly limited to the governance of the newly created District of Columbia. To be sure the Cohen brothers claimed the law authorized them to sell tickets in Virginia, but a more restricted reading of the statute was readily available to Marshall. A restrictive, that is to say, a nonconfrontational, reading of that act appears all the more reasonable when it is recalled that the Virginia law in question appeared to come under the general category of police legislation, the authority all, including Marshall, assumed states to possess, allowing them to legislate for the general well-being of their people. Laws governing lotteries could readily be seen as police legislation. In any case, the statute under which the Cohens were convicted was a criminal law, the ultimate in local law and one heretofore exempt from Section 25 review. The wording of both Section 25 and the Eleventh Amendment also presented problems for the Cohen brothers, and discretionary latitude for Marshall. First, Section 25 provided for appeal only from the *highest* court in the state, which condition was not met in *Cohens*. Regarding the Eleventh Amendment, there was a real question whether the Cohen brothers were suing the state, which suits were prohibited by the Eleventh Amendment, since they were appealing a criminal conviction brought against them by the state. To uphold the Court's jurisdiction, Marshall would

---

57. Hobson's editorial introduction to the case set forth the issues with admirable clarity. PJM, 9: 106–13.

then have to read Section 25 broadly and the Eleventh Amendment narrowly. He did both and with persuasive force. But the fact remains that the interpretive play in the statute and the amendment would have allowed him to go the other way had he chosen to do so—shades of *Marbury*.

Why then did he decide to take on Virginia and by what means, to what end, and with what consequences? Marshall's most conspicuously legalistic constitutional opinion was also his most political—no doubt the two aspects of his opinion were very much connected. Although he had a plausible legal way out of the case, circumstances beyond his control left him little real choice. By the time the case reached the Court, it had become so thoroughly politicized that not to respond would have appeared to be capitulation. Not only had the political press of Virginia challenged the Court openly, but the Virginia legislature had joined the fray with its instructions to counsel. There was no doubt in Marshall's mind that Jefferson had put his imprimatur on the proceedings, and there was the Roane rivalry to contend with as well. Hampden had been answered in the papers, to be sure, but the Court had yet to address officially the ongoing challenge of Virginia jurists to its appellate authority. And the danger was spreading. National newspapers, for the first time in history, had devoted coverage to the debate over *McCulloch* and could be expected to do the same with *Cohens*. More serious was the escalating struggle between Ohio and the Court over the bank decision in the pending case of *Osborn v. Bank of the United States,* which challenged the authority of the Court to enforce its decision in *McCulloch* under Section 25. As he made clear to Story, Marshall viewed widespread challenge to the jurisdiction as a challenge to the Union itself. Circumstances called for a definitive answer—to Roane the lawyer, Jefferson the politician, and states' rights theorists wherever they were.[58]

Cohens was fashioned for the crisis at hand, but it was also vintage Marshall, in its language, which radiated impartiality and reason, and in its carefully planned rhetorical strategy, wherein lawyerly "proof" was preceded by self-evident and unprovable generalizations. The chief justice opened rhetorically by restating the arguments made by the counsel of Virginia:

> They maintain that the nation does not possess a department capable of restraining, peaceably, and by authority of law, any attempts which may

58. Marshall anticipated a showdown over *Cohens* as early as February 1821 and expressed his desire to Bushrod Washington "that the court be as full as possible when it is decided." Marshall to Washington, 8 February 1821, ibid., 101. His reaction to Virginia's reaction is recounted in Marshall to Story, 15 June 1821, ibid., 167–68.

be made, by a part, against the legitimate powers of the whole; and that the government is reduced to the alternative of submitting to such attempts, or of resisting them by force. They maintain the constitution of the United States has provided no tribunal for the final construction of itself, or the laws or treaties of the nation; but that this power may be exercised in the last resort by the courts of every state in the Union.[59]

To quote, Marshall assumed, was to damn; and to state Virginia's arguments in their baldest form was also to signal what the Court's response would be. That response, the chief justice assured his readers, stemmed not from the Court's aggrandizing power but from its sense of legal and moral obligation. The words, which he invited his readers to read through republican glasses, were familiar ones to Court watchers: "If such be the constitution, it is the duty of the court to bow with respectful submission to its provisions. If such be not the constitution, it is equally the duty of the court to say so; and to perform that task which the American people have assigned to the judicial department." The message was that law, not judges, ruled; that the Court, despite the charges of aristocracy leveled against it, derived its authority, no less than did the political branches, from the sovereign people speaking, as only they could speak, in a written constitution.[60]

Having put his and the Court's republican honor on the line, Marshall turned abruptly to Virginia's objections to the Court's assertion of jurisdiction under Section 25. He might have confronted that section straight off but instead, following the logic of Story's argument in *Martin v. Hunter's Lessee,* chose to rest his case first on the text of the Constitution, particularly Articles 3 and 6. Virginia claimed a "sovereign independent state" could not be sued against its will; Article 3 granted the federal courts jurisdiction over cases in which the state was a party. Indeed, he said, by ratifying the Constitution, "it shall appear, that the state has submitted to be sued, then it has parted with this sovereign right of judging, in every case, on the justice of its own pretensions, and has intrusted that power to a tribunal in whose impartiality it confides," that is, to the Supreme Court. And why, Marshall asked, did they do so? Because, he said, in oft-quoted words:

The American states, as well as the American people, have believed a close and firm union to be essential to their liberty and to their happi-

59. 6 Wheaton 377.
60. Ibid.

ness. They have been taught by experience, that this union cannot exist, without a government for the whole; and they have been taught by the same experience, that this government would be a mere shadow, that must disappoint all their hopes, unless invested with large portions of that sovereignty which belongs to independent states. Under the influence of this opinion, and thus instructed by experience, the American people, in the conventions of their respective states, adopted the present constitution.[61]

In addition to being eloquent and quotable rhetoric, this brief passage was central to Marshall's argument because it established, by the authority of the written text of the Constitution, the general principle that states could be sued and that the Supreme Court could hear such suits. In addition, it permitted him to discourse again on the theory of divided sovereignty he had expounded in *McCulloch* and in the newspaper war with Roane and Brockenbrough.

In the earlier discussions, Marshall aimed to refute the "consolidationist" accusation and to minimize the powers of the national government, even while he was enlarging them though implied powers. In *Cohens,* he emphasized the "supremacy," a word he used several times in two paragraphs, of the national government. Sovereignty was still divided between nation and the states, to be sure, but his emphasis was now on Article 6, which made federal law supreme over state law. In that article, he said, "is the authoritative language of the American people; and, if gentlemen please, of the American states. It marks, with lines too strong to be mistaken, the characteristic distinction between the government of the union, and those of the states. The general government, though limited as to its objects, is supreme with respect to those objects. This principle is a part of the constitution; and if there be any who deny its necessity, none can deny its authority."[62]

Thus far, two principles essential to the Court's powers had been set forth: First, the Court's powers resided in the text of the Constitution, which had been agreed to not only by the American people but the states themselves; second, the portion of sovereignty granted to the national government was, again by the authority of the text of the Constitution, supreme. The third principle, which followed logically from the first two, concerned the appellate powers of the Supreme Court. If the Constitution was supreme, if it created a national

61. Ibid., 380–81.
62. Ibid., 381–82.

government that was supreme in its granted sphere of powers, and if the Court was granted the power to try constitutional cases coming from state courts, then it too, in those cases was supreme. It was literally the *Supreme* Court of the United States. The purpose of the Court, said Marshall, according to the Constitution itself, was "the maintenance of these principles in their purity":

> It is authorized to decide all cases of every description, arising under the constitution or laws of the United States. From this general grant of jurisdiction no exception is made of those cases in which a state may be a party. When we consider the situation of the government of the Union and of a state, in relation to each other; the nature of our constitution; the subordination of the state government to that constitution; the great purpose for which jurisdiction over all cases arising under the constitution and laws of the United States, is confided to the judicial department; are we at liberty to insert in this general grant, an exception of those cases in which a state may be a party? Will the spirit of the constitution justify this attempt to control its words?[63]

In the course of justifying the Court's jurisdiction, Marshall had defined its role in sweeping republican language: Its domain was constitutional principle; in the spirit and language of the Constitution, it was the keeper of the flame. He went on to argue in language bound to inflame Virginia that the Court was uniquely suited to this high purpose, especially when compared to state judiciaries. It was a matter of historical fact, he continued, that "different states may entertain different opinions on the true construction of the constitutional powers of congress" and that "they will legislate in conformity to their opinion, and may enforce those opinions by penalties." Turning to state courts, with an eye on Spencer Roane and the Virginia Court of Appeals, he said, "It would be hazarding too much, to assert that the judicatures of the states will be exempt from the prejudices by which the legislatures and people are influenced, and will constitute perfectly impartial tribunals." This was especially true since judges in many states were "dependent for office and for salary, on the will of the legislature." The Constitution could not be placed in the keeping of such institutions, Marshall stated. It "is framed for ages to come, and is designed to approach immortality, as nearly as human institutions can approach it. Its course cannot always be tranquil. It is exposed to storms and tempests, and its

---

63. Ibid., 382–83.

framers must be unwise statesmen indeed, if they have not provided it, so far as its nature will permit, with the means of self-preservation from the perils it may be destined to encounter. No government ought to be so defective in its organization, as not to contain within itself, the means of securing the execution of its own laws against other dangers than those which occur every day." The federal judiciary, at the head of which was the Supreme Court, was the means chosen by the Framers to secure the execution of the laws of the national government "and of preserving them from all violation, from every quarter, so far as judicial decisions can preserve them."[64]

There are no references in this opening statement to Section 25 or the Eleventh Amendment, for rhetorical reasons, one must assume. Marshall opened instead with the simple proposition that the Supreme Court has been created by the American people as the special guardian of the Constitution and of the federal Union. To drive home this point, he argued further, taking his cue from Story's expansive and much-contested opinion in *Martin v. Hunter's Lessee*, that even without Section 25, the Court's authority as the final interpreter-protector was established by Article 3 of the Constitution. Virginia argued that Article 3 suits against the state could come only under original jurisdiction, which had not been done in *Cohens*. Marshall countered in fourteen pages of intricate argumentation that Article 3 was intended to cover all contingencies, including those in *Cohens*. Nowhere were his rhetoric, his legal logic, or his interpretive skills more forcefully displayed—or his contempt for Virginia theorists. He admitted that most suits involving states would come under original jurisdiction, but insisted that states could also be sued under appellate jurisdiction, provided only that the subject matter in the case involved a question of constitutional or federal law: "The truth is, that where the words confer only appellate jurisdiction, original jurisdiction is most clearly not given; but where the words admit of appellate jurisdiction, the power to take cognizance of the suit originally does not necessarily negative the power to decide upon it on an appeal, if it may originate in a different court." Heads, the Court wins; tails, Virginia loses. The general rule of construction, according to Marshall, was this: "Every part of the article must be taken into view, and that construction adopted, which will consist with its words, and promote its general intention. The court may imply a negative from affirmative words, where the implication promotes, not where it defeats the intention." Virginia's argument that the Court could not rightfully entertain *Cohens* because it was an appellate case

64. Ibid., 385–88.

brought under Section 25, not an original jurisdiction case, went down in flames.[65]

Having rejected Virginia's interpretation of Article 3, Marshall then turned to the state's remaining objections to the Court's jurisdiction. The first centered on the Eleventh Amendment, which said that "The judicial power of the United States shall not be construed to extend to one of the United States, by citizens of another state." Arguing this time for a broad interpretation of the Constitution, Virginia contended that the amendment was intended, out of respect for the dignity and sovereignty of the state, to prohibit all suits in federal courts brought by individuals, whether or not they were citizens of other states or foreign countries as the amendment read. Uncharacteristically, Marshall now argued for a narrow interpretation. The true meaning of the amendment, he said, was to be found in the specific problem that gave rise to it: the case of *Chisholm v. Georgia,* in which Georgia had been sued by citizens of South Carolina to recover debts against the state. This amendment, on both first impression and extended inquiry, he said, was "intended for those cases, and for those only, in which some demand against a state is made by an individual, in the courts of the Union." He willingly conceded "a general interest might well be felt in leaving to a state the full power of consulting its convenience in the adjustment of its debts, or of other claims upon it." Even so, he continued, "no interest could be felt in so changing the relations between the whole and its parts, and so strip the government of the means of protecting, by the instrumentality of its courts, the constitution and laws from active violation." In any case, he insisted, the amendment did not apply to cases like *Cohens,* which originated not as a suit by an individual against the state but as an action brought by the state against an individual and appealed by the individual to another court. When the individual based his appeal on the Constitution or a federal law, that court, Marshall argued, was appropriately the Supreme Court of the United States—this brought Marshall finally to Section 25, which provided precisely for such appeals.[66]

Section 25 of the Judiciary Act of 1789, passed by the First Congress—by a majority composed largely of men who had served in the convention that framed the Constitution—was arguably one of the most important statutes passed by that Congress or any other. Because it provided appeal from state court interpretations of federal law, it was the one essential link to national

65. Ibid., 397–98.
66. Ibid., 407–8.

sovereignty, the sine qua non of a unified system of constitutional law. For precisely that reason, it became the focal point of the struggle between Virginia and the Marshall Court in 1816, and the starting point of the states' rights logic of John C. Calhoun after 1823. In *Cohens,* Marshall found himself on the front line of a major constitutional battle, indeed, the fault line of a major constitutional realignment. Virginia premised its position on "the supposed total separation of the judiciary of a state from that of the Union, and their entire independence of each other." This "hypothesis" was, as Marshall correctly perceived, merely another manifestation of states' rights theory, which argued that the national government was the mere agent of states, who, as parties to the contract, retained absolute sovereignty. Marshall's theory of divided sovereignty recognized that states had sovereign powers that the Court was bound to respect. Now, he asked Virginia to acknowledge those areas in the Constitution that affirmed the supremacy of the national government and bound Americans together as a nation:[67]

> That the United States form, for many, and for most important purposes, a single nation, has not yet been denied. In war, we are one people. In making peace, we are one people. In all commercial regulations, we are one and the same people. In many other respects, the American people are one; and the government which is alone capable of controlling and managing their interests in all these respects, is the government of the Union. It is their government, and in that character, they have no other. America has chosen to be, in many respects, and to many purposes, a nation; and for all these purposes, her government is complete; to all these objects it is competent. The people have declared, that in the exercise of all powers given for these objects, it is supreme. It can, then, in effecting these objects, legitimately control all individuals or governments within the American territory. The constitution and the laws of a state, so far as they are repugnant to the constitution and the laws of the United States, are absolutely void. These states are constituent parts of the United States; they are members of one great empire—for some purposes sovereign, for some purposes subordinate.[68]

The doctrine here is familiar, but the words warrant notice because they display not only Marshall's rhetorical skills but the passion of his convictions. In

67. Ibid., 413.
68. Ibid., 413–14.

an age that cherished great preaching, Marshall was a great preacher and a great believer, and the two were inextricably connected. His peroration also fit his argument. By declaiming on the great nation-building purpose of the Constitution, he laid an emotional foundation for his justification of the Court's appellate authority. The Supreme Court and the nation were bound together, and if the Court were to do its duty, the reach of its jurisdiction had to equal the reach of the nation's law: "We think, that in a government, acknowledgedly supreme, with respect to the objects of vital interest to the nation, there is nothing inconsistent with sound reason, nothing incompatible with the nature of government, in making all its departments supreme, so far as respects those objects, and so far as is necessary to their attainment. The exercise of the appellate power over those judgments of the state tribunals which may contravene the constitution or laws of the United States, is, we believe, essential to the attainment of those objects." The Supreme Court provided for in Article 3, it followed inexorably, was inseparable from the supreme law provided for in Article 6. The Founding Fathers, wise from the experience of the Articles of Confederation period, deliberately made it that way; "contemporaneous exposition," verified their intent. Chief among contemporaneous expositions of the intent of the Framers, standing right alongside *The Federalist*, was the Judiciary Act of 1789, most particularly Section 25.[69]

Given the centrality of Section 25 in the case at hand, one would expect an extensive discussion of it. But Marshall dispensed with it summarily, referring readers who wanted more to Story's opinion in *Martin v. Hunter's Lessee*. In fact, Marshall followed Story's *Martin v. Hunter's Lessee* argument, which is to say he rested the Court's appellate powers on the wording of the Constitution, amplified for effect by his own rendition of Revolutionary War history. It made for stirring rhetoric, but it was also brilliant strategy. To have emphasized Section 25, to have suggested even faintly that the Court's appellate authority rested solely on that statute would have encouraged the Court's enemies to repeal the statute, which they could do by a simple majority vote of Congress. Instead, Marshall, like Story, rested the case on the Constitution itself. Section 25 then became evidence of the Framers' intent. And compelling evidence it was, since, as he noted, "in the congress which passed that act were many eminent members of the convention which formed the constitution." Moreover, Marshall added, in a statement hard to prove but impossible to refute, "not a single individual, so far as is known, supposed that part of the act

69. Ibid., 414–15, 417–19.

which gives the supreme court appellate jurisdiction over the judgments of the state courts, in the cases therein specified, to be unauthorized by the constitution." Behind Marshall's reading of the Constitution were these eminent legislators, and to them must be added all the eminent state judges ("whose talents and character would grace any bench") who had acknowledged the appellate jurisdiction of the Court. Roane and Jefferson stood alone in their obstinacy, perhaps, as Marshall intimated, because their ideas, if followed, would destroy the Constitution and the federal Union. The gauntlet was down, and it didn't matter that the Court went with Virginia on the merits of the case, which it did almost as an afterthought.[70]

Cohens was Marshall's last and greatest statement on the nature of the federal Union and the republican responsibilities of the Court. But it did not settle the matter. Nor did it silence Roane, who instantly answered *Cohens* in a series of essays in the *Richmond Enquirer,* published between May 15 and July 13, this time writing as "Algernon Sidney." "Somers" and "Fletcher of Salturn," whose identities are not known, also joined the assault. These various essays are notable for their assertions concerning the inevitable subjectivism of judicial decisions and their ad hominem assault on Marshall, who is depicted as a traitor to Virginia. As Somers put it, Marshall "may have performed his *noviate* there . . . but the moment he passes the federal threshold, he looks back with indifference on the scenes of his juvenile experience; discards his former allegiance; and enters with all the enthusiasm of a new convert." Roane's criticisms, which echoed Jefferson's, were especially personal: Marshall's "most awful" opinion, in addition to being completely wrong was "unusually tedious, and tautologous," which it was. It was replete with "premises which cannot be conceded" and took for granted "the very points which are to be proved." Roane professed to want "no insurrections, no rebellions, no revolutions," but he summoned the Spirit of '98 and the spirit of the American Revolution to aid Virginians in their renewed struggle against tyranny. And he promised that Virginia judges would not be bowled over "by the breath of a single man" but would hold the ground staked out by Jefferson.[71]

Marshall in effect had been expelled from his own state for disloyalty. He was distressed but chose not to respond, and when Roane died unexpectedly

70. Ibid., 423, 420–21.

71. The essays attacking *Cohens* appeared in the *Richmond Enquirer* between 15 May and 13 July 1821; quotes are from the *Enquirer,* 15 and 25 May 1821, and from Roane's "Algernon Sidney" essays numbers 2 and 3 in the *Enquirer* of 29 May and 1 June 1821; Roane's argument on the Eleventh Amendment appeared in the *Enquirer* on 8 June 1821.

on September 4, 1822, the great debate between the two men was over for good. By that time, however, the arguments on both sides had taken on a life of their own—in Virginia, and in the course of the 1820s and early 1830s, in the nation at large. Marshall feared the worst. Indeed, at one point in *Cohens,* he prophesied that the struggle with Virginia, should it become "universal" among the other states, might end in a union-destroying war: "The people made the constitution, and the people can unmake it." If there were a general "determination" to destroy the Union, he said, "its effects will not be restrained by parchment stipulations; the fate of the constitution will not then depend on judicial decisions." Marshall glimpsed here what the 1820s would make more clear: that the Court would not, in its ultimate relationship with democratic politics, have the final word. He can be forgiven for concluding that a Court that was not final was no court at all. Historians armed with retrospective wisdom know that he was wrong.[72]

A Republican Court in a Democratic Polity

It might appear Marshall won his great duel with Roane and the Virginia theorists. After all, *McCulloch* still stands as a source national authority and as a universal touchstone of constitutional interpretation. *Cohens* endures as the definitive statement on the Court's appellate authority. Connecting these two landmark decisions into a coherent statement on the nature of sovereignty and the meaning of the Constitution, as well as the republican duties of the Court, was Marshall's series of brilliant polemic essays, written with passion and genius in the heat of battle, and in the midst of his regular duties on circuit. With the authority of the Court behind him and presumably the force of the nation-state as well, it might be assumed that the golden age of the Marshall Court was indeed the golden age of American nationalism.

This familiar interpretation, which relies heavily on what Marshall said rather than what happened as a consequence of what he said, needs to be modified. If the 1820s saw "the awakening of American nationalism," it also witnessed an even more dramatic resurgence of states' rights and sectional self-consciousness. Rather than clinching a victory for nationalism, Marshall's opinion in *McCulloch* set in motion the forces of states' rights that charted the direction of antebellum history. *McCulloch* did, of course, put constitutional

72. 6 Wheaton 389.

footing under the Bank of the United States, which functioned effectively for several more years, thanks to the ability of Nicholas Biddle, who became its president in 1823. What Marshall's law established, however, Jacksonian politics and Andrew Jackson himself undid. President Jackson's suspicion of banks, like much else in his political persuasion, was rooted in personal experience. But it didn't help that the bank gave preferential treatment to his opponents in the election campaign of 1828 or that a sizeable chunk of the bank stock was held by British investors. More important still was the convenience of the "Monster Bank" as a political symbol of aristocracy in an age of growing egalitarianism. Clay and Webster, Jackson's political rivals in 1832, sealed the bank's fate, as well as their presidential ambitions, when they made early recharter an issue in the election. Though it lived on after 1836 as the Bank of Pennsylvania, Biddle's Bank of the United States, and with it the idea of a central regulatory banking institution of any kind, was effectively dead, at least until the Civil War, and in reality until the creation of the Federal Reserve System in 1913.[73]

Gone also in a practical sense with the emergence of the Jacksonian Democrats was Marshall's celebrated doctrine of implied powers. The party of Jackson, which did so much to set the permanent political agenda during the antebellum period, believed, as did Jefferson, whose ideas the party borrowed, that the best government was the least. The defeat of John Quincy Adams in 1828 doomed Clay's American System, except as an *unsuccessful* election issue. While Congress retreated from national planning, the new Jacksonian majority on the Taney Court reasserted the constitutional primacy of states' rights. Implied powers, in short, was not called on significantly again by the Court until the surge of national legislation in the 1880s. It was entirely consistent with Jacksonian constitutional principles, too, that Taney's opinion in *Dred Scott v. Sandford* (1857) should have voided an act of Congress. Not coincidentally, that decision also put to rest the possibility that Marshall's doctrine of implied powers announced in 1819 would be put to antislavery uses.[74]

In other ways, too, political resistance diminished the authority of the Marshall Court's decisions. Some state challenges were beat back, most noticeably in *Osborn v. Bank of the United States* where the Court faced down Ohio over

---

73. Hammond, *Banks and Politics,* chs. 13 and 14.

74. On the temporary demise of *McCulloch,* see R. Kent Newmyer, "John Marshall and the Southern Constitutional Tradition," in *An Uncertain Tradition: Constitutionalism and the History of the South,* eds. Kermit L. Hall and James W. Ely Jr. (Athens, Ga., 1989). *Dred Scott v. Sandford,* 19 Howard 393.

the enforcement of *McCulloch*. Even when the Court's decisions were left standing, their effect could be diluted or postponed by state obstruction. Often the Court modified early decisions itself under pressure through the familiar common-law process of distinguishing and clarification of terms. In some cases, outright resistance was successful, an early example being New Jersey's disregard for Marshall's opinion in *New Jersey v. Wilson*. In 1823 in the circuit case of *Elkison v. Deliesseline,* Justice William Johnson "hung himself on a democratic snag," to use Marshall's memorable words, when he ruled that South Carolina's Negro seaman law was unconstitutional, a decision that was never enforced or reviewed by the Court. In the same year, Kentucky grassroots democracy successfully nullified the impact of *Green v. Biddle,* which struck down Kentucky claimant laws designed to protect actual settlers against absentee owners. Continued resistance to *Green* persuaded the Court to silently reverse itself, via a statute of limitations argument, in *Hawkins v. Barney's Lessee*. More well known, but not atypical, was Georgia's defiance of the Marshall Court's later decisions in the Georgia Indian cases.[75]

The message in all this—in the political and legal dissipation of *McCulloch* and the considerable and varied state resistance to the Court's appellate authority and to its substantive rulings as well—was that law was not autonomous, that the word of the Court was not always final, and that constitutional law was unavoidably connected to politics. Given the origins and nature of the Constitution, it could hardly have been otherwise. Certainly the factors the Framers at Philadelphia attempted to answer were as much political, and economic, as legal. The document they submitted to the states for ratification reflected this reality. The Constitution was supreme law, and the Supreme Court it created was a legal institution. But the Court was also dependent on the political branches—on Congress in matters of structure, on the Senate and the president in matters of appointments, and on the executive in matters regarding execution. A Court that was given the power to interpret a Constitution that was political was bound to be enmeshed in politics. Nowhere was this more apparent than in the constitutional clash between state and nation. Con-

---

75. *New Jersey v. Wilson,* 7 Cranch 164; Steven R. Boyd, "The Contract Clause and the Evolution of American Federalism, 1789–1815," *William and Mary Quarterly,* 3d ser., 44 (1987): 529–48. Kentucky's opposition to *Green v. Biddle* is discussed in Warren, *Supreme Court,* 1: ch. 16. *Hawkins v. Barney's Lessee,* 5 Peters 457. Henry Clay's role in *Green v. Biddle,* and the case itself, is discussed with admirable clarity in Maurice G. Baxter, *Henry Clay the Lawyer* (Lexington, Ky., 2000). For Marshall on Johnson's circuit opinion, see his letter to Story, 26 September 1823, PJM, 9: 338.

sidering how imperfectly the line was drawn by the Founding Fathers, how they backed away from clarity to achieve agreement, it can be appreciated just how political was the law Marshall and his Court aimed to administer and clarify. Long before Tocqueville said it, Marshall realized that in America every major political question sooner or later, in one way or another, turns into a constitutional one. When he admitted in *Cohens* that the people who made the Constitution can also destroy it, he acknowledged the *political* vulnerabilities of supreme law.[76]

The real question is what he did with his wisdom about the connectedness of constitutional law and democratic politics. What he *professed* to do was to separate the two and make the Court first and foremost a legal institution. This was the central theme of his jurisprudence—proclaimed in *Marbury,* acted on in *McCulloch,* defended against Roane, and reaffirmed in *Cohens.* Indeed, all his major constitutional decisions operated on the premise that the Court was bound by the law of the Constitution to do what it was doing; that it was guided by legal, not political, reasoning by the intent of the Framers. These pronouncements, on and off the Court, were not single, isolated episodes but ought to be seen as a coherent response to the larger developments of the new age, especially to the newly emerging democratic polity represented by the rise of political parties and the emergence of the Jacksonian Democrats. Marshall intuited what historians have come to understand more clearly: that the Richmond Junto used the Court issue to consolidate the Republican Party in Virginia, which, thanks to the organizing genius of Martin Van Buren, joined with the Albany Regency in 1827 to form the Democratic Party of Andrew Jackson. The new party was professedly egalitarian, and it refashioned Jeffersonian ideology to make the point. Like Jefferson, it believed that the best government was the one that governed least. National planning, like that championed by Henry Clay and J. Q. Adams, was out; state pluralism and states' rights were in. So were political parties and professional politicians. Brokerage was their forte. Operating on the principle that half a loaf is better than none, the newly arisen tribe of professional politicians worked to attract enough voters to dominate legislatures, win executive offices at the state level, and ultimately capture the presidency itself. Old deferential leaders "stood" for office; modern politicians "ran," and what they chased was political power. It was a new and

76. On the complexity of federalism in the Constitution, see Jack N. Rakove, *Original Meanings: Politics and Ideas in the Making of the Constitution* (New York, 1996), ch. 7.

different way to govern. Jefferson called it democracy; Marshall called it demagoguery. In the new age, political compromise rather than republican truth became the guiding spirit of the Constitution.[77]

By fashioning the Court as a legal institution, by viewing judges as republican statesmen above the fray, Marshall set himself against this new way of doing constitutional business. His plan, as Virginia critics hurried to point out, was unavoidably elitist—in the political vernacular of the times, aristocratic; in the historian's view, deferential. Even friends of Marshall conceded the point, as did William Ellery Channing, who defended Marshall's opinion in *McCulloch* on the same ground that he defended the role of the learned clergy to expound scripture, that is, the God-given right of the learned to exegete the text for the unregenerate. Even Marshall seemed at times to concede the point, as when in his debate with Roane he expressed hope that the people would trust the Court with the power he claimed it had. Trust, of course, was the watchword and justification of the old deferential system of politics Marshall knew as a young man in Virginia, the glue that bound followers to the natural elite. It is not surprising that in his defense of *McCulloch,* he put his reputation on the line to make the point.

It was not just trust on one side and noblesse oblige on the other that Marshall relied on to justify and restrain the Court's powers. Rather, it was legal science, as the lawyers of the early Republic understood that concept and as he had practiced it for nearly two decades in the courts of Virginia. And the heart of early national legal science was the taught tradition of the common law. The Framers who did most to shape the institutional contours of the federal court system in the Constitution were profoundly influenced by common-law training and experience. So were those members of the First Congress who passed the Judiciary Act of 1789 and the several Process Acts of the 1790s, which defined the working rules for the federal courts. No one, least of all John Marshall, could ignore the fact that interpreting a written constitution that was supreme law was a unique and distinctly American undertaking. Still, the whole idea of a separate system of courts, proceeding by the adversarial method and applying generally agreed-upon rules by agreed-upon procedures,

77. On the Virginia-New York axis and the emergence of the Jacksonian Democratic Party see Robert Remini, *The Election of Andrew Jackson* (Philadelphia, 1963). Herbert Agar, *The Price of Union* (Boston, 1950) explores the compromise function of the American party system; also see Peter B. Knupfer, *The Union as It Is: Constitutional Unionism and Sectional Compromise, 1787–1861* (Chapel Hill, N.C., 1991).

originated in the common law. Marshall's constitutional world, as Charles Hobson has shown so clearly, rested on a common-law foundation.[78]

Marshall's conception of republican judging also rested on common-law premises. Specifically, it drew on the well-developed tradition of statutory interpretation, one which, as Jefferson Powell has persuasively shown, was readily applicable to the text of the written Constitution. In this tradition, interpretation was not only acceptable but indispensable. In common-law hermeneutics, judges who interpreted statutes and other written instruments of the law did not *make* law wholesale in the process of applying it retail. What kept judging objective was the master principle of stare decisis, which bound judges to previous decisions when the factual situation was similar, plus the countless rules of construction and substantive legal principles established in centuries of case law. Probably no practicing common-law judge thought these principles were applied automatically and with absolute objectivity. On the other hand, few doubted that the common-law system provided consistent and workable rules, free of judicial whimsy and gross subjectivity. The simple fact that 90 percent or more of the Supreme Court justices' work involved common-law cases made it all the easier to believe that the same objective judging applied to constitutional cases as well.[79]

One could argue that the common law itself was biased in favor of property; that those who had the most were automatically privileged by the system. One might even suggest, that Marshall's bias in favor of large speculators, including himself, was a case in point. Still, the evidence points to the fact that Marshall sincerely believed in the theory of objective judging he set forth in *Marbury* and elaborated in his defense of the Court in the 1820s. He hoped no doubt, following percolate-up principle in *Federalist 51*, that justices would be republican statesmen because they were the best, brightest, and most honorable. But legal science helped make disinterested statesmen of able judges who were all too human. Principled judging did not have to be perfect, either, since the Court was competing for republican laurels with state legislatures. Scholars know all too little about the actual process of lawmaking at the state level in this period, or in Congress, for that matter. But Marshall knew firsthand, as

78. Forrest McDonald, *Novus Ordo Seclorum: The Intellectual Origins of the Constitution* (Lawrence, Kans., 1985) treats the common-law aspects of the Constitution; on the common-law background of Marshall's constitutionalism, see Charles F. Hobson, *The Great Chief Justice: John Marshall and the Rule of Law* (Lawrence, Kans., 1996), ch. 2.

79. On the common-law tradition of constitutional interpretation, see H. Jefferson Powell, "The Original Understanding of Original Interpretation," *Harvard Law Review* 98 (March 1985): 885–948.

did Madison, and he had no respect for what he saw. Possibly, structural reforms improved the legislative process at the state level in the early Republic, as they did in Congress. But the overriding development, as Marshall correctly perceived, was the emergence of political parties. The driving principle of party was power, which was linked functionally to compromise, all of which was at serious odds with the republican tradition of disinterested statesmanship Marshall associated with the Court.[80]

What impact did Marshall's belief in republican, i.e., disinterested, judging have on the Court and its battle for survival in the new democratic age? The definitive history of the anti-Court movement of the 1820s has yet to be written; in any case, it is impossible to trace precisely the impact ideas have on history. But certain things do seem clear, the first being that the debate between Marshall and Virginia—from the Virginia and Kentucky Resolutions and *Marbury* on, but most intensively during the Roane-Marshall debate from 1819 to 1821—set the stage for what followed. What did follow was an outpouring of measures for curbing judicial power, for undoing the position Marshall advocated in *Marbury, McCulloch,* and *Cohens.* Roane proposed the state courts, *sans* Section 25, as the corrective. Jefferson worked behind the scenes, urging Justice William Johnson to reintroduce seriatim opinions and dissents as a way of undercutting Marshall's dominance, which the South Carolinian did in fact do. Senator Richard Johnson from Kentucky joined in the demand for institutional curbs on judicial review. Even Marshall's cousin Humphrey Marshall joined the feeding frenzy. Several state legislatures joined in with anti-Court resolutions and a wide range of reforms designed to curb the Court's interpretive powers. John Bannister Gibson of the Pennsylvania Supreme Court added intellectual respectability to the attack, though it should be noted that his blast against Marshall's conception of judicial review in *Eakin v. Raub* (1825) appeared in a dissenting opinion. State opposition carried into Congress, too, which debated various measures for curbing the Court. One of the most revealing suggestions—since it was based on the premise that all constitutional adjudication was political—was to make the Senate the final judge in constitutional cases involving federalism. Another was to create a special court composed of the chief justices of all the states, giving it final authority in such cases.[81]

Most of these measures barely got off the ground, and all crashed for want

---

80. Joseph Story justifies judicial review à la Marshall by reference to legal science in his *Commentaries on the Constitution of the United States* . . . (Boston, 1891), 1: book 3, chs. 4 and 5, also ch. 38.

81. The anti-Court movement is treated in Warren, *Supreme Court,* ch. 17.

of support. The most threatening was the attempt spearheaded by Virginia to repeal Section 25, which could be done by a simple legislative majority and which would make the supreme court of each state court the final authority on the Constitution. One man who watched the process of this movement carefully—and learned from it—was John C. Calhoun of South Carolina. Calhoun began his career as a nationalist and shifted to states' rights only when state interests in South Carolina demanded it. As late as 1823, he was so bold as to support Marshall's decision regarding that section in *Cohens.* States' rights sentiment, prompted by the Charleston slave rebellion in 1822, changed his mind. He ended up backing the movement to curb the Court's appellate powers, and when that failed, he crafted his own method of asserting state control over constitutional interpretation—known familiarly as the theory of nullification—which was adopted by the South Carolina legislature in 1828 and put into action in 1831.

Calhoun took over where Roane and Virginia left off. Like them, he believed, as he put it to Virgil Maxcy in 1831, that the issue was between the Supreme Court and the people of the states. Working from the tradition begun in 1798, indeed in the ratification debates, Calhoun came forward with a device that made the states (Calhoun would say the people of the state) the final authorities on the Constitution. Acting through specially called constitutional conventions, states could challenge the constitutionality of an act of Congress by declaring it null and void within the state. If the national government let the nullification stand, then ipso facto, the law was void, presumably not only in the state that nullified it but in other states as well. Alternately, Congress could initiate an amendment authorizing itself to enact the disputed law, say a protective tariff, and if a sufficient number of states ratified, the constitutional contract, as Calhounites referred to the Constitution, was in effect redrawn. Each state, a party to the contract in Calhoun's formulation, then had a choice. The state could ratify or not. If one-fourth plus one failed to do so, those states in effect would have exercised a veto. In this way, a minority of slaveholding states had a concurrent veto over the majority. If the amendment were ratified, any state that did not accept the new constitution would thus secede from the Union. Building on the assumption that the Constitution was a contract created by sovereign states, Calhoun supplied what early theorists like Taylor, Jefferson, and Madison had only hinted at: a mechanism of implementation that claimed to be both peaceful and constitutional.[82]

82. For Calhoun and the nullifiers, see Charles M. Wiltse, *John C. Calhoun, Nullifier, 1829–1839* (Indianapolis and New York, 1949), especially ch. 8; for a collection of relevant documents,

The pending showdown between Marshall and the Court and the forces of states' rights, which Calhoun predicted, came in 1832 when South Carolina applied Calhoun's theory by nullifying the Tariffs of 1828 and 1832. What happened would appear to be a decisive victory for Marshall's view of the Court as the final interpreter of the Constitution: first, because no other state north or south joined South Carolina at the nullification barricade; second, because President Jackson threatened to use federal troops to suppress South Carolina's resistance to federal law. The fact that Jackson was elected on a states' rights platform and had opposed Marshall's version of constitutional nationalism made his action all the more significant. Equally telling in this regard was the fact that James Madison, whose ideas and authority had contributed to Calhoun's doctrine, now in the last years of his life threw his support to the Court. Madison, it will be recalled, had called Marshall into action in defense of the Constitution and of judicial review in the Virginia ratifying convention—and praised him for his efforts. As president, he had backed the Marshall Court in its bitter confrontation with Pennsylvania in 1809. Madison was also the author of the Virginia Resolution of 1798 and the Virginia Report of 1799. He had serious constitutional objections to Marshall's opinion in *McCulloch* and to the broad concept of judicial power on which it was based. When confronted with the radical, unhinging implications of nullification, however, Madison shifted course yet again. Calhoun had taken both Jackson and Madison to the precipice, and after gazing into the abyss, they withdrew to moderate ground. An imperfect Court was better than a perfectly logical constitutional system that almost certainly would destroy the Union.[83]

Thanks to Marshall's fans, however, especially the New England publicists who came to his defense in the 1820s, it was not an imperfect Court, or a less-than-perfect chief justice, that made it into American textbooks. New England "sectional nationalists," as one insightful scholar has called them, had the final word on Marshall and his enemies. What they said and wrote contributed both to the myth of Marshall and the myth of the Supreme Court. Never mind that New England's law-abiding statesmen retreated into states' rights after losing to Jefferson in 1800, that they defied national law on a massive scale during the War of 1812, and took their section to the brink of secession in the Hartford Convention. New England rediscovered nationalism in the 1820s, when it

---

see Ross M. Lence, ed., *Union and Liberty: The Political Philosophy of John C. Calhoun* (Indianapolis, 1992).

83. William W. Freehling, *Prelude to Civil War: The Nullification Controversy in South Carolina, 1816–1836* (New York, 1996). On Madison's opposition to nullification, see McCoy, *Last of the Fathers*, ch. 4.

suited the region's economic interests. When New England capitalists joined the national market revolution, they gained a new appreciation of Marshall and the Court. In the several years after 1815, for example, the *North American Review* (the leading journal of the period, with a circulation of 3,200 in 1830) contained no fewer than seven essays and reviews praising Marshall and his Court and criticizing his critics. Even more important, the leading lawyers of New England came to his defense, none more effectively than Daniel Webster. Webster identified himself with New England, New England with the nation, and the nation with Marshall's constitutional nationalism. When the "godlike" Webster thundered, New England, indeed the nation, listened. And he spoke consistently before the Court, where he contributed to Marshall's thinking. Now he spoke in behalf of the Court, and never more effectively than in the Webster-Hayne debate of 1830. There, with the help of Justice Story, Webster set out to prove to the nation that John Marshall's Court was the last best hope of national union against the unhinging doctrines of John C. Calhoun.[84]

Webster was a host, but it was really Marshall's colleague Story who had the final word, one much amplified by his reputation on the Court and his position as Dane Professor at Harvard Law School. Working with Nathan Dane and Josiah Quincy, Story brought the law school back from the dead in the same year Jackson attained the presidency. The school's avowed purpose was to train elite lawyers, equipped with up-to-date commercial law and nationalist constitutional principles to counteract the new professional states' rights politicians. To this end, Story wrote his *Commentaries on the Constitution* in three volumes in 1833. He dedicated this remarkable work to John Marshall, whose interpretation of the Constitution was "destined to enlighten, instruct, and convince future generations"—and more to the task at hand, "dissipate the illusions of ingenious doubt and subtle argument and impassioned eloquence" of his southern critics. Marshall responded with gratitude and expressed the hope that the *Commentaries* would rescue the country from states' rights madness. And that was its avowed purpose. Written in the midst of the nullification crisis, the massive work was a direct response to Calhoun's theory of nullification. To that end, it was also a massive justification of Marshall's view of the Court as final republican interpreter of the Constitution. Following Marshall

84. The most insightful book on New England conservatives in the 1820s is Harlow W. Sheidley's *Sectional Nationalism: Massachusetts Conservative Leaders and the Transformation of America, 1815-1836* (Boston, 1998); also see Newmyer, *Justice Joseph Story*, ch. 5.

and quoting his opinions copiously, Story justified judicial review on the ground that the justices were uniquely situated institutionally and intellectually to exercise it objectively. Like Marshall, he believed that the intent of the Framers was set forth in the words of the Constitution for the guidance of the justices. Armed with the science of the law, the Court could apply those principles fairly and equitably, and to aid them in that noble enterprise, he listed nineteen specific "Rules of Interpretation," most of which came directly from Marshall's opinions, particularly those from the 1820s.[85]

Story's *Commentaries* remained *the* text on the Constitution for the remainder of the nineteenth century and into the twentieth as well. As much as anything, except the Supreme Court reports themselves, the book established the lasting reputation of John Marshall and his view of the Court as an institution above politics. At the very moment of its inception, however, this view was out of sync with the realities of history—and Marshall himself stood witness to the fact. His republican vision of the Court, like Story's and Tocqueville's too, was that the Court, armed with constitutional truth and legal science, would curb democracy, the "tyranny of the majority," as Tocqueville put it. But rather than standing above the political process, the Marshall Court increasingly became a part of it, an integral part, no less. The anti-Court movement of the 1820s and early 1830s tells the story. What it tells is that the Court survived—but not because South Carolina conceded to the wisdom of Marshall, which it most assuredly did not, or because Jackson converted to Marshall's view of the Constitution, which he did not. What happened instead was that the Court saved itself: first, by maneuvering deftly and conceding to the states a good bit of what they demanded, which Marshall's federalism, properly understood, allowed it to do. What mainly placated the Court's enemies, however, was that they gradually gained a voice on the Court itself—loud enough, if we are to believe Marshall, to "revolutionize" the institution from the inside out. Marshall did not give up the battle for republican truth, but he recognized that the Court, which was supposed to be above and indeed to control politics, had itself been politicized. This did not mean the Court had lost its power, as Marshall concluded, but only that its decisions were not final. For Marshall, it was not an easy truth to live with.

85. Story, *Commentaries on the Constitution*, book 3, ch. 5: "Rules of Interpretation." Also see Newmyer, *Justice Joseph Story*, chs. 5, 8.

CHAPTER SEVEN

Conservative Nationalist *in the* Age *of* Jackson

> I yield slowly and reluctantly to the conviction that our constitution cannot last. I had supposed that North of the Potowmack a firm and solid government, competent to the security of national liberty might be preserved. Even that now seems doubtful. The case of the south seems to me to be desperate. Our opinions are incompatible with a united government even among ourselves. The union has been prolonged thus far by miracles. I [believe] they cannot continue.
>
> —*Marshall to Story, September 22, 1832.*

M ARSHALL'S DESPAIRING letter to Story appears to be excessively gloomy—until one recognizes he was right in his description of things as they were and in his prophecy of things to come. He had survived a dozen years of states' rights agitation in Virginia, aimed largely at him and his Court. He had witnessed the electoral defeat of his friend John Q. Adams by a man half as qualified and by means of a party organization that signified the demise of deferential statesmanship. In the state constitutional convention of 1829–1830, he would see Virginians divide over slavery. He would hear them threaten war, with each other or with the free states—whichever threatened their way of life. In the Webster-Hayne debate, he listened to the unhinging rhetoric of Colonel Robert Hayne of South Carolina defend the unhinging constitutional doctrines of Calhoun, which were already being implemented in South Carolina. He watched as President Jackson challenged his ruling in *Mc-*

Culloch and ignored the Court's decision in the Cherokee Indian case of *Worcester v. Georgia* (1832). When he stepped forth to champion a radical new national government in 1788, Marshall was on the victorious cutting edge of history. Now, in the final years of his life, he was on the losing side. He had not changed, but the times had. American history had turned the "young man of the Revolution" into a beleaguered conservative.

His conservatism, like his nationalism, was more complicated than it appeared, partly because he was a conservative in America, where radical change was endemic and seemingly irresistible, and partly because he was a conservative in Virginia, where conservatism was increasingly associated with slavery and states' rights constitutionalism. He was snookered. Conservatism was on the run nationally; in Virginia, it was running in the wrong direction. Marshall the conservative had no place to turn but the Supreme Court. He had always sought to make it a republican institution, now he saw it as a conservative one, the sheet anchor against the tyranny of the majority and the idiocy of states' rights ideologues. The only problem—and it put his leadership to the ultimate test—was the Court's vulnerability to the very forces he wanted it to contain. To be a Burkean in America, it would appear, one not only had to create institutions before they could be revered but also had to create them out of materials that were largely democratic.

An American Conservative at the Virginia Constitutional Convention of 1829–1830

In understanding Marshall's conservatism, as with most everything else in his public philosophy, one falls back unavoidably on actions rather than words. Not only did he not philosophize on the subject, he most often did not bother even to explain his actions. Like surveyors, which Marshall once was, historians must locate him by triangulation, perhaps by using John Randolph and John Adams as base points in the computations. Even a brief glance at the terrain to be mapped warns of its complexity, starting with Marshall's ambivalent attitude toward change itself. Radical political change called Marshall the conservative into action, yet he was by no means opposed to all change. Indeed, some of the changes he accepted were profoundly transformative. He was born a citizen of the British Empire, which he soon fought to destroy. As a constitutional nationalist, he was on the cutting edge of change. On the Court and off, he labored to create a national market, which would radically transform the way Americans lived. Judged by his position on these policies, Marshall, like Hamilton, qualifies as a radical reformer—this is not to mention his economic individualism, which put him at odds with philosophical conservatives like Burke, who cherished class and institutions as bulwarks of tradition.[1]

In accepting and, selectively, even championing change, Marshall the conservative made some very practical concessions to the realities of American experience, which was not an unconservative thing to do. What he feared was not change but chaos, disorder, history out of control, or more accurately perhaps, history out of the control of statesmen like himself. And chaos is what he increasingly saw around him, first in the 1790s, when with the help of Jefferson and his party, French ideas invaded America. In the 1820s, the same radical democratic ideas—still championed by Jefferson, as Marshall believed—threatened to unleash chaos by destroying the two things designed to keep it at bay: the Constitution and the Supreme Court. With Jackson's election, the presidency became part of the problem rather than part of the solution. With both the national government and the states having gone over to the enemy, only the Supreme Court was left to hold the barbarians at bay, assuming it could escape the contagion of democracy.

Events were not only making Marshall a conservative but were forcing him to own up to the fact. Nowhere was this more apparent than in the Virginia state constitutional convention of 1829–1830, and nowhere were the nuances of his conservatism more manifest. The convention was called to reform the constitution of 1776. Created as an ad hoc response to revolutionary necessity, this constitution had been the subject of criticism almost from the beginning—for never have been submitted to the people for ratification, for not providing for an amending process, and for vesting too much power in the legislature and too little in the executive branch. Two things precipitated the call for the convention of 1829 after years of successful resistance to reform. One was the suffrage and apportionment provisions of the old constitution, which privileged the slaveholding Tidewater and Piedmont counties; the other was the phenomenal growth of the free-white population in the Shenandoah Valley and the trans-Allegheny west. By 1828, when the state legislature finally authorized the calling of a convention, these factors resulted in the disfranchisement of some

---

1. On conservatism in general, see Russell Kirk, *The Conservative Mind, from Burke to Santayana* (Chicago, 1953); on American conservatism, Clinton Rossiter, *Conservatism in America* (New York, 1955). On southern conservatism, see Norman K. Risjord, *The Old Republicans: Southern Conservatism in the Age of Jefferson* (New York, 1965), and Russell Kirk, *Randolph of Roanoke: A Study in Conservative Thought* (Chicago, 1951).

31,000 taxpaying adult men. More serious still were the inequities between eastern and western Virginians resulting from the provision of the old constitution apportioning representatives on the basis of slave property. With a white population of 348,873, the slaveholding Tidewater and Piedmont counties had 134 delegates to the house and 15 to the senate; while the transmontane, largely free western counties, with a total white population of 254,196, had only 80 house delegates and 9 senators.[2]

Thus were political democracy and the institution of slavery inseparably connected in the debates of the convention. To defuse the politically explosive issue, arguments were made that slavery would inevitably make its way into the Shenandoah Valley and across the mountains, but no one really believed them. The western delegates, who held few, if any, slaves saw slave representation in the east as the chief source of their political oppression and slavery itself as hostile to their way of life. With almost no exceptions, eastern delegates believed that expanded suffrage and a democratic apportionment would permit the more numerous west to end slavery and emancipate the slaves. Increasingly, western Virginia looked to and identified with the northern states—and with internal improvements, banks, and a national market—while the east looked to itself and ultimately to the "southern way." East blamed west for talking and thinking like Yankees, and hotheads, such as Benjamin W. Leigh, threatened to fight if westerners moved against slavery. After a decade of states' rights demagoguery, many, including Marshall, were inclined to take the threat seriously.[3]

As Virginians debated the coming convention in the spring of 1828, Marshall "grieved" to his son James about "the turbulence of the times." In December of that year, he referred again, this time to John Randolph of Roanoke, to the growing agitation and division of opinion in the legislature over calling and structuring the convention. He predicted correctly that the division between "the great slave holding counties" of the east and the democrats of the west would generate "much exasperation and discontent"; where the confrontation would end, he was unable to say. The one thing he was sure of was that he did not want to be involved, except as a private citizen. On hearing in early March 1829 that he was being "held up as a candidate for the convention," he

2. On the convention of 1829, see Robert P. Sutton, *Revolution to Secession: Constitution Making in the Old Dominion* (Charlottesville, Va., 1989), especially ch. 2 on the Constitution of 1776 and ch. 4 on the convention of 1829–1830. Charles Henry Ambler's *Sectionalism in Virginia from 1776 to 1861* (Chicago, 1910) is still indispensable; the figures appear at 137–38.

3. Ambler, *Sectionalism*, ch. 5; Sutton, *Revolution to Secession*, ch. 4.

assured his wife that he had "no desire to be in the convention and do not mean to be a candidate." Three weeks later, he reaffirmed this decision to the Committee of Richmond Citizens, which wanted to draft him. Three days after that, he reluctantly agreed to "go if chosen" but only out of "deference" to his fellow citizens. They insisted, and he caved, acting, as he recounted the episode to Story, "like the girl addressed by a gentleman she does not positively dislike, but is unwilling to marry. She is sure to yield to the advice and persuasion of her friends." With the convention less than a week away, he said he still felt "vain regrets at being a member. The chief though not the only cause of these regrets is that *non sum qualis eram*—I can no longer debate. Yet I cannot apply my mind to anything else."[4]

Reluctant though it was, Marshall's participation speaks to several points, the first being his continued popularity in Richmond. For all of his misgivings, he was still deeply engaged with the great issues of the day and, as it turned out, on the side of the "old conservatives." In fact, he had taken his stand against radical democratic reform, and the chaos it promised, even before the convention assembled in October. He explained his opposition to democratic suffrage to James Mercer Garnett, who represented the Tidewater counties of King William, King and Queen, Essex, Caroline, and Hanover at the convention, in unusual detail. Marshall was, he confessed at the outset, not a champion of the "natural rights of Man," a position he associated with Jefferson. "These rights exist in a state of nature," he admitted without much conviction, "but are surrendered, as it seems to me, when he enters into a state of society, in exchange for social rights and advantages." Both "life and liberty," then "may be controuled by society, and are exercised by its permission." While that control might be used wantonly, he said, "still the power exists, and its exercise must be regulated by the wisdom of society." This, according to Marshall, applied to "the exclusion of females, minors, free people of colour &c" and to the limits placed on suffrage and representation, the two great issues before the convention. The question of who gets to participate in government and on what terms, he said, was a matter "of expediency, not of right." Determining expediency was not a matter of counting heads or talking abstractions, but rather had to "take into view all of the great objects for which government

4. In order: Marshall to James Marshall Jr., 7 April 1828, PJM, typescript; Marshall to Randolph, 24 December 1828, ibid; Marshall to Mary W. Marshall, 5 March 1829, ibid; Marshall to the Committee of Richmond Citizens, 25 March 1829, ibid; Marshall to Story, 11 June, 30 September 1829, ibid.

is instituted." "Security against external force" is one object of "primary magnitude,"and it "devolves," he declared, "mainly on the government of the Union." "Personal" security, he stated, was another objective and a matter for the states to determine.[5]

What concerned Marshall most, what was central to his conservatism, was not personal security so much as the rights of property. Power and property, he believed, must be united, and indeed, if they were separated, they almost surely would be reunited—"by means which cannot be avowed." The surest way to protect property by uniting it with power, he declared, was to begin "at the foundation at the right of suffrage." Virginia's government had to represent interests; indeed, it had to reflect them. And the dominant interests in Virginia were land and slavery. It followed then, Marshall reasoned, that the "right of suffrage" must continue to rest "on the basis of an interest in land"—on the freehold suffrage as provided by the old constitution. Thus, he said, "in the representative we may expect to see the image—the improved image, but still the image, of his constituents." Marshall conceded that "among the destitute of the race may be found intelligence, honor, and inflexible principle." But "in framing a constitution," he said, the people "must act on general principles," one of them being that property be represented and protected, including property in slaves. Marshall spoke for the eastern interests in this instance as well as when he went on to insist that slavery "is among the most productive funds for taxation." Since "it bears a great portion of the burthen of government," he stated, slave property "has peculiar claims to consideration in the formation of that body which is to be entrusted with the power of imposing taxes." To frame a constitution on the basis of democratic suffrage alone, given the population differential between east and west, he claimed, would make slave property insecure and shake the very foundation of Virginia's social order. With social chaos looming, he determined, the new constitution must protect slavery and rally the support of the eastern slaveholding planters, this from the man who was a leading figure in the Virginia branch of the American Colonization Society, the father of a man who would in two years champion the gradual abolition of slavery in Virginia.[6]

What Marshall witnessed before and during the convention, what fueled his conservatism and defined his strategy, was the mounting threat of violence as each side entrenched behind a barricade of nonnegotiable demands. More

5. Marshall to Garnett, 20 May 1829, PJM, typescript.
6. Ibid.

frightening still was the fact that the ideological line separating eastern from western Virginia was precisely the one dividing free states from slave states. Marshall did not go to Richmond only out of deference to his fellow citizens; neither did he plan to play a mere symbolic role once he got there. Rather he chose to use what remaining energy and influence he had to hold at bay the hotheads on both sides. He succeeded not just because of his "intense earnestness"—the "leading trait of his manner" at the convention, according to Hugh Grigsby—but because as always he knew when to stand back and when to step forth. Despite his strong opposition to political democracy, he did not engage in the debate about the democratization of suffrage and representation until the extreme democrats and extreme conservatives had reached a standoff over whether slave property should be represented. The situation appeared desperate when the chief justice of the United States spoke briefly but movingly in support of a compromise and "the spirit of conciliation." He helped turn the tide. In the end, the convention retained freehold suffrage and compromised apportionment so that the house was based on white population only and the senate on a mixed slave-white count, using the federal compromise, wherein one slave counted as three-fifths of a white person. Because this compromise increased the number of representatives from the Shenandoah Valley, that section joined the east in support of the old constitution. It was a constitution, Marshall admitted, that was less than perfect, but it held back chaos for the time being. But chaos was sure to come, as Marshall observed sadly to Story, because the slave holders of the Old Dominion were enmeshed in the institution and could not let go.[7]

Albert Beveridge used Marshall's role in the convention to define him as "the supreme conservative." Given Marshall's views on suffrage, as expressed to Garnett before the convention, his identification with the conservative Tidewater during the convention, and his final support of a constitution that preserved conservative power, it seems a valid assessment. Some important qualifications are in order, however. Marshall may not have liked the democratic measures pushed by radical democrats such as Philip Doddridge from the northern valley, but he could not have ignored the fact that it was the west that supported state and federal internal improvements against eastern opposi-

7. Marshall to Story, 30 September 1829, ibid. Grigsby on Marshall in Hugh Blair Grigsby, *The Virginia Convention of 1829–30* (New York, 1969), 15; *Proceedings and Debates of the Virginia State Convention of 1829–1830* (Richmond, Va., 1830), 497. On Marshall's despondency, see his letter to Story, 22 September 1832, PJM, typescript.

tion and in general looked favorably on national union. Marshall's views on slavery were also at odds with those of the young conservative firebrands at the convention, who promised to die defending the institution. Ever the practical man, he joined the conservatives to facilitate a rational compromise acceptable to both extremes. This was the role he always played: a principled but practical-minded conservative with an innate distrust of ideological purity. Like the modern politicians he hated, he realized that half a loaf was better than none.[8]

Marshall was not just a pragmatic conservative, but a principled one as well, a Burkean who believed that institutions developed naturally over the years in response to the needs of society should be cherished and defended. Whether Marshall consciously patterned his behavior at the convention after Burke is doubtful, but his actions follow a Burkean trajectory just the same: his decision to join the east in its battle against democracy, his willing acceptance of slavery as a given of Virginia life, and generally his unwillingness to stand in judgment on the imperfect world around him. It was in defending Virginia's old county court system, however, that he most explicitly endorsed the conservative principle that imperfect practice is better than perfect theory. As the chairman of the convention's Committee on the Judiciary, he played a decisive role in the convention's final decision to retain the county court system without change. Reformers at the convention, citing Jefferson as authority, criticized the system as inefficient and unrepublican, the dilapidated vestige of colonial aristocracy, which violated separation of powers at every turn. As a young lawyer in the 1780s, Marshall said pretty much the same thing. Now with so much else up for grabs in Virginia, he circled the Burkean wagons. The old court system might be "ill organized" for some purposes, he conceded, for example, in matters of chancery, and perhaps some modest reform was in order. But, he insisted, the system "must be preserved." The justices of the peace, he said, are "the best men in their respective counties," who "act in the spirit of peace-makers, and allay, rather than excite the small disputes and differences which will sometimes arise among neighbours." Because of their efforts, he declared confidently, in "no part of America," was there "less disquiet and less of ill-feeling between man and man." Social order and good feelings, as the convention itself proved, were hard to come by in the new age.[9]

8. Albert J. Beveridge, *The Life of John Marshall* (Boston, New York, 1916–1919), 4: ch. 9. Ambler divided the conservatives at the convention into old and new, putting Marshall with the former, *Sectionalism*, 149–50, 165.

9. For Marshall's speech, see *Proceedings and Debates of the Convention*, 504–5.

Marshall's speech on the county courts, as Hugh Grigsby points out, was brief but able, more a display of authority than persuasive argument. With Marshall's defense of judicial tenure, however, "he came forth in all his strength," to again cite Grigsby. At issue was the provision of the proposed new constitution that provided for the removal of judges—one of several schemes put forth to curb the state courts by making them more responsive to the legislature and to the electorate. Marshall spoke frequently against these measures, taking on some of Virginia's best lawyers and politicians in the process, including Littleton W. Tazewell, Philip P. Barbour (whom Jackson appointed to the Supreme Court in 1836), and his old nemesis William B. Giles. It may seem strange that Marshall defended the judicial independence of Virginia judges so passionately when he had contended with them most of his professional life—as a lawyer and plaintiff in the Fairfax litigation, as the chief justice asserting the power of the United States Supreme Court to review their decisions, and in the newspaper duel with Roane and Brockenbrough. Still the fact remained that he had spent twenty happy years of his life in that system, learning his law there under Wythe and Pendleton. Most important, perhaps, he feared legislative supremacy at the state level more than judicial authority. Now that Roane was gone and Jefferson as well, the hope of a rapprochement between federal and state courts may have seemed a real possibility. In any case, since the independence of the judiciary was essential to the administration of justice by the courts, it was a principle good in any venue, state or federal.[10]

Marshall's argument against the legislative removal of judges was part of his defense of the constitutional status quo in the Old Dominion, another effort to hold reform at bay. He was also defending the independence of the Supreme Court of the United States, and from the same enemies—a point that becomes readily apparent, as Grigsby observed, since the question of judicial tenure in the Virginia convention "was virtually the same as that presented in Congress in 1802 on the repeal of the judiciary act." The connection was even more meaningful for Marshall since leaders in the early attack on the Supreme Court, John Randolph and William B. Giles, opposed him in the judiciary debate in 1829, which, according to Grigsby, was the most brilliant of the convention. In truth, Marshall had been defending the Court against Virginia politicians going back to the Virginia and Kentucky Resolutions of 1798, if not to the ratifying convention of 1788. He had put forth the vision of an independent judiciary, armed with legal science and objective law, as an essential fea-

10. *Proceedings and Debates of the Convention,* 615–17.

ture of republican government. Even as he spoke in Richmond, the movement to repeal Section 25 was gathering steam around the country, as were other schemes to curb the independence of the federal courts. With Jackson in the presidency, the party spirit, which had permeated the political branches, now threatened the Supreme Court itself. Under Marshall's leadership, the Court had helped create the nation; now it would have to become the conservative instrument for the nation's preservation. But first, it would have to preserve itself.[11]

Judicial Strategy for Hard Times
(Or the Imperatives of a Sitting Chief Justice)

As a Burkean conservative in America, Marshall faced a uniquely American dilemma: the network of institutions Burke fell back on as a check on radicalism, those he approached with "trembling and reverence," simply did not exist in America, especially at the national level. There was no national church but instead a plethora of sects at war with one another. If they shared a common denominator, it was evangelical democracy, not Burkean conservatism. There were pockets of self-conscious class privilege—witness the Virginia constitutional debates of 1829–1830—but there was no national aristocracy capable of curbing the democratic impulse. More to the point, Tocqueville notwithstanding, there was no national bench and bar as in England. Mainly there was the Constitution, but it was a mere skeleton—an "experiment," as the founding generation liked to call it. Only with the fleshing out of the real institutions of government after 1789 had it come slowly to life. Even then, there was no guarantee that it would be a conservative anchor to the democratic ship of state.[12]

The chief justice did what Madison predicted in *Federalist* 51: He identified with the office and, indeed, infused it with his personality. Prideful ambition was not the point. With democracy and states' rights thinking dominant in the political branches and the states, he came to see the Court in conservative ideo-

11. Grigsby, *Virginia Convention,* 15–16.
12. See Paul C. Nagel, *One Nation Indivisible: The Union in American Thought, 1776–1861* (New York, 1964), on the experimental nature of the Constitution. Stanley Elkins discusses the lack of national institutions and the character of American slavery in *Slavery: A Problem in American Institutional and Intellectual Life* (Chicago, 1968). On the democratic denominator of American Protestantism, see Perry Miller, *The Life of the Mind in America: From the Revolution to the Civil War* (New York, 1965), Book 1.

logical terms, as the conservator and last best hope of union under the Constitution. It was, however, a hope that rested on two assumptions: first, that partisan politics could be kept off the Court and out of its law and, second, that the decisions of a *unified* Court would be accepted by the American people as final and authoritative. In the age of Jackson, however, neither of those assumptions proved true. Increasingly with new appointments after 1823, the Court began to reflect the new age, which is to say it was increasingly divided, argumentative, and riven along sectional and ideological lines. Marshall's final years were spent trying to rally this divided and contentious Court to its republican duties and a divided and fearful American people to the Court. In neither effort was he entirely successful, but neither did he fail entirely, as he mistakenly concluded he had. The Court that emerged at the end of his tenure remained a formidable institution and even a conservative one, but the position it came to occupy in the democratic polity was not what Marshall had in mind.

Unfortunately for historians who want to reconstruct his efforts to save the Court from its enemies and itself, there are no tell-all memoirs, no intra-Court memoranda, no clerks willing to tell all. Rather, its inner workings have to be pieced together from spare official records, supplemented by snippets of personal correspondence of the justices, Court reporters, and leading members of the Supreme Court bar. Marshall's own surviving papers are especially, and no doubt deliberately, barren when it comes to Court business. Even without an explicit accounting, however, it is clear that several factors combined to shape his theory of judging and his role as chief justice. One was his belief in the intent of the Framers, the idea that the written Constitution placed in the Court's keeping contained fundamental principles intended to last for generations to come and adequate to "the various *crises* of human affairs." As the Court's leading strategist, he also understood its peculiar vulnerabilities to the political branches, to party politics, to the states, and finally to the fickle opinion of the people themselves, whose lack of precise information about the law made them receptive to quick-fix demagoguery. Marshall had already taken accurate measure of the new and more virulent external forces of states' rights in the 1820s, which sought to curb the Court and transform the Constitution. With the new appointments beginning in 1823, he came to realize that the final battle over states' rights and the role of the federal judiciary would be fought out in the Court itself as a new generation of justices challenged his authority and the constitutional principles he assumed were self-evident and unassailable.[13]

13. For the internal history of the Marshall Court, scholars are greatly in the debt of the authors of the Marshall volumes in the *Oliver Wendell Holmes Devise History of the Supreme Court*

Before tracing its radical transformation after 1823, it should be noted that the Marshall Court had never been static. As personnel and issues changed so did the dynamics of the Court, so also did Marshall's influence as chief justice. Measured by the proportion of opinions written, the general absence of dissents and concurrences, he was most dominant during the crucial precedent-setting first decade of his tenure. The reasons for this are several. The small size of the Court, six until 1807, probably had something to do with the success of his unifying agenda and with his commanding position as chief justice. More important—the "real cause," according to Justice William Johnson—was the absence of powerful minds among his colleagues. According to Johnson's brutally frank assessment, "Cushing was incompetent. Chase could not be got to think or write—Patterson [*sic*] was a slow man and willingly declined the trouble, and the other two [Bushrod Washington and Marshall] . . . are commonly estimated as one judge." If Johnson was right, then the weakness of Marshall's early colleagues helped him strengthen the Court as an institution and consolidate his own authority. To do this, however, he had to know what needed to be done. And the way he went about doing it—that is, through collective deliberation—was no less important, and, perhaps, even more remarkable since he probably had more leeway than he took.[14]

Thanks to Marshall's leadership and sense of timing, the early Court settled on a way of doing business that prepared it to meet the challenges of its most creative and stable period—from 1811, when Madison appointed Story and Duvall to the Court, to 1823, when Livingston's death and Smith Thompson's appointment ushered in a period of internal change. The living and working conditions of the Court during this period were particularly congenial to Marshall's style of leadership. Like members of Congress, the judges were interlopers in the hostile environment of Washington City, where Goose Creek flooded every spring (giving real meaning to separation of powers), where disease threatened, and where inconvenience was a way of life. Officials of the new government fled when their official duties were completed. The justices were among the last to arrive, usually showing up for the winter term in early February, and the first to depart, generally leaving in late March in time for their

---

of the United States. Herbert A. Johnson, coauthor of the first volume on the Marshall Court, has gathered his insights on Marshall as leader of the Court in *The Chief Justiceship of John Marshall, 1801–1835* (Columbia, S.C., 1997).

14. Johnson to Jefferson, 10 December 1822, Jefferson Papers, MSS, Library of Congress, as quoted in Donald G. Morgan, *Justice William Johnson, The First Dissenter: The Career and Constitutional Philosophy of a Jeffersonian Judge* (Columbia, S.C., 1954), 181–82. Ch. 10 of Morgan's biography contains an excellent account of the internal divisions on the Court in the 1820s.

spring circuits. During their short stay, the justices, who regularly left their families back home, shared a common boardinghouse, where they slept, ate, and worked. The informality of the setting was a perfect fit for Marshall's personality, and for his collegial approach to leadership.[15]

The austerity of the Court during this period is hard to imagine, especially for those familiar with the modern institution, ensconced in its marble, electronically wired palace, where each justice has access to a printing press, is equipped with a spacious office, a secretarial staff, and three or four bright young law clerks to conduct research and help write opinions. In Marshall's day, justices did it all and rose or fell on the basis of what they did. It was not only their written opinions that counted, but their daily interaction with the bar and among themselves. Interaction there assuredly was, and the arena was so intimate that one's flaws, as well as strengths, were known by all. Indeed, the working and living arrangements of the justices were as confined as was the social space of Washington City. During the first eight years of Marshall's tenure, the Court heard cases in a room on the first floor of the Capitol originally designated for Senate committee hearings, a room as cramped and constricted as Jefferson wanted the Court itself to be. The room was so small that the justices had to robe in public view. There was no separate conference room, either, but since the justices lived in the same boardinghouse, conference discussions easily spilled over, making the line between business and pleasure difficult to draw. No one knows for certain what business transpired in the boardinghouse, but it is likely that concepts were clarified and conflicts resolved during and after meals, when the madeira made its customary rounds.[16]

Marshall made arrangements for communal living himself, and as chief justice, he benefited most from them. The intimate environment and informal procedures privileged precisely those traits of mind and heart he possessed in such abundance. In the days before regularly printed briefs, oral arguments were

15. Herbert Johnson discusses the "four phases of the Marshall Court," with illustrative statistics, in his *Chief Justiceship of Marshall,* ch. 3. See also Donald M. Roper's pioneering article, "Judicial Unanimity and the Marshall Court—A Road to Reappraisal," *American Journal of Legal History* 9 (1964): 118–34. Consult James S. Young, *The Washington Community, 1800–1828* (New York, 1966) on the layout of Washington City during this period and the importance of boardinghouse political culture. Note that Young does not treat the Court.

16. George Lee Haskins and Herbert A. Johnson, *Foundations of Power: John Marshall, 1801–1815* (New York, 1981), 80–82. The boardinghouse arrangements are discussed in G. Edward White, *The Marshall Court and Cultural Change, 1815–1835,* 160–66, 184–86, 189–91. Also see Robert G. Seddig, "John Marshall and the Origins of Supreme Court Leadership," *University of Pittsburgh Law Review* 36 (summer 1975): 785–833.

particularly important and often went on for several days. This informal way of proceeding put a premium on listening, remembering, and resolving quickly—qualities Marshall honed to a sharp edge as a lawyer in Richmond. His analytical acumen, precisely because it was balanced by a sensitivity to those less gifted, was ideally suited to the informal judicial conferences, where cases were resolved with unusual dispatch and where the points raised in oral argument could easily be lost. His quickness with the pen, so amply demonstrated in his essay-writing contest with Roane, was a great advantage, too, when opinions were delivered hard on the heels of oral argument. Had he not been able to write so quickly and so persuasively, he could not have assumed the responsibility of speaking so often for his brethren, even if he wanted to. Here for once, numbers do tell the story. From 1801 to 1804, Marshall wrote for the majority in every case on which he sat; from 1805 to 1810, he was almost as dominant. He shared the honors more often from 1811 to 1823—which reflected both the ability of his new colleagues and his recognition of that ability—but he still wrote most of the major constitutional opinions. Even when decisions were collective in nature, which was often, Marshall had the last word, so to speak. As with the Committee of Detail at the Constitutional Convention of 1787, putting concepts into words often meant shaping the concepts themselves.[17]

Like other great chief justices, then, Marshall had to compete for respect. In an age when the justices shared a linguistic and conceptual universe shaped by the common law, it helped that he was an outstanding common lawyer. But his personality was hardly less important to his success as chief justice than his mind, and no less perfectly suited to the peculiar circumstances of the Court. Story, who visited Washington in 1808 as an agent for the New England Mississippi Land Company, saw the Court in action and was captivated by the way Marshall mixed congeniality and humility with legal ability. His "genius," as Story summed it up, was "vigorous and powerful, less rapid than discriminating, and less vivid than uniform in its light. He examines the intricacies of a subject with calm and persevering circumspection, and unravels the mysteries with irresistible acuteness." The same man Story ranked with David Hume in terms of "subtle logic" also had the plainest of manners and an "unaffected modesty," which "diffused itself through all his actions." His language was "chaste" and plain, his conversation sometimes hesitant and "drawling," and

17. For a detailed analysis of Marshall's opinions as compared to the other justices in various periods, see Seddig, "John Marshall and the Origins of Supreme Court Leadership."

his laugh "too hearty for an intriguer." His "good temper and unwearied patience," said Story, "are equally agreeable on the bench and in the study." What Jefferson and other of Marshall's detractors called manipulation and personal aggrandizement, Story saw as the unpretentious genius of a natural-born leader, who was perfectly at home in his life's work.[18]

Essential to the Court's productivity was Marshall's sensitivity to the unique abilities and special expertise of his colleagues. At this time, Supreme Court justices rode circuit and were expected to be experts in the kind of law that went with their circuits. Thus were William Johnson and Marshall, whose circuits embraced the southern states, experts in real property law and the law of slavery, among other things. Thomas Todd (1807–1826), whose circuit included Kentucky, was especially versed in the intricate and hotly contested land law of that state. Bushrod Washington, who sat with district judge Joseph Hopkinson in Pennsylvania, had to be knowledgeable in commercial and maritime law. Henry Brockholst Livingston and, after him, Smith Thompson, both from New York, specialized in various aspects of commercial-maritime law as befit their circuit. Story, from the New England circuit, was appointed by Madison in 1811, over the protest of Jefferson, in large part because he had established himself as his section's leading authority on maritime and commercial matters.[19]

Regional appointments to the Court, mirroring the regional nature of American jurisprudence, made the Court a remarkably representative institution and, ironically, a national one as well. The Court's deliberations were also more cacophonous than the individual personalities of the justices alone would have made them. But disparate talents, strong personalities, and regional law made collective decision making not only essential but unavoidable. Evidence suggests, and Marshall testified to the fact, that collective deliberation, already explicit in the circuit court crisis of 1802, quickly became the Court's modus operandi. Several justices, including Marshall, also shared information about their circuit decisions in search of uniformity. But it was, as Story suggested, mainly Marshall as chief justice who inspired cooperation, if not unanimity.

18. Story to Samuel P. P. Fay, 25 February 1808, in *Life and Letters of Joseph Story . . .* , ed. W. W. Story (London, England, 1851), 1: 166–67.

19. White's *Marshall Court*, chs. 4 and 5, contains excellent biographical sketches of the leading lawyers who practiced before the Marshall Court after 1815 and also the justices who sat with Marshall. Also see R. Kent Newmyer, "Justice Joseph Story on Circuit and a Neglected Phase of American Legal History," *American Journal of Legal History* 14 (April 1970): 112–35; and Mary K. Tachau, *Federal Courts in the Early Republic: Kentucky, 1789–1816* (Princeton, N.J., 1978).

Confident in his own abilities, and humble about them, he could draw out, and on, his colleagues. Joseph Story, the resident scholar on matters of admiralty, maritime law, commercial law, and most everything else was a case in point. Marshall's flattering inquiries to his young colleague not only harnessed Story's genius to the collective work of the Court but also deepened his affection for the chief justice. Intellectually, the Marshall-Story axis was the key to the dynamics of the Marshall Court. Not surprisingly, it was Story more than anyone who perpetuated the remembrance of Marshall's greatness.[20]

Personality differences aside, collegiality, mutual consultation and respect, along with a shared sense of common purpose, characterized the Marshall Court during its glory days. In an age that still looked to the Revolution for legitimation, it helped immensely that the Court's leader was intimately connected with that defining moment—as a combat veteran, as a friend and biographer of Washington, and as a ratifier of the Constitution he was called on to interpret. Sharing the Revolutionary moment did not, of course, mean that the justices agreed precisely on its meaning, but there was a generational dimension to Marshall's success as leader of the Court. Johnson, whose father was an active patriot, shared the republican tradition with Marshall, along with a strong preference for congressional power. Bushrod Washington, Marshall's oldest friend on the Court, was a soldier of the Revolution and a member of the Virginia ratifying convention; like Marshall, he was there at the creation. Washington was not afraid to disagree with his chief and did so on a number of occasions, but Marshall could count on him as a stalwart soldier in the ongoing campaign to secure the Revolution. Young Story, too, was brought up to cherish the memory of the Revolution and that of his father, who served as a physician in George Washington's army. Indeed, Marshall was to Story what George Washington was to Marshall and Bushrod Washington. These three were united in a vision of the Court as the keeper of the nationalist flame. It was a vision they shared with the American people, at least until the Court's time of troubles.[21]

General support for the Court, along with the Court's internal unity, disappeared with remarkable suddenness in the years after 1823. Fortunately, however, its operating procedures and its habits of harmony, and the recognition

20. The working life of the Marshall Court is treated fully and authoritatively in Haskins and Johnson, *Foundations of Power*, 74–106, and White, *Marshall Court*, 157–200.

21. R. Kent Newmyer, *Supreme Court Justice Joseph Story: Statesman of the Old Republic* (Chapel Hill, N.C., 1985), especially ch. 3.

of Marshall as the first among equals, were solidly in place. Working procedures and assumptions based on three decades of experience, dating back to the 1790s, allowed the chief justice and his colleagues a measure of maneuverability in fending off disaster in the 1820s. Basic to all else was the assumption, after *Marbury,* that the Court was first and foremost a legal institution whose procedures set it apart from and above the political branches. As a corollary to that rule, the painful lesson driven home by the Chase impeachment, was the need for justices to avoid personal involvement in the world of politics. Marshall was particularly wary. As an active participant in Washington City's social life, he did, as a matter of course, follow political developments, especially those that concerned the Court. His Republican enemies accused him of being a closet Hamiltonian, and some of his Federalist friends even floated his name as a possible presidential candidate for that party in the election of 1812. But neither insult nor blandishment called him out of retirement, though he did reluctantly serve as a delegate to the Virginia convention in 1829, where party politics were not at issue. He also voted for John Quincy Adams in 1828, which was a vote against Jackson. That the public attention given that vote, which he was entitled to as a private citizen, should have distressed him so much only underscores his disengagement from politics. Given his conviction on the matter, one can also understand his distress on learning that Smith Thompson and John McLean, his new colleagues, had not given up their presidential ambitions. For Marshall, it was further evidence that the Court was changing and that his view of republican judging might even be subverted by the justices themselves. As it turned out, Thompson and McLean were the least of his problems.[22]

Even though Marshall had little control over the political activities of his colleagues, except by way of example, there were means at hand by which the Court could minimize its vulnerability to political attack. One such means was control over its own docket and with this, the timing of its decisions. There was of course nothing approaching modern certiorari jurisdiction (which came in 1925), which allows the Court almost total control over the cases it decides. In contrast, most of the cases heard by the Marshall Court came under obligatory jurisdiction, that is to say, they were authorized by either statutory or constitutional mandate. The Court did, however, have two ways of maneuvering

---

22. Marshall expresses chagrin concerning the article about his vote in the *Marylander* in his letter to John H. Pleasants, 29 March 1828, PJM, typescript. For his doubts about McLean, whom he came to respect, see Marshall to Story, 15 October 1830, PJM, typescript.

within this rather stringent formulaic system. One was a pro forma division between the Supreme Court justice on circuit and the federal district judge with whom he sat. An agreed-upon division automatically sent the case forward, thus permitting the justices en banc to control the timing of their decision and at the same time avoid the limited scope of a circuit ruling, which was law only for the circuit in which it was decided. An example of this strategy came in the Dartmouth College case when Story divided pro forma with the district judge in order to bring a broader case before the Court should the first one go against the old college. Marshall, as noted above, also massaged the docket in *Martin v. Hunter's Lessee* by personally drawing up and forwarding the writ of error, even though he later recused himself from the case. In cases such as *Fletcher v. Peck* and possibly even *McCulloch v. Maryland,* the justices also agreed to hear cases that were collusive in nature and thus technically in violation of the case-controversy requirement of Article 3, Section 2, clause 1. In addition, the Court could, and after *Green v. Biddle* in 1823 did, refuse to decide constitutional cases if it was unable to muster a majority of the justices. Such informal rules could not relieve the Court of its duty to decide, but the latitude they allowed did permit it to maximize its decision-making authority—and avoid or postpone decisions that divided the Court or were certain to invite resistance and possibly congressional recrimination. Finally, and most important, the justices had considerable control over the doctrinal scope of their decisions—whether they were decided on broad constitutional grounds, as in *McCulloch;* whether they avoided bright line decisions, as when Marshall avoided ruling on the exclusivist power of Congress in *Gibbons;* or whether they maneuvered within precedent to avoid unworkable results, as with Marshall's refusal to apply the full force of *Gibbons* in *Willson v. The Black-bird Creek Marsh Co.* in 1829. As the Court's chief spokesman in constitutional cases, Marshall's influence in this regard was preeminent.[23]

Marshall's ability to mobilize the majority and to speak for it, even when the justices composing it were not in perfect accord, was the hallmark of his chief justiceship. And it was this authority that came increasingly under assault as a new generation of justices appeared on the scene in the 1820s and as veterans such as William Johnson reasserted themselves. The outward sign of inward change was death of Livingston in 1823 and the appointment in his place

23. For Marshall's questionable profession ethics in drafting the writ in *Martin v. Hunter's Lessee,* see White, *Marshall Court,* 167–68. For Story in *Dartmouth College,* see Newmyer, *Justice Joseph Story,* 129–31.

of Smith Thompson of New York, the first new member of the Court since 1811. Thompson was not a states' rights jurist compared to later Jacksonian appointees, but he was no knee-jerk nationalist either, and his assumption of judicial duties was hampered further by his political ambition. Much more disruptive of the Court's unity and Marshall's authority was the emergence of William Johnson as "the great dissenter." Johnson had been appointed by Jefferson in 1804 with the hope that he would dilute Marshall's nationalism and check his authority. Given Johnson's acerbic personality and general crustiness, there was reason to think he might do just that. The son of a Rhode Island blacksmith, he moved to South Carolina before the Revolution, attended Princeton, where he was an honors student, and then returned to Charleston to study law with Marshall's friend C. C. Pinckney. Thanks to a provident marriage and his own ability and ambition, Johnson quickly attained full standing in South Carolina's slaveholding elite, which may explain his defection from Federalism to the party of Jefferson. At the time of his appointment, he was a justice on the South Carolina Constitutional Court, with a reputation for independence. That quality made him a bit of a loose cannon on the early Marshall Court. On one hand, and much to Jefferson's consternation, he was a strong advocate of implied powers, which he was willing to extend even to federal internal improvements. He also upheld congressional power over commerce, even when the issue of slavery was involved—as it was in his circuit court decision in *Elkison v. Deliesseline,* which invalidated South Carolina's law requiring that Negro seamen on vessels docked at Charleston be imprisoned on grounds of public safety. Consistent with his concern for individual liberties, he was also highly suspicious of executive power, even when that power was wielded by Republican presidents. On the other hand, and more to Jefferson's liking, he was more receptive to state legislative activism than either Marshall or Story. Most important and comporting with his general faith in legislative government on both the state and national level, Johnson was critical of Marshall's expansive definition of judicial authority. It was mainly on this point that Jefferson persuaded him to speak out against Marshall's "dominance" of the Court.[24]

If Johnson was looking for an excuse to speak out, it came with Jefferson's letter of October 27, 1822, which prompted a twenty-one-page reply on December 10. Jefferson complained, as he had in earlier letters, later ones, too,

24. Johnson's career on the Marshall Court is analyzed in Morgan, *Justice William Johnson.* *Elkison v. Deliesseline,* 8 Fed. Cas. 493 (No. 4,366) (C.C.D.S.C.).

about the dangers of excessive judicial nationalism, but it was mainly his biting attack on Marshall's leadership that resonated with Johnson. To counter Marshall, and silently to subvert the Court's interpretive authority, Jefferson urged Johnson to reintroduce the practice of seriatim opinions—which practice, incidentally, the Virginia Court of Appeals under the leadership of Spencer Roane had just abandoned. What bothered Jefferson, what, he said, "has long weighed on my mind," was "the habitual mode of making up and delivering the opinions of the supreme court of the US." The practice of a single majority opinion written by one justice—John Marshall, that is to say—Jefferson declared, obscured the real views of the justices: "For nobody knows what opinion any individual member gave in any case, nor even that he who delivers the opinion, concurred in it himself. Be the opinion therefore ever so impeachable, having been done in the dark it can be proved on no one." Whether impeachable or not, he said, "the practise is certainly convenient for the lazy, the modest & the incompetent." Jefferson, with *Marbury* on his mind and possibly *Batture* as well, also blasted Marshall "for travelling out of his case to prescribe what the law would be in a moot case not before the court."[25]

Jefferson's letter is interesting in that it confirms what Marshall himself admitted, namely, that the Marshall Court operated collectively. But it also pointed to the fact that the chief justice was the guiding spirit of its collectivity. In either case, Johnson now took up the challenge, announcing in his concurrence in *Gibbons v. Ogden* that he conceived it his public duty "to maintain my opinions in my own way." As his biographer noted, from 1823 until his death in 1834, Johnson was responsible for nine out of eleven of the concurrences delivered and eighteen of the forty-two dissenting opinions. He did not change his mind on broad congressional power in these final years, and when his own state of South Carolina implemented nullification, he spoke out courageously against it as a "silly and wicked delusion." He did, however, develop a more tolerant attitude toward state economic regulation, even when it resulted, as it did in *Ogden v. Saunders,* in a more restrictive interpretation of the Contract Clause. In the final analysis, however, his independence impacted less on doctrine than it did on the internal operation of the Court. Johnson was one of the first to abandon the practice of living together and, more important,

---

25. For Jefferson's mobilization of Johnson against Marshall, see generally Morgan, *Justice William Johnson,* ch. 9; Jefferson to Johnson, 27 October 1822, in *The Works of Thomas Jefferson,* ed. Paul L. Ford (New York, 1904–1905), 12: 246–52; Jefferson to Johnson, 12 June 1823, ibid., 256, for the traveling outside the record quote.

as a veteran justice in dissent, he made the practice of living apart increasingly *de rigeur* for the new appointees, who had their own reasons for paring Marshall's nationalism.[26]

The five new justices who made their appearance in the last twelve years of Marshall's tenure differed widely in ability and constitutional persuasion. Smith Thompson, who replaced Livingston in 1823, was very politically minded and had a sizeable streak of independence and a penchant for moderate states' rights constitutional doctrine. Robert Trimble of Kentucky replaced Thomas Todd in 1826, served only two years before his death, and had almost no impact except to further disrupt the stability of the Court by his untimely death. John McLean from Ohio was more influential. Although Jackson wanted to shift the Court away from Marshall's nationalism, he apparently appointed McLean less for his constitutional ideology than from the desire to remove him as postmaster general, where he refused to implement the new president's policy of appointments. Having served six years on the Ohio Supreme Court, McLean might have been expected to be sympathetic to state rights. He turned out instead to be a moderate nationalist, who after Marshall's death increasingly allied himself with Story. On the other hand, Henry Baldwin from Pennsylvania, appointed by Jackson in 1830 to replace Bushrod Washington, did disrupt the Court, not only by virtue of his states' rights constitutionalism but because of the onset of mental instability. For both reasons, Baldwin became a chronic dissenter and Marshall's most vocal critic among the justices. His presence further disrupted the Court's communal living arrangements and added to its institutional inefficiency.[27]

As a sitting chief justice, Marshall was obliged to keep this increasingly discordant group on task. Deciding the cases on the docket in a timely fashion was difficult enough, but when the justices were ideologically divided and personally contentious it was a trial and a tribulation. More challenging still was the preservation of the principles of constitutional nationalism set forth in the previous decisions of the Court. In this effort, Marshall counted heavily on

26. *Gibbons v. Ogden,* 9 Wheaton 223. Morgan sums up Johnson's opinions succinctly in "William Johnson," in *The Justices of the United States Supreme Court, 1789–1969: Their Lives and Major Opinions,* eds. Leon Friedman and Fred L. Israel (New York, 1969), 1: 367. For Johnson on nullification, ibid., 371.

27. Brief essays on Marshall's colleagues are found in Friedman and Israel, *Justices of the Supreme Court,* vol. 1; also see White's scholarly vignettes in his *Marshall Court,* ch. 5. On Smith Thompson, see Donald M. Roper, *Mr. Justice Thompson and the Constitution* (New York, 1987).

Bushrod Washington and Joseph Story. Story remembered Washington as a "learned judge," who was "wise, impartial, and honest," and, paradoxically, as "a good old-fashioned federalist, of the school of the days of Washington." Bushrod Washington was Marshall's oldest and dearest friend on the Court, the only justice in the 1820s who outranked him in terms of seniority. Contrary to Jefferson, the two men did not always agree—witness Washington's disagreement with Marshall in *Huidekoper's Lessee* and, more important, in *Ogden v. Saunders*. The two men, however, were bound together by the Revolution, the shared culture of the Northern Neck, and a reverence for George Washington. It was Bushrod, as the executor of George Washington's papers, who got Marshall involved in the biography. Marshall consulted Bushrod Washington regarding his decision to answer Roane and relied on him to get his essays into print. Like Marshall, he was there at the creation of the Constitution "and steadily and uniformly supported it through every change in its fortunes." In the 1820s, with the Court under siege, he was there for the chief justice.[28]

So was Story; indeed, the working friendship of Marshall and Story was a central feature of the Court during its golden age and in the time of troubles that followed. Story appreciated Marshall almost to the point of idolatry. But the scholarly New Englander also presented a problem for Marshall in terms of the Court's unity. Story was exceedingly generous, gregarious to a fault, and easy to live with. But he was also exceedingly ambitious and had the legal learning to match, which he did not always carry modestly. His inclination was to push his nationalist doctrines to extremes and back them up with copious authorities. Marshall and Story did not always agree either—witness the latter's single-minded effort to expand the federal criminal common-law jurisdiction and his sharp disagreement with Marshall over neutral rights and national interest in *The Nereide*. They parted company, too, in cases involving the international slave trade. Still, Story's unyielding nationalism, his scholarship, and his friendship were things Marshall could count on. While it was not true, as rumor had it, that Marshall made decisions and then turned to Story for authorities to back them up, it was true that he leaned on his younger colleague for advice and willingly followed his lead in areas such as admiralty and private corporation law. If Story's nationalism was occasionally ahead of Mar-

28. Story, "Sketch of the Character of Bushrod Washington . . . ," in *The Miscellaneous Writings of Joseph Story,* ed. William W. Story (Boston, 1852), 809–11.

shall's, it worked to the latter's advantage to have a point man on the divided Court. After the death of Bushrod Washington in 1829, Story became Marshall's chief confidant and most effective ally.[29]

In his effort to fend off external enemies and get the work out the door, Marshall had no choice but to continue the tradition of collective decision making—to facilitate compromise when it was possible and minimize personal rancor when it wasn't. As chief justice, only he could do some things, as for example defend the Court's decision, and his opinion, in *McCulloch*. He could also call into play the discretionary authority the rules of the Court and his reputation among his colleagues allowed. A case in point was the decision, in response to Henry Clay's request, to reargue the controversial Kentucky land case of *Green v. Biddle*. Marshall no doubt took the lead as a result of that case in persuading his colleagues to implement the majority rule in constitutional decisions, a decision that helped defuse the anti-Court sentiment. When implemented in the years after 1831, that rule resulted in the postponement of decisions in the great constitutional disputes over contracts, commerce, and corporations until the first term of the Taney Court.[30]

Assigning opinions, which fell to the chief justice when he was in the majority, also opened up the possibility of maximizing the impact of decisions—or minimizing damage. Marshall, it should be noted, did not originate the practice of opinions being delivered by the chief justice, but he clearly recognized the institutional advantages of the practice. Even after the onset of internal division on the Court in 1823, he continued to speak for the majority in the most important and controversial cases. This was true in *Gibbons*, where the Court bucked the tide by expanding constitutional nationalism; it was also true in cases such as *Willson v. Black-bird Creek*, *Providence Bank v. Billings* (1830), and *Barron v. Mayor of Baltimore* (1833), where it reined in its earlier nationalism. Even when Marshall did not speak for the Court, there is strong circumstantial evidence he influenced the outcome by his assignment of the justice

29. See Newmyer, *Justice Joseph Story* on the Marshall-Story relationship. Story's "Life, Character, and Services of Chief Justice Marshall" in *Miscellaneous Writings*, 639–97, though biased, is full of insights into Marshall the man and the judge. The Marshall-Story letters are conveniently reprinted in *The Proceedings of the Massachusetts Historical Society*, 2d ser., vol. 14.

30. White unravels the internal disputes on the Court in *Green v. Biddle* in his *Marshall Court*, 642–48. Efforts to reform the Court, including the amendment of Senator Johnson of Kentucky requiring a majority of seven in decisions involving the validity of state and congressional acts, are discussed in Charles Warren, *The Supreme Court in United States History*, new and rev. ed. (Boston, 1926), 1: ch. 17.

who would write for the Court. Thus, when he recused himself in the great case of *Martin v. Hunter's Lessee*, he assigned the case to Story, of whose opinion he heartily approved (perhaps because it was even more aggressively nationalist than his own). Story's separate concurrence in *Dartmouth College*, was so complementary to Marshall's that one might reasonably infer they collaborated on the matter. When the Court itself was against the wall and needed to speak forcefully, it was Marshall who generally wrote for the majority. And when the majority had a point to make to the dissenters and needed some punch, as in *Craig v. Missouri* (1830), it was Marshall who delivered. His boldest use of his authority as chief justice came in the Cherokee Indian cases, where he as much as guaranteed the Court's jurisdiction (while denying the same), signaled what its response might be when it heard the case, encouraged the dissents of Thompson and Story in order to get the issues on the table, and then wrote the opinion for the majority that addressed them.[31]

That Marshall continued to speak for an increasingly divided Court strongly suggests that he was responsible for working out compromises among the justices that preserved at least a semblance of unity, as well as the bedrock principles of constitutional nationalism previously established. Adjusting old law to new circumstances without abandoning principle, however, became progressively more difficult with changing personnel. Even at the peak of the Court's unity, it was no easy matter—witness the case of *Sturges v. Crowninshield*. There were no dissenting opinions in that case, and Marshall spoke for the Court in ruling that a New York law that altered a contract retrospectively violated the Contract Clause of the Constitution. Only in 1827, when the Court divided bitterly over the same issue, did it become clear that it also had been divided in 1819. What Marshall had done—and it was one of the options open to him as leader of the Court—was to settle the case but not the law. When he had to compromise his own doctrinal principles to maintain unity, as he did in *Sturges,* he did it so as not to contradict them or forestall further exposition of them when the occasion presented itself.[32]

Perhaps the most telling example of Marshall's dexterity in fusing various doctrinal differences into a single workable decision for the Court was *Gibbons v. Ogden.* His opinion for the Court spoke decisively and eloquently

31. For the origin of the practice of chief justices speaking for the majority, see ibid., 654 n. 1. Story's opinion is discussed in Newmyer, *Justice Joseph Story,* 106–14.

32. *Willson v. The Black-bird Creek Marsh Co.,* 2 Peters 245; *Providence Bank v. Billings,* 4 Peters 514; *Barron v. Mayor of Baltimore,* 7 Peters 243; *Craig v. Missouri,* 4 Peters 410.

about the need for economic unity, and he struck a decisive blow for it when he voided the New York monopoly. In light of the quotable national rhetoric in his opinion and its market-enhancing consequences, one might miss the fact that Marshall struck down the New York law not because it conflicted with the Commerce Clause of the Constitution, which he defined in famously broad terms, but because it conflicted with the Federal Licensing Act of 1787. As a result, the great question of whether the Commerce Clause of the Constitution was exclusive in nature or whether it was concurrent with state authority and came into play only in cases of direct conflict between state and federal statutes was left unsettled. By not accepting the doctrine of exclusivism yet not rejecting it, Marshall brought Story, who liked exclusivism, into the same fold as Smith Thompson, who didn't. Johnson, who favored exclusive commerce powers, could not be persuaded to remain silent, but he wrote a separate concurring opinion, not a dissent. John Marshall, practical judge that he was, got his national market and considerable doctrinal maneuverability in future cases, which he found exceedingly useful in the face of growing states' rights sentiment on the Court, and off, after 1827.

In fact, one can look at the post-1827 period of Marshall's tenure as being nothing but compromise and finesse if one is generous or capitulation and retreat from doctrinal purity altogether if one follows the ungenerous logic of William Crosskey. At first glance, this appears to be true in regard both to his Commerce Clause opinions and those on the Contract Clause. In the Commerce Clause cases, Marshall seems to be all over the place, and nowhere in particular. In *Brown v. Maryland* (1827), for example, he was boldly creative in expanding, or possibly finessing, *Gibbons,* holding that the Commerce Clause prohibited states from taxing interstate goods as long as they remained in the original package, but permitted state taxation at the retail level. Witness his equally dextrous rendition of the Commerce Clause in *Willson v. Black-bird Creek,* in which a state-authorized bridge that obstructed a tidal river was held *not* to interfere with interstate commerce, though it might without much trouble have been found to do so under the *Gibbons* ruling. Common sense and practical compromise, not doctrinal purity, was the order of the day, from both an institutional and a political point of view.[33]

Doctrinal maneuvering to quell states' rights opposition on and off the

---

33. William Crosskey, *Politics and the Constitution in the History of the United States,* 2 vols. (Chicago, 1953). In ch. 13 of vol. 2 of this massive work, Crosskey sets forth his unitary view of national power in the Constitution, the one from which Marshall allegedly departed.

Court seemed to be the pattern in the Contract Clause cases as well during this period. In *Providence Bank v. Billings,* the question concerned whether the Providence Bank was exempt from a state tax levied on the bank's real assets on the ground that the right to tax was not specifically mentioned in its charter. Lawyers for the bank presented arguments that were dear to Marshall and that in fact were drawn from his opinions. Marshall's opinion in this case reaffirmed *McCulloch*—that the power to tax could destroy—but he then did what he refused to do in *McCulloch,* which was to give the benefit of the doubt to the state legislature in cases where contractual language was ambiguous. In words that were soon to be quoted with approval by a Jacksonian majority and a Jacksonian chief justice, Marshall proclaimed that "the taxing power is of vital importance, that it is essential to the existence of government." While states might relinquish that power, he declared, it can never be assumed they have done so in the absence of specific language. It was, he said, a matter of community rights: If the "whole community," that is, the people of a state, "is interested in retaining it undiminished, that community has a right to insist that its abandonment ought not to be presumed in a case in which the deliberate purpose of the State to abandon it does not appear." The power to tax may imply the power to destroy, he said, but it also "resides in government as a part of itself, and need not be reserved when property of any description, or the right to use it in any manner, is granted to individuals or corporate bodies. However absolute the right of an individual may be, it is still in the nature of that right that it may bear a portion of the public burdens, and that portion must be determined by the legislature. This vital power may be abused; but the constitution of the United States was not intended to furnish the corrective for every abuse of power which may be committed by state governments."[34]

Though not ordinarily thought to be one of Marshall's "great" opinions, *Providence Bank* stands as a revealing example of the way he dealt with doctrinal adjustment and internecine disputes among the brethren. Here, Marshall spoke for a unanimous Court that was anything but unanimous about states' rights and the Contract Clause. To get everyone aboard, while accommodating his own doctrinal priorities, was no easy job. First he distinguished all of his own opinions cited by counsel to void the tax, refusing to apply any of them to the case at hand. Where he had previously spoken consistently about the sacred nature of individual property rights, he now spoke of the rights of community, indeed, of states. Where in *McCulloch* he had reasoned by implica-

---

34. *Providence Bank v. Billings,* 4 Peters 561, 563.

tion—both in finding congressional authority to charter the Bank of the United States, then in prohibiting the state from taxing it—he now not only refused to read property rights into the bank's charter by implication but made a principle of his refusal to do so. Whereas in previous opinions he refused to give the benefit of the doubt to state legislatures, he now acknowledged legislative power in the crucial realm of taxation "to be an original principle, which has its foundation in society itself." To concede rhetorically, as he did, that the Constitution "was not intended to furnish the corrective for every abuse of power which may be committed by the state governments" was also a most uncharacteristic note to sound. One can readily see why the *National Gazette,* of March 13, 1830, referred to his opinion approvingly as "opportune" and why the states' rights Court of Roger Taney made it the leading precedent of its new Contract Clause jurisprudence, as announced in the Charles River Bridge case in 1837. According to the calculations of one careful scholar, Marshall appears to have agreed generally with that pro-state, pro-legislative position when the bridge case was first argued in 1831. Indeed, looking collectively at the late Marshall Court's decisions—the meandering course of the Commerce Clause decisions, the shift in some Contract Clause cases (*Ogden v. Saunders, Providence Bank*), the fragile majority in others (*Craig*), and the retreat under fire in cases such as *Jackson v. Lamphire* (1830) and *Beaty v. Lessee of Knowler* (1830)—it seems clear that the shift in constitutional law usually associated with the Taney Court in 1837 really began in the final years of Marshall's tenure and to some extent with his compliance.[35]

Indeed, it might be argued, and was in fact argued at length by William Crosskey, that Marshall, rather than being the nationalizing tyrant Jefferson accused him of being, was really a supremely political judge—so political, said Crosskey, that he backed off not only from his own decisions but from the unitary nationalism of the Framers as well. Crosskey's conclusion that Marshall's "Chief Justiceship was a period of constitutional decay" has been discredited, but his massive scholarship has its uses. Crosskey was wrong to assume that the Framers had established a unitary nationalist state, but he was correct when he concluded that Marshall was not a consolidationist. This is precisely what Marshall himself said in his argument with Roane. To put the matter

---

35. *National Gazette,* 13 March 1830, quoted in Warren, *Supreme Court,* 1: 715. *Jackson v. Lamphire,* 3 Peters 280; *Beaty v. Lessee of Knowler,* 4 Peters 152; *U.S. v. Corredondo,* 6 Peters 691; See Stanley I. Kutler, *Privilege and Creative Destruction: The Charles River Bridge Case* (Philadelphia, 1971), app., for an analysis of Marshall's position on the Charles River Bridge case.

somewhat differently, Marshall's success in leading the Court in its time of troubles was due not only to his astute leadership but also to the fact that his constitutional jurisprudence made adjustment possible. Tactics and doctrine merged so that he did not have to abandon the principles set forth in the nationalist period of his tenure to accommodate the states' rights challenges of his final years. There were some cases in which compromise was not possible, where the justices split sharply, as in *Craig,* and hopelessly, as they did in the great constitutional cases that were held over until 1837. But while Marshall lived, the badly divided Court did adjust old law to the new age without a permanent surrender of principles. Despite the bold improvisation in *Brown v. Maryland* and the ad hoc application in *Willson,* the core nationalism of *Gibbons* remained intact. Neither did *Providence Bank* obliterate the doctrine of implied powers.[36]

What the Marshall Court seems to have done in its final years, then, is what the Taney Court institutionalized in *Cooley v. Board of Wardens:* It applied and adjusted doctrine case by case and avoided expansive and controversial doctrinal innovation. This was not glorious stuff. *Providence Bank* doesn't measure up to *Dartmouth College; Brown v. Maryland* and *Willson v. Blackbird Creek* pale beside *Gibbons. McCulloch* was already on the shelf, and remained there for another half century. By bending a little, Marshall preserved a lot. Scholars like Crosskey, who wanted to tidy up history, and working lawyers, who need to do so, might be frustrated by the flexibility of the Marshall Court's jurisprudence during this period. But it was flexibility, along with tactical savvy, that permitted Marshall to salvage so much of his constitutional nationalism in an age hostile to it. It's an unprovable counterfactual statement to say that Marshall's timely strategic retreat foiled his enemies, but it's a good guess that it did. At any rate, they were foiled. Unlike so many other conservatives of the early period who only talked conservative principles, John Marshall actually secured them institutionally. Neither Washington, John Adams, nor Alexander Hamilton, nor Spencer Roane or Jefferson for that matter could claim as much. What about the Founders themselves? They probably would have been greatly pleased, since the balanced federalism Marshall called on was pretty much what they had in mind. So at least Marshall believed.[37]

36. Crosskey states his case in "John Marshall," in *Mr. Justice,* eds. Allison Dunham and Philip B. Kurland (Chicago, 1956), 3–34.

37. *Cooley v. Board of Wardens,* 12 Howard 299. On that case, see R. Kent Newmyer, *The Supreme Court under Marshall and Taney* (New York, 1968), 105–7.

Slavery and the Limits of Paternalism

Slavery has not figured prominently in most accounts of Marshall's life or his work, but he was involved in the institution in several important and revealing ways. As a small urban slaveholder in Richmond, he lived with the institution on a daily basis and, however marginally, was encompassed by its hegemonic reach. He also participated in Virginia's increasingly heated debate about the "slave problem," indirectly as a member of the Virginia constitutional convention and directly as an active member and one of twelve vice-presidents of the Virginia branch of the American Colonization Society. Domestic slavery was not a central feature of the Court's jurisprudence during Marshall's tenure, nonetheless he was involved in the administration of slave law, both at the full session of the Court and sitting at circuit in the slave states of Virginia and North Carolina. Unavoidably, his private involvement with the institution and his constitutional duty to maintain it were inseparable, at least on a human level.

The intersection between Marshall's private role and public duty locates him for better *and* worse squarely in the tradition of southern paternalism, the system of authority that defined social relationships in terms of patriarchal authority and fatherly responsibility. Paternal values infused social relationships—between husbands and wives, fathers and children, masters and servants or apprentices—and the law, which recognized and governed, thus justified, those relationships as both inevitable and beneficial. For southern masters seeking to define and justify their relationship with slaves, the paternalist tradition was perfect. For judges and lawmakers, such as Marshall, it was a tradition that helped to soften and obscure the harsh realities of the system they were oath-bound to administer. Paternalism, to put it another way, was the connecting link between the various facets of Marshall's life: the family man who looked after his wife, children, and extended family with tender solicitude; the kind and solicitous master of domestic slaves; the chief justice who was gradually, if unconsciously, assuming the role of the father of American Constitutional law; and finally, the conservative who preferred an imperfect world to the promises of radical reform.[38]

38. On patriarchy in Marshall's Virginia, see Christopher L. Doyle, "Lord, Master, and Patriot, St. George Tucker and Patriarchy in Republican Virginia, 1772–1851" (Ph.D. diss., University of Connecticut, 1997); also Bertram Wyatt-Brown, *Southern Honor: Ethics and Behavior in the Old South* (New York, 1982).

Marshall experienced slavery primarily as an urban slaveholder, which is not surprising given that he was a citizen of the largest slaveholding state in the South (Virginia had roughly 400,000 slaves for most of the antebellum period) and a resident of the largest slaveholding city in the state, where 68 to 76 percent of all residents were slaveholders and where 38.6 percent of the total population were slaves. The sparse records indicate that Marshall's household slaves numbered 11 or 12 throughout the course of his life. The modest dwellings of these slaves, visible in some of the old photographs of the Marshall residence, are nowhere in evidence now. But the men and women who lived there in his day cleaned the house, cooked the meals, and attended the sumptuous table for which the Marshalls were well known in Richmond. Given Polly's long illness and Marshall's frequent absences, trusted house slaves no doubt played an important part in the rearing and care of the children. All evidence shows that Marshall treated them kindly in return. To William W. Gray, he recounted how, when "a female slave of my family was affected . . . with a swollen and ulcerated leg . . . ," he "called in the aid of eminent physicians, who attended her without at all improving her situation." On another occasion, when he found himself trouserless on circuit in North Carolina, he did administer "a little scolding" to his manservant Peter, who forgot to pack the essential item. But the butt of his humor, as Marshall recounted the episode to Polly, was not Peter but himself. That he had a close bond with "my faithful servant Robin" is strongly suggested by the fact that Marshall willed Robin the choice of freedom "if he chuses to conform to the laws on that subject." This may not appear to have been much of a choice, since the Virginia slave statute of 1806 required manumitted slaves to leave the state within twelve months of manumission or be re-enslaved. As it turned out, Robin chose to remain the slave of Marshall's daughter Mary, but Marshall treated him as a rational man capable of deciding his own fate. As the leading scholar on American slave law noted, "Other than those who freed slaves, testators who allowed slaves the choice of masters came the closest to recognizing their humanity in that they acknowledged a will, however constrained, in the slave."[39]

39. I have relied on Marianne Buroff Sheldon, "Black-White Relations in Richmond, Virginia, 1782–1820," *Journal of Southern History* 45 (February 1979): 27–44, especially 27–29. For urban slavery in general, see Richard C. Wade, *Slavery in the Cities: The South, 1820–1860* (New York, 1964). Marshall to William W. Gray, 30 May 1831, PJM, typescript. On the trouser episode, see Marshall to Mary W. Marshall, 2 January 1803, PJM, 6: 145–46. On the manumission in Marshall's will of 9 April 1832, see PJM, typescript. Thomas D. Morris comments on the significance of willing slaves the choice of freedom in his *Southern Slavery and the Law, 1619–1860* (Chapel Hill, N.C., 1996), 100.

As an urban slaveholder in a city known for its liberal treatment of slaves, Marshall had the moral luxury of not participating directly in the dehumanizing and often brutal aspects of plantation slavery. There is no hint that he whipped his slaves to keep order, as did Thomas Jefferson; nor did financial exigency force him to break up slave families by selling them into the Deep South, as was the case with many Virginians, including Bushrod Washington. There is, however, some evidence Marshall was involved at least indirectly in plantation slavery. For example, he advised his son James, regarding the purchase of slaves, that those "intended to be reserved for the family should be sold with the others and purchased in my name." In the same will that gave Robin Spurlock the choice of freedom, Marshall mentioned that he had already given his son Edward the slaves that had worked his, Edward's, plantation—which suggests he may have done the same with his other sons who employed slaves to work their land. Even his eldest son, Thomas, who had the courage to speak out against forced exportation of slaves in the Virginia legislative debates in 1831 and 1832, owned 45 slaves. Marshall also willed his Richmond slaves, with the exception of Robin Spurlock and his "Cooke Henry," to his daughter Mary; additionally, "a tract of land on Chickahominy, with all the slaves[,] stock, and plantation utensils, thereon" went to his nephew.[40]

Unfortunately, what little we know about Marshall's personal involvement in slavery tells us little about his view of the institution as a whole. Significantly, he was not among those Virginians who condemned it on moral grounds. Even during the heyday of post-Revolutionary liberalism in Virginia, when reform talk was plentiful and when manumission was at its peak, he showed little interest in the subject. He wrote no "dissertations" condemning slavery, as did St. George Tucker in 1796. Unlike Jefferson, he did not search for explanations or justifications. Marshall's concern, generalizing from his actions during this early period, was about the stability of society, not the dehumanization of enslaved Africans. As a judge on the Richmond Court of Hustings during the 1780s with jurisdiction over urban African Americans, slave and free, he was directly involved in the problem of maintaining social order. Like other Virginians, he was alerted to the dangers of slave rebellion by

40. See Marshall to James K. Marshall, 19 May 1834, PJM, typescript; Marshall's last will and testament, PJM, typescript. Thomas Marshall's role in the slavery debates as well as his slaveholding is discussed in Alison Goodyear Freehling, *Drift toward Dissolution: The Virginia Slavery Debate of 1831–1832* (Baton Rouge, 1982), 123, and table for ch. 5 in app.

the successful slave uprising in Santo Domingo in 1791. As an officer in the state militia and commander of the Richmond militia unit, he was alerted about possible slave uprisings, such as those rumored to be taking place in Northhampton and Charles City Counties in 1792. Like other Virginians, he was concerned about the large number of arsons in the 1790s that were attributed to slaves. One such act came close to home when William, a thirteen-year-old house servant recently purchased by Marshall's brother-in-law Rawleigh Colston, set fire to the plantation causing some £2,000 damage. Colston wrote Marshall a long letter about the episode, noting several others of a similar nature in the vicinity. The court condemned the boy to death, but Colston was upset that his lawyer had recommended clemency. He need not have worried since the execution was quickly carried out. Whether Marshall intervened on the side of retributive justice as Colston wanted, is unknown. What is known is that Marshall was part of the Richmond public safety committee formed to guarantee social order and allay public fears after the abortive rebellion led by the slave Gabriel in 1800.[41]

Marshall never put together his thoughts on the slavery issue as he experienced it in the 1790s. The closest he came was a brief comment about the bloody slave rebellion in Santo Domingo in 1791, which appeared in volume 5 of his biography of Washington, written well after the brutal repression of Gabriel's Rebellion. The passage deserves to be quoted at length for what it says about Marshall's views on race and race relations, about French philosophy, and about his conservative approach to social reform:

Early and bitter fruits of that malignant philosophy, which, disregarding the actual state of the world, and estimating at nothing the miseries of a vast portion of the human race, can coolly and deliberately pursue, through oceans of blood, abstract systems for the attainment of some fancied untried good, were gathered in the French West Indies. Instead

41. For slave rebellions in eighteenth-century Virginia, see Gerald W. Mullin, *Flight and Rebellion: Slave Resistance in Eighteenth-Century Virginia* (New York, 1972); on Gabriel's Rebellion, Douglas R. Egerton, *Gabriel's Rebellion: The Virginia Slave Conspiracies of 1800 and 1802* (Chapel Hill, N.C., 1993). St. George Tucker's "dissertation" and his hypocrisy on the issue of slavery is treated in Doyle, "Lord, Master, and Patriot," ch. 3. See Rawleigh Colston to Marshall, 5 August 1796, PJM, 3: 36–38. On this episode, also see Philip J. Schwarz, *Twice Condemned: Slaves and the Criminal Law of Virginia, 1705–1865* (Baton Rouge, 1988), 210–11. On Marshall and the security measures taken in Richmond, see James Wood to Marshall, 23 August 1793, PJM, 2: 200.

of proceeding in the correction of any abuses which might exist, by those slow and cautious steps which gradually introduce reform without ruin, which may prepare and fit society for that better state of things designed for it, and which, by not attempting impossibilities, may enlarge the circle of happiness, the revolutionists of France formed the mad and wicked project of spreading their doctrines of equality among persons, between whom distinctions and prejudices exist to be subdued only by the grave. The rage excited by the pursuit of this visionary and baneful theory, after many threatening symptoms, burst forth on the 23d day of August 1791, with a fury alike destructive and general.[42]

Judging from this telling passage, Marshall believed that at least some of the evils of slavery might be ameliorated by conservative reforms. He neither condemned nor defended slavery itself, but simply accepted it, along with racial prejudice and social inequality, as a part of "the actual state of the world." But the state of the world was changing. "Hints of possible slave unrest" during the War of 1812 kept the issue of social control alive, and with the debate over the Missouri Compromise of 1820, the issue burst forth with new urgency. Then came the abortive Denmark Vesey Rebellion in Charleston, South Carolina, in 1822 and, most threatening of all, Nat Turner's bloody uprising in South Hampton County, Virginia, in 1831. Fears of race war concentrated attention. So did the declining economic viability of slavery in Virginia, which cast doubt on the economic future of the entire state. Virginians developed piecemeal solutions to the economic crisis. Some, especially those in the Northern Neck, diversified crops and paid new attention to scientific farming and new markets. Others solved the cash-flow problem by selling off slaves into the Deep South, where cotton had taken hold and field hands were in demand. Others raised slaves to be sold. Increasing numbers of Virginia planters rented out slaves in Richmond to work as artisans and as operatives in the new tobacco factories or the Tredegar iron works. These expedients, however, were both ineffectual and problematic. Selling slaves into the Deep South destroyed slave families and flat-out countered the paternalistic obligations many Southerners took seriously. Renting slaves out for wages was problematic, too, since it created an urban slave population that threatened white artisan labor and presented serious problems of social control, especially when rented slaves

42. John Marshall, *The Life of George Washington*, 2d ed., revised and corrected (Philadelphia, 1832), 2: 239.

mixed with the growing population of freed slaves living in urban areas. None of the palliatives solved the economic problem. Nor did they settle or even address the dilemma that haunted Virginians: whether slavery, which was inextricably connected with every aspect of their society, could coexist with the emerging liberal capitalist economy men like Marshall worked tirelessly to create. It was precisely this connection that caused Virginia agrarians to reject *McCulloch* so vehemently. As for Marshall, he may not have opposed slavery in Virginia, but he did oppose those men who defended it by recourse to radical states' rights theorizing. Increasingly it was impossible for him to remain on the sidelines.[43]

He entered the public debate, at least indirectly, by becoming a lifetime member of the American Colonization Society (ACS) and by serving as president of the Richmond and Manchester Auxiliary, the most prestigious affiliate of the national association. Exactly what this involvement meant, however, is as ambiguous as the ACS itself. Organized in 1816 with a number of southerners as charter members, its primary aim was to colonize free blacks outside the territorial boundaries of the United States, which location after considerable debate became the new African state of Liberia. From the beginning, however, there was considerable uncertainty as to whether the society favored emancipation or merely wanted to get rid of free blacks. Its organizer, the Reverend Finley of New Jersey, was motivated primarily by a Christian concern for the degraded status of freed Negroes in New Jersey, which he hoped to remedy by deportation to Africa; indeed, he saw an African state peopled by American blacks as a first step in the Christianization, and commercialization, of Africa. The national statesmen Finley assembled in Washington in 1816 to develop a constitution for the society, however, were badly divided. Some, like Finley, were Christian idealists with a strong antislavery bias, who saw the society as the opening wedge of general emancipation. Most of the southerners who attended the organizational meeting, however, were mainly interested in transporting free blacks out of the country so that domestic slavery would be more secure and racial intermixture less likely.[44]

Given its ambivalent goals, it is not surprising the society was denounced—by northern abolitionists as racist and ineffectual and by southern

43. For developments in the 1820s, consult William W. Freehling, *Prelude to Civil War: The Nullification Controversy in South Carolina, 1816–1836.* On the hiring-out practice, see Wade, *Slavery in the Cities,* especially ch. 2.

44. See P. J. Staudenraus, *The African Colonization Movement, 1816–1865* (New York, 1961), 12–35; also Early Lee Fox, *The American Colonization Society* (Baltimore, 1919), 46–50.

critics as part of an insidious campaign to destroy slavery. The South need not have feared. Almost from the beginning, the ACS was short of money and long on internal disputes about strategy and goals. While proslavery radicals and northern abolitionists both assailed it, Congress increasingly ignored it. Worst of all, blacks wisely showed little interest in trading present difficulties in the only home they knew for unknown ones in a foreign country. Tellingly, the Virginia legislature endorsed the institution, not because it would free slaves but as a means of securing the institution by facilitating the deportation of free blacks who might foment rebellion if they remained. During the long history of the ACS, only about 12,000 free blacks emigrated, which was about twice as many as were created each year by natural increase among the slave population.

Marshall never clarified his motives for joining the ACS or his general feelings about emancipation. In two long letters to the Marquis de Lafayette written in 1825 and 1827, however, he did address the questions indirectly. The Frenchman was interested in the future of emancipation in America and knowing of Marshall's membership in ACS wrote to get his view of Benjamin Lundy's *A Plan for the Gradual Abolition of Slavery in the United States, without Danger or Loss to the Citizens of the South,* published in Baltimore in 1825. Lundy, the Quaker antislavery editor of the *Universal Emancipator* in Philadelphia, was an early champion of the communitarian movement in the United States. His plan was to purchase slaves, free them, and then put them to work in collective communities, the profits from which would be used to purchase freedom for more slaves.[45]

Marshall was opposed to almost everything about Lundy's plan, starting with the assumption about the perfectibility of human nature on which it rested. As a lifelong champion of economic individualism, Marshall could not agree either with Lundy's faith in the perfecting virtues of collective enterprise, the purported advantages, as he put it to Lafayette, of "united over individual labour." Perhaps such a scheme might work, he conceded, in "small societies for a limited time" where "enthusiasm" might temporarily carry the day. But, he said, it could not "animate so large a mass as must be acted upon to effect the abolition of slavery in the United States by the labour of the slaves." The lesson of American experience, said Marshall, referring to the failure of early communal societies such as Plymouth and early Jamestown, was "that the sur-

---

45. See Marshall to Lafayette, 26 August 1825, PJM, 10: 199–201; and 2 May 1827, PJM, typescript.

est stimulus to labor is the certainty of enjoying its profits." Even more damning were the reformer's economic calculations about the profitability of
slavery, on which emancipation rested. The problem, as Marshall put it, was
Lundy's calculation of the value of slave labor itself, specifically his assumption
"that any given number of persons between nine and fifty will by the net produce of their labour replace the purchase money given for them with interest
in five years." If that were the case, Marshall calculated, then slaveholders
would be rich men all, and slavery itself would be economically viable. Neither
proposition, he concluded, was true: "The general fact is known to be that it
requires a combination of industry skill and economy in a proprietor of slaves
to accumulate even a moderate fortune in the course of a long life. In truth, the
profits of their labour, in the general, will barely support a family and rear up
the young slaves." Were Lundy's plan to be implemented in the states of Maryland and Virginia, where success would be most likely according to Lundy,
Marshall said, "the net profits of their labour would probably not liberate
them as fast as they multiply." Obviously, the problem would be infinitely
greater in the Deep South, where slavery was more profitable, thus the cost of
buying freedom greater, and where "jealousy" on the subject of abolition
would constitute "a great impediment."[46]

In a second letter to Lafayette, on May 2, 1827, Marshall followed through
with his distinction between the border states and the Deep South, holding out
the possibility that some form of limited emancipation might be possible in the
former. Clearly this was his desire. As he put it, "[I declare] without hesitation
that in Maryland, Virginia, Kentucky, and Missouri and even in Tennessee, and
North Carolina unless it be immediately on the seaboard, white labour might
be substituted for black with advantage. The positive prosperity and happiness
of these states, as well as their relative power and weight in the union, would, I
confidently believe, be promoted by this change." Marshall was also guardedly
optimistic about the newly established colony of Liberia, which he thought was
"rapidly advancing to a state of solidity and permanent prosperity which will
make it so great an object to our people of colour to migrate thither as to justify the hope that the colonization society may so be relieved from the expense
of transporting those who wish to remove to that country. They receive rich
lands which they can cultivate in safety; and the prospect of a profitable commerce is very flattering. Under these circumstances, the hope that voluntary
emigration will releive [*sic*] us from our free coloured people may, I trust be

46. Marshall to Lafayette, 26 August 1825, PJM, 10: 199–201.

indulged without the charge of being over sanguine." But he was overly sanguine. Like Robin Spurlock, African Americans, slave and free, wisely showed little interest in Liberia.[47]

Despite Marshall's guarded optimism about Liberia and his hope of limited emancipation in the border states, the questions remain of whether he really believed that emancipation in some form or other was within reach and whether his membership in the ACS signified that belief. On this subject, his conscience pulled him one way; practical reason and a knowledge of southern history the other. He appears to have believed that emancipation, if linked with the self-interest of the planter, was possible, thus limiting it to those areas where slavery was unprofitable. But even here, he had qualifications. Believing that self-liquidating schemes like Lundy's were impractical, Marshall was forced to conclude that financial incentives from the federal government were essential. As he explained to Lafayette in his letter of August 26, 1825, he was particularly intrigued with the plan of Rufus King of New York, which proposed using money from the sale of public land to finance both the emancipation of slaves and their transportation out of the country. In Marshall's opinion, this was the only plan "which promises to be in any degree adequate to its object." Even so, there were serious obstacles to its success, as Marshall admitted. The idea that federal funds would be used to compensate owners, as southern opponents pointed out, rested on a broad exercise of congressional authority under the doctrine of implied powers, which principle they violently opposed. Even if this problem could be resolved, there still remained widespread southern opposition and political hostility to any form of emancipation. As Marshall noted in 1827, "An excessive jealousy of the free states, and an extreme apprehensions of the domestic evils which might grow out of any measure having even a remote tendency to effect the object, stifles any attempt towards it." This was true, he noted, not only in the Deep South but in the border states as well. The attainment of emancipation, he concluded pessimistically, even if it were compensated, peaceful and limited to those states where slavery was losing money, "is attended with such difficulties as to impress despair rather than hope on the minds of those who take a near view of the subject."[48]

Given this harshly realistic assessment, one wonders why Marshall bothered with the ACS. Perhaps it was an act of desperation, maybe even self-

47. Marshall to Lafayette, 2 May 1827, PJM, typescript.
48. Marshall to Lafayette, 26 August 1825, PJM, 10: 199–201.

deception, though he was not given to that trait. A harsher explanation, one supported indirectly by his correspondence, is that he, like so many other Virginians, was attracted to the racist logic of that organization. For whatever else it would do or not do, the ACS would rid Virginia and other southern states of free black people, who, Marshall concluded, "can not be safely located on any lands within the United States." His conviction that a "secure asylum" in Africa would be as "beneficial for them" as it was "safe for us," was confirmed by Nat Turner's Rebellion. Writing to the Reverend R. R. Gurley, secretary of the ACS, on December 14, 1831, four months after that event, Marshall noted hopefully that "the excitement produced by the late insurrection" might well induce the states, with the prompting of state organizations of the society, to provide "permanent" funding to support emancipation and transportation. This was all the more essential, he added, because federal funding would be defeated by the South on constitutional grounds. Perhaps the only hope in that direction, he said, and it was not strong, was that funds from the sale of federal land might be used, since Congress already possessed the "power to dispose of, and make all needful rules and regulations respecting the territories or the property belonging to the U. States." In any case, he concluded, returning to the point made to Lafayette in 1827, the "removal of our colored population is, I think, a common object, by no means confined to the slave States, although they are more immediately interested in it. The whole Union would be strengthened by it, and relieved from a danger, whose extent can scarcely be estimated."[49]

When all was said and done, the transportation of blacks out of the country appeared to be, if not Marshall's major concern, then certainly his most pressing goal. Even if it were voluntary, which Marshall and his son insisted it must be, deportation rested on an inescapable racist premise that blacks and whites could not live side by side on free and equal terms. This principle was accepted almost universally by the ruling elite, regardless of political persuasion, as part of the hegemonic culture of slavery that permeated the Old Dominion. While it is impossible to prove, it is reasonable to assume that Marshall's decision to side with the slave interests in the Virginia constitutional convention in some subtle way was influenced by that culture. Like many other Virginians of his day, Marshall was opposed intellectually to slavery but accepted it as an unalterable fact of life. Like them, he had the wolf by the ears and feared to let go.

49. Marshall to Lafayette, 2 May 1827; Marshall to the Rev. R. R. Curley, Secretary of the ACS, 14 December 1831, PJM, typescript.

Slavery, Federalism, and the Rule of Law

Given Marshall's intellectual opposition to slavery, one might expect his judicial opinions on the subject would favor freedom, at least in those cases where the law or the facts allowed him some discretion. Such was not the case. Whether that discrepancy marks him as a hypocrite or reveals his commitment to the rule of law as he perceived it is difficult to determine. In either case, the problem of relating his private and political stance on slavery to his slave law is fraught with difficulties. Chief among them is the fact that at no time during Marshall's tenure did the Court confront the constitutionality of slavery directly. There were no slave rendition cases, such as *Prigg v. Pennsylvania* (1841), where the Court was forced to admit that the Constitution protected southern slavery; there were no cases remotely resembling *Dred Scott v. Sandford,* which made slavery the supreme law of the land governing new territories, perhaps the free states as well. Marshall wrote only one major opinion on slavery, *The Antelope,* and it dealt exclusively with the international law aspects of the foreign slave trade. Since in that case, he was writing for a badly divided Court, it is difficult to confidently ascertain his position. The challenge in this case, indeed, in all others, is to establish the range of real options open to Marshall—as chief justice, whose duties were to unite and often speak for a divided Court, and as an interpreter of a Constitution that was itself a slave document.

Because slavery was dealt with piecemeal in the Constitution—without mentioning the word—and because it was bound up with the contested issue of federalism, scholars and contemporaries alike have argued about its constitutional status. All concede that the Constitution recognized the institution when it authorized Congress to prohibit the foreign slave trade after twenty years, when it applied the three-fifth rule to the slave population in apportioning representatives and direct taxes, when it provided for the return of "fugitives from justice," and when it gave Congress the power to establish "needful rules and regulations" for the governance of the territories. That these several provisions added up to a recognition of slavery is clear. What is not clear is whether and to what extent they made slavery into a national institution. One interpretation is that the Constitution did not make slavery a national institution but simply recognized that on the state level it was a fact of life, which had to be grudgingly acknowledged in the federal system. The fact that states could and did abolish slavery without reference to the Constitution would seem to support this notion. Abolitionist constitutional theorists such as Lysander

Spooner, and some modern scholars as well, went further to argue that by *not* explicitly making slavery a national institution, the Framers actually intended to privilege freedom. The view that won out as the slavery issue made its way to the Supreme Court—implicitly in *Prigg* and explicitly in *Dred Scott*—was that the Constitution made slavery the supreme law of the land. On this point alone, William Lloyd Garrison, Wendell Phillips, and John C. Calhoun could agree; most scholars now appear to agree with them.[50]

Since Marshall had no opportunity to rule directly on the constitutional status of slavery, and since he did not comment in any of his extrajudicial writings on that issue, there is no way of knowing precisely where he stood on this central constitutional issue. Inferential reasoning does not settle the question either. For example, one might infer that Marshall's doctrine of implied powers armed Congress with enough power to damage slavery severely, if not actually kill it—and this was one of the main reasons southern states' rightists opposed *McCulloch* so strenuously. Still, his property-minded Lockean view of the Constitution clearly included property in slaves. One thing at least is clear: Among the powers Marshall conceded to states in his system of divided sovereignty was the constitutionally protected right to establish slavery. In this, as in many other things, Marshall considered himself bound by the intent of the Framers, who were willing to enslave African Americans in order to establish a national Union.[51]

Marshall made no effort to escape the harsh realities of that compromise. As circuit judge in Virginia and North Carolina and as chief justice charged with reviewing circuit decisions on appeal, he regularly confronted the statute and common law of the states that reduced human beings to items of private property. Such cases were not new to Marshall. As a practicing lawyer in Richmond for more than two decades, he dealt with them routinely and unavoidably. If he fretted about the moral implications of administering the slave law, he did not say so in any of his extant correspondence. Perhaps, as John Noonan Jr. has suggested, the "mask of the law," which reduced the issue of human freedom into routine legal questions concerning wills, contracts, promissory notes, secured transactions, and the like, permitted Marshall, like other judges,

---

50. For the antislavery interpretation of the Constitution during the antebellum period, see William M. Wiecek, *The Sources of Antislavery Constitutionalism in America, 1760–1848* (Ithaca, N.Y., 1977).

51. Perhaps no contemporary scholar was more explicit on this than Marshall's friend Story, who discussed the slavery compromises as the price paid for union in his *Commentaries on the Constitution of the United States . . .* (Boston, 1891), 1: 466–71.

to escape the moral dilemma. Just as important, no doubt, was the fact that slave law for Marshall and other southern judges was merely another dimension of familiar social terrain they routinely traversed in their daily lives. For whatever reason, the chief justice of the United States never flinched from his sworn judicial obligation. Neither, it would appear, did he make any effort to extend the area of freedom, even when the indeterminacy in the common law of slavery allowed him leeway to do so.[52]

A case in point is *Mima Queen v. Hepburn* (1813), which came from the District of Columbia on a writ of error. The case involved a petition for freedom brought by Mima Queen and her daughter Louisa, slaves of one John Hepburn of Washington County, D.C. They claimed freedom on the ground that their distant maternal ancestor, Mary Queen, had been a free woman. To support this claim, their lawyers relied on hearsay evidence, evidence, that is, that did not proceed "from the personal knowledge of the witness, but from the mere repetition of what he has heard others say." In *Mima Queen,* one Richard Disney "deposed that he had heard a great deal of talk about Mary Queen, the ancestor of the plaintiffs, and had heard diverse persons say, that Captain Larkin brought her into this country, and that she had a great many fine clothes," evidence presumably that she could not have been a slave. More directly to the point was the testimony of Caleb Clark, who deposed that he had heard his mother say that Mary Queen was free. In addition, he also deposed he had heard his mother say that his father spoke of Mary as a free person. The circuit court admitted the first part of Clark's deposition but denied the admissibility of double hearsay. The jury verdict, following the court's instructions on hearsay evidence, went against the Queens.[53]

The legal issue drawn up by the writ of error, which came before the full Court, concerned the admissibility of hearsay evidence in personal freedom suits. Counsel defined the issue clearly. Arguing that there was no difference regarding evidence between suits for personal freedom and other claims at law, Walter Jones pressed for a restricted use of all hearsay evidence. As he put it, "The admission of hearsay is an exception to the general rule of evidence, and therefore, must be confined strictly to the excepted cases, which are prescription, custom and pedigree," all questions of a general nature. Hearsay evidence

---

52. John T. Noonan Jr., *Persons and Masks of the Law: Cardozo, Holmes, Jefferson, and Wythe as Makers of the Masks* (New York, 1976). The best book on southern slave law is Morris, *Southern Slavery and the Law.*

53. 7 Cranch 290. The definition of hearsay appears in *Black's Law Dictionary,* 4th ed. (Saint Paul, Minn., 1951), 852.

used to prove a *fact,* he claimed, was not admissible, which eliminated Disney's deposition attesting to Mary Queen's status as a free person. The problem with this position, as counsel for the Queens noted, was that such evidence was almost always the only kind available in suits for freedom. Moreover, counsel pointed out, and it was a point of considerable importance, "such evidence as this is always admitted in the courts of Maryland, under whose laws this case was tried, and its use had been sanctioned by the authority of the highest court of that state."[54]

Mima Queen put Marshall to the test. Not only did it confront him with a real choice, but the consequences of that choice in human terms was painfully evident. The legal choice was between two rules governing the admissibility of hearsay evidence: the first, designed to maximize the security of private property, banned hearsay absolutely as evidence of specific facts; the second, which had taken shape in slave states such as Maryland, admitted hearsay in personal freedom suits because it was generally the only kind available. The first choice meant a life of slavery for the Mima Queen and her daughter; the latter meant freedom.

Marshall spoke for a bare majority of four—Johnson and Todd were absent, and Duvall dissented—but he spoke forcefully, without hesitation or equivocation. As he saw it, the "one general principle," which determined all the questions before the Court, was "that hearsay evidence is incompetent to establish any specific fact, which fact is, in its nature, susceptible of being proved by witnesses, who speak from their own knowledge." He conceded there were exceptions to this rule as in "cases of pedigree, of prescription, of custom, and in some cases of boundary" and also in "matters of general and public history, which may be received without that full proof which is necessary for the establishment of a private fact." There was, however, no exception to the inadmissibility of hearsay, regarding "specific facts," such as the status of Mary Queen, and he was not about to introduce "fresh exceptions to an old and well-established rule, the value of which is felt and acknowledged by all." As Marshall the common lawyer put it, quoting "a great judge," "All questions upon the rules of evidence are of vast importance to all orders and degrees of men; our lives, our liberty and our property are all concerned in the support of these rules, which have matured by the wisdom of ages, and are now revered for their antiquity, and the good sense in which they are founded." Even more pointedly, he said, "If the circumstance that the eye-witnesses of any fact be

54. 7 Cranch 292–93.

dead, should justify the introduction of testimony to establish that fact from hearsay, no man could feel safe in any property, a claim to which might be supported by proof so easily obtained."[55]

It was a harsh decision and difficult not to judge harshly—not only by modern standards but by contemporary ones. It should be fairly noted that the common law was hostile to hearsay evidence for the Lockean reasons Marshall frankly stated. It is also true that, except for Duvall, the whole Court agreed with his ruling, including Justice Story, who was the leading scholar on the Court. Still, there was no reason why the admission of hearsay evidence in personal liberty cases could not be distinguished from the general rules governing other types of property. This, as Duvall pointed out in his dissent, was precisely what Maryland courts had done. In his words, the "reason for admitting hearsay evidence upon a question of freedom is much stronger than in cases of pedigree, or in controversies relative to the boundaries of land. It will be universally admitted, that the right to freedom is more important than the right of property." Moreover, he added, "people of color, from their helpless condition, under the uncontrolled authority of a master, are entitled to all reasonable protection. A decision that hearsay evidence, in such cases, shall not be admitted, cuts up by the roots all claims of the kind, and puts a final end to them, unless the claim should arise from the fact of recent date, and such a case will seldom, perhaps never occur."[56]

Marshall had a choice; he chose to uphold property rights for human beings when he might have chosen freedom, and he did so in the name of objective law. "However the feelings of the individual may be interested on the part of a person claiming freedom," he stated, "the court cannot perceive any legal distinction between the assertion of this, and of any other right, which will justify the application of a rule of evidence to cases of this description, which would be inapplicable to general cases, in which a right to property may be asserted." To reach this conclusion, Marshall ignored the position of Maryland courts on the question of double hearsay. If he ignored state law on matters of evidence, however, he accepted it in regard to slavery itself. If slavery was first and foremost the creation of state law, it was still the constitutional duty of the federal judiciary to protect it.

55. Ibid., 295, 296.
56. Ibid., 298–99. See Donald M. Roper, "In Quest of Judicial Objectivity: The Marshall Court and the Legitimation of Slavery," *Stanford Law Review* 21 (February 1969): 532–39.

As a humane slave master who rewarded his personal slave with the choice of freedom, he may have been uneasy with that fact. He may have conceded, as in *Boyce v. Anderson* (1829), that for purposes of assessing the liability of a common carrier, a slave "in the nature of things and in his character . . . resembles a passenger, not packages of goods." This modest concession to the humanity of slaves, however, was in the final analysis prompted more by the legal logic of tort law than by philosophical considerations. In this sense, it was typical of much of state slave law, including Virginia's, in which slaves were alternately considered real property or chattels depending on the convenience of the owners. This is not to say that the humanity of the slaves was entirely alien to the law of all the southern slave states for all of antebellum history. But as Thomas Morris has shown conclusively, the economic interests of owners and the necessity of social control always trumped humanity when there was a choice. As much as slaves asserted their humanity, southern lawyers and judges rarely, if ever, deviated from this cardinal principle of American slave law. John Marshall was no exception.[57]

Alongside *Mima Queen, The Antelope* stands as Marshall's most revealing opinion concerning slavery. Here, too, thanks to the arguments of counsel and the circuit opinion of Story in *U.S. v. La Jeune Eugenie* (1822), there was an element of choice. *The Antelope,* an international law case on appeal from the federal circuit court in Georgia, dealt with the foreign slave trade. The facts were complicated. The Spanish slaver *Antelope* was captured off the coast of Africa by the *Arraganta,* a privateer that had been provisioned and manned in Baltimore, from which it departed with an American captain and a crew that was partly American. Some of the slaves on board the *Arraganta* were transferred to the *Antelope,* where they joined other slaves who had been taken previously from other vessels said to be Portuguese. Both vessels then set sail for South America. When the *Arraganta* was wrecked off the coast of Brazil, the surviving crew and slaves were boarded on the *Antelope,* which was subsequently captured by an American revenue cutter off the coast of Florida, presumably with the intent of smuggling slaves into the United States in violation of federal law. The captured vessel and cargo were libeled by the vice-consuls of Spain and Portugal in the federal circuit court of Georgia. The vice-consuls argued that since the vessel was in the possession of the United States and since

---

57. *Boyce v. Anderson,* 2 Peters 150–56, quote at 155. Morris, *Southern Slavery and the Law,* 97. On slavery and state tort law, Morris, *Slavery and the Law,* ch. 17.

it was commanded by an American captain, the United States was obliged by treaty to return those Africans who had been taken on by the *Antelope* from vessels sailing under their respective flags.[58]

The case presented a number of complicated questions of fact and law, but the main issue concerned the status of the Africans themselves: Were they slaves or free men and women, and what law determined their status? The captain of the *Antelope* disingenuously—he planned to sell the Africans into slavery in the United States—claimed that he was legally entitled to take the Africans off Spanish and Portuguese vessels because they were being held in violation of the law of nations that outlawed slavery. On circuit, Justice Johnson ruled that the law of nations had not outlawed the slave trade but that municipal law governed since neither Spain nor Portugal had outlawed the trade. By this reckoning, the nearly two hundred Africans aboard those vessels remained the property of those governments and were ordered to be returned to their Spanish and Portuguese owners. The remaining Africans, sixteen in number (to be chosen by lot) were deemed property of the United States and were to be freed and sent to Liberia.[59]

The Antelope pitted freedom against property rights. Arguing for freedom, William Wirt, attorney general of the United States, and Francis Scott Key, counsel in the *Mima Queen,* mobilized authority and precedent to prove that the law of nations prohibited the international slave trade. By their reckoning, the Africans seized by the *Antelope* were free at the time of seizure and could not now be claimed as slaves under the laws of Spain and Portugal. Key's argument on that point was less than convincing, however, and a close reading suggests that he did not quite convince himself. He was certain, however, that "a great moral and legal revolution" was "now going on in the world respecting this trade" and that "the time must come, when it will cease to have a legal existence, by the universal concurrence of nations." Indeed, he continued, the time *had* come, or might come if the Court could be persuaded. Citing Story's circuit opinion in *La Jeune Eugenie,* he insisted that the international community had outlawed the trade not by convention but by various separate municipal acts against it, in "the treaties of Paris and Ghent; by the acts and

---

58. *The Antelope,* 10 Wheaton, 66; *U.S. v. La Jeune Eugenie,* 26 Fed. Cas. 832 (No. 15,551) (C.C.D.Mass., 1822). For a penetrating account of the case, see John T. Noonan Jr., *The Antelope: The Ordeal of the Recaptured Africans in the Administrations of James Monroe and John Quincy Adams* (Berkeley, Calif., 1977).

59. On the circuit litigation and Johnson's brutal calculations about the human cargo, see Noonan, *The Antelope,* 62–68. The circuit court's decision was not reported.

conferences at the congresses of Vienna, London and Aix la Chapelle; by the treaties between Great Britain and Spain and Portugal; by the negotiations between the United States and Great Britain; and by the reports of the committees of the house of commons, and the house of representative in congress." Like Story, Key argued that the individual action of nations, and not even all nations, was tantamount to the collective action ordinarily thought to be necessary to create enforceable rules of international law. This collective action, moreover, applied to Spain and Portugal even though they were not among those nations acting against the trade. Key's point was the same he argued in *Mima Queen:* In close cases, the benefit of the doubt goes to freedom, and the burden of proof falls on those who support slave law. The tide of world law was turning against the slave trade, and Key urged Marshall and his colleagues to get ahead of the wave.[60]

John Berrien of Georgia and Charles J. Ingersoll of Philadelphia, representing the governments of Spain and Portugal, were as brutally frank as Key and Wirt were idealistic. First, they argued, there was no international law condemning the slave trade, which meant that the slaves taken by the privateer *Arraganta* and found aboard the *Antelope* at the time of its capture remained slaves under the municipal laws of Spain and Portugal. Following Johnson's ruling, the Africans were simply property that should be returned to the owners. As Berrien bluntly put it, the people of the United States had no rights "to enforce against these foreigners their own speculative notions on this subject." Then followed a series of rhetorical and bitterly sarcastic questions: "Would it become the United States to assume to themselves the character of censors of the morals of the world of this subject?" Did Americans "consider themselves as the ministers of heaven, called to wipe out from the nations this stain of this iniquity?" And how, Berrien continued, pointing his fingers at opposing counsel, at the Court, indeed at his fellow Americans, could the United States take such a "lofty" moral position when Americans were slave traders for "more than thirty years," when they still were "extensively slave-owners." He continued, "If the slave trade be robbery, you were robbers, and are yet clinging to your plunder. For more than twenty years, this traffic was protected by your constitution; exempted from the whole force of your legislative power; its fruits yet lie at the foundation of that compact. The principle by which you continue to enjoy them, is protected by that constitution, forms a basis for your representatives, is infused into your laws, and mingles itself with the sources of

60. 10 Wheaton 75–76.

authority." His advice? "Relieve yourselves from these absurdities, before you assume the right of sitting in judgment on the morality of other nations. But this you cannot do. Paradoxical as it may appear, they constitute the very bond of your union. The shield of our constitution protects them from your touch."[61]

Whether arguments of counsel were fashioned with the chief justice in mind, they brought the issues facing him into sharp focus and in ways that played to his prejudices and values. Key as much as admitted that positive law was not yet on the side of freedom, as Berrien and Marshall, too, were quick to notice. But he spoke to "the great moral and legal revolution going on in the world" as revealed in the separate actions of sovereign nations. For a judge who believed in sovereignty and a man who believed in freedom, it was a tempting handle. Berrien, for the other side, played to Marshall's contempt for feel-good arguments and moral speculation. With the sneer at the hypocrisy of his opponents, he homed in on the fact that American law was slave law; union rested on the willingness of the Court to say so. The choice, as counsel on both sides appeared to concede, was between moral law in the making or slave law as it actually was.

Speaking for a unanimous Court, Marshall noted the "momentous importance" of the case, in which "the sacred rights of liberty and of property come in conflict with each other." He also admitted the difficulty of the case, since law was in transition and precedents both American and English could be cited on both sides of the question. Throughout the opinion, he made reference to the gross immorality of the international slave trade, how "the feelings of justice and humanity, regaining their ascendancy" had been increasingly aroused against it in the United States and Great Britain, and how both countries "have used all their influence to bring other nations into the same system, and to interdict this trade by the consent of all." He conceded, too, that the slave trade was "contrary to the law of nature" and "that every man has a natural right to the fruits of his own labor . . . and that no other person can rightfully deprive him of those fruits, and appropriate them against his will."[62]

In paying deference to the arguments of Key and Wirt, Marshall expressed his philosophical opposition to slavery, a position corresponding to that stated in private correspondence and to his activities in the ACS. But he also stated at the outset of his opinion that "this court must not yield to feelings which might

61. Ibid., 84, 86.
62. Ibid., 114–16, 120.

seduce it from the path of duty, and must obey the mandate of the law." A jurist, in contrast to a moralist, he declared in another place, must search for answers "in those principles of action which are sanctioned by the usages, the national acts, and the general assent, of that portion of the world of which he considers himself as a part, and to whose law the appeal is made," that is, to international law. That law, he concluded, as distinct from the municipal laws of the nations composing the international community of nations, sanctions the slave trade. The governing principle—and here he was consistent with his earlier rulings on international law—was the sovereign equality of all nations: "It results from this equality, that no one can rightfully impose a rule on another. Each legislates for itself, but its legislation can operate on itself alone. A right, then, which is vested in all, by the consent of all, can be divested only by consent; and this trade, in which all have participated must remain lawful to those who cannot be induced to relinquish it. As no nation can prescribe a rule for others, none can make a law of nations; and this traffic remains lawful to those whose governments have not forbidden it." It followed, said Marshall, "that a foreign vessel engaged in the African state-trade, captured on the high seas, in time of peace, by an American cruiser, and brought in for adjudication, would be restored." It did not matter that the Spanish and Portuguese owners could not identify specific Africans or distinguish them from other slaves taken aboard the *Arraganta* in its privateering ventures. Ownership was settled by a Court-imposed ratio, and those ordered back into slavery were to be chosen by lot, which meant that the Court abandoned all effort to determine the legal status of individual Africans. Those Africans fortunate enough to win the lottery were disposed of according to American law, which meant they would be shipped to Liberia as free men and women.[63]

John Marshall had adhered to the law as he saw it, and a brutish law it was, mitigated only, if at all, by the fact that his strict reading of the evidence resulted in a total denial of Portuguese claims and a significant reduction in those of Spanish owners. The Court's decision may have looked liberal when compared to Johnson's circuit holding, but the bottom line was that property trumped freedom again. What does that say about Marshall's jurisprudence? One explanation for his decision might be drawn from his statement to Story regarding Justice William Johnson's circuit opinion in *Elkison v. Deliesseline:* that by striking down the state's Negro seaman law, Johnson had "hung himself on a democratic snag in a hedge composed entirely of thorny state rights

63. Ibid., 114, 121–23, 131–32.

in South Carolina" and that he was not about to do the same. This flip statement in a private letter to a close friend seems to validate the view of Marshall
as a thoroughly political judge who cynically traded principle for expediency.
The more tragic truth is that he did not have to abandon his legal objectivity
to uphold slavery and the slave trade.[64]

Marshall adhered to the law of slavery with a rigor that is painful to observe. He did so not because he admired slavery or thought it best for America
or Virginia (he didn't), not because southern states' rightists threatened to dis-
mantle his Court (which they did), and not because he had to deal with the
collective sentiments of his colleagues on the Court, all of whom believed that
slavery was embedded in American law. He did it because he agreed with them
and because his system of federalism deferred to the states on the question of
slavery. Like James Madison, Joseph Story, John Berrien, and John Calhoun,
he realized that the positive law of the Constitution sanctioned the institution;
that the constitutional compromises on slavery made union possible. He truly
believed what he said in *The Antelope*: that it was possible to separate morals
from law and that it was his duty to follow the law as he found it and the intent
of the Framers as he perceived it. If anything softened the grimly inhuman implications of this position, it was that he championed a broad construction of
congressional power, which might someday be used to abolish the institution.
However, the fact remained that slave law was the price of union. When the
bill came due, Marshall paid it in full.

Holding the Line for Principle and Morality:
Georgia, Jackson, and the Cherokee Indian Cases

Perhaps it was inevitable that Marshall and Jackson should have crossed
swords. Marshall's model presidents were Washington, John Adams, and John
Quincy Adams, and Jackson was at odds with all three in terms of policy, style,
and personality. Even so, the story is more complicated than it appears. There
was no personal enmity between the two men. If Jackson's remarks on the
death of the chief justice are an indication, he had a deep respect for Marshall's
character and his accomplishments even while he disagreed with some of his

---

64. Noonan discusses the numbers, ibid., 116. Marshall to Story, 26 September 1823, PJM,
9: 338.

decisions. If Marshall disliked the states' rights orientation of the new party, he in turn appreciated Jackson's firm stand against the nullifiers. Jackson may well have recognized, too, that the Marshall Court had made significant concessions to the states in the area of slavery and in cases such as *Ogden v. Saunders, Providence Bank v. Billings,* and *Willson v. Black-bird Creek.* Finally, there was *Barron v. Baltimore,* where Marshall spoke for the majority in ruling that the Bill of Rights did not apply to the states. This was a commonly accepted view at the time, to be sure, but the ironic fact that Marshall's last constitutional opinion was a concession to state power reminds one, as it must have reminded contemporaries, that his nationalism had considerable states' rights play in the joints and that his federalism, like that of the Framers, was rooted in historical reality. If Marshall was not a consolidating ideologue and Jackson not a states' rights fanatic, then they could and did meet on some common American ground.[65]

Even so, that was not the end of the matter. Jackson may not have looked on the Court with contempt and may indeed have felt obliged to respect its decisions. But indirectly he did what all American presidents have done when given the chance—appoint justices who agreed with him. Marshall had held his own against the Court's external foes, but with the appointment process, the doctrines of states' rights democracy invaded the Court via the Constitution itself. He did not live to see the full impact of Jackson's six appointments, but the appearance of John McLean (1829) and Henry Baldwin (1830), on top of the changes already underway, was a signal of things to come. What came in *Craig v. Missouri,* as Marshall saw it, was a rebellion against the old law and, by necessary implication, against his leadership. *Craig* came from the Missouri Supreme Court on a writ of error. It involved the constitutionality of a state statute establishing loan offices that were authorized to issue certificates receivable by the state in payment for taxes and as payment of state salaries and fees; with proper security, they might also be lent at interest to citizens of the state. Hiram Craig and the other defendants in the case, plaintiffs on appeal, were issued certificates on the basis of their promissory note, which they refused to redeem on the ground that the loan office act was unconstitutional. The case raised two questions, both of which touched matters central to Marshall's jurisprudence. The first concerned the right of the Supreme Court to hear the case under Section 25; the second asked whether loan office certificates backed by the state violated the constitutional prohibition against the state emission of paper money in Article 1, Section 10.[66]

Marshall assumed both questions had been settled definitively: the paper money question by the clear mandate of Article 1, Section 10, as informed by the historical record of the Articles of Confederation period; and Section 25 by two major decisions of the Supreme Court. Missouri Senator William Benton, who was also leading the effort to repeal Section 25 in the Senate, was not persuaded. A writ of error issued to the Supreme Court of Missouri, he declared, sounding every bit like the late Spencer Roane, was an insult to a "free, sovereign, and independent State." "Such a course," he continued, now sounding like John C. Calhoun, "was not calculated to promote harmony, and to secure a continuance of the Union. If, in questions of this kind . . . the character of a sovereign State shall be made the subject of such imputation, this peaceful tribunal would not be enabled to procure the submission of the States to its jurisdiction; and contests about civil rights would be settled amid the din of arms, rather than in these halls of national justice." On the paper money question, Benton contended that the "language of the Constitution should be strictly construed, as it is a limitation on the sovereignty of a State." By his states' rights reckoning, loan office certificates, though they circulated with the backing of the state, were not formally legal tender and constituted a legitimate exercise of the state's power to borrow money.[67]

Speaking for a bare majority, Marshall marched to his conclusions with more than the usual dispatch. On the Section 25 question, the only obstacle he encountered was the fact that in trying the plea of *non assumpsit,* which carried the constitutional question along with it, the Supreme Court of Missouri had, with the agreement of the parties, dispensed with jury trial and gone directly to judgment. While the record did not reveal it in the usual manner, i.e., in the charge to the jury, there was no doubt the lower court had upheld a state law, which was challenged on constitutional grounds, thus bringing it clearly within the purview of Section 25. For Marshall, it was a matter of form only.[68]

Not so with the "great question" of whether the loan office act authorized the issuance of paper money in violation of Article 1, Section 10, which prohibited states from issuing "bills of credit." This question took Marshall back to

66. *Craig v. Missouri,* 4 Peters 410.
67. Ibid., 420, 422, 421.
68. Ibid., 428–30.

the Articles of Confederation period, where he often went in search of constitutional meaning. In this case, the words in dispute and the history that accounted for them were indisputably clear. Colonial and Revolutionary War experience defined bills of credit as "a paper medium, intended to circulate between individuals and between government and individuals, for the ordinary purposes of society." Because of its fluctuating value, such paper money exposed "individuals to immense loss" and gave rise to "ruinous speculations," Marshall said, so as to "destroy all confidence between man and man. To cut up this mischief by the roots, a mischief which was felt through the United States and which deeply affected the interest and prosperity of all, the people declared in their constitution that no state should emit bills of credit. If the prohibition means anything, if the words are not empty sounds, it must comprehend the emission of any paper medium by a state government for the purpose of common circulation." This broad definition, he concluded in a couple pages of finely tuned analysis, clearly embraced the state loan office certificates. After returning again, and at length, to the history of paper money in colonial and Revolutionary War America, Marshall declared the act of Missouri to be unconstitutional.[69]

For Marshall, the Constitution itself was on the line in *Craig,* and the deeply troubling problem was that the Court, which was supposed to defend it and whose "path was marked out by duty," was bitterly divided. In a case that seemed to be open and shut, he spoke for only four justices. Johnson, who embodied the new spirit of dissent, agreed with Marshall on the Court's jurisdiction and on the fact that the case was "of the most vital importance to the interests of this Union." Johnson believed, however, that the loan office certificates "are of a truly amphibious character," which is to say they partook as much of loans as they did paper money. In such cases, following the rule of thumb set forth earlier by Jefferson and Roane, Johnson gave the benefit of doubt to the state. He was doubtful even about the court's jurisdiction in the case, though he refused to argue the point. On the merits, however, he concluded from his reading of history that loan office certificates were not bills of credit within the meaning of the Constitution. Since they resembled bank notes—and since bank notes were not prohibited by Article 1, Section 10—neither were loan office certificates, he reasoned. Justice McLean, the first of Jackson's appointees, was even more fundamentally at odds with Marshall's definition of bills of credit. The new justice gave two main reasons for uphold-

69. Ibid., 432, 434–36.

ing Missouri's law, and one flatly contradicted the other. His first point was that the Missouri statute did not specifically make the loan office certificates legal tender and so they could not be paper money; his second was that the law in question was an emergency measure passed to offset a critical shortage of specie brought on by the failure of state banks and the "utter worthlessness of the currency." How the loan office certificates could take the place of a failed currency without *being* currency he did not say. Having convinced himself that there was some doubt whether the loan office certificates were paper money, McLean then concluded with Johnson that the benefit of the doubt went to the state. McLean would later support Marshall's and Story's brand of constitutional nationalism, but his logic in *Craig* gave no comfort to the beleaguered chief justice.[70]

Marshall carried the day in *Craig*, but he looked on his precarious victory as the beginning of the end. In a series of letters to Joseph Story, each more gloomy than the previous one, he recorded the decline of contract doctrine and, indeed, of the Court itself. "I find our brother McLean could not acquiesce in the decision of the Court in the Missouri case," he wrote on October 15, 1830, regarding *Craig*. "I am sorry for this, and am sorry too to observe his sentiments on the 25th sec. of the judicial act. I have read the last volume of Mr. Peters, the three dissenting opinions delivered in that case, and think it requires no prophet to predict that the 25th section is to be repealed, or to use a more fashionable phrase, to be nullified by the Supreme Court of the United States. I hope the case in which this is to be accomplished will not occur during my time, but accomplished it will be at no very distant period."[71]

Marshall was wrong about the demise of Section 25, but he was right to view *Craig* as an omen. It was not just that his victory in the case was a narrow one or that three justices dissented openly on a constitutional question for the first time in his tenure. Rather it was that the Court divided over something so fundamental and elemental as the paper money prohibition in Article 1, Section 10. Contractual sanctity went to the heart of Marshall's jurisprudence. More fundamental still was his belief that fair-minded judges aided by time-tested rules of interpretation could ascertain the meaning of constitutional language. If they divided on the meaning of a provision so obvious as paper money, what could they agree on? Judging from the 1830 and 1831 terms of the Court, the answer was less and less. The "revolutionary spirit" among the

---

70. Ibid., 438, 444; 449–50, and 437–38 for the path of duty quote.
71. Marshall to Story, 15 October 1830, PJM, typescript.

justices was beginning to take a toll. First, there was the abandonment of communal living, which was not only a personal insult but also both a cause and a symptom of a more fundamental fragmentation. As Marshall put it, "If the Judges scatter ad libitum the docket, I fear, will remain quite compact, losing very few of its causes; and the few it may lose will probably be carried off by seriatim opinions." Some of the growing inefficiency of the Court was due to the personal problems of the justices, for example, Baldwin's growing paranoia and progressive deafness or Johnson's ill health. But the heart of the matter was the irreconcilable division among the justices over the meaning of the Constitution. A sign of the problem was Marshall's inability to mobilize a majority on the three great constitutional causes docketed in the early 1830s. Like *Craig*, all three cases raised the question of whether the states ought to get the benefit of the doubt in constitutional disputes over federalism. All three cases were continued for want of agreement until the first term of the new Court under Chief Justice Taney, when all were decided in favor of the states.[72]

To complicate matters further, Marshall himself was stricken physically and emotionally. Early in 1831, he suffered the first of a series of gallstone attacks, which would require painful operations without anaesthesia and which would finally bring him down. More devastating to him than his own illness was the death of his wife on Christmas Day, 1831. Though the sad event could not have come as a total surprise, it was nonetheless a crushing blow that left him totally inconsolable. He continued to perform his duties, but he was increasingly distracted. He also seemed more careless than usual of his own health, as when Edward Everett encountered him on the way to the Court on a bitter March day without coat or hat. William Wirt noted on another occasion that the chief justice was "badly shaved this morning" and "came into the court with a quantity of egg on his underlip & chin." Conscious that he was "a bird of passage," he grew increasingly introspective and retrospective. In 1832, he drew up his last will and testament and began to speculate about his successor on the Court, planning to make his continuance in office contingent on the coming presidential election. His hope was that a Whig president, such as Webster or Clay, would name Story to succeed him. Indeed, there is strong circumstantial evidence Marshall sought to bring about that result by giving the Whigs what he hoped would be a surefire campaign issue. Intended or not, that

---

72. Marshall to Story, 26 June 1831; and Marshall to Story, 3 May 3, 1831, ibid. The three cases as decided were *New York v. Miln*, 11 Peters 102; *Briscoe v. Commonwealth Bank of Kentucky*, 11 Peters 257; and *Charles River Bridge v. Warren River Bridge*, 11 Peters 420.

was the consequence of his two remarkable opinions in the Cherokee Indian cases of 1831 and 1832.[73]

The Cherokee Indian cases were the climax of three decades of struggle with the forces of states' rights, the final battle in Marshall's "campaign of history." This was true in several respects. First, the litigation occurred simultaneously with the nullification controversy in South Carolina and must be seen as part of a massive frontal attack on Marshall's concept of national union. In some ways, the threat from Georgia was even greater than from South Carolina, since the Court was a principle player in the action. More important, the president was allied with Georgia against the Court and with the states' rights party in Congress, which supported his policy of Indian removal. Marshall's political opponents seemed to be closing in for the kill. Against them, he called forth all the resources he had: his stature as chief justice, the discretionary control over the Court's docket that came with that office, and his knowledge of the Court's vulnerabilities and strengths vis-à-vis his political enemies. Aware that he might lose, Marshall was determined to go down fighting for judicial authority, for principled adjudication, and for the beleaguered Cherokees.

As with slavery, Marshall's thoughts about Native Americans had taken shape before he was required to define their position in law. As with slavery, he was also torn between a concern for human rights and a recognition of the cultural obstacles to their realization. As a Virginian and a frontiersman, he had grown up with the problem, and the lessons he learned were harsh ones, which is to say, the history of race relations between white settlers and Native Americans in colonial Virginia was mainly one of deception and aggression on the part of a relentlessly advancing Anglo civilization, marked by bloody warfare in which both sides shared in the barbarities. In June of 1755, three months before Marshall was born, Native Americans massacred nine families in nearby Frederick County. Native Americans and frontiersmen were still fighting on the northwest frontier of Virginia during his youthful days in Fauquier County, and frontier safety was still an issue at the Virginia ratifying convention of 1788. Not surprisingly, Marshall grew up thinking of Native Americans as "savage," warlike, and expert "with the tomahawk and the scalping knife," words he used to describe them in his biography of Washington. When allied with Great Britain, France, and Spain, as they had been at various

73. Wirt to Elizabeth Wirt, 1 February 1830, Wirt Papers, Box 116, Maryland Historical Society, Baltimore; Edward Everett to Mrs. Everett, 25 February 1831, Everett Papers, Massachusetts Historical Society, Boston; Marshall to Story, 26 June 26, 1831, PJM, typescript.

times, he saw them as enemies of the new nation. At the same time, especially when it was clear that ultimate victory would go to the better-armed and more numerous English, he saw Native Americans as victims in need of protection from the white man's rapacity. While serving in the Virginia House of Delegates in 1784, he even supported a bill, introduced by Patrick Henry, that encouraged intermarriage with Native Americans—though he also believed that the prejudices of Anglo-Virginia "operate too powerfully for them." As a young lawyer in the Indian slave case of *Hannah v. Davis* three years later, he argued, victoriously as it turned out, that the Virginia statute law prohibited the enslavement of Native Americans.[74]

Marshall's fullest personal statement on Native Americans came three years before he encountered the first of the Cherokee cases, in response to Joseph Story's speech, "History and Influence of the Puritans." Story's point, which he mistakenly found embedded in Puritan policy, was that the Native Americans by the right of prior discovery and the principles of public law and Christian morality were entitled to the land they occupied. Marshall held Story's scholarship in the highest regard, and he had great admiration for the Puritans as well, but he could not agree with his friend's legal argument; indeed, he had already repudiated it in *Johnson v. McIntosh*. In 1828, however, Marshall was prompted to say that a fundamental change in policy was in order. As he explained to Story, the Indians had been "a fierce and dangerous enemy whose love of war made them sometimes the aggressors, whose numbers and habits made them formidable, and whose cruel system of warfare seemed to justify every endeavor to remove them to a distance from civilized settlements." But now that they were doomed to extinction, Marshall reasoned, public safety and morality were no longer at odds. The time had come, he said, for the American people "to give full indulgence to those principles of humanity and justice which ought always to govern our conduct towards the aborigines when this course can be pursued without exposing ourselves to the most afflicting calamities. That time, however, is unquestionably arrived, and every oppression now exercised on a helpless people depending on our magnanimity and justice for the preservation of their existence impressed a deep stain on the American character. I often think with indignation on our disreputable con-

74. Beveridge, *Life of John Marshall*, 1: 1, as reported in *Pennsylvania Journal and Weekly Advertiser*, 24 July 1755. Marshall, *Life of Washington*, 1: 279. For other references, see Marshall's letter to Augustine Davis printed in the *(Richmond) Virginia Gazette and General Advertiser*, 13 November 1793. Marshall to James Monroe, 2 December 1784, PJM, 1: 131. On *Hannah v. Davis*, PJM, 1: 218–21.

duct (as I think) in the affair of the Creeks of Georgia; and I look with some alarm on the course now pursuing in the Northwest."[75]

Marshall's reference to Georgia had to do with its forceful removal of the Creek Indians, beginning in 1824; the alarming events in the "Northwest" referred to the state's effort to do the same to the Cherokees, who occupied several million acres in the state's northwest corner. The legal right of the Cherokees to this land seemed fully secured by a series of treaties with the federal government, especially the Treaty of Hopewell (1785) and the Treaty of Holston (1791). Along with several federal statutes, these treaties encouraged the Indians to give up their native traditions in favor of American "civilization." Thus encouraged, the Cherokees, led by a mixed-blood elite, turned to domestic agriculture and developed a written language and a written constitution. Ironically, it was this very progress of Americanization, along with perennial land greed and the discovery of gold on Cherokee lands, that prompted Georgia to move against them. Two state laws, the first passed December 20, 1828 (nine days before Marshall wrote to Story about the Indians), and a second on December 19, 1829, set the state in direct defiance of the treaty of 1791 and ultimately of the Marshall Court. According to Charles Warren, the resulting clash with Georgia was "the most serious in the history of the Court."[76]

Marshall blamed Georgia, Andrew Jackson, and states' rights constitutional theorists for the crisis, and he had a point. But neither he nor the Court, nor President Adams for that matter, were innocent bystanders in the process of dispossessing the Native Americans of their lands and their way of life. A case in point, one that may conceivably have had some influence on Georgia's actions against the Creeks and Cherokees, was Marshall's opinion for the Court in *Johnson v. McIntosh*. Although both parties in the case were whites, that decision was the Court's first major statement on Native American land ownership, one that has had lasting impact in American law. At issue was the title to some 50 million acres of land lying in the state of Illinois between the Illinois and Wabash Rivers. The plaintiff claimed title from a purchase and conveyance from tribes northwest of the Ohio River in 1773 and 1775; the defendant claimed title under a grant from the United States. The central in-

75. Story's speech of 18 September 1828 is reprinted in *Miscellaneous Writings*, 408–74, quote at 457; Marshall to Story, 29 October 1828, PJM, typescript. *Johnson v. McIntosh*, 8 Wheaton 543.

76. William McLoughlin and Walter H. Conser Jr., "The Cherokees in Transition," *Journal of American History* 64 (1977): 678–703. Marshall to Story, 29 October 1828, PJM, typescript. Warren, *Supreme Court*, 1: 729.

quiry, in Marshall's words, was "confined to the power of Indians to give, and of private individuals to receive, a title, which can be sustained in the courts of this country." That issue turned in part on the question of whether Indians could legally own land in the first place and, if so, how.[77]

Marshall signaled the direction of his thinking in his opening statement, declaring that it was the undisputed "right of society to prescribe those rules by which property may be acquired and preserved." It followed, he reasoned, that the title to lands must "depend entirely on the law of the nation in which they lie" and, ominously for the Native Americans, "not simply [on] those principles of abstract justice, which the Creator of all things has impressed on the mind of his creature man, and which are admitted to regulate, in a great degree, the rights of civilized nations." Natural justice, it followed, he said, must give way to positive law and positive law followed in the conqueror's footsteps. The governing principle in American law, as in the English law on which it was based, he said, was "that discovery gave title to the government by whose subjects, or by whose authority, it was made . . . [and] which title might be consummated by possession." Apparently uncomfortable with this harsh ruling, he went on to note that Native Americans were "the rightful occupants of the soil, with a legal as well as just claim to retain possession of it, and to use it according to their own discretion." At one point, he even expressed the hope, as he had in 1784, that the Native Americans might be assimilated with whites. But the bottom line remained, he determined, that the "rights to complete sovereignty, as independent nations, were necessarily diminished, and their power to dispose of the soil, at their own will, to whomsoever they pleased, was denied by the original fundamental principle, that discovery gave exclusive title to those who made it." The principle, he said, that the "history of America, from its discovery to the present day, proves"—and Marshall gave a fourteen-page account of that history—was that the Native Americans held land by right of occupancy only; further, "that the exclusive power to extinguish that right, was vested in that government which might constitutionally exercise it." The right of the Illinois tribes to hold their land by occupancy was strongly affirmed and presumably would have to be respected by those European powers who claimed by the doctrine of discovery. To put it another way, the doctrine of discovery did not destroy Native American claims to the land but rather was meant to settle the competing claims of rival European powers. Sovereign nations that claimed by discovery and maintained authority by conquest were still morally and legally

77. *Johnson v. McIntosh*, 8 Wheaton 572.

obliged to respect the Native American right of occupancy. At the same time—and here Marshall modified the general principle to suit "the actual state of things"—the right of occupancy did not include the right of "transferring the absolute title to others." Native Americans might sell to non–Native Americans, but if they did, the latter in effect became incorporated into the community of Native Americans and could hold the purchased land under the laws of that community, that is to say, by occupancy. The right of occupancy could be extinguished only by the sovereign power, presumably by peaceful purchase. Applying this principle to the case at hand, Marshall affirmed the judgment of the district court of Illinois and held for defendants.[78]

What of the Cherokees of Georgia, whose fate would soon be thrown onto the scales of American justice? There is no way of knowing precisely what, if anything, Georgians bent on driving the Cherokee off their land made of *McIntosh*. A close reading suggests that Marshall himself was conflicted. In one paragraph, he spoke hopefully about the "general rule, that the conquered shall not be wantonly oppressed." He even looked forward to the day when Native Americans would be assimilated with whites, when, as "new subjects," they would be governed "equitably as the old," and when "confidence in their security should gradually banish the painful sense of being separated from their ancient connections." In the next paragraph, however, he observed with equal assurance that "the tribes of Indians inhabiting this country were fierce savages, whose occupation was war, and whose subsistence drawn chiefly from the forest. To leave them in possession of their country, was to leave the country a wilderness; to govern them as a distinct people, was impossible, because they were as brave and as high-spirited as they were fierce, and were ready to repel by arms every attempt on their independence."[79]

Georgians might have found some comfort in Marshall's apparent ambivalence and his tacit recognition that American civilization and Native American culture were headed for a showdown. Sharp-eyed Georgia lawyers might even have drawn a parallel between Marshall's conflicted statements in *McIntosh* and his ambivalent reference to the Cherokee lands in *Fletcher v. Peck*, wherein he briefly acknowledged the legal claims of the Cherokees to their land and at the same time noted that Native American title "is not such as to be absolutely repugnant to seizing in fee on the part of Georgia." Ambivalence aside, the main thrust of Marshall's opinion in *McIntosh* was at odds with Georgia's pol-

---

78. Ibid., 572–74.
79. Ibid., 589–90.

icy of expropriation, since it clearly recognized that Native Americans had a rightful claim to the land they occupied. Moreover, the doctrine that only the controlling sovereign could extinguish that claim could be construed as a protection for the Native Americans, assuming the goodwill of the government, of course. If Cherokee territory within the state was protected by federal treaty, which it was, then it must also have been clear to Georgians that their claim to Cherokee land was precarious.[80]

This said, it cannot be denied that a selective reading of *McIntosh* could yield some ominous implications—for the Cherokees and, indeed, all American Indians. By holding that the Cherokee land title rested exclusively on positive law, the Court deprived the Native Americans of a natural-law argument in defense of their fundamental rights. And by basing Native American land law on positive law, the Court put the Native Americans at the mercy of those who made that law. For Georgians, it was the state of Georgia, but ultimately it was the sovereign American people, who believed they had a God-given right to claim the continent for themselves and their version of civilization. By reelecting Andrew Jackson in 1832, the American people joined Georgia in settling the fate of the Cherokee people.[81]

The process of dispossession and annihilation began when Georgians, backed by state law, swarmed into Native American territory in search of gold and land. For a moment, it appeared that President Adams would call out federal troops to resist the invasion, but Jackson's election ended that possibility. When the new president announced in his inaugural address that he favored removal of the Native Americans beyond the Mississippi River and when the Jacksonian majority in Congress answered with the Indian Removal Act of 1830, it was clear that the last best hope for the Cherokees was the Marshall Court. The resulting litigation set the Court on a collision course against Georgia and the administration. Supporting the Court and the Cherokees was an impressive array of legal talent. The chief counsel for the Cherokees was William Wirt, one of the brightest ornaments of the Supreme Court bar. As attorney general in the Monroe administration, he had issued an opinion in 1824 denying that the Cherokees were a sovereign nation. Now he put his talents at their disposal. Joining him was John Sergeant of Philadelphia, in-house counsel ·

80. For Marshall's statement, *Fletcher v. Peck*, 6 Cranch 142–43; Johnson's dissent regarding Georgia's fee simple claim appears at ibid., 146.

81. On the complex meaning and misuse of *McIntosh*, see Milner S. Ball's insightful analysis in "Constitution, Court, Indian Tribes," *American Bar Foundation Research Journal*, 1987, No. 1, especially 23–29.

for the second Bank of the United States, which, like the Cherokees, was under attack by Jackson. Supporting Wirt and Sergeant informally with legal advice and moral support were Webster, Henry, Clay, and the great legal scholar James Kent. Not coincidentally, Wirt, Sergeant, Clay, and Webster would all enter the lists against Jackson in the election of 1832: Webster and Clay as contending candidates for the National Republican Party; Wirt as presidential candidate for the Antimasonic Party; and Sergeant as vice-presidential candidate on the Clay ticket. Justice Story appeared to be a part of this informal coalition, too. It was not coincidental that his speech in defense of the rights of Native Americans, to which Marshall responded appeared in September 1828, by which time Georgia's campaign against the Cherokees and Jackson's against Adams were in full swing.[82]

Clearly, law and politics were intertwined from the beginning of the Cherokee litigation. The question, given Marshall's conviction that the Court ought to stick to law and avoid politics, now asked was whether they could now be separated. Wirt's and Sergeant's arguments in *Cherokee Nation v. Georgia* (1831), the first of the cases, supplied Marshall with the legal ammunition to resolve the dilemma. Wirt's strategy, developed in close consultation with John Ross, the principal chief of the Cherokees, began to unfold on December 27, 1830, when Wirt served notice to the governor and the attorney general of Georgia that a motion in equity would be filed asking the Supreme Court to enjoin the state from enforcing its laws against the Cherokees. The main point of the bill was that "the Cherokee Nation of Indians" was "a foreign state, not owing allegiance to the United States, nor to any State of this Union, nor to any prince, potentate or State, other than their own." Furthermore, Wirt stated, their character as "a sovereign and independent state," as well as title to their territory, "had been repeatedly recognized, and still stands recognized by the United States, in the various treaties subsisting between their nation and the United States." The Cherokee land may have been, as Wirt put it, granted to them by "the Great Spirit, who is the common father of the human family," but they were protected against the incursions of Georgia by federal treaties, which were the supreme law of the land.[83]

---

82. For Story's conservative activities and his use of Harvard Law School as a corrective to Jacksonian Democracy, see Newmyer, *Justice Joseph Story,* especially ch. 5. Also see Joseph C. Burke, "The Cherokee Cases: A Study in Law, Politics, and Morality," *Stanford Law Review* 21 (February 1969): 500–31.

83. *Cherokee Nation v. Georgia,* 5 Peters 1 at 3. On Georgia's response, Beveridge, *Life of John Marshall,* 4: 540, cites Phillips, *Georgia and State Rights,* in the *Annual Report of the American Historical Association* (1901), 2: 71. On the removal crisis, see also William G. McLoughlin, *Cherokee Renascence in the New Republic* (Princeton, N.J., 1986), ch. 20.

The strategy was brilliant if novel. Arguing that the Cherokees were a foreign nation as well as a sovereign state meant that the case could be brought under original jurisdiction, which meant that the states could not delay the litigation as they could do in Section 25 cases. It also meant that the Court could render a decision in time to figure in the presidential campaign of 1832. Thanks to Wirt's strategy, the case involved President Jackson as much as it did Georgia. If the Cherokees held their land by treaty, then the president would be obliged by his oath of office to uphold their rights against Georgia. His refusal to do so—not an unforeseen possibility—would make a splendid campaign issue for Clay, Wirt, or Daniel Webster, all of whom were anxious to challenge Jackson's states' rights constitutionalism in the name of humanitarian principles. The issue was the tyranny of "King Andrew" versus the rule of law.

If Wirt put Jackson on the spot, he also placed Marshall and the Court in an extremely precarious position. Just its hearing the case rekindled Georgia's long-standing hostility to the Court, which went back to 1793 and *Chisholm v. Georgia.* As in that case, Georgia refused to appear before the Court—not only in *Cherokee Nation v. Georgia,* which came under original jurisdiction, but also in *Worcester v. Georgia,* which was a Section 25 case. Georgia in fact let the Court know exactly what it might expect when the state executed a Cherokee by the name of Corn Tassel in December 1830 in direct defiance of a writ of habeas corpus issued by the Supreme Court and signed personally by Marshall. The message was unmistakable: A decision by the Court in favor of the Cherokees would be treated with contempt. There were other problems, too. A ringing nationalist decision in 1831 might divide the Court further and almost certainly would strengthen the hand of the South Carolina nullifiers. Finally, there was the *McIntosh* precedent to be dealt with, or avoided. After ruling that the Cherokees held title to their land by occupancy only, that they were legally at the mercy of the English who conquered them and to the Americans who inherited the bloody bequest from England at the time of independence, it would defy legal logic to declare them to be a foreign nation with the same sovereign rights as Great Britain, Spain, or France. Clearly Marshall would have to do some deft maneuvering if the Cherokees were going to get their day in court.[84]

He did just that in *Cherokee Nation v. Georgia* and *Worcester v. Georgia*

---

84. For a discussion of the Tassel case, see Jill Norgren, *The Cherokee Cases: The Confrontation of Law and Politics* (New York, 1996), 95–98. Norgren provides an excellent brief account of the Cherokee litigation and its impact on American Indian law. For the Marshall trilogy in the modern context, see Charles F. Wilkinson, *American Indians, Time, and the Law: Native Societies in a Modern Constitutional Democracy* (New Haven, Conn., 1987).

—the two cases have to be considered in tandem because that is the way Marshall conceived them. His rather chaotic opinion for a divided Court in the first case was not auspicious for the Native Americans, but it was clear from his opening statement of sympathy that something was in the wind. "If the courts were permitted to indulge their sympathies," he noted, "a case better calculated to excite them can scarcely be imagined. A people, once numerous, powerful, and truly independent, found by our ancestors in the quiet and uncontrolled possession of an ample domain, gradually sinking beneath our superior policy, our arts and our arms, have yielded their lands by successive treaties, each of which contain a solemn guarantee of the residue, until they retain no more of their formerly extensive territory than is deemed necessary to their comfortable subsistence." From Marshall's saying the Cherokees claimed under "successive treaties, each of which contain a solemn guarantee," it would appear he spoke to the merits of the controversy, indeed, settled it decisively. But leaving that legal possibility suspended, Marshall went on quickly to note that he was not speaking on the merits of the case. He could not do so, he ruled, because the Court had no authority to hear the case under original jurisdiction as the Cherokees were not a state of the Union, which Wirt conceded, nor a foreign state, as he had argued.[85]

Technically, Marshall should have stopped with his denial of jurisdiction, but he went on to expound on the jurisdictional dilemma facing the Cherokees. In search of a workable solution to an unprecedented problem, he started, as he so often did, with the facts. The Cherokees, he reasoned, were not intended by the Framers to be either a state of the Union or a foreign nation. But they were a "State"; they were also "a distinct political society separated from others, capable of managing its own affairs and governing itself." More to the point, they could negotiate treaties with the United States, which the Court was obliged to recognize and which it had consistently done. Marshall conceded that there were some anomalies. For example, he said, the Cherokees "acknowledge themselves in their treaties to be under the protection of the United States; they admit that the United States shall have the sole and exclusive right of regulating the trade with them, and managing all their affairs as they think proper." Clearly, Marshall pointed out, the Native Americans were not being treated as sovereign states or foreign nations. That point was even more apparent in light of Article 1, Section 8, clause 3 of the Constitution, which granted power to Congress to regulate commerce "with the Indian tribes." Such a grant

85. 5 Peters 15.

of power put the tribes in a subjugated position and even raised questions about their capacity to negotiate Article 2 treaties, so clearly Indian tribes were not seen by the Framers as sovereign foreign states or as states of the Union. But if not, what were they? What legal category described distinct political societies with the power of self-government and the right to make treaties that have the force of supreme law but who, in those same treaties, were recognized as "dependent" on the United States and whose trade with the United States could be regulated by Congress?[86]

Marshall's much-cited answer to the question was that Native Americans in general and the Cherokees in particular "may, more correctly, perhaps, be denominated domestic dependent nations," who were "in a state of pupilage" and who stood in relation to the United States as "a ward to his guardian." At first glance, this doctrinal improvisation appeared to be a mere play on words; worse, it was insultingly paternalistic. In either case, it seemed to denigrate the Cherokees in the eyes of the law. Not only did the "domestic dependent nation" concept lead to a denial of jurisdiction, but the word and idea of "dependency" was given a solid foundation in Native American law. Indeed, the whole opinion with its hesitancy, its lack of supporting argument, conveyed the impression that the old chief justice was slipping. That impression was strengthened by the fact that he was unable to unite the Court behind him. Johnson was particularly harsh in his separate concurrence. Following his "practise of giving an opinion on all constitutional questions," Johnson not only denied jurisdiction to the Cherokees but gratuitously referred to them as "a people so low in the grade of organized society" that they hardly counted. "Must every petty kraal of Indians, designating themselves a tribe or nation, and having a few hundred acres of land to hunt on exclusively," he asked, "be recognized as a State?" In his view, the whole case "is one of a political character altogether, and wholly unfit for the cognizance of a judicial tribunal." In the same tone, Johnson also rebuked Marshall for talking about the merits of the case in the process of denying jurisdiction. Baldwin, now a constant critic of the chief justice, added a dissent, which was characteristically pompous, ponderous, and largely irrelevant. Adding further to the chaos of the decision, Justice Thompson, joined silently by Story, entered a long dissent, which, following Wirt's argument, went the entire distance with the Cherokees on both jurisdictional and substantive grounds.[87]

86. Ibid., 16–20.
87. Ibid., Marshall at 17, Johnson at 21, 25, 28.

Taken as an isolated statement of doctrine, *Cherokee Nation* appeared to be a significant defeat not only for the Cherokees but for the Court and Marshall personally. But the decision was a bridge to *Worcester v. Georgia* in 1832, when the unified Court gave the Cherokees one last chance for survival. The link connecting the two cases was the "domestic dependent nations" concept, which Marshall fashioned from experience and the facts of history. The record of two centuries of relations between Anglo-Americans and Native Americans as he presented it, and as in fact it was, was full of unresolved tension between empowerment and dependency. From early settlement onward, the Native Americans were simultaneously respected and feared, admired for their nobility and denigrated as savages, respected as discrete self-governing political entities with the authority to negotiate with England and treated as hapless and helpless victims. Marshall refused to tidy this history, which is to say his concept of "domestic dependent nation" was both realistic and ambiguous. Native American tribes viewed themselves as nations and had been consistently denominated as such. But no one seriously spoke of them as foreign states. They had been truly independent, but by 1831, the force of American arms and numbers had made them dependent, though not yet for sustenance, not for wisdom, self-government, or civilization. They were, however, dependent on the words of federal treaties, which guaranteed them the positive legal right to the lands they had occupied for ages. Marshall's "domestic, dependent, nations" concept recognized the reality of this dependency. It also bespoke the power of the Cherokees to negotiate treaties with the federal government as they had done with England before independence and with the United States thereafter. Dependent or not, title to their land was protected by treaties with the United States government, which treaties were protected by the Constitution against state violation. This was "a mere question of right," Marshall determined, and as such, it "might perhaps be decided by this court, in a proper case, with proper parties." To be certain the American people got the last point, Marshall not only encouraged Thompson and Story to dissent on the merits but urged Thompson to write his dissent, which he did at length with Story's silent concurrence.[88]

Marshall had pushed to the outer limits of his authority, if not beyond. *While* denying jurisdiction, he signaled how the jurisdictional problem might be solved. *After* denying jurisdiction, he went on to comment on the substantive issues in the case; then, using his authority as chief justice, he got Thomp-

88. Ibid., 20.

son and Story to address those issues in a full opinion. What was needed next was to get the case before the Court by some other route than original jurisdiction. While Wirt, Sergeant, and the Cherokees were pondering that problem, it was solved for them when two divinely inspired New England missionaries insisted on preaching to the Native Americans in defiance of state law. Upon refusing to leave, the missionaries were tried in the Superior Court of Gwinnett County, found guilty, and sentenced to four years hard labor. Rather than accept a pardon from the governor, they retained Wirt, who appealed the decision of the Gwinnett County court via a writ of error to the Supreme Court. On the merits, Wirt contended that the state law under which Worcester and Butler were convicted violated Cherokee property rights, which were guaranteed by federal treaty.

To an unusual degree, *Worcester v. Georgia* was Marshall's own case. It was also his ordeal by fire. He was, as Story attested, still in the slough of despondency over the death of his wife the previous Christmas. The gallbladder ailment that would kill him was acting up again after a brief remission. On top of these troubles, the disarray among the justices was now full blown and out in the open. Across the land, the Court's external enemies were on the move: in South Carolina, in Virginia, in Congress, and at the bar of the Supreme Court. Everywhere there was talk about the fragility of federal union and the threat of impending civil war. In seeking liberty under American law for themselves, the beleaguered Cherokees, much like Dred Scott in the case named after him, had generated a massive showdown between the champions of states' rights and those who believed with Daniel Webster that it was "liberty and union now and forever," or as Marshall saw it, liberty and union now or never. He circulated the final edition of his Washington biography to friends to remind them what was at stake. The old but still "principled soldier" of the Revolution was ready to meet the enemy one last time.

He read his opinion to a hushed audience in a voice that was barely audible, but the words he spoke were forceful and uncompromising. This time, he was supported by all of his colleagues except McLean, whose concurrence did not deviate significantly from Marshall's opinion. *Worcester* was one of Marshall's longest and most thoroughly researched opinions, evidence he was still in full command of his faculties. After acknowledging the importance of the issues, he moved on quickly to justify the Court's jurisdiction under Section 25. His language was moderate, but his position was unyielding and unusually thorough: Worcester was imprisoned under a state law averred to be in direct violation of federal treaties; he claimed under those treaties, and the highest court of Georgia with final jurisdiction in the matter, in this case, the Superior Court of Gwinnett County, ruled against him. The case was made to order for Section 25. The Court had issued the writ to the Gwinnett County court, and the clerk of that court, upon receipt of the writ, apparently not mindful of the state's determination to stonewall the litigation, had forwarded the records of the trial court as required by law. The Supreme Court, Marshall declared, as was his wont to do in controversial cases, had no choice but to do its duty, "however unpleasant." He concluded the jurisdictional overture with a protest of innocence, which seemed calculated to cover his tracks in *Cherokee Nation.* In words that directly contradict his action in that case, he said, "Those who fill the judicial department have no discretion in selecting the subjects to be brought before them."[89]

The substantive issue in *Worcester* was whether Georgia's laws declaring sovereignty over the Cherokees violated federal treaties guaranteeing them possession. Marshall addressed the question first by reaffirming his reasoning in *McIntosh:* that law followed history, that colonial history was the story of conquest and dominance, which led to the legal principle that discovery backed by force divested the Indians of all innate claims to their homeland. By preserving the distinction between "is" and "ought," by denying the innate morality of law, by tying Native American law to the outcome of history, to "the actual state of things," to "power, war, conquest," Marshall's legal positivism appeared to have doomed the Cherokees yet again. Instead, it established the dispositive point that the Cherokees were capable of establishing treaty relations with the United States, cognizable by the Constitution and the Supreme Court and binding on Georgia as supreme law of the land. He cited Vattel, who conveniently defined treaties between nations as moral contracts of a binding nature. Vattel did not, however, refer to Native Americans as treaty-making nations. Marshall eased into this conclusion, not by reference to law but, as in *McIntosh* and *Cherokee Nation,* by extrapolating from colonial history, about which, as Washington's biographer, he could claim some expertise.

He made two main points first, that the English had traditionally established treaty relations with the Native Americans and that this power belonged exclusively to the United States under the Constitution. Second, and hardly less important, was the fact that the Crown had treated Native American tribes with respect as befitted the fact that they were self-governing communities em-

89. *Worcester v. Georgia,* 6 Peters 536, 541.

powered, like other nations, to shape their destiny. Sovereignty on one side and dependence on the other did not preclude self-government. As Marshall put it, our history "furnishes no example, from the first settlement of our country, of any attempt on the part of the crown to interfere with the internal affairs of the Indians, further than to keep out the agents of foreign powers, who, as traders or otherwise, might seduce them into foreign alliances. The king purchased their lands when they were willing to sell, at a price they were willing to take; but never coerced a surrender of them. He also purchased their alliance and dependence by subsidies, but never intruded into the interior of their affairs, nor interfered with their self-government, so far as respected themselves only." It followed, Marshall reasoned, that the Native American's power to make treaties included, and was premised on, the power of self-government. What applied to England also applied to the United States.[90]

From his long discourse on the historical record, Marshall extracted two principles, one normative and the other legal and constitutional. The normative principle, established in treaty relations first between the Native Americans and Great Britain and then between the United States and the Native Americans, was both humane and practical. It held that the best way to ensure peace with the Native Americans was to respect them as self-governing nations and to guarantee their collective rights, including a right to the territory they occupied. Such was the specific intent of the Treaty of Holston (1790), the seventh article of which solemnly guaranteed "to the Cherokee all their lands not hereby ceded." Marshall found the same guarantee in all of the acts of Congress passed to regulate trade and intercourse with the Native Americans: "All these acts, and especially that of 1802, which is still in force, manifestly consider the several Indian nations as distinct political communities, having territorial boundaries, within which their authority is exclusive, and having a right to all the land within those boundaries, which is not only acknowledged, but guaranteed by the United States." Also relevant to the situation of the Cherokees, said Marshall, was the act of Congress passed in 1819, which "avowedly contemplates the preservation of the Indian nations as an object sought by the United States, and proposes to effect this object by civilizing and converting them from hunters into agriculturists."[91]

The legal principle, first adumbrated as an obiter dictum in *Cherokee Nation,* Marshall now presented as the law of the land:

90. Ibid., 547–48.
91. Ibid., 556–57.

The Indian nations had always been considered as distinct, independent political communities. . . . The very term 'nation,' so generally applied to them, means 'a people distinct from others.' The constitution, by declaring treaties already made, as well as those to be made, to be the supreme law of the land, has adopted and sanctioned the previous treaties with the Indian nations, and consequently admits their rank among those powers who are capable of making treaties. The words 'treaty' and 'nation' are words from their own language, selected in our diplomatic and legislative proceedings, by ourselves, having each a definite and well understood meaning. We have applied them to the other nations of the earth; they are applied to all in the same sense.

It did not matter, either, said Marshall, citing Vattel again, that the terms of the treaty were such as to make the Cherokees dependent: It is "the settled doctrine of the law of nations . . . that a weaker power does not surrender its independence—its right to self-government, by associating with a stronger and taking its protection. A weak State in order to provide for its safety, may place itself under the protection of one more powerful without stripping itself of the right of government, and ceasing to be a State." It followed then, he argued, and the Court so ruled, that the laws passed by Georgia in 1828, which claimed sovereignty over Cherokee lands guaranteed by federal treaties and confirmed in numerous federal statutes, were null and void as repugnant to the Constitution, and so was the ruling of the Superior Court of Gwinnett County condemning Samuel Worcester to four years of hard labor.[92]

The reaction to the Court's decision was instantaneous and predictable. Opponents of Jackson, located mainly in New England, celebrated it as a great victory for the Cherokees and moral vindication of the Court. The Jacksonians, especially the radical states' rights wing of the party, blasted the decision as yet another example of judicial tyranny and national consolidationism. Georgians denounced the decision and proceeded to ignore it, assuming that Jackson stood fully behind them. Historians over the years went along with the assumption, quoting the president as having said, "John Marshall has made his decision, now let him enforce it." As it turns out, these famous words were never spoken, which leads one to wonder whether the president, who moved so forcefully against nullification in South Carolina, would have countenanced it in Georgia. As it turned out, he was never put to the test. Due to a glitch in

92. Ibid., 559–60.

federal statute law, the Court's formal reversal order to the Gwinnett County court was never issued. Technically, Georgia did not have to defy the Court, and Jackson did not have to take a public stand.[93]

Still, the fact remains that the administration worked in various other ways to defeat the intention of the decision and humble the Court. The president had gone on record, favoring removal of all Native American tribes beyond the Mississippi River, and Congress had supported him with the Indian Removal Act of 1830, which laid down general terms governing the negotiation of removal. In light of this policy, Jackson could hardly have supported *Worcester.* Being silent when he should have openly backed the Court spoke volumes. There were other problems, too, starting with the fact that the Cherokees themselves were divided as to whether, or how, they should continue to resist. Many, particularly those who resisted the policy of assimilation and the rule of the mixed-breed elite who presided over the process, were tantalized by the possibility that migration west might be the best way to preserve traditional ways. There was also the realization among elite Cherokees that the Court's decision was meaningless without the president's willingness to back it by force. That possibility, faint at best, became even more unlikely when it became clear that any pressure on Jackson to intervene against Georgia might detract from his willingness to use force against nullification in South Carolina. The Court's decision was also undercut by the fact that several lawyers hired by the Cherokees to defend the land titles were secretly working for Jackson and removal, which did not stop the lawyers from presenting exorbitant bills. Several leading supporters of the Native Americans, including Worcester himself, also advised that a favorable treaty of removal might be preferable to pointless resistance. In December 1835, the Treaty of New Echota, providing for Cherokee removal, was signed. On the way to the promised land beyond the Mississippi, several thousand Cherokee men, women, and children perished. When the survivors arrived, they found themselves at odds with other tribes already in possession of the land.[94]

From the Cherokees' point of view—which is the one that counts most— Marshall's opinion, like the treaties they were now legally entitled to negotiate, was worth no more than the paper it was written on. For those who want to assess the chief justice and his Court, however, the opinion is revealing. At first

93. On the nonenforcement of *Worcester,* see Norgren, *Cherokee Cases,* 122–30.
94. The full story of Cherokee removal is movingly recounted in Thurman Wilkins, *Cherokee Tragedy: The Story of the Ridge Family and the Decimation of a People* (New York, 1970).

glance, it appears to prove what critics have always maintained: that Marshall was essentially a political judge with a genius for dominating the Court. Indeed, after his remarkable performance in *Cherokee Nation,* rumor circulated that "judges Marshall, Thompson and Story, and Messrs. Clay, Webster, Sergeant and Everett, had held a caucus, at which it was determined that the Cherokee case should be decided 'solely upon political grounds!'" Clay, Webster, and Everett, of course, denied such a meeting (in a letter dated April 10, 1832). They probably told the literal truth. But given Marshall's discretionary powers as chief justice, his authority, and well-honed working relationship with key members of the Court and the bar, he did not have to caucus openly to shape the work of the Court or to maximize the legal and political clout of its decisions. Circumstances, along with the words and fit of his two opinions, tell us that he worked to shape the outcome of the case.[95]

There is compelling circumstantial evidence, too, that he hurried the litigation so as to make Jackson's Indian policy an issue in the presidential election of 1832. Marshall's encouragement of the dissenters and his suggestion to Thompson to write out his dissent and have it printed fits into this scenario. So does the well-known fact that Marshall wanted Jackson defeated so that he might resign from the Court with the knowledge that his successor would be of the right persuasion. Story deserved the honor and wanted the job, and he understood that the election of 1832 would settle the matter. As he put it to George Ticknor regarding *Worcester,* "The Court has done its duty. Let the nation now do theirs." As it turned out, the American people did not oblige. Instead, they ignored the plight of the Cherokees, elected Old Hickory to a second term, and left the Court to fend for itself. Given Marshall's conservative distrust of popular government and the general pessimism of his final years, it is amazing that he thought they might do anything different. Perhaps he didn't.[96]

In any case, Marshall, like Story, was determined that the Court should do its duty, which was to develop a coherent body of decisional law that adhered as closely as possible to the intent of the Framers. Although it may not seem so in light of Marshall's tactical maneuvers, his substantive rulings in the Cherokee cases were true to that standard. Indeed, one is struck by the coherence and doctrinal interconnectedness of both Cherokee opinions and *McIntosh* as well. By refusing to apply natural law to Native American rights in the latter, by em-

95. As reported in *Niles' Weekly Register,* 28 April 1832.
96. Story to Professor Ticknor, 8 March 1832, in *Life and Letters of Joseph Story,* 2: 83.

phasizing sovereignty instead, he pushed doctrinal development in the direction of positive law rights based on the constitutional treaty power he developed in the two Cherokee cases. The "domestic, dependent nations" concept set forth in *Cherokee Nation* connected all three cases. It could be argued that he invented that concept to get what he wanted, that is, to enable the Cherokees to negotiate binding treaties with the United States, which by virtue of the supremacy clause could then be used to put Georgia in its place. Marshall wanted to do that, of course, but he did not manufacture the "domestic dependent nations" doctrine out of thin air. Rather he based law on history, fashioned it from what he called "the actual state of things," from the examples that "our history furnishes," from "the history of the day." Long usage informed constitutional meaning, just as it informed the common law. Both *Cherokee Nation* and *Worcester* were consistent with other of Marshall's decisions in that they rejected abstract theory and limited doctrinal innovation by consistent rules of construction based on history and practice.[97]

The Cherokee opinions were a fitting climax to his chief justiceship. He used the powers of that office boldly and expansively, as he had from *Marbury* on, with an eye always to presenting the Court to the American people as an institution dedicated to the rule of law. For him, the Court was now the last best hope for the Republic as it rushed precipitously toward democracy. As Marshall viewed this epic drama, the Court was pitted against states steeped in self-interest, backed by presidents who had surrendered republican *noblesse* for partisan popularity and political power. It was the last campaign in a long war, and he knew the odds were against him; in truth, he did lose. Georgia flouted the *Worcester* decision, President Jackson left the Court twisting in the breeze, and the American people put their imprimatur on the defeat in 1832. Still the aging chief justice went out fighting. If he took liberties to get the issues before the Court (shades of *Marbury*), he dealt with them rationally and *legally* once they got there. In an age when racism, land greed, and arrogance mingled to destroy an innocent people unnecessarily, he worked to put the Court on the side of justice. Admittedly, the ramshackle functionalism of *Cherokee Nation* and *Worcester* was a far cry from the grand style of his greatest opinions. Sadly, the decisions did not protect the Cherokees in their struggle to survive as a people. Those opinions did, however, reaffirm the Court's position as a legal institution and, perhaps, as a republican one as well. The aging chief justice presided over the entire process while he was suffering from his wife's

97. 6 Peters 546, 547, 551.

death and contemplating his own, while his beloved Court was disintegrating before his eyes, and while his enemies were everywhere ascendent. In this his final battle in "the campaign of history," the old soldier of republicanism went down valiantly. Given the odds against him, it may have been his finest moment.

A Judge *for* All Seasons

[Marshall] has done more to establish the Constitution of the United States on sound construction than any other man living.

—*John Quincy Adams*

He would have been deemed a great man in any age, and of all ages.

—*Joseph Story*

If American law were to be represented by a single figure, skeptic and worshipper alike would agree without dispute that the figure could be one alone, and that one, John Marshall.

—*Oliver Wendell Holmes Jr.*

H OLMES WAS RIGHT: The evidence that John Marshall is *the* representative figure of American law is overwhelming. What was true in 1901 remains true today. There is a paradox involved, however, the kind Holmes himself loved to ponder as something that "would take the scum off your mind." The paradox is that Marshall's reputation for greatness appears to exceed the scope of his juridical accomplishments. "If I were to think of John Marshall simply by numbers and measure in the abstract," Holmes opined, "I might hesitate in my superlatives." He had a point. Concede that Marshall was a workhorse for the Court, that he spoke for the majority in 49 percent of all the cases heard during his tenure and in 59 percent of all the constitutional law decisions, and in almost all of the leading ones. The fact still remains that only a handful of these opinions were truly memorable. As Holmes put it, "Remove a square inch of mucous membrane, and the tenor will sing no more." Take away any three of Marshall's great opinions—say *Marbury, McCulloch,* and *Gibbons*—and it would be difficult to argue that he was *the* constitutional lawgiver of all times. Keep in mind, also, that his circuit opinions, though competent, were not notable for pioneering new doctrine, as, for example, were those of Story on the New England circuit. Beyond Marshall's opinions, there is mainly the massive biography of George Washington in its various editions. Although it is better history than once was thought, it is remembered, when it is, more for what it reveals about Marshall than about Washington. In any case, the biography has little bearing on Marshall's legal reputation. Unlike other famous statesmen of the early Republic, Marshall's extant correspondence is decidedly minimalist, more like Lincoln's slender opus than that of Jefferson, Adams, Madison, Hamilton, or Washington. Nor was Marshall a legal educator as was his teacher George Wythe, or David Hoffman of Maryland, or his colleague Story. This leaves only the eleven polemical essays written in defense of *McCulloch*. Brilliant and revealing of Marshall's legal acuity as they are, they do not warrant comparison in terms of legal learning to St. George Tucker's edition of Blackstone's *Commentaries,* James Kent's four-volume *Commentaries on American Law,* or Story's dozen volumes of legal and constitutional commentaries. Even in the area of constitutional law, there was some measure of truth in Holmes's assessment that "after Hamilton and the Constitution itself," Marshall had little truly original to offer and not much beyond "a strong intellect, a good style, personal ascendancy in his court, courage, justice and convictions of his party."[1]

Beyond this grudging concession, Holmes offered little to resolve the paradox of Marshall's greatness, except for one keen heuristic insight: that like other great men, Marshall "represented a great ganglion in the nerves of society" and was "a strategic point in the campaign of history, and part of his greatness consists in his being *there*." Like others of the founding generation, Marshall was fortunate to have lived in an age that not only permitted but invited bold and creative statesmanship. Like Erick Erickson's young man Luther, however, Marshall was not only energized by the remarkable age in which he lived but modified its rich legacy, and, to steal a phrase from Benjamin Cardozo, he molded it creatively "in the fire of his own intense convictions." Contrary to his own modest assessments of his career, what Marshall created has

---

1. Oliver Wendell Holmes Jr., *Collected Legal Papers* (New York, 1920), 267, 269. Figures from Robert G. Seddig, "John Marshall and the Origins of Supreme Court Leadership," *University of Pittsburgh Law Review* 36 (summer 1975): 805.

to a remarkable degree withstood the ravages of time. Not only has his reputation for greatness survived, but it has, if anything, taken on mythical proportions. It is the myth of Marshall's greatness that now needs to be explicated, if it can be.[2]

John Marshall on John Marshall

The chief justice died in Philadelphia July 6, 1835, a few months short of eighty years of age, brought down by the ailment that had plagued him for several years. Present during the final hours were his sons, except for Thomas, who, unbeknownst to his father, died in a freak accident on his way to join his brothers. Marshall's death was not a surprise. Though he continued to perform his duties on the Court, it was clear to family and friends and to Marshall himself that the end was approaching. He had long since put his affairs in order, with an eye as always to providing for his family. On April 9th, 1832, after the death of his wife, he revised his earlier will, which had come down hard on James for his improvident ways. John Marshall bequeathed the family place at Oak Hill, plus other lands, to Thomas. Other extensive holdings, including "the slaves on the land," were parceled out fairly to Jaquelin, James Keith, and Edward Carrington. The Chickahominy plantation, "with all the slaves stock, and plantation utensils, thereon," and his Richmond properties, along with "slaves and household furniture," went in trust to his daughter Mary and her children, "so as to protect her and them from distress, whatever casualties may happen." Smaller bequests, including bank stock and land, went to various nephews and grandchildren, including 1,000 acres "to each of my grandson's [*sic*] named John." To his "faithful servant Robin," Marshall bequeathed emancipation "if he chuses to conform to the laws on that subject requiring that he should leave the state, or if permission can be obtained for his continuing, to reside in it." If Robin chose Liberia, he was to receive a hundred dollars; if he chose to remain a slave, he could choose his master from among the Marshall children.[3]

With his family generously provided for, Marshall was free to continue his work on the Court and grapple with his own illness, which he did without

2. Holmes, *Legal Papers*, 267–68. Benjamin N. Cardozo, *The Nature of the Judicial Process* (New Haven, Conn., 1921), 170.

3. Marshall's revised "last will & testament," 9 April 1832, PJM, typescript.

complaint and, according to Story, with a stubborn disregard of his doctor's orders. Throughout his waning years, as throughout his life, he remained casual about his reputation. He labored to complete the two-volume edition of the Washington biography and even began to plan for a one-volume student edition, but he seemed less concerned about his reputation as a biographer than about spreading the word of Washington's relevance to the new age. One slight vanity was his quaint and touching wish that at least one of his grandsons should be named John. Friend and foe alike, however, attested to his modesty, his "plain and unpretending" manner, and his republican simplicity.[4]

This is not to suggest he doubted his own ability. He could not have sallied forth so valiantly in defense of his version of constitutional truth and justice, or stayed the course so long, had he been plagued with self-doubt. The substance and tone of his opinions bespoke his conviction and his determination to educate posterity to republican verities, to leave future generations a Constitution that was adequate to the "various *crises* of human affairs." But his opinions, though they bore the imprint of his genius, were also, as he acknowledged, collective efforts. He was determined to shun "paltry vanity," as he once put it, and made no effort to save his papers, doubting whether the written record of his life was "worth communication or preserving." True to his word, he pored over his "old papers" in the spring of 1833 "to determine how many of them were worthy of being committed to the flames." The letters that survived, found mostly in the papers of others, are devoid of puffery and self-justification, or even self-explanation. There are a couple brief autobiographical letters, plus a somewhat fuller one to Story, written at his request. There are the impressive journals Marshall kept while he was in Paris, relating mainly to the XYZ negotiations. But there is no personal diary, no memoir or journal, like those kept by Washington, John Adams, and John Quincy Adams, recording his thoughts or explaining himself to posterity. Unlike Webster, he did not quest for fame. Jefferson listed his greatest accomplishments on his tombstone; Marshall wanted only his name and dates, those of his parents, and, no doubt most important to him, the fact that he was the husband of Mary Willis Ambler. At his request, he was buried beside her in the "New Burying Ground" on Shockoe Hill.[5]

4. Story to Richard Peters, 20 May 1835, in *Life and Letters of Joseph Story*, ed. W. W. Story (London, England, 1851) 2: 194.

5. For a brief history of the *Marshall Papers* project, see S. Dean Olson, "A Collection after All These Years," *William and Mary Magazine* (fall 1997), 28–31. For quote, see Marshall to Story, 24 April 1833, PJM, typescript.

Marshall's self-abnegation, so apparent in all he did and said, stemmed from a quality rare among the great men of the early Republic: he was a genuinely modest man. The more famous he became, the more modest he grew. What Thomas Babington Macaulay said of John Hampden fits Marshall exactly: He was "an almost solitary instance of a great man who neither sought nor shunned greatness, who found glory only because glory lay in the plain path of duty." Nowhere is this more apparent than in the final years of his correspondence. As the end of his life approached, letters of admiration from old friends and admirers poured in; honors of all sorts, too numerous to list, were bestowed in recognition of his life's work. For him, it was a period of introspection and retrospection. There were tender and solicitous letters to Polly, and on the anniversary of her death in 1832, the heart-wrenching "Eulogy for Mary W. Marshall," celebrating the remembrance of their love and their life together. Old friendships assumed a new meaning—witness his generous words of praise to his political opponent James Monroe for a life lived in honorable service to his country. With Lafayette, another veteran of the American Revolution, Marshall shared his thoughts on slavery, emancipation, and the American Colonization Society. The irascible Timothy Pickering wrote to pay his respects and, characteristically, to pass judgment on American society past and present. Marshall responded kindly, though he did not hesitate to express his "real veneration & respect for Mr. [John] Adams," whom Pickering continued to savage. Past disagreements were forgotten and forgiven, no doubt, when Pickering praised "the Supreme Federal Judiciary" as "the high Controlling *Authority,* the *Moral Scepter,* of the Nation." Marshall also went out of his way to make peace with another Salem resident, Samuel P. P. Fay, whom he had written under the mistaken notion that his son Edward had become engaged to Fay's daughter. Reading Marshall's delicate and diplomatic apology, one can understand why he succeeded so brilliantly in the XYZ mission.[6]

Marshall also responded patiently to the inquiries of friends and strangers

6. Thomas Babington Macaulay, *Critical and Historical Essays* (London, England, 1966), 1: 103. Marshall to Monroe, 13 December 1824; 7 March 1825, PJM, 10: 134; also Marshall to Monroe, 7 March 1825, PJM, 10: 151. Marshall's correspondence to his wife (typescript, PJM) is printed in Frances Norton Mason, *My Dearest Polly: Letters of Chief Justice John Marshall to His Wife, with Their Background, Political and Domestic, 1779–1831* (Richmond, Va., 1961). His "Eulogy" of 25 December 1832 (typescript, PJM) appears on 243–44 of Mason's book. Marshall to Pickering, 31 May 1824, PJM, 10: 90. Pickering to Marshall, 2 January 1828 [misdated 1827 by Pickering], PJM, typescript. Marshall to Fay, 15 September 1826, PJM, 10: 302–3; Marshall to Fay, 15 October 1826, PJM, 10: 309–11.

and to the various materials sent him, ranging from Horace Binney's eulogy of Chief Justice Tilghman to Alexander Smyth's proposal to limit the term of president to one term, which in light of Andrew Jackson, Marshall thought might be worth a try. Everyone wanted the great man's blessing, which he seemed so willing to bestow. Marshall wrote as a "Virginian" in response to James M. Garnett's address to the Agricultural Society at Fredericksburg about the "causes & remedies" of Virginia's "present discontents." It is not clear what Garnett liked most, agricultural reform or female education, but Marshall liked both causes. He sat for several portraits by well-known painters such as Rembrandt Peale, John Wesley Jarvis, Chester Harding, and Henry Inman. He received fellow Washington scholar and future president of Harvard Jared Sparks, who came away in awe of Marshall's republican personality, the blending into a consistent whole, as Sparks put it, of "all things about him—his house, grounds, office, himself," and how they all "bear marks of a primitive simplicity and plainness rarely to be seen combined."[7]

And on it went. What the correspondence reveals is what Sparks described, a humble great man at peace with himself and with those around him. One of Marshall's last letters, to John Marshall Jr., distilled a life experience for the edification of his grandson: "Happiness is pursued by all; though too many mistake the road by which this greatest good is to be successfully followed. Its abode is not always in the palace or the cottage. Its residence is the human heart, and its inseparable companion is a quiet conscience. Of this Religion is the surest and safest foundation."[8]

If Marshall's conscience was quiet in the assurance he had done his best, it also troubled him deeply that it was not enough to save the country he loved so much. Indeed, behind his disregard of reputation was his sincere belief that his life's work was a failure, that the Court was weakened beyond repair and that without the Court to defend it, the Constitution itself was doomed. Fame goes to history's winners, and Marshall saw himself on the losing side as the American people repudiated his conservative version of the Revolution in their mad embrace of political democracy. The more he feared the irrationality of the electorate and the demagogic excess of politicians north and south of the

7. See Andrew Oliver, *The Portraits of John Marshall* (Charlottesville, Va., 1977), 48–53, 55–62, 63–82, 134–163. Marshall to Binney, 19 November 1827, PJM, typescript; Marshall to James M. Garnett, 17 December 1830, PJM, typescript; Marshall to Thomas W. White, 29 November 1824, PJM, 10: 124–25. "Interview with Jared Sparks," Richmond, 1 April 1826, PJM, 10: 283–84.

8. Marshall to John Marshall Jr., 7 November 1834, PJM, typescript.

Mason-Dixon Line, the closer he clung to the conservative wisdom of the eighteenth century. His law-and-order Revolution had turned radical. What was once the "revolutionary center" was fast becoming the revolutionary fringe, and that is where Marshall placed himself. For the most part, his view was accurate.

What was true of politics was also true of constitutional law. Increasingly the "sovereign people" of the states, armed with "local knowledge" and urged into action by political parties, called the shots. With the help of Martin Van Buren's organizing genius, Jeffersonian-Jacksonian democracy had prevailed over Marshallian conservatism. The Court, which in Marshall's scheme of things was supposed to curb popular democracy, had been "revolutionized" by it. During his last years in office, he experienced the beginning of the transformation of constitutional law the Taney Court would carry to completion. Increasingly he feared the civil war that finally came. In one important respect, the war itself was the final blow to Marshall's dream of a law-abiding, Court-obeying republic. Perhaps there is no sadder or more telling symbol of the failure than one of Alexander Gardner's photographs: the shallow grave of a soldier at the foot of a battle-shattered tree, the tree silhouetted against the sky. Beneath the tree's fractured branches stand several soldiers, leaning battle-weary on their rifles or standing strangely at attention. The photograph was taken after Antietam's bloody work was done. The dead soldier, from the Twenty-eighth Pennsylvania Volunteers, was Private John Marshall. The unfortunate soldier was not a namesake, but in an age famous for remembering famous men, he easily could have been. In any case, the image conveys a sad truth: What Marshall had feared, what he had worked to avoid, had come to pass. The rule of law as a rational way of settling disputes had given way, first to emotion and ideological extremism in the North and South, then to the lord of battles. The Union he hoped to preserve by adhering to the Constitution had gone to war over its meaning. His own state, indeed his own grandchildren, fought *against* the nation he had fought to create. Out of the bloody conflict would come a new birth of freedom, to be sure, and the Union, stronger for having endured the stress of civil war, would endure. But the new age was light-years removed from Marshall's world and hostile to much that was dear to him. Ironically, it was this pulsating, chaotic age that bestowed on him its highest honors and the fame he doubted would be his.[9]

9. The photograph of Marshall's grave appears in Michael Kernan's "The Pictures that Stunned the North," *Civilization* (March/April 1995), 70–71. The John Marshall in the picture

The Marshall Myth and the Modern Nation-State

Marshall died thinking he had become marginalized, and judging by the course of antebellum history and law, in some ways he had. Ironically, however, it was during this period that the myth of his greatness began to take shape. Admittedly, the mythmakers had much to work with. Such qualities as decency, modesty, kindness, patriotism, and genius count immensely, and friend and foe alike agreed that he had all of them in abundance. It would be difficult to find another statesman of his period who was so universally loved as a person and equally difficult to identify another statesman whose personal qualities so neatly meshed with the transitional age in which he lived. Marshall was a born aristocrat, whose democratic demeanor fit the democratic age he disliked so much. He was an American who loved Virginia, a southerner celebrated by the North. He was a genuinely great man who was genuinely modest, a combination that was "irresistibly winning," as even his old foes at the *Richmond Enquirer* conceded in their touching eulogy. The Americans who lined the roads to celebrate his triumphant return from France and the XYZ mission got the point early on: In a country still unsure of itself or its destiny, one that was moving from a traditional social order to a new egalitarian one, he was a natural-born American hero. The more he refused the accolade, the more he was revered. This is not yet to mention his life's work on the Supreme Court and the mysterious way he blended his republican personality with the institution over which he presided for thirty-four years. Less than two weeks after his death, the outpouring of grief and praise in all sections of the country over his death prompted the *National Gazette of Philadelphia* to conclude the whole nation held its dead chief justice "in almost universal veneration." Even as the political debate heated up about who should replace him, evidence was pouring in that "the fame of a good man" would be impervious to "censure." Marshall was on his way to becoming not just a national hero but a national institution, in both respects, according to some, second only to Washington. For Americans inclined to think in providential terms, it must have seemed entirely appropriate that the famed Liberty Bell, which once tolled independence,

---

was a fifty-year-old Irish immigrant who enlisted in July 1861. For more on the photograph, see William A. Frassanato, *Antietam: The Photographic Legacy of America's Bloodiest Day* (New York, 1978), 171–74. Mason noted in *My Dearest Polly,* 320, that of the five sons of Marshall's son James, four "served in the army that marched to oppose the military invasion of the State of Virginia."

cracked while tolling Marshall's death and went entirely silent sixteen years later ringing the anniversary of Washington's birth.[10]

In reading the many eulogies praising Marshall's work, one might forget that his jurisprudence, in contrast to his character, was not universally admired. Indeed, in the months and years following his death, periodicals and newspapers across the nation hotly debated key aspects of his constitutional legacy. Ironically, however, even the chief justice's detractors contributed to the myth of his greatness, none more so than Thomas Jefferson and other Virginia states' rightists who opposed Marshall every step of the way. The point they made publicly and privately, year after year from his appointment in 1801 on, was that he had single-handedly and single-mindedly made the Supreme Court over in his own image and used it to create a consolidated, that is to say, a Hamiltonian, nation-state with a judge-made Constitution to match. Marshall mythmakers such as Beveridge had only to praise the qualities in Marshall that contemporary critics condemned.[11]

Southern critics also contributed to the Marshall mythology by calling forth the commercial interests north of the Mason-Dixon Line to defend him and, in the process, put their own gloss on his jurisprudence and his reputation. Take, for example, the great commercial city of Philadelphia, whose populace first welcomed back the conquering hero of XYZ and whose lawyers dominated the Supreme Court bar for many years. No professional group was more distinguished or better placed to know Marshall and none more ardent in his praise. The great men and distinguished lawyers of the city gathered in the county courtroom for the memorial service presided over by Stephen DuPonceau, Philadelphia's legal scholar-in-residence. Leading the chorus of mournful praise were Horace Binney and John Sergeant, two of the city's most influential lawyers. Members of the bar association turned out to pay their final respects as

10. For the eulogy in *Richmond Enquirer,* see 10 July 1835, as cited in Albert J. Beveridge, *The Life of John Marshall* (Boston, New York, 1916–1919), 4: 589. The *National Gazette,* Thursday, 23 July 1835. On the Liberty Bell story, see "Liberty Bell," in *The Dictionary of American History,* ed. James Truslow Adams (New York, 1940), vol. 3. Also the Reverend John B. Stoudt, *The Liberty Bells of Pennsylvania* (Philadelphia, 1930), and the Franklin Institute, *Report of the Committee for the Preservation of the Liberty Bell* (Philadelphia, December 1962).

11. Less than two weeks after Marshall's death, the Whiggish *National Gazette,* 13 July 1835, blasted the Democratic *New York Evening Post* for its criticism of Marshall's jurisprudence and its call for a Democratic chief justice. One of the most interesting evaluations of the shift in jurisprudence after 1837 is found in the *North American Review* 46 (January 1838): 126–56. For the debate over the Marshall legacy and the future of the Court, see Charles Warren, *The Supreme Court in United States History,* new and rev. ed. (Boston, 1926), 2: ch. 21.

Marshall's body was transported to the boat that would carry it home to Richmond. The conservative press, which praised the honest republican lawyer for putting Talleyrand in his place, now praised the dead chief justice for rescuing the nation and making it safe for capitalism. So did the legal profession and the commercial press of New York City. James Kent, the "American Blackstone," said it all when he journeyed to Richmond in May to pay his final respects. Kent wrote to Jeremiah Smith, one of New England's most formidable common lawyers, about the experience, and Smith spoke for both men and no doubt for most northern lawyers. Marshall's views of national affairs and national law were "perfectly just in themselves," he declared, and "now come to us confirmed by the dying attestation of the greatest and best of men." Where commerce, industry, and capitalism flourished, it would seem, so did the memory and reputation of John Marshall.[12]

Nowhere was the celebratory prose more lavish or the mythmaking machinery better oiled than in New England. The more Virginia criticized Marshall, the more New England loved him. Massachusetts led the way and with much reason. After all, it was native son John Adams who appointed Marshall to the Court and who considered it one of the most important accomplishments of his accomplished life. John Quincy Adams shared his father's views, praising and defending Marshall whenever he got the chance, which happened often in the 1820s. New England capitalists such as the Cabots and Lowells— and the Appletons, Lees, and Jacksons—paid Marshall the ultimate compliment by putting his ideas about corporations into practice in the Merrimack Valley. The formidable intellectual establishment of Massachusetts chimed in, too, especially in the 1820s, when New England conservatives mobilized to stamp out the Jeffersonian democratic states' rights heresy. In this conservative, countercultural revolution, Marshall and his nationalist law figured prominently. Articles and reviews praising him were regular features of the influential *North American Review,* the voice of New England conservatism, after the journal's creation in 1815. Leading intellectuals, such as Jared Sparks, and religious leaders, such as William Ellery Channing, joined the chorus of praise.[13]

Primarily, however, it was the legal community of New England and Massa-

---

12. For Kent and Smith on Marshall, see Beveridge, *Life of John Marshall.* 4: 586–87.

13. Harlow W. Sheidley, *Sectional Nationalism: Massachusetts Conservative Leaders and the Transformation of America, 1815–1836* (Boston, 1998). Also R. Kent Newmyer, *Justice Joseph Story: Statesman of the Old Republic* (Chapel Hill, N.C., 1985), ch. 5.

chusetts that canonized Marshall. Its partiality is not surprising, given the fact that its members contributed significantly to his opinions in such cases as *Fletcher, Dartmouth College, McCulloch,* and *Gibbons,* to mention only some. Webster provided grist for Marshall's mill in the latter three opinions, and in *Gibbons,* he shared nearly equal billing. Mainly, however, it was Joseph Story who took charge of Marshall's reputation. Story did not live to complete the full biography of Marshall he hoped to write, but while he lived, he spread the word of Marshall's good works; and as New England's leading jurist, as the dominant figure on the New England judicial circuit, as Dane Professor at Harvard Law School, and as part of the elite junto that ran Harvard University, Story was in a position to be heard. Story was a big talker, but he was also a careful listener, and he paid attention when Marshall shared information about his life. It was Story who persuaded Marshall to write an autobiographical letter in 1827, the most extensive personal account that exists. Story used the information in a review of Marshall's *History of the Colonies* (1824), which appeared in the *North American Review* (January 1828) as "Chief Justice Marshall's Public Life and Services" and which plugged Marshall more than his history. Throughout the 1820s, Story used his influence on and off the Court to defend and praise Marshall. It is impossible to reconstruct Story's innumerable conversations during this period or his lectures to Harvard Law School students, but it is certain they were fulsome in Marshall's praise. Story's eulogy on Marshall's death, delivered before the Suffolk Bar on October 15, 1835, was the most touching and informative of all the many memorials past and present. Widely circulated in pamphlet form, it was reprinted in William W. Story's *The Miscellaneous Writings of Joseph Story* (1852) and again in John Dillon's three-volume collection of essays celebrating the centennial of Marshall's ascension to the Court in 1901.[14]

More important in furthering Marshall's fame, was Story's three-volume *Commentaries on the Constitution* (1833), written to refute his states' rights critics. Story dedicated the work to Marshall in a long, heartfelt letter of praise, predicting, "Posterity will assuredly confirm, by its deliberate award, what the present age has approved as an act of undisputed justice." Marshall was the epic hero of this epic work. Story cited his opinions often and at length, no

---

14. Marshall's letter to Story is printed as *An Autobiographical Sketch by John Marshall,* ed. John Stokes Adams (Ann Arbor, Mich., 1937). Adams traces the provenance of the letter in his introduction. For Story's review-essay, see *North American Review,* new ser., 16 (January 1828): 1–40. John F. Dillon, ed., *John Marshall: Life, Character, and Judicial Services . . .* (Chicago, 1903), 3: 327–80.

small advantage to lawyers who did not have access to the Supreme Court Reports. Marshall's opinions also figured prominently in Story's nineteen rules of construction, which were designed to keep the Court in harmony with the intent of the Framers and guarantee its nonpolitical legal character. Story's interpretation of the Court as the salvation of the Republic put Marshall's lifetime work into words. In its various editions, including ones for students and lay adults, Story's *Commentaries* remained the leading text on the Constitution well into the twentieth century. Readers over the years came away believing that Marshall's name was synonymous with constitutional wisdom. Thus when one aspiring Philadelphia lawyer named Henry B. Pearson set out in 1840 to "render" the great truths of the Constitution "plain and easy" to the youth of America, he planned his book as an intimate dialogue between the benevolent and all-wise chief justice and his fictional "son in law Horace." Indeed, in the years from 1815 to 1860 no fewer than five popular textbooks for students celebrated Marshall as the model judicial statesman. Adults got the same romantic message in Henry Flanders's *Lives of the Chief Justices of the Supreme Court of the United States* (1858), which portrayed Marshall as judge of Olympian wisdom who stood above the partisan struggles of the age.[15]

By fusing Marshall with the Supreme Court and the Court with the Constitution, Story and other antebellum mythmakers laid the foundation of his enduring fame. In the grand sweep of things, however, it was the Civil War that clinched the matter. Marshall sought desperately to avoid just such a war, but it was natural to argue that the man who fought and judged for the new nation would have supported a war to preserve it. Beveridge made the connection when he noted the similarities between Lincoln and Marshall. Lincoln worked to preserve what Marshall proclaimed in his opinions. When Lincoln's chief justice Salmon P. Chase declared in *Texas v. White* (1869) that the Union and the states that composed it were indestructible, he vindicated not just Marshall's constitutional principles but his life's work. Harvard Law School's James Bradley Thayer made the point in his *John Marshall,* published in 1901. "It was Marshall's strong constitutional doctrine," declared Thayer, "explained in detail, elaborated, powerfully argued, over and over again, with unsurpassable earnestness and force, [and] placed permanently in our judicial

---

15. The eight-page prospectus of Pearson's unpublished book is in the Rare Book Department of the Free Library of Philadelphia (thanks to Morris Cohen of Yale Law School for the reference). Maxwell Bloomfield, *American Lawyers in a Changing Society, 1776–1876* (Cambridge, Mass., 1976), 157–58, treats Marshall's popularity and his symbolic importance to lawyers who were trying to upgrade the image of the legal profession.

records . . . that saved the country from succumbing, in the great struggle of forty years ago, and kept our political fabric from going to pieces." An attachment to states' rights and a deep commitment to federalism had not disappeared, of course, but secession and the threat of it was dead. On the wane, too, was southern resistance to the market culture of the newly united United States. Increasingly, the New South replaced the Old South and set out to beat the industrial North at its own game. Southern history was becoming American history, and both were catching up with John Marshall and sweeping him along to posthumous greatness.[16]

With the cultural rapprochement between North and South, Marshall's reputation became truly national—Holmes's undisputed "representative figure of American law." Even the defeated South joined the chorus of praise. This is not to say that southerners abandoned states' rights or even the constitutional ideas of John C. Calhoun, which inspire serious discussion to this day. There were southerners immediately after the war who saw the irony of praising Marshall the lawgiver after four years of law-defying war. One such was Innes Randolph, who wrote the following poem in 1869 about the dedication of Marshall's statue in Richmond, the capital of the defeated confederacy.

We are glad to see you, John Marshall, my boy,
    So fresh from the chisel of Rodgers;
Go take your stand on the monument there,
    Along with the other old codgers;
With Washington, Jefferson, Henry, and such,
    Who sinned with a great transgression
In their old-fashioned notions of freedom and right
    And their hatred of wrong and oppression.
You come rather late to your pedestal, John,
    And sooner you ought to have been here,
For the volume you hold is no longer the law,
    And this—is no longer Virginia.
The old Marshall law you expounded of yore
    Is now not at all to the purpose,

16. *Texas v. White,* 7 Wallace 700. On Lincoln and Marshall, see Beveridge, *Life of John Marshall,* 4: 92, 93, 344; for Beveridge's criticism of Lincoln, see John Braeman, *Albert J. Beveridge: American Nationalist* (Chicago, 1971), especially 304–7. James Bradley Thayer, *John Marshall* (Boston, 1901), 58.

And the Martial Law of the Brigadier
   Is stronger than habeas corpus.
   So keep you the volume shut with care
For the days of the law are over;
   And it needs all your *brass* to be holding it there
With "Justice" inscribed on the cover.
   Could life awaken the limb of bronze
And blaze in the burnished eye,
   What would you do with your moment of life?
Ye men of the days gone by!
   Would ye chide us or pity us? blush or weep?
Ye men of the days gone by!
   Would Jefferson roll up the scroll he holds
Which time has proven a lie?
   Would Marshall close the volume of law
And lay it down with a sigh?[17]

The main point, however, is not that Randolph sneered at Marshall's faith in the rule of law, but that a statue to him was erected in the former capital of the Confederacy. Richmond was Marshall's home, and even when it was the intellectual capital of states' rights, he was always loved. But a cursory sampling of the literature suggests that Marshall was invited into the pantheon of legal giants only gradually by southerners. During 1820s and 1830s, southern theorists of all persuasions jumped on the anti-Marshall bandwagon. Indeed, three years after Marshall's death, a writer in the *Southern Literary Messenger* listed Virginia's legal greats without even mentioning his name. After the Civil War, legal reformers continued to attack the "moldy monstrosities" of his procorporate, procapitalist opinions. By the time Alexander Stephens published his *Constitutional History of the Late War between the States* (1868–1870), however, things were changing. Since Stephens was mainly interested in refuting Unionist constitutional theory, he could hardly have praised the Marshall Court; indeed, he hardly mentioned the Supreme Court. Nevertheless, the old chief justice did make a cameo appearance—as a champion of moderate federalism who deserved a place of eminence alongside Roger Taney. Judging by Henry St. George Tucker's attack on the General Welfare Clause doctrine in the *American Bar Association Journal* in 1927, southern theorists preferred to

17. Quoted in Oliver, *Portraits of Marshall*, 183–85.

target Story rather than Marshall, perhaps because it was mainly Story's *Commentaries* that kept Marshall's ideas current. In any case, by that time, if not long before, the chief justice had joined Washington and Madison on Virginia's all-star team of national heroes.[18]

If the Civil War settled the federalism issue in Marshall's favor, postwar economic history did the same for his law-based economic preferences. Again he looked prophetic. The growth of a national railroad system free from state interference was bolstered by resuscitating the national market potential of *Gibbons v. Ogden,* just as *Dartmouth College* was frequently cited to defeat state economic regulation. Marshall and his Court also contributed subtly to the rise of substantive due process by building the assumption into American public law that the private business corporation was just another enterprising individual whose property needed protection from the encroachment of the state. Marshall's Contract Clause decisions, though less important after the transformation of the Due Process Clause of the Fourteenth Amendment than before, remained relevant until the *Blaisdell* decision in 1934, when the Court bent Article 1, Section 10, to the necessities of the Great Depression. Though *Lockner v. New York* (1905) turned on the Due Process Clause of the Fourteenth Amendment, its contract preferences were clearly those of Marshall.[19]

Marshall's incorporation into the conservative constitutional construct of the late nineteenth century helped consolidate his mythic status. But it also produced a growing body of criticism, which would not so much detract from his reputation as it would alter it. As Paul W. Kahn has shown, the main thrust of constitutional theory after the Civil War was away from Marshall's "maintenance theory" of constitutional law that the role of the Court was to preserve the Constitution of 1787 against all comers by adhering to the intent of the Framers as expressed in the text of the document. After the Civil War, under the intellectual impact of Darwinian science and the practical consequences of business consolidation, the Constitution was increasingly looked upon as a work in process; the process according to some was, or should be, communal and democratic in nature, not judicial. Like Holmes, Thayer saw Marshall as

18. Alexander H. Stephens, *A Constitutional View of the Late War between the States: Its Causes, Character, Conduct, and Results* . . . (Philadelphia, 1868–1870), 2: 261. Henry St. George Tucker, "Judge Story's Position on the So-Called General Welfare Clause," *American Bar Association Journal* 13 (July–August 1927): 363–68, 465–69. Richard B. Davis, *Intellectual Life in Jefferson's Virginia, 1790–1830* (Knoxville, Tenn., 1972), 363.

19. *Home Building and Loan Association v. Blaisdell,* 290 US 398; *Lockner v. New York,* 198 US 45.

a man of his own age; Thayer was also among the first to acknowledge that "we seem to be living in a different world from Marshall's." The Court under Marshall aimed its nationalist decisions at the Union-busting implications of states' rights radicalism, while the late nineteenth-century Court aimed to destroy the legislative will of the people, which aimed to curb corporate excess. While Thayer did not criticize Marshall and, indeed, found much to praise, he vigorously opposed the judicial excesses of the late nineteenth-century Court done in Marshall's name. Like Holmes and Frankfurter after him—and John Bannister Gibson earlier, whose critique of Marshall Thayer cited with approval—Thayer argued that the Court worked best when it restrained itself.[20]

Other less moderate critics of Marshall soon chimed in. One such was Gustavus Myers, whose socialist *History of the Supreme Court* (1912) depicted the Marshall Court as part of the economic class struggle. More influential was Charles Beard's *An Economic Interpretation of the Constitution* (1913), which claimed that the Constitution was largely the creation of a consolidated capitalist class. It followed logically that if Marshall adhered to the intent of the Framers as he claimed to do, then he was also part of the capitalist conspiracy. In fact, Beard argued exactly that position in *The Supreme Court and the Constitution,* which appeared one year before *Economic Interpretation.* Moreover, judicial review itself was part of the Framers' intent, put in place, Beard argued, to implement capitalist policy objectives he believed permeated the Constitution itself. Edward Corwin, soon to become the nation's leading authority on the Court, appeared to agree. By arguing that Marshall deliberately went out of his way in *Marbury* to declare Section 13 unconstitutional, Corwin suggested, as Jefferson had claimed earlier, that Marshall had taken personal charge of American constitutional history. Corwin also claimed that Marshall's decision in the Burr treason trial was politically motivated. The Jeffersonian overtones of Corwin's scholarship became explicit, and less scholarly, in Vernon Parrington's *Main Currents in American Literature* (1927). Parrington viewed all of American history as the unfolding of Jeffersonian democracy and accordingly dismissed Marshall as a politically motivated judge whose main legacy was to give lawyers a monopoly on constitutional interpretation and fix a Hamiltonian Constitution on an unwilling populace. This was also

20. Thayer's views on the Court and the Constitution are treated in Paul W. Kahn, *Legitimacy and History: Self-Government in American Constitutional Theory* (New Haven, Conn., 1992), ch. 3, especially 85–89. Thayer's essay on Marshall is reprinted in *James Bradley Thayer, Oliver Wendell Holmes, and Felix Frankfurter on John Marshall,* with a contribution by Mark De Wolfe Howe (Chicago, 1967), quote at 83.

the main thrust of two major studies of the Supreme Court, one by Louis B. Boudin in 1932 and the second by Charles Grove Haines in 1960—both written from a Jeffersonian point of view.[21]

Despite many keen insights and some needed perspective on Marshall and his Court, these latter-day Jeffersonians did not carry the day. One might even argue that the more irrelevant Marshall appeared to the modern age, the more mythical he became. Thus, at the very time Thayer of Harvard was attempting to put Marshall back in his own age, John Fiske of Yale was elevating him to mythical status. Fiske, like Thayer, believed in evolution. His grand theme was Anglo-Saxon liberty under law, which he saw as the end product of a process that began in the Teutonic forests of northern Germany and climaxed in America, from whence it would presumably conquer the world. The determining moment in this great drama, as Fiske explained in his *Critical Period in American History* (1888), was the framing and ratification of the Constitution. Marshall was too young to figure as a central character in this happening, though he makes his debut at that time as a young patriot marked for destiny. But as chief justice, according to Fiske, Marshall was the original genius who melded the theories of Jefferson and Hamilton into "a new form of political organization," with judicial review as its foundation. By the time of his death in 1901, Fiske concluded, in the words of his biographer, that Marshall's contributions "were not inferior in value, to those of Washington, in giving birth to the nation itself." This appeared to be the unanimous conclusion of the legal luminaries who celebrated the centennial anniversary of Marshall's ascension to the Court in 1901. The published edition of these memorial speeches, which include earlier eulogies by Story, Horace Binney, and others, marks the end of one century of hagiography and the beginning of another.[22]

The dominant figure in the second century of Marshall studies was Albert Beveridge, whose four-volume life-and-times biography appeared in 1919. The

21. For a discussion of Beard's work, see Alan F. Westin's excellent introduction to *The Supreme Court and the Constitution*, by Charles A. Beard (Englewood Cliffs, N.J., 1962). Edward S. Corwin, "The Establishment of Judicial Review," *Michigan Law Review* 9 (December 1910): 102 ff., (February 1911), 283 ff., and *John Marshall and the Constitution* (New Haven, Conn., 1921). Vernon Louis Parrington, *Main Currents in American Thought: An Interpretation of American Literature from the Beginning to 1920* (New York, 1927–1930). See Louis B. Boudin, *Government by Judiciary* (New York, 1932); and Charles Grove Haines, *The Role of the Supreme Court in American Government and Politics* (New York, 1960), a book that challenged the pro-Marshall works by Charles Warren and Albert Beveridge.

22. John Spencer Clark, *The Life and Letters of John Fiske* (Boston, 1917), 2: 491–93. Dillon, *John Marshall*

character of Beveridge, as well as the quality of his scholarship, helps explain the commanding authority his larger-than-life view of Marshall came to have. As a young man growing up in hardscrabble times in Illinois, Beveridge came to view Marshall—along with Lincoln—as the embodiment of his personal values and those of America as well. Like Marshall and Lincoln, Beveridge was both a lawyer and a politician. As senator from Illinois, he blended the ideals of democratic reform—first, as a reform-minded Republican, then, after 1912, as a member of the Progressive Party—with ideas of racial supremacy, which spilled over into an aggressive America-first imperialism. When he lost the congressional election of 1912, he became a full-time biographer of Marshall. The project became the focus of his life—a surrogate profession, as well as a vindication of the progressive, nationalist, imperialist values that had gone down in defeat at the polls, as had Marshall's. In Beveridge's skilled hands, Marshall became the embodiment of a triumphant but beleaguered Anglo-American culture. With Marshall's "martial blood," his preference for English culture, and American law and order, the fit seemed perfect.[23]

Despite his bias (perhaps because of it), Beveridge was a force to reckon with. He was a dogged researcher, who set out to write the "definitive" biography, based on the demanding standards of the new "scientific history." Before he was finished, he had consulted not only an impressive corpus of Marshall materials but many of the leading political scientists and historians of the age as well. James Franklin Jameson, the acknowledged leader of the profession and champion of the "New History," was one of the first to lend his support. Among others who critiqued Beveridge's work and celebrated it upon publication were Charles Beard, Edward Corwin, and Max Farrand of Yale, who had just published *The Framing of the Constitution* and would go on to edit Madison's *The Records of the Federal Convention of 1787*. Samuel Eliot Morison at Harvard, already on his way to professional prominence, lent his name to the project, as did the ubiquitous Harold Laski. Even William E. Dodd, whose assessment of Marshall was conditioned by a strong liking for Jefferson, got on board. With backers such as these, it is not surprising that Beveridge's *Life of John Marshall* was awarded the Pulitzer Prize for biography in 1920.[24]

Though never without its critics, Beveridge's biography commanded the field of Marshall scholarship for much of the twentieth century. According to

23. See Beveridge, *Life of John Marshall,* 17, and ch. 1 generally, on Marshall's English ancestry.
24. John Braeman, *Albert Beveridge,* especially ch. 19.

Beveridge's dramatic rendering, Marshall was as relevant to the modern age as he had been to his own. Marshall was a nationalist and internationalist; so were Theodore Roosevelt and Woodrow Wilson. The production miracle of modern America, as well as the laissez-faire capitalism of J. P. Morgan and J. D. Rockefeller, appeared to rest on the legal foundation laid by Marshall. For those who looked to an activist Court to strike down "socialist" regulation of property at both the state and national level, Marshall showed the way in *Marbury, Cohens,* and his Contract Clause opinions. Marshall's love of English culture resonated with an age in which England and America reaffirmed their cultural affinity. The martial side of Marshall's career—as a soldier, as a champion of military preparedness, as a frank defender of American sovereignty and American interests—also assumed a new relevance as the United States joined Great Britain in a great war against Germany, which happened precisely when Beveridge was putting the finishing touches on volumes 3 and 4 of the biography. It didn't hurt either, in an age that saw the reunification of the North and South, that Marshall the southerner should be harnessed to the chariot of twentieth-century national and international greatness Beveridge saw as the manifest destiny of America.

Beveridge's Marshall was a ready-made symbol for what many modern Americans wanted to see in their lawmakers, perhaps in themselves. The less they actually saw of John Marshall's world, it seemed, the more they admired John Marshall. The evidence of his mythic status cannot be easily catalogued, but the common themes of the tributes to him, combined with their scope and diversity, is telling. The streets, schools, and towns named after him are too numerous to mention, and there is at least one hotel. There is Franklin and Marshall College in Lancaster, Pennsylvania, and Marshall University in Huntington, West Virginia, named in his honor, it would appear, more for his conservative role in the Virginia constitutional convention of 1829–1830 than for his constitutional nationalism. There is the John Marshall School of Law in Chicago, the Cleveland-Marshall College of Law in Cleveland, Ohio, and the Marshall-Wythe School of Law in Williamsburg, Virginia. Numerous clubs, scholarships, fellowships, and honorary distinctions of various sorts bear his name. His portraits, painted by the great painters of the age, as well as countless imitators, are everywhere: in the beautiful East Room of the Supreme Court Building, at various other places of prominence in the nation's capital, and almost invariably in the country's leading law schools. Marshall's likenesses in marble and bronze appear in almost every size and shape, from larger-than life-statues to affordable desk-size replicas. There is a much-admired, and much-imitated, bust by Hiram Powers. On a grander scale is William Wetmore Story's great figure of Marshall the lawgiver, once located on the front lawn of the Capitol and now resting in a place of honor in the Supreme Court Building. A recent larger-than-life bronze by William Bahrends adorns the central campus of Marshall University. The list goes on, from the commemorative John Marshall silver spoon, to the giant stained-glass window in Saint John the Divine's Cathedral in New York City (where Marshall joins Hammurabi, Solon, and Joseph Story), to the modern commemorative postage stamps. After two centuries, it seems clear Marshall belongs to the American people, in whose name he so often spoke.

Leading political scientists, historians, and legal scholars—beginning with Roscoe Pound's 1936 list of great American judges—have unanimously agreed with Beveridge, and with Holmes before him and Story before him, that Marshall was the greatest of the great, a judge for all ages. Scholars attending the bicentennial of Marshall's birth in 1955, sponsored by the College of William and Mary, reaffirmed his greatness even while gaining critical perspective on it. The recent outpouring of scholarship—starting first and foremost with the publication of *The Papers of John Marshall* at the College of William and Mary and ranging from dozens of learned articles to superb short studies of his jurisprudence, major biographies, and monumental volumes about his Court—is a tribute to his stature and importance. The coming bicentennial of his ascension to the Court will almost certainly consolidate his reputation further by making it more generally known.[25]

Given the tendency of scholars to revise, reconsider, and debunk, it is remarkable that Marshall's reputation, unlike that of some of his contemporaries, seems largely impervious to criticism. Nor have changing times taken a toll. Consider the remarkable irony, for example, that Marshall should have been so universally celebrated in the late 1930s, exactly at the time the Supreme Court, often citing his opinions in *Gibbons* and *McCulloch* for authority, was fundamentally altering the nonregulatory, property-loving, individualistic society he valued. Taken out of context, Marshall's memorable statement in *McCulloch* that the Constitution was intended to meet the "varied *crises* of the American people" became the hallmark of the new open-ended approach to

25. For the various listings of great American judges, see John V. Orth, "John Marshall and the Rule of Law," *South Carolina Law Review* 49 (spring 1998): 633–49. The papers presented at the 1955 conference with an introduction by Chief Justice Earl Warren praising Marshall are published in *Chief Justice John Marshall: A Reappraisal*, ed. W. Melville Jones (Ithaca, N.Y., 1956).

constitutional interpretation he would surely have opposed. What he would have thought about the New Deal and the New Deal Court had he actually lived to see them cannot be determined. But the historical Marshall was closer to the "four horsemen of the Apocalypse" than the post-1937 Court, which put a constitutional foundation under the liberal, regulatory welfare state. Marshall feared undue legislative meddling in economic matters; believed in the sanctity of contract; in balanced, perhaps even dual, federalism; in stare decisis; and in the meaning of language, which allowed him to understand the intent of the Framers. None of these things he took for granted as the foundation blocks of constitutional law had much meaning after 1937. About the only point of real continuity between his age and the modern one, it would seem, was that the Supreme Court was still at the center of the constitutional process—and the constitutional storm.

Where Myth and Reality Intersect:
The "Great Chief Justice" and the Supreme Court

No one would argue that the American Revolution, either in its origins or conclusion, was monolithically constitutional in nature, but recent scholarship shows that constitutional ideas permeated every aspect of it, even the fighting. Among the world's great revolutions, none was more productive of legal ideas and institutions. Marshall tapped into the legal-constitutional dimension of the Revolution in several ways—as a soldier, a lawyer-legislator in Virginia, a ratifier of the Constitution, and then in the 1790s as a Federalist defender of Revolutionary truth as he saw it. In that turbulent partisan decade, he concluded that only constitutional law and legal institutions could save the Republic from party-based, states' rights radicalism. His jurisprudence rested on a Burkean foundation, but unlike Burke, Marshall had to create legal institutions rather than preserve them. Chance, contingency, and the friendship of John Adams gave him the opportunity to do so. As chief justice, he brought the republican and conservative legal legacy of the Revolution to bear on the institutional development of the Supreme Court. Never in American history was Emerson's statement more apt, that "an institution is the lengthened shadow of one man."[26]

26. Ralph Waldo Emerson, "Self-Reliance," in *Essays: First Series* (1841), as quoted in *American Heritage Dictionary of American Quotations,* selected and annotated by Margaret Miner and Hugh Rawson (New York, 1997), 248.

Despite the impression conveyed by worshipful biographers and the allegations of his enemies, Marshall did not create the Supreme Court single-handedly any more than he originated judicial review. Wisely, he built on the English common tradition of rule of law. More specifically, he consulted the Framers themselves—building on the logic of Article 3, which put a constitutional foundation under the Court and connected it directly to the sovereign people, and of Article 6, which made the Constitution supreme law of the land. He drew heavily on the Judiciary Act of 1789, which explicitly gave the Court the authority to review state judicial decisions regarding federal questions, and on the Process Acts of the 1790s, which outlined the Court's mode of operation. More directly, he built on the formative labors of the Jay and Ellsworth Courts, which bequeathed to him a functioning institution of great potential. *Marbury* is a case in point. The genius of that opinion was the fact that it was *not* boldly original or doctrinally conclusive. Rather, Marshall built from existing materials, seized the appropriate moment to act, and stated only so much as the moment allowed and no more. For all of its political savvy, the decision promised that the Court would be a legal, not a political, institution. Probably no modern scholar would insist that Marshall was entirely immune from the politics that swirled around him in that case or in others. Often, to reach the law, he had to think and behave politically, if for no other reason than to fend off his enemies. But even in its most "political moments,"—*Marbury* comes to mind, as does *McCulloch,* and the Georgia Cherokee cases—the Court's "politics" differed fundamentally from those of Congress and the executive branch. More than any other institution that competed for power and the respect of the American people during the early Republic, the Court under Marshall embodied the first principle of republican government that law, not men, should rule. It was a principle associated unavoidably with the intent of the Framers.

It is a bit heretical these days to argue that there was a time when the Framers' intent had real meaning, but there was such a time, and the phrase did have such. Marshall referred to intent in his opinions; he believed what he said, and what he said and believed was grounded in the history of the period. It is the historical reality of intent, more even than his unique concept of nationalism or his concept of balanced federalism, that locates Marshall in his own age and distinguishes his jurisprudence from ours. Modern constitutional relativism is part of a pervasive cultural cynicism that looks skeptically on systems of moral values and doubts the "meaning of meaning," to quote the title of the 1924 article that helped launch linguistic indeterminacy in modern legal theory.

More important than indeterminacy in language, physics, ethics, and philosophy in producing legal relativism, however, has been the constantly shifting meaning given to the Constitution by a constantly shifting and highly politicized Supreme Court. It is hard to believe that the words of the Constitution reveal one true meaning when they have been cited to support such diverse things as laissez-faire capitalism, the New Deal corporate welfare state, and the modern revolution in civil rights. The changing Court that molded the same Constitution to such changing policy goals cannot persuasively claim to be above politics. The fact that Marshall is seemingly cited on both sides of every question—and sometimes, as in *U.S. v. Lopez* (1995), in the same case—seems to implicate him in our indeterminate and highly politicized legal culture, especially since the charge of politics was leveled against him during his own age.[27]

While those allegations cannot be entirely disregarded, it is instructive to recall that the lawyers, jurists, and politicians of Marshall's age, even those who accused him of being political, believed that the Constitution had a true meaning. For them, one interpretation of the Constitution was not as good as the next. This is not to say Marshall and his contemporaries believed the Founding Fathers spoke with absolute clarity about everything. He was not a constitutional literalist. But he did believe a single constitutional meaning could be derived from the text, even when it was not immediately clear what meaning the Framers intended. Two interrelated things help account for his faith in the possibility of an objective interpretation of constitutional language. The first was the common-law tradition of statutory interpretation he shared with other lawyers and judges of the period. The second was a natural-law interpretive tradition that was deeply rooted in Western history, one that included and informed the thinking of continental and English jurists of the seventeenth and eighteenth centuries such as Grotius, Vattel, Rutherford, and Blackstone. Marshall appeared to accept without question, and without careful examination, their collective belief that law had an objective existence and that its meaning could be ascertained by time-tested rules of interpretation, the same Story extracted from Marshall's opinions in his *Commentaries on the Constitution.* Marshall's use of *intent* in his opinions was not a smoke screen

27. For some of the best current scholarship on the problem of original intent, see Jack N. Rakove, ed., *Interpreting the Constitution: The Debate over Original Intent* (Boston, 1990). For the sharp disagreement among the justices over Marshall's opinion in *Gibbons,* see *U.S. v. Lopez,* 514 US 549.

designed to hide his policy preferences or the lawmaking implications of his opinions but rather emanated from his belief in the fundamental assumptions of the early national legal culture.[28]

This is not to say Marshall claimed to have read the minds of the Framers; he did not. Nor could he have, since the records of the Philadelphia Convention and the state ratifying conventions were not available to him. What he did have—and it was basic to the meaning of *intent,* as he used the concept—was a consanguinity to the Framers. Belonging to the first generation of interpreters, "being *there*" at the beginning, had advantages other than getting to write on a clean slate. One of the greatest was that Marshall and his colleagues were asked to supply constitutional answers to the same questions addressed by the Framers. No axiom of constitutional interpretation was more decisive for Marshall than reference to the deficiencies of the Articles of Confederation, the same that the Constitution was designed to correct. Marshall not only shared a common interpretive tradition with the Framers, then, he shared the political history from which the Constitution was fashioned. To understand what this meant, and how it separates his age from ours, one has only to compare the effort of the Marshall Court to settle matters concerning contracts, paper money, slavery, and the emerging national market with those of the modern Court asked to find authority for desegregation, abortion rights, gay rights, and equal voting rights in the Fourteenth Amendment of 1868, which was designed primarily to grant a modicum of civil equality to newly freed slaves.

Marshall not only consolidated the power of the Court to interpret the Constitution (the real meaning of judicial review), then, but he did so when it was possible to ascertain with some assurance what the words of the Constitution meant. One cannot claim Marshall was omniscient or that everything he did was equally circumscribed by the text of the Constitution. Least confining was international law, which permitted Marshall and the Court to fashion a body of law that blended market-oriented policy with the natural-law tradition of the continental jurists, the same he consulted for rules of interpretation. The constitutional text did not define Native American "nations" either, which led Marshall to forge doctrine from experience, custom, and history, the same things the Framers consulted. What is striking, even in Marshall's most cre-

---

28. The common-law tradition of interpretation is discussed brilliantly by H. Jefferson Powell, "The Original Understanding of Original Intent," *Harvard Law Review* 98 (March 1985): 885–948, reprinted in *Interpreting the Constitution,* 53–116. Robert Lowry Clinton explores the broader natural-law interpretive tradition in *God and Man in the Law: The Foundations of Anglo-American Constitutionalism* (Lawrence, Kans., 1997).

ative moments, is how closely his view of federalism followed the contours laid down in the Constitution. Who except the radical states' rightists could deny that the Constitution was a document meant to "energize" the national government, to give it the powers governments of a sovereign nation ordinarily have. This meant curbing state power to issue paper money, to destroy contracts, and, in general, to obstruct the growth of a national market. The Framers took on state sovereignty, as the ratifying debates conclusively show, and Marshall followed their lead. His jurisprudence, like theirs, also recognized the historical limits of nationalism, leaving a large reservoir of traditional power in the hands of the states, including control over the institution of slavery. His concept of federalism, like that of Madison and the other Framers, was not a perfectly tidy arrangement, but neither was early national history.[29]

Recognizing Marshall's deep affinity with the Framers helps locate him in the sweep of American history. His lack of originality, which troubled Holmes, is not a problem but a virtue. What Marshall did was to work creatively within the framework provided by the Framers. By expounding, legitimating, and maintaining their ideas, his opinions and their Constitution came to be perceived as one and the same. Great symbolic advantage accrued in this fact for both Marshall and the Court, but there was a problem. The problem was that the Framers' Constitution, which he approached legally, was also partly political. It was the supreme law of the land, as Article 6 proclaims, *and* a bundle of political compromises—between large states and small, between the free states and the slave states, and, indeed, between Federalists and Anti-Federalists. Marshall made his constitutional debut in *Marbury* by casting the Court as a legal institution, and he expanded and justified its powers building on that premise. But the political features of the Constitution could not be readily legalized, especially the compromise between states' rights and nationalism that permeated so much of it. It was that part of the Constitution the political branches claimed as their domain; it was that part the parties of Jefferson and Jackson were bent on privileging. Having lost in the battle for ratification, the defenders of states' rights and localism retreated to fight over interpretation. They had some considerable history on their side. One might even argue that local culture, which lay at the basis of states' rights theory, was always dominant; that the nationalism of the Constitution was a creation of a handful of

---

29. Jack N. Rakove does justice to the historical complexities constitution making, including Madison's federalism, in his *Original Meanings: Politics and Ideas in the Making of the Constitution* (New York, 1996).

bold visionaries who seized the brief window of opportunity created by Revolution. It wasn't just that the Constitution was "a roof without walls" but that it was superimposed on a culture that was essentially local and would remain so for decades. Marshall understood the problem but hoped that the memory of the Revolution and the growing economic advantages of national union and national market would forge permanent bonds for the Union. Ironically, it was the growth of a national market and national capitalism located mainly in the North that fueled the southern states' rights movement, leading to the Civil War and putting Marshall on the losing side of antebellum history.

To recognize that Marshall was somehow an accomplice in his own undoing is to acknowledge that he was not a status quo conservative. To be sure, his belief in the intent of the Framers puts him back in the Revolutionary War period. But the Revolution was not simply the conservative law-abiding event Marshall thought it was, nor was the Constitution that completed the Revolution exclusively conservative in its meaning and operation. The document that laid the conservative foundations of judicial review also contained the seeds of popular democracy, without the benefit of amendment, just as the Revolution set in motion the egalitarian transformation of American society. Likewise, the growth of national commerce, which the Constitution promoted, transformed the way Americans lived. Also the sovereign people continued to play an active role in constitution making. Marshall approved of them and cited them copiously when they created the Constitution of 1787. When they took charge of constitutional change in the 1820s, however, it was another matter; when they took over the Court, through the appointment process, it looked to Marshall like the beginning of the end.

What this popular shift in constitutional law meant, among other things— what Marshall witnessed in his last years and what the Taney Court completed—was that the Supreme Court did not have a monopoly on constitutional interpretation. Doctrines change over time and sometimes disappear, even Marshall's. As modern scholars have shown, it is not always the Court that initiates the changes. The bitter lesson Jefferson and Jackson taught Marshall was that the Court does not have the final word on the Constitution. Understandably, he concluded that a changed Court was no Court at all. What he did not fully appreciate was that the Court as an institution did not have to be final to remain at the center of American constitutional government. More than any other man, Marshall put it there—by associating it with the Revolution, through his person; with the Constitution, through the intent of the Framers; and by making it work as an institution. Holmes put the matter in words:

"When we celebrate Marshall we celebrate at the same time and indivisibly the inevitable fact that the oneness of the nation and the supremacy of the national Constitution were declared to govern the dealings of man with man by judgments and decrees of the most august of courts." The great chief justice put his stamp on the Court as an institution, and when the Court goes about its work, it keeps his fame alive. No other institution of government is so well equipped to perform this chore. To be sure, the other branches celebrate themselves, too. Presidents occasionally cite other presidents, and political parties search for presidential forebears. The Senate and the House are mindful of their own heroes and their own traditions. But stare decisis, along with West Law and LEXIS-NEXIS, makes John Marshall uniquely relevant. Over its long history, the Supreme Court has cited Marshall's great opinions thousands of times. Sometimes the opinions cited have been misunderstood, and sometimes they have been cited to further policy goals that would have made the old chief justice cringe. But his name and his ideas still command attention in the actual work of the Court as it serves the American nation he loved.[30]

30. Oliver Wendell Holmes Jr., *Collected Legal Papers* (New York, 1920), 268.

Essay on the Sources

In attempting to place Marshall in the context of early national history, I have been the beneficiary of a rich body of scholarship. My indebtedness to the labors of others, as I hope to point out here, goes far beyond the works cited in my footnotes. In this brief essay, I will refer to the sources—some primary, some secondary, some old, and some new—that have most influenced my understanding of Marshall and the world in which he lived and worked.

MARSHALL IN HIS OWN WORDS

Marshall's judicial opinions remain the basic source of his life's work. Though they have been cited literally thousands of times and written about endlessly, I have tried to read them, along with arguments of counsel, with an open mind. It is amazing how revealing they can still be. Marshall's most important constitutional opinions, along with a representative sampling of his circuit-court opinions are included (with useful scholarly introductions) in *The Papers of John Marshall*, 10 vols. to date (Chapel Hill, N.C., 1974–), under the current editorship of Charles F. Hobson.

These papers—sponsored by the College of William and Mary, and the Institute of Early American History and Culture under the auspices of the National Historical Publications and Records Commission—have been central to my biography. For whatever reason, Marshall showed little interest in preserving his papers for posterity—and even may have destroyed some of them. Those that survived are widely scattered. Building on the pioneering bibliographic efforts of Irwin S. Rhodes, the editors of *The Papers of John Marshall* have not only identified and assembled these materials but have provided the scholarly context that makes them readily accessible to scholars. The footnotes are a gold mine of references to other primary sources and to relevant secondary literature, while the editorial essays on various aspects of Marshall's private and public life constitute both a guide to the use of the documents and a running narrative on his life. Among those essays I have found indispensable are those dealing with Marshall's land speculation and his Virginia law practice. Without editorial guidance in these areas, I would surely have been lost in an impenetrable thicket.

Several other primary sources on Marshall have been essential to my research. The first, yet to be printed in *The Papers of John Marshall,* is Marshall's autobiographical letter written sometime in 1827 to Joseph Story at Story's request and reprinted as *An Autobiographical Sketch by John Marshall,* John Stokes Adams, ed. (Ann Arbor, Mich., 1937). Another indispensable source of Marshall's ideas in his own words is his *The Life of George Washington,* 5 vols. (Philadelphia, 1805–1807). Marshall was not pleased with this edition and spent much of the rest of his life correcting and revising. Considerations of space and focus led me to omit the story of Marshall's publishing venture (for which see vol. 6 of *The Papers of John Marshall*), but I have often drawn on his biography as a source of his ideas—about Washington, about the nature of the Revolution, about the 1790s and his alienation from Virginia politics, and about his growing animus toward Jefferson. Unless otherwise indicated, I have cited from Marshall's final revision, the one he most approved of: *The Life of George Washington,* 2d ed., revised and corrected, 2 vols. (Philadelphia, 1832). Another critical source of Marshall's ideas, again in his own words, is the series of anonymous essays that appeared in the *Alexandria (Virginia) Gazette,* written in defense of his opinion in *McCulloch v. Maryland.* Marshall's essays, along with those of his critics William Brockenbrough and Spencer Roane, are reprinted with a valuable scholarly introduction in *John Marshall's Defense of McCulloch v. Maryland,* Gerald Gunther, ed. (Stanford, Calif., 1969). As a glance at chapter 6 will indicate, I have profited greatly from Gunther's scrupulous scholarship.

Finally, let me mention several other widely differing "primary" sources I have relied on. One that defies easy categorization is *The Marshall Family* by William McClung Paxton (1885; reprint, Baltimore, 1988). This book, as the subtitle informs us, is a genealogical chart of the Marshall family with "Sketches of Individuals and Notices of Families Connected with Them." The information in this volume, some of which is anecdotal in nature, is not always easy to verify, but it remains a unique source of information about Marshall and his family in the Virginia setting. For those including myself who believe a picture is worth a thousand words, there is *The Portraits of John Marshall,* Andrew Oliver (Charlottesville, Va., 1977), which treats more than a hundred Marshall portraits, plus several of his wife, Mary Willis Marshall.

Finally, there are two editions of primary documents dealing with key episodes in Marshall's career. The most recent is *The Documentary History of the Ratification of the Constitution,* Merrill Jensen et al., eds., 18 vols. to date (Madison, Wis., 1976–); vols. 8, 9, and 10, edited by John P. Kaminski and Gaspare J. Saladino, cover ratification in Virginia. In addition to including Marshall's three speeches at the convention, which are also printed in *The Papers of John Marshall,* this admirable work includes a wide range of supplementary documents, including newspapers and private correspondence on the ratification struggle, supplemented by scholarly essays by the editors. It is the indispensable starting point for any full understanding of Marshall's constitutional thinking. Two other essential sources are *Reports of the Trials of Colonel Aaron Burr* (1808; reprint, New York, 1969), by David Robertson, which after nearly two centuries still radiates the passions of that unique moment in American history; and *Proceedings and Debates of the Virginia State Convention of 1829–1830* (1830; reprint, 2 vols., New York, 1971), which reports Marshall's speeches at the Virginia constitutional convention of 1829.

SECONDARY WORKS

The secondary scholarship on Marshall is voluminous, and I make no claim to have read it all. While I have learned from other scholars over the years, I have made no effort to address, much less to resolve, their varying interpretations of Marshall—though occasionally I make general reference to them. Here permit me to mention some of the works that have influenced my thinking about Marshall (some well before I undertook to write about him). One such was Joseph Story's "Character and Services of Chief Justice Marshall: A Discourse Pronounced on the 15th of October, 1835, at the Request of the Suffolk Bar," in *The Miscellaneous Writings of Joseph Story,* William W. Story, ed. (Boston, 1852), 639–97. Story was Marshall's closest and most important ally on the Court, and he understood Marshall's work, probably his character, too, better than any living man. Though passionately favorable to his dead friend, Story's discourse, in my mind, still stands as one of the best essays ever written on Marshall. Spending so much time with Joseph Story attuned me to his love of the chief justice—and also warned me against admiring him too much.

Though I run the risk of being too much identified with dead conservatives,

I would also like to pay my respects to Albert J. Beveridge's *The Life of John Marshall*, 4 vols. (Boston, New York, 1916–1919). It is fashionable now to disparage Beveridge for his anachronistic and exceedingly worshipful approach to his subject. Still I am grateful to him for introducing me to Marshall many years ago. Many Marshall biographers over the years, including this one, have drawn on Beveridge's work even while parting interpretive company with him. Jean Edward Smith's *John Marshall: Definer of a Nation* (New York, 1996), the most recent full biography, avoids Beveridge's biases is especially good on Marshall's private life. Among the few works that have withstood the ravages of time and the changing fads of historical scholarship is Samuel J. Konefsky's *John Marshall and Alexander Hamilton: Architects of the Constitution* (New York, 1964). This marvelously humane book is as fresh today as it was nearly forty years ago. Also worthy of note are three shorter books about Marshall. In order of publication they are: *The Jurisprudence of John Marshall*, Robert K. Faulkner (Princeton, N.J., 1968); *The Great Chief Justice: John Marshall and the Rule of Law*, Charles F. Hobson (Lawrence, Kans., 1996); and *The Chief Justiceship of John Marshall, 1801–1835*, Herbert A. Johnson (Columbia, S.C., 1997). Both Faulkner and Hobson analyze Marshall's jurisprudence with admirable learning and clarity. Johnson focuses on Marshall's contributions to the development of the Court as an institution. More sharply focused is Robert Lowry Clinton's *Marbury v. Madison and Judicial Review* (Lawrence, Kans., 1989). Clinton demystifies Marshall's most famous decision by putting it in the context of its own time. Christopher Wolfe's *The Rise of Modern Judicial Review: From Constitutional Interpretation to Judge-Made Law* (New York, 1986) continues the contextualization process by locating *Marbury*, judicial review, and Marshall himself in the long sweep of American judicial history. Both books have helped me put Marshall in historical perspective.

SECONDARY ACCOUNTS: CONSTITUTIONAL AND LEGAL HISTORY

In recovering the unique constitutional and legal world of John Marshall, I have drawn on so many scholars that it is all but impossible to credit them all. The following have been especially relevant to the enterprise. On the Virginia context of Marshall's legal and professional life, two works stand out: *Faithful Magistrates and Republican Lawyers: Creators of Virginia Legal Culture, 1680–1810*, A. G. Roeber (Chapel Hill, N.C., 1981); and *Edmund Pendleton,*

1721–1803: A Biography, David John Mays, 2 vols. (Cambridge, Mass., 1952). Though it doesn't treat Virginia, John Murrin's "The Legal Transformation: The Bench and Bar of Eighteenth-Century Massachusetts," in *Colonial America: Essays in Politics and Social Development,* Stanley N. Katz, ed. (Boston, 1971), has been very suggestive. By far the clearest and most authoritative treatment of Marshall's legal practice, appears in volume 5 of *The Papers of John Marshall,* edited by Charles F. Hobson. His concise and scholarly editorial introductions make the arcane documents readily accessible to ordinary historians such as myself.

Though not constitutional history in the formal sense, Gordon S. Wood's *The Creation of the American Republic, 1776–1787* (Chapel Hill, N.C., 1969) has been central to my understanding of Marshall's early constitutional experience—his Federalist perspective on republican ideology and his lifelong distrust of state government. Like Wood, Marshall viewed the Constitution of 1787 as the completion of the Revolution. Also impressive for its interpretive punch and for the scope of its scholarship is Forrest McDonald's trilogy on the constitution-making process: *We the People: The Economic Origins of the Constitution* (Chicago, 1958); *E Pluribus Unum: The Formation of the American Republic, 1776–1790* (Boston, 1965); and *Novus Ordo Seclorum: The Intellectual Origins of the Constitution* (Lawrence, Kans., 1985). More strictly legal in focus, but equally impressive for its comprehensive analysis, is John Phillip Reid's *Constitutional History of the American Revolution,* 3 vols. (Madison, Wis., 1986–1993). McDonald educated me about the interrelated political, economic, and intellectual aspects of constitution making, while Reid persuaded me more than ever to consider the Revolution as a source of Marshall's constitutional education.

Several other works have informed my understanding of Marshall's constitutional jurisprudence. Jennifer Nedelsky, *Private Property and the Limits of American Constitutionalism: The Madisonian Framework and Its Legacy* (Chicago, 1990) explores the Lockean fusion of liberty and property in the Constitution so central to Marshall's jurisprudence. In exploring this theme, especially in chapter 5, I have found the argument of C. B. Macpherson, *The Political Theory of Possessive Individualism: Hobbes To Locke* (Oxford, England, 1962) to be especially relevant. Finally, Jack Rakove's *Original Meanings: Politics and Ideas in the Making of the Constitution* (New York, 1996) captures the complexity of constitutional thought in a way that is especially suggestive for the study of Marshall—especially his federalism. Also relevant to that subject are two seminal books on law in action at the state level, both published under the auspices of the Committee on Research in Economic History: *Commonwealth: A Study of the Role of Government in the American Economy: Massachusetts, 1774-1861,* by Oscar and Mary Flug Handlin (New York, 1947); and *Economic Policy and Democratic Thought: Pennsylvania, 1776–1860,* by Louis Hartz (Cambridge, Mass., 1948). Some of the Marshall Court's decisions circumscribed the extensive state economic intervention described in these volumes, and some were used in the course of the nineteenth century to justify laissez-faire economic policy. But what impressed me most—using Hartz's and the Handlins' discussion of state mercantilism as the benchmark—was how much of the extensive state regulation, and regulatory authority, Marshall's jurisprudence actually left in place.

On the subject of state-federal relations, my thinking has also been influenced by the long-forgotten great work on administrative history by Leonard D. White, especially the first three volumes of his four-volume opus: *Federalists: A Study in Administrative History* (New York, 1948); *Jeffersonians: A Study in Administrative History* (New York, 1951); *Jacksonians: A Study in Administrative History* (New York, 1954). In these volumes, White describes a rich tradition of administrative innovation at the state level, which was not interrupted by the Marshall Court's decisions. White also sees a complex pattern of administrative cooperation between the states and the federal government—a pattern that Marshall's effort to achieve a workable balance between federal and state power readily accommodated.

Among the general works most useful to me in studying Marshall—not surprisingly—have been those devoted to the institution over which he presided. Heading the list are the relevant volumes in the *Oliver Wendell Holmes Devise History of the Supreme Court of the United States,* the multivolume history of the Court endowed by Justice Holmes on his death and published by Macmillan, New York. Easing my labors every step of the way have been the two volumes in this series on the Marshall Court: *Foundations of Power: John Marshall, 1801–1815,* by George Lee Haskins and Herbert A. Johnson (New York, 1981); and *The Marshall Court and Cultural Change, 1815–1835,* by G. Edward White with the aid of Gerald Gunther (New York, 1988). These hefty volumes include an in-depth analysis of the Court's decisions, a detailed exposition of its internal working procedures, and sharply etched vignettes of the justices and key members of the Supreme Court bar. In addition to being encyclopedic reference works, these volumes have proved to be a rich source of interpretive ideas.

Also useful to me have been the older general histories of the Court. Charles

Warren's *The Supreme Court in United States History,* 2 vols., new rev. ed. (Boston, 1926) is especially good on the popular reception of the Court's opinions. Viewing Marshall and his Court from a Jeffersonian perspective, thus serving to correct the bias of both Warren and Beveridge, is Charles Grove Haines's *The Role of the Supreme Court in American Government and Politics, 1789–1835* (New York, 1960). Worthy of mention also, is William W. Crosskey's *Politics and the Constitution in the History of the United States,* 2 vols. (Chicago, 1953–1980). Crosskey's controlling thesis—that Marshall retreated from the unitary nationalism of the Framers—is badly flawed, as many scholars have pointed out, but his argument set me thinking. What Crosskey treats as Marshall's deviation from constitutional truth, I tend to see as the essence of his constitutional jurisprudence—and of his perceptive reading of the Framers' intent as well.

SELECT WORKS ON EARLY NATIONAL HISTORY

One of the primary objectives of my book is to locate Marshall and his jurisprudence in the broader historical context—the "circumstances of which he was a part," in Holmes's words. A number of historians have helped me do this, but two in particular stand out for the interpretive ideas they have supplied. The first is Gordon S. Wood, *The Radicalism of the American Revolution* (New York, 1992); the second is Charles Sellers, *The Market Revolution: Jacksonian America, 1815–1846* (New York, 1991). Wood argues that the Revolution unleashed the forces of egalitarian democracy that ultimately transformed every aspect of American society; Sellers argues that the forces of market capitalism were equally transformative. Marshall, as I see it, responded both personally and jurisprudentially to the historical developments Wood and Sellers describe. As a Federalist politician and a republican jurist, he spent his whole adult life trying to restrain the egalitarian transformation Wood describes. As chief justice he worked simultaneously to liberate the economic energy of American entrepreneurs and to create a national market in which they could operate efficiently—one that would bind the sections together in self-interest. Sellers's concept of market helped me contextualize Marshall's jurisprudence—and provided the common policy denominator that connected Marshall's "nationalist" opinions with those dealing with contract individualism. Also helpful in this regard—and in relating Marshall's republicanism and his liberalism—is Steven Watts, *The Republic Reborn: War and the Making of Liberal America, 1790–1820* (Baltimore, 1987).

Like almost every other statesman of his age, Marshall thought of himself as a republican. In trying to understand what that pervasive, and illusive, concept meant, I have drawn on J. G. A. Pocock's *The Machiavellian Moment: Florentine Political Thought and the Atlantic Republican Tradition* (Princeton, N.J., 1975); Bernard Bailyn's *The Ideological Origins of the American Revolution* (Cambridge, Mass., 1967); and Wood's previously mentioned *Creation of the American Republic;* also Robert E. Shalhope's "Republicanism and Early American Historiography," *William and Mary Quarterly* 39 (April 1982): 334–56; Daniel T. Rodgers's "Republicanism: The Career of a Concept," *American Historical Review* 97 (June 1992): 11–38; and Joyce Appleby's "Republicanism in Old and New Contexts," *William and Mary Quarterly* 43 (1986): 20–34. Appleby's argument that classical liberalism and republicanism were not at odds, as some historians have insisted, is especially applicable to Marshall.

Marshall's version of republican ideology took him into the Federalist Party—which has taken me into the extensive literature on that subject. The definitive work on the origins of the Federalist Party in the 1790s—and on that turbulent decade in general—is *The Age of Federalism,* by Stanley Elkins and Eric McKitrick (New York, 1993). On the Federalist Party in New England, the standard work is *To the Hartford Convention: The Federalists and the Origins of Party Politics in Massachusetts, 1789–1815,* by James M. Banner Jr. (New York, 1970). *The Adams Federalists,* by Manning J. Dauer (Baltimore, 1968), has been especially relevant, since John Marshall was one of the moderates the author describes. John Howe's "Republican Thought and the Political Violence of the 1790s," *American Quarterly* 19 (summer 1967): 148–65, also remains fruitful reading after all these years. Howe's argument helped me understand how men such as Jefferson and Marshall could both be republicans—yet disagree fundamentally about what republican ideology stood for. The political arena in which those two clashed in the 1790s is set forth in Richard R. Beeman's *The Old Dominion and the New Nation, 1788–1801* (Lexington, Ky., 1972); in reconstructing Marshall's political career, Beeman's book has been indispensable. Also very useful as background to the continued clash between the two men is Leonard W. Levy's *Jefferson and Civil Liberties: The Darker Side* (Cambridge, Mass., 1963). National party developments—the tradition Marshall reacted against politically and jurisprudentially—is the subject of Richard Hofstadter's *The Idea of a Party System: The Rise of a Legitimate Opposition in the United States, 1780–1840* (Berkeley, Calif., 1969).

Among the books I have found most instructive about the antebellum South, even though they are not frequently cited in my footnotes, are the following: on the southern constitutional tradition, *An Uncertain Tradition: Constitutionalism and the History of the South,* edited by Kermit L. Hall and James W. Ely Jr. (Athens, Ga., 1989); on antebellum slavery and slave law, *Roll, Jordan, Roll: The World the Slaves Made,* by Eugene D. Genovese (New York, 1976); *Southern Slavery and the Law, 1619–1860,* by Thomas D. Morris (Chapel Hill, N.C., 1996), and *Prelude to Civil War: The Nullification Controversy in South Carolina, 1816–1836,* by William W. Freehling (New York, 1966); and on antebellum southern society in general, *Southern Honor: Ethics and Behavior in the Old South,* by Bertram Wyatt-Brown (New York, 1982). Finally, to see the Old South through the eyes of one of its great champions—and most insightful critics as well—I have turned to William C. Bruce's *John Randolph of Roanoke, 1773–1833,* 2 vols. (1922; reprint, New York, 1970). Robert Dawidoff's *The Education of John Randolph* (New York, 1979) also captures the backward-looking romanticism of Marshall's friend and ideological opponent.

Index

The Index contains references to the discussions of legal cases. For a complete listing of the pages on which cases are mentioned, please use the List of Cases.

List of Cases